Handbook of Child and Adolescent Obsessive-Compulsive Disorder

Titles of Related Interest

Handbook of Child and Adolescent Obsessive-Compulsive Disorder

Edited by

Eric A. Storch
Gary R. Geffken
Tanya K. Murphy
University of Florida

2007
LAWRENCE ERLBAUM ASSOCIATES, PUBLISHERS
Mahwah, New Jersey   London

Lawrence Erlbaum Associates, Inc., Publishers
10 Industrial Avenue
Mahwah, New Jersey 07430
www.erlbaum.com

Cover design by Tomai Maridou

Library of Congress Cataloging-in-Publication Data

Handbook of child and adolescent obsessive-compulsive disorder / [edited by] Eric A. Storch, Gary R. Geffken, and Tanya K. Murphy.
    p. cm.
    Includes bibliographical references and index.
    ISBN 978-0-8058-5766-5 — 0-8058-5766-4 (cloth)
    ISBN 978-0-8058-6254-6 — 0-8058-6254-4 (pbk.)
    ISBN 1-4106-1600-5 — 1-4106-1600-2 (e book)
    1. Obsessive-compulsive disorder in children—Treatment—Handbooks, manuals, etc. 2. Obsessive-compulsive disorder in adolescence—Treatment—Handbooks, manuals, etc. I. Storch, Eric A. II. Geffken, Gary R. III. Murphy, Tanya.
    [DNLM: 1. Obsessive-Compulsive Disorder—diagnosis. 2. Adolescent. 3. Child. 4. Obsessive-Compulsive Disorder—therapy. 5. Psychotherapy—methods. WM 176 C737 2007]
    RJ506.O25C66 2007
    618.92'85227—dc22
                                     2006018647
                                                  CIP

Books published by Lawrence Erlbaum Associates are printed on acid-free paper, and their bindings are chosen for strength and durability.

Printed in the United States of America
10 9 8 7 6 5 4 3 2 1

EAS: For Jill, my dream come true.

Contents

Foreword

The past decades have witnessed numerous advances in the treatment of obsessive-compulsive disorder (OCD). As happens with many conditions, the literature on children has lagged behind that of adults. The editors of this collection on pediatric OCD recognized the need for a new text on the topic given advances in knowledge in many areas of research. With growing awareness that childhood onset OCD is common and may represent a meaningful subtype of OCD with unique management challenges, a volume dedicated to the condition is justified and timely. Advances in efficacy of psychopharmacological intervention in pediatric OCD and concerns about side effect profiles of antidepressants in children and adolescents emerged after publication of existing texts. Likewise, new information has emerged from controlled trials with cognitive behavioral therapy (CBT). Given that these are the two evidence-based treatments for OCD, this merits an updated review.

In addition to treatment, we have also seen significant advances in the assessment and neurobiology of pediatric OCD. Genetic, neuroimaging and immunological advances are all included. This text exemplifies the highest level of integration on evidence based healthcare for pediatric OCD and captures the background of thought on OCD leading to this comprehensive and in-depth integration of scientific discovery. Research relevant to the settings of the family, school and primary care is covered in this text, as are OCD spectrum disorders and comorbidities. This book meets the need to disseminate information to the international community of psychiatry, psychology, neuroscience, family practice and pediatric medicine, nursing, and pedagogy. Antiquated and outdated knowledge of pediatric OCD hinders the recognition of this condition and referral of those children suffering with this condition for appropriate treatment.

Our understanding of OCD has grown exponentially in recent decades. This area of scientific inquiry will continue to flourish. At this time, the editors of this book have developed the most comprehensive collection of writings by leading researchers. The book will undoubtedly guide researchers and practitioners to formulate new questions that will further elucidate this condition.

—*Wayne Goodman, MD*
Professor and Chairman
Department of Psychiatry, University of Florida

Preface

As adults, we recall our childhood days of avoiding stepping on cracks so as not to "break our mother's back," or insisting that our father check under the bed every night to insure the absence of monsters. Repetitive play, superstitions, and ritualistic games are typical aspects of child development. However, practitioners are faced with the question of what to do when these superstitious and ritualistic behaviors stop being normal and cross the line into more clinically relevant, worrisome behavior.

Previously thought rare, obsessive-compulsive disorder (OCD) in children and adolescents has been identified as one of the most common psychiatric illnesses affecting youth with point-prevalence rates of 1% to 4% of the general youth population. Without clinical attention, OCD is associated with significant social, academic, and familial impairment, and tends to persist into adulthood.

Over the past two decades, practitioners have witnessed a great expansion in understanding about the etiology, neurobiology, treatment, and assessment of childhood OCD. For example, evidence from controlled trials has accumulated suggesting that cognitive-behavioral therapy (CBT), with or without medication, is the front-line treatment for pediatric OCD. Similarly, tremendous advances in knowledge about pharmacological interventions and mechanisms of action have been made. Yet, despite these significant advances, a compilation of the extant knowledge base does not exist. As a result, the dissemination of information about effective treatments, etiology, and accurate assessment has been hindered greatly. Although several books or chapters discuss the nature and treatment of pediatric OCD within the context of a larger text that covers a broad range of childhood psychopathology, these volumes generally do not cover in great depth many of the topics that the present text covers. When conceptualizing this edited collection, we included topics that span the spectrum of issues linked to childhood OCD in an effort to make this book applicable for a wide audience. With this in mind, particular strengths of this work include the wide breadth of coverage and utility for numerous disciplines, including psychiatrists, psychologists, social workers, pediatricians, graduate students in mental health professions, and other mental health professionals.

The chapters contained in this volume were designed to provide comprehensive, current reviews about the phenomenology, neurobiology, assessment, and treatment of childhood OCD in a manner that captures the complexities of this condition as well as uncovering areas in need of future study. The text covers Diagnosis and Assessment, Etiology, Treatment, and School and Family Issues.

Dr. Alvarenga and colleagues open the volume with a detailed history of OCD, focusing on early perceptions of OCD, significant milestones in the field, and future directions. In chapter 2, Dr. Moore and colleagues review the epidemiology and phenomenology of pediatric OCD, with special attention to comorbid conditions commonly occurring in the context of OCD. Drs. Douglas Shytle and Berney Wilkinson discuss psychiatric conditions that are commonly found in youth with OCD in chapter 3. Dr. Lisa Merlo and her colleagues provide an overview of recent advances in assessment in chapter 4, including an introduction to several new assessment instruments that are included in reproducible forms.

In Etiology, Dr. Jonathan Abramowitz and his colleagues (chap. 6) explore psychological theories relevant to OCD and its etiology. In chapter 7, Dr. Tanya Murphy and colleagues review the history, potential etiology, clinical features, and currently accepted treatments for Pediatric Autoimmune Neuropsychiatric Disorders Associated with Streptococcus (PANDAS). In chapter 8, Drs. Paul Arnold and Margaret Richter provide a comprehensive and critical review of the literature regarding the probabilistic genetic determinants of OCD.

Dr. Eric Storch and his colleagues cover Treatment with a discussion of the nature and application of cognitive-behavioral therapy. This chapter is notable for its pragmatic nature and inclusion of reproducible handouts. Dr. Daniel Geller provides a comprehensive review in chapter 10 of neuropsychiatric models of pediatric OCD and their relation to pharmacological management. Dr. Geller includes detailed information about medication treatment of childhood OCD with particular attention to relevant outcome data. In chapter 11, Drs. Kimberli Treadwell and David Tolin address clinical challenges common to treating pediatric OCD patients, focusing on issues such as noncompliance, comorbidity, and family issues. In chapter 12, Dr. Julia Berkman and her colleagues present a model for the treatment of early-onset OCD, highlighting the role of family members in intervention.

Finally, Family and School, addresses factors relevant to working with pediatric patients. In chapter 13, Drs. Lara Farrell and Paula Barrett review the literature on family interactions among OCD patients, highlighting the role of family factors in predicting treatment outcome and symptomatic relapse. Dr. Deborah Ledley and Ms. Radhika Pasupuleti, in chapter 14, analyze the problems youth with OCD routinely encounter in the school setting, such as academic problems, stigma, isolation and peer victimization. A significant strength of this chapter is the discussion of clinical strategies specific to the school and recommendations to professionals on assisting families with working with schools on education plans. Finally, in chapter 15, Dr. David Rettew reviews guidelines for the assessment and treatment of OCD within a primary care setting. Particularly innovative is the inclusion of an assessment template that will enable primary care practitioners to identify and connect patients with appropriate treatment approaches.

Each of the chapters within this volume contains a wealth of knowledge. Perhaps the greatest contribution of this textbook, however, is the synergy with which it addresses the complexity of childhood OCD and emphasizes the elements inherent to the condition. As editors, it is our hope that the reader is left to consider issues inherent to effective assessment and treatment. It is crucial for health care professionals, both within and outside the mental health profession, to collaborate in patient care and educate the other about their field. With this in mind, our wish is that this text will serve bridge disciplines and stimulate additional discussion and scholarship on childhood OCD.

About the Editors

Eric A. Storch, PhD, received his doctorate in Clinical Psychology from Columbia University. He is currently an Assistant Professor in the Departments of Psychiatry and Pediatrics. Dr. Storch's research interests are in childhood and adult OCD, peer relationships, and measurement evaluation. He has published more than 85 peer-reviewed papers focused on OCD, anxiety disorders, and related topics, and made numerous presentations at professional meetings. He is highly regarded in psychological treatment for OCD, particularly with regards to treatment refractory cases. He also has a special interest in the development and validation of OCD assessment measures.

Gary K. Geffken, PhD, is an Associate Professor of Clinical Psychology in the Department of Psychiatry at the University of Florida Health Science Center with additional academic appointments in Pediatrics, and Clinical and Health Psychology. Dr. Geffken has special expertise in the psychological treatment of Obsessive Compulsive Disorder. He directs the Cognitive-Behavioral Therapy Program of the Department of Psychiatry's Treatment Program for Refractory Obsessive-Compulsive Disorder. He has published numerous scientific studies and chapters primarily on the psychological and family issues of children.

Tanya K. Murphy, MD, is an Associate Professor in the Department of Psychiatry at the University of Florida, Dr. Murphy is a board-certified child psychiatrist who also holds a Master of Science in Clinical Investigation. She is Director of the Pediatric Anxiety and Tic Disorder Clinic at the University of Florida in Gainesville, Florida. Dr. Murphy's current research efforts are aimed at understanding the role of infections and immune dysfunction in the onset of childhood psychiatric disorders. She is a member of the National

Tourette Syndrome Association Medical Advisory Board and Regional Obsessive-Compulsive Foundation Scientific Advisory Board. The author of several book chapters and journal articles, she is also a reviewer for multiple prestigious journals.

1

Obsessive-Compulsive Disorder: A Historical Overview

Pedro G. Alvarenga
Ana G. Hounie
Marcos T. Mercadante
Euripedes C. Miguel
Maria Conceição do Rosario
University of São Paulo Medical School

Obsessions have an intriguing connection with human beings. They can develop from any thought, feeling, fear, or image and therefore can be present in our daily expressions of art, love, science and religion. Obsessive-compulsive disorder (OCD) is sometimes called the disease of doubt: Patients often doubt their thoughts, their senses, and their own beliefs (Rosario-Campos et al., 2001). Very frequently, they end up feeling trapped by the lack of certainty. OCD is also known as the disease of secrets (Rosario-Campos, et al., 2001). Patients hide their symptoms for shame or fear of being criticized. Some spend years looking for help, often without success.

In general, psychiatric concepts have changed over time. The same has happened with the definitions and knowledge related to OCD. For instance, once thought to be a rare disorder, we currently know that OCD affects 1% to 3% of the world population, independent of gender, religion or socioeconomic status (Karno & Golding, 1991; Kessler et al., 2005). The main objective of this chapter is to give an overview of the history of OCD.

INITIAL DESCRIPTIONS OF OCD

Ancient descriptions suggest that obsessive-compulsive (OC) symptoms have been a matter of concern throughout human history. For example, today what is called compulsive behavior could be represented by a metaphor based on the ancient myth of Sisyphus. As a punishment from the gods in the underworld, Sisyphus was compelled to roll a big stone up a steep hill; but before it reached the top of the hill the stone always rolled down, and Sisyphus had to begin all over again. This cycle continued on and on for eternity. In addition, OC symptom descriptions have been identified, quite consistently, since the 17th century. At that time, obsessions and compulsions were often described as symptoms of religious melancholy and sufferers were considered to be possessed by outside forces (Jenike et al., 1998; Salzman & Thaler, 1981). The *Malleus Maleficarum* ("The Witch Hammer"), first published in 1486 by the Dominicans, contains what has been considered the first description of OCD (Shapiro, Shapiro, Young, & Feinberg, 1988). The *Malleus* served as a guidebook during the Inquisition, helping the inquisitors in the identification, prosecution, and dispatching of Witches (Del Porto, 1994; Kramer & Sprenger, 1486/1991). In the 10th chapter of this guidebook, the authors described how men can be obsessed by the devil and compelled to act against their own thinking (Kramer & Sprenger, 1486/1991). In 1553, Inácio de Loyola described his own "scruples" that forced him to give exhaustive confessions (Loyola, 1991). In his 1691 sermon on religious melancholy, John Moore, Bishop of Norwich, England, described a phenomena he observed in people he referred to as obsessed individuals. He explained that these individuals experience "naughty, and sometimes blasphemous thoughts that start in their minds, while they are exercised in the worship of God, despite all their endeavors to stifle and suppress them" (Mora, 1969, pp. 163–174). Not surprisingly, the most popular treatment method at that time was exorcism, which sometimes reportedly resulted in therapeutic benefits (Krochmalik & Menzies, 2003).

EARLY PSYCHIATRIC DESCRIPTIONS OF OCD
IN EUROPEAN PSYCHIATRY

By the first half of the 19th century, along with other changes in medical thinking, OCD shifted from the religious to the scientific field of enquiry. Modern concepts of OCD began to evolve in Europe, when psychiatry was strongly influenced by intellectual streams coursing through philosophy, physiology, chemistry and other biological sciences (Del Porto, 1994). OC symptoms were first considered to be a type of "insanity" or madness (Berrios, 1995, pp. 3–13). Obsessions in which insight was preserved were gradually distinguished from delusions, in which insight was not preserved. Compulsions were also distinguished from impulsions, which included a great number of paroxysmal and stereotyped behaviors (Del Porto, 1994). During that period of time, psychiatrists disagreed about whether the grounds of OCD lay in disorders of the will, the emotions, or the intellect (Berrios, 1995; Del Porto, 1994).

In 1838, Jean-Etienne Dominique Esquirol, the favorite student of Philippe Pinel at the Salpêtrière Hospital, first described a psychiatric disorder quite similar to the contemporary concept of OCD (the case report of "Mademoiselle F."). He classified it as a form of monomania, a kind of partial insanity (Esquirol, 1838). Esquirol moved between defining OCD as a disorder of the intellect or the will (Esquirol, 1838). Pinel, along with his disciple, hypothesized that the origins of this mental illness resided in the "passions of the soul" and believed this "madness" did not fully and irremediably affect patient's reasoning (Del Porto, 1994). Esquirol (1838) argued that, because his patients were aware that their obsessions were irresistible, they possessed a certain degree of insight, calling the obsessions "*délire partiel*" (partial delusions).

Across Europe, early medical descriptions, which correspond to contemporary definitions of OCD, focused on different aspects of the disorder. English psychiatrists emphasized the religious perspective and melancholic features, whereas the French school identified loss of will and anxiety as the principal symptoms of the disorder. Dagonet (1870, pp. 5–32, 215–259), for example, considered compulsions as a form of "*folie impulsive*" (impulsive insanity) in which violent and irresistible impulses overcame the subjects' will and were manifested through obsessions and compulsions. Magnan (1893, pp. 109–426) described the "*folie des dégénérés*" (degenerative insanity), indicating cerebral pathology due to defective heredity.

The emergence of the "neurosis" concept was first introduced by Cullen in 1777, and further developed when Morel defined OCD as "*délire émotif*" (delusion of the emotions), which he believed to be originated from a pathology of the autonomic nervous system (Morel, 1866, pp. 385–402, 530–551). Morel was the first author to place OCD among disorders of emotion due to its anxiety component, reinforcing the "neurotic" aspects of the disorder. Towards the end of the 19th century, Legrand du Saulle, based on a clinical observational study, described OCD as "insanity with insight," warning, however, that psychotic symptoms could be present sometimes (Legrand du Saulle, 1875). Moreover, other terms to define OCD throughout the 19th century were employed by French psychiatrists: "*Manie sans délire*" (mania without delusion); "*folie raisonnante*" (reasonable madness); "*idée fixes*" (unchangeable ideas); "*idée irresistible*" (irresistible ideas); "*délire de toucher*" (touching delusion); "*délire avec conscience*" (delusion with conscience); and "*folie de doute*" (doubt insanity; Berrios, 1989, pp. 283–295, 1995; Del Porto, 1994).

Whereas the emotive and volitional aspects of OCD were emphasized in France, German writers considered it, along with paranoia, as an intellectual disorder and deemed irrational thoughts as neurological events with cognitive representation. In 1868, Griesenger published three cases of "*Grubelnsucht*," characterized as a ruminatory and questioning illness (Bergener, 1987). Westphal (1878, pp, 734–750) ascribed obsessions to a disordered intellectual function and used the term "*Zwangsvorstellung*" (compelled presentation or idea). In fact, Westphal was the first to describe OCD as it is currently defined in the classification manuals, including integrity of intelligence, absence of affective causal pathology, inability to suppress the intrusive thoughts, and recognition of the bizarreness of the representations. Interestingly, he also considered heritability as a prominent etiological factor. In England, the term "*Zwangsvorstellung*' was translated as "obsession," whereas in the United States it was translated as "compulsion." The term *obsessive-compulsive* emerged as an agreement between the two definitions (Berrios, 1995; Del Porto, 1994).

JANET AND THE PSYCHASTHENIA CONCEPT

In the last quarter of the 19th century, there was a shift towards a more psychological view of psychiatric disorders and the definition of OCD as "neurasthenia" emerged (Berrios, 1995; Laplanche & Pontallis, 2001). First coined by George Miller Beard in 1869, the "neurasthenia" concept included OC symptoms, as well as numerous other psychiatric symptoms such as fatigue, anxiety, headache, impotence, neuralgia, and depression, among others. It was explained as resulting from the exhaustion of the central nervous system's storage of energy attributed to civilization (Beard, 1869). In the beginning of the 20th century, both Pierre Janet (1859–1947) and Sigmund Freud (1856–1939) isolated OC symptoms from neurasthenia. Influenced by Morel and Legrand du Saulle, Pierre Janet (1903) proposed that obsessional patients possessed an abnormal personality, with features such as anxiety, excessive worrying, lack of energy, and doubting. They described the successful treatment of compulsions and rituals with techniques consistent with the later development of behavior therapy (Pitman, 1987; Rachman & Hodgson, 1980).

   Based on a study of 325 patients (with obsessions, compulsions, tics, and body dysmorphic features), Janet suggested that obsessions and compulsions were primitive psychological operations derived from diverted nervous energy (Janet, 1903). Thus, in his classical work, "*Les Obsessions et la Psychasthenie*," Janet proposed that obsessions and compulsions arise in the third (final) stage of the psychasthenic illness and described the important role played in the psychasthenic mental state by symptoms defined as "forced agitations" separated into a mental group (obsessions), a motor group (tics) and an emotional group (dysmorphophobia; Janet, 1903). This symptomatology is very similar to the current descriptions of the obsessive-compulsive spectrum (Stein & Hollander, 1995). The first stage of psychastenia would correspond to what it is now called obsessive-compulsive personality disorder. The second stage (forced agitations) would be represented by some symptoms of the OC spectrum disorders. Despite the relevance of this contribution for the understanding of the psychopathology of OCD, 100 years later, *"Les Obsessions et la Psychasthenie"* has not been translated into English.

FREUD AND THE PSYCHOANALYTICAL PERSPECTIVE

Sigmund Freud explored the human mind and developed his approach to psychology as a comprehensive method and a therapeutic technique to treat neurosis and other mental disorders. His idea that the mind works through unconscious processes and that the main cause of neurosis is the repression of painful memories sequestered from consciousness holds a central place in psychology today (Laplanche & Pontallis, 2001). Different from the descriptive work produced at his time, Freud was searching for ways of understanding the etiology of the disorders he observed, and how the symptoms evolved, in a similar way to the challenges faced by modern neuroscience.

In 1895, the term *obsessive neurosis "Zwangsneurose"*) was first mentioned in Freud's paper about "anxiety neurosis" (Freud, 1895/1976, pp. 83–85). In his study, *"Further Remarks on the Neuro-psychoses of Defense,"* Freud proposed a revolutionary theory for the existence of obsessional thinking in which he defined obsessive ideas as "transformed self-reproaches that have re-emerged from repression and that always relate to some sexual act that was performed with pleasure in childhood" (Freud, 1896/1976, pp. 181–185). Freud developed a concept of obsessive neurosis that influenced and then drew on his ideas of mental structure, mental energies, and defense mechanisms. This concept included intellectualization and isolation (warding off the effects associated with the unacceptable ideas and impulses), undoing (carrying out compulsions to neutralize the offending ideas and impulses) and reaction formation (adopting character traits exactly opposite of the feared impulses; Laplanche & Pontallis, 2001).

A great proportion of Freud's thinking about obsessive neurosis was formulated in 1909 with his famous description of the case of "The rat man," in which Freud described the psychoanalytical treatment of a 29-year old man who developed certain impulses (*Zwangshandlung*) against aggressive and sexual obsessions since his early childhood. Later in his life, the patient came across a senior military officer who conveyed a particularly sadistic method of punishment that involved confining rats and placing them in the victim's anus (Freud, 1909/1976). At this moment, Freud's patient reportedly started obsessing that his dead father and a young lady he liked could have suffered this type of torture. Although the patient expressed horror as he mentioned it in his analysis, Freud interpreted it as one of "horror at pleasure of his own desires, of which he himself was unaware." The precipitating cause of this man's obsessions was never clearly identified by Freud or by the patient himself, but Freud correlated them to the patient's ambivalent feelings (hate–love) about his father and his doubts concerning sexual orientation (Del Porto, 1994). Later, in "*Totem and Taboo*," Freud illustrated OC symptoms from social and anthropological perspectives, in which compulsions, like primitive rituals, were assumed to be human efforts to magically modify the external world and to prevent catastrophes (Freud, 1913/1976).

In 1926, Freud reformulated his theories about the origin of OC symptoms. Thus, in the article "Inhibition, Symptom, and Anxiety," Freud postulated that OC symptoms, as well as melancholia, derived from the ego's fear of the superego punishment (Freud, 1926/1976). Thus, contrary to his previous publications, Freud considered that obsessive-compulsive neurosis existed as a syndrome separated from the "anal-erotic" character, defined by scrupulous, rigid and controlling traits of personality (Laplanche & Pontallis, 2001). Nevertheless, according to Freud, an "anal character" could predispose to the development of OC symptoms, a description that brings up the concept of a "continuum" between these disorders. These definitions have some resemblance with the current differentiation between OCD (obsessional neurosis) and obsessive-compulsive personality disorder (Krochmalik & Menzies, 2003).

All descriptions just discussed referred to adult patients. During that period of time, there was a belief that obsessions could only be present in people with a high degree of knowledge about themselves, and therefore could not be present in children. Contrary to these ideas, a recent epidemiological study reported that about half of the subjects interviewed met criteria for a *DSM–IV* disorder sometime in their life, with first onset usually in childhood or adolescence (Kessler et al., 2005). Most importantly, median age of onset was much earlier for anxiety disorders, compared to the other disorders assessed (Kessler et al., 2005). In the following, we present an overview of OCD descriptions in children and adolescents through history.

DESCRIPTIONS OF EARLY-ONSET OCD

In 1903, Pierre Janet reported the case of a 5-year-old boy presenting with "repetitive thoughts," similar to "mental tics" (Leonard & Rapoport, 1991). This is considered to be the first description of OCD in childhood. In his book *Obsessive Children*, Adams described 49 children with OC symptoms, highlighting the higher proportion of boys in his sample (39 boys and 10 girls; Adams, 1973). In 1965, Skoog reported that "obsessive neurosis" started earlier than most of the psychiatric problems. At least in his sample, 15.5% of the patients had had the onset of the OC symptoms before the age of 19. Among these, in 10% of the patients, the symptoms started before age 14 and for 6% of them the OC symptom onset was before age 10 (Skoog, 1965).

Until the 1980s, descriptions of OCD in children and adolescents were rare and limited by small sample sizes. It was only in 1989 that the NIMH published the first longitudinal study of OCD children and adolescents using specific diagnostic criteria defined by the DSM–III (American Psychological Association [APA], 1980). They interviewed 5596 students from eight different schools and found prevalence rates of 0.4% (Flament et al., 1989). The authors emphasized that the rates would probably be underestimated because some of the more severe cases could not be attending school or could be among the 557 students that did not return their questionnaires (Flament et al., 1989). Zohar et al. (1992) reported, in Israeli adolescents, a prevalence of 3.5% for OCD, including subclinical cases (Zohar et al., 1992). Valleni-Basilie et al. (1994) found even higher prevalence rates with 3% meeting criteria for OCD and 19% for the presence of OC symptoms. Another epidemiological study of the prevalence of self-reported OCD at age 18 including 930 individuals found a 1-year prevalence rate of 4% (Douglass, Moffitt, Dar, McGee, and Silva, 1995).

More recent studies of children and adolescents with OCD have also reported, compared to adults, higher prevalence of OCD in boys, higher comorbidity with tic disorders, and higher rates of both OCD and tics among their first-degree family members. For instance, Swedo, Rapoport, Leonard, Lenane, and Cheslow (1989) described that 20% of the initial NIMH sample developed tics, even though having tics was an exclusion criteria for participating in the study. The aforementioned clinical and epidemiological studies—which showed that OCD is, in fact, a common disorder affecting adults, adolescents, and children from different countries, independent of race, religion or socioeconomical status—changed the history of OCD. Some other heuristic changes in the history of OCD are presented in the following section.

DEVELOPMENT OF CLASSIFICATION MANUALS

Classification manuals were developed as an attempt to facilitate communication between clinicians and researchers, and also as a demand from insurance companies and mental health systems. Even though some manuals, such as the *Research Diagnostic Criteria* (RDC: Spitzer, Endicott, and Robbins, 1978) already existed, it was only in 1980, with the publication of the DSM–III (APA, 1980) that more precise meanings were introduced to terminology. The DSM–III proposed categorical diagnoses, divided in discrete mental disorders defined by observable criteria and with an atheoretical perspective to the validity of individual categories (Maser & Paterson, 2002). With its operational criteria, greater reliability in diagnosis was achieved and a significant number of studies on psychopathology were conducted. Therefore, whereas the DSM–III was based largely on consensus among experts, successive revisions had the benefit of an increasingly large empirical literature (Maser & Paterson, 2002).

The DSM–III and the newer versions, the DSM–III–R (APA, 1987), the DSM–IV (APA, 1994), and the DSM–IV–TR (APA, 2000) became the most widely used classification manuals. Even though the *International Classification of Diseases, 10th Edition,* (ICD–10), developed by the World Health Organization (WHO) is considered by physicians to be the official medical classification system in most countries, the *DSM–IV* (Andrews, Slade, & Peters, 1999) and the *DSM–IV–TR* are more popular among mental health professionals. This may be due to the influence of American psychiatry on specialized journals for research publication. The influence of the *DSM–III–R* has been so strong that even the WHO developed the ICD–10 based on the *DSM* system.

The classification of OCD is very similar across manuals. However, OCD is classified in the *DSM–IV–TR* as an anxiety disorder, whereas in ICD–10 it is a stand-alone disorder. For a definite OCD diagnosis, ICD–10 requires that obsessional symptoms or compulsive acts (or both) must be present on most days for at least 2 consecutive weeks and be a source of distress or interference with activities. The obsessional symptoms should have the following characteristics: (1) they must be recognized as the individual's own thoughts or impulses; (2) there must be at least one thought or act that is still resisted unsuccessfully, even though other symptoms may be present that the sufferer no longer resists; (3) the thought of carrying out the act must not in itself be pleasurable; and (4) the thoughts, images, or impulses must be unpleasantly repetitive (World Health Organization [WHO], 1992).

Both the *DSM–IV* and the *DSM–IV–TR* maintain that an individual must experience a significant disturbance in normal functioning, or engage in obsessive-compulsive activity for at least 1 hour per day, to be given a diagnosis of OCD. Further, the individual must recognize the irrationality of thoughts and behaviors; though this criterion is not required for children and adolescents (APA, 1994; 2000). A specification of poor insight may be added to the diagnosis of OCD when an individual does not recognize that the obsessions and compulsions are excessive or unreasonable (APA, 1994; 2000). The *DSM–IV* and the *DSM–IV–TR* also incorporated the definition of "mental rituals," now described as a compulsion. Contrary to the *DSM–III* (APA, 1980) and ICD–10 (WHO, 1992), the *DSM–IV* and the *DSM–IV–TR* do not require the exclusion of other axis-I diagnoses such as Tourette's syndrome, schizophrenia, and mood disorders to the diagnosis of OCD (Jenike et al., 1998). Additionally, in ICD–10 and previous *DSM* definitions, a diagnosis of OCD implied that the individual could generally recognize that his or her fears were irrational or unreasonable throughout the life of his or her disorder. It was only in the *DSM–IV* that a "poor insight" subtype was added in order to account for a number of individuals who appear to fail to accept the senselessness of their OC symptoms (Marazziti et al., 2002).

In summary, it is possible to say that the development of the *DSM* has been a landmark in psychiatry. Nevertheless, it has some shortcomings. For instance, they have to meet the needs not only of the clinical and research community but also the needs from insurance companies and welfare systems. This creates complexity that could limit the acceptance of some improvements in the classification of patients, such as the use of a dimensional perspective for diagnosis.

TREATMENT RESPONSE AND NEUROBIOLOGICAL FINDINGS

Another landmark in the history of OCD was the demonstration of efficacy of both behavior therapy and the serotonin re-uptake inhibitors in the treatment of OCD patients. These reports gave clues to the neurobiological pathways involved in the etiology of OCD. For instance, in 1966, Meyer reported the successful treatment of two OCD cases with behavioral therapy (Meyer, 1966). Since then, there have been numerous studies showing the efficacy of both behavior therapy and cognitive-behavioral therapy in adults (Cordioli et al., 2003; Foa et al., 2005; Marks, 1981) and also children and adolescents (Barrett, Healy, & March, 2003; Barrett, Healy-Farrell, & March, 2004; March et al., 2004; Piacentini, 1999) with OCD.

In 1967, intravenous clomipramine was reported to be successful in the treatment of 10 to 15 OCD cases (Thoren et al., 1980). The efficacy and specificity of serotoninergic antidepressants in the treatment of OC symptoms (Hollander, 1998; Pigott, Sheila, & Seay, 1999) and the evidence of abnormalities in platelet serotonin transporter (Sallee, Richman, Beach, Sethuraman, & Nesbitt, 1996) reinforced the hypothesis that serotoninergic pathways are implicated in the genesis of OC symptoms.

There is also a consistent body of information implicating specific cortico-basal ganglia circuits in OCD. The primary source of this data is neuroimaging studies, including functional neuroimaging studies. Baxter (1992) proposed an interesting theory suggesting that OC symptoms derive from dysfunction of the cerebral loops, originating, respectively, from the orbitofrontal cortex (OFC) and anterior cingulated cortices, projecting into the caudate nucleus and reaching the thalamic relay. More recent studies have reinforced this theory. Aouizerate et al. (2004) reported increased activity in the OFC bilaterally or in the right side, frequently associated with an increased functional activity in the bilateral anterior cingulated cortices, the bilateral or right head of the caudate nucleus and the bilateral or right thalamus. Provocation tests using fMRI found bilateral activation of the OFC, anterior cingulated cortices, caudate nucleus and amygdala (Breiter et al., 1996). Studies with magnetic resonance spectroscopy found decreased levels of the neuronal loss marker N-acetyl-aspartate in the cingulated gyrus, right or left striatum and left and right thalamus in patients with OCD (Aouizerate et al., 2004).

In the 1980s, clinical, genetic, treatment response, and neuroimaging studies have demonstrated the association between at least a subgroup of OCD patients and other childhood disorders, such as tic disorders and

Sydenham's chorea. This was a milestone in the history of OCD and was followed by two lines of research. One of them investigated the association between OCD and tics and the other one tried to explore the immunological hypothesis for OCD etiology.

The association between OCD and TS has been suggested since the original descriptions of Gilles de la Tourette in 1885 (Tourette, 1885), and has been reinforced by clinical (Miguel et al., 1997); genetic (Grados, Walkup, & Walford, 2003; Leckman et al., 2003; Paul, Alsobrook, Goodman, Rasmussen, & Leckman, 1995; Rosario-Campos et al., 2005); and treatment response studies (Diniz et al., 2004). Interestingly, the link between Sydenham's chorea and tics had been described in the 19th century (Kushner, 1998). Recently, environmental factors have been implicated in the genesis of OCD. In the past 10 years, a group of prepubertal children with abrupt onset of OCD and tics following infection by specific strains of ß-hemolytic streptococci has been identified (Swedo et al., 1997). The association between streptococcal infection and these neuropsychiatric disorders has been attributed to antibodies directed against invading bacteria that cross-react with basal ganglia structures and other findings involving immunological markers (Mercadante, 2001). Swedo and colleagues name this subgroup of neuropsychiatric disorders with the acronym PANDAS (Pediatric Autoimmune Neuropsychiatric Disorders Associated with Streptococcus; Swedo et al., 1998). The validity of PANDAS as an independent entity has been discussed. Although potentially promising for these highly selected patients, active immunomodulatory therapies require further validation by controlled double-blind protocols (Singer, 1999).

Regarding an evolutionary and ethologic perspective, contemporary research has been correlating a variety of ritualistic and grooming behaviors in animals with OCD and related disorders. Based on phenomenological aspects and pharmacological response, Rapoport, Ryland, and Kriete (1992) proposed that canine acral lick dermatitis could be an animal model of OCD. Furthermore, Leckman and Mayes (1994) considered some normal cognitive, affiliative, grooming, and reproductive behaviors mediated by oxytocin in rodents to contain elements that are similar to OC symptoms. Anecdotal data and a recently completed cerebrospinal fluid study provided evidence that some subtypes of OCD are related to oxitocin dysfunction. Based on these findings, Leckman and Mayes (1994) hypothesized that preoccupations and behaviors associated with early phases of romantic love and early parental love could be considered normal physiological behaviors bridging a continuum with OCD.

CONCLUSIONS

The literature has come a long way since the initial descriptions of OC symptoms as a punishment by the Greek gods or as evil influences on the patient's soul. Although the pathophysiology of OCD remains unknown, the advances in psychiatry and neuroscience have provided strong evidence for a neurobiological basis of the disorder. Some of these advances include more accurate epidemiological studies, the development of classification manuals and the improvement in technology used in genetic, neuroimaging, and treatment response studies.

Currently, OCD is viewed as a heterogeneous neuropsychiatric disorder, with different clinical presentations reflecting possible different subtypes. In the search for putative OCD genes, the more promising strategies have focused on early-onset OCD patients, OCD patients with tics, and also on specific OC symptom dimensions (Miguel et al., 2005; Rosario-Campos et al., 2005). Another strategy to differentiate the OCD phenotype has been the study of spectrum disorders associated with OCD.

Furthermore, it is important to note that even though research has evolved considerably since the early descriptions of OCD, it is clear that we will not be able to understand the mechanisms underlying OCD or to find genes and etiological factors if we rely only on technological tools. Based on the history of OCD, it is possible to optimize the power of the modern approaches, allowing us to more appropriately approach the current challenges. Similar to clinicians hundreds of years ago, we see value in observing patients in a very comprehensive and exhaustive manner. Although our technology has improved, we see the continuing importance of observing, listening and taking care of the ones who have the disease.

REFERENCES

Adams, P. L. (1973). *Obsessive children: A sociopsychiatric study*. New York: Brunner-Mazel.

American Psychiatric Association. (1980). *Diagnostic and statistical manual of mental disorders* (3rd ed.). Washington, DC: Author.

American Psychiatric Association. (1987). *Diagnostic and statistical manual of mental disorders* (3rd ed., text revision). Washington, DC: Author.

American Psychiatric Association. (1994). *Diagnostic and statistical manual of mental disorders* (4th ed.). Washington, DC: Author.

American Psychological Association. (2000). *Diagnostic and statistical manual of mental disorders* (4th ed., text revision). Washington, DC: Author.

Andrews, G., Slade, T., & Peters, L. (1999). Classification in psychiatry: ICD–10 versus DSM–IV. *British Journal of Psychiatry, 174*, 3–5.

Aouizerate, B., Guehl, D., Cuny, E., Rougier, A., Boulac, B., Tignol, J., et al. (2004). Pathophysiology of obsessive-compulsive disorder: A necessary link between phenomenology, neuropsychology, imagery and physiology. *Progress in Neurobiology, 72*, 195–221.

Barrett, P., Healy, L., & March, J. S. (2003). Behavioral avoidance test for childhood obsessive-compulsive disorder: A home-based observation. *American Journal of Psychotherapy, 57*, 80–100.

Barrett, P., Healy-Farrell, L., & March, J. S. (2004). Cognitive-behavioral family treatment of childhood obsessive-compulsive disorder: A controlled trial. *Journal of the American Academy of Child and Adolescent Psychiatry, 43*, 46–62.

Baxter, L. R. (1992, December). Neuroimaging studies of obsessive compulsive disorder. *Psychiatric Clinics of North America, 15*(4), 871–884.

Beard, G. M. (1869). *Sexual neurasthenia (nervous exhaustion). Its hygiene, causes, symptoms and treatment.* New York.

Bergener, M. (1987, May). Classical texts-newly read. Wilhelm Griesinger: Pathology and therapy of psychiatric disease, a pioneer in humane psychiatry. *Psychiatrische Praxis, 14*(3), 105–108.

Berrios, G. E. (1989). Obsessive-compulsive disorder: its conceptual history in France during the 19th century. *Comprehensive Psychiatry, 30,* 283–295.

Berrios, G. E. (1995). *Historia dos trastornos obsesivos* [History of obsessive disorders]. In J. V. Ruiloba, & G. E Berrios (Eds.), *Estados obsesivos* [Obsessive states] (2nd ed., pp. 3–13). Barcelona: Masson.

Breiter, H. C., Rauch, S. L., Kwong, K. K., Baker, J. R., Weisskoff, R. M., Kennedy, D. N., et al. (1996). Functional magnetic resonance imaging of symptom provocation in obsessive-compulsive disorder. *Archives of General Psychiatry, 53,* 663–674.

Cordioli, A. V., Heldt, E., Braga Bochi, D., Margis, R., Basso de Sousa, M., Fonseca Tonello, J. et al. (2003). Cognitive-behavioral group therapy in obsessive-compulsive disorder: A randomized clinical trial. *Psychotherapy and Psychosomatics, 72,* 211–216.

Dagonet, H. (1870). *Des impulsions dans la folie et de la folie impulsive* [Impulsive in madness and obsessive insanity]. *Annales Médico-Psychologique, 4,* 5–32, 215–259.

Del Porto, J. A. (1994). *Distúrbio obsessivo-compulsivo: fenomenologia clínica de 105 pacientes e estudo de aspectos trans-históricos e trans-culturais* [Obsessive-compulsive disorder: Clinical phenomenology of 105 patients] (pp. 3–46). São Paulo: Escola paulista de Medicina.

Diniz, J. B., Rosario-Campos, M. C., Shavitt, R. G., Curi, M., Hounie, A. G., Brotto, S. A., et al. (2004). Impact of age at onset and duration of illness on the expression of co-morbidities in obsessive-compulsive disorder. *Journal of Clinical Psychiatry, 65,* 22–27.

Douglass, H. M., Moffitt, T. E., Dar, R., McGee, R., & Silva, P. (1995). Obsessive-compulsive disorder in a birth cohort of 18-year-olds: Prevalence and predictors. *Journal of the American Academy of Child and Adolescent Psychiatry, 34,* 1424–1431.

Esquirol, J. E. D. (1838). *Des maladies mentales considérées dous les rapports médical, hygiénique et médicq-légal* [Mental illnesses considered by medical, hygenic and medico-legal aspects]. Paris: Ed. Balliere, Librarie de l'Académie de Médicine.

Flament, M. F., Whitaker, A., Rapoport, J. L., Davies, M., Berg, C. Z., Kalikow, K., et al. (1988). Obsessive compulsive disorder in adolescence: An epidemiological study. *Journal of the American Academy of Child and Adolescent Psychiatry, 27,* 764–771.

Foa, E. B., Liebowitz, M. R., Kozak, M. J., Davies, S., Campeas, R., Franklin, M. E., et al. (2005). Randomized, placebo-controlled trial of exposure and ritual prevention, clomipramine, and their combination in the treatment of obsessive-compulsive disorder. *American Journal of Psychiatry, 162,* 151–161.

Freud, S. (1895/1976). *Obsess-es e fobias. Seu mecanismo psíquico e sua etiologia. The Brazilian standard edition of the complete psychological works of Sigmund Freud* (Vol. 3). Rio de Janeiro: Imago ed.

Freud, S. (1896/1976). *Novos comentários sobre as neuropsicoses de defesa* [Further remarks on the neuro-psychoses of defense]. *The Brazilian standard edition of the complete psychological works of Sigmund Freud* (Vol. 3, pp. 83–85). Rio de Janeiro: Imago ed.

Freud, S. (1909/1976). *Notas sobre um caso de neurose obsessiva. The Brazilian standard edition of the complete psychological works of Sigmund Freud* (Vol 10). Rio de Janeiro: Imago ed.

Freud, S. (1913/1976) *Totem e Tabu* [Totem and taboo]. *The Brazilian standard edition of the complete psychological works of Sigmund Freud* (Vol. 8). Rio de Janeiro: Imago ed.

Freud, S. (1926/1976). *Inibições, Sintomas e Ansiedade* [Inhibitions, symptoms and anxiety]. *The Brazilian standard edition of the complete psychological works of Sigmund Freud* (Vol. 20, pp. 134–146). Rio de Janeiro: Imago ed.

Grados, M. A., Walkup, J., & Walford, S. (2003). Genetics of obsessive-compulsive disorders: New findings and challenges. *Brain Development, 25*(S1), 55–61.

Hollander, E. (1998). Treatment of obsessive-compulsive spectrum disorders with SSRIs. *British Journal of Psychiatry, 173*(S35), 7–12.

Janet, P. (1903). *Les obsessions et la psychasthenie*. Paris: Alcan.

Jenike, M. A., Baer, L., & Minichiello, W. E. (1998). An Overview of obsessive compulsive disorder. In M. A. Jenike, L. Baer, & W. E. Minichiello (Eds), *Obsessive-compulsive disorders—Practical management* (3rd ed., pp. 3–11). New York: Mosby.

Karno, M., & Golding, J. M. (1991). Obsessive compulsive disorder. In L. N. Robins, & D. A. Regier (Eds.), *Psychiatric disorders in America. The epidemiologic catchment area study* (pp. 204–209). New York: The Free Press.

Kessler, R. C., Berglund, P., Demler, O., Jin, R., Merikangas, K. R., & Walters, E. E. (2005). Lifetime prevalence and age-of-onset distributions of DSM–IV disorders in the National Comorbidity Survey Replication. *Archives of General Psychiatry, 62,* 593–602.

Kramer, H., & Sprenger, J. (1486/1991). *Malleus maleficarum*. São Paulo: Ed. Rosa dos Ventos.

Krochmalik, A., & Menzies, R. G. (2003). The classification and diagnosis of obsessive-compulsive disorder. In R. G. Menzies & P. de Silva (Eds), *Obsessive-compulsive disorder: Theory, research and treatment* (pp. 4–20). West Sussex, UK: Wiley.

Kushner, H. I. (1998). Freud and the diagnosis of Gilles de la Tourette's illness. *History of Psychiatry, 9,* 1–25.

Laplanche, J., & Pontallis, I. (2001). *Vocabulário de Psicanálise* [The language of psycho-analysis] (4th ed., pp. 185–186, 295–315, 394–415). São Paulo: Martins Fontes.

Leckman, J. F., & Mayes, L. C. (1999). Preoccupations and behaviors associated with romantic and parental love. Perspectives on the origin of obsessive-compulsive disorder. *Child and Adolescent Psychiatric Clinics of North America, 8,* 635–665.

Leckman, J. F., Goodman, W. K., North, W. G., Chappell, P. B., Price, L. H., Pauls, D. L., et al. (1994). The role of central oxytocin in obsessive compulsive disorder and related normal behavior. *Psychoneuroendocrinology, 19,* 723.

Leckman, J. F., Pauls, D. L., Zhang, H., Rosario-Campos, M. C., Katsovich, L., Kidd, K. K., et al. (2003). Obsessive-compulsive symptom dimensions in affected sibling pairs diagnosed with Gilles de la Tourette syndrome. *American Journal of Medical Genetics: Part B Neuropsychiatric Genetics, 116,* 60–68.

Legrand du Saulle, H. (1875). *La folie du doute (avec délire du toucher)* [Double insanity]. Paris, France: Adrien Delahaye.

Leonard, H. L., & Rapoport, J. L. (1991). Obsessive-compulsive disorder. In J. M. Wiener, & M. K. Dulcan (Eds.), *Textbook of child and adolescent psychiatry* (pp. 323–329). Arlington, VA: American Psychiatric Publishing Inc.

Loyola, I. (1991). *Autobiografia* [Autobiography] (pp. 32–38). São Paulo: Ed. Loyola. (Original work published 1553)

Magnan, V. (1893). Des héréditaires dégénérés [Hereditary insanities]. In *Recherches sur les centres nerveux* [Research in the nervous system] (2nd ed., pp. 109–426). Paris, France: Masson-Press.

Marazziti, D., Dell'Osso, L., Di Nasso, E., Pfanner, C., Presta, S., Mungai, F., et al. (2002). Insight in obsessive-compulsive disorder: A study of an Italian sample. *European Psychiatry, 17,* 407–410.

March, J. S., Foa, E. B., Gammon, P., Chrisman, A., Curry, J., Fitzgerald, D., et al. (2004). Cognitive-behavior therapy, sertraline, and their combination for children and adolescents with obsessive-compulsive disorder: The Pediatric OCD Treatment Study (POTS) randomized controlled trial. *Journal of the American Medical Association, 292,* 1969–1976.

Marks, I. M. (1981). Review of behavioral psychotherapy. I: Obsessive-compulsive disorders. *American Journal of Psychiatry, 138,* 584–592.

Maser, J. D., & Patterson, T. (2002). Spectrum and nosology: Implications for DSM–V. *Psychiatric Clinics of North American, 25,* 855–885.

Mercadante, M. T. (2001). *Transtorno obsessivo-compulsivo: Aspectos neuroimunológicos* [Neurobiological findings in obsessive-compulsive disorder]. *Revista Brasileira de Psiquiatria, 23*(S2), 31–34.

Meyer, V. (1966). Modifications of expectations in cases of obsessional rituals. *Behaviour Research and Therapy, 4,* 273–280.

Miguel, E. C., Baer, L., Coffey, B. J., Rauch, S. L., Savage, C. R., O'Sullivan, R. L., et al. (1997). Phenomenological differences appearing with repetitive behaviours in obsessive-compulsive disorder and Gilles de la Tourette's syndrome. *British Journal of Psychiatry, 170,* 140–145.

Miguel, E. C., Leckman, J. F., Rauch, S., Rosario-Campos, M. C., Hounie, A. G., Mercadante, M. T., et al. (2005). Obsessive-compulsive disorder phenotypes: Implications for genetic studies. *Molecular Psychiatry, 10,* 258–275.

Mora, G. (1969). The scrupulosity syndrome. *International Journal of Clinical Psychology, 5,* 163–174.

Morel, B. A. (1866). *Du délire emotif. Névrose du systéme nerveux ganglionaire viscéral* [The emotional delusion. Neurosis of the visceral ganglionar nervous system]. *Archives Génefor a les de Médecine,* 385–402, 530–551.

Pauls, D. L., Alsobrook, J. P., Goodman, W., Rasmussen, S., & Leckman, J. F. (1995). A family study of obsessive-compulsive disorder. *American Journal of Psychiatry, 152,* 76–84.

Piacentini, J. (1999). Cognitive behavioral therapy of childhood OCD. *Child and Adolescent Psychiatric Clinics of North America, 8,* 599–616.

Pigott, T. A., Sheila, M., & Seay, S. M. (1999). A Review of the efficacy of selective serotonin reuptake inhibitors in obsessive-compulsive disorder. *Journal of Clinical Psychiatry, 60,* 101–106.

Pitman, R. K. (1987). Pierre Janet on obsessive-compulsive disorder: Review and commentary. *Archives of General Psychiatry, 44,* 226–232.

Rachman, S. G., & Hodgson, R. J. (1980). *Obsessions and compulsions.* Englewood Cliffs, NJ: Prentice Hall.

Rapoport, J. L., Ryland, D. H., & Kriete, M. (1992). Drug treatment of canine acral lick. An animal model of obsessive-compulsive disorder. *Archives of General Psychiatry, 49,* 517–521.

Rosario-Campos, M. C., Leckman, J. F., Mercadante, M. T., Shavitt, R. G., & Prado, H. S. (2001, November). Adults with early-onset obsessive-compulsive disorder. *The American Journal of Psychiatry, 158*(11), 1899–1903.

Rosario-Campos, M. C., Leckman, J. F., Curi, M., Quatrano, S., Katsovitch, L., Miguel, E. C., et al. (2005). A family study of early-onset obsessive-compulsive disorder. *American Journal of Medical Genetics: Part B, Neuropsychiatric Genetics, 136,* 92–97.

Sallee, F. R., Richman, H., Beach, K., Sethuraman, G., & Nesbitt, L. (1996). Platelet serotonin transporter in children and adolescents with obsessive-compulsive disorder or Tourette's syndrome. *Journal of the American Academy of Child and Adolescent Psychiatry, 35,* 1647–1656.

Salzman, L., & Thaler, F. (1981). Obsessive-compulsive disorder: A review of the literature. *American Journal of Psychiatry, 138,* 286–296.

Shapiro, A. K., Shapiro, E., Young, J. G., & Feinberg, T. E. (1988). *Gilles de la Tourette Syndrome.* New York: The Raven Press.

Singer, H. S. (1999). PANDAS and immunomodulatory therapy. *Lancet, 354,* 1137–1138.

Skoog, G. (1965). Onset of anancastic conditions. *Acta Psychiatrica Scandinavica, 41*(S184), 1–84.

Spitzer, R. L., Endicott, J., & Robins, E. (1978). Research diagnostic criteria: Rationale and reliability. *Archives of General Psychiatry, 35,* 773–782.

Stein, D. J., & Hollander, E. (1995). Obsessive-compulsive spectrum disorders. *Journal of Clinical Psychiatry, 56,* 265–266.

Swedo S. E., Leonard, H. L., Mittleman, B. B., Allen, A. J., Rapoport, J. L., Dow, S. P., et al. (1997). Identification of children with pediatric autoimmune neuropsychiatric disorders associated with streptococcal infections by a marker associated with rheumatic fever. *American Journal of Psychiatry, 154,* 110–112.

Swedo, S. E., Leonard, L. H., Garvey, M., Mittleman, B. B., Allen, A. J., Perlmutter, S., et al. (1998). Pediatric autoimmune neuropsychiatric disorders associated with streptococcal infections: Clinical description of the first 50 cases. *American Journal of Psychiatry, 155,* 264–271.

Swedo, S. E., Rapoport, J. L., Leonard, H., Lenane, M., & Cheslow, D. (1989). Obsessive-compulsive disorder in children and adolescents. Clinical phenomenology of 70 consecutive cases. *Archives of General Psychiatry, 46,* 335–341.

Thoren, P., Asberg, M., Bertilsson, L., Mellstrom, B., Sjoqvist, F., & Traskman, L. (1980). Clomipramine treatment of obsessive-compulsive disorder. II. Biochemical aspects. *Archives of General Psychiatry, 37,* 1289–1294.

Tourette, G. (1885). Étude sur une affection nerveuse caractérisé par de L'Incoordination motrice accompagnée d'echolalie et de coprolalie [Study of a neurosis characterized by motor abnormalities with echolalia and coprolalie]. *Archives of General Neurology, 9*(19), 158.

Valleni-Basile, L. A., Garrison, C. Z., Jackson, K. L., Waller, J. L., McKeown, R. E., Addy, C. L., et al. (1994). Frequency of obsessive-compulsive disorder in a community sample of young adolescents. *Journal of the American Academy of Child and Adolescent Psychiatry, 33,* 782–791.

Westphal, K. (1878). Uber zwangsvorstellungen [Compelled ideas]. *Arch psychiatr nervenkrank, 8,* 734–750.

World Health Organization. (1992). *Classification of Mental and Behavioral Disorders, Tenth Edition (ICD–10).* Geneva: World Health.

Zohar, A. H., Ratzoni, G., Pauls, D. L., Apter, A., Bleich, A., Kron, S., et al. (1992). An epidemiological study of obsessive-compulsive disorder and related disorders in Israeli adolescents. *Journal of the American Academy of Child and Adolescent Psychiatry, 31,* 1057–1061.

2

Obsessive-Compulsive Disorder in Children and Adolescents: Diagnosis, Comorbidity, and Developmental Factors

Phoebe S. Moore
Amy Mariaskin
John March
Duke University

Martin E. Franklin
University of Pennsylvania School of Medicine

Obsessive-compulsive disorder (OCD) is a prevalent, distressing, and functionally impairing anxiety disorder of childhood. By late adolescence, the lifetime prevalence of childhood OCD is estimated to fall between 2% and 3% (Rapoport et al., 2000), while point prevalence estimates indicate that, at any given moment, between ½% and 1% of children suffer from OCD (Flament et al., 1988). The disorder is highly disruptive to the normal developmental trajectory, causing impairment in school performance, friendships, family relationships, and vocational functioning (Adams, Waas, March, & Smith, 1994; Piacentini, Bergman, Keller, & McCracken, 2003). In many to most cases, symptoms wax and wane through adolescence and into adulthood, indicating a need for early intervention (Stewart et al., 2004).

Despite the relatively high prevalence rates, detection and diagnosis in the community is surprisingly low (Fireman, Koran, Leventhal, & Jacobson, 2001; Heyman et al., 2001). Thus, educating clinicians about diagnosis, common developmental variations, correlates, and comorbidities is essential to prevent developmental derailment and long-term negative outcomes for youngsters with OCD. This chapter reviews the epidemiology and phenomenology of pediatric OCD, with special attention to comorbid conditions commonly occurring in the context of OCD. It also addresses the need for a developmental model of pediatric OCD and reviews psychosocial factors that may relate to etiology and course of the disorder through childhood and into adulthood. In order to illustrate some of the complexities involved in evaluating pediatric OCD, we include a hypothetical case example.

DIAGNOSIS

As described in the fourth edition, text revision of the *Diagnostic and Statistical Manual of Mental Disorders* (*DSM–IV–TR*), OCD is characterized by recurrent obsessions and/or compulsions that cause marked distress and/or interference in one's life (American Psychiatric Association [APA], 2000). To merit a diagnosis of OCD, an affected youngster must have either obsessions or compulsions, although the great majority has both (Storch et al., 2004). Obsessions are recurrent and persistent thoughts, images, or impulses that are typically ego-dystonic, intrusive, and, for the most part, are acknowledged as senseless. Obsessions are generally accompanied by negative affects, such as fear, disgust, doubt, or a feeling of incompleteness, and so are distressing to the affected individual. Like adults, young persons with OCD typically attempt to ignore, suppress, or neutralize obsessive thoughts and associated feelings by performing compulsions, which are repetitive, purposeful behaviors performed in response to an obsession, often according to certain rules or in a stereotyped fashion. Compulsions, which can be observable repetitive behaviors, such as washing, or covert mental acts, such as counting, exist at least in part because they serve to neutralize or alleviate obsessions and accompanying distress in the short run.

Because there are many normal OC-like behaviors, *DSM–IV–TR* specifies that OCD symptoms be distressing, time-consuming (more than 1 hour a day), or significantly interfere with school, social activities, or important relationships. *DSM–IV–TR* also specifies that affected individuals recognize at some point in the illness that obsessions originate within the mind and are not simply excessive worries about real problems; similarly, compulsions must be seen as excessive or unreasonable. Persons of all ages who lack insight receive the designation: "poor insight type." Although most children and adolescents do recognize the senselessness of OCD, the requirement that insight be preserved is waived for children. This adaptation is based in the finding that children and adolescents see OCD symptoms as reasonable more frequently than do adults (Geller et al., 2001).

Finally, to be clear about the origin of the symptoms, the DSM–IV also requires that the specific content of the obsessions cannot be related to another Axis I diagnosis, such as thoughts about food resulting from an eating disorder, guilty thoughts (ruminations) originating with depression, or delusional thought content related to psychosis.

EPIDEMIOLOGY

As with adults, OCD is substantially more common in children and adolescents than once thought, with a 6-month prevalence of clinically significant OCD in approximately 1 in 200 children and adolescents (Flament et al., 1988; Rutter, Tizard, & Whitmore, 1970), although some think that the prevalence is somewhat higher (Douglass, Moffitt, Dar, & McGee, 1995; Valleni-Basile et al., 1996). Prevalence estimates in childhood are slightly lower than those in adulthood, which range from 0.4% to 3.5% in national and international epidemiological samples (Angst et al., 2004; Horwath & Weissman, 2000). Among adults with OCD, one third to one half develop the disorder during childhood (Rasmussen & Eisen, 1990), implying that the childhood-onset form of OCD foreshadows considerable adult morbidity.

Unfortunately, children and adolescents with the disorder often go unrecognized. In Flament's epidemiological survey, only 4 of the 18 children found to have OCD were under professional care (Flament et al., 1988). Not one of the 18 had been correctly identified as suffering from OCD, including the 4 children in mental health treatment. Fireman et al. (2001), using outpatient diagnostic data on more than 1.7 million subscribers (over age 6) to look at prevalence rates for OCD, found a 1-year prevalence of only 0.084%, suggesting that OCD in both pediatric and adult populations is under-recognized and undertreated in clinical care. An epidemiological study in the United Kingdom found that the great majority (88%) of the children they identified with OCD were neither detected as OCD nor treated (Heyman et al., 2001). These data lend support to Jenike's characterization of OCD as a "hidden epidemic" (Jenike, 1989, p. 539). Reasons that have been advanced for the underdiagnosis and undertreatment of OCD in children and adolescents include OCD-specific factors (secretiveness and lack of insight), health care provider factors (such as incorrect diagnosis and either lack of familiarity with or unwillingness to use proven treatments), and general factors (such as lack of access to treatment resources).

In a clinical sample, the modal age of onset of OCD was 7 years and the mean age at onset was 10 years in clinical samples (Swedo, Rapoport, Leonard, Lenane, & Cheslow, 1989). Boys appear more likely to have a prepubertal onset, whereas girls are more likely to have OCD start during adolescence (Tukel et al., 2005). In the Flament et al. (1988) epidemiological study, the ratio of males to females was 1:1, implying (1) that the male:female ratio equalizes in adolescence, or (2) that there is an ascertainment bias in the clinical samples, or both. For unclear reasons, OCD is more common in Caucasian than African-American children in clinical samples, although epidemiological data in adults suggest no differences in prevalence as a function of ethnicity or geographic region (Rasmussen, 1994). It is possible that this discrepancy between clinical and epidemiological samples is based in difficulty with recruiting minority families into child mental health treatment centers.

PHENOMENOLOGY

Common obsessions and compulsions seen in pediatric OCD are presented in Table 2.1. In the pediatric population, the most common obsessions are fear of contamination, harm to self, harm to a familiar person, and symmetry/exactness urges. Corresponding compulsions in children are washing and cleaning, followed by checking, counting, repeating, touching, and straightening (Swedo et al., 1989). Another study found elevations of hoarding compulsions in children and adolescents (Geller et al., 2001). In almost every case, these symptoms can be driven by one or more negative affects, including fear, doubt, disgust, rudimentary urges, and "just so" feelings, which some have labeled sensory incompleteness (Goodman, Rasmussen, Foa, & Price, 1994). For example, washing rituals may be a reaction to contamination fears or a response to feeling "sticky." The former is cognitive-phobic in origin; the latter may occur in response to a sensorimotor dysesthesia or without an obvious trigger. Whatever their origin, most children experience washing and checking rituals at some time during the course of the illness.

OCD symptoms frequently change over time, often with no clear progression pattern. Many if not most children have more than one OCD symptom at any one time, and many will have experienced almost all the classic OCD symptoms by the end of adolescence (Rettew, Swedo, Leonard, Lenane, &

TABLE 2.1
Common OCD Symptoms in Children and Adolescents

Common Obsessions	*Common Compulsions*
Contamination	Washing
Harm to self or others	Repeating
Aggressive themes	Checking
Sexual ideas / urges	Touching
Scrupulosity / religiosity	Counting
Symmetry urges	Ordering / arranging
Need to tell, ask, confess	Hoarding
	Praying

Rapoport, 1992). Those with only obsessions or compulsions are very rare (Swedo et al., 1989). This is especially so now that *DSM–IV* makes a clear distinction between obsessions and mental rituals, thereby reducing the number of patients misclassified as pure obsessionals but who, in fact, have mental rituals. Examples of mental rituals are prayers, counting, and "do-overs" of harm obsessions in which the harm is "undone."

A clinically useful detailed symptom checklist accompanies the Children's Yale-Brown Obsessive Compulsive Scale (CY-BOCS; Scahill et al., 1997), and should be a regular part of the initial assessment and maintenance care of every patient with OCD (see the following section).

NATURAL HISTORY

The main concern with early-onset OCD is its deleterious effect on the child's developmental trajectory. OCD can interfere severely with role functioning, affecting everything from academics to friendships to family relationships. Left untreated, OCD not only tends to persist but is linked to the development of other psychiatric disorders. For example, young boys with OCD and no tics are at clear risk for later development of tic disorders (Leonard, Lenane, Swedo, Rettew, & Cheslow, 1992). Thus, in addition to the risk of OCD symptoms persisting into adulthood and causing impairment, pediatric OCD can severely divert the course of normal development, leading to long-term deficits across many areas of functioning.

Before the arrival of modern pharmacotherapy and cognitive-behavior therapy, the outcome of treatment was dismal. Currently, although OCD often remains a chronic mental illness in adult (Rasmussen & Eisen, 1990) and pediatric patients (Leonard et al., 1993), most patients achieve meaningful symptom relief with well-delivered, comprehensive treatment. The recent publication of findings from the first randomized, controlled clinical trial comparing medication (sertraline, a selective serotonin reuptake inhibitor) to cognitive-behavior therapy in a pediatric population showed excellent effects of both modalities, with an especially good outcome for patients who received both treatments (Pediatric OCD Treatment Study Team [POTS], 2004). Therefore, children and adolescents who receive treatment can expect meaningful improvement that can substantially and positively impact the developmental trajectory.

Successful treatment by definition interrupts, even if only temporarily, the natural history of OCD. Though the relative merits of pharmacotherapy and CBT have not been fully resolved, CBT seems the more durable treatment (Barrett, Farrell, Dadds, & Boulter, 2005; Franklin, Tolin, March, & Foa, 2001; March & Mulle, 1995; March, Mulle, & Herbel, 1994). Because relapse commonly follows medication discontinuation (Leonard et al., 1991), adding CBT may limit relapse when medications are discontinued (March, Mulle, & Herbel, 1994; Sallinen, Nangle, & O'Grady, 2004).

DEVELOPMENTAL CONSIDERATIONS

In recent years, many studies have been published concentrating on the phenomenology, concomitants, and treatment outcomes for children with OCD. However, the very task of identifying the disorder in children presents a number of challenges for clinicians as ritualistic and superstitious behavior is normative to some extent in early childhood (Leonard, Goldberger, Rapoport, Cheslow, & Swedo, 1990; Snider & Swedo, 2000; Zohar & Felz, 2001). These behaviors, which bear a superficial resemblance to true obsessive-compulsive symptoms, seem to peak between the ages of 2 and 5, though they may be present in varying degrees throughout childhood and adolescence (Evans et al., 1997). Given that identifying continuities and discontinuities between normal and abnormal development is essential in applying a developmental psychopathology framework to disorder (Rutter & Sroufe, 2000), it behooves researchers to understand the differences between those behaviors that are normative and those that indicate risk for future disorder.

The current *DSM–IV–TR* (American Psychiatric Association [APA], 2000) does not list separate criteria for OCD as it manifests in children. Although there is no unique entry for pediatric OCD, the manual does contain a caveat stating that children need not realize that their compulsions are irrational. Recognizing pediatric OCD as a distinct disorder entity, with unique risk factors, symptom profiles, and prognoses, is imperative in terms of guiding future research programs. In addition, the recognition of commonly co-occurring disorders is an important step toward integrating these comorbidities into treatment protocols.

In fact, a number of distinct correlates and manifestations appear to distinguish pediatric OCD from the disorder as it appears in adulthood. For example, pediatric samples tend to be marked by a male preponderance, whereas in adult samples the reported sex ratios either show a slight overrepresentation of females or a roughly equal rate of occurrence (Geller et al., 2001; Jaisoorya, Reddy, & Srinath, 2003; Riddle et al., 1990; Swedo et al., 1989). Childhood-onset OCD may also have a greater risk associated with heritability, as relatives of child probands display higher rates of disorder than do those of adults who develop the disorder (Lenane et al., 1990; Nestadt et al., 2000; Pauls, Alsobrook, Goodman, Rasmussen, & Leckman, 1995). This finding, though consistent and compelling, may also be related to proposed connections between the development of childhood-onset OCD and characteristics of the family environment (Barrett, Shortt, & Healy, 2002; Carter & Pollock, 2000; Waters & Barrett, 2000).

Developmental differences in the phenomenology of the disorder have been found as well. As just noted, harm obsessions and hoarding compulsions are more common in children and adolescents with the disorder than in their adult counterparts (Geller et al., 2001). Conversely, sexual obsessions are less common in the younger age groups than in the adult patients. In addition, comorbidity presents differently for children with OCD and adults with the adult-onset type of the disorder, with children experiencing more concomitant ADHD and tics (see the following section).

Additionally, because many children lack insight about their obsessions and compulsions and may attribute a "magical" quality to them, there is variability in the extent to which a child feels that his or her behavior is inappropriate (Snider & Swedo, 2000). Although the research shows that children with OCD do show reduced insight (Geller et al., 2001), the issue may be a bit more complex. This pattern of findings may, at least in part, represent an artifact of (1) difficulty maintaining insight during acute "attacks" of OCD, or (2) confounding of insight and secretiveness due to fear of punishment or simple embarrassment. Careful, developmentally appropriate assessment of the child's level of insight is important to good clinical formulation.

ASSESSMENT OF PEDIATRIC OCD

An adequate assessment of pediatric OCD should include a comprehensive evaluation of current and past OCD symptoms, current OCD symptom severity and associated functional impairment, and a survey of comorbid psychopathology. In addition, the strengths of the child and family should be evaluated, as well as their knowledge of OCD and its treatment. There are many self-report and clinician-administered instruments that can be used to guide this type of assessment. A complete discussion of the psychometric properties of these measures is located in chapter 4 of this text. A useful clinical approach is to mail several relevant self-report questionnaires for the family to complete prior to the intake visit, then review these materials prior to meeting with the child. If it is apparent from these materials that comorbid depression or other anxiety problems besides OCD are prominent, a focus on these symptoms in addition to OCD is indicated in the intake.

For surveying history of OCD symptoms and current symptom severity, the standard is the Children's Yale-Brown Obsessive Compulsive Scale checklist and severity scale (CY-BOCS; Scahill et al., 1997). Before administering this scale, it is important to determine whether the child should be interviewed with or without the parent present. In the Pediatric OCD Treatment Study (POTS; Pediatric OCD Treatment Study Team, 2004), a conjoint interview format was used, directing questions to the child but soliciting parental feedback as well. In nonresearch settings there is more flexibility, and the decision to interview the child alone or with a parent present can be made by discussing these choices with the parent in advance, observing the child and family's behavior in the waiting area, and even during the interview if necessary. For example, if it becomes clear that a patient is reluctant to discuss certain symptoms with a parent present (e.g., sexual obsessions), the therapist can skip that item on the CY-BOCS checklist and save some time at the end of the interview to revisit these potentially sensitive issues alone with the patient. The key focus of the clinical application of the CY-BOCS is to obtain all relevant information in the most valid way possible, Therefore, whether to include a parent is a clinical decision based on whether the evaluator thinks that the parental presence will enhance or decrease validity of assessment.

Prior to administering the CY-BOCS, the therapist should explain the concepts of obsessions and compulsions, using examples if the child and/or parent have difficulty grasping the concepts. This discussion represents a good opportunity to tell children and adolescents about the prevalence, nature, and treatment of OCD, which may increase their willingness to disclose their specific symptoms. Children may be particularly vulnerable to feeling as if they are the only ones on Earth with obsessive fears of hurting a loved one, so prefacing the examples with, "I once met a kid who …" may dispel this myth and minimize the accompanying sense of isolation. During the intake, it is also important to observe the child's behavior and inquire if certain behaviors (e.g., unusual movements, vocalizations) are compulsions designed to neutralize obsessions or to reduce distress. Tic disorders are commonly comorbid with OCD, and it is important to try to make a differential diagnosis as compulsions and tics may be targeted by different treatment procedures. Further, as mentioned earlier, some children who are aware of their obsessional content may be fearful of saying the fears aloud. Surveying common obsessions with a checklist instead of asking the child to disclose the fears tends to help with this problem, as does encouragement on the part of the therapist (e.g., "Lots of the kids I see have a hard time talking about these kinds of fears"). In general, allowing flexibility in terms of how the child discusses or discloses his obsessions can be very helpful. Thus, for example, the child can be encouraged to write down the fears, or nod their heads as the therapist describes examples of similar fears in order to help the child share their OCD problems. In this way, it is conveyed to the child and family that the difficulty associated with disclosure is understood and that there is empathy available from the clinician. It can also be useful use examples from children that the therapist had evaluated in the past (e.g., "I remember a few months ago when a kid about your age told me she would be scared to touch her dog for fear she might lose control and hurt him"), although it is important to let the children and families know that the therapist is careful not to violate confidentiality when citing such examples.

Although the CY-BOCS usually represents the heart of the assessment, and is generally the tool used to gauge progress in treatment, it is also important to assess for commonly comorbid conditions. One excellent tool is the Anxiety Disorders Interview Schedule—Child and Parent Report versions (Silverman & Albano, 1996) and the Yale Global Tic Severity Scale (Leckman et al., 1989), which can be used to gain a comprehensive picture of the child's clinical status. Common comorbid conditions, reviewed in the next section, may affect treatment outcome and should be carefully considered in the treatment plan.

COMORBIDITY

Childhood OCD is associated with a number of comorbid conditions, including tic disorders, ADHD, other anxiety disorders, and mood disorders. Studies have consistently documented that the majority of children with OCD will also receive another lifetime psychiatric diagnosis (Flament et al., 1990; Geller, Biederman, Griffin, Jones, & Lefkowitz, 1996; Geller et al., 2001). Differential diagnosis between OCD and other psychiatric illnesses can be difficult as the disorder shares some features with other disorders (March, Franklin, Leonard, & Foa, 2004). For example, care must be taken to ensure that the attention problems resultant from preoccupation with obsessions and compulsions is not labeled as ADHD without a thorough diagnostic evaluation. In addition to psychiatric diagnoses, children with OCD are at risk of developing secondary physical problems associated with their illness, such as eczema from repeated washing, lesions from skin-picking, and enuresis and encopresis from refusal to void bodily waste (Snider & Swedo, 2000).

Despite the many studies documenting comorbid disorders associated with pediatric OCD, few have examined contemporaneous disorders within the context of prospective designs. Therefore, although much is known about psychopathology that co-varies with childhood-onset OCD, the specific sequence of these disorders is poorly understood. Uncovering common chronological patterns in the appearance of different disorders would help to elucidate shared etiologies and would potentially increase predictive power. In the following section, we review the current knowledge base on comorbidity in pediatric OCD.

Tic Disorders and Tourette's Syndrome

Tic disorder and Tourette's disorder are the most often cited comorbid psychiatric illnesses for OCD as it presents in children. Comorbidity rates for this type of disorder may be as high as 80% in childhood-onset cases of OCD (Leonard et al., 1992). Some researchers have even proposed that, because the rate of co-occurring OCD and tics is so high in children, childhood-onset OCD may be a tic-related subtype of the disorder, distinct from adult-onset due to this connection (Eichstedt & Arnold, 2001). Studies have demonstrated that familial rates of OCD are elevated for probands with Tourette's disorder, suggesting that the two may have a common genetic component that interacts with other factors to determine phenotypic expression, as one disorder or the other (Pauls et al., 1995). In one study, males younger than 15 years were much more likely to display comorbid tics than older boys or girls in the sample (Becker, Jennen-Steinmetz, Holtmann,

El-Faddagh, & Schmidt, 2003), supporting previous evidence that tic-related OCD is marked by a preponderance of males (Leckman et al., 1995). All of these findings point to a very close relationship between the two disorders that is, as yet, poorly understood.

In one prospective longitudinal study examining the development of OCD, Peterson and colleagues found that certain temporal patterns emerged between the development of obsessive-compulsive symptoms and the development of tic disorders (Peterson, Pine, Cohen, & Brook, 2001). A large sample of more than 700 children was followed from childhood through adolescence and into adulthood. Prevalence rates of psychiatric disorder were ascertained at four time-points over a period of 15 years: one in childhood, two in adolescence, and one in early adulthood. Results indicated that the presence of tics in childhood and early adolescence predicted an increase in obsessive-compulsive symptoms in late adolescence and adulthood, a finding that has been noted by other researchers (Leckman & Cohen, 1999). Furthermore, young adolescents with both OCD and tics were more likely than those with tics alone to experience a persistence of tics into adulthood.

Other Anxiety Disorders

Estimates vary, but the prevalence rate of other anxiety disorders in children with OCD may be as high as 50%–60% (Geller et al., 2001; Zohar, 1999). Geller and colleagues (1996) found that overanxious disorder (now classified in DSM–IV–TR as "generalized anxiety disorder") and separation anxiety disorder were the most common comorbid anxiety disorders. Rasmussen and Eisen (1990) found that these disorders tended to precede the appearance of obsessive-compulsive symptoms. It is not yet clear whether anxiety disorders are risk factors for OCD per se, or whether the expression of anxiety disorders is connected to a common etiological mechanism that gives rise to both OCD and its comorbid correlates. Temporal connections between the onset of OCD and the onset of anxiety disorders have been noted, such that children with an earlier diagnosis of a comorbid anxiety disorder had a later onset of OCD than those children without such a history (Hanna, 1995). Social phobia has been observed in subjects with OCD, though the reported rates at which it covaries with OCD have ranged from 2–25%, depending on the age group of the participants studied (Diniz et al, 2004; Geller et al. 2001). A longer duration of OCD was positively related to the appearance of social phobia in one sample, a relationship that is in accordance with the shame, secrecy, and functional impairment commonly experienced by children with OCD (Diniz et al., 2004).

Mood Disorders

The concordance of depression and pediatric OCD has been well demonstrated in multiple research programs (Douglass et al., 1995; Hanna, 1995;

Peterson et al, 2001; Swedo et al., 1989). In one study, children and adolescents with OCD were compared to three other groups: a group of healthy controls, a group of children with conduct disorder, and a group of children with anxiety disorders other than OCD. At age 11 years, the OCD group exhibited a higher level of depressive symptoms than the healthy controls and at ages 15 and 18 years, the OCD group was more depressed than any of the others (Douglass et al., 1995). Data from this study also suggest that depression in early adolescence is a possible predictor of risk for developing OCD in young adulthood. Comorbidity rates of major depressive disorder in clinical samples range from 10% to 26% (Hanna, 1995; Swedo et al., 1989). This prevalence rate is striking but is lower than that estimated in adulthood. For example, Rasmussen and Eisen (1990) found that approximately two thirds of adult patients with OCD also met criteria for major depressive disorder. The duration of OCD may also be related to the development of depression, with longer durations elevating risk for a major depressive episode (Diniz et al., 2004).

The connections between childhood-onset OCD and depressive symptoms are not entirely surprising given the putative consequences of having OCD. In fact, some researchers have commented that OCD is depressogenic in nature and may serve as an impetus for the appearance of depressive cognitions (Carter & Pollock, 2000; Swedo et al., 1989). Although far less research has been done examining the connections between bipolar disorder and OCD, especially in children and adolescents, one study suggested that patients who develop both bipolar disorder and OCD tend to have earlier onsets of OCD than do patients without the comorbidity (Masi et al. 2004).

Attention-Deficit Hyperactivity Disorder

The concordance of attention-deficit hyperactivity disorder (ADHD) and OCD has been documented in multiple research programs, both cross-sectional and longitudinal in design. Moreover, true comorbid OCD and ADHD may confer additional impairment over that found in individuals with OCD alone, specifically in the areas of social functioning, school problems, and self-reported depression (Sukhodolsky et al., 2005). Children with OCD may display attentional abnormalities and impulsive behaviors that are not best attributed to ADHD. Thus, a very careful inquiry into the nature and presentation of such symptoms is imperative before implementing a dual diagnosis (Geller et al., 2002). It is estimated that as many as 30% of individuals with childhood OCD also meet criteria for ADHD (Geller et al., 1996). In longitudinal analyses, the presence of ADHD in adolescence was associated with an increase in obsessive-compulsive symptoms in early adulthood (Peterson et al., 2001). This pattern has also been documented in younger populations as more than 80% of children with comorbid OCD and ADHD experienced the onset of their ADHD prior to the OCD (Geller et al., 2002).

Disruptive Behavior Disorders

Disruptive behavior disorders, such as conduct disorder and oppositional-defiant disorder, also co-occur with OCD in childhood at an increased rate relative to control populations. This finding refutes the notion that obsessive-compulsive children exhibit the rigid perfectionist personality characteristics popularly associated with the disorder (King, Leonard, & March, 1998). In fact, correlations between OCD and obsessive-compulsive personality disorder (OCPD) characteristics have been negligible in pediatric populations (Allsopp & Verduyn, 1990). Differential diagnosis between OCD and oppositional defiant disorder can be difficult at times, as the rigidity of compulsive behavior can mimic oppositional behavior in children. This difficulty notwithstanding, there does appear to be a true elevation of behavioral disorders in children with OCD as compared to other children, affecting as many of quarter of these children (Geller et al., 1996; Hanna, 1995). This subgroup merits special clinical attention, as comorbid oppositional-defiant disorder has been found to adversely impact response to medication treatment (Geller et al., 2003).

Other Comorbid Disorders

Several other categories of comorbid disorder have been found to be linked with OCD, either in pediatric or adult samples. Eating disorders and body dysmorphic disorder (BDD) have also been associated with pediatric OCD in a handful of studies (Becker et al., 2003; King et al., 1998; Yaryura-Tobias, Neziroglu, & Kaplan, 1995). In a German sample of adolescents, females over the age of 15 were much more likely to exhibit concurrent eating disorders than what would be expected in a nonclinical sample (Becker et al., 2003).

Rates of trichotillomania and impulse control disorders such as skin-picking are also elevated in samples of children and adults with OCD (Fontenelle, Mendlowicz, & Versiani, 2005; King et al., 1995; Stewart, Jenike, & Keuthen, 2005). The differential diagnosis between these behaviors and compulsive behaviors made in the context of OCD is important, as treatment approaches may vary for impulse-control symptoms. Treatment approaches such as habit reversal are usually indicated to address the pulling, picking, or nail-biting behaviors (e.g., Michael, 2004; Romaniuk, Miltenberger, & Deaver, 2003).

Pediatric anxiety disorders in general predict substance abuse in later adolescence and adulthood (Essau, Conradt, & Petermann, 2002). Substance and alcohol use should thus be carefully evaluated in any child or adolescent with OCD.

DIFFERENTIAL DIAGNOSIS: A CASE EXAMPLE

The challenge of case formulation and differential diagnosis is illustrated here via a case example. In this case, although initial symptoms (e.g., family conflict; distressing ego-dystonic thoughts) may suggest disruptive behavior disorder or even psychotic symptoms, the skillful clinician can detect and develop the clinical picture of adolescent OCD with harm obsessions and checking compulsions.

Case Description

Emily, age 15 years, presented with her parents to the University Clinic, with the initial complaint of family conflict. In the course of the intake evaluation, it became clear that Emily was experiencing intrusive images of herself harming her younger sister, Kayla, age 8 years. When these images would occur, usually in the context of feeling angry at Kayla over some small issue, Emily would become extremely upset and would lock herself in her room crying. Her parents were inferring from her behavior that Emily harbored "repressed anger" toward Kayla and that she had an intention to hurt her sister, and responded by taking Kayla out of the house when any conflict between the sisters appeared to be brewing. In addition, they were taking extreme measures to "maintain safety" in the home, keeping all sharp objects and "potential weapons" under lock and key in a cabinet in the kitchen. Emily was deeply distressed by these thoughts and by her parents' interpretation, as she herself reported no wish to harm her sister. The parents' goal at the initial session was to understand why Emily felt so much anger toward her sister. Emily's goal was to make her parents understand that she did not wish ill toward her sister, and to get help "getting the pictures out of [her] head."

Case Formulation and Differential Diagnosis

This initial case presentation should (but in many clinics might not) immediately generate a working hypothesis of OCD, because the patient is reporting bothersome, intrusive thoughts that are not concordant with his or her own reported wishes/desires. It is easy to get side-tracked by the issues of family conflict and "repressed anger," but the alert clinician should detect an unusual aspect to the conflict that is based in the patient's intrapsychic experience (rather than the parents' reactions to it or interpretations of it.) Although OCD should be a primary working hypothesis, in the course of the evaluation, the clinician should be sure to evaluate for any disruptive behavior disorder (such as oppositional defiant disorder or even conduct disorder), as well as rule out any thought disorder or psychosis. In addition, any abuse or trauma history and any post-traumatic symptoms should be carefully evaluated.

A detailed exploration of the nature of the obsessions is indicated, and in this case it is recommended that the patient be interviewed alone. It is important to establish in this interview the unwanted nature of the violent image.

clinician should rule out the case where the patient is excited by violent images or expresses any intention toward acting out the images. In addition, the presence of any psychotic symptoms should be evaluated; although un-common, it is important to be sure that there is no disturbance of thought process or reality testing. A careful evaluation of how the image interacts with the patient's anger level is also important in this case, as the intrusions are generally triggered by some angry affect on the part of the patient. The clinician should carefully disentangle normative, ego-syntonic fantasies that occur in the context of anger (e.g., thinking "I'd like to just hit her!" or imag-ining a minor violent act like slapping or pinching) from obsessional, ego-dystonic content (e.g., elaborated images of extreme or gruesome violence).

The clinician's stance in this interview can be crucial to getting the infor-mation needed. It is vitally important that the clinician be matter-of-fact about the patient's obsessions, conveying the message that the clinician has heard such things before, even in much more frightening variations from other patients. In other words, it should be conveyed that the patient's expe-rience is "old hat" to the clinician. An example of dialogue follows:

Therapist: I've met a lot of kids like you, who get thoughts they don't like or want to have. Sometimes the thoughts can get pretty scary. Can you tell me a bit about the thoughts you get about your sister?

Emily: It's hard to talk about.

Therapist: I know that it can be hard to talk about it. However, I also know that what your brain is coming up with in these moments has nothing to do with what *you* want or wish.

Emily: I really don't want it! That's why I go in my room. There's just some-thing wrong with me, that I think these things!

Therapist: What I think is happening here is that you are getting something called an *obsession,* which is a medical term for a kind of brain hiccup that some kids get. *Obsessions* are thoughts that you don't want to have, that have nothing to do with who you are or what you want. I've seen kids who get all kinds of scary images—images about hurt-ing their loved family members or pets, images about hurting them-selves, or wrecking things. They don't *want* to get these thoughts— it's just that their brain is kind of misfiring and giving them these im-ages. Is that what you are experiencing?

Emily: Yes. I get these images of hurting my sister with knives or hitting her with things. I even one time imagined hanging her from the banister of the stairs. Do other kids really get thoughts like that?

Therapist: Absolutely. I've heard all kinds of things like that from other kids. And you know what? None of them has ever done anything violent like the images that bother them!

This element of normalization, combined with some reassurance by the clinician about the actual (low) risk of having obsessions, can be very helpful in giving the patient hope and allowing the patient to share important information with the clinician. Note the strong contrast between the clinician's response and the family's response—there is no judgment here, nor attributions of hidden anger or risk of violence in the patient. Both the patient and the family are confounding thought content with behavior (or probability of behavior), and the therapist makes it clear very early with both her words and her behavior that the patient's intrusive thoughts, although upsetting, are not meaningful in terms of her motivations, wishes, desires, or personality; nor do they make her a risk to her sister.

Given that the patient certainly has obsessions and compulsions (the compulsion is to get physically away from the younger sister so she cannot harm her), it is important to assess for any additional symptoms of OCD. As just noted, an assessment tool such as the CY-BOCS can be extremely useful here. Patients usually have symptoms from several domains (e.g., washing, checking, morality, etc.), and a careful assessment of Emily reveals that she has some additional symptoms beyond the violent intrusions. She frequently does visual checks to make sure her sister is physically safe, and becomes distressed if her sister is hard to locate. She also has some symptoms of doubt, feeling frequently unsure of herself and often asking her parents for reassurance repeatedly about whether she is correct (e.g., about homework assignments, family rules, etc.). Finally, she has some mild contamination symptoms, fearing that she will spread toxins to her family members, and she avoids touching surfaces that may have chemicals on them and washes for 5 or more minutes when she touches something that she thinks may have a toxic residue. These additional OCD symptoms lend support to the working diagnosis of OCD and help to rule out disruptive behavior disorder and psychosis.

A full assessment will need to evaluate for the presence of other anxiety disorders, mood disorders, and attentional and behavioral issues. In this evaluation, we find that Emily has some distress and sad moods associated with her OCD symptoms, but no full-blown mood disorder, nor any comorbid anxiety disorders or eating concerns. Once the assessment is complete, and the differential diagnosis thus confirmed, treatment can proceed.

PSYCHOSOCIAL RISK FACTORS IN PEDIATRIC OCD

Understanding the epidemiology, phenomenology, and comorbidity patterns of pediatric OCD is crucially important to good diagnosis. In addition, other factors may influence the development of OCD in children and adolescents. These factors can range from the biological (e.g., genes, exposure to streptococcus) to the psychosocial. Biological factors are reviewed elsewhere in this volume; here we focus on psychosocial factors, both intrapersonal and interpersonal, that are associated with childhood OCD. Understanding these factors, which can affect risk and course of the illness, can help inform the thoughtful clinician with case formulation and treatment planning.

Temperament

Carter and Pollock (2002) have suggested that children who develop OCD may exhibit certain temperamental features, such as emotional reactivity or behavioral inhibition. Temperament could explain why some children who are exposed to other risk factors, such as trauma or harsh family environments (see the following section), develop OCD and others do not. Because one of the major differences between ritualistic behavior as it presents in typical children and the compulsions that characterize OCD is the level of distress associated with rituals, it would be expected that children with OCD would exhibit more negative emotionality than others. Some parents of children with obsessive-compulsive disorder have reported that their children seemed to be more fearful or to exhibit obsessive-compulsive personality characteristics throughout their childhood, whereas others report no such connection (King, Leonard, & March, 1998). A problem with asking parents about their retrospective recall of their children is that responses are bound to be influenced by the child's current behavior and diagnostic status.

In the only systematic investigation of temperament in pediatric OCD, elevated levels of behavioral inhibition and emotionality were found in a sample of children and adolescents with the disorder when compared to nonclinical age- and sex-matched controls (Ivarsson & Winge-Westholm, 2004). Behavioral inhibition, which has been associated with a wide range of anxious pathology (Kagan, 1997), is a measure of fearful and inhibited behavior in novel situations. Emotionality, on the other hand, is essentially a measure of negative emotional reactivity akin to difficult temperament in infancy. Further analyses revealed that two clusters of children emerged in the OCD group, an "Inhibited/Shy" group and an "Uninhibited" group. The former group was characterized by high scores on shyness and low scores on emotionality, sociability, and activity. The second group was characterized by a reversal of this pattern with high scores on emotionality, sociability, and activity, and low scores on shyness. This suggests that although certain temperamental profiles may be more likely in OCD than in control subjects, children with the disorder display a great deal of heterogeneity with respect to shyness, emotionality, sociability, and activity level. Further, no group differences were found with respect to the two temperament groups and symptom profiles.

A relationship was also found between inhibited or fearful temperament and subclinical obsessive-compulsive behavior in a community sample of 228 children (Zohar & Felz, 2001). Because these studies are cross-sectional, it is difficult to ascertain whether these characteristics predated the onset of the disorder and thus whether temperament can be considered a true risk factor for OCD. Although theoretically believed to be stable over time (Buss & Plomin, 1975), the influence of environmental factors is likely to change presentation of these behaviors over time. Therefore, temperament as it pertains to OCD is likely most potent when combined with other stressors or disorder correlates.

Cognition

Because most children and adolescents afflicted with OCD exhibit both obsessions and compulsions, and because obsessions are cognitive in nature, it makes sense that cognitive models of the disorder have received a fair amount of attention. In 1995, a group of international experts in the field formed the Obsessive Compulsive Cognitions Working Group to pool knowledge and methods and investigate the role of dysfunctional beliefs in OCD (Obsessive Compulsive Cognitions Working Group, 1997). A main focus of the group was to ascertain if there existed any cognitive styles that reliably discriminated individuals with the disorder from both control subjects and others with anxiety disorders. Findings from this study, as well as other cognitive theories to account for obsessive-compulsive behavior are outlined in the following section.

Although ritualistic behavior is elevated in children with OCD and may be a sign of disorder in certain circumstances, having routines and displaying a desire to have "things just so" is somewhat normative in young children. As many as two thirds of preschoolers exhibit concerns with sameness or symmetry (King et al., 1998). In fact, ritualistic behavior is considered to be adaptive in terms of developing a sense of control and mastery during these years and has been associated with positive outcomes (Carter & Pollock, 2000; Evans et al., 1997). Therefore identifying any qualitative differences in the cognitions driving the ritualistic behavior between disordered and nondisordered children would be a helpful prognostic tool. Evidence suggests, however, that the difference in these cognitions and behaviors is likely more of a quantitative than a qualitative disparity. *Magical thinking*, a term that has been invoked to describe beliefs about causal relationships between unconnected thoughts or behaviors and events in the external world (Bolton, Dearsley, Madronal-Luque, & Baron-Cohen, 2002), for example, is equally common in children with and without the disorder. Likewise, the intensity of superstitious beliefs, which appear on the surface very similar to obsessive-compulsive behavior, does not distinguish children with the affliction from their healthy counterparts (Leonard et al., 1990). Carter and Pollock (2000) have suggested that one reliable difference between the rituals of children with and without OCD is that rituals are associated with distress in the disorder, whereas they are generally pleasurable in other children.

One cognitive style that has been associated with OCD is inflated responsibility. This belief dictates that individuals overestimate their own responsibility over potential harm. Salkovskis (1989) proposed that this inflated responsibility is the link between the presence of an intrusive thought and the ensuing anxiety associated with it. That is, without the appraisal of responsibility for preventing potential harm, the individual experiencing an intrusion would have no reason to be anxious and feel compelled to "undo" the thought with a compulsion.

Related to this belief is the notion that individuals with OCD over-attribute importance to their thoughts. Whereas nondisordered individuals experience intrusive thoughts and are able to dismiss them, those with OCD attribute a great deal of importance to these thoughts. In fact, the term *"thought–action fusion"* (TAF) was coined to describe the belief that some afflicted individuals hold that having a thought about an aversive event elevates the likelihood of the imagined event happening (Rachman, 1993), and its functional impact can be seen through the case example of Emily that was just described. Thought–action fusion also leads individuals to believe that imagining an immoral act is as "wrong" as actually committing the act. Studies with psychologically healthy adults have shown that TAF triggers thought suppression that leads to intrusions and distress, two features that resemble OCD (Rassin, Muris, Schmidt, & Merckelbach, 2000).

In a study of the cognitive features of children with OCD, it was demonstrated that both overestimation of responsibility and TAF distinguished children with OCD from nonclinical controls but not from other anxious children (Barrett & Healy, 2003). Although these factors constitute correlates that are anxiety-specific, another cognitive feature was measured that distinguished OCD subjects not only from nonclinical controls but also from other anxious children. This measure, cognitive control, indexes the extent to which children feel able to control their intrusive thoughts. Given that persistent unwanted thoughts are part of the actual criteria of OCD, it is not surprising that this link was found. Future research may inform the field about the processes that bolster the perceived uncontrollability of obsessions, such the overuse of thought suppression as a (generally ineffective) strategy for combating intrusions. For example, in one study both perceived control and thought suppression surrounding stressful events were associated with OCD (McLaren & Crowe, 2003). Although the researchers were not working with a pediatric sample, the results demonstrate a relationship between the combination of high thought suppression and low perceived control over stressful life events and obsessive-compulsive symptoms.

An interesting question about cognitive style concerns the role of other psychological and biological factors in the genesis of such styles. That is, the presence of many of the beliefs associated with OCD is presumed to be precipitated by anxiety or to serve as a means of ameliorating anxiety. For example, it has been proposed that perfectionism results from the impulse to alleviate anxiety associated with possible negative outcomes. This suggests that the cognitive styles and beliefs just listed may be in part a result of emotional reactivity or physiological arousal and that the beliefs themselves do not represent a "starting point" on the pathway to disorder.

Family and Peer Factors

One of the major hypothesized differences between the development of OCD in children and in adults is that the family environment plays a substantial role for the former (Steketee & Van Noppen, 2003; Waters, Barrett, & March, 2001). Various aspects of the family, from emotion expression to specific childrearing strategies, have been positively associated with anxiety in cross-sectional designs. However, the existing evidence specifically linking childhood-onset OCD to familial factors is lacking, as very few studies have attempted to examine these questions (Waters & Barrett, 2000). In addition to the cross-sectional studies of OCD and general family factors, family involvement in the maintenance of the disorder has been noted throughout the years in descriptions of the presentation of the disorder (e.g., Allsopp & Verduyn, 1990; Amir, Freshman, & Foa, 2000). Treatment programs for pediatric OCD have also benefited from the inclusion of family members as active "co-therapists" (March & Mulle, 1998; Steketee & Van Noppen, 2003). Because the results from family studies indicate that there are modest correlations between family factors and OCD, and because there have been no studies examining familial influence within a longitudinal design, it seems appropriate and parsimonious to state that family factors are neither necessary nor sufficient for the development of the disorder. Therefore, family influence may be conceptualized as one of many potential risk factors for the etiology of the disorder and a powerful factor in the maintenance of the disorder.

In one study of 83 children and their families, parental interaction style and affect were examined in four groups: those with a child with OCD, those with a child with a non-OCD anxiety disorder, those with a child with externalizing disorder, and control families with psychopathology-free children (Barrett, Shortt, & Healy, 2002). All families were given the task of completing two 5-minute discussions of hypothetical situations designed to evoke a low level of anxiety. It was demonstrated that the OCD group differed from all other groups with respect to a number of parental characteristics. More specifically, mothers and fathers in this group demonstrated less confidence in their child's ability, rewarded independence less often, and used problem-solving strategies less often than parents in other groups. That these parents can be differentiated from all other groups, including other anxious subjects, suggests that these parental qualities may play an important role in the appearance of or the maintenance of OCD symptoms. However, because all data was collected postdiagnosis, it is likely that parental behavior is in part influenced by the disorder itself in addition to potentially influencing it. Indeed, children with OCD may be compromised in their ability to cope with anxiety-provoking situations and parents may attempt to compensate by taking a more active role in such situations (thereby restricting independence and exhibiting lowered confidence).

It has also been suggested by a number of researchers (e.g., Allsopp & Verduyn, 1990; Frost, Steketee, Cohn, & Griess, 1994; Hoover & Insel, 1984) that perfectionism in parents raises the propensity toward obsessive-compulsive symptoms in children. The proposed mechanism for this is simply that children adopt and internalize the perfectionist standards for themselves, which in turn generate anxiety and a compulsive desire to control the environment. Correlational studies have yielded mixed results in this area. More specifically, in one study fathers of nonclinical subjects with compulsive tendencies were rated higher on a scale of perfectionism than were those of noncompulsive controls (Frost et al., 1994). In a retrospective study of case note reviews conducted by Allsopp and Verduyn (1990), perfectionism and precision in family members were the attributes most commonly mentioned by adolescent patients with OCD when describing family members. Notably however, there was no control group of other psychiatric patients against which these frequencies were compared. In addition to these other characteristics, lower parental warmth and closeness was noted in one sample of adolescents with OCD as compared to a nonclinic control (Valleni-Basile et al., 1995), although this information was provided by self-report and involved neither observational coding nor input from parents.

Expressed emotion (EE), a measure of parental hostility, criticism, and overinvolvement, has also been examined in families of children with pediatric OCD, though not very extensively. One hundred and twenty-eight families participated in one such study that compared families with children who had (1) OCD, (2) an externalizing disorder, or (3) no psychopathology (Hibbs et al., 1991). Expressed emotion was measured on the basis of a parent's 5-minute description of his or her child. Although no differences were found between the clinical groups, parents in the OCD group received higher ratings on this construct than did control parents. This finding has been replicated (Leonard et al., 1993) and points to a family correlate that may be nonspecific for psychopathology in general.

Maternal control has been isolated as an area of disparity between mothers of anxious and non-anxious children (Rapee, 1997). Control has been defined in a variety of ways but some of the behaviors that fall under this umbrella are overprotectiveness, failure to encourage autonomy, and restrictiveness. Many findings have emerged supporting the connections between maternal control and anxiety (for a review, see Rapee, 1997), but few of the studies used to come to these conclusions included families of subjects with OCD. In one study that compared depressed, obsessive-compulsive and panic-disordered adolescents, maternal overprotectiveness differentiated panic and OCD from depression but not from one another (Merkel, Pollard, Wiener, & Staebler, 1993). In recent work (Moore, Whaley, Sigman, & Garcia, unpublished manuscript), observations of mother–child dyads showed that mothers of children with OCD resembled those with other anxiety disorders on psychological control; both clinical groups showed lower levels of maternal autonomy granting than did a normal comparison group. Therefore, maternal control may be considered an anxiety-specific, but not an OCD-specific, correlate.

The influence of peers is less well understood as it pertains to the development and maintenance of pediatric OCD. In the aforementioned Allsopp and Verduyn (1990) study, it was found that 75% of adolescents being treated for OCD mentioned difficulties maintaining satisfactory peer networks over the course of their therapy. The difference was more marked for males with the disorder, 96% of whom mentioned absent or poor peer relationships (as opposed to 46% for females). Interestingly, most of these subjects noted that the peer difficulties predated the appearance of obsessive-compulsive symptoms, suggesting that poor social relations may be a common antecedent in the disorder. Although the detrimental effect of obsessive-compulsive symptoms on peer relationships is well documented (Langley, Bergman, McCracken, & Piacentini, 2004; Piacentini, Bergman, Keller, & McCracken, 2003; Storch et al., 2005), this particular temporal pattern (peer difficulty predating OCD) warrants further research with the inclusion of contemporaneous and potentially confounding factors such as comorbid disorder and temperament. Additionally, because anxiety disorders are in general often associated with compromised social skills or relationships (American Psychiatric Association, 2000), peer difficulties are likely not a risk factor that is particular to OCD. However, it is clear that the peer problems, particularly peer victimization, is an important link between pediatric OCD and other emotional and behavioral problems (Storch et al., 2006). Thus, victimization and the possibility of bullying and teasing should be evaluated and addressed in treatment.

Stress and Traumatic Life Events

Although a hypothesized connection between the experience of trauma and the subsequent development of OCD has been in the literature since the very earliest accounts of the disorder, research addressing this theory has been scant. From a classical conditioning point of view, the development of obsessions themselves could be a result of the pairing of thoughts, impulses, or images with a highly aversive stimulus such as a trauma. The compulsions, by ameliorating the distress caused by the obsessions, would then be reinforced by means of negative reinforcement. Although behaviorist perspectives such as this have been implemented in treatments for the disorder (March & Mulle, 1998) by employing exposure and response prevention techniques, the role of such processes in the genesis of the disorder has not received much attention.

It has been suggested that the intrusive nature of obsessions in OCD shares much in common with post-traumatic stress disorder (PTSD), a disorder that develops after exposure to traumatic life events (de Silva & Marks,

2001). Additionally, some evidence has accumulated regarding the relation-ship between exposure to stress and increases in intrusive thoughts (Rachman, 1997; Rachman & de Silva, 1978). Taken together, these find-ings point to the potential role of extreme stress or trauma as an impetus for the appearance of obsessive-compulsive symptoms. de Silva and Marks (2001) presented a number of case studies in a recent article detailing the os-tensible link between trauma and OCD. However, the subjects in this report were all adults and no data were available on the relative frequency of cases in which trauma may be an etiological factor. Trauma histories have also been noted in individuals with the disorder who were sexually or physically abused or neglected, though these subjects were also adults and the age of onset was not specified (Lochner et al., 2002).

It is likely that trauma can play a role in the development of OCD in cer-tain cases. However, it is very clear that trauma is a risk factor for a great number of psychiatric illnesses and that such a risk would not be specific to OCD, as many individuals experience trauma without developing OCD. Prospective research is needed to address the factors that could serve as vul-nerabilities to developing OCD after exposure to a trauma (e.g. tempera-ment, subclinical OC symptoms prior to the event, etc.).

Summary

It is clear that a number of psychosocial factors may increase risk, both for developing OCD (e.g., temperament, trauma) and for maintaining or exac-erbating the course of OCD (e.g., family factors, cognitive factors) in child-hood and adolescence. Clinicians treating children with OCD, or treating children at risk for OCD (e.g., a young child of a parent with OCD who is en-gaging in larger-than-normal amounts of childhood ritualizing) can extend their understanding of the exacerbating and ameliorating factors in the child's life—both internal and external aspects—by attending to these fac-tors. In addition, these factors can be a target for intervention, particularly those factors that likely affect course such as family interaction patterns and cognitive style.

TOWARD A DEVELOPMENTAL MODEL
OF PEDIATRIC OCD

Because it is estimated that up to half of all cases of obsessive-compulsive disorder have their genesis in childhood (Rasmussen & Eisen, 1990), future research is needed to address the life course of pediatric-onset OCD. Differ-entiating between childhood-onset adult OCD, childhood-onset child-hood-limited OCD and adult-onset subtypes (see Jaisoorya et al., 2003) may yield a clearer picture of the developmental features and natural course of the disorder. At present, there is a paucity of research that addresses risk factors that may be specific to OCD, rather than general to broader categories of dysfunction such as anxiety or psychopathology. In order to clarify unique antecedents and mechanisms in the etiology and maintenance of this disorder, future studies addressing these questions may benefit from the inclusion of participants with other psychopathology in addition to nonclinical peers.

Overall, it appears that childhood OCD is a heterogeneous disorder with a multitude of pathways to disorder expression. Multideterminism of disorder is consistent with a developmental psychopathology view as the pathways leading to a disorder may be very different based on the individuals and his or her environment (Rutter & Sroufe, 2000). For example, evidence suggests that the combination of a preexisting autoimmune abnormality and exposure to streptococci may be one distinct pathway to disorder. Another potential pathway seems to differentially affect prepubertal boys and is associated with comorbid tics and hyperactivity.

There exists a need for well-designed prospective longitudinal studies to help map out the antecedents and consequences of the onset of OCD in childhood and adolescence. Although epidemiological studies have yielded a detailed picture of the prevalence, sex ratio, and average age of onset for childhood OCD, a more detailed inquiry into the mechanisms of disorder etiology and maintenance is warranted.

REFERENCES

Adams, G. B., Waas, G. A., March, J. S., & Smith, M. C. (1994). Obsessive-compulsive disorder in children and adolescents: The role of the school psychologist in identification, assessment, and treatment. *School Psychology Quarterly, 94,* 274–294.

Allsopp, M., & Verduyn, C. (1990). Adolescents with obsessive-compulsive disorder: A case note review of consecutive patients referred to a provincial regional adolescent psychiatry unit. *Journal of Adolescence, 13,* 157–169.

American Psychiatric Association. (2000). *Diagnostic and statistical manual of mental disorders* (4th ed., text revision). Washington DC: Author.

Amir, N., Freshman, M., & Foa, E. B. (2000). Family distress and involvement in relatives of obsessive-compulsive disorder patients. *Journal of Anxiety Disorders, 14,* 209–217.

Angst, J., Gamma, A., Endrass, J., Goodwin, R., Ajdacic, V., Eich, D., et al. (2004). Obsessive-compulsive severity spectrum in the community: Prevalence, comorbidity, and course. *European Archives of Psychiatry and Clinical Neuroscience, 254,* 156–164.

Barrett, P., Farrell, L., Dadds, M., & Boulter, N. (2005). Cognitive-behavioral family treatment of childhood obsessive-compulsive disorder: Long-term follow-up and predictors of outcome. *Journal of the American Academy of Child and Adolescent Psychiatry, 44,* 1005–1014.

Barrett, P. M., & Healy, L. J. (2003). An examination of the cognitive processes involved in childhood obsessive-compulsive disorder. *Behaviour Research & Therapy, 41,* 285–299.

Barrett, P., Shortt, A., & Healy, L. (2002). Do parent and child behaviours differentiate families whose children have obsessive-compulsive disorder from other clinic and non-clinic families? *Journal of Child Psychology & Psychiatry, 43,* 597–607.

Becker, K., Jennen-Steinmetz, C., Holtmann, M., Ei-Faddagh, M., & Schmidt, M. H. (2003). Comorbidity of obsessive-compulsive disorders in childhood and adolescence. *Zeitschrift fur Kinder- und Jugendpsychiatrie und Psychotherapie, 31,* 175–185.

Bolton, D., Dearsley, P., Madronal-Luque, R., & Baron-Cohen, S. (2002). Magical thinking in childhood and adolescence: Development and relation to obsessive compulsion. *British Journal of Developmental Psychology, 20,* 479–494.

Buss, A. H., & Plomin, R. (1975). *A temperament theory of personality development.* New York: Wiley.

Carter, A. S., & Pollock, R. A. (2000). Obsessions and compulsions: The developmental and familial context. In A. J. Sameroff & M. Lewis (Eds.), *Handbook of developmental psychopathology* (2nd ed., pp. 549–566). Dordrecht: Kluwer.

de Silva, P., & Marks, M. (2001). Traumatic experiences, post-traumatic stress disorder and obsessive-compulsive disorder. *International Review of Psychiatry, 13,* 172–180.

Diniz, J. B., Rosario-Campos, M. C., Shavitt, R. G., Curi, M., Hounie, A. G., Brotto, S. A., & Miguel, E. C. (2004). Impact of age at onset and duration of illness on the expression of comorbidities in obsessive-compulsive disorder. *Journal of Clinical Psychiatry, 65,* 22–27.

Douglass, H. M., Moffitt, T. E., Dar, R., & McGee, R. (1995). Obsessive-compulsive disorder in a birth cohort of 18-year-olds: Prevalence and predictors. *Journal of the American Academy of Child & Adolescent Psychiatry, 34,* 1424–1431.

Eichstedt, J. A., & Arnold, S. L. (2001). Childhood-onset obsessive-compulsive disorder: A tic-related subtype of OCD? *Clinical Psychology Review, 21,* 137–157.

Essau, C., Conradt, J., & Petermann, F. (2002). Course and outcome of anxiety disorders in adolescents. *Journal of Anxiety Disorders, 16,* 67–81.

Evans, D. W., Leckman, J. F., Carter, A., Reznick, J., Henshaw, D., King, R. A., et al. (1997). Ritual, habit, and perfectionism: The prevalence and development of compulsive-like behavior in normal young children. *Child Development, 68,* 58–68.

Fireman, B., Koran, L. M., Leventhal, J. L., & Jacobson, A. (2001). The prevalence of clinically recognized obsessive-compulsive disorder in a large health maintenance organization. *American Journal of Psychiatry, 158,* 1904–1910.

Flament M. F., Koby, E., Rapoport, J. L., Berg, C. J., Zahn, T., Cox, C., et al. (1990). Childhood obsessive-compulsive disorder: A prospective follow-up study. *Journal of Child Psychology and Psychiatry, 31,* 363–380.

Flament, M. F., Whitaker, A., Rapoport, J. L., Davies, M., Berg, C. Z., Kalikow, K., et al. (1988). Obsessive-compulsive disorder in adolescence: An epidemiological study. *Journal of the American Academy of Child & Adolescent Psychiatry, 27,* 764–771.

Fontenelle, L. F., Mendlowicz, M. V., & Versiani, M. (2005). Impulse control disorders in patients with obsessive-compulsive disorder. *Psychiatry and Clinical Neurosciences. 59,* 30–37.

Franklin, M. E., Tolin, D. F., March, J. S., & Foa, E. B. (2001). Treatment of pediatric obsessive-compulsive disorder: A case example of intensive cognitive-behavioral therapy involving exposure and ritual prevention. *Cognitive & Behavioral Practice, 8,* 297–304.

Frost, R. O., Steketee, G., Cohn, L., & Griess, K. (1994). Personality traits in subclinical and non-obsessive-compulsive volunteers and their parents. *Behaviour Research & Therapy, 32,* 47–56.

Geller, D. A., Biederman, J., Faraone, S., Agranat, A., Cradock, K., Hagermoser, L., et al. (2001). Developmental aspects of obsessive-compulsive disorder: Findings in children, adolescents, and adults. *Journal of Nervous & Mental Disease, 189,* 471–477.

Geller, D. A., Biederman, J., Faraone, S., Cradock, K., Hagermoser, L., Zaman, N., et al. (2002). Attention-deficit/hyperactivity disorder in children and adolescents with obsessive-compulsive disorder: Fact or artifact? *Journal of the American Academy of Child and Adolescent Psychiatry, 41,* 52–58.

Geller, D. A., Biederman, J., Griffin, S., Jones, J., & Lefkowitz, T. R. (1996). Comorbidity of juvenile obsessive-compulsive disorder with disruptive behavior disorders. *Journal of the American Academy of Child and Adolescent Psychiatry, 35,* 1637–1646.

Geller, D. A., Biederman, J., Stewart, S. E., Mullin, B., Farrell, C., Wagner, K., et al. (2003). Impact of comorbidity on treatment response to paroxetine in pediatric obsessive-compulsive disorder: Is the use of exclusion criteria empirically supported in randomized clinical trials? *Journal of Child and Adolescent Psychopharmacology, 13*(2), S19–S29.

Goodman, W., Rasmussen, S., Foa, E., & Price, L. (1994). Obsessive-compulsive disorder. In R. Prien & D. Robinson (Eds.), *Clinical evaluation of psychotropic drugs: Principles and guidelines* (pp. 431–466). New York: Raven Press.

Hanna, G. L. (1995). Demographic and clinical features of obsessive-compulsive disorder in children and adolescents. *Journal of the Academy of Child and Adolescent Psychiatry, 34,* 19–27.

Heyman, I., Fombonne, E., Simmons, H., Ford, T., Meltzer, H., & Goodman, R. (2001). Prevalence of obsessive-compulsive disorder in the British nationwide survey of child mental health. *British Journal of Psychiatry, 179,* 324–329.

Hibbs, E. D., Hamburger, S. D., Lenane, M., Rapoport, J. L., Kruesi, M. J. P., Keysor, C. S., et al. (1991). Determinants of expressed emotion in families of disturbed and normal children. *Journal of Child Psychology & Psychiatry, 32,* 757–770.

Hoover, C. F., & Insel, T. R. (1984). Families of origin in obsessive-compulsive disorder. *Journal of Nervous & Mental Disease, 172,* 207–215.

Horwath, E., & Weissman, M. (2000). The epidemiology and cross-national presentation of obsessive-compulsive disorder. *Psychiatric Clinics of North America, 23,* 493–507.

Ivarsson, T., & Winge-Westholm, C. (2004). Temperamental factors in children and adolescents with obsessive-compulsive disorder (OCD) and in normal controls. *European Child & Adolescent Psychiatry, 13,* 365–372.

Jaisoorya, T. S., Reddy, Y., & Srinath, S. (2003). Is juvenile obsessive-compulsive disorder a developmental subtype of the disorder? Findings from an Indian study. *European Child & Adolescent Psychiatry, 12,* 290–297.

Jenike, M. A. (1989). Obsessive-compulsive and related disorders: A hidden epidemic [editorial; comment]. *New England Journal of Medicine, 321,* 539–541.

Kagan, J. (1997). Temperamental contributors to the development of social behavior. In D. Magnusson,(Ed.), *The lifespan development of individuals: Behavioral, neurobiological, and psychosocial perspectives: A synthesis* (pp. 376–393). New York: Cambridge University Press.

King, R. A., Leonard, H., & March, J. (1998). Practice parameters for the assessment and treatment of children and adolescents with obsessive-compulsive disorder. *Journal of the American Academy of Child & Adolescent Psychiatry, 37,* 27S–45S.

King, R. A., Scahill, L., Vitulano, L. A., Schwab-Stone, M., Tercyak, K. P., & Riddle, M. A. (1995). Childhood trichotillomania: Clinical phenomenology, comorbidity, and family genetics. *Journal of the American Academy of Child & Adolescent Psychiatry, 34,* 1451–1459.

Langley, A. K., Bergman, R. L., McCracken, J., & Piacentini, J. (2004). Impairment in childhood anxiety disorders: Preliminary examination of the child anxiety impact scale—parent version. *Journal of Child and Adolescent Psychopharmacology, 14,* 105–114.

Leckman, J. F., & Cohen, D. J. (1999). *Tourette's syndrome-tics, obsessions, compulsions: Developmental psychopathology and clinical care.* Hoboken, NJ: Wiley.

Leckman, J. F., Grice, D. E., Barr, L. C., de Vries, A. L. C., Martin, C., Cohen, D. J., et al. (1995). Tic-related versus non-tic-related obsessive-compulsive disorder. *Anxiety, 1,* 208–215.

Leckman, J. F., Riddle, M. A., Hardin, M. T., Ort, S. I., Swartz, K. L., Stevenson, J., et al. (1989). The Yale Global Tic Severity Scale: Initial testing of a clinician-rated scale of tic severity. *Journal of the American Academy of Child and Adolescent Psychiatry, 28,* 566–573.

Lenane, M. C., Swedo, S. E., Leonard, H., Pauls, D. L., Sceery, W., & Rapoport, J. L. (1990). Psychiatric disorders in first degree relatives of children and adolescents with obsessive-compulsive disorder. *Journal of the American Academy of Child & Adolescent Psychiatry, 29,* 407–412.

Leonard, H. L., Goldberger, E. L., Rapoport, J. L., Cheslow, D. L., & Swedo, S. E. (1990). Childhood rituals: Normal development or obsessive-compulsive symptoms? *Journal of the American Academy of Child & Adolescent Psychiatry, 29,* 17–23.

Leonard, H. L., Lenane, M. C., Swedo, S. E., Rettew, D. C., & Cheslow, D. L. (1992). Tics and Tourette's disorder: A 2- to 7-year follow-up of 54 obsessive-compulsive children. *American Journal of Psychiatry, 149,* 1244–1251.

Leonard, H. L., Swedo, S. E., Lenane, M. C., Rettew, D. C., Cheslow, D. L., Hamburger, S. D., et al. (1991). A double-blind desipramine substitution during long-term clomipramine treatment in children and adolescents with obsessive-compulsive disorder. *Archives of General Psychiatry, 48,* 922–927

Leonard, H. L., Swedo, S. E., Lenane, M. C., Rettew, D. C., Hamburger, S. D., et al. (1993). A 2- to 7-year follow-up study of 54 obsessive-compulsive children and adolescents. *Archives of General Psychiatry, 50,* 429–439.

Lochner, C., du Toit, P. L., Zungu-Dirwayi, N., Marais, A., van Kradenburg, J., Seedat, S., et al. (2002). Childhood trauma in obsessive-compulsive disorder, trichotillomania, and controls. *Depression & Anxiety, 15,* 66–68.

March, J. S., Franklin, M. E., Leonard, H. L., & Foa, E. B. (2004). Obsessive-compulsive disorder. In T. L. Morris & J. S. March, (Eds.), *Anxiety disorders in children and adolescents* (pp. 212–240). New York: Guilford.

March, J., & Mulle, K. (1995). Manualized cognitive-behavioral psychotherapy for obsessive-compulsive disorder in childhood: A preliminary single case study. *Journal of Anxiety Disorders, 9,* 175–184.

March, J. S., & Mulle, K. (1998). *OCD in children and adolescents: A cognitive-behavioral treatment manual.* New York, NY: Guilford.

March, J. S., Mulle, K., & Herbel, B. (1994). Behavioral psychotherapy for children and adolescents with obsessive-compulsive disorder: An open trial of a new protocol-driven treatment package. *Journal of the American Academy of Child and Adolescent Psychiatry, 33,* 333–341.

Masi, G., Perugi, G., Toni, C., Millepiedi, S., Mucci, M., Bertini, N., et al. (2004). Obsessive-compulsive bipolar comorbidity: Focus on children and adolescents. *Journal of Affective Disorders, 78,* 175–183.

McLaren, S., & Crowe, S. F. (2003). The contribution of perceived control of stressful life events and thought suppression to the symptoms of obsessive-compulsive disorder in both non-clinical and clinical samples. *Journal of Anxiety Disorders, 17,* 389–403.

Merkel, W. T., Pollard, C., Wiener, R. L., & Staebler, C. R. (1993). Perceived parental characteristics of patients with obsessive-compulsive disorder, depression, and panic disorder. *Child Psychiatry & Human Development, 24,* 49–57.

Michael, K. D. (2004). Behavioral treatment of trichotillomania: A case study. *Clinical Case Studies, 3,* 171–182.

Moore, P., Whaley, S., Sigman, M., & Garcia, A. *Maternal behavior in families of children with obsessive-compulsive disorder.* Unpublished manuscript.

Nestadt, G., Samuels, J., Riddle, M., Bienvenu, O. J., Liang, K.-Y., LaBuda, M., et al. (2000). A family study of obsessive-compulsive disorder. *Archives of General Psychiatry, 57,* 358–363.

Obsessive Compulsive Cognitions Working Group. (1997). Measurement of cognitions in obsessive-compulsive disorder. *Behavior Research and Therapy, 35,* 667–682

Pauls, D. L., Alsobrook, J. P., Goodman, W., Rasmussen, S., & Leckman, J. F. (1995). A family study of obsessive-compulsive disorder. *American Journal of Psychiatry, 152,* 76–84.

Pediatric OCD Treatment Study Team. (2004). Cognitive-behavior therapy, sertraline, and their combination for children and adolescents with obsessive-compulsive disorder: The pediatric OCD treatment study (POTS) randomized controlled trial. *Journal of the American Medical Association, 292,* 1969–1976.

Peterson, B. S., Pine, D. S., Cohen, P., & Brook, J. S. (2001). Prospective, longitudinal study of tic, obsessive-compulsive, and attention-deficit/hyperactivity disorders in an epidemiological sample. *Journal of the American Academy of Child & Adolescent Psychiatry, 40,* 685–695.

Piacentini, J., Bergman, R. L., Keller, M., & McCracken, J. (2003). Functional impairment in children and adolescents with obsessive-compulsive disorder. *Journal of Child & Adolescent Psychopharmacology, 13,* S61–S69.

Rachman, S. (1993). Obsessions, responsibility and guilt. *Behaviour Research & Therapy, 31,* 149–154.

Rachman, S. (1997). A cognitive theory of obsessions. *Behaviour Research & Therapy, 35,* 793–802.

Rachman, S., & de Silva, P. (1978). Abnormal and normal obsessions. *Behaviour Research & Therapy, 16,* 233–248.

Rapee, R. M. (1997). Potential role of childrearing practices in the development of anxiety and depression. *Clinical Psychology Review, 17,* 47–67.

Rapoport, J. L., Inoff-Germain, G., Weissman, M. M., Greenwald, S., Narrow, W. E., Jensen, P. S., et al. (2000). Childhood obsessive-compulsive disorder in the NIMH MECA Study: Parent versus child identification of cases. *Journal of Anxiety Disorders, 14,* 535–548.

Rasmussen, S. A. (1994). Obsessive compulsive spectrum disorders. *Journal of Clinical Psychiatry, 55,* 89–91.

Rasmussen, S. A., & Eisen, J. L. (1990). Epidemiology of obsessive-compulsive disorder. *Journal of Clinical Psychiatry, 53,* 10–14.

Rassin, E., Muris, P., Schmidt, H., & Merckelbach, H. (2000). Relationships between thought-action fusion, thought suppression and obsessive-compulsive symptoms: A structural equation modeling approach. *Behaviour Research & Therapy, 38,* 889–897.

Rettew, D. C., Swedo, S. E., Leonard, H. L., Lenane, M. C., & Rapoport, J. L. (1992). Obsessions and compulsions across time in 79 children and adolescents with obsessive-compulsive disorder. *Journal of the American Academy of Child & Adolescent Psychiatry, 31,* 1050–1056.

Riddle, M. A., Scahill, L., King, R., Hardin, M. T., Towbin, K. E., Ort, S. I., Leckman, J. F., & Cohen, D. J. (1990). Obsessive-compulsive disorder in children and adolescents: Phenomenology and family history. *Journal of the American Academy of Child & Adolescent Psychiatry, 29,* 766–772.

Romaniuk, C., Miltenberger, R., & Deaver, C. (2003). Long-term maintenance following habit reversal and adjunct treatment for trichotillomania. *Child & Family Behavior Therapy, 25*, 45–59.

Rutter, M., & Sroufe, L. A. (2000). Developmental psychopathology: Concepts and challenges. *Development & Psychopathology, 12*, 265–296.

Rutter, M., Tizard, J., & Whitmore, K. (1970). *Education, health, and behavior.* London: Longmans.

Salkovskis, P. M. (1989). Cognitive behavioural factors and the persistence of intrusive thoughts in obsessional problems. *Behaviour Research and Therapy, 27*, 677–682.

Sallinen, B., Nangle, D., & O'Grady, A. (2004). Case study: Successful medication withdrawal using cognitive-behavioral therapy for a preadolescent with OCD. *Journal of the American Academy of Child & Adolescent Psychiatry, 43*, 1441–1444.

Scahill, L., Riddle, M. A., McSwiggin-Hardin, M., Ort, S. I., King, R. A., Goodman, W. K., et al. (1997). Children's Yale-Brown Obsessive Compulsive Scale: Reliability and validity. *Journal of the American Academy of Child and Adolescent Psychiatry, 36*, 844–852.

Silverman, W. K., & Albano, A. M. (1996). *The Anxiety Disorders Interview Schedule for DSM–IV—Child and Parent versions.* San Antonio, TX: Physiological Corporation.

Snider, L. A., & Swedo, S. E. (2000). Pediatric obsessive-compulsive disorder. *JAMA: Journal of the American Medical Association, 284*, 3104–3106.

Steketee, G., & Van Noppen, B. (2003). Family approaches to treatment for obsessive-compulsive disorder. *Revista Brasileira de Psiquiatria, 25*, 43–50.

Stewart, S. E., Geller, D. A., Jenike, M., Pauls, D., Shaw, D., Mullin, B., et al. (2004). Long-term outcome of pediatric obsessive-compulsive disorder: A meta-analysis and qualitative review of the literature. *Acta Psychiatrica Scandinavica, 110*, 4–13.

Stewart, S. E., Jenike, M. A., & Keuthen, N. J. (2005). Severe obsessive-compulsive disorder with and without comorbid hair pulling: Comparisons and clinical implications. *Journal of Clinical Psychiatry, 66*, 864–869.

Storch, E. A. *Peer victimization in children with obsessive-compulsive disorder: Relations with social-psychologist adjustment.* Unpublished manuscript.

Storch, E. A., Heidgerken, A., Adkins, J., Cole, M., Murphy, T., & Geffken, G. R. (2005). Peer victimization and the development of obsessive-compulsive disorder in adolescence: A case report. *Depression and Anxiety, 21*, 41–44.

Storch, E. A., Ledley, D. R., Lewin, A. B., Murphy, T. K., Johns, N. B., Goodman, W. K., & Geffken, G. R. (2006). Peer victimization in children with obsessive-compulsive disorder: Relations with social-psychological adjustment. *Journal of Clinical Child and Adolescent Psychology, 35*, 446–455.

Storch, E., Murphy, T., Geffken, G., Soto, O., Sajid, M., Allen, P., et al. (2004). Psychometric evaluation of the Children's Yale-Brown Obsessive-Compulsive Scale. *Psychiatry Research, 129*, 91–98.

Sukhodolsky, D. G., do Rosario-Campos, M. C., Scahill, L., Katsovich, L., Pauls, D. L., Peterson, B. S., et al. (2005). Adaptive, emotional, and family functioning of children with obsessive-compulsive disorder and comorbid attention deficit hyperactivity disorder. *American Journal of Psychiatry, 162*, 1125–1132.

Swedo, S. E., Rapoport, J. L., Leonard, H. L., Lenane, M., & Cheslow, D. L. (1989). Obsessive-compulsive disorder in children and adolescents: Clinical phenomenology of 70 consecutive cases. *Archives of General Psychiatry, 46*, 335–341.

Tukel, R., Ertekin, E., Batmaz, S., Alyanak, F., Sozen, A., Aslantas, B., et al. (2005). Influence of age of onset on clinical features in obsessive-compulsive disorder. *Depression and Anxiety, 21*, 112–117.

Valleni-Basile, L. A., Garrison, C. Z., Jackson, K. L., Waller, J. L., McKeown, R. E., Addy, C. L., et al. (1995). Family and psychosocial predictors of obsessive-compulsive disorder in a community sample of young adolescents. *Journal of Child & Family Studies, 4,* 193–206.

Valleni-Basile, L. A., Garrison, C. Z., Waller, J. L., Addy, C. L., McKeown, R. E., Jackson, K. L., & Cuffe, S. P. (1996). Incidence of obsessive-compulsive disorder in a community sample of young adolescents. *Journal of the American Academy of Child & Adolescent Psychiatry, 35,* 898–906.

Waters, T. L., & Barrett, P. M. (2000). The role of the family in childhood obsessive-compulsive disorder. *Clinical Child & Family Psychology Review, 3,* 173–184.

Waters, T. L., Barrett, P. M., & March, J. S. (2001). Cognitive-behavioral family treatment of childhood obsessive-compulsive disorder: Preliminary findings. *American Journal of Psychotherapy, 55,* 372–387.

Yaryura-Tobias, J. A., Neziroglu, F. A., & Kaplan, S. (1995). Self-mutilation, anorexia, and dysmenorrhea in obsessive-compulsive disorder. *International Journal of Eating Disorders, 17,* 33–38.

Zohar, A. H. (1999). The epidemiology of obsessive-compulsive disorder in children and adolescents. *Child & Adolescent Psychiatric Clinics of North America, 8,* 445–460.

Zohar, A. H., & Felz, L. (2001). Ritualistic behavior in young children. *Journal of Abnormal Child Psychology, 29,* 121–128.

3

Obsessive-Compulsive Spectrum Disorders

R. Douglas Shytle
Berney Wilkinson
University of South Florida College of Medicine

Since the earliest descriptions of obsessive–compulsive disorder (OCD) in the Western world, clinicians have recognized the heterogeneous nature of the syndrome. For example, as early as 1866, Falret (Falret, 1866) made the distinction between *folie du doute* (madness of doubt) and délire du toucher (delusion of touching; Hantouche & Lancrenon, 1996; Mataix-Cols, Rosario-Campos, & Leckman, 2005). Since then, several attempts have been made to classify persons with OC symptoms into homogeneous, usually mutually exclusive, subgroups (Mataix-Cols et al., 2005). These classificatory attempts have had various levels of success in terms of being related to patterns of neurobiological variables, genetic transmission, and treatment response. Despite this heterogeneity, the current classification systems—the *Diagnostic and Statistical Manual of Mental Disorders* (DSM–IV–TR)—still regard OCD as a single entity (American Psychological Association, 2000).

Nevertheless, there are many other disorders that have characteristics involving repetitive thoughts and behaviors, like those that occur in people with OCD. These disorders are sometimes called Obsessive-Compulsive Spectrum Disorders (OCSD) because of these similarities (McElroy, Phillips, & Keck, 1994). In fact, some experts believe that these disorders may all have similar underlying neurobiological causes as OCD. For example, neuroimaging studies report similar brain activity between OCD and certain OCSD and many also respond similarly to medication and cognitive-behavioral therapy (Mataix-Cols et al., 2005). As well as having similarities to OCD, OCSD are

47

also commonly comorbid with OCD and vice versa. This chapter covers the characteristics and treatment of OCSD that can occur in children.

TOURETTE'S DISORDER

Perhaps the best known OCSD is Tourette's disorder (TD). TD (also known as Tourette's Syndrome) is a neuropsychiatric condition characterized by multiple, repeated, uncontrollable body motor and vocal tics. A tic is described as a sudden, rapid, recurrent, nonrhythmic, stereotyped motor movement or vocalization (American Psychological Association, 2000).

Although the *DSM–IV–TR* (American Psychological Association, 2000) delineates four kinds of tic disorders, TD is the most severe in terms of intensity of symptoms and incidence of comorbid conditions (Zinner, 2000). To meet criteria for TD, one must experience multiple motor and one or more vocal tics, though not necessarily concurrent, nearly every day for at least 1 year with no "tic-free" periods that last more than 3 months. In addition, the onset of the tics must occur before the age of 18 years. Although typical age of onset is about age 6 or 7 years, some have reported that as many as 58% of individuals with TD had symptom onset after age 10 (Leckman, 2002). Symptoms typically become more frequent and variable as the child ages, with tics and associated symptoms generally peaking by about age 12, and in many cases the symptoms subside around early adulthood. Other tic disorders include Chronic Motor or Vocal Tic Disorder, Transient Tic Disorder, and Tic Disorder Not Otherwise Specified. Diagnostic criteria for Chronic Motor or Vocal Tic Disorder is similar to TD, except that the individual experiences either one or multiple motor or vocal tics, but not both (American Psychological Association, 2000). To meet diagnostic criteria for Transient Tic Disorder, one must experience one or multiple motor and/or vocal tics nearly every day for at least 4 weeks, but for no longer than 12 consecutive months (American Psychological Association, 2000).

TD was once considered a relatively rare disorder, with estimates indicating that 4 in every 10,000 people in the United States have symptoms associated with TD (American Psychological Association, 2000). However, some studies show that the rate may be as high as 1 in 95 boys and 1 in 759 girls (Comings, Himes, & Comings, 1990). More recently, various researchers have reported prevalence rates ranging from 1%–3% (Hornse, Banerjee, Zeitlin, & Robertson, 2001; Kadesjo & Gillberg, 2000; Olson, 2004). Therefore, TD appears to be an increasingly more common psychiatric disorder affecting as many as 1% of all children and adolescents.

TOURETTE'S DISORDER AND OCD

Tourette's Disorder is frequently found to be comorbid with OCD (Robertson, 1991; Robertson, Banerjee, Eapen, & Fox-Hiley, 2002). The rates of comorbidity between TD and OCD range from 30% to 70% (Carter, Pauls, Leckman, & Cohen, 1994; Geller, Biederman, Faraone, Bellordre, et al., 2001; Grad, Pelcovitz, Olson, Matthews, & Grad, 1987; Kadesjo & Gillberg, 2000; Nee, Polinsky, & Ebert, 1982; Robertson et al., 2002; Walkup et al., 1988).

It has also been found that a tic history among individuals with OCD was likely to distinguish a genetically meaningful subtype. For example, there appears to be an association between tics, male gender, early age of onset, and disruptive behavior disorders in younger OCD patients (Geller, Biederman, Faraone, Agranat, et al., 2001). Also, a range of studies comparing OCD patients with and without tics has reported interesting differences in symptomatology and the rates of specific obsessions and compulsions (Holzer et al., 1994; Leckman et al., 1994; Miguel et al., 1997; Miguel et al., 1995). In a comparison of patients with OCD alone and those with both OCD and TS, for example, the former group was more likely to have (1) contamination obsessions and compulsions, (2) fear of not saying the right thing, and (3) body dysmorphic disorder However, the latter group was more likely to have (1) obsessions with the need for symmetry accompanied by magical thinking, (2) fear of doing something embarrassing or of blurting out an obscenity, (3) intrusive violent or sexual images and thoughts, (4) touching compulsions, (5) blinking or staring rituals, (6) self-injurious compulsions, (7) hoarding, and (8) counting (George, Trimble, Ring, Sallee, & Robertson, 1993). These findings were also supported by Petter and colleagues (Petter, Richter, & Sandor, 1998) who found that individuals with OCD and TD reported significantly more symptoms associated with the need for symmetry, nonviolent images, and counting compulsions than individuals with OCD without TD. Other studies reached similar conclusions differentiating pure OCD from OCD with tics (Holzer et al., 1994; Leckman et al., 1994; Leckman, Peterson, Pauls, & Cohen, 1997; Miguel et al., 1997; Miguel et al., 1995; Pitman, Green, Jenike, & Mesulam, 1987) with one exception (Cath et al., 2001).

There is also some evidence of increased aggression and externalizing behaviors when a child has TD that is accompanied by other comorbid disorders, particularly ADHD, OCD, and Oppositional Defiant Disorder (ODD; Budman, Bruun, Park, & Olson, 1998). Budman and colleagues (Budman et al., 1998) reported that in 12 TD patients with comorbid ADHD and OCD, rage and aggressive symptoms were related more to the presence of the comorbid disorders than to tic severity. Similarly, studies have reported that groups with OCD with comorbid TD report more ADHD symptoms during childhood than groups with OCD without TD (Leonard et al., 1992). Additional research is needed to discern whether there is an increased likelihood of aggressive behaviors in children with TD and OCD.

Stephens and Sandor (1999) compared four groups of participants; 10 TD-Only, 14 TD + ADHD, 9 TD + ADHD + OCD, and 6 healthy controls. Parents were asked to complete several questionnaires and forms to quantitatively define their child's behavior. Their results show that the TS-Only group did not differ significantly from the control group on any measure of aggressive behavior. However, the TD + ADHD and TD + ADHD + OCD groups had an increased risk for aggressive behavior over the TD-Only group. Interestingly, the TD + ADHD + OCD group reported more severe tics than the other groups, which makes it difficult to conclude whether the comorbidity increases the likelihood of aggressive behavior or if the tic severity increases aggressive behavior.

In OCD family studies, OCD probands had tics in at least 17% of adult patients and increased rates of tics in their first-degree relatives (Holzer et al., 1994; Pauls, Alsobrook, Goodman, Rasmussen, & Leckman, 1995). Overall, OCD family studies have found that earlier age of onset of OCD and male gender in probands were associated with increased tic disorders in relatives, suggesting that tic disorders constitute an alternate expression of the familial OCD phenotype (Nestadt et al., 2000; Pauls et al., 1995). Conversely, in TD family-genetic studies, OC symptoms were found to be a possible alternate phenotype among female members of TD families (Pauls & Leckman, 1986; Pauls, Raymond, Stevenson, & Leckman, 1991; Santangelo et al., 1994).

Clinical research has also documented this bidirectional overlap between TS and OCD from phenomenological, comorbidity, and familial-history perspectives (Coffey et al., 1998). For example, one of the three obsessive-compulsive (OC) symptom clusters identified by Baer (Baer, 1994)— "symmetry/hoarding"—was significantly related to a lifetime history of TD or chronic tic disorder. These findings suggest that TD patients with comorbid OCD may represent a meaningful OCD subtype. Interestingly, tics were found more useful than obsessions or compulsions in distinguishing relatives of patients with OCD from relatives of control subjects.

Regional cerebral blood flow patterns in individuals with OC behavior in families affected by TD are comparable to their relatives with TD, and differ from individuals with primary OCD but with no family history of tic disorders (Moriarty et al., 1997). Together with previously discussed data, this finding supports the hypothesis that at least some forms of OCD are genetically related to TD (Pauls, Leckman, Towbin, Zahner, & Cohen, 1986). Such a hypothesis would explain the frequent comorbidity of OCD and TS, the familial relationships between the two disorders, and the neurochemical overlap in their treatment.

INTERVENTIONS FOR TOURETTE'S DISORDER

In order to treat TD patients optimally, the clinician needs to integrate educational, psychological and pharmacological approaches (Miguel, Shavitt, Ferrao, Brotto, & Diniz, 2003). The most effective psychological interventions are cognitive-behavior therapy (CBT; see chap. 9) and habit-reversal training (HRT).

Medical interventions for TD vary greatly. Currently, only two medications, both neuroleptics, are approved for TD by the FDA, Orap® (pimozide) and Haldol® (haloperidol). Although these medications are very effective at reducing tic symptoms, when used alone they often do not help reduce OCD symptoms (McDougle et al., 1995; McDougle, Goodman, & Price, 1994; Zohar et al., 1992), and they are not frequently used as they have negative side effects that prescribing physicians typically want to avoid including cognitive dulling and tardive dyskinesia.

A number of placebo-controlled studies have demonstrated the efficacy of clomipramine (McDougle, 1997; Montgomery, Montgomery, & Fineberg, 1990; Simeon, Thatte, & Wiggins, 1990) and most of the SSRIs in the treatment of OCD (Miguel et al., 2003). The SSRIs that have been found to be effective include fluvoxamine, sertraline, fluoxetine, paroxetine, and citalopram (Miguel et al., 2003). The therapeutic effects of SSRIs in OCD are in marked contrast to norepinephrine uptake inhibitors, such as desipramine and nortriptyline, which have been found to be ineffective (Zohar & Insel, 1987).

Although treatment with SSRIs is effective for most patients with OCD, few patients become totally asymptomatic and about 30%–40% show no significant improvement after adequate trials with such treatments (Ackerman, Greenland, Bystritsky, Morgenstern, & Katz, 1994; Rosario-Campos et al., 2001). The presence of tics may predict a worse response to SSRI monotherapy, McDougle et al. studied 33 OCD patients with and 33 without tics treated with fluvoxamine (McDougle et al., 1993; McDougle, Goodman, & Price, 1994). Clinical improvement occurred in 52% in the OCD-alone group compared to only 21% of the OCD + tics group. However, preliminary results of two unpublished studies, one with clomipramine and the other employing an SSRI, did not find a significant difference in treatment response between those with pure OCD versus those with OCD + tics (Miguel et al., 2003). Clearly, more studies are necessary to verify if the tic-related OCD has a worse prognosis.

Although available data indicate that neuroleptics alone are ineffective in treating OCD (McDougle et al., 1993; McDougle, Goodman, & Price, 1994; Zohar, Zohar-Kadouch, & Kindler, 1992), the addition of typical neuroleptics to SSRIs was found to be of benefit in an open study with pimozide (McDougle et al., 1990; McDougle, Southwick, & Rohrbaugh, 1990), and in a controlled trial with haloperidol (McDougle et al., 1994). Moreover, haloperidol addition to fluvoxamine was especially effective for OCD patients with comorbid tic disorders, but was ineffective for patients without tics, suggesting that tic-related OCD is a clinically meaningful subtype (McDougle et al., 1994).

Cognitive-behavior therapy (CBT) is the psychological treatment of choice for pediatric OCD (Butler, Chapman, Forman, & Beck, 2006; James, Soler, Weatherall, & James, 2005; Piacentini & Langley, 2004) mainly through the employment of exposure and response prevention (ERP). During an exposure, the patient is placed in contact with objects or situations she or he fears in order to elicit anxiety or distress. Response prevention consists of not allowing the patient to engage in usual rituals or other anxiety-reducing behaviors in response to exposure. With repetitive ERP, anxiety decreases through the process of physiologic habituation and the compulsive behaviors decrease through a process know as extinction. Although this technique has a success rate in OCD ranging from 60% to 80%, compliance rate is only about 50%, and for some patients, ERP corrects their obsessions or belief distortions only modestly (Butler, Chapman, Forman, & Beck, 2006; Cartwright-Hatton, Roberts, Chitsabesan, Fothergill, & Harrington, 2004; Piacentini, 1999; Piacentini & Bergman, 2000). Two studies suggest that group behavior therapy may also be effective for pediatric OCD (with or without tics) and less costly (Himle, Fischer, Van Etten, Janeck, & Hanna, 2003; Van Noppen BL, 1998). The cognitive approach can be very helpful in managing overestimation of danger and overvalued ideas, pathological doubting, family and interpersonal problems resulting from OCD, or when the patient is too anxious to engage in behavior therapy.

The technique of habit-reversal training (HRT) may be promising for TD patients with comorbid OCD because their repetitive behaviors are often triggered by sensory phenomena (Miguel et al., 2003). Using this technique, the patient learns to identify the urge preceding the tic or compulsion and to produce a physical response opposite to the repetitive behavior, which should be socially unnoticeable and compatible with normal behavior (Miguel et al., 2003).

Individuals with TD may also receive psychosocial interventions to help reduce tics and OCD symptoms and increase self-monitoring skills. As Harrington (1998) points out, interventions focus mainly on patient education and on helping patients and families manage the comorbid conditions associated with TD. For the school-age child, these generally include possible emotional, educational, and behavioral impairments that can interfere with normal social development and school performance. Such impairments are not insignificant and nearly all patients with TD have one or more comorbid conditions (Zinner, 2000). It is this high incidence of comorbid psychopathology, furthermore, that presents young patients and their parents with formidable challenges to school performance (Hagin, Beecher, Pagano, & Kreeger, 1982; Wodrich, Benjamin, & Lachar, 1997), as well as social interactions with peers (Bawden, Stokes, Camfield, Camfield, & Salisbury, 1998; Kurlan et al., 1996).

In a study by Cooper (1996), parents of children with OCD were asked what interventions were helpful to them. The intervention reported most frequently (89%) was drug treatment for the patient. However, nearly 84% of the parents reported that individual therapy for them was a useful intervention. In addition, almost 25% of the sample reported family therapy, self-help groups, and group therapy were useful. Finally, 57% of the respondents reported that workshops and classes on OCD were needed most by the family. It is clear that education about the disorder, either TS or OCD, is a very useful intervention desired by families.

TRICHOTILLOMANIA

The defining characteristic of trichotillomania (TTM) is the recurrent, compulsive pulling out of one's own hair, resulting in observable hair loss. The scalp and face are usually the primary locations for hair-pulling; however, trichotillomania may involve any part of the body with hair. The most common hair-pulling sites are the scalp, eyebrows, and eyelashes. Less common locations for hair-pulling include the pubic area, perirectal region, or any other body region. An individual with trichotillomania may use his or her fingernails, as well as tweezers, pins, or other mechanical devices to pull out hair; this may result in permanent skin damage. The hair-pulling is often described as a compulsion that is disturbing to the person, much in the same way as someone suffering from OCD is distressed by a compulsion.

Diagnostic criteria for TTM, applied to both adults and children, have been established and are published in the 4th edition of the *DSM–IV–TR* (American Psychological Association, 2000). TTM is included under other disorders of "impulse control" such as pyromania, kleptomania, and pathologic gambling. These conditions share in common a sense of tension before performing a given act and gratification and/or relief after completion. However, many patients with TTM, especially children, deny this tension/gratification phenomenon and therefore do not meet *DSM–IV* criteria for the disorder (Oranje, Peereboom-Wynia, & De Raeymaecker, 1986). Thus, it has been suggested that TTM be included under anxiety disorders, because it shares some OC features. A new diagnostic category (displacement activity disorder) that would include TTM as well as other "nervous habits" such as skin-picking and nail-biting have been proposed previously (Lochner et al., 2005; McElroy, Hudson, Pope, Keck, & Aizley, 1992; McElroy, Phillips, & Keck, 1994).

Aberrant grooming behaviors consisting of hair-pulling, nail-biting, and skin-picking have been found to be significantly more frequent in the familial OCD subgroups (Hanna, Fischer, Chadha, Himle, & Van Etten, 2005). For example, a family study of OCD found a lifetime prevalence of 4% for TTM in adults with OCD (Bienvenu et al., 2000). However, the prevalence of TTM is probably grossly underestimated because of the secretiveness so characteristic of the disorder as well as under-recognition by medical professionals.

Recent neuropsychological studies in OCSD have demonstrated that cognitive inhibition deficits appeared specific to OCD. For example, one study found that strategy implementation deficits, suggestive of cognitive inflexibility, and fronto-striatal dysfunction, appear integral to the neuropsychological profile of OCD, but not TTM (Bohne, Keuthen, Tuschen-Caffier, & Wilhelm, 2005; Chamberlain, Blackwell, Fineberg, Robbins, & Sahakian, 2006).

Like tics in TD, hair-pulling is usually, but not always, proceeded by a certain level of tension and a strong "urge." In addition, hair-pulling is usually, but not always, followed by a sensation of relief or pleasure. Hair-pulling is usually done alone, often while reading, watching TV, driving or talking on the phone, or while grooming in the bathroom. An episode may occur in response to stress or be triggered by a negative mood state, but may also occur while an individual is calm and relaxed. Sometimes hair-pulling is done as a conscious behavior, but it is frequently done as an unconscious habit.

Individuals with TTM often attempt to camouflage the hair loss that accompanies the disorder. Common camouflaging techniques include the use of scarves, hats, and false eyelashes. In extreme cases, individuals with TTM may avoid social situations in an effort to prevent others from seeing the hair loss.

Interventions for Trichotillomania

Pharmacotherapy for TTM is not well established, due to a lack of controlled long-term studies, especially in children. Although SSRIs seem to be the safest and best-established medication choices, positive treatment response is not consistent in the literature and is often disrupted by significant relapse (Walsh & McDougle, 2005).

The primary treatment modality for TTM is CBT (Keijsers et al., 2006; Woods, Wetterneck, & Flessner, 2005). As described earlier for OCD with tics, HRT challenges the problem in a two-fold process. First, the individual with TTM learns to be more consciously aware of situations and events that trigger hair-pulling episodes. Second, the individual learns to utilize alternative behaviors in response to these situations and events.

There are a number of other therapeutic techniques that can be used as adjuncts to HRT (Keijsers et al., 2006; Woods, Wetterneck, & Flessner, 2005). Among these are Stimulus Control techniques and ERP. Stimulus Control techniques involve utilizing specific physical items as "habit-blockers" to restrict the ability to pull hair. ERP, which is the primary treatment for OCD and many OCSD, is most valuable if the individual with TTM is already aware of the specific situations and events that trigger hair-pulling episodes, and has already made significant recovery using HRT.

COMPULSIVE SKIN-PICKING

The primary characteristic of compulsive skin-picking (CSP) is the repetitive picking at one's own skin to the extent of causing damage (Wilhelm et al., 1999). Usually, but not always, the face is the primary location for skin-picking. However, CSP, also known as dermatillomania or neurotic excoriation, may involve any part of the body. Individuals with CSP may pick at normal skin variations such as freckles and moles, at actual pre-existing scabs, sores or acne blemishes, or at imagined skin defects that nobody else can observe. Individuals with CSP may use their fingernails, as well as their teeth, tweezers, pins or other mechanical devices. As a result, CSP may cause bleeding, bruises, infections, and/or permanent disfigurement of the skin.

As stated earlier, aberrant grooming behaviors were significantly more frequent in family studies of OCD (Hanna et al., 2005). CSP, in particular, occurred in 33% of the familial subgroup but in none of the sporadic subgroup. A family study of OCD found a lifetime prevalence of 25% for pathologic nail-biting, 24% for pathologic skin-picking, and 4% for TTM in adults with OCD (Bienvenu et al., 2000). The rates of pathologic skin-picking and pathologic grooming disorders overall were significantly increased in first-degree relatives in that study. Furthermore, among all relatives, the prevalence of pathologic skin- picking was significantly greater in those with OCD than in those without OCD (Cullen et al., 2001). Uncontrolled clinical series suggest that pathologic skin-picking is associated with a high lifetime prevalence of OCD (Arnold et al., 1998; Wilhelm et al., 1999). Another descriptive study found that pathologic skin-picking and TTM occurred at higher rates in OCD patients than in patients with either panic disorder or social phobia (Richter, Summerfeldt, Antony, & Swinson, 2003). A family study of TTM found a trend for an elevated rate of OCD in the first-degree case relatives (Lenane et al., 1992).

Skin-picking is also a common characteristic of Prader-Willi syndrome (PWS). PWS is characterized by hypotonia at birth, hypogonadism, early childhood obesity, and mental deficiency (Warnock & Kestenbaum, 1992). Other behavioral symptoms that become prominent during adolescence and adulthood include temper outbursts, stealing and hoarding food. The skin-picking behavior observed in individuals with PWS is quite common and can lead to persistent sores and infections, even requiring hospitalization. In one case report two patients with PWS who displayed repetitive skin-picking were both treated successfully with different doses of the SSRI fluoxetine (Warnock & Kestenbaum, 1992).

As with other OCSDs, skin-picking is sometimes preceded by a certain level of tension and a strong "itch" or "urge." Likewise, skin-picking may be followed by a feeling of relief or pleasure. A CSP episode may be a conscious response to anxiety or depression, but is frequently done as an unconscious habit. Individuals with CSP often attempt to camouflage the damage caused to their skin by using make-up or wearing clothes to cover the subsequent marks and scars. In extreme cases, individuals with CSP may avoid social situations in an effort to prevent others from seeing the scars, scabs, and bruises that result from skin-picking.

Because CSP has OC features that are quite similar to OCD, TD and TTM, CSP is sometimes found in individuals with these disorders, as well as in patents with certain medical conditions. For example, body dysmorphic disorder and a preoccupation about their skin's appearance precipitated CSP in about 30% of patients (Arnold et al., 1998). Though not currently listed in the *DSM–IV–TR* (American Psychological Association, 2000), some researchers believe it merits distinction as a separate diagnostic entity (Arnold et al., 1998).

As with the other OCSDs, the primary CBT modality for CSP depends on the level of awareness the individual has regarding the problem. If the CSP is generally an unconscious habit, HRT is used, but if the individual with CSP is already aware of the specific situations and events that trigger skin-picking episodes, ERP is used.

BODY DYSMORPHIC DISORDER

Body dysmorphic disorder (BDD) is currently classified by the *DSM–IV–TR* as a somatoform disorder (American Psychological Association, 2000). The main feature of this disorder is the obsession over an imagined physical defect or anomaly in a person of normal appearance. Although any part of the body can be obsessed about or simply being unattractive, the most common symptom is usually over a perceived facial flaw, such as a big nose. BDD can be very debilitating. For example, one study showing that as many as one third of its sufferers becomes homebound. The sufferer becomes obsessed with worry and rituals much like a person suffering from OCD. In the same way an OCD sufferer will check the stove numerous times to see if its turned off, a sufferer of BDD will repeatedly look at their appearance in the mirror. Some studies have shown a 12% lifetime comorbidity rate with BDD for people suffering from OCD. Studies have also shown that between 37%–56% of people with BDD have a family history of OCD.

There has been a major push recently for BDD to be removed from its current grouping with the somatoform disorders in *DSM–IV–TR*. For example, Mayou et al. (Mayou, Kirmayer, Simon, Kroenke, & Sharpe, 2005) proposed that the whole somatoform category be abandoned altogether in future editions of the *DSM*. Under their scheme, BDD would be grouped along with OCD, reflecting the clinical, demographic and treatment response similarities between BDD and OCD.

Only a few studies have directly compared patients who have BDD with those who have OCD. Frare, Perugi, Ruffolo, and Toni (2004) compared three groups: 79 patients with OCD only, 34 patients with BDD only, and 24 patients with both OCD and BDD (Frare et al., 2004). Both BDD groups were younger, had an earlier symptom onset, and were more often unemployed and unmarried than the pure OCD group. In terms of comorbidities, the BDD + OCD group had the highest rates of bipolar disorder, bulimia, social phobia, and alcohol and other drug problems, whereas the OCD group had the lowest levels of comorbidity, with those with BDD only having intermediate levels. These authors concluded that BDD is "not a simple clinical variant of OCD," and that it is also related to other disorders such as mood, social anxiety, and the eating disorders (Frare et al., 2004).

However, there are some key differences between the disorders in terms of phenomenology and the precise nature of the belief (Castle & Groves, 2000; Jefferys & Castle, 2003). For example, in BDD the beliefs are ego-syntonic (synchronous with the sense of self) rather than dystonic (alien to the self) as is necessary for an OCD diagnosis. Moreover, there are high rates of delusional conviction in BDD that are typically not present in OCD.

Treatment of BDD

BDD patients have a poor quality of life, are socially isolated, depressed, and have a high risk of committing suicide. They often have needless dermatological treatment and cosmetic surgery (Phillips et al., 2006; Veale, 2004). The condition is easily trivialized and stigmatized. As with other OCSDs, there is evidence for the benefit of CBT and SSRIs in high doses for at least 12 weeks in adults (Veale, 2004). Although these studies were controlled, they were small and not conducted in adolescent patients. Surprisingly, there is little evidence of any benefit of antipsychotic drugs or other forms of psychotherapy, despite some studies showing approximately 50% of BDD patients are delusional (Phillips, 2005; Phillips, Menard, Pagano, Fay, & Stout, 2006).

OTHER POSSIBLE OBSESSIVE-COMPULSIVE SPECTRUM DISORDERS

In addition to TD, TTM, CSP, and BDD, there are other conditions that share characteristics with OCD. These disorders include depersonalization disorder, pervasive developmental disorders, pyromania, and kleptomania. Although these disorders are classified in various categories within the *DSM–IV–TR*, they each have underlying urges and behaviors that are consistent with other OCSD.

Depersonalization Disorder

Listed in the *DSM–IV–TR* as a dissociative disorder (American Psychological Association, 2000), depersonalization disorder is defined by a feeling of being detached from ones mind or body (as if the person were floating outside of their body). People often feel as if they are not in control of their body or speech, and can demonstrate a lack of affect. The actual experience of depersonalization is fairly common among normal functioning people, and also occurs during drug use. Individuals suffering from depersonalization disorder report that the symptoms are severe, frequent, unwanted, and interfering with one's life. Depersonalization disorder frequently occurs during other disorders such as schizophrenia and depression, and therefore is not diagnosed when the depersonalization appears only during episodes of these other disorders. OCD and depersonalization disorder have similar onset and a similarly chronic course (Torch, 1978). In much the way a person suffering from OCD suffers from unwanted, repetitive thoughts, so to does a person suffering from depersonalization disorder.

In one study of 30 adult male and female patients, the mean age at onset of depersonalization disorder was 16 years old and the illness had a chronic course that was usually continuous but sometimes episodic (Simeon et al., 1997). Severe distress and high levels of interpersonal impairment with major depression and anxiety disorders are common, but none specifically related to the depersonalization. In addition, a wide variety of personality disorders was manifested including avoidant, borderline, and obsessive-compulsive. Although not highly traumatized, the patients with depersonalization disorder reported significantly more childhood trauma than the normal comparison subjects.

Depersonalization is typically treatment refractory with only serotonin reuptake inhibitors and to a lesser extent, benzodiazepines being of any therapeutic benefit (Simeon et al., 1997). Despite the relatively high rates of reporting these symptoms, little research has been conducted into psychotherapy for this disorder. In a recent open study (Hunter et al., 2005), 21 adult subjects with DPD were treated individually with cognitive-behavioral therapy (CBT). The therapy involved helping the patients reinterpret their symptoms in a nonthreatening way as well as reducing avoidances, safety behaviors, and symptom monitoring. Significant improvements in standardized measures of dissociation, depression, anxiety and general functioning were found at post-treatment and 6-month follow-up. In addition, there were significant reductions in clinician ratings on the Present State Examination (Wing, Cooper, & Sartorius, 1974), and nearly 30% of subjects no longer met criteria for DPD at the end of therapy. Although these initial results are encouraging, further trials with more rigorous research methodology and larger sample sizes are warranted to determine the specificity of CBT for treating DPD.

Autism/Asperger's Disorder

Autism is a pervasive developmental disorder that begins in early childhood. It is characterized by severe deficits in the ability to communicate and interact with others. Also present in autism are repetitive behaviors and a limited range of interests, which is similar to an OCD presentation. Asperger's disorder is also classified as a pervasive developmental disorder, however, communication is not impaired and individuals are typically higher functioning in comparison to those with autism.

OC behaviors are common and disabling in autistic-spectrum disorders (ASD) but little is known about how they compare with those experienced by people with OCD (Russell, Mataix-Cols, Anson, & Murphy, 2005). In a recent study, symptoms of 40 adults with high-functioning ASD were compared with a gender-matched group of adults ($n = 45$) with a primary diagnosis of OCD using the Yale-Brown Obsessive-Compulsive Scale and Symptom Checklist (Russell, Mataix-Cols, Anson, & Murphy, 2005). When OCD symptoms were carefully distinguished from stereotypic behaviors and interests usually displayed by those with ASD, the two groups had similar frequencies of OC symptoms, with somatic obsessions and repeating rituals being more common in the OCD group. The OCD group had higher OC symptom severity ratings but up to 50% of the ASD group reported at least moderate levels of interference from their symptoms. These researchers concluded that OC symptoms are common in adults with high-functioning ASD and are associated with significant levels of distress.

Pyromania

Pyromania is an impulse control disorder that involves intentionally setting a fire for gratification (American Psychological Association, 2000). Prior to setting a fire the person typically obsesses and experiences some tension. Following the compulsive act of starting the fire, the individual feels relief and gratification. The fire setting is not done for any personal reasons, such as revenge, anger, monetary gain, and so on, nor is it done in a state of psychosis. Merely it is an obsession that must be acted on.

Kleptomania

Kleptomania is an impulse control disorder characterized by the impulsive need to steal (American Psychological Association, 2000). Like pyromania, the act is not performed for personal reasons, such as monetary gain or revenge (in fact, a person with kleptomania will sometimes replace the item they steal after the fact), nor is it done because of another disorder, such as antisocial personality disorder or bipolar disorder. Similar to OCD or pyromania, the person obsesses about stealing and feels tension and anxiety. On acting compulsively by stealing, a kleptomaniac feels temporary relief from their obsession.

SUMMARY

Obsessive-compulsive disorder is an anxiety disorder characterized by obsessive thoughts that evoke distressing anxiety. The anxiety caused by the obsessive thoughts is typically relieved through the performance of a simple or complex compulsive behavior. Further, there are disorders from other diagnostic categories that share many of the same obsessive-compulsive (OC) symptoms. These disorders are frequently referred to as Obsessive-Compulsive Spectrum Disorders (OCSD). Although the specific obsessive thoughts and compulsive behaviors vary across the OCSDs, the underlying urges and anxieties are very similar. Treatment for these disorders varies and may include medications, psychosocial interventions, and cognitive-behavioral therapy.

However, it should be pointed out that much of the extant data on OCSDs covered in this chapter was derived from adult studies and extrapolated to children and this may be problematic for developmental reasons. For example, in a recent systematic evaluation of the effects of age on the expression of clinical features of OCD, Geller et al. (2001) found evidence of developmental heterogeneity in which specific correlates were associated with symptoms in different age groups. For example, OCD in childhood and adolescence was male preponderant and associated with a higher frequency of aggressive obsessions, hoarding and saving compulsions, multiple obsessions and compulsions, and poor insight compared with adult OCD. Sexual and religious obsessions were selectively more prevalent in adolescents compared with either children or adults. In addition, children with OCD had higher rates of Tourette's disorder and separation anxiety disorder than older age groups, but mood disorders were similarly elevated in both adolescents and adults with OCD. Adults with OCD also had higher rates of substance use and eating disorders than either children or adolescents. These findings support a hypothesis of developmental discontinuity between pediatric and adult OCD across the life cycle and should be considered when conducting research on OCSDs.

Nevertheless, studies of the phenomenology, psychobiology, family relationships, and treatment response of OCD support the view that OCD is not simply a homogenous entity. Eventually, perhaps, we will be able to delineate specific subtypes of OCD that allow the correlation of particular symptomatic presentations, psychobiological mechanisms, and treatment response.

REFERENCES

Ackerman, D. L., Greenland, S., Bystritsky, A., Morgenstern, H., & Katz, R. J. (1994). Predictors of treatment response in obsessive-compulsive disorder: Multivariate analyses from a multicenter trial of clomipramine. *Journal of Clinical Psychopharmacology, 14*, 247–254.

American Psychological Association. (2000). *Diagnostic and Statistical Manual of Mental Disorders: DSM–IV–TR* (4th ed.). Washington, DC: Author.

Arnold, L. M., McElroy, S. L., Mutasim, D. F., Dwight, M. M., Lamerson, C. L., & Morris, E. M. (1998). Characteristics of 34 adults with psychogenic excoriation. *Journal of Clinical Psychiatry, 59*, 509–514.

Baer, L. (1994). Factor analysis of symptom subtypes of obsessive-compulsive disorder and their relation to personality and tic disorders. *Journal of Clinical Psychiatry, 55 Supplemental*, 18–23.

Bawden, H. N., Stokes, A., Camfield, C. S., Camfield, P. R., & Salisbury, S. (1998). Peer relationship problems in children with Tourette's disorder or diabetes mellitus. *Journal of Child Psychology and Psychiatry, 39,* 663–668.

Bienvenu, O. J., Samuels, J. F., Riddle, M. A., Hoehn-Saric, R., Liang, K. Y., Cullen, B. A., et al. (2000). The relationship of obsessive-compulsive disorder to possible spectrum disorders: Results from a family study. *Biological Psychiatry, 48,* 287–293.

Bohne, A., Keuthen, N. J., Tuschen-Caffier, B., & Wilhelm, S. (2005). Cognitive inhibition in trichotillomania and obsessive-compulsive disorder. *Behaviour Research and Therapy, 43,* 923–942.

Budman, C. L., Bruun, R. D., Park, K. S., & Olson, M. E. (1998). Rage attacks in children and adolescents with Tourette's disorder: A pilot study. *Journal of Clinical Psychiatry, 59,* 576–580.

Butler, A. C., Chapman, J. E., Forman, E. M., & Beck, A. T. (2006). The empirical status of cognitive-behavioral therapy: A review of meta-analyses. *Clinical Psychologist Review, 26,* 17–31.

Carter, A. S., Pauls, D. L., Leckman, J. F., & Cohen, D. J. (1994). A prospective longitudinal study of Gilles de la Tourette's syndrome. *Journal of the American Academy of Child and Adolescent Psychiatry, 33,* 377–385.

Cartwright-Hatton, S., Roberts, C., Chitsabesan, P., Fothergill, C., & Harrington, R. (2004). Systematic review of the efficacy of cognitive behaviour therapies for childhood and adolescent anxiety disorders. *British Journal of Clinical Psychology, 43,* 421–436.

Castle, D. J., & Groves, A. (2000). The internal and external boundaries of obsessive-compulsive disorder. *Australian and New Zealand Journal of Psychiatry, 34,* 249–255.

Cath, D. C., Spinhoven, P., Hoogduin, C. A., Landman, A. D., van Woerkom, T. C., van de Wetering, B. J., et al. (2001). Repetitive behaviors in Tourette's syndrome and OCD with and without tics: What are the differences? *Psychiatry Research, 101,* 171–185.

Chamberlain, S. R., Blackwell, A. D., Fineberg, N. A., Robbins, T. W., & Sahakian, B. J. (2006). Strategy implementation in obsessive-compulsive disorder and trichotillomania. *Psychological Medicine, 36,* 91–97.

Coffey, B. J., Miguel, E. C., Biederman, J., Baer, L., Rauch, S. L., O'Sullivan, R. L., et al. (1998). Tourette's disorder with and without obsessive-compulsive disorder in adults: Are they different? *Journal of Nervous and Mental Disease, 186,* 201–206.

Comings, D. E., Himes, J. A., & Comings, B. G. (1990). An epidemiologic study of Tourette's syndrome in a single school district. *Journal of Clinical Psychiatry, 51,* 463–469.

Cooper, M. (1996). Obsessive-compulsive disorder: Effects on family members. *American Journal of Orthopsychiatry, 66*(2), 296–304.

Cullen, B. A., Samuels, J. F., Bienvenu, O. J., Grados, M., Hoehn-Saric, R., Hahn, J., et al. (2001). The relationship of pathologic skin picking to obsessive-compulsive disorder. *Journal of Nervous and Mental Disease, 189,* 193–195.

Falret, J. P. (1866). Discussion sur la folie raisonnante [Discussion on the reasoning of madness] (Vol. V). *Annals of Medical Psychology, 24,* 382–426.

Frare, F., Perugi, G., Ruffolo, G., & Toni, C. (2004). Obsessive-compulsive disorder and body dysmorphic disorder: A comparison of clinical features. *European Psychiatry, 19,* 292–298.

Geller, D. A., Biederman, J., Faraone, S., Agranat, A., Cradock, K., Hagermoser, L., et al. (2001). Developmental aspects of obsessive-compulsive disorder: Findings in children, adolescents, and adults. *Journal of Nervous and Mental Disease, 189,* 471–477.

Geller, D. A., Biederman, J., Faraone, S. V., Bellordre, C. A., Kim, G. S., Hagermoser, L., et al. (2001). Disentangling chronological age from age of onset in children and adolescents with obsessive—compulsive disorder. *International Journal of Neuropsychopharmacology, 4*, 169–178.

George, M. S., Trimble, M. R., Ring, H. A., Sallee, F. R., & Robertson, M. M. (1993). Obsessions in obsessive-compulsive disorder with and without Gilles de la Tourette's syndrome. *American Journal of Psychiatry, 150*, 93–97.

Grad, L. R., Pelcovitz, D., Olson, M., Matthews, M., & Grad, G. J. (1987). Obsessive-compulsive symptomatology in children with Tourette's syndrome. *Journal of the American Academy of Child and Adolescent Psychiatry, 26*, 69–73.

Hagin, R. A., Beecher, R., Pagano, G., & Kreeger, H. (1982). Effects of Tourette's syndrome on learning. *Advances in Neurology, 35*, 323–328.

Hanna, G. L., Fischer, D. J., Chadha, K. R., Himle, J. A., & Van Etten, M. (2005). Familial and sporadic subtypes of early-onset obsessive-compulsive disorder. *Biological Psychiatry, 57*, 895–900.

Hantouche, E. G., & Lancrenon, S. (1996). Modern typology of symptoms and obsessive-compulsive syndromes: Results of a large French study of 615 patients. *L'Encephale, 22,* Spec. No. 1, 9–21.

Harrington, R. G. (1998). Tourette syndrome. In L. Phelps (Ed.), *Health related disorders in children and adolescents: A guidebook for understanding and educating* (pp. 641–651). Washington, DC: American Psychological Association.

Himle, J. A., Fischer, D. J., Van Etten, M. L., Janeck, A. S., & Hanna, G. L. (2003). Group behavioral therapy for adolescents with tic-related and non-tic-related obsessive-compulsive disorder. *Depression and Anxiety, 17*, 73–77.

Holzer, J. C., Goodman, W. K., McDougle, C. J., Baer, L., Boyarsky, B. K., Leckman, J. F., et al. (1994). Obsessive-compulsive disorder with and without a chronic tic disorder. A comparison of symptoms in 70 patients. *British Journal of Psychiatry, 164*, 469–473.

Hornse, H., Banerjee, S., Zeitlin, H., & Robertson, M. (2001). The prevalence of Tourette's syndrome in 13–14-year-olds in mainstream schools. *Journal of Child Psychology and Psychiatry, 42*, 1035–1039.

Hunter, E. C., Baker, D., Phillips, M. L., Sierra, M., & David, A. S. (2005). Cognitive-behaviour therapy for depersonalisation disorder: An open study. *Behavioral Research Therapy, 43*, 1121–30.

James, A., Soler, A., Weatherall, R., & James, A. (2005). Cognitive behavioural therapy for anxiety disorders in children and adolescents. *Cochrane Database of Systematic Review*, CD004690.

Jefferys, D. E., & Castle, D. J. (2003). Body dysmorphic disorder—a fear of imagined ugliness. *Australian Family Physician, 32*, 722–725.

Kadesjo, B., & Gillberg, C. (2000). Tourette's disorder: Epidemiology and comorbidity in primary school children. *Journal of the American Academy of Child and Adolescent Psychiatry, 39*, 548–555.

Keijsers, G. P., van Minnen, A., Hoogduin, C. A., Klaassen, B. N., Hendriks, M. J., & Tanis-Jacobs, J. (2006). Behavioural treatment of trichotillomania: Two-year follow-up results. *Behaviour Research and Therapy, 44*(3), 359–370.

Kurlan, R., Daragjati, C., Como, P. G., McDermott, M. P., Trinidad, K. S., Roddy, S., et al. (1996). Non-obscene complex socially inappropriate behavior in Tourette's syndrome. *Journal of Neuropsychiatry and Clinical Neurosciences, 8*, 311–317.

Leckman, J. F. (2002). Tourette's syndrome. *Lancet, 360*, 1577–1586.

Leckman, J. F., Grice, D. E., Barr, L. C., de Vries, A. L., Martin, C., Cohen, D. J., et al. (1994). Tic-related vs. non-tic-related obsessive-compulsive disorder. *Anxiety, 1*, 208–215.

Leckman, J. F., Peterson, B. S., Pauls, D. L., & Cohen, D. J. (1997). Tic disorders. *Psychiatry Clinics of North America, 20*, 839–861.

Lenane, M. C., Swedo, S. E., Rapoport, J. L., Leonard, H., Sceery, W., & Guroff, J. J. (1992). Rates of obsessive-compulsive disorder in first degree relatives of patients with trichotillomania: A research note. *Journal of Child Psychology and Psychiatry, 33*, 925–933.

Leonard, H. L., Lenane, M. C., Swedo, S. E., Rettew, D. C., Gershon, E. S., & Rapoport, J. L. (1992). Tics and Tourette's disorder: A 2- to 7-year follow-up of 54 obsessive-compulsive children. *American Journal of Psychiatry, 149*, 1244–1251.

Lochner, C., Seedat, S., du Toit, P. L., Nel, D. G., Niehaus, D. J., Sandler, R., et al. (2005). Obsessive-compulsive disorder and trichotillomania: A phenomenological comparison. *BMC Psychiatry, 5*, 2.

Mataix-Cols, D., Rosario-Campos, M. C., & Leckman, J. F. (2005). A multidimensional model of obsessive-compulsive disorder. *American Journal of Psychiatry, 162*, 228–238.

Mayou, R., Kirmayer, L. J., Simon, G., Kroenke, K., & Sharpe, M. (2005). Somatoform disorders: Time for a new approach in DSM–V. *American Journal of Psychiatry, 162*, 847–855.

McDougle, C. J. (1997). Update on pharmacologic management of OCD: Agents and augmentation. *Journal of Clinical Psychiatry, 58*(12), 11–17.

McDougle, C. J., Barr, L. C., Goodman, W. K., Pelton, G. H., Aronson, S. C., Anand, A., et al. (1995). Lack of efficacy of clozapine monotherapy in refractory obsessive-compulsive disorder. *American Journal of Psychiatry, 152*, 1812–1814.

McDougle, C. J., Goodman, W. K., Leckman, J. F., Barr, L. C., Heninger, G. R., & Price, L. H. (1993). The efficacy of fluvoxamine in obsessive-compulsive disorder: Effects of comorbid chronic tic disorder. *Journal of Clinical Psychopharmacology, 13*, 354–358.

McDougle, C. J., Goodman, W. K., Leckman, J. F., Lee, N. C., Heninger, G. R., & Price, L. H. (1994). Haloperidol addition in fluvoxamine-refractory obsessive-compulsive disorder. A double-blind, placebo-controlled study in patients with and without tics. *Archives of General Psychiatry, 51*, 302–308.

McDougle, C. J., Goodman, W. K., & Price, L. H. (1994). Dopamine antagonists in tic-related and psychotic spectrum obsessive-compulsive disorder. *Journal of Clinical Psychiatry, 55*, 24–31.

McDougle, C. J., Goodman, W. K., Price, L. H., Delgado, P. L., Krystal, J. H., Charney, D. S., et al. (1990). Neuroleptic addition in fluvoxamine-refractory obsessive-compulsive disorder. *American Journal of Psychiatry, 147*, 652–654.

McDougle, C. J., Southwick, S. M., & Rohrbaugh, R. M. (1990). Tourette's disorder and associated complex behaviors: A case report. *Yale Journal of Biology and Medicine, 63*, 209–214.

McElroy, S. L., Hudson, J. I., Pope, H., Jr., Keck, P. E., Jr., & Aizley, H. G. (1992). The DSM–III–R impulse control disorders not elsewhere classified: Clinical characteristics and relationship to other psychiatric disorders. *American Journal of Psychiatry, 149*, 318–327.

McElroy, S. L., Phillips, K. A., & Keck, P. E., Jr. (1994). Obsessive-compulsive spectrum disorder. *Journal of Clinical Psychiatry, 55*, 33–51.

Miguel, E. C., Baer, L., Coffey, B. J., Rauch, S. L., Savage, C. R., O'Sullivan, R. L., et al. (1997). Phenomenological differences appearing with repetitive behaviours in obsessive-compulsive disorder and Gilles de la Tourette's syndrome. *British Journal of Psychiatry, 170*, 140–145.

Miguel, E. C., Coffey, B. J., Baer, L., Savage, C. R., Rauch, S. L., & Jenike, M. A. (1995). Phenomenology of intentional repetitive behaviors in obsessive-compulsive disorder and Tourette's disorder. *Journal of Clinical Psychiatry, 56*, 246–255.

Miguel, E. C., Shavitt, R. G., Ferrao, Y. A., Brotto, S. A., & Diniz, J. B. (2003). How to treat OCD in patients with Tourette syndrome. *Journal of Psychosomatic Research, 55*, 49–57.

Montgomery, S. A., Montgomery, D. B., & Fineberg, N. (1990). Early response with clomipramine in obsessive-compulsive disorder—a placebo controlled study. *Progress in Neuropsychopharmacology and Biological Psychiatry, 14,* 719–727.

Moriarty, J., Eapen, V., Costa, D. C., Gacinovic, S., Trimble, M., Ell, P. J., et al. (1997). HMPAO SPET does not distinguish obsessive-compulsive and tic syndromes in families multiply affected with Gilles de la Tourette's syndrome. *Psychological Medicine, 27,* 737–740.

Nee, L. E., Polinsky, R. J., & Ebert, M. H. (1982). Tourette syndrome: Clinical and family studies. *Advances in Neurology, 35,* 291–295.

Nestadt, G., Samuels, J., Riddle, M., Bienvenu, O. J., Liang, K. Y., LaBuda, M., et al. (2000). A family study of obsessive-compulsive disorder. *Archives of General Psychiatry, 57,* 358–363.

Olson, S. (2004). Neurobiology. Making sense of Tourette's. *Science, 305,* 1390–1392.

Oranje, A. P., Peereboom-Wynia, J. D., & De Raeymaecker, D. M. (1986). Trichotillomania in childhood. *Journal of the American Academy of Dermatology, 15,* 614–619.

Pauls, D. L., Alsobrook, J. P., Goodman, W., Rasmussen, S., & Leckman, J. F. (1995). A family study of obsessive-compulsive disorder. *American Journal of Psychiatry, 152,* 76–84.

Pauls, D. L., & Leckman, J. F. (1986). The inheritance of Gilles de la Tourette's syndrome and associated behaviors. Evidence for autosomal dominant transmission. *New England Journal of Medicine, 315,* 993–997.

Pauls, D. L., Leckman, J. F., Towbin, K. E., Zahner, G. E., & Cohen, D. J. (1986). A possible genetic relationship exists between Tourette's syndrome and obsessive-compulsive disorder. *Psychopharmacology Bulletin, 22,* 730–733.

Pauls, D. L., Raymond, C. L., Stevenson, J. M., & Leckman, J. F. (1991). A family study of Gilles de la Tourette syndrome. *American Journal of Human Genetics, 48,* 154–163.

Petter, T., Richter, M. A., & Sandor, P. (1998). Clinical features distinguishing patients with Tourette's syndrome and obsessive-compulsive disorder from patients with obsessive-compulsive disorder without tics. *Journal of Clinical Psychiatry, 59,* 456–459.

Phillips, K. A. (2005). Placebo-controlled study of pimozide augmentation of fluoxetine in body dysmorphic disorder. *American Journal of Psychiatry, 162,* 377–379.

Phillips, K. A., Menard, W., Pagano, M. E., Fay, C., & Stout, R. L. (2006). Delusional versus nondelusional body dysmorphic disorder: Clinical features and course of illness. *Journal of Psychiatric Research, 40*(2), 95–104.

Phillips, K. A., Didie, E. R., Menard W., Pagano, M. E., Fay, C., & Weisberg, R. B. (2006). Clinical features of body dysmorphic disorder in adolescents and adults. *Psychiatry Research, 141,* 305–314.

Piacentini, J. (1999). Cognitive-behavioral therapy of childhood OCD. *Child and Adolescent Psychiatry Clinics of North America, 8,* 599–616.

Piacentini, J., & Bergman, R. L. (2000). Obsessive-compulsive disorder in children. *Psychiatry Clinics of North America, 23,* 519–533.

Piacentini, J., & Langley, A. K. (2004). Cognitive-behavioral therapy for children who have obsessive-compulsive disorder. *Journal of Clinical Psychology, 60,* 1181–1194.

Pitman, R. K., Green, R. C., Jenike, M. A., & Mesulam, M. M. (1987). Clinical comparison of Tourette's disorder and obsessive-compulsive disorder. *American Journal of Psychiatry, 144,* 1166–1171.

Richter, M. A., Summerfeldt, L. J., Antony, M. M., & Swinson, R. P. (2003). Obsessive-compulsive spectrum conditions in obsessive-compulsive disorder and other anxiety disorders. *Depression and Anxiety, 18,* 118–127.

Robertson, M. M. (1991). The Gilles de la Tourette syndrome and obsessional disorder. *International Clinical Psychopharmacology*, 6(3), 69–82.

Robertson, M. M., Banerjee, S., Eapen, V., & Fox-Hiley, P. (2002). Obsessive-compulsive behaviour and depressive symptoms in young people with Tourette syndrome. A controlled study. *European Child and Adolescent Psychiatry*, 11, 261–265.

Rosario-Campos, M. C., Leckman, J. F., Mercadante, M. T., Shavitt, R. G., Prado, H. S., Sada, P., et al. (2001). Adults with early-onset obsessive-compulsive disorder. *American Journal of Psychiatry*, 158, 1899–1903.

Russell, A. J., Mataix-Cols, D., Anson, M., & Murphy, D. G. (2005). Obsessions and compulsions in Asperger syndrome and high-functioning autism. *British Journal of Psychiatry*, 186, 525–528.

Santangelo, S. L., Pauls, D. L., Goldstein, J. M., Faraone, S. V., Tsuang, M. T., & Leckman, J. F. (1994). Tourette's syndrome: What are the influences of gender and comorbid obsessive-compulsive disorder? *Journal of the American Academy of Child and Adolescent Psychiatry*, 33, 795–804.

Simeon, D., Gross, S., Guralnik, O., Stein, D. J., Schmeidler, J., & Hollander, E. (1997). Feeling unreal: 30 cases of DSM–III–R depersonalization disorder. *American Journal of Psychiatry*, 154, 1107–1113.

Simeon, J. G., Thatte, S., & Wiggins, D. (1990). Treatment of adolescent obsessive-compulsive disorder with a clomipramine-fluoxetine combination. *Psychopharmacology Bulletin*, 26, 285–290.

Stephens, R. J., & Sandor, P. (1999). Aggressive behaviour in children with Tourette syndrome and comorbid attention-deficit hyperactivity disorder and obsessive-compulsive disorder. *Canadian Journal of Psychiatry*, 44, 1036–1042.

Torch, E. M. (1978). Review of the relationship between obsession and depersonalization. *ACTA Psychiatrica Scandinavica*, 58, 191–198.

Van Noppen BL, P. M., Marsland, R., & Rasmussen, S. (1998). A time-limited behavioral group for the treatment of obsessive-compulsive disorder. *Journal of Psychotherapy Practice and Research*, 7, 272–280.

Veale, D. (2004). Body dysmorphic disorder. *Postgraduate Medical Journal*, 80, 67–71.

Walkup, J. T., Leckman, J. F., Price, R. A., Hardin, M., Ort, S. I., & Cohen, D. J. (1988). The relationship between obsessive-compulsive disorder and Tourette's syndrome: A twin study. *Psychopharmacology Bulletin*, 24, 375–379.

Walsh, K. H., & McDougle, C. J. (2005). Pharmacological strategies for trichotillomania. *Expert Opinion on Pharmacotherapy*, 6, 975–984.

Warnock, J. K., & Kestenbaum, T. (1992). Pharmacologic treatment of severe skin-picking behaviors in Prader-Willi syndrome. Two case reports. *Archives of Dermatology*, 128, 1623–1625.

Wilhelm, S., Keuthen, N. J., Deckersbach, T., Engelhard, I. M., Forker, A. E., Baer, L., et al. (1999). Self-injurious skin picking: Clinical characteristics and comorbidity. *Journal of Clinical Psychiatry*, 60, 454–459.

Wing, J. K., Cooper, J. E., & Sartorius, N. (1974). *Measurement and classification of psychiatric symptoms. Instruction manual for the PSE and CATEGO program* (p. 233). New York: Cambridge University Press.

Wodrich, D. L., Benjamin, E., & Lachar, D. (1997). Tourette's syndrome and psychopathology in a child psychiatry setting. *Journal of the American Academy of Child and Adolescent Psychiatry*, 36, 1618–1624.

Woods, D. W., Wetterneck, C. T., & Flessner, C. A. (2005). A controlled evaluation of acceptance and commitment therapy plus habit reversal for trichotillomania. *Behaviour Research and Therapy*.

Zinner, S. H. (2000). Tourette disorder. *Pediatrics in Review*, *21*, 372–383.

Zohar, A. H., Ratzoni, G., Pauls, D. L., Apter, A., Bleich, A., Kron, S., et al. (1992). An epidemiological study of obsessive-compulsive disorder and related disorders in Israeli adolescents. *Journal of the American Academy of Child and Adolescent Psychiatry*, *31*, 1057–1061.

Zohar, J., & Insel, T. R. (1987). Drug treatment of obsessive-compulsive disorder. *Journal of Affective Disorders, 13*, 193–202.

Zohar, J., Zohar-Kadouch, R. C., & Kindler, S. (1992). Current concepts in the pharmacological treatment of obsessive-compulsive disorder. *Drugs, 43*, 210–218.

4

Assessment of Pediatric Obsessive-Compulsive Disorder

Lisa J. Merlo
Eric A. Storch
Jennifer W. Adkins
Tanya K. Murphy
Gary R. Geffken
University of Florida

Pediatric obsessive-compulsive disorder (OCD) is relatively common, affecting an estimated 2%–4% of children and adolescents (Douglass, Moffitt, Dar, McGee, & Silva, 1995; Maina, Albert, Bogetto, & Ravizza, 1999; Rapoport & Inoff-Germain, 2000), though more children likely go undiagnosed or misdiagnosed. For most children, OCD is quite debilitating and results in academic difficulties, social problems, and disruptions in the home/family environment (Piacentini, Bergman, Keller, & McCracken, 2003). The prevalence and severity of pediatric OCD have resulted in increased attention from researchers and clinicians alike in the realms of assessment and treatment (see Lewin, Storch, Adkins, Murphy, & Geffken, 2005, for a review). This chapter focuses on the assessment of pediatric OCD, giving special attention to descriptions of commonly used measures, as well as an overview of challenges and critical issues in pediatric OCD assessment.

SYMPTOMATOLOGY AND PHENOMENOLOGY

Obsessive-compulsive disorder, in both adult and pediatric populations, is characterized by recurrent "obsessions" and/or repetitive/ritualistic "compulsions" that result in significant distress and impaired functioning (American Psychiatric Association, 2000). Obsessions refer to intrusive thoughts, images, sounds, or impulses that the individual experiences as distressing. Generally, the content of obsessions is disturbing to the individual, causing her or him to experience significant anxiety. In addition, though some obsessions appear more neutral in content, their frequency of intrusion may impair the individual's ability to concentrate effectively. Among pediatric patients, the presentation of OCD symptoms is heterogeneous and may include idiosyncratic symptoms.

The majority of patients also acknowledge participation in compulsive behaviors. Compulsions are repetitive/ritualistic behaviors or mental acts that serve to prevent or reduce the experience of anxiety. Patients frequently engage in these behaviors in response to an obsession. For example, a child who experiences obsessive thoughts about being contaminated may exhibit repetitive, ritualized hand-washing or bathing routines. Compulsive behaviors are distinguished from typical responses by their excessive or irrational nature (American Psychiatric Association, 2000). Like obsessions, the nature of compulsive behaviors varies from one individual to the next, and may change over time. Though less common, about 15% of children display only obsessions or compulsions (Storch Murphy, Geffken et al., 2005).

Just as individual differences in symptom expression are typical, the level of distress and impairment exhibited by children with OCD can vary widely. Many children will endorse multiple symptoms (Flament, Whitaker, Rapoport, & Davies, 1988); however, not all children will recognize that their obsessions and compulsions are bizarre or excessive (Practice Parameters, 1998). In fact, recent evidence has suggested that some children report that they enjoy engaging in OCD behaviors and/or seem undistressed by them (Geffken et al., 2005). This subtype of OCD, labeled "ego-syntonic," is most frequently seen among young children with primarily compulsive symptoms. However, despite the child's lack of distress, the symptoms frequently interrupt family functioning and cause difficulty for those who live with the patient (Geffken et al., 2005).

For other children, the OCD symptoms cause significant impairment in social, academic, familial, and daily functioning. Many children have difficulty interacting appropriately with peers and experience teasing/bullying due to their strange behaviors. Others find that the compulsions and avoidance prevent them from participating in many activities with peers. Youngsters frequently have difficulty concentrating in school and may be impaired in their ability to complete assignments on time due to compulsive re-reading or rewriting. Some children become so distressed by their symptoms, either before or during school, that they miss important lessons due to excessive tardiness or absences. Children's ability to function effectively in the home is often compromised as well. Many parents report that their child experiences "meltdowns" when the OCD symptoms are not accommodated, and children often report feeling "stuck" because the OCD is preventing them from completing day-to-day tasks (e.g., bathing, eating, chores, etc.).

PROGNOSIS

Left untreated, the course of pediatric obsessive-compulsive disorder is generally chronic and unremitting, with 13%–87% (mean = 41%) of children demonstrating long-term persistence of their symptoms (Stewart et al., 2004). Symptoms tend to fluctuate over time, and often become exacerbated in times of stress (American Psychiatric Association, 2000). Children with this disorder remain at higher risk for other psychiatric problems in adulthood (Bolton, Luckie, & Steinberg, 1995; Hanna, 1995). Accurate diagnosis of OCD and the identification of a qualified treatment provider remain two major obstacles to treatment of OCD (Hollander et al., 1996). However, with treatment, prognosis for patients with OCD is positive. Children who receive pharmacological, psychological, or combined treatments generally demonstrate significant long-term improvement (Stewart et al., 2004). Thus, accurate assessment and diagnosis of OCD are critical factors in the prognosis of children who suffer from this disorder.

STRUCTURED ASSESSMENT

Pediatric OCD can be difficult to identify given the significant symptom overlap between OCD and other psychiatric and neurological disorders (i.e., Generalized Anxiety Disorder and other anxiety disorders, depressive disorders, autism-spectrum disorders, and Tourette's Disorder), and, therefore, differential diagnosis can be challenging. In order to facilitate the assessment of OCD in children and adolescents, several structured methods have been developed. The use of diagnostic interviews, clinician-administered inventories, self-report measures, and/or parent-report measures can complement traditional clinical interviews and provide quantitative data to support the diagnosis. Descriptions and psychometric properties of commonly used measures are reviewed in the following section. Assessment measures are grouped by category and listed in chronological order of their introduction. Strengths and weaknesses of each measure are listed in Appendix A.

Psychosocial and Medical History

As with all comprehensive evaluations, assessment for pediatric OCD should include a detailed psychosocial and medical history. Clinicians should consider a diagnosis of OCD when the patient exhibits or complains of intrusive thoughts, anxiety-based avoidance of certain places or objects, excessive reassurance-seeking, or repetitive behaviors/rituals. In addition, the clinician should inquire about any family history of OCD and/or other anxiety disorders, as OCD is more common among relatives of individuals with anxiety disorders (Black, Gaffney, Schlosser, & Gabel, 2003). With regard to medical history, strong consideration should be given to a diagnosis of OCD if the child or adolescent patient displays behavioral changes (i.e., develops obsessions or compulsions) after exposure to the streptococcal virus. These behavior changes may reflect Pediatric Autoimmune Neurological Disorders Associated with Streptococcus (PANDAS)—onset symptoms of OCD (Murphy, Petitto, Voeller, & Goodman, 2001; Murphy et al., 2004).

Diagnostic Interviews

In order to facilitate assessment, several structured diagnostic interviews have been developed, which consist of specific questions based on the criteria outlined in the *Diagnostic and Statistical Manual of Mental Disorders, 4th Edition* (DSM–IV: American Psychiatric Association, 1994). This structure adds to the utility of the interviews by including questions to ensure that each criterion is met and to facilitate differential diagnosis with questions assessing for rule-out criteria. In general, diagnostic interviews have demonstrated good reliability and validity. In addition, children are typically able to participate in these interviews without concerns that negative consequences will result from their answers (Hodges, 1993). However, diagnostic interviews are time-consuming, averaging 45–75 minutes for administration. Thus, they are not recommended for basic screening purposes, and their use may be impractical in certain settings (e.g., medical clinics where all patient contacts, including psychological consults, are brief; practices with a high percentage of patients who do not have adequate insurance coverage to reimburse extensive, time-consuming psychological testing). In addition, these interviews require extensive training to ensure proper administration, and parent-reports and child-reports should not be viewed as interchangeable (Hodges, 1993). Though interviews can be administered conjointly or separately, when discrepancies arise it is generally best to consider parent-reports more heavily when interpreting reports of observable behaviors and child self-reports more heavily when interpreting reports of subjective experiences (Herjanic & Reich, 1982).

Anxiety Disorders Interview Schedule for DSM–IV: Child and Parent Version. The most commonly used structured interview for the assessment of pediatric OCD is the *Anxiety Disorders Interview Schedule for DSM–IV: Child & Parent Versions* (ADIS–C/P: Silverman & Albano, 1996). This measure is a clinician-administered, structured interview, which was developed from *DSM–IV* (American Psychiatric Association, 2000) diagnostic criteria. The majority of questions in the *ADIS–C/P* focus on anxiety disorders; however, the *ADIS–C/P* also includes screening questions to rule out the presence of other related disorders (i.e., disruptive behavior disorders, psychotic disorders, and eating disorders). The interview is structured by disorder, and detailed questions regarding each disorder are administered only if the preliminary criteria are endorsed. Parents and children are generally interviewed separately, and the clinician combines data obtained from both informants, using clinical judgment to assign diagnoses and severity ratings. According to *DSM–IV* criteria, diagnoses are based on symptom endorsement, as well as a severity rating of at least 4 (on a scale of 0–8) assessing the patient's level of impairment/distress. The *ADIS–C/P* takes approximately 45–75 minutes to administer depending on the degree of symptom severity and number of diagnoses.

Previous research has shown the *ADIS–C/P* to be a reliable assessment device. For anxiety disorder diagnoses, intraclass correlation coefficients (ICCs) ranged from .82 to .95 (Wood, Piacentini, Bergman, McCracken, & Barrios, 2002), indicating excellent inter-rater reliability. Additionally, *ADIS–C/P* diagnoses have demonstrated excellent test–retest reliability across all anxiety disorders (Silverman, Saavedra, & Pina, 2001), with 1–2 week kappa coefficients ranging from .80 to .92 for diagnoses based on the combined parent/child data. Although the stability of diagnoses based on child interviews alone and parent interviews alone appear somewhat lower (kappa = .63 to .80 and .65 to .88, respectively), these reliabilities are still adequate. Questions regarding the validity of data obtained using the *ADIS–C/P* relate to the relatively low agreement (i.e., kappa = .24 to −.37) observed between parent-report and child-report in a sample of clinic-referred children (Silverman et al., 2001). One possible explanation for these findings that the authors introduce is the likelihood that clinicians generally weigh parent-reports more heavily than child self-reports of symptoms when making diagnostic decisions (Grills & Ollendick, 2002; 2003).

Schedule for Affective Disorders and Schizophrenia for School-Age Children. The *Schedule for Affective Disorders and Schizophrenia for School-Age Children—Present & Lifetime* version (*K–SADS–PL*: Kaufman, Birmaher, Brent, & Rao, 1997) is another clinician-administered, semi-structured interview that was based on *DSM–IV* diagnostic criteria. It was developed as a revision of the *K–SADS—Present Episode* version (Chambers, Puig-Antich, & Hirsch, 1985), and improves on the original measure by including: (1) an assessment of both current and lifetime symptomatology, (2) sections regarding important childhood disorders that had previously been omitted, (3) clarification of certain probes and scoring criteria, (4) impairment ratings to facilitate diagnostic decisions, and (5) correspondence to *DSM–IV* criteria. Clinicians administer the *K–SADS–PL* to parents and children separately, and use clinical judgment to assign diagnoses based on data obtained from both informants. In general, clinicians tend to weigh parent-report of observable behaviors and child self-report of subjective experiences more heavily in making diagnostic decisions (Herjanic & Reich, 1982). The K-SADS begins with a 10–15 minute Introductory Interview, which should be utilized to build rapport with the respondent and establish a base of knowledge for further probing. Next, clinicians administer a series of screening items in order to determine which supplemental questions should be given.

These diagnostic supplements—affective disorders; psychotic disorders; anxiety disorders; behavioral disorders; and substance abuse, eating, and tic disorders—are given after the screening is completed. Symptom and impairment ratings generally correspond to a 4-point scale ranging from 0—"no information available" to 3—"threshold criteria met."

Clinicians score each of the 32 child psychiatric disorder diagnoses as "Definite," "Probable (at least 75% of symptom criteria met)," or "Not present." Administering the K–SADS–PL to nonreferred children and their parents takes about 40 minutes each, whereas it frequently takes about 75 minutes each to administer the K–SADS–PL to psychiatric patients and their parents (Kaufman, 1997).

The K–SADS–PL has generally demonstrated strong psychometric properties, with excellent inter-rater reliability across all diagnoses for assessment of both current diagnoses and past diagnoses (Kaufman et al., 1997). The K–SADS–PL has also demonstrated good to excellent test–retest reliability of common diagnoses, with kappas ranging from .55 to 1.00 across present and lifetime diagnoses. In addition, it has displayed concurrent validity with several other measures of psychopathology in children (e.g., Child Behavior Checklist, Conner's rating scales) as well as other child diagnostic interviews (e.g., Child Assessment Schedule, Interview Schedule for Children, Diagnostic Interview Schedule for Children Version 2.1).

Clinician Rating Scales

Clinician-rated inventories require trained clinicians to make informed ratings of the patient's level of impairment and distress. These ratings are generally believed to be more reliable and valid than parent- or child-report because the clinician can draw on his or her clinical experience and assign ratings to the patient in comparison to other patients he or she has seen. As a result, response bias tends to be less problematic with these measures. Two clinician-administered measures that are commonly used in the assessment of pediatric OCD are described in the following section.

Children's Yale-Brown Obsessive-Compulsive Scale.   The Children's Yale-Brown Obsessive-Compulsive Scale (CY-BOCS; Scahill, Riddle,

McSwiggin-Hardin, & Ort, 1997) is a clinician-rated, semi-structured inventory of pediatric OCD symptoms and severity. This measure was adapted from the well-validated Yale-Brown Obsessive-Compulsive Scale (Goodman, Price, Rasmussen, & Mazure, 1989a, 1989b), which is commonly used with adult patients. The CY-BOCS follows the same format and is designed to assess OCD-related symptoms and impairment over the previous week. The CY-BOCS consists of two subscales: Obsessions Severity (5 items) and Compulsions Severity (5 items), which are combined to yield a Total Score. Items are rated on a 5-point Likert scale, with those assessing the severity of symptoms (i.e., distress, frequency, interference, and resistance) ranging from 0—"None" to 4—"Extreme," and those assessing the child's control over his/her symptoms ranging from 0—"Complete control" to 4—"No control." The CY-BOCS can be administered to the child and parent(s), either separately or jointly, based on the clinician's judgment. Scores are determined by the clinician on the basis of the child-report, parent(s) report, and behavioral observations. Individual item scores are summed to provide an Obsessions Severity score (range = 0–20), Compulsions Severity score (range = 0–20), and Total Score (range = 0–40).

The CY-BOCS is often referred to as the "gold standard" in assessment of pediatric OCD and remains the most commonly used measure. It has demonstrated high internal consistency, with Total Score alphas ranging from .87 (Scahill et al., 1997) to .90 (Storch et al., 2004a), and alphas of .80 and .82 for the Obsession and Compulsion Severity scores, respectively (Storch et al., 2004a). Inter-rater agreement for the subscales and total score range from good to excellent (intraclass correlation coefficients [ICCs] = .66 – .91), and the CY-BOCS has demonstrated adequate 6-week test–retest reliabilities for the Obsession Severity score (ICC = .70), Compulsion Severity score (ICC = .76), and Total Score (ICC = .79). Convergent and divergent validity of the CY-BOCS has been demonstrated, with researchers finding stronger associations to other measures of obsessional thinking and compulsive symptoms than to measures of general anxiety, depression, tic severity, aggression, or ADHD (Scahill et al., 1997; Storch et al., 2004a). Finally, the CY-BOCS has repeatedly demonstrated good sensitivity to treatment effects (Benazon, Ager, & Rosenberg, 2002; Geller et al., 2003; Piacentini, Bergman, Jacobs, McCracken, & Kretchman, 2002; Scahill et al., 1997; Storch, Geffken, Adkins, Murphy, & Goodman, in press). However, the use of the Obsession Severity, Compulsion Severity, and Total scores has recently been criticized, as factor analytic studies of the CY-BOCS (MacKay et al., 2003; Storch, Murphy, Geffken et al., 2005) and the Y-BOCS (Amir, Foa, & Coles, 1997; Arrindell, de Vlaming, Eisenhardt, van Berkum, & Kwee, 2002; MacKay, Danyko, Neziroglu, & Yaryura-Tobias, 1995; MacKay et al., 2003; Storch et al., 2005) have found support for two separate 2-factor solutions: (1) Obsession and Compulsion factors, and (2) Severity and Disturbance factors. Although no study has found support for the use of a Total Score, the Severity and Disturbance factors contribute to the prediction of clinician-rated impairment (Storch, Murphy, Geffken et al., 2005). It appears that both sets of factors represent unique constructs (MacKay et al., 2003). Thus, relying on the Total Score could underestimate symptom severity in "primarily obsessional" or "primarily compulsive" patients, especially given that approximately 20% of pediatric OCD patients exhibit clinically significant differences in the severity of obsessive symptoms and compulsive symptoms they experience (Storch, et al., 2004a).

Yale Children's Global Stress Index.   Findley and colleagues developed the Yale Children's Global Stress Index (YCGSI: Findley et al., 2003) as an objective, clinician-rated measure of psychosocial stress in children and adolescents. The YCGSI is administered to both parents and children in two parts. First, the clinician obtains information related to significant life events that the child has experienced by administering the Life Events Questionnaire (Masten, Neemann, & Andenas, 1994) to the child or the Family Inventory of Life Events (McCubbin, Patterson, & Wilson, 1991) to the parent. The clinician follows with the YCGSI—Selected Events Interview form, which assesses the type and degree of stress experienced during the respondent's three most significant life events, and the interview generally lasts about 20–30 minutes. An example question is "How has this event affected your relationships?" Next, the clinician combines data obtained from the parent and child interviews in order to make the YCGSI ratings. The YCGSI includes ratings of global "objective threat" (defined as "the degree of stress most people would experience under similar contextual circumstances"), as well as the child's experienced level of stress resulting from the significant life event. A distinction is also made for assessing the level of stress experienced by the child "without including an increase in stress that was clearly secondary to increases in tic or obsessive-compulsive symptoms" (Findley et al., 2003). Ratings are assigned based on a 5-point scale ranging from 0—"None: Notable events, but not stressful" to 4—"Extreme: Stressful events affecting the child associated with permanent changes or lasting extended periods of time."

Although the YCGSI was developed as a general measure of psychosocial distress, it was validated on a group of children diagnosed with OCD or Tourette's syndrome (TS). In this validation study, the YCGSI demonstrated good inter-rater reliability (kappa = .75) and was associated with measures of significant life events, daily stress, and symptoms of depression (Findley et al., 2003). A comparison of OCD and TS patients with a control group further indicated that clinical patients experienced greater degrees of stress than nonpatients (Findley et al., 2003).

Inventories and Questionnaires

Child self-report and parent-report inventories and questionnaires are frequently utilized in the assessment of pediatric OCD due to their many advantages. For example, these measures can generally be completed quickly and independently. And, because they can usually be administered to multiple individuals at once, self- or parent-report measures are useful screening tools that can be utilized to identify potential research participants or treatment candidates from a larger group. These measures are also typically sensitive to treatment, and can be used to track progress across time. Given that some patients and parents display tendencies to under-report (or over-report) symptoms when speaking directly to a clinician, the use of questionnaire measures may help to guard against this problem. On the other hand, individuals' lack of care or comprehension when responding to specific items may affect their ratings on these measures, as might their general response style. For example, various patients and parents may have different interpretations of choices such as "sometimes" or "often." Finally, the sometimes idiosyncratic nature of pediatric OCD may lead to an underestimate of the child's impairment, due to omission of specific/idiosyncratic symptoms from the measures. New and commonly used inventories and questionnaires that are completed by children and/or their parents are listed in the following section.

Child Self-Report Measures

Leyton Obsessional Inventory—Child Version. Citing the need to develop a self-report method of assessing pediatric OCD symptoms, Berg, Rapoport, and Flament (1986) developed the 44-item Leyton Obsessional Inventory—Child Version (LOI–CV) card-sorting task, which was based on a modified version of the original 69-item adult Leyton Obsessional Inventory (Cooper, 1970) card sort. The authors excluded items that were believed to be irrelevant to children, and added several child-related items (e.g., items related to schoolwork). A sample item is "Do you ever do papers over just to make sure that they are perfect?" Items fall into the general categories of Persistent thoughts, Checking, Fear of dirt and/or dangerous objects, Cleanliness, Order, Repetition, and Indecision. The administration of the LOI–CV entails three distinct steps and yields three scores: (1) "Yes" score, (2) "Resistance" score, and (3) "Interference" score. Children are presented with a stack of cards listing one question per card, and endorse symptoms by dropping the relevant cards into the "yes" slot of an answer box. The "Yes" score is obtained by summing the number of items endorsed in the "yes" slot. Next, "Resistance" is assessed using five keycards ranging from 0—"Sensible: My thoughts and habits are quite sensible and reasonable" to 3—"Try very hard to stop: What I do bothers me a lot and I try very hard to stop." The child is asked to place each card that was endorsed in step 1 onto the keycard that matches his/her feelings about the specific item. Scores for each item are summed to provide the "Resistance" score. Finally, this step is repeated using four keycards that designate levels of interference ranging from 0—"No interference: My habit does not stop me from doing other things I want to do" to 3—"Interferes a lot: This stops me from doing a lot of things and wastes a lot of my time." As in step 2, only items that were originally scored as a "Yes" response are sorted in step 3. The Interference score is determined by summing the scores for each item. The LOI–CV is administered to the child independently and can be time-intensive, especially if the child's obsessions or rituals interfere with completion of the task. However, it also provides clinicians with opportunities for behavioral observations during the assessment.

The LOI–CV has demonstrated excellent 5-week test–retest reliabilities in a clinical sample (Berg et al., 1986). Inter-rater reliability is also reported to be excellent for the total "Yes" scores (ICC = .96, $p < .0001$), the "Resistance" scores (ICC = .97, $p < .0001$), and the "Interference" scores (ICC = .94, $p < .0001$). Berg and colleagues (1986) demonstrated treatment sensitivity of the LOI–CV, and reported significant levels of change following pharmacotherapy on the "Yes" score ($t = 2.19, p < .05$), "Resistance" score ($t = 2.12, p < .05$), and "Interference" score ($t = 2.24, p < .05$). The LOI–CV has demonstrated concurrent validity as well (Murphy, Pickar, & Alterman, 1982; Rapoport & Mikkelson, 1980; Thorâen, Asberg, Cronholm, Jornestedt, & Traskman, 1980).

Leyton Obsessional Inventory—Child Version, Survey Form. The Survey Form of the Leyton Obsessional Inventory—Child Version (Berg, Whitaker, Davies, & Flament, 1988), which was based on the LOI–CV card-sorting task (Berg et al., 1986), was the first child self-report questionnaire assessing pediatric OCD symptoms to be developed. The authors selected 20 of the original 44 items for the measure because they distinguished students in a clinical group from normal controls or were representative of common obsessional symptoms. Items, such as "Do you often feel like you have to do certain things even though you know you don't really have to?" are rated as "yes" or "no." Interference from each symptom is assessed with a follow-up question, and is rated on a 4-point scale, ranging from 0—"This habit does not stop me from doing other things I want to do" to 3—"This stops me from a lot of things and wastes a lot of my time." The LOI–CV Survey Form was validated within an epidemiological study of 5,596 high school students (Berg et al., 1988; Flament et al., 1988).

The LOI–CV Survey Form demonstrated good internal consistency (α = .81), and a stable factor structure, which accounted for 47% of the total variance. The factors consisted of: (1) general obsessive, (2) dirt-contamination,

(3) numbers-luck, and (4) school. Test–retest reliability coefficients for the LOI–CV Survey Form are inconsistent, ranging from good to poor, based on child age (King, Inglis, Jenkins, & Myerson 1995). Obsessive-symptom test–retest rates are best for 14–16 year-olds ($r = .83$), followed by 11–13-year-olds ($r = .75$) and 8–10-year-olds ($r = .51$). Test–retest rates for interference are highest in 11–13-year-olds ($r = .81$), followed by 8–10-year-olds ($r = .65$) and 14–16-year-olds ($r = .57$). The LOI–CV Survey Form has demonstrated adequate concurrent validity. In addition, the authors reported that, using a cutoff score of 25 or higher on the Interference ratings, the LOI–CV has a sensitivity rate of 75% and specificity rate of 84% (Flament et al., 1988). However, other research has demonstrated high false-positive rates using the LOI–CV Survey Form (Wolff & Wolff, 1991), and the LOI–CV Survey Form does not appear to be sensitive to treatment effects (Geller et al., 2003).

LOI–CV Short Form. More recently, a shortened screener version of the Leyton Obsessional Inventory—Child Version, Survey Form has been developed for use in epidemiological research and clinical practice (Bamber, Tamplin, Park, Kyte, & Goodyer, 2002). The short form consists of 11 items, which load on 3 distinct factors that were derived from the original survey form (i.e., Compulsions, Obsessions/Incompleteness, and Concern with Cleanliness). Items are scored a 4-point Likert-type scale ranging from 0—"never" to 3—"always." The LOI–CV Short Form has demonstrated adequate psychometric properties, with adequate internal consistency for the total scale ($\alpha = .86$), Compulsions factor ($\alpha = .73$), Obsessions/Incompleteness factor ($\alpha = .79$), and Concern with Cleanliness factor ($\alpha = .75$). The LOI–CV Short Form has also demonstrated adequate sensitivity (78%) and specificity (70%), using a cut-off score of 5 (Bamber et al., 2002). However, the Short Form is primarily meant to be used as a screener and does not contain items uniquely designed to assess distress or functional impairment caused by symptoms of pediatric OCD.

Thought–Action Fusion Scale. The Thought–Action Fusion Scale (TAF: Shafran, Thordarson, & Rachman, 1996) is 19-item, self-report scale that was developed to assess cognitive biases that are common in patients with OCD. It consists of a "morality bias" subscale (12 items, e.g., "If I wish harm on someone, it is almost as bad as doing harm") and a "probability bias" subscale (7 items, e.g., "If I think of myself falling ill, this increases the risk that I will fall ill"). Items on the TAF are rated on a 5-point Likert type scale ranging from 0—"disagree strongly" to 4—"agree strongly." Higher scores are indicative of stronger cognitive biases.

Research has demonstrated that the TAF possesses satisfactory psychometric properties, with internal consistency coefficients ranging from $\alpha < .75$ (Rassin, Merckelbach, Muris, & Schmidt, 2001) to $\alpha < .85$

(Shafran et al., 1996). There is evidence that the TAF displays adequate test–retest reliability (Rassin et al., 2001), and convergent validity has been demonstrated with significant correlations between the TAF and other measures of obsessional and depressive symptoms (Rassin et al., 2001; Shafran et al., 1996).

Children's Automatic Thoughts Scale.   The Children's Automatic Thoughts Scale (CATS: Schniering & Rapee, 2002) is a 40-item youth self-report measure that assesses negative beliefs related to both internalizing and externalizing problems in children and adolescents. The items consist of common worries/obsessions experienced by children with OCD (e.g., "Kids will think I'm stupid" and "It's my fault that things have gone wrong"). The authors generated items through extensive interviews with youth suffering from various psychological disorders. Items were then pilot-tested and factor-analyzed to yield the final measure. Respondents rate the frequency with which they have experienced each thought (e.g., "I'm going to have an accident") over the past week on a 5-point scale ranging from 0—"not at all" to 4—"all the time." The measure is comprised of four separate subscales of cognitive content: (1) physical threat, (2) social threat, (3) personal failure, and (4) hostility. Ratings for each item are summed to provide a total score.

The CATS has demonstrated excellent internal consistency, with $\alpha = .95$ for the total scale, and α ranging from .85 to .92 for the subscales (Schniering & Rapee, 2002). The authors also report excellent 1–3-month test–retest reliability (ICC = .87 to .91 for the subscales and ICC = .91 for the total score). Discriminant validity for each subscale of the CATS was demonstrated with statistically significant differences in comparisons of normative and clinical (e.g., anxious, depressed, and/or behavior disordered) samples (Schniering & Rapee, 2002).

Metacognitions Questionnaire—Adolescent Version.   Adapted from the adult version, the Metacognitions Questionnaire—adolescent version (MCQ–A: Cartwright-Hatton et al., 2004) is a 30-item scale, designed to measure metacognitive beliefs (e.g., beliefs about thought monitoring and worrying) in youth. The scale measures beliefs about thinking and thinking processes, and many of the items correspond to common obsessions observed among pediatric OCD patients. The items are grouped into five subscales, including (1) Positive Beliefs About Worry, (2) Cognitive Confidence, (3) Superstition, Punishment, and Responsibility, (4) Cognitive Self-Consciousness, and (5) Uncontrollability and Danger. Participants are asked to rate how strongly they agree with each statement (e.g., "I should be in control of my thoughts all of the time") on a 4-point scale, ranging from 1—"do not agree" to 4—"agree very much." The MCQ–A is similar in item content and scoring to the adult short version (MCQ-30; Wells & Cartwright-Hatton, 2004), though the language was slightly modified to improve its utility with youth.

The MCQ–A has demonstrated excellent internal consistency for the full scale (α = .91)and acceptable internal consistency for the individual subscales (range of α = .66 to .88). The authors also report adequate construct validity and discriminant validity for the MCQ–A (Cartwright-Hatton et al., 2004).

Children's Florida Obsessive-Compulsive Inventory.   The Children's Florida Obsessive-Compulsive Inventory (C-FOCI: Storch, Murphy, Geffken et al., in press) was developed as a quick, focused screening instrument for pediatric OCD (see Appendix B). The measure includes a symptom checklist (17 items) as well as an impairment scale (5 items). The items were generated by the authors through review of published reports of pediatric OCD symptoms (Berg et al., 1988; Hanna et al., 2002; Scahill et al., 1997; Thomsen & Jensen, 1991), as well as the authors' clinical experiences. Children endorse checklist symptoms by indicating "yes"—1 or "no"—0, based on whether they have experienced each of the symptoms in the past month. There are separate subscales for Obsessions and Compulsions, with example items including, "Have you worried a lot about terrible things happening, such as harm coming to a loved one because you weren't careful enough?" (obsessions) and "Have you felt driven to perform certain acts over and over again, such as checking light switches, water faucets, the stove, or door locks?" (compulsions). Subscale scores are computed by summing the number of "yes" responses in each category, and a Total Score is obtained by adding the Obsessions scale score to the Compulsions scale score. Higher scores on these subscales are indicative of more symptoms, though not necessarily more severe symptoms. The impairment questions assess the extent to which the child's symptoms interfere with daily functioning and are rated on a 5-point Likert-type scale ranging from 0—none to 4—Extreme. A sample item is "How much distress do these thoughts and behaviors cause you?" The C-FOCI can generally be completed in 5–10 minutes.

The C-FOCI has generally demonstrated good psychometric properties (Storch, Murphy, Geffken et al., in press), with adequate internal consistency coefficients of α = .86, .77, and .83 for the Total Score scale, Obsessions subscale, and Compulsions subscale, respectively. Convergent and divergent validity were demonstrated with significant correlations found between the C-FOCI and other measures assessing OCD impairment (i.e., CY-BOCS, TODS–PR), but not with measures of general anxiety (i.e., MASC) or depression (i.e., Children's Depression Inventory). It has also been demonstrated that individuals diagnosed with OCD endorse significantly more items on the C-FOCI than do individuals from a normative sample. A cut-off score of 1 symptom is used to determine the presence of OCD, based on research indicating acceptable sensitivity and specificity with this criterion (Storch, Murphy, Geffken et al., in press).

Parent-Report Measures

Family Accommodation Scale. Due to the prevalence of familial in-volvement in the maintenance of OCD symptoms, Calvocoressi and col-leagues developed the Family Accommodation Scale (FAS; Calvocoressi et al., 1995) to assess the extent to which family members participate in OCD obsessions and rituals. This measure is completed by a family member of the identified patient. It consists of nine items that assess the degree to which family members accommodated the child's participation in obsessions and compulsions during the previous month (e.g., by providing reassurance or objects necessary for completion of compulsions, decreasing behavioral ex-pectations or modifying family activities or routines, and/or helping the child avoid objects, places, or experiences that may cause him or her distress). An example item is "How often did you provide items for the patient's compul-sions?" In addition, four items assess the level of distress that family members experience as a result of accommodating the child and the level of dis-tress/impairment experienced by the child when family members refuse to participate in the OCD-related behaviors. An example item is "Has the pa-tient become distressed/anxious when you have not provided assistance? To what degree?" All items are scored on a 5-point Likert-type scale, and the en-tire FAS can be completed in approximately 5 minutes.

Research (Calvocoressi et al., 1995; Geffken, Storch, Duke, Lewin, Mo-naco, & Goodman, 2006) has demonstrated that the FAS has adequate-to-good internal consistency for the 9-item total family accommodation score ($\alpha = .76–.80$). In addition, inter-rater reliability on individual items of the FAS ranges from adequate to excellent (ICC = .72 to 1.0). More research is needed to examine convergent and discriminant validity of the FAS in fami-lies of children suffering from OCD.

Obsessive-Compulsive Scale of the Child Behavior Checklist. Given the frequency with which the Child Behavior Checklist (CBCL: Achenbach, 1991) is administered to both normative and clinical samples of children, it had remained an untapped resource in the screening of pediatric OCD for many years. However, Nelson and colleagues (2001) recognized this potential and used factor analytic techniques to derive a measure of pe-diatric OCD from existing items. They began with 11 items that they hypoth-esized to predict OCD, and the end result was an 8-item subscale. Sample items include "Repeats certain acts over and over; compulsions" and "wor-ries." Consistent with the instructions for the CBCL, items are rated 0—"not true," 1—"somewhat or sometimes true," or 2—"very true or often true."

Psychometric properties of the derived subscale are generally good, with an internal consistency coefficient of $\alpha = .84$. In addition, the CBCL Obses-sive-Compulsive Scale has demonstrated adequate sensitivity (ranging from 75.3% to 84.9%) and good specificity (ranging from 82.2% to 92.5%) in identifying children who suffer from OCD (Nelson et al., 2001). However, using confirmatory and exploratory factor analyses, Storch and colleagues found that a 6-item scale provided a better fit. This revision (the OCS-R) demonstrated adequate reliability (α = .75) and was significantly related to the CY-BOCS (Storch, Murphy, Bagner, et al., 2006).

Tourette's Disorder Scale. The Tourette's Disorder Scale—Parent-Rated version (TODS–PR: Shytle et al., 2003) is a 15-item parent-report checklist that assesses the presence of several symptoms commonly seen in children with Tourette's Disorder. Examples of these symptoms include obsessions, compulsions, tics, inattention, hyperactivity, aggression, and emotional disturbances. Due to the significant symptom overlap often observed among Tourette's and OCD patients (i.e., obsessions and compulsions), the measure can be utilized with pediatric OCD patients as well. Factor-analytic studies have supported the presence of an Obsessive-Compulsive Disorder (OCD) factor in the TODS–PR, as well as factors representing Aggression, ADHD, and Tics (Shytle et al., 2003; Storch et al., 2004b). However, there are questions related to the composition of this factor, as there has been some discrepancy in the results from different research groups. Further research is needed to clarify the underlying OCD factor composition. The TODS–PR takes approximately 5 minutes to complete.

Research (Shytle et al., 2003; Storch et al., 2004b) has demonstrated good internal consistency for the TODS–PR Total Score (α = .92), and the 4-item OCD factor scale (α = .81). Convergent validity has been demonstrated among the 4-item TODS–PR Obsessive-Compulsive Disorder Factor score and the CY-BOCS Total Score, Obsession severity score, and Compulsion severity score, as well as the Clinical Global Impression (CGI) scale. The discriminant validity of the 4-item TODS–PR OCD Factor scale has not been adequately supported, as it also correlates significantly with depressive symptoms (p < .001). Given the high levels of comorbidity seen in children with depressive and anxiety disorders, these results are not unexpected. However, these data imply that the TODS–PR may be less useful for questions of differential diagnosis (Johns, Storch, Geffken, & Murphy, in press).

OCD Disturbance Scale. Citing years of clinical experience with pediatric OCD patients, Geffken and colleagues noted that some children did not find their OCD symptoms particularly distressing, despite the fact that the patients' parents would often disagree. The OCD Disturbance Scale (Geffken et al., 2005) was developed to assess the degree to which OCD symptoms are ego-syntonic or ego-dystonic to pediatric OCD patients (see Appendix C). This parent-report measure consists of 25 items that were rationally-derived. Respondents rate each item on a scale of 1—"never" to 4— "always." The Ego-Syntonic subscale includes items such as "There is an oppositional quality to my child's OCD," whereas the Ego-Dystonic subscale

contains items such as "My child is embarrassed about having OCD." In preliminary reports (Geffken et al., 2005), the OCD Disturbance Scale has displayed adequate internal consistency as well as evidence of both convergent
and divergent validity. As expected, higher scores on the Ego-Syntonic
subscale were related to lower scores on child-rated OCD-related distress
and higher scores on parent-reports of child-externalizing behavior.

Preliminary data (Geffken et al., 2005) suggests that the OCD Disturbance Scale generally displays good psychometric properties. Internal con-
sistencies ranged from $\alpha = .64$ (for the Ego-Syntonic factor) to $\alpha = .77$ (for
the Ego-Dystonic Factor). The OCD Disturbance Scale also demonstrated
good convergent validity with other measures of OCD severity (e.g.,
CY-BOCS, CY-BOCS-CR and CY-BOCS-PR).

Child-and-Parent-Report Measures

Child Obsessive-Compulsive Impact Scale. Although several questionnaires have been developed to assess the presence of pediatric OCD
symptoms, until recently, no measures were available to adequately measure
the extent to which pediatric OCD causes impairment in child functioning.
The Child Obsessive-Compulsive Impact Scale (COIS: Piacentini & Jaffer,
1999) was developed to assess impairment in specific areas of psychosocial
functioning due to symptoms of pediatric OCD. This instrument is a
56-item, self-report or parent-report measure, which asks the child and/or
parent to respond to the prompt, "In the past month, how much trouble have
you [your child] had doing the following because of OCD?" Items were generated by the authors on the basis of interviews and focus groups with pediatric OCD patients and their parents. The items address common difficulties
in school activities (16 items), social activities (19 items), and home/family
activities (17 items). Example items include "Getting to classes on time during the day" and "Getting ready for bed at night." Respondents rate the extent to which OCD interferes with the child's ability to participate fully and
successfully in each area using a 4-point scale ranging from "not at all" to
"very much." The four final questions assess global impairment related to
school, social activities, going places, and home/family activities.

The COIS has demonstrated good internal consistency and construct validity (Piacentini et al., 2002), and has displayed convergent validity with
other measures of OCD symptom severity and functional impairment
(Piacentini et al., 2003). Prior research has suggested that parents and children may endorse different areas of functioning as problematic. In general, it
appears that parents report more problems in home/family activities and
school/academic problems, whereas children tend to report more problems
in situations where their parents are not usually present (e.g., getting to class
on time) or where obsessions/mental rituals cause impairment (e.g., watching television: Piacentini et al., 2003). The COIS appears to be useful as a

pre-treatment prognostic indicator (Piacentini et al., 2002) and is sensitive to treatment effects (Liebowitz et al., 2002; Piacentini et al., 2003). It can be completed in approximately 10 minutes.

Children's Obsessional Compulsive Inventory. The Children's Obsessional Compulsive Inventory (ChOCI: Shafran et al., 2003) is a 44-item measure that was originally developed to provide a psychometrically sound alternative to the LOI–CV. The ChOCI includes separate forms for child self-report and for parent-report, and consists of 19 items assessing compulsive symptoms (e.g., "I feel I must check my homework over and over and over again") and 13 items assessing obsessive symptoms (e.g., "I often have horrible thoughts about my family being hurt that upset me very much"). All items are rated on a 3-point scale ranging from 1—"not at all" to 3—"a lot." The authors generated the symptom checklist items from a revised version of the Maudsley Obsessional Compulsive Inventory (Thordarson, Rachman, & Radomsky, 1996). The ChOCI also contains two sections (6 items each) assessing the child's level of impairment related to (1) compulsions and (2) obsessions. These "impairment" sections were based on the CY-BOCS (Scahill et al., 1997) Obsession and Compulsion Severity scores. The ChOCI thus consists of four subscales: (1) Compulsive symptoms, (2) Impairment associated with compulsions, (3) Obsessional symptoms, and (4) Impairment associated with obsessions. Subscale scores are determined by summing the responses to each item within the scale, and a Total Impairment Score is calculated by summing the two impairment subscales. The measure can be completed in approximately 15 minutes and takes about 5 minutes to score.

The ChOCI has demonstrated adequate psychometric properties (Shafran et al., 2003), with high internal consistency coefficients (i.e., $\alpha > .80$) reported for each of the four subscales, and item-total correlations for the impairment scales all significant ($p < .05$). Parent- and child-reports of compulsion-related impairment were significantly correlated ($r = .53, p < .01$), whereas reports of obsession-related impairment were not. This finding likely resulted from the fact that obsessions are not easily observable by others. The ChOCI has also demonstrated convergent validity with the CY-BOCS Total Score A cut-off of 17 on Total Impairment Score has demonstrated adequate sensitivity and specificity in determining a diagnosis of OCD (Shafran et al., 2003).

Children's Yale-Brown Obsessive-Compulsive Scale—Child-Report and Parent-Report. The Children's Yale-Brown Obsessive-Compulsive Scale—Child-Report (CY-BOCS-CR) and Parent-Report (CY-BOCS-PR: Storch, Geffken, Murphy, & Goodman, 2004) were developed to be used as self- or parent-report measures of pediatric OCD severity. These measures were closely modeled after the original CY-BOCS clinician-administered inventory (Scahill et al., 1997), and consist of two subscales (five items each) assessing the distress and impairment caused by obsessions and compulsions. As in the clinician-rated instrument, items assess: (1) time devoted to obsessions/compulsions, (2) functional impairment caused by obsessions/compulsions, (3) level of distress related to obsessions/compulsions, (4) attempts to resist obsessions/compulsions, and (5) success in resisting obsessions/compulsions. A sample item is, "How much do these thoughts bother or upset you [your child]?"). Responses are scored on a 5-point Likert-type scale ranging from 0—"not at all" to 4—"They bother me so much it is hard to do anything." Scores are summed within subscales to yield distinct scores for Obsessions and Compulsions.

Preliminary analyses suggest that the CY-BOCS-CR and CY-BOCS-PR are useful instruments in the assessment of OCD severity (Storch, Geffken, Murphy, & Goodman, 2004). Although a full analysis of their psychometric properties is needed to validate their use with clinical and/or research populations, the measures have demonstrated concurrent validity within a small sample. Both measures demonstrated significant correlations with the clinician-administered version of the CY-BOCS ($r \sim .60-.70$).

Teacher Rating Scale

Most children spend a large portion of their day in school-related activities (e.g., preparing for school, attending classes, completing homework). As a result, those who suffer from OCD frequently display symptoms that interfere with their academic functioning. Given that cognitive-behavioral treatment is tailored specifically to the patient's symptoms and areas of functional impairment, it is important to obtain information related to the patient's school functioning. Teachers are important resources who have been underutilized in the identification and assessment of pediatric OCD, and use of a teacher-rated assessment measure would allow clinicians to obtain important information about the child's functioning outside of the home environment.

Florida Obsessive-Compulsive Student Inventory (FOCSI). Although we are not aware of any published teacher-rated measure of pediatric OCD symptoms, Merlo and Storch (2005) have developed a 30-item questionnaire to address this need. The Florida Obsessive-Compulsive Student Inventory consists of two sections: a checklist of symptoms that the teacher might observe (15 items) and a school-impairment rating scale (15 items). Teachers are instructed to respond according to the child's behavior over the past week in order to simplify assessment of symptom change over time (e.g., pre-treatment vs. post-treatment). An example item from the symptom checklist is, "Has this student displayed a tendency to perform certain acts over and over again, such as erasing and re-writing notes, worksheet answers, test responses, or essays?"

These items are scored "yes" or "no." An example item from the impairment rating is, "How much have the symptoms you endorsed on the first page caused this student problems in being prepared for classes (e.g., having supplies and assignments ready when needed)." Response choices for the impairment rating scale range from 0—"Not at all" to 3—"Very much." The items were modified from existing measures (e.g., the Child's Florida Obsessive-Compulsive Inventory (Storch, Murphy, Geffken et al., in press), the Children's Obsessive-Compulsive Impact Scale (Piacentini & Jaffer, 1999), and the Children's Yale-Brown Obsessive-Compulsive Scale (Scahill et al., 1997) or based on the authors' clinical experiences with this population. Although psychometric properties of the measure are currently unknown, the authors are conducting research to evaluate the reliability, validity, and utility of this measure for clinical and normative samples.

ADJUNCTIVE MEASURES

Given the relatively high levels of comorbidity among pediatric OCD and other disorders (e.g., depression, ADHD, generalized anxiety disorder), the inclusion of other screening instruments can provide a valuable complement to OCD-specific measures in a comprehensive assessment. Helpful adjunctive screening measures are described next.

Child-Report Measures

Children's Depression Inventory. Given the frequency of depression and depressive symptoms in pediatric OCD patients, a screening for clinically significant mood disturbance is important. The Children's Depression Inventory (CDI; Kovacs, 1992) is a 27-item self-report measure of depressive symptoms. Respondents choose one sentence, from a group of three, which best describes them over the past 2 weeks. Items are rated 0–2, depending on the severity of their response (e.g., 0—"I like myself," 1—"I do not like myself," 2—"I hate myself"). Item scores are summed to yield a Total Score, in addition to several subscale scores. The CDI is appropriate for children aged 7–17, and has demonstrated strong psychometric properties (Kovacs, 1992).

Multidimensional Anxiety Scale for Children. Screening for the presence of more generalized anxiety is also a useful addition to assessment of pediatric OCD. The Multidimensional Anxiety Scale for Children (MASC; March & MHS staff, 1997) is a 39-item, self-report measure of anxiety symptoms in children. The MASC contains for basic subscales: (1) physical symptoms, (2) harm avoidance, (3) social anxiety, and (4) separation/panic. In addition, the Inconsistency Index helps to identify random/careless response behaviors. Respondents rate each item (e.g., "I feel tense or uptight") on a 4-point scale ranging from 0—"Never true about me" to 3—"Often true about me." The MASC is appropriate for children aged 8–19, although younger children may need help reading the items. Scores are age-and-gender-corrected, and the MASC has demonstrated good psychometric properties (March et al., 1997).

Parent-Report Measures

Child Behavior Checklist.   The Child Behavior Checklist (CBCL; Achenbach, 1991) is a 113-item parent-report questionnaire comprised of symptoms commonly seen in children with psychological and psychiatric conditions. Example items include "Fails to finish things he/she starts" and "Disobedient at home." Items are rated 0—"not true," 1—"somewhat or sometimes true," or 2—"very true or often true." The CBCL yields age-corrected scores on scales assessing Internalizing Problems, Externalizing Problems, and Total Problems. T-scores greater than 70 are indicative of clinically significant problems. The CBCL also includes subscales designed to assess adaptive functioning. The CBCL is one of the most commonly used measures in child/adolescent assessment and has demonstrated excellent psychometric properties (Achenbach, 1991). The most recent version of the CBCL is divided into "school age (6–18)" and a "preschool age (1.5–5 years)" forms. Child self-report and teacher-report forms are also available.

Behavior Assessment System for Children.   Like the CBCL, the Behavior Assessment System for Children (BASC: Reynolds & Kamphaus, 1992) is a multi-item, parent-report measure designed to assess the presence of common pediatric psychological/psychiatric symptoms. Parents rate each of 131 items (e.g., "Is easily distracted" and "Calls other children names") on a 4-point scale ranging from 0—"Never" to 3—"Almost always." Separate forms are available for Preschool (ages 4–5), School-age (ages 6–11) and Adolescent (ages 12–18) patients. The BASC provides age-and-gender-corrected scores on Internalizing Problems, Externalizing Problems, Total Problems, and School Problems, as well as an Adaptive Skills Composite. Child self-report and teacher-report forms are also available. The BASC has demonstrated good psychometric properties (Reynolds & Kamphaus, 1992).

CONCLUSIONS AND FUTURE DIRECTIONS

Pediatric OCD often results in academic difficulties, social problems, and disruptions in the home/family environment (Piacentini et al., 2003). It affects a relatively large number of children, and is associated with continued impairment in adulthood (Flament, Koby, Rapoport, & Berg, 1990; Thomsen & Mikkelsen, 1995). As a result, clinicians and researchers have begun to focus more attention to improving methods of assessment and treatment.

In fact, in the past 5 years, at least 11 new measures have been developed that are useful in the assessment of pediatric OCD symptoms in community and clinical samples (e.g., YGSI, LOI–CV Short Form, CBCL OCD Scale, CATS, ChOCI, MCQ–A, TODS–PR, C-FOCI, CY-BOCS-PR & CY-BOCS-CR, OCD Disturbance Scale, and FOCSI).

The main goals of this chapter were to (1) review commonly used measures in the assessment of pediatric OCD, (2) introduce newly developed instruments for pediatric OCD assessment, and (3) outline and critique contemporary methods of pediatric OCD assessment. We discussed various methods of assessment, including diagnostic interviews, clinician-administered measures, child self-report measures, parent-report measures, and a teacher-report measure. In general, each method categorically demonstrated utility in clinical and research endeavors, as well as good psychometric properties. However, each method also demonstrated unique strengths. For example, diagnostic interviews are most comprehensive, incorporate both parent- and child-report, and are useful for differential diagnosis. Clinician-rated inventories decrease the effects of participant response bias or lack of understanding of the items, and provide a relatively objective measure of impairment. Youth self-report measures and parent-report measures are useful for screening, can be completed quickly and easily, and can be re-administered to assess post-treatment change. Finally, the teacher-report measure provides a method for assessing symptom presence and related impairment during school.

Each method of assessment has weaknesses as well. For example, diagnostic interviews can be extremely time-consuming, expensive to administer, and require extensive training. Clinician-rated measures also require training and respondents may feel uncomfortable admitting to symptom presence or impairment when responding to questions posed by a clinician versus on a pen-and-paper questionnaire. However, self-report and parent-report measures can sometimes be confusing to respondents, and are not appropriate for young children or adults who do not read well. In addition, questionnaires may be too specific to adequately reflect the level of symptoms and impairment experienced by children who demonstrate idiosyncratic symptoms. Finally, teacher-reports are sometimes difficulty to obtain and may be viewed as burdensome. Although many advances have been made in pediatric OCD assessment, further research is needed to refine existing measures and increase the quality of information obtained from these instruments and the efficiency with which it is gathered. For example, more information is needed regarding how best to interpret response variation between patients and across time. Currently, most measures of pediatric OCD do not adequately account for patients who present with multiple mild symptoms or patients who present with one or two symptoms that cause severe impairment. Thus, future research should examine ways to best account for differences in quantity of symptoms versus severity of symptoms when assessing patient improvement. In addition, although changes on clinician-reported ratings (e.g., CY-BOCS) are currently considered the best indicator of treatment outcome, this method is time-consuming for both the patient and clinician. Thus, future research should continue to promote the development and improvement of treatment-sensitive self- or parent-report measures of patient impairment. Finally, because OCD symptoms frequently change over time, research should continue the validation of existing measures across both child and adolescent samples, in order to ensure that the instruments are appropriate for both age levels.

APPENDIX A

Strengths and Weaknesses of Common Assessment Measures for Pediatric OCD

Measure	Strengths	Weaknesses
Anxiety Disorders Interview Schedule for Children	• Facilitates diagnostic decisions • Focuses primarily on anxiety disorders • Parallel child and parent versions	• Time-consuming • Requires extensive training • Must be individually-administered
Schedule for Affective Disorders and Schizophrenia for School-Age Children	• Facilitates diagnostic decisions • Screens for all psychiatric disorders • Combines parent & child reports	• Very time-consuming • Requires extensive training • Must be individually-administered
Children's Yale-Brown Obsessive-Compulsive Scale	• More objective than self- report • Experienced clinician makes ratings • Relatively quick & easy to administer • "Gold standard"	• Requires training • Must be individually-administered
Yale Children's Global Stress Index	• Clinician-rated • Measures general psychosocial stress • Compares experienced threat to objective threat	• Administration is time-consuming and somewhat complicated • Not developed specifically for OCD • Must be individually-administered
Leyton Obsessional Inventory—Child Version	• First child-report measure for OCD assessment • Allows for behavioral observations	• Time-consuming • Must be individually-administered • Somewhat complicated
Leyton Obsessional Inventory—Child Version Survey Form	• First child-report questionnaire for OCD assessment	• May not be as sensitive to treatment effects • May result in false positives
Leyton Obsessional Inventory—Child Version Short Form	• Good screening measure • Quick & easy to administer	• Does not assess distress/impairment • Not sufficient for diagnostic decisions

Instrument	Strengths	Limitations
Thought-Action Fusion Scale	• Helpful in identifying obsessions & dysfunctional cognitions • May facilitate cognitive interventions	• Not useful for diagnostic decisions
Children's Automatic Thoughts Scale	• Helpful in identifying obsessions & dysfunctional cognitions • May facilitate cognitive interventions	• Not useful for diagnostic decisions
Meta-Cognitions Questionnaire—Adolescent version	• Helpful in identifying obsessions & dysfunctional cognitions • May facilitate cognitive interventions	• Not useful for diagnostic decisions
Children's Florida Obsessive-Compulsive Inventory	• Contains symptom checklist as well as impairment ratings • Quick & easy to administer	• More data are needed about psychometric properties of impairment ratings
OCD Disturbance Scale	• Assesses for ego-syntonic sub-type of OCD and child distress	• Not useful for diagnostic decisions
Family Accommodation Scale	• Assesses family involvement in OCD and identifies family issues to target during intervention • Quick & easy to administer	• Not useful for diagnostic decisions
Child Behavior Checklist—Obsessive-Compulsive Scale	• Included within most commonly-administered parent-report questionnaire • Useful for screening purposes	• Does not assess distress/impairment • Not sufficient for diagnostic decisions
Tourette's Disorder Scale—Parent Report	• Quick & easy to administer • Screens for related disorders	• Factor structure remains unclear • Not useful for diagnostic decisions
Child Obsessive-Compulsive Impact Scale	• Assesses impairment in child functioning • Quick & easy to administer	• Parent and child reports may be inconsistent

Measure	Strengths	Weaknesses
Children's Obsessional Compulsive Inventory	• Contains symptom checklist as well as impairment ratings	• More lengthy than some other questionnaires
Children's Yale-Brown Obsessive-Compulsive Scale—Child Report & Parent Report	• Provides information on symptom severity • Quick & easy to administer	• Child & parent report are more subjective
Florida Obsessive-Compulsive Student Inventory	• Only teacher-rated measure of OCD symptoms • Includes checklist of symptoms & impairment ratings	• Data are needed about psychometric properties

APPENDIX B

The Children's Florida Obsessive Compulsive Inventory

General Instructions: The questions below are designed to help your doctors evaluate anxiety symptoms. Keep in mind, a high score on this questionnaire does not necessarily mean you have an anxiety disorder—only an evaluation by a health professional can make this determination. Answer these questions as accurately as you can.

Instructions: Please circle YES or NO for the following questions, based on your experience in the past MONTH:

Have you been bothered by unpleasant thoughts or images that repeatedly enter your mind, such as:

1.	Concerns with contamination (dirt, germs, chemicals, radiation) or getting a serious illness such as AIDS?	YES	NO
2.	Overconcern with keeping objects (clothes, toys, books) in perfect order or arranged exactly?	YES	NO
3.	Images of death or other horrible events?	YES	NO

Have you worried a lot about terrible things happening, such as:

4.	Fire, burglary or flooding of the house?	YES	NO
5.	Accidentally hitting a pedestrian with your car or letting it roll down a hill?	YES	NO
6.	Spreading an illness (giving someone AIDS)?	YES	NO
7.	Losing something valuable?	YES	NO
8.	Harm coming to a loved one because you weren't careful enough?	YES	NO

Have you felt driven to perform certain acts over and over again, such as:

9.	Excessive or ritualized washing, cleaning or grooming?	YES	NO
10.	Checking light switches, water faucets, the stove, or door locks?	YES	NO
11.	Counting, arranging; evening-up behaviors (making sure socks are at same height)?	YES	NO
12.	Repeating routine actions (in/out of chair, going through doorway, relighting cigarette) a certain number of times or until it feels *just right*?	YES	NO
13.	Needing to touch objects or people?	YES	NO
14.	Unnecessary rereading or rewriting?	YES	NO
15.	Examining your body for signs of illness?	YES	NO

16. Avoiding colors ("red" means blood), numbers ("13" is unlucky) or   YES   NO
    names (those that start with "D" signify death) that are associated
    with scary events or thoughts?

17. Needing to "confess" or repeatedly asking for reassurance that you   YES   NO
    said or did something correctly?

PART B Instructions: The following questions refer to the repeated thoughts, images, urges or behaviors identified in Part A. Consider your experience during the past month when selecting an answer.

Circle the most appropriate number from 0 to 4.

In the past month ...

	0	1	2	3	4
1. On average, how much *time* is occupied by these thoughts or behaviors each day?	None	Mild (less than 1 hour)	Moderate (1 to 3 hours)	Severe 3 to 8 hours)	Extreme (more than 8 hours)
2. How much *distress* do they cause you?	None	Mild	Moderate	Severe	Extreme (disabling)
3. How hard is it for you to *control* them?	Complete control	Much control	Moderate control	Little control	No control
4. How much do they cause you to *avoid* doing anything, going anyplace or being with anyone?	No avoidance	Occasional avoidance	Moderate avoidance	Frequent and extensive avoidance	Extreme avoidance (house-bound)
5. How much do they *interfere* with school, work or your social or family life?	None	Slight interference	Definitely interferes with functioning	Much interference	Extreme interference (disabling)

For clinician use:

Sum on Part B

(Add Items 1 to 5): _____

APPENDIX C

THE OCD DISTURBANCE SCALE

This page has sentences that tell how about your child's Obsessive-Compulsive Disorder (OCD) symptoms. We would like to know how true these sentences are about your child. Please read each sentence carefully. Then decide if **1**—The sentence is **Never true** about your child. **2**—The sentence is **Sometimes true** about your child. **3**—The sentence is **Often true** about your child. **4**—The sentence is **Always true** about your child. Circle the letter than shows your answer. Please remember that there are no right or wrong answers.

	Never	Sometimes	Often	Always
1. My child seems bothered about having OCD.	1	2	3	4
2. My child asks me for help when dealing with his/her OCD.	1	2	3	4
3. I am more bothered by my child's symptoms than he/she is.	1	2	3	4
4. My child's OCD is most intense when a family member is present.	1	2	3	4
5. My child's OCD is worse at home (as compared to school).	1	2	3	4
6. My child is embarrassed about having OCD.	1	2	3	4
7. My child would be relieved if his/her OCD was cured?	1	2	3	4
8. My child gets rewards from having OCD such as missing school or attention.	1	2	3	4
9. My child argues with me about OCD related issues.	1	2	3	4
10. My child seems to enjoy OCD symptoms that bother me and other family members.	1	2	3	4
11. My child gets upset when his/her OCD symptoms are interrupted or prevented.	1	2	3	4
12. My child's OCD involves repetitive reassurance seeking.	1	2	3	4
13. My child gets out of chores and other responsibilities because of his/her OCD.	1	2	3	4
14. Family members are always doing things for my child with OCD to relieve symptoms.	1	2	3	4

	Never	Sometimes	Often	Always
15. My child's OCD interferes with peer relations.	1	2	3	4
16. My child's OCD interferes with school.	1	2	3	4
17. My child's OCD interferes with family functions.	1	2	3	4
18. We are frequently late for events because of my child's OCD.	1	2	3	4
19. My child cries and is often irritable because of his/her OCD.	1	2	3	4
20. My child is not upset by his/her OCD.	1	2	3	4
21. There is an oppositional quality to my child's OCD.	1	2	3	4
22. My child has trouble falling asleep sometimes because of his/her OCD.	1	2	3	4
23. My child has intense distressing ideas or thoughts.	1	2	3	4
24. My child wastes a lot of time because of his/her OCD.	1	2	3	4
25. My child enjoys engaging in repetitive ritualistic behaviors.	1	2	3	4

APPENDIX D

THE CHILDREN'S YALE-BROWN
OBSESSIVE-COMPULSIVE SCALE—PARENT REPORT

Please circle the letter that best describes your child over the **past week**.

Please answer the next 5 questions about the **obsessions or thoughts** your child cannot stop thinking about. Obsessions are thoughts, ideas, or pictures that keep coming into your child's mind even though he or she does not want them to.

1. How much time does your child spend thinking about these things in a day?
   a. None
   b. Less than **1** hour a day
   c. Between **1 to 3** hours a day
   d. Between **3 to 8** hours a day
   e. More than **8** hours a day

2. How much do these thoughts get in the way of school or doing things with his or her friends?
   a. They don't get in the way
   b. They get in the way a little
   c. They get in the way sometimes
   d. They get in the way a lot
   e. They keep him/her from doing everything

3. How much do these thoughts bother or upset your child?
   a. Not at all
   b. They bother him/her a little
   c. They bother him/her some
   d. They bother him/her a lot
   e. They bother him/her so much that it is hard to do anything

4. How hard do your child try to stop the thoughts or ignore them?
   a. He/she always tries to resist the thoughts
   b. He/she tries to resist the thoughts most of the time
   c. He/she tries to resist the thoughts sometimes
   d. He/she usually don't try to resist the thoughts, but wants to
   e. He/she does not try to resist the thoughts

5. When your child tries to fight the thoughts, can he or she beat them?
   a. He/she always can beat or stop them
   b. He/she can usually beat or stop them
   c. He/she can sometimes beat or stop them
   d. He/she does not beat or stop them very often
   e. He/she never beats or stops them

Please answer the next 5 questions about the **<u>compulsions or habits</u>** your child cannot stop doing. Compulsions are things that your child feels he or she has to do although he or she may know that they do not make sense. Sometimes your child may try to stop from doing them but this might not be possible. Your child might feel worried or angry or scared until he or she has finished what he or she has to do.

6. How much time does your child spend doing these things in a day?
   a. None
   b. Less than **1** hour a day
   c. Between **1 to 3** hours a day
   d. Between **3 to 8** hours a day
   e. More than **8** hours a day

7. How much do these habits get in the way of school or doing things with his or her friends?
   a. They don't get in the way
   b. They get in the way a little
   c. They get in the way sometimes
   d. They get in the way a lot
   e. They keep him/her from doing everything

8. How upset would your child feel if he or she could not do his or her habits?
   a. Not upset at all
   b. He/she would feel a little upset or scared
   c. He/she would feel pretty upset or scared
   d. He/she would feel very upset or scared
   e. He/she would feel as upset or scared as possible

9. How hard does your child try to stop or fight the habits?
   a. He/she always tries to resist the habits
   b. He/she tries to resist the habits most of the time
   c. He/she tries to resist the habits sometimes
   d. He/she usually does not try to resist the habits, but wants to
   e. He/she does not try to resist the habits

10. When your child tries to fight the habits, can he or she beat them?
    a. He/she always can beat or stop them
    b. He/she can usually beat or stop them
    c. He/she can sometimes beat or stop them
    d. He/she does not beat or stop them very often
    e. He/she never beats or stops them

THE CHILDREN'S YALE-BROWN
OBSESSIVE-COMPULSIVE SCALE—CHILD REPORT

Please circle the letter that best describes you over the **past week**.

Please answer the next 5 questions about the **obsessions or thoughts** you cannot stop thinking about. Obsessions are thoughts, ideas, or pictures that keep coming into your mind even though you do not want them to.

1. How much time do you spend thinking about these things in a day?
   a. None
   b. Less than **1** hour a day
   c. Between **1 to 3** hours a day
   d. Between **3 to 8** hours a day
   e. More than **8** hours a day

2. How much do these thoughts get in the way of school or doing things with your friends?
   a. They don't get in the way
   b. They get in the way a little
   c. They get in the way sometimes
   d. They get in the way a lot
   e. They keep me from doing everything

3. How much do these thoughts bother or upset you?
   a. Not at all
   b. They bother me a little
   c. They bother me some
   d. They bother me a lot
   e. They bother me so much that it is hard to do anything

4. How hard do you try to stop the thoughts or ignore them?
   a. I always try to resist the thoughts
   b. I try to resist the thoughts most of the time
   c. I try to resist the thoughts sometimes
   d. I usually don't try to resist the thoughts, but I want to
   e. I don't try to resist the thoughts

5. When you try to fight the thoughts, can you beat them?
   a. I always can beat or stop them
   b. I can usually beat or stop them
   c. I can sometimes beat or stop them
   d. I don't beat or stop them very often
   e. I never beat or stop them

Please answer the next 5 questions about the **<u>compulsions or habits</u>** you cannot stop doing. Compulsions are things that you feel you have to do although you may know that they do not make sense. Sometimes you may try to stop from doing them but this might not be possible. You might feel worried or angry or scared until you have finished what you have to do.

6. How much time do you spend doing these things in a day?
    a. None
    b. Less than **1** hour a day
    c. Between **1 to 3** hours a day
    d. Between **3 to 8** hours a day
    e. More than **8** hours a day

7. How much do these habits get in the way of school or doing things with your friends?
    a. They don't get in the way
    b. They get in the way a little
    c. They get in the way sometimes
    d. They get in the way a lot
    e. They keep me from doing everything

8. How upset would you feel if you could not do your habits?
    a. Not upset at all
    b. I would feel a little upset or scared
    c. I would feel pretty upset or scared
    d. I would feel very upset or scared
    e. I would feel as upset or scared as possible

9. How hard do you try to stop or fight the habits?
    a. I always try to resist the habits
    b. I try to resist the habits most of the time
    c. I try to resist the habits sometimes
    d. I usually don't try to resist the habits, but I want to
    e. I don't try to resist the habits

10. When you try to fight the habits, can you beat them?
    a. I always can beat or stop them
    b. I can usually beat or stop them
    c. I can sometimes beat or stop them
    d. I don't beat or stop them very often
    e. I never beat or stop them

APPENDIX F

THE FLORIDA OBSESSIVE-COMPULSIVE STUDENT INVENTORY.

Part A Instructions: Please circle YES or NO for the following questions, based on your experiences with the above-named student <u>over the past week</u>.

Has this student displayed a tendency to have upsetting thoughts or perform certain acts over and over again, such as:

Yes / No   1. Erasing and re-writing notes, worksheet answers, test responses, or essays even when there is nothing wrong with them?

Yes / No   2. "Getting stuck" and unnecessarily re-reading the same sentence or paragraph?

Yes / No   3. Needing to touch, tap, or rub certain objects or people repeatedly?

Yes / No   4. Excessive / ritualized washing or restroom trips (e.g., repetitive handwashing)?

Yes / No   5. Counting, arranging, or "evening-up" behaviors (e.g., making sure the left and right side are balanced)?

Yes / No   6. Collecting useless items or inspecting garbage before it is thrown out (e.g., saving old school papers that are no longer needed)?

Yes / No   7. Checking his/her backpack, desk, or assignment book repeatedly?

Yes / No   8. Making excessive lists (e.g., "to do" lists)?

Yes / No   9. Needing to "confess" or repeatedly asking for reassurance that s/he did something correctly?

Yes / No   10. Avoiding certain colors (e.g., "red" means blood), numbers (e.g., "13" is unlucky), or names?

Yes / No   11. Refraining from stepping on lines in the tile, cracks on the pavement, etc.?

Yes / No   12. Seeming overly concerned with contamination (e.g., avoids touching or being near objects that might be "dirty" or have "germs"?

Yes / No   13. Focusing excessive energy or concern on keeping objects in perfect order or arranged exactly?

Yes / No   14. Worrying that s/he may cause or may have caused something bad to happen?

Yes / No   15. Other (please specify) _____

Part B Instructions: Please rate how much the symptoms you endorsed on the first page have caused this student problems *over the past week.* *If the question does not apply,* please mark "None at all."

	None at All	Just a Little	Quite a Bit	Very Much
1. Being prepared for classes (e.g., having supplies and assignments ready when needed)	____	____	____	____
2. Getting to classes on time during the day	____	____	____	____
3. Staying in class (e.g., not going to school office) during the school day	____	____	____	____
4. Remaining at school for the entire day	____	____	____	____
5. Paying attention in class/concentrating on his or her work	____	____	____	____
6. Giving oral reports or reading aloud	____	____	____	____
7. Writing in class/taking notes	____	____	____	____
8. Taking tests or exams	____	____	____	____
9. Turning in homework	____	____	____	____
10. Earning good grades	____	____	____	____
11. Participating in physical activities	____	____	____	____
12. Doing fun things during free time or recess	____	____	____	____
13. Eating lunch with other students	____	____	____	____
14. Going to school outings or field trips	____	____	____	____
15. Other (please specify):	____	____	____	____

_____

REFERENCES

Achenbach, T. M. (1991). *Manual for the child behavior checklist / 4–18 and 1991 profile*. Burlington, VT: University of Vermont Department of Psychiatry.

Amir, N., Foa, E. B., & Coles, M. E. (1997). Factor structure of the Yale-Brown Obsessive Compulsive Scale. *Psychological Assessment, 9*, 312–316.

Arrindell, W. A., de Vlaming, I. H., Eisenhardt, B. M., van Berkum, D. E., & Kwee, M. G. T. (2002). Cross-cultural validity of the Yale-Brown Obsessive Compulsive Scale. *Journal of Behavior Therapy and Experimental Psychiatry, 33*, 159–176.

American Psychiatric Association. (1994). *Diagnostic and Statistical Manual of Mental Disorders* (4th ed.). Washington, DC: Author.

American Psychiatric Association. (2000). *Diagnostic and Statistical Manual of Mental Disorders* (4th ed., text revision). Washington, DC: Author.

Bamber, D., Tamplin, A., Park, R. J., Kyte, Z. A., & Goodyer, I. M. (2002). Development of a Short Leyton Obsessional Inventory for children and adolescents. *Journal of the American Academy of Child & Adolescent Psychiatry, 41*, 1246–1252.

Benazon, N. R., Ager, J., & Rosenberg, D. R. (2002). Cognitive-behavior therapy in treatment-naive children and adolescents with obsessive-compulsive disorder: An open trial. *Behavior Research and Therapy, 40*, 529–539.

Berg, C. J., Rapoport, J. L., & Flament, M. (1986). The Leyton Obsessional Inventory—Child Version. *Journal of the American Academy of Child & Adolescent Psychiatry, 25*, 84–91.

Berg, C. Z., Whitaker, A., Davies, M., & Flament, M. F. (1988). The survey form of the Leyton Obsessional Inventory—Child Version: Norms from an epidemiological study. *Journal of the American Academy of Child & Adolescent Psychiatry, 27*, 759–763.

Black, D. W., Gaffney, G. R., Schlosser, S., & Gabel, J. (2003). Children of parents with obsessive-compulsive disorder—A 2-year follow-up study. *Acta Psychiatrica Scandinavica, 107*, 305–313.

Bolton, D., Luckie, M., & Steinberg, D. (1995). Long-term course of obsessive-compulsive disorder treated in adolescence. *Journal of the American Academy of Child & Adolescent Psychiatry, 34*, 1441–1450.

Calvocoressi, L., Lewis, B., Harris, M., Trufan, S. J., Goodman, W. K., & McDougle, C. J. (1995). Family accommodation in obsessive-compulsive disorder. *American Journal of Psychiatry, 152*, 441–443.

Cartwright-Hatton, S., Mather, A., Illingworth, V., Brocki, J., Harrington, R., & Wells, A. (2004). Development and preliminary validation of the Metacognitions Questionnaire—Adolescent Version. *Journal of Anxiety Disorders, 18*, 411–422.

Chambers, W. J., Puig-Antich, J., & Hirsch, M. (1985). The assessment of affective disorders in children and adolescents by semistructured interview: Test–retest reliability of the Schedule for Affective Disorders and Schizophrenia for School-Age Children, Present Episode Version. *Archives of General Psychiatry, 42*, 696–702.

Cooper, J. (1970). The Leyton Obsessional Inventory. *Psychological Medicine, 1*, 48–64.

Douglass, H., Moffitt, T. E., Dar, R., McGee, E., & Silva, P. (1995). Obsessive-compulsive disorder in a birth cohort of 18-year-olds: Prevalence and predicators. *Journal of the American Academy of Child and Adolescent Psychiatry, 34*, 1424–1431.

Findley, D. B., Leckman, J. F., Katsovich, L., Lin, H., Zhang, H., & Grantz, H. (2003). Development of the Yale Children's Global Stress Index (YCGSI) and its application in children and adolescents with Tourette's syndrome and obsessive-compulsive disorder. *Journal of the American Academy of Child & Adolescent Psychiatry, 42*, 450–457.

Flament, M. F., Koby, E., Rapoport, J. L., & Berg, C. J. (1990). Childhood obsessive-compulsive disorder: A prospective follow-up study. *Journal of Child Psychology & Psychiatry, 31*, 363–380.

Flament, M. F., Whitaker, A., Rapoport, J. L., & Davies, M. (1988). Obsessive compulsive disorder in adolescence: An epidemiological study. *Journal of the American Academy of Child & Adolescent Psychiatry, 27*, 764–771.

Geffken, G. R., Storch, E. A., Duke, D., Lewin, A., Monaco, L., & Goodman, W. K. (2006). Hope and coping in family members of patients with obsessive compulsive disorder. *Journal of Anxiety Disorders, 20*, 614–629.

Geffken, G. R., Storch, E. A., Lewin, A., Adkins, J., Merlo, L. J., & Murphy, T. K. (2005, March). *Development of the Pediatric OCD Disturbance Scale: Assessing ego-syntonic OCD.* Paper presented at the Anxiety Disorders Association of America Annual Meeting, Seattle, WA.

Geller, D. A., Biederman, J., Stewart, S. E., Mullin, B., Martin, A., & Spencer, T. (2003). Which SSRI? A meta-analysis of pharmacotherapy trials in pediatric obsessive-compulsive disorder. *American Journal of Psychiatry, 160*, 1919–1928.

Goodman, W. K., Price, L. H., Rasmussen, S. A., & Mazure, C. (1989a). The Yale-Brown Obsessive Compulsive Scale: II Validity. *Archives of General Psychiatry, 46*, 1012–1016.

Goodman, W. K., Price, L. H., Rasmussen, S. A., & Mazure, C. (1989b). The Yale-Brown Obsessive Compulsive Scale: II Validity. *Archives of General Psychiatry, 46*, 1006–1011.

Grills, A. E., & Ollendick, T. H. (2002). Issues in parent–child agreement: The case of structured diagnostic interviews. *Clinical Child and Family Psychology Review, 5*, 57–83.

Grills, A. E., & Ollendick, T. H. (2003). Multiple informant agreement and the anxiety disorders interview schedule for parents and children. *Journal of the American Academy of Child & Adolescent Psychiatry, 42*, 30–40.

Hanna, G. L. (1995). Demographic and clinical features of obsessive-compulsive disorder in children and adolescents. *Journal of the American Academy of Child & Adolescent Psychiatry, 34*, 19–28.

Hanna, G. L., Piacentini, J., Cantwell, D. P., Fischer, D. J., Himle, J. A., & Van Etten, M. (2002). Obsessive-compulsive disorder with and without tics in a clinical sample of children and adolescents. *Depression and Anxiety, 16*, 59–63.

Herjanic, B., & Reich, W. (1982). Development of a structured psychiatric interview for children: Agreement between child and parent on individual symptoms. *Journal of Abnormal Child Psychology, 10*, 307–324.

Hodges, K. (1993). Structured interviews for assessing children. *Journal of Child Psychology & Psychiatry & Allied Disciplines, 34*, 49–68.

Hollander, E., Kwon, J. H., Stein, D. J., Broatch, J., Rowland, C. T., & Himelein, C. A. (1996). Obsessive-compulsive and spectrum disorders: Overview and quality of life issues. *Journal of Clinical Psychiatry, 19*, 134–144.

Johns, N., Storch, E. A., Geffken, G. R., & Murphy, T. K. (in press). Convergent and divergent validity of the Tourette's Disorder Scale—Parent-Rated Version. *Child Study Journal*.

Kaufman, J., Birmaher, B., Brent, D., & Rao, U. (1997). Schedule for Affective Disorders and Schizophrenia for School-Age Children-Present and Lifetime version (K–SADS–PL): Initial reliability and validity data. *Journal of the American Academy of Child & Adolescent Psychiatry, 36*, 980–988.

King, N., Inglis, S., Jenkins, M., & Myerson, N. (1995). Test–retest reliability of the survey form of the Leyton Obsessional Inventory-Child Version. *Perceptual and Motor Skills, 80*, 1200–1202.

Kovacs, M. (1992). *Children's Depression Inventory Manual.* Toronto: Multi-Health Systems.

Lewin, A., Storch, E. A., Adkins, J., Murphy, T. K., & Geffken, G. R. (2005). Current directions in pediatric obsessive-compulsive disorder. *Pediatric Annals, 34,* 2–7.

Liebowitz, M., Turner, S., Piacentini, J. C., Beidel, D., Clarvit, S., & Davies, S. (2002). Fluoxetine in children and adolescents with OCD: A placebo-controlled trial. *Journal of the American Academy of Child & Adolescent Psychiatry, 41,* 1431–1438.

MacKay, D., Danyko, S., Neziroglu, F., & Yaryura-Tobias, J. A. (1995). Factor structure of the Yale-Brown Obsessive-Compulsive Scale: A two dimensional measure. *Behavior Research and Therapy, 33,* 865–869.

MacKay, D., Piacentini, J., Greisberg, S., Graae, F., Jaffer, M., & Miller, J. (2003). The Children's Yale-Brown Obsessive-Compulsive Scale: Item structure in an outpatient setting. *Psychological Assessment, 15,* 578–581.

Maina, G., Albert, U., Bogetto, F., & Ravizza, L. (1999). Obsessive-compulsive syndromes in older adolescents. *Acta Psychiatrica Scandinavica, 100,* 447–450.

March, J. S., & MHS Staff. (1997). *Multidimensional anxiety scale for children technical manual.* Toronto: Multi-Health System.

Masten, A. S., Neemann, J., & Andenas, S. (1994). Life events and adjustment in adolescents: The significance of event independence, desirability, and chronicity. *Journal of Research on Adolescence, 4,* 71–97.

McCubbin, H. I., Patterson, J. M., & Wilson, L. R. (1991). Family Inventory of Life Events and Changes—Form C. In H. I. McCubbin & A. I. Thompson (Eds.), *Family assessment inventories for research and practice* (pp. 79–98). Madison: University of Wisconsin.

Merlo, L. J., & Storch, E. A. (2005). *Development and preliminary validation of the Florida Obsessive-Compulsive Student Inventory.* Unpublished manuscript.

Murphy, D. L., Pickar, D., & Alterman, I. S. (1982). Methods for the quantitative assessment of depressive and manic behavior. In E. L. Burdock, A. Sudilousky & S. Gershon (Eds.), *The behavior of psychiatric patients* (pp. 355–392). New York: Marcel Decker.

Murphy, T. K., Petitto, J. M., Voeller, K. S., & Goodman, W. K. (2001). Obsessive compulsive disorder: Is there an association with childhood streptococcal infections and altered immune function? *Seminars in Clinical Neuropsychiatry, 6,* 266–276.

Murphy, T. K., Sajid, M., Soto, O., Shapira, N. A., Edge, P., & Yang, M. (2004). Detecting pediatric autoimmune neuropsychiatric disorders associated with streptococcus in children with obsessive-compulsive disorder and tics. *Biological Psychiatry, 55,* 61–68.

Nelson, E. C., Hanna, G. L., Hudziak, J. J., Botteron, K. N., Heath, A. C., & Todd, R. D. (2001). Obsessive-Compulsive Scale of the Child Behavior Checklist: Specificity, sensitivity, and predictive power. *Pediatrics, 108,* 1–5.

Piacentini, J. C., Bergman, R. L., Jacobs, C., McCracken, J. T., & Kretchman, J. (2002). Open trial of cognitive behavior therapy for childhood obsessive-compulsive disorder. *Journal of Anxiety Disorders, 16,* 207–219.

Piacentini, J. C., Bergman, R. L., Keller, M., & McCracken, J. (2003). Functional impairment in children and adolescents with obsessive-compulsive disorder. *Journal of Child and Adolescent Psychopharmacology, 13S-1,* S61–S69.

Piacentini, J. C., & Jaffer, M. (1999). *Measuring functional impairment in youngsters with OCD: Manual for the Child OCD Impact Scale (COIS).* Los Angeles: UCLA Department of Psychiatry.

Practice Parameters for the Assessment and Treatment of Children and Adolescents With Obsessive-Compulsive Disorder. (1998). *Journal of the American Academy of Child & Adolescent Psychiatry, 37,* 27S–45S.

Rapoport, J. L., & Inoff-Germain, G. (2000). Treatment of obsessive-compulsive disorder in children and adolescents. *Journal of Child Psychology & Psychiatry, 41,* 419–431.

Rapoport, J. L., & Mikkelson, E. (1980). Clinical controlled trial of chlorimipramine in adolescents with obsessive-compulsive disorder. *Psychopharmacology Bulletin, 16,* 61–63.

Rassin, E., Merckelbach, H., Muris, P., & Schmidt, H. (2001). The thought–action fusion scale: Further evidence for its reliability and validity. *Behavior Research and Therapy, 39,* 537–544.

Reynolds, C. R., & Kamphaus, R. W. (1992). *Behavior Assessment System for Children Manual.* Circle Pines, MN: American Guidance Services, Inc.

Scahill, L., Riddle, M. A., McSwiggin-Hardin, M., & Ort, S. I. (1997). Children's Yale-Brown Obsessive Compulsive Scale: Reliability and validity. *Journal of the American Academy of Child & Adolescent Psychiatry, 36,* 844–852.

Schniering, C. A., & Rapee, R. M. (2002). Development and validation of a measure of children's automatic thoughts: The Children's Automatic Thoughts Scale. *Behaviour Research and Therapy, 40,* 1091–1109.

Shafran, R., Frampton, I., Heyman, I., Reynolds, M., Teachman, B., & Rachman, S. (2003). The preliminary development of a new self-report measure for OCD in young people. *Journal of Adolescence, 26,* 137–142.

Shafran, R., Thordarson, M. A., & Rachman, S. (1996). Thought-action fusion in obsessive-compulsive disorder. *Journal of Anxiety Disorders, 10,* 379–391.

Shytle, R. D., Silver, A. A., Sheehan, K. H., Wilkinson, B. J., Newman, M., & Sanberg, P. R. (2003). The Tourette's Disorder Scale (TODS): Development, reliability and validity. *Assess, 10,* 273–287.

Silverman, W. K., & Albano, A. M. (1996). *The Anxiety Disorders Interview Schedule for DSM–IV: Child and Parent versions.* San Antonio, TX: Psychological Corporation.

Silverman, W. K., Saavedra, L. M., & Pina, A. A. (2001). Test–retest reliability of anxiety symptoms and diagnoses with anxiety disorders interview schedule for *DSM–IV*: Child and parent versions. *Journal of the American Academy of Child & Adolescent Psychiatry, 40,* 937–944.

Stewart, S. E., Geller, D. A., Jenike, M., Pauls, D., Shaw, D., & Mullin, B. (2004). Long-term outcome of pediatric obsessive-compulsive disorder: A meta-analysis and qualitative review of the literature. *Acta Psychiatrica Scandinavica, 110,* 4–13.

Storch, E. A., Geffken, G. R., Adkins, J. W., Murphy, T. K., & Goodman, W. K. (in press). Sequential cognitive-behavioral psychotherapy for children with obsessive-compulsive disorder with an inadequate medication response: A case series of five patients. *Depression and Anxiety.*

Storch, E. A., Geffken, G. R., Murphy, T. K., & Goodman, W. K. (2005). *Child- and parent-report versions of the Children's Yale-Brown Obsessive-Compulsive Scale.* Unpublished manuscript.

Storch, E. A., Murphy, T. K., Bagner, D. M., Johns, N., Baumeister, A., Goodman, W. K, et al. (2006). Reliability and validity of the Child Behavior Checklist Obsessive-Compulsive Scale. *Journal of Anxiety Disorders, 20,* 473–485.

Storch, E. A., Murphy, T. K., Geffken, G. R., Soto, O., Sajid, M., Allen, P., et al. (2004a). Psychometric evaluation of the Children's Yale-Brown *Obsessive Compulsive Scale. Psychiatry Research, 129,* 91–98

Storch, E. A., Murphy, T. K., Geffken, G. R., Soto, O., Sajid, M., Allen, P., et al. (2004b). Further psychometric properties of the Tourette's Disorder Scale—Parent Rated Version (TODS–PR). *Child Psychiatry and Human Development, 35,* 107–120.

Storch, E. A., Murphy, T. K., Geffken, G. R., Soto, O., Sajid, M., & Allen, P. (in press). Development of the Children's Florida Obsessive-Compulsive Inventory (C-FOCI). *Journal of Behavior Therapy and Experimental Psychiatry.*

Storch, E. A., Murphy, T. K., Geffken, G. R., Soto, O., Sajid, M., Bagner, D. M., Allen, P., Killany, E. M., & Goodman, W. K. (2005). Factor structure of the Children's Yale-Brown Obsessive-Compulsive Scale. *Journal of Clinical Child and Adolescent Psychology, 34,* 312–319.

Storch, E. A., Shapira, N. A., Dimoulas, E., Geffken, G. R., Murphy, T. K., & Goodman, W. K. (2005). The Yale-Brown Obsessive Compulsive Scale: The dimensional structure revisited. *Depression and Anxiety, 22,* 28–35.

Thomsen, P. H., & Jensen, J. (1991). Dimensional approach to obsessive-compulsive disorder in childhood and adolescence. *Acta Psychiatrica Scandinavica, 83,* 183–187.

Thomsen, P. H., & Mikkelsen, H. U. (1995). Course of obsessive-compulsive disorder in children and adolescents: A prospective follow-up study of 23 Danish cases. *Journal of the American Academy of Child & Adolescent Psychiatry, 34,* 1432–1440.

Thorâen, P., Asberg, M., Cronholm, B., Jornestedt, L., & Traskman, L. (1980). Clomipramine treatment of obsessive-compulsive disorder. *Archives of General Psychiatry, 37,* 1281–1285.

Thordarson, D. T., Rachman, S., & Radomsky, A. (1996). *A revision of the Maudsley Obsessive Compulsive Inventory.* Paper presented at the American Association for Behavior Therapy.

Wells, A., & Cartwright-Hatton, S. (2004). A short form of the Metacognitions Questionnaire: Properties of the MCQ-30. *Behavior Research and Therapy, 42,* 385–396.

Wolff, R. P., & Wolff, L. S. (1991). Assessment and treatment of obsessive-compulsive disorder in children. *Behavior Modification, 15,* 372–393.

Wood, J. J., Piacentini, J. C., Bergman, R. L., McCracken, J., & Barrios, V. (2002). Concurrent validity of the anxiety disorders section of the Anxiety Disorders Interview Schedule for *DSM–IV*: Child and Parent Versions. *Journal of Clinical Child and Adolescent Psychology, 31,* 335–342.

5

Psychological Theories of Obsessive-Compulsive Disorder

Jonathan S. Abramowitz
University of North Carolina at Chapel Hill

Steven Taylor
University of British Columbia

Dean McKay
Fordham University

Obsessive-compulsive disorder (OCD) is an anxiety disorder that can affect children, adolescents, and adults of any age. This chapter explores the major psychological theories that have been put forward to explain the nature of OCD and its etiology. In discussing these models, the foundation of which primarily includes clinical observations and laboratory research with adults, we highlight considerations for the explanation of OCD as observed in pediatric samples. We begin with a look at the clinical presentation of OCD, as exemplified by three children with typical presentations of the disorder. These cases are used to illustrate aspects of the theoretical models discussed further below:

Bob, a 12-year-old boy, suffered from obsessional thoughts of making mistakes when completing schoolwork. For example, while working on math problems, he would often get the idea that perhaps he had added, subtracted, or multiplied incorrectly, or that he had copied a number incorrectly from the output of his calculator. Such thoughts evoked subsequent ideas and images of bad grades, punishment from his parents, social embarrassment, and being "a failure" in life. These concerns evoked high levels of doubt and distress. Driven by the desire to reduce the distress evoked by these persistent doubts about mistakes, Bob reluctantly re-checked all of his schoolwork multiple times. Even if initial checks revealed no apparent errors, he would review mathematical computations, spelling, and so forth, up to 10 times. When Bob presented for treatment, he was unable to complete assignments in class in the allotted time, and was spending in excess of 5 hours re-checking his homework each night.

Ilene, who was 16, struggled with fears of contamination. She knew that other people sometimes worried about dirt and germs, but she was different. Ilene felt a strong need to wash her hands in order to prevent herself from becoming blind. Beginning in the fifth grade, she thought that if she touched items belonging to her grandmother, who had a visual impairment, she would lose her own sight. As a result, she would try to avoid her grandmother and anything that belonged to her; and would wash her hands if contact did occur. As Ilene grew older, the problem worsened to the point that she washed even when she heard words such as "blind," read about people with vision problems, or came into contact with anything associated with a visually impaired person. If it was difficult for Ilene to wash her hands immediately, she would maintain a mental list of obsessional triggers so that later she could wash away the "blindness germs". When Ilene came to our clinic for treatment, her hands were raw from all the time spent washing (up to 6 hours per day).

Howard, a 10-year-old boy in the fourth grade, had problems with recurrent distressing thoughts about his mother having a car accident and dying, and ritualistic counting and repeating behaviors. Whenever he had thoughts of an accident, he engaged in repetitive behaviors to try to "prevent something awful from happening." Examples included getting dressed over and over, opening and closing doors repeatedly, going through doorways, and chewing food. Howard thought that if he didn't perform these behaviors "just right," or if the "bad" thought was in his head while he performed the behaviors, his mother would have an accident and it would be his own fault. He also counted when completing rituals to ensure that these behaviors were performed the "correct" number of times (i.e., odd numbers of repetitions were unacceptable). Sometimes, Howard used mental rituals to deal with the upsetting intrusions. For example, he mentally replaced thoughts of accidents with "good" thoughts, which he believed would protect his mother from injury. Although Howard could function at school, he was beginning to avoid social situations because of embarrassment. His obsessional thoughts and rituals were taking up to 3 hours per day.

THE NATURE OF OCD

OCD is characterized by obsessions, compulsions or, (most often) both (American Psychiatric Association, 2000). Obsessions are intrusive and recurrent, unwanted, distressing thoughts, ideas, doubts, images, impulses, or urges, which are subjectively resisted. They most often concern mistakes (as in the case of Bob), unacceptable thoughts (as described by Howard), contamination (e.g., Ilene), and responsibility for harm (e.g., Howard). In adults, obsessions are experienced as senseless or inappropriate—although this is not always the case in children—and often have a bizarre quality or are contrary to the person's world view (e.g., a deeply religious individual who has recurrent images of Jesus with an erection on the cross).

Compulsions are urges to perform behaviors or mental acts (rituals) in a repeated or stereotyped manner. The rituals are usually carried out directly in response to a specific obsession, such as Bob's checking his homework to allay obsessional doubts about mistakes. Compulsions are often performed according to certain self-imposed rules, such as repeating an action a set number of times (e.g., Howard's avoidance of odd numbers of repetitions). They may be overt (e.g., retracing one's steps multiple times through a doorway) or covert (e.g., mentally replacing a "bad" thought with a "good" one). Although compulsive rituals are excessive, or not realistically connected to what they are intended to prevent, the patient usually can articulate a link between obsessional fears and compulsive rituals (e.g., "I must touch the wall 10 times to prevent my mother from dying"). In children, however, the senselessness of the obsessions and compulsions might not be recognized.

Studies of adults suggest that OCD is highly heterogeneous (McKay et al., 2004). The major symptom dimensions or "subtypes" that have been consistently identified include (a) contamination obsessions and decontamination (washing, cleaning) rituals; (b) obsessions about harm and mistakes, and checking compulsions; (c) unacceptable obsessional thoughts (sexual, sacrilegious, violent) and mental rituals; (d) obsessions with things being symmetrical and ordering rituals, and (e) hoarding symptoms (Abramowitz, Franklin, Schwartz, & Furr, 2003). Research and clinical observations indicate that the presentation of OCD in pediatric patients is similar to that displayed by adults (Geller et al., 1998), although recent analyses suggest that magical ideation plays a greater role in pediatric presentations (McKay et al., 2006).

Subclinical obsessional and compulsive phenomena are common in the general adult population (Muris, Merckelbach, & Clavan, 1997). In fact, nonclinical adults regularly report experiencing intrusive unwanted thoughts concerning violence and harm, contamination, order, and doubt—the same themes commonly expressed in the clinical obsessions of OCD patients (Rachman & de Silva, 1978). These similarities suggest that the study of normal obsessions and compulsions may shed light on the mechanisms of their clinical counterparts. The major differences between normal and clinical obsessions and compulsions appear to be in their frequency, intensity, and duration, with clinical obsessions being more severe (Rachman & de Silva, 1978).

Although numerous theories have been proposed to explain the complex clinical picture of OCD, few have been empirically studied. Fewer still offer a developmental perspective on the mechanisms hypothesized to underlie the disorder. In many cases, theories have little or no empirical support (e.g., psychoanalytic theories), cannot account for the heterogeneity of OCD, or have very limited explanatory power. We have asserted elsewhere (Taylor, McKay, & Abramowitz, 2005) that a valuable theoretical model of OCD should be able to explain the following:

1. The nature of obsessions and compulsions (and their interrelations), their origins, and clinical course.
2. The symptom heterogeneity of OCD (i.e., why are some sufferers, for example, obsessed with contamination, whereas others have intrusive religious obsessions, and still others have harming obsessions and checking compulsions?
3. The distinction between OCD and other disorders with similar clinical features (i.e., the model must have *specificity*).
4. Why some treatment techniques are effective (e.g., exposure and response prevention), whereas others are largely ineffective (e.g., relaxation training).

We now turn to an examination of the most promising of the psychological theories of OCD: learning (conditioning) models, cognitive deficit models, and cognitive-behavioral models. In considering the models reviewed in this chapter, we discuss the basic tenets of each model, along with the relevant empirical research, developmental considerations, and treatment implications. The chapter closes with an evaluation of the extent to which each approach accomplishes the goals of a valuable theoretical model, and how well it addresses issues relevant to OCD in children and adolescents.

LEARNING (CONDITIONING) MODELS OF OCD

Summary of the Model

The principal conditioning model of OCD is based on Mowrer's (1960) two-stage theory of the acquisition and maintenance of fear. In the first stage of the model, a neutral stimulus acquires the ability to evoke fear through classical conditioning in much the same way that specific phobias are thought to develop: A previously neutral stimulus (the conditioned stimulus, or CS) is paired with an aversive stimulus (the unconditioned stimulus, or UCS; e.g., via a traumatic experience), so that the CS comes to elicit a conditioned fear response (CR). As a result of this associative learning process, specific situations (e.g., using the bathroom), objects (e.g., door handles, knives), and thoughts, images, doubts, or impulses (e.g., thoughts of curse words) that pose no *objective* threat come to evoke fear.

The second stage of the model (operant conditioning) proposes that avoidance behaviors develop to reduce the obsessional anxiety and are then negatively reinforced by the reduction in distress that they engender. However, unlike in phobias where we primarily observe fear cues that are external and that can be passively avoided (e.g., elevators, snakes), obsessional fear in OCD is often evoked by ubiquitous cues such as internal cognitive stimuli (e.g., intrusive thoughts as in the case of Howard) and other generally unavoidable situations (e.g., one's grandmother as in the case of Ilene). In response to these stimuli, individuals with OCD therefore resort to *active avoidance* strategies such as compulsive rituals that provide the desired immediate escape from obsessional fear. However, by virtue of their anxiety-reducing properties, rituals are negatively reinforced and therefore are used whenever obsessional fear arises. Moreover, rituals and avoidance terminate exposure to the conditioned stimulus and prevent the natural extinction of conditioned fear that would otherwise occur with prolonged and repeated exposure. Thus, these habitual responses are maladaptive in the long-term in that they maintain the conditioned obsessional fear.

Empirical Status

Whereas some claims of the conditioning model are supported by clinical observation and empirical research, other claims are not. A major problem is that neither empirical research nor clinical observations support a classical conditioning explanation for the *development* of obsessional fear. First, OCD onset is typically gradual, which is in contrast to the immediate (traumatic) onset that would be predicted by the classical conditioning theory. Second, children tend not to ascribe the onset of their OCD symptoms to specific (traumatic) conditioning experiences. In adults, when traumatic events are reported, they often precede the onset of OCD symptoms by long periods of time. Third, many children exhibit multiple types of obsessions as well as the development of new obsessions that do not correspond with new or multiple traumatic conditioning experiences. Thus, it appears that classical conditioning alone can not account for the acquisition of obsessions.

In contrast, there is substantial evidence that operant conditioning (negative reinforcement) plays a role in the *maintenance* of OCD. A series of experimental studies demonstrated that exposure to obsessional stimuli evokes subjective distress and urges to perform compulsive behaviors in adults with OCD (Rachman & Hodgson, 1980). Rituals such as checking and washing compulsions lead to short-term reduction in distress (e.g., Rachman, de Silva, & Roper, 1976; Roper, Rachman, & Hodgson, 1973). In rare instances compulsive behavior (particularly checking) is associated with *increased* distress (during or following the behavior). This is readily explained by patients' intense frustration with their inability to control these behaviors. Overall, then, negative reinforcement (i.e., escape from anxiety) provides an excellent explanation for the persistence of compulsive rituals, neutralization, and avoidance behavior in OCD.

Developmental Considerations

There has been no empirical work addressing the conditioning model of OCD in children. However, the principles of classical and operant conditioning apply to children's behavior as well as to that of adults. In anxiety disorders in general, it has been suggested that proneness to avoidance coping facilitates the development of anxious avoidance (Ollendick, Vasey, & King, 2001). This could occur in the form of observational learning, if a parent or caregiver relies on avoidance, or if the child shows this coping preference. In the case of pediatric and adult OCD, they are phenomenologically similar. Clinical observations of children who are able to articulate the relationship between obsessions and compulsions report that their obsessional thoughts evoke distress and that the "purpose" of their rituals is to reduce this discomfort. Therefore, we can assume that the strengths and limitations of the conditioning model as it applies to adults would be relevant also in the case of children with OCD.

Treatment Implications

Conditioning models have led to a highly effective treatment for OCD, known as exposure and response prevention (ERP). This involves evoking obsessional fear via systematic confrontation with feared stimuli (e.g., floors, odd numbers) under low-risk circumstances; and prolonging this exposure until anxiety reduction occurs naturally (habituation). Depending on the form of the feared stimulus (e.g., situations, objects, doubts, images, ideas, impulses), habituation might require exposure *in vivo*—actual confrontation with specific objects or situations, and/or exposure in *imagination*—confrontation with fear-evoking intrusive cognitions. Regardless of the exposure media, repeated trials in which habituation occurs facilitates the extinction of fear.

Response prevention entails refraining from behaviors or mental acts (e.g., compulsive rituals, neutralizing) that would reduce anxiety before it declines naturally. It is necessary to implement continuous response prevention in tandem with exposure because performance of anxiety-reducing behaviors would terminate exposure to the feared situation and consequently interfere with the habituation of obsessional anxiety. The beneficial effects of exposure and response prevention have been demonstrated in many treatment outcome studies of adult and pediatric samples (Abramowitz, Whiteside, & Deacon, 2005; Kozak & Coles, 2005).

Evaluation of the Model

With respect to explaining the nature of OCD symptoms, their origins, and clinical course, the conditioning model is only partially helpful. Indeed, obsessions typically evoke anxiety and compulsive rituals typically reduce anxiety. However, whereas the model accounts for the *maintenance* of obsessional fear via the habitual performance of rituals, it cannot account very well for the *origins* of obsessional fear. With respect to symptom heterogeneity, the conditioning model might explain why some patients present with contamination fears and washing rituals, whereas others have blasphemous obsessions and prayer rituals, but it does not account for the fact that most patients evidence multiple types of obsessions, or that the themes of obsessions and rituals may shift over time without the occurrence of additional conditioning experiences.

With respect to specificity, the functional relationship between obsessions and compulsions specified by the conditioning model distinguishes OCD from other disorders often considered to have similar clinical features (Hollander, Friedberg, Wasserman, Yeh, & Iyengar, 2005). For example, repetitive behaviors in impulse control disorders (e.g., hair-pulling in trichotillomania) are not triggered by the kinds of obsessional fears that trigger compulsive rituals in OCD; that is hair-pulling is not performed to remove fears of disasters. Instead, hair-pulling is triggered by general stress or boredom (Stanley, Swann, Bowers, & Davis, 1992). Similarly, impulsive sexual behavior (e.g., chronic pornography use) appears to be maintained by *positive* reinforcement (i.e., this behavior brings about physically pleasurable feelings), as opposed to *negative* reinforcement that is observed in OCD (Schwartz & Abramowitz, 2003).

The most significant legacy of the conditioning model is how it has informed the treatment of OCD. ERP was derived directly from learning theory and elegant experimental research; and it remains the most effective treatment for OCD across the lifespan. Moreover, the conditioning model predicts the *ineffectiveness* of alternate treatment procedures such as thought stopping, aversive conditioning, and progressive muscle relaxation, which do not reduce OCD symptoms (e.g., Fals-Stewart, Marks, & Schafer, 1993). Yet, despite the impact of conditioning models on current treatments, the inability of this theoretical approach to explain the onset of OCD has led researchers and theorists to shift their focus onto the possible cognitive bases of obsessions and compulsions, as we explore next.

COGNITIVE DEFICIT MODELS

Summary of the Models

Cognitive deficit models of OCD are based on the hypothesis that obsessions and compulsions result from abnormally functioning neuropsychological and cognitive processes, such as working memory. For example, perhaps compulsive checking arises as a consequence of *not being able to remember* whether or not one has locked the door, turned off the oven, or unplugged the iron. Conceivably, compulsive washing could arise due to a problem with not *being able to forget or dismiss ideas* about dirt, germs, or illnesses. Perhaps impairments in other neuropsychological processes (e.g., organizational or executive functions) account for the apparent failure of cognitive control, difficulty making decisions, and otherwise abnormal responding to environmental stimuli as observed in OCD. Cognitive deficits assumed to underlie OCD are *functional* as opposed to *neurobiological* (McNally, 2000). That is, they are not thought to be correlated with specific structural or functional brain anomalies—although information-processing abnormalities are certainly compatible with neurobiological processes. Put another way, cognitive deficits are akin to a problem with the computer *software*, rather than in the *hardware*.

The most familiar cognitive deficit model of OCD is Reed's (1985) cognitive-structural model, which proposes that people with OCD have an impaired ability to organize and integrate experiences and memories. Therefore, when confronted with classification tasks, people with OCD try to compensate by over-structuring their lives and by using strict categorical limits and time markers. The result is a tendency to over-define categories of stimuli and form an excessive number of categories, each with very few characteristics. Reed suggested that uncertainty about the properties of a stimulus, situation, or action is reflected in the persistent doubt present in OCD (e.g., *uncertainty* over whether one was exposed to contaminants, injured another person, etc.). In an attempt to reduce this doubt, the individual engages in compulsive rituals such as checking, washing, assurance-seeking, and repeating activities.

Empirical Status

The vast majority of research on cognitive deficits in OCD has been conducted with adult patients. Therefore, the extent to which such deficits appear in children and adolescents remains largely unknown. In the following, we review studies on a number of cognitive functions hypothesized to cause the signs and symptoms of OCD.

Organizational Deficits. In an early study, Persons and Foa (1984) had individuals with and without OCD sort cards with different words relating to a particular idea (e.g., temperature) into categories of their own choosing. Results indicated that OCD patients took more time and invented more categories to sort the cards into than did the nonpatients. Persons and Foa concluded that, consistent with the cognitive-structural model, OCD patients have a general "complex-concepts deficit" in which they make finer distinctions among items as compared to nonpatients. A number of later studies using card-sorting tasks, however, did not find results consistent with the presence of such a deficit (Tallis, 1995). Thus, it seems that a general deficit in category formation is unlikely to account for OCD symptoms.

Working Memory Deficits. A meta-analysis by Woods, Vevea, Chambless, and Bayen (2002) found small to medium effect sizes suggesting that compulsive checkers do not perform quite as well as noncheckers on tests of short-term/working memory, as well as on various forms of episodic long-term memory. Woods et al. (2002) noted, however, that numerous variables could give rise to the apparent memory deficits in checkers, and they cautioned against inferring any causal relationships.

Some theorists have proposed that individuals with OCD have a memory deficit only in situations relevant to their obsessional fears. This would explain, for example, why a patient who fears burglaries might spend hours re-checking that doors to the outside (e.g., the garage door) are securely locked, yet has no urges to check closet or bathroom doors. However, results from the few studies that have examined this *selective memory* hypothesis suggest that patients actually have enhanced memory for threat-relevant (OCD-related) information. In one study, Radomsky and Rachman (1999) had healthy individuals and OCD patients with washing compulsions look at everyday (neutral) objects, such as a ruler, that had been touched with either a "clean" cloth or a "dirty" cloth. In a subsequent surprise recall test, the OCD patients recalled more "contaminated" objects than "clean" objects, and they recalled fewer "clean" objects than did the nonpatient participants. Radomsky, Rachman, and Hammond (2001) replicated their earlier findings in a study with compulsive checkers. Together, these two studies suggest that individuals with OCD have a selectively *better* memory for anxiety-relevant, than for irrelevant, events. These findings are consistent with what is known about the body's natural fight-or-flight response, in which attentional resources are automatically shifted toward threatening stimuli.

Reality Monitoring Deficits.   If abnormal working memory per se is not the problem in OCD, perhaps obsessions and compulsions are caused by deficits in *reality monitoring*—the ability to discriminate between memories of actual and imagined events (Johnson & Raye, 1981). It seems plausible that ritualistic checking, for example, is prompted by problems discerning whether an action (e.g., locking the door) was really carried out or merely imagined. However, studies examining the reality monitoring skills of OCD patients report inconsistent results. Most studies suggest that OCD is not characterized by a deficit in reality-monitoring skills (Constans, Foa, Franklin, & Matthews, 1995). In their meta-analytic review, Woods et al. (2002) found virtually no differences in reality monitoring between OCD patients and control groups across five reality monitoring studies (effect sizes of .02 and .03).

Cognitive Inhibition.   The intrusive, repetitious, and seemingly uncontrollable quality of obsessional thoughts has led some researchers to hypothesize that OCD patients have deficits in cognitive inhibition. In other words, perhaps they have trouble *forgetting* disturbing information. Wilhelm, McNally, Baer, and Florin (1996) tested this hypothesis using a directed forgetting paradigm in which OCD patients and healthy control participants were presented with a series of negative, positive, and neutral words; and given instructions to either remember or to forget each word after it was presented. Tests of recall and recognition showed that OCD patients had more difficulty forgetting negative material relative to positive and neutral material, whereas control subjects did not. Tolin, Hamlin, and Foa (2002) replicated and extended this finding by demonstrating that relevance to OCD, rather than general threat-relevance, predicted impaired forgetting.

Developmental Considerations

Research on neuropsychological and cognitive deficits in children with OCD is sparse, and the available studies largely have not found differences between children affected with OCD and those unaffected (Rosenberg et al., 1997). For example, Beers et al. (1998) found that children with OCD performed normally on a number of measures of executive functioning, including some previously shown to be impaired in adults with OCD (e.g., the Wisconsin Card-Sorting Test). One explanation for these null results is that these cognitive deficits emerge during the course of development in a manner that parallels the normal cognitive development. Such problems may not be apparent in childhood OCD because children do not have fully matured prefrontal cortical networks and, consequently, show less developed executive functioning (Savage & Rauch, 2000). Further, it has been demonstrated that compulsive behaviors are associated with normal development and diminish with normal brain development (Evans, Lewis, & Iobst, 2004).

Many executive and memory functions, including sustained attention, planning, problem solving, and semantic organization, show the greatest progression after age 12 (Levin et al., 1991).

Evaluation of the Models

The research provides only weak support for cognitive deficits in OCD. Meta-analytic findings on memory in OCD suggest that any effects are fairly minimal (Woods et al., 2002). In most studies, patients actually perform quite normally on memory tests. The most consistent finding is that compared to nonpatients, individuals with OCD have less *confidence* in their own memory (Foa, Amir, Gershuny, Molnar, & Kozak, 1997). In their meta-analysis, Woods et al. (2002) reported large effect sizes of 0.74 and 0.92 for memory confidence, further supporting this view. But, reduced confidence in one's (normally functioning) memory is not a deficit per se; rather, it is an erroneous interpretation (i.e., *bias*; "I recall seeing that I made no spelling errors, but I can't trust that my memory is accurate"). There is experimental evidence that compulsive checking results, at least in part, from decreased memory confidence, particularly in situations where there is the perception of responsibility for mistakes (Radomsky et al., 2001; Tolin et al., 2001). Fearing responsibility for negative outcomes, people with OCD become highly concerned about their memory and try to compensate by checking.

Another limitation of cognitive deficit models (as with biological deficit models such as those that posit serotonergic dysregulations or defective brain structures or functions) is that they are unable to explain the heterogeneity of OCD symptoms. For example, general deficit theories cannot account for the development of contamination fears, as opposed to fears of religious sin, in a given child. Moreover, mild neuropsychological "deficits" (i.e., differences between affected adults and healthy controls) have been reported in people with a number of mood, eating, and anxiety disorders (Alarcon, Libb, & Boll, 1994). Thus, these models do not differentiate OCD from other adult disorders and do not account for why the deficits give rise to OCD instead of these other conditions (i.e., the models lack specificity). Finally, with regard to treatment, cognitive deficit models predict that effective therapy for OCD should involve cognitive rehabilitation training to reverse deficits in processes such as memory, reality monitoring, and cognitive inhibition. However, there is no evidence for the effectiveness of such treatments in adults or children (in fact, these have not been studied). Deficit models also cannot account for the effectiveness of ERP.

In summary, despite its intuitive appeal, the conceptualization of OCD as arising from general cognitive deficits does not appear to add to the understanding or treatment of the disorder in either adults or children. Apparent memory and other processing deficits are better accounted for by *cognitive biases* in which obsessional anxiety leads to preferential processing of threat relevant stimuli. In the case of compulsive checking, it is likely that reduced confidence in memory, and therefore concern over whether the seeming memory problems will lead to misfortune, are evoked by the perception that one may be (or may come to be) responsible for negative outcomes. Hence, checking results as a way of reducing doubts that have arisen because of mistaken beliefs about one's memory, ability to manage doubts and uncertainty, and pathological estimates of responsibility for harm.

CONTEMPORARY COGNITIVE-BEHAVIORAL MODELS

Summary of the Models

Cognitive-behavioral models of OCD posit that dysfunctional beliefs and interpretations of normally occurring intrusive thoughts give rise to obsessions and compulsions. The basis of all of these models (several of them have been delineated [e.g., Rachman, 1997; Salkovskis, 1985, 1989] and their similarities outweigh the differences) is the well-established finding (discussed in the beginning of this chapter) that mental intrusions (i.e., thoughts, images, and impulses that intrude into consciousness) are normal experiences that almost everyone has from time to time (i.e., normal obsessions; Rachman & deSilva, 1978). Such normal intrusions are thought to develop into highly distressing and time-consuming clinical obsessions when the intrusions are appraised as highly significant and as posing a threat for which the individual is personally responsible. Thus, the individual becomes preoccupied with the unwanted thought, and with trying to control the thought. Misinterpretations of one's thoughts might include any appraisal of the intrusive thought as personally significant or threatening. For example, the belief that thinking about bad behavior is morally equivalent to performing the corresponding behavior (e.g., "Thinking about hurting someone is as bad as actually injuring them"). An international group of researchers interested in the cognitive basis of OCD, the Obsessive-Compulsive Cognitions Working Group (OCCWG: Frost & Steketee, 2002), identified various domains of "core beliefs" thought to underlie the development of obsessions from normal intrusive thoughts in adults. These are summarized in Table 5.1.

To illustrate, consider Howard's unwanted thoughts of his mother dying in a car accident. Most people would consider such an idea as meaningless and harmless ("mental noise"), and then brush it aside as inconsequential. However, the cognitive-behavioral model proposes that such an intrusion will develop into a clinical obsession if the person attaches to it a high degree of importance in a way that leads to an escalation in negative emotion. For example, if Howard believes that "My thoughts about mom having an accident reveal that I'm an awful son" or "I must be extra careful to make sure this doesn't happen." Habitual appraisal of intrusive thoughts in this manner

TABLE 5.1

Types of Dysfunctional Beliefs Associated with OCD

Belief Domain	Description
Inflated responsibility	Belief that one has the special power to cause, and/or the duty to prevent, negative outcomes
Over importance of thoughts (thought-action fusion)	Belief that the mere presence of a thought indicates that the thought is significant. For example, the belief that the thought has ethical or moral ramifications, or that thinking the thought increases the probability of the corresponding behavior or event
Need to control thoughts	Belief that complete control over one's thoughts is both necessary and possible
Overestimation of threat	Belief that negative events are especially likely and would be especially awful
Perfectionism	Belief that mistakes and imperfection are intolerable
Intolerance for uncertainty	Belief that it is necessary and possible to be completely certain that negative outcomes will not occur

evokes distress and motivates the person to try to suppress the unwanted thought and to attempt to prevent any harmful events associated with the intrusion. In Howard's case, he engaged in compulsive rituals to (in his own mind) reduce the probability of accidents.

From the cognitive-behavior perspective, passive avoidance behavior and compulsive rituals are conceptualized as maladaptive efforts to prevent or remove intrusions, and to prevent feared consequences of intrusions. There are several ways in which avoidance and rituals are counterproductive. First (borrowing from conditioning models), because these strategies are effective (in the short-term) in providing the desired reduction in obsessional distress, they are negatively reinforced and thus evolve into strong habits. Second, (also borrowing from the behavioral approach) because they provide an immediate reduction in anxiety, these strategies prevent the natural abatement of the fear response that typically occurs when individuals stay in feared situations for longer periods of time. Third, avoidance and rituals are thought to lead to an increase in the frequency of obsessions by serving as reminders of obsessional intrusions, and thereby triggering their reoccurrence. For example, compulsively checking paperwork can trigger additional intrusions about possible mistakes (as in the example of Bob). Finally, performing rituals is thought to preserve dysfunctional beliefs and misinterpretations of obsessional thoughts. That is, when feared consequences do not occur after the performance of a ritual, the person attributes this to their having ritualized. As an example, when Ilene does not lose her sight, she attributes this to her washing rituals, rather than to the irrationality of her fear of catching "blindness germs."

In summary, cognitive-behavioral models posit that when a person appraises an otherwise normally occurring mental intrusion as highly meaningful (e.g., as posing a threat for which he or she is responsible), the person becomes distressed and attempts to remove the intrusion and prevent the feared consequences. This paradoxically increases the frequency of intrusions and they escalate into persistent and distressing clinical obsessions. Compulsive rituals maintain the intrusions and prevent the self-correction of mistaken (catastrophic) appraisals, setting the individual up for a vicious cycle of intrusion → misinterpretation → anxiety → rituals → intrusion, and so on.

Empirical Status

Cognitive-behavioral models of OCD have stimulated a wealth of research that has provided support for these formulations. Studies indicate that adults and children with OCD, as compared to clinical and nonclinical controls, have elevated scores on measures of the dysfunctional beliefs and interpretations listed in Table 5.1 (OCCWG, 2003, 2005). Two studies have examined OCD-related dysfunctional beliefs in children, each with a focus on the tendency to overestimate the importance of intrusive thoughts (i.e., thought–action fusion or TAF). Barrett and Healy (2003) found that in a sample of 7- to 13 year-olds, idiographic assessment of TAF allowed distinction between children with OCD and nonclinical children, but not between children with OCD and those with other anxiety disorders. Difficulty controlling intrusive thoughts, however, did differentiate children with OCD from those with other anxiety disorders. In a nonclinical adolescent sample, Muris, Meesters, Rassin, Merckelbach, and Campbell (2001) found that TAF was related to symptoms of both OCD and other anxiety disorders. When trait anxiety was controlled for, TAF remained significantly associated with only OCD. Together, these findings suggest that a tendency to endorse TAF may exist before adulthood and thus may contribute to the development or maintenance of pediatric OCD (and perhaps other forms of psychopathology).

Studies with adult samples report that OCD-related dysfunctional beliefs and appraisals are correlated with measures of OCD symptom severity. Moreover, the correlations with OCD symptoms tend to be larger than correlations with measures of general distress (depression and general anxiety), and the correlations with OCD symptoms remain significant even when controlling for the effects of general distress (OCCWG, 2003). This indicates that the cognitive phenomena in Table 5.1 have a somewhat specific relationship to OCD in adults.

Several laboratory experiments have manipulated OCD-related cognitions, particularly responsibility appraisals, in order to assess the effects on compulsive behavior (Lopatka & Rachman, 1995; Rachman, Shafran, Mitchell, Trant, & Teachman, 1996; Rassin, Merckelbach, Muris, & Spaan, 1999). To illustrate, Rassin et al. (1999) attached 45 psychologically naïve adolescents (high school students) to bogus electrical equipment that, the adolescents were told, would monitor all of their thoughts for 15 minutes. To induce dysfunctional beliefs about the importance of thoughts, participants assigned to the experimental condition were told that thinking the word "apple" would automatically result in an electric shock to another person whom they had met earlier (a confederate of the experimenter). Participants were also informed that by pressing a certain button immediately after having an "apple" thought, they could prevent the shock. This was intended to be akin to a compulsive ritual aimed at removing an intrusive obsessional thought. Subjects in the control group were told only that the electrical equipment would monitor their thoughts. Results indicated that during the 15-minute monitoring period, the experimental group reported more intrusive "apple" thoughts, more guilt, greater subjective discomfort, and more intense resistance to thoughts about apples compared to the control group. Moreover, there was a strong association between the number of reported "apple" thoughts and the number of button presses. Thus, experimentally induced dysfunctional beliefs (i.e., the belief that one's thoughts can produce harmful and preventable consequences) evoked intrusive distressing thoughts and ritualistic behavior akin to OCD symptoms.

Also in accord with the hypothesis that OCD is maintained by compulsive rituals and efforts to suppress intrusive thoughts, experimental evidence suggests that repetitive checking increases doubt and uncertainty (van den Hout & Kindt, 2003). Experimental studies of non-OCD participants suggests that attempts to suppress unwanted thoughts often (but not invariably) leads to a paradoxical increase in the frequency of these thoughts (Abramowitz, Tolin, & Street, 2001). Given the degree that OCD sufferers strive to avoid their unwanted thoughts, this suggests that deliberate attempts to suppress obsessions should paradoxically increase the frequency of obsessions. There is inconsistent evidence for this occurring in OCD, although research indicates that people with OCD symptoms are more likely to try to suppress their unwanted, intrusive thoughts (Purdon, 1999).

Developmental Considerations

Cognitive-behavioral models predict that OCD symptoms would arise only after the child has developed a *capacity* to think in ways that are thought to underlie OCD (e.g., to have dysfunctional beliefs about personal responsibility). Children incapable of metacognition (i.e., thinking about ones thoughts), for example, would not be expected to develop severe obsessional symptoms. The observation that children as young as 5 to 7 years old can develop obsessive-compulsive symptoms, and research suggesting that the ability to feel responsible normally arises during these same years (Sameroff & Haith, 1996), are both consistent with the view that inflated sense of responsibility plays a role in childhood OCD. Similarly, the capacity for magical thinking, and the use of magic when imagining solutions to problems, arises somewhat early in cognitive development (Piaget, 1973). This is consistent with the observation that obsessions and compulsive in young people with OCD often have a magical component (as in Ilene's fear of blindness germs and Howard's use of repetitive behavior to prevent car accidents). Metacognition, on the other hand, develops over a broader age range (perhaps not until early adolescence), and often as a function of intellectual development (Alexander, Fabricius, Fleming, Zwahr, & Brown, 2001). Therefore, a very young child might not possess the necessary level of cognitive development to appraise his or her own thoughts in catastrophic ways (as in TAF).

Treatment Implications

The cognitive-behavioral model has clear implications for the treatment of OCD. Cognitive-behavior therapy (CBT; e.g., Salkovskis, 1985) was developed to help patients to (a) modify their erroneous interpretations of intrusive thoughts and other obsessional stimuli, and (b) eliminate avoidance and ritualistic behaviors that serve as barriers to the self-correction of the erroneous interpretations. The main task of CBT is to foster an appraisal of unpleasant intrusive thoughts as normal (i.e., "mental noise") and therefore not demanding of further action. As developed for adults, CBT involves the use of four treatment procedures. First, patients are educated about the normalcy of intrusive thoughts, the ways in which misinterpreting such stimuli lead to obsessions, and the ways in which obsessional fear is maintained. Second, cognitive restructuring procedures similar to those used in the treatment of depression (Beck, Rush, Shaw, & Emery, 1979) are implemented to help patients identify and correct distorted beliefs about thoughts and other obsessional stimuli. Exposure and response prevention, the third and fourth procedures, are incorporated as in traditional behavior therapy. However, in CBT, these exercises might be framed as "behavioral experiments" to test appraisals and beliefs, in addition to being used to foster habituation of obsessional fear (Abramowitz, 2006).

A cognitive-behavioral treatment package has been developed specifically for childhood OCD (March & Mulle, 1998). This model relies primarily on ERP, with some limited cognitive therapy procedures. One of the major developmental adjustments involves separating OCD from the child (i.e., "talking back to OCD," referred to as "cultivating non-attachment,"). Unlike cognitive strategies used with adults, where behavioral experiments are prominently featured, this particular approach relies on a variety of self-statements that allow the child to minimize the significance of the obsessional symptom when it arises. Attention is paid to cognitive distortions that are typical among adults with OCD, such as inflated responsibility or overestimation of threat. However, strategies that are intended to minimize the significance of the obsession are relied on more heavily in this case.

Evaluation of the Model

The cognitive-behavioral approach to OCD provides a clearly articulated, comprehensive, logically sound, and empirically verifiable account of the nature of obsessions, compulsions, and related features. Implicit in this model is the notion that obsessions have their origins in normal intrusive thoughts, and that compulsive rituals are predictable responses for someone who perceives threat. Thus, this approach implicates normal human learning principles (i.e., conditioning) and normal cognitive processes. It accounts for the nature and etiology of OCD with greater parsimony than do models that appeal to the presence of chemical imbalances, disease states, or general deficits in attempting to explain the nature and etiology of OCD. Even the kinds of biased thinking implicated in the transformation of normal intrusions into obsessions are not in themselves "disturbed" because everyone makes incorrect judgments about situations and stimuli from time to time. When faced with a perceived threat, it is highly adaptive to take action to avoid or reduce the anticipated danger. Thus, avoidance and rituals in OCD are neither mysterious nor uniquely pathological. This behavior is, however, self-preserving in that it prevents the person from correcting their faulty beliefs and judgments that underlie obsessional fear.

Cognitive-behavioral models also account for the heterogeneity of OCD symptoms. Indeed, this approach predicts that the content of a person's obsessions are determined by the themes that are important in the person's value system (Rachman, 1998). For example, if one is very religious and believes that it is sinful to think blasphemous thoughts, the occurrence of blasphemous thoughts will be particularly unacceptable. Thus, it is no wonder that we typically observe contamination obsessions among people who pride themselves on cleanliness, aggressive obsessions among gentle people, obsessions concerned with mistakes among careful people, homosexual obsessions among heterosexuals, and blasphemous obsessions among strongly religious people. Similarly, the model also predicts the clinically observed constraints on the themes of obsessions. Indeed, although we frequently observe obsessions about mistakenly harming vulnerable people (e.g., the very young and the very old), we do not run into obsessions about mistakenly harming people like Arnold Schwarzenegger. This is because we know that people like Arnold can protect themselves, whereas infants and the very elderly cannot. Models that rely on general deficits, whether cognitive or neurological, cannot account for this aspect of OCD. Additional study of the relationship between cognitive development and the development of implicated cognitive distortions would be relevant in evaluating the relevance of the cognitive-behavioral model to the development of OCD in children.

CONCLUSIONS

OCD in children is, in many ways, similar to that in adults. However, there are some noteworthy differences, such as the greater likelihood that insight into the senselessness of one's compulsions will be lacking in children. This suggests that a model of pediatric OCD must take developmental factors into consideration, such as age-related changes in moral development (especially as related to the development of responsibility beliefs) and the ability to reason about causal relationships (as relevant to thought–action fusion). Of the three classes of theories reviewed in this chapter, the contemporary cognitive-behavioral models show the most promise in explaining OCD in adults and in children. These models have also led to a highly effective treatment for the disorder. Yet despite a good deal of empirical support, cognitive-behavioral models are "works in progress," and will require further refinement. For example, they have been developed without reference to the growing body of research on possible biological and genetic factors in OCD. The models also are not sufficiently integrated with theory and research on child development, such as cognitive development. A more comprehensive understanding of OCD will likely arise if theorists and researchers are willing to tackle the challenging task of integrating cognitive-behavioral models with theory and research from the fields of child development, neuroscience, and genetics.

REFERENCES

Abramowitz, J. S. (2006). *Understanding and treating obsessive-compulsive disorder: A cognitive-behavioral approach.* Mahwah, NJ: Lawrence Erlbaum Associates.

Abramowitz, J. S., Franklin, M. E., Schwartz, S. A., & Furr, J. M. (2003). Symptom presentation and outcome of cognitive-behavioral therapy for obsessive-compulsive disorder. *Journal of Consulting and Clinical Psychology, 71,* 1049–1057.

Abramowitz, J. S., Tolin, D. F., & Street, G. P. (2001). Paradoxical effects of thought suppression: A meta-analysis of controlled studies. *Clinical Psychology Review, 21,* 683–703.

Abramowitz, J. S., Whiteside, S., & Deacon, B. J. (2005). The effectiveness of treatment for pediatric obsessive-compulsive disorder: A meta-analysis. *Behavior Therapy, 36,* 55–64.

Alarcon, R. D., Libb, J. W., & Boll, T. J. (1994). Neuropsychological testing in obsessive-compulsive disorder: A clinical review. *Journal of Neuropsychiatry & Clinical Neurosciences, 6,* 217–228.

Alexander, J. M., Fabricius, W. V., Fleming, V. M., Zwahr, M., & Brown, S. A. (2001). The development of metacognitive causal explanations. *Learning and Individual Differences, 13,* 227–238.

American Psychiatric Association. (2000). *Diagnostic and statistical manual of mental disorders* (4th ed., text revision). Washington, DC: Author.

Barrett, P., & Healy, L. (2003). An examination of the cognitive processes involved in childhood obsessive-compulsive disorder. *Behaviour Research and Therapy, 41*, 285–299.

Beck, A. T., Rush, A. J., Shaw, B. F., & Emery, G. (1979). *Cognitive therapy of depression.* New York: Guilford.

Beers, S. R., Rosenberg, D. R., Dick, E. L., Williams, T., O'Hearn, K., Birmaher, B., et al. (1998). Neuropsychological study of frontal lobe function in psychotropic-naive children with obsessive-compulsive disorder. *American Journal of Psychiatry, 156*, 777–779.

Constans, J., Foa, E., Franklin, M. E., & Matthews, A. (1995). Memory for actual and imagined events in obsessive-compulsive checkers. *Behaviour Research and Therapy, 33*, 665–671.

Evans, D. L., Lewis, M. D., & Iobst, E. (2004). The role of the orbitofrontal cortex in normally developing compulsive-like behaviors and obsessive-compulsive disorder. *Brain and Cognition, 55*, 220–234.

Fals-Stewart, W., Marks, A. P., & Schafer, J. (1993). A comparison of behavioral group therapy and individual behavior therapy in treating obsessive-compulsive disorder. *Journal of Nervous and Mental Disease, 181*, 189–193.

Foa, E., Amir, N., Gershuny, B., Molnar, C., & Kozak, M. (1997). Implicit and explicit memory in obsessive-compulsive disorder. *Journal of Anxiety Disorders, 11*, 119–129.

Frost, R. O., & Steketee, G. S. (2002). *Cognitive approaches to obsessions and compulsions: Theory, assessment, and treatment.* Oxford, UK: Elsevier.

Geller, D., Biederman, J., Jones, J., Park, K., Schwartz, S., Shapiro, S., et al. (1998). Is juvenile obsessive-compulsive disorder a developmental subtype of the disorder? A review of the pediatric literature. *Journal of the American Academy of Child & Adolescent Psychiatry, 37*, 420–427.

Hollander, E., Friedberg, J., Wasserman, S., Yeh, C., & Iyengar, R. (2005). The case for the OCD spectrum. In J. Abramowitz & A. C. Houts (Eds.), *Concepts and controversies in obsessive-compulsive disorder* (pp. 95–118). New York: Springer.

Johnson, M. K., & Raye, C. L. (1981). Reality monitoring. *Psychological Review, 88*, 67–85.

Kozak, M. J., & Coles, M. E. (2005). Treatment for OCD: Unleashing the power of exposure. In J. Abramowitz & A. C. Houts (Eds.), *Concepts and controversies in obsessive-compulsive disorder* (pp. 283–304). New York: Springer.

Levin, H., Culhane, K., Hartmann, J., Evanovitch, K., Mattson, A., Harward, H., et al. (1991). Developmental changes in performance on tests of purported frontal lobe functioning. *Developmental Neuropsychology, 7*, 377–395.

Lopatka, C., & Rachman, S. (1995). Perceived responsibility and compulsive checking: An experimental analysis. *Behaviour Research and Therapy, 33*, 673–684.

March, J. S., & Mulle, K. (1998). *OCD in children and adolescents: A cognitive-behavioral treatment manual.* New York, NY: Guilford.

McKay, D., Abramowitz, J. S., Calamari, J. E., Kyrios, M., Radomsky, A. S., Sookman, D., et al. (2004). A critical evaluation of obsessive-compulsive disorder subtypes: Symptoms versus mechanisms. *Clinical Psychology Review, 24*, 283–313.

McKay, D., Piacentini, J., Greisberg, S., Graae, F., Jaffer, M., & Miller, J. (2006). The structure of childhood obsessions and compulsions: Dimensions in an outpatient sample. *Behaviour Research and Therapy.*

McNally, R. J. (2000). Information-processing abnormalities in obsessive-compulsive disorder. In W. K. Goodman, M. V. Rudorfer, & J. D. Maser (Eds.), *Obsessive-compulsive disorder: Contemporary issues in treatment.* (pp. 105–116). Mahwah, NJ: Lawrence Erlbaum Associates.

Mowrer, O. (1960). *Learning theory and behavior.* New York: Wiley.

Muris, P., Meesters, C., Rassin, E., Merckelbach, H., & Campbell, J. (2001). Thought–action fusion and anxiety disorders symptoms in normal adolescents. *Behaviour Research and Therapy, 39,* 843–852.

Muris, P., Merckelbach, H., & Clavan, M. (1997). Abnormal and normal compulsions. *Behaviour Research and Therapy, 35,* 249–252.

Obsessive-Compulsive Cognitions Working Group. (2003). Psychometric validation of the Obsessive Beliefs Questionnaire and the Interpretation of Intrusions Inventory: Part I. *Behaviour Research and Therapy, 41,* 863–878.

Obsessive-Compulsive Cognitions Working Group. (2005). Psychometric validation of the Obsessive Belief Questionnaire and Interpretation of Intrusions Inventory: Part 2, Factor analyses and testing of a brief version. *Behaviour Research and Therapy, 43,* 1527–1542.

Ollendick, T. H., Vasey, M. W., & King, N. J. (2001). Operant conditioning influences in childhood anxiety. In M. W. Vasey & M. R. Dadds (Eds.), *The developmental psychopathology of anxiety* (pp. 231–252). New York: Oxford.

Piaget, J. (1973). *The child's conception of the world.* London: Granada Publishing. (Original work published 1929)

Persons, J. B., & Foa, E. B. Processing of fearful and neutral information by obsessive-compulsives. *Behaviour Research and Therapy, 22,* 259–265.

Purdon, C. (1999). Thought suppression and psychopathology. *Behaviour Research and Therapy, 37,* 1029–1054.

Rachman, S. (1997). A cognitive theory of obsessions. *Behaviour Research and Therapy, 35,* 793–802.

Rachman, S. (1998). A cognitive theory of obsessions: Elaborations. *Behaviour Research and Therapy, 36,* 385–401.

Rachman, S., & de Silva, P. (1978). Abnormal and normal obsessions. *Behaviour Research and Therapy, 16,* 233–248.

Rachman, S., & de Silva, P., & Roper, G. (1976). The spontaneous decay of compulsive urges. *Behaviour Research and Therapy, 14,* 445–453.

Rachman, S., & Hodgson, R. J. (1980). *Obsessions and compulsions.* Englewood Cliffs, NJ: Prentice Hall.

Rachman, S., Shafran, R., Mitchell, D., Trant, J., & Teachman, B. (1996). How to remain neutral: An experimental analysis of neutralization. *Behaviour Research and Therapy, 34,* 889–898.

Radomsky, A. S., & Rachman, S. (1999). Memory bias in obsessive-compulsive disorder (OCD). *Behaviour Research and Therapy, 37,* 605–618.

Radomsky, A. S., Rachman, S., & Hammond, D. (2001). Memory bias, confidence and responsibility in compulsive checking. *Behaviour Research and Therapy, 39,* 813–822.

Rassin, E., Merckelbach, H., Muris, P., & Spaan, V. (1999). Thought–action fusion as a causal factor in the development of intrusions. *Behaviour Research and Therapy, 37,* 231–237.

Reed, G. (1985). *Obsessional experience and compulsive behavior: A structural approach.* Orlando, FL: Academic Press.

Roper, G., Rachman, S., & Hodgson, R. (1973). An experiment on obsessional checking. *Behaviour Research and Therapy, 11,* 271–277.

Rosenberg, D. R., Averbach, D. H., O'Hearn, K. M., Seymour, A. B., Birmaher, B., & Sweeney, J. A. (1997). Oculomotor response inhibition abnormalities in pediatric obsessive-compulsive disorder. *Archives of General Psychiatry, 54,* 831–838.

Salkovskis, P. M. (1985). Obsessional-compulsive problems: A cognitive-behavioural analysis. *Behaviour Research and Therapy, 23,* 571–583.

Salkovskis, P. M. (1989). Cognitive-behavioural factors and the persistence of intrusive thoughts in obsessional problems. *Behaviour Research and Therapy, 27,* 677–682.

Sameroff, A., & Haith, M. (Eds.). (1996). *The five to seven year shift: The age of reason and responsibility.* Chicago: University of Chicago Press.

Savage, C. R., & Rauch, S. L. (2000). Cognitive deficits in obsessive-compulsive disorder. *American Journal of Psychiatry, 157,* 1182.

Schwartz, S. A., & Abramowitz, J. S. (2003). Are nonparaphilic sexual addictions a variant of obsessive-compulsive disorder? A pilot study. *Cognitive and Behavioral Practice, 10,* 373–378.

Stanley, M., Swann, A., Bowers, T., & Davis, M. (1992). A comparison of clinical features in trichotillomania and obsessive-compulsive disorder. *Behaviour Research and Therapy, 30,* 39–44.

Tallis, F. (1995). *Obsessive-compulsive disorder: A cognitive and neuropsychological perspective.* New York: Wiley.

Taylor, S., McKay, D., & Abramowitz, J. (2005). Is obsessive-compulsive disorder a disturbance of security motivation? Comment on Szechtman and Woody (2004). *Psychological Review, 112,* 650–657.

Tolin, D. F., Abramowitz, J., Brigidi, B., Amir, N., Street, G., & Foa, E. (2001). Memory and memory confidence in obsessive-compulsive disorder. *Behaviour Research and Therapy, 39,* 913–927.

Tolin, D. F., Hamlin, C., & Foa, E. B. (2002). Directed forgetting in obsessive-compulsive disorder: Replication and extension. *Behaviour Research and Therapy, 40,* 792–803.

van den Hout, M., & Kindt, M. (2003). Repeated checking causes memory distrust. *Behaviour Research and Therapy, 41,* 301–316.

Wilhelm, S., McNally, R., Baer, L., & Florin, I. (1996). Directed forgetting in obsessive-compulsive disorder. *Behaviour Research and Therapy, 34,* 633–641.

Woods, C. M., Vevea, J. L., Chambless, D. L., & Bayen, U. J. (2002). Are compulsive checkers impaired in memory? A meta-analytic review. *Clinical Psychology: Science and Practice, 9,* 353–366.

6

Neurobiology, Neuropsychology, and Neuroimaging of Child and Adolescent Obsessive-Compulsive Disorder

David R. Rosenberg
Frank P. MacMaster
Yousha Mirza
Phillip C. Easter
Christian J. Buhagiar
Wayne State University and the Children's Hospital of Michigan

Until recently, obsessive-compulsive disorder (OCD) was considered a rare and untreatable illness primarily of pedantic interest. We have since learned that OCD is a severe and typically chronically disabling disorder affecting 1%–3% of the world's population (Rasmussen & Eisen, 1994), with as many as 80% of all cases having pediatric onset (Pauls, Alsobrook, Phil, Goodman, Rasmussen, & Leckman, 1995). There are considerable advantages in studying pediatric patients with OCD to delineate the developmental neurobiology of the illness. Such an approach can also minimize potentially confounding factors, such as treatment effects and longer term illness duration (Rosenberg & Keshavan, 1998). Empirically supported cognitive-behavioral therapy and pharmacotherapy with serotonin reuptake inhibitors (SRI's) are widely available for pediatric patients with OCD (March & Leonard, 1996; Pediatric OCD Treatment Study [POTS], 2004). Because its clinical phenomenology/nosology and treatment have been well described in childhood OCD, the illness has become a prime area for new and innovative neurobiologic study. OCD also appears to have fewer ambiguities in its expression across the lifetime compared to conditions such as unipolar and bipolar disorder (Rosenberg, Russell, & Fougere, 2005). Thus, there is an unprecedented opportunity to combine comprehensive assessment and treatment with neurobiologic (e.g., neuroimaging and genetic) studies to enhance our understanding of the mechanisms underlying the pathogenesis and treatment response of the illness (see Rosenberg & MacMillan, 2002, and Rosenberg et al., 2005 for reviews).

NEUROANATOMIC MODELS OF OCD

The reader is referred to Fitzgerald, MacMaster, Paulson, and Rosenberg (1999) for a detailed review of the neurobiology of childhood OCD. A brief overview is presented here (see Fig. 6.1). Specific alterations in fronto-cortical-striatal-thalamic circuits have been repeatedly observed in patients with OCD (see Rosenberg & MacMillan, 2002, for review). Even before the advent of neuroimaging technology, evidence for basal ganglia abnormalities in OCD existed. Von Economo reported postmortem alteration of the globus pallidus in OCD-associated post-encephalitic Parkinsonism (Schilder, 1938). Basal ganglia disorders including Huntington's disease, post-streptococcal Sydenham's chorea (SC), neuroacanthocytosis, and progressive supranuclear palsy are associated with increased obsessive-compulsive behaviors (see Fitzgerald, MacMaster, et al., 1999 for review). It should be noted, however, that basal ganglia disease is not always associated with ob-

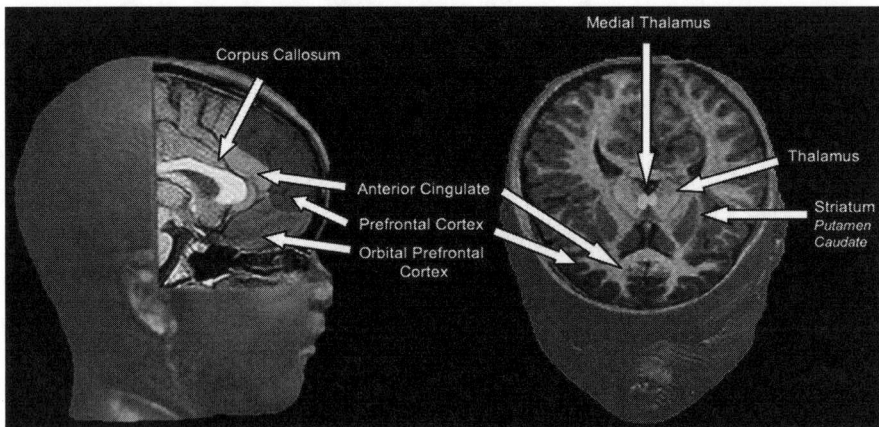

Figure. 6.1.   Brain regions implicated in the pathophysiology of obsessive-compulsive disorder. Adapted from "Brain Anatomy and Chemistry May Predict Treatment Response in Pediatric Obsessive-Compulsive Disorder," by D. R. Rosenberg, S. N. MacMillan, & G. J. Moore, 2001, *International Journal of Neuropsychopharmacology, 4,* pp. 179–190. Reprinted with permission of the author.

sessive-compulsive behaviors, with conditions like Parkinson's disease and Wilson's disease less associated with OCD symptoms than other basal ganglia diseases (Cummings, 1993). Thus, it is likely that alterations in neuronal systems projecting to basal ganglia, rather than specific anatomic abnormalities within the basal ganglia may result in obsessive-compulsive behaviors (Fitzgerald, MacMaster, et al., 1999).

This is especially relevant given the growing body of research suggesting a model for OCD based on potentially reversible abnormalities in fronto-striatal circuitry (Alexander, Crutcher, & DeLong, 1990; Baxter et al., 1996; Cummings, 1993; Insel, 1992; Mega & Cummings, 1994; Modell, Mountz, Curtis, & Greden, 1989). Five fronto-striatal circuits have been delineated and include (1) motor, (2) oculomotor, (3) dorsolateral prefrontal, (4) ventral (lateral orbital) prefrontal, and (5) limbic anterior cingulate and medial orbital (Alexander et al., 1990). These circuits, thought to be anatomically and likely functionally distinct, progress through distinct parts of frontal cortex, basal ganglia, substantia nigra and the thalamus in a self-repeating loop (Alexander et al.,1990). Two of these pathways interact to regulate output from frontal cortex to insure appropriate behavioral responses to external stimuli (Alexander et al., 1990; Baxter et al., 1996; Cummings, 1993). The "direct" pathway facilitates thalamic stimulation of the cortex, whereas the "indirect" pathway inhibits the thalamus permitting the cortex to shift sets and respond to novel stimuli. It has been proposed that OCD may result from excessive neural tone in the direct pathway relative to the indirect pathway (Baxter et al., 1996).

Although still controversial, accumulating data suggests that functional aspects of ventral prefrontal, dorsolateral prefrontal, and limbic circuitry are critically involved in the pathogenesis of OCD. Nonetheless, components of all five circuits are likely involved to some extent and have been implicated in neuroimaging studies in OCD.

Oculomotor response inhibition is correlated with decreased cerebral blood flow in ventral prefrontal cortex, anterior cingulate cortex, medial temporal cortex, and ventral striatum (Sweeney et al., 1996). Rosenberg et al. (1997) found a selective deficit in oculomotor response inhibition in psychotropic-naïve pediatric patients with OCD (see Fig. 6.2). Oculomotor response inhibition abnormalities were associated with increased OCD symptom severity and with anterior cingulate volume abnormalities in pediatric patients with OCD (Rosenberg & Keshavan, 1998). In contrast, patients with OCD and controls did not differ on neurocognitive tasks, such as delayed response and preparatory set mediated by dorsolateral prefrontal cortex (Fuster, 1989; Rosenberg, Averbach, et al., 1997; Rosenkilde, 1979). Rosenberg, Averbach, et al. (1997) hypothesized that response inhibition deficits in pediatric patients with OCD might underlie the clinical phenomenology of OCD, for example, the inability to inhibit inappropriate thoughts, ideas, and behaviors. Advances in neuroimaging technology are allowing for

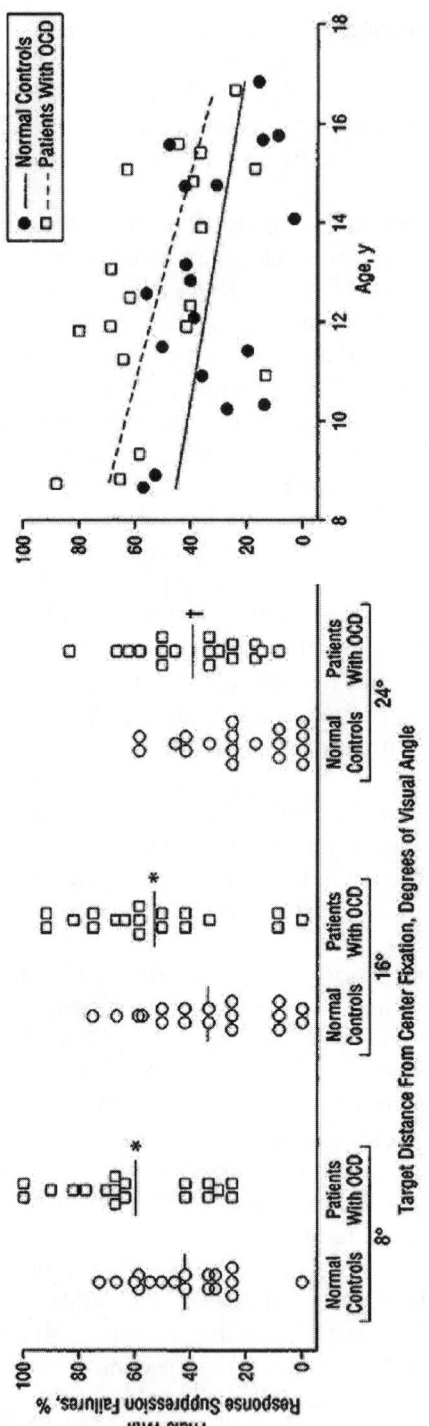

Figure 6.2. (A) Mean response suppression failures of nondepressed, psychotropic medication-naïve pediatric patients with obsessive-compulsive disorder (OCD) and normal controls performing the antisaccade task. Lines through distributions represent mean value. Asterisks indicate $P = 0.01$, dagger, $P = 0.02$. (B) Response suppression failures as a function of age for nondepressed, psychotropic medication-naïve pediatric patients with OCD (squares) and normal (circles) controls performing the antisaccade task. Note the marked inverse correlation between age and total number of response suppression errors in patients with OCD and a trend for such an effect in controls. Adapted from "Oculomotor Response Inhibition Abnormalities in Pediatric Obsessive-Compulsive Disorders," by D. R. Rosenberg, D. H. Averbach, K. M. O'Hearn, et al., 1997, *Archives of General Psychiatry, 54*, p. 831. Reprinted with permission of the author.

unprecedented advances in our understanding of the mechanisms involved in the pathophysiology of the illness and its treatment response.

STRUCTURAL BRAIN IMAGING

Structural neuroimaging studies have demonstrated alterations in cortico-striatal-thalamic circuits implicated in the pathogenesis of OCD (Table 6.1).

Basal Ganglia

The basal ganglia may represent a primary site of pathology in OCD (Rauch, Whalen, Dougherty, & Jenike, 1998). Reduced basal ganglia volumes have been reported in psychotropic-naïve pediatric patients with OCD, which were correlated with increased anterior cingulate volumes (Luxenberg et al., 1988; Rosenberg, Keshavan, O'Hearn, et al., 1997; Szeszko, MacMillan, McMeniman, Chen, et al., 2004). Increased ventricular brain ratios have been reported in pediatric patients with OCD compared to healthy controls, which would be predicted with decreased basal ganglia volume (Behar et al., 1984). Behar et al. did not, however, report information on basal ganglia volume. In contrast, Giedd et al. (1995) and Giedd, Rapoport, Garvey, Perlmutter, and Swedo (2000) found significantly larger basal ganglia volumes in pediatric patients with pediatric autoimmune neuropsychiatric disorders associated with Group A Streptococcal infections (GAS). Peterson et al. (2000) also found that recurrent and chronic GAS infections were associated with increased basal ganglia volumes that correlated with increased antibody titers of antistreptolysin O and antideoxyribonuclease B. Especially intriguing is that immunotherapy, for example, plasmapharesis has been found to be effective in pediatric autoimmune neuropsychiatric disorders associated with streptococcus (PANDAS; Allen, Leonard, & Swedo, 1995) and symptom exacerbation and resolution may be associated with increased and decreased basal ganglia volumes, respectively (Giedd, Rapoport, Leonard, Richter, & Swedo, 1996). Thus, findings of increased basal ganglia volumes in PANDAS patients and decreased basal ganglia volumes in presumed non-autoimmune pediatric OCD suggest that disruption of the neural network in the basal ganglia may be more critical in the evolution of OCD symptoms as opposed to a particular direction of neuroanatomic change.

Prefrontal Cortex

Rosenberg, Keshavan, O'Hearn, et al. (1997) found no significant differences in total prefrontal cortical gray or white matter volume between psychotropic-naïve pediatric patients with OCD versus age and sex-matched healthy controls. However, measurement of total prefrontal cortex may have "averaged out" more subtle abnormalities in specific circuits. Follow-

TABLE 6.1
Structural Imaging in Pediatric Patients With Obsessive-Compulsive Disorder

Brain Region	Pediatric Finding	References
Prefrontal Cortex	A) Normal	A) Rosenberg, Keshavan, O'Hearn, et al., 1997
Orbital Prefrontal Cortex	A) Normal	A) Farchione et al., unpublished data
Anterior Cingulate	A) Increase in Gray Matter B) Increase in Gray Matter, no difference in White Matter	A) Rosenberg & Keshavan, 1998 B) Szeszko, MacMillan, McMeniman, Chen, et al., 2004
Dorsolateral Prefrontal Cortex	A) Normal	A) Rosenberg & Keshavan, 1998; Szeszko, MacMillan, McMeniman, Chen, et al., 2004
Temporal Lobe (TL) Structures	A) Normal TL, superior temporal gyrus, hippocampus, and amygdala B) Increased left amygdala volume which decreased after 12 weeks of treatment with paroxetine	A) Rosenberg & Keshavan, 1998 B) Szeszko, MacMillan, McMeniman, Lorch, et al., 2004
Corpus Callosum	A) Increased B) Decreased signal intensity	A) Rosenberg, Keshavan, Dick, et al., 1997b) MacMaster et al., 1999
Intracranial Volume	A) Normal B) No change pre/post paroxetine treatment	A) Rosenberg, Keshavan, O'Hearn, et al., 1997; Gilbert et al., 2000; Szeszko, MacMillan, McMeniman, Chen, et al., 2004 B) Gilbert et al, 2000
Caudate	A) Decreased B) Normal C) Increased D) Decreased basal ganglia with plasmapheresis E) Increased basal ganglia volumes correlated with increased antibody titers of antistreptolysin O and antideoxyribonuclease B	A) Luxenberg et al., 1998 B) Rosenberg, Keshavan, O'Hearn, et al., 1997; Szeszko, MacMillan, McMeniman, Chen, et al., 2004 C) Giedd et al., 1995*, 2000* D) Giedd et al., 1996* E) Peterson et al., 2000*

136

Brain Region	Pediatric Finding	References
Putamen	A) Decreased B) Normal C) Increased	A) Rosenberg, Keshavan, O'Hearn, et al., 1997 B) Szeszko, MacMillan, McMeniman, Chen, et al., 2004 C) Giedd et al., 1995*, 2000*
Globus Pallidus	A) Decreased	A) Szeszko, MacMillan, McMeniman, Chen, et al., 2004
Lenticulate Nucleus	A) Increased B) Normal	A) Rosenberg et al., 1997c B) Luxenberg et al., 1988
Thalamus	A) Increased then decreased in size following 12 weeks of paroxetine treatment B) No significant change following cognitive behavioral therapy	A) Gilbert et al., 2000 B) Rosenberg, Benazon, et al., 2000
Ventricles	A) Increased B) Normal	A) Rosenberg, Keshavan, O'Hearn, et al., 1997; Behar et al., 1984 B) Luxenberg et al., 1988
Pituitary	A) Decreased	B) MacMaster et al., 2005

*Sydenham's OCD patients (pediatric autoimmune neuropsychiatric disorders [PANDAS] associated with Group A ß-hemolytic streptococcal infection)

up investigation by Rosenberg, Keshavan, Dick, Bagwell, MacMaster, and Birmaher (1997) found that the genu region of the corpus callosum was significantly larger in 21 psychotropic-naïve pediatric patients with OCD compared to age and sex-matched controls. MacMaster, Keshavan, Dick, and Rosenberg (1999) also found increased signal intensity in the genu of the corpus callosum in pediatric patients with OCD compared to controls. As depicted in Fig. 6.3, the corpus callosum connects the cerebral hemispheres and the genu connects right and left ventral prefrontal cortex (de Lacoste, Kirkpatrick, & Ross, 1985; Seltzer & Pandya, 1986). Thus, increased genu size and signal intensity might suggest increased size of ventral prefrontal cortical regions. Rosenberg and Keshavan (1998) reported localized increased anterior cingulate volume in treatment-naïve pediatric patients with OCD versus age and sex-matched controls. Increased anterior cingulate volume was correlated with increased OCD symptom severity but not with illness duration. The normative increase in anterior cingulate volume with age was absent in patients with OCD (Fig. 6.4). No significant dif-

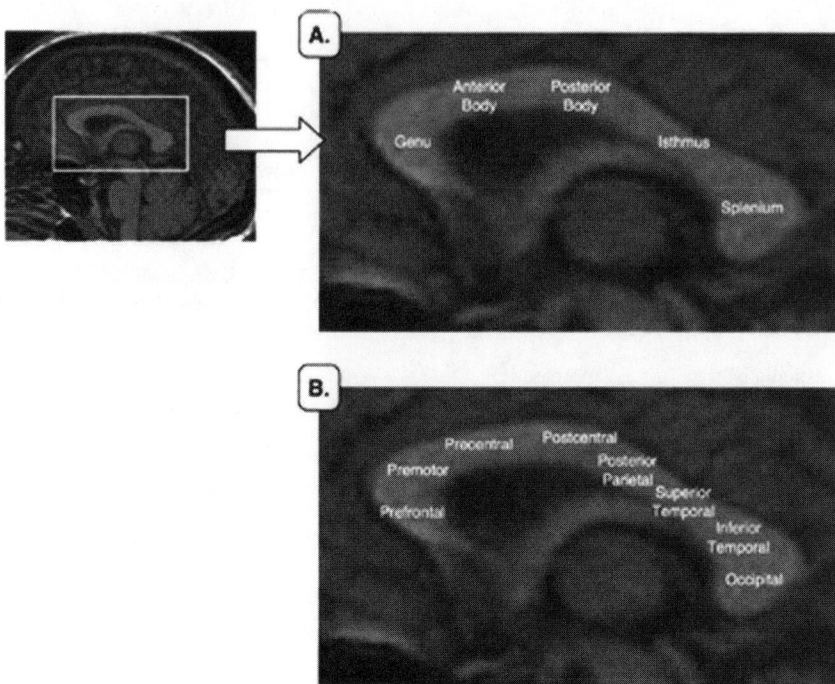

Figure 6.3.   Schematic drawing of the regional subdivisions of the corpus callosum (A) and of commissural pathways in the corpus callosum (B). Adapted from "Corpus Callosal Morphology in Treatment-naïve Pediatric Obsessive-Compulsive Disorder," by D. R. Rosenberg, M. S. Keshavan, E. L. Dick, et al., 1997, *Progress in Neuropsychopharmacology and Biological Psychiatry, 21*, pp. 1269–1283. Also adapted with permission from "The Topography of Commissural Fibers," by B. Seltzer & D. Pandya. In H. H. Jasper, F. Lepore, & M. Pito, 1986, (Eds.), *Two Hemispheres, One Brain. Functions of the Corpus Callosum* (pp. 47–73). New York, NY: Liss. 1, genu; 2, anterior body; 3, posterior body; 4, isthmus; 5, splenium.

ferences in posterior cingulate volume or dorsolateral prefrontal cortex were observed between pediatric patients with OCD and controls. Szeszko, MacMillan, McMeniman, Chen, et al. (2004) replicated and extended these results by demonstrating increased anterior cingulate gray, but not white matter volume (Figs. 6.5 and 6.6). Increased anterior cingulate volumes were correlated with reduced basal ganglia volumes in pediatric patients with OCD (Rosenberg & Keshavan, 1998; Szeszko et al., 2004).

Rosenberg and Keshavan (1998) hypothesized that increased ventral prefrontal cortical volumes correlated with reduced basal ganglia volumes in pediatric patients with OCD might suggest a neural network dysplasia characterized by alterations in postnatal pruning. Therefore, increased anterior cingulate volume in pediatric patients with OCD might reflect delayed or reduced neural pruning, whereas reduced striatal volume might reflect in-

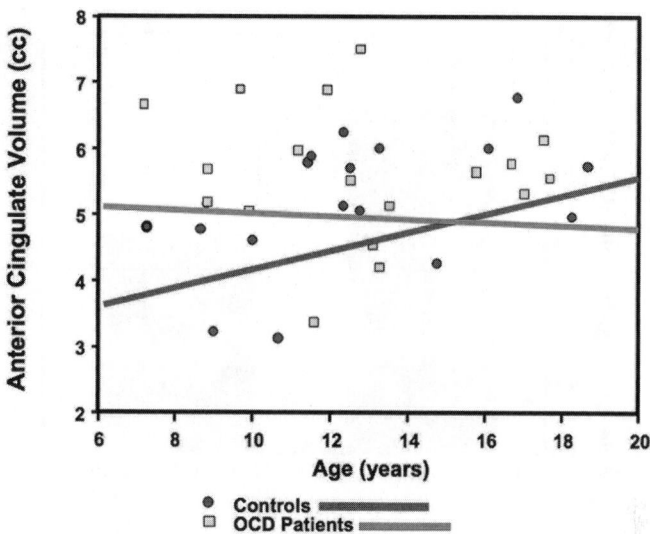

Figure 6.4.   Anterior cingulate volume versus age in pediatric obsessive-compulsive disorder patients and healthy comparison subjects. Note that the age-related increase in anterior cingulate volume observed in healthy children is absent in pediatric patients with obsessive-compulsive disorder (Controls—circles, OCD patients—squares). Adapted from "Toward a Neurodevelopmental Model of Obsessive-Compulsive Disorder," by D. R. Rosenberg & M. S. Keshavan, 1998, *Biological Psychiatry, 43*, pp. 623–640. Reprinted with permission of the author.

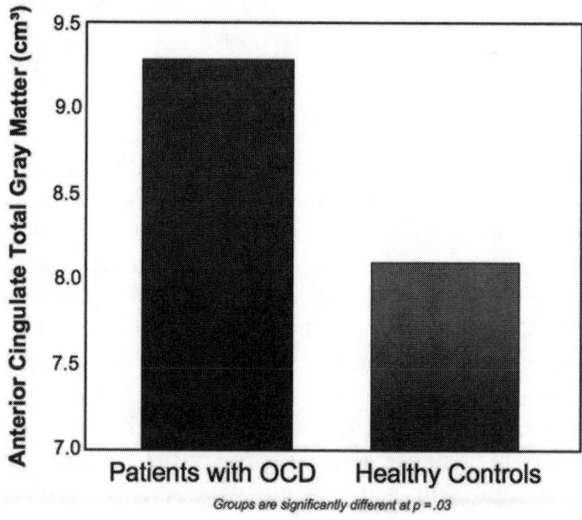

Figure 6.5.   Anterior cingulate gray matter volume in psychotropic drug naïve OCD patients and healthy controls. Adapted from "Brain Structural Abnormalities in Psychotropic Drug-naïve Pediatric Patients With Obsessive-Compulsive Disorder," by P. R. Szeszko, S. MacMillan, M. McMeniman, S. Chen, et al., 2004, *American Journal of Psychiatry, 161*, pp. 1049–1056.

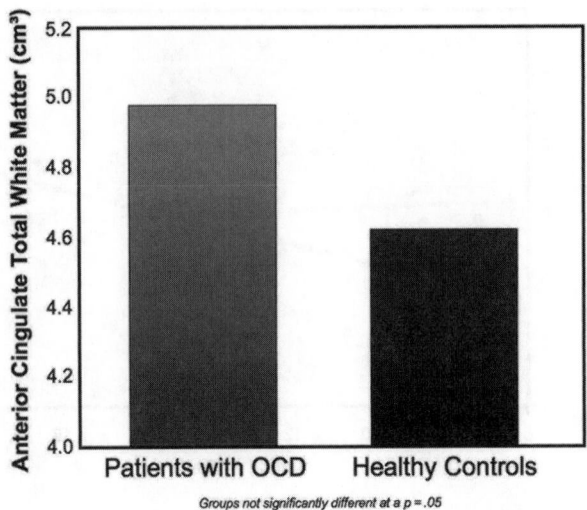

Figure 6.6.   Anterior cingulate white matter volume in psychotropic drug naïve OCD patients and healthy controls. Adapted from "Brain Structural Abnormalities in Psychotropic Drug-naïve Pediatric Patients With Obsessive-Compulsive Disorder," by P. R. Szeszko, S. MacMillan, M. McMeniman, S. Chen, et al., 2004, *American Journal of Psychiatry, 161*, pp. 1049–1056.

creased pruning. This is discussed in detail elsewhere (Keshavan, 1997; Rosenberg & Keshavan, 1998).

Thalamus

Increased anterior cingulate volumes correlated with reduced striatal volumes suggesting potential structural alterations in the thalamus, which serves as the final subcortical input to frontal cortex, stimulating cortical output when released from the inhibitory tonic influence of the striatum (Baxter et al., 1996). Using volumetric magnetic resonance imaging (MRI), Gilbert et al. (2000) found increased thalamic volumes in 21 psychotropic-naïve pediatric patients with OCD compared to 21 age- and sex-matched healthy pediatric controls (Fig. 6. 7). After 12 weeks of mono-drug therapy with the selective serotonin reuptake inhibitor (SSRI), paroxetine, thalamic volume decreased in pediatric patients with OCD to volumes that were not significantly different from healthy controls. Decrease in thalamic volume was correlated with reduction in OCD symptom severity. In contrast, no significant changes were observed in thalamic volume in psychotropic-naïve pediatric patients before and after 12 weeks of cognitive-behavioral therapy (CBT), none of whom received medication during this study (Rosenberg, Benazon, Gilbert, Sullivan, & Moore, 2000; Fig. 6.8). Intracranial volume,

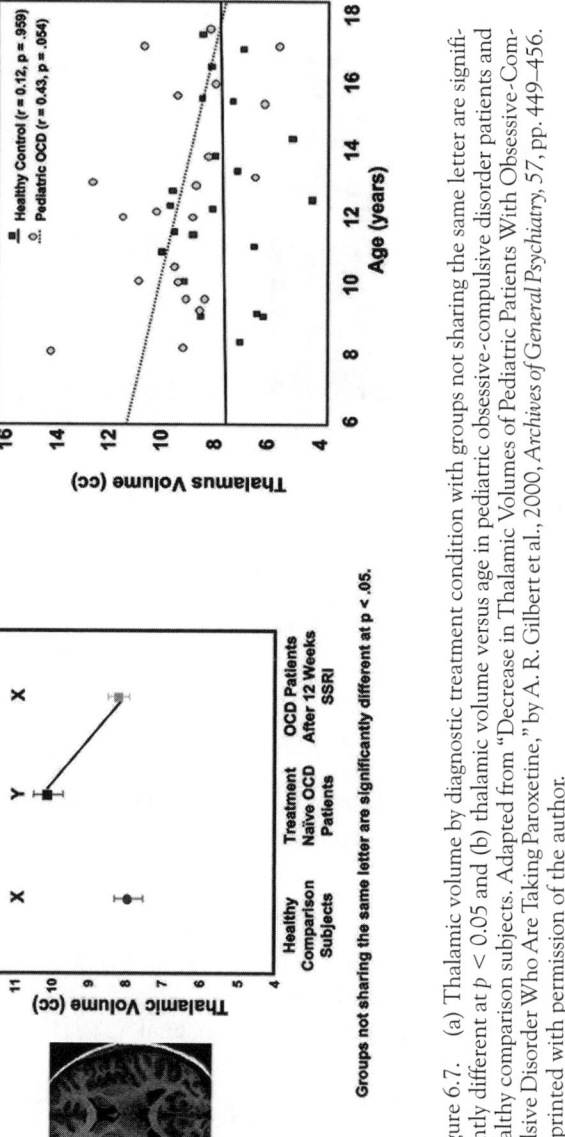

Figure 6.7. (a) Thalamic volume by diagnostic treatment condition with groups not sharing the same letter are significantly different at $p < 0.05$ and (b) thalamic volume versus age in pediatric obsessive-compulsive disorder patients and healthy comparison subjects. Adapted from "Decrease in Thalamic Volumes of Pediatric Patients With Obsessive-Compulsive Disorder Who Are Taking Paroxetine," by A. R. Gilbert et al., 2000, *Archives of General Psychiatry, 57*, pp. 449–456. Reprinted with permission of the author.

caudate volume, and ventral prefrontal cortical volumes did not change pre–post SSRI or CBT (Benazon, Moore, & Rosenberg, 2003; Gilbert et al., 2000; Rosenberg, Benazon, et al., 2000; Rosenberg, MacMaster, Keshavan, Fitzgerald, Stewart, & Moore, 2000). Changes in thalamic volume, therefore, appeared to be specific to SSRI versus CBT and suggest that alterations in thalamic volume may represent a potential anti-OCD medication effect

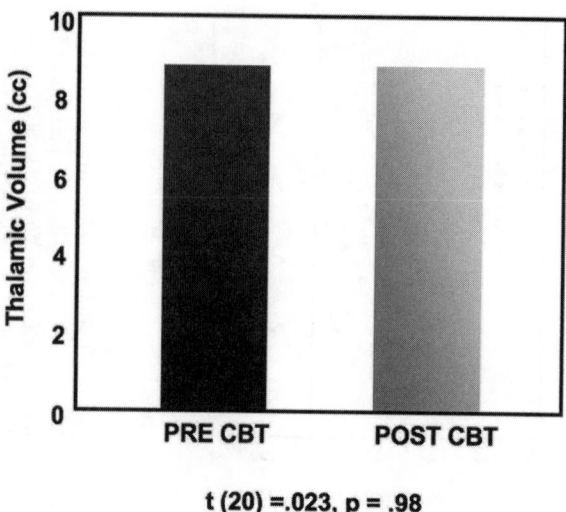

Figure 6.8.   Left (A) and right (B) thalamic volumes before and after treatment. Lines indicate means. OCD, obsessive-compulsive disorder; CBT, cognitive behavioral therapy. Adapted from "Thalamic Volume in Pediatric Obsessive-Compulsive Disorder Patients Before and After Cognitive Behavioral Therapy," by D. R. Rosenberg, N. R. Benazon, A. Gilbert, A. Sullivan, & G. J. Moore, 2000, *Biological Psychiatry, 48*, pp. 294–300. Reprinted with permission of the author.

(Gilbert et al., 2000). Giedd et al. (1995, 2000) also found no differences in thalamic volume between PANDAS patients and controls.

Other Brain Regions

Despite the attractiveness of the fronto-striatal-thalamic model of OCD, other brain regions have been implicated in the pathogenesis of OCD. Investigation by Rosenberg, Keshavan, O'Hearn, et al. (1997) suggested potential amygdala abnormalities in pediatric patients with OCD. The amygdala has rich connections with prefrontal and basal ganglia circuits (Sah, Faber, Lopez De Armentia, & Power, 2003). Szeszko, MacMillan, McMeniman, Lorch, et al. (2004) found increased left amygdala: right amygdala volume ratios in pediatric patients with OCD compared to healthy controls. After SSRI treatment, a significant decrease in left but not right amygdala volume was noted (Fig. 6.9). Decrease in amygdala volume after SSRI treatment was not, however, correlated with change in OCD symptom severity but with higher dose and cumulative exposure to paroxetine. This underscores the complexity of pre–post treatment studies. MacMaster et al. (2006) also recently found reduced pituitary volume in psychotropic-naïve pediatric patients with OCD compared to age- and sex-matched controls (Fig. 6.10).

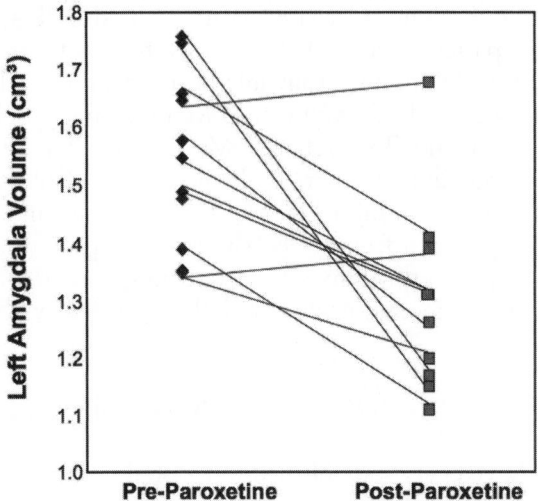

Figure 6.9. Left amygdala volume changes in each patient after treatment. Adapted from "Amygdala Volume Reductions in Pediatric Patients with Obsessive-Compulsive Disorder Treated with Paroxetine: Preliminary Findings," by P. R. Szeszko, S. MacMillan, M. McMeniman, E. Lorch, et al., 2004, *Neuropsychopharmacology*, 29, 826–832. Reprinted with permission of the author.

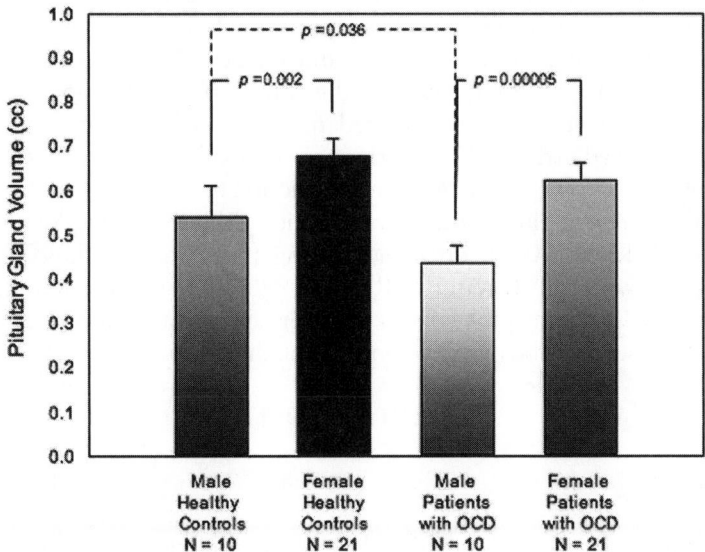

Figure 6.10. Reduced pituitary volume in psychotropic-naïve pediatric patients with OCD compared to age and sex matched controls. Adapted from "Pituitary Volume in Pediatric Obsessive-Compulsive Disorder," by F. P. MacMaster et al., 2006, *Biological Psychiatry*. Reprinted with permission of the author.

Decreased pituitary volume associated with increased OCD symptom severity in pediatric patients with OCD is consistent with prior reports of dysregulation of the limbic-hypothalamic-pituitary-adrenal (LHPA) axis in OCD (Altemus et al., 1992; Catapano, Monteleone, Fuschino, Maj, & Kemali, 1992; Catapano, Tortorella, Di Martino, & Maj, 1995; Leckman, Goodman, North, Chappell, Price, Pauls, et al., 1994; Monteleone, Catapano, Del Buono, & Maj, 1994; Monteleone, Catapano, Tortorella, & Maj, 1997; Swedo, Leonard, et al.,1992) and suggest a potential effect of this dysregulation on pituitary volume. Indeed, changes in endocrine function have been shown to affect pituitary morphology previously (Gonzalez et al., 1988).

FUNCTIONAL NEUROIMAGING

To date, there have been no published functional neuroimaging studies in pediatric patients with OCD. This contrasts with the adult literature where positron emission tomography (PET) and functional MRI (fMRI) studies have demonstrated abnormalities in glucose metabolism, regional cerebral blood flow, and activation in fronto-striatal-thalamic circuits that are associated with severity of illness and treatment response (Baxter, 1994; Baxter et al., 1992; Breiter et al., 1996; Rauch et al., 1994; Swedo, Pietrini, et al., 1992).

As robust as PET imaging is, due to concerns regarding radiation exposure, it is not often feasible in studies of children. Evidence is growing, however, that PET imaging studies may indeed be safe and within ethical boundaries (Ernst, 1999). Given that the clinical phenomenology/nosology and treatment have been well described in childhood OCD, functional imaging studies in pediatric OCD are a ripe area for exploration. Probes do need to be delineated to explore cognitive dysfunction in pediatric OCD. Possible areas of interest include studies of conflict (Maltby, Tolin, Worhunsky, O'Keefe, & Kiehl, 2005), error monitoring (Fitzgerald et al., 2005) and symptom provocation (Breiter & Rauch, 1996). The main requirement of fMRI studies is that the probe needs to be very specific and tap into cognitive processes thought to be dysfunctional in the disorder.

NEUROCHEMISTRY

Serotonin

The serotonin hypothesis for OCD has spawned largely from clinical trials demonstrating the superiority of serotonin reuptake inhibitors to placebo in the treatment of pediatric and adult OCD (March et al., 1998; POTS, 2004). To date, the SRI's are the only medications ever shown to be superior to placebo in children and adults with OCD (Insel, 1990; Rapoport, Leonard,

Swedo, & Lenane, 1993; Swedo, Rapoport, Leonard, Lenane, & Cheslow, 1989). Platelet and cerebrospinal fluid (CSF) studies have suggested serotonergic alterations in OCD (Asberg, Thoren, & Bertilsson, 1982; Bastani, Arora, & Meltzer, 1991; Flament, Rapoport, Murphy, Berg, & Lake, 1987; Insel, Mueller, Alterman, Linnoila, & Murphy, 1985; Marazziti, Hollander, Lensi, Ravagli, & Cassano, 1992; Sallee, Richman, Beach, Sethuraman, & Nesbitt, 1996; Swedo, Leonard, et al., 1992; Thoren et al., 1980; Vitiello et al., 1991; Weizman et al., 1986) although contradictory reports exist (Insel et al., 1985; Leckman et al., 1995; Marazziti et al., 1992; Weizman et al., 1986). Platelet and CSF serotonin measures provide only a very peripheral index of brain function and may be complicated by their variability with height, diet, season, activity level, and menstrual period (Insel & Winslow, 1992). Pharmacologic challenge studies have also shown some promise but also have inconsistent results and provide a peripheral window into brain function (for review, see Fitzgerald, MacMaster, et al., 1999). Positron emission tomography (PET) allows for the in vivo measurement of serotonin synthesis and receptors but its putative ionizing radiation risks make it less attractive for use in pediatric populations, particularly healthy controls, and for repeated studies in pediatric populations. Advances in PET technology, for example, 3D PET, which can reduce radiation exposure, may make this technique more feasible for implementation in pediatric populations.

Dopamine

Peripheral markers and pharmacologic challenge have shown dopamine (DA) dysregulation in adults with OCD (Butler, Anderson, & Venton, 1983; Karayiorgou et al., 1997; Marazziti et al., 1992, 1997; Young, Laws, Sharbrough, & Weinshilboum, 1985). Nonetheless, measurements of the dopamine metabolite, homovanillic acid in the CSF of pediatric (Swedo, Leonard, et al., 1992) and adults with OCD (Insel et al., 1985; Leckman et al., 1995; Thoren et al., 1980) have not found significant differences from healthy controls. Oades, Ropcke, and Eggers (1994) did find increased homovanillic acid levels in the urine of young, unmedicated patients with OCD. Augmentation of SRI response in patients who have not responded or incompletely responded has been reported with addition of D2 receptor blocking agents, for example, haloperidol, particularly in patients with co-morbid tics (McDougle et al., 1994). McDougle et al. (2000) also found augmentation with the atypical neuroleptic, risperidone to be superior to augmentation with placebo in treatment-refractory OCD patients. Fitzgerald, Stewart, Tawile, and Rosenberg (1999) noted additional clinical improvement in an open-label case series of SRI treatment-refractory pediatric OCD patients after augmentation with risperidone.

Although not entirely consistent, studies of peripheral markers, pharmacologic challenge and treatment response in OCD suggest that possible dopamine excess may be involved in the pathogenesis of OCD (Creese & Iversen, 1974; Eilam, Golani, & Szechtman, 1989; Ellinwood, 1969; Frye & Arnold, 1981; Koizumi, 1985; Schiorring, 1975; Wallach, 1974). For example, OCD symptoms have been observed following levodopa treatment of tardive dyskinesia (Neale & Oltmanns, 1988). Indirect support for this also comes from oculomotor studies in OCD patients. Dopamine innervation to dorsolateral prefrontal cortex has been found to play a key role in mediating oculomotor delayed response (Daniel et al., 1991; Sawaguchi, & Goldman-Rakic, 1991). Pediatric OCD patients have demonstrated enhanced performance compared to healthy controls on oculomotor delayed response tasks as well as other delayed-response tasks (Rosenberg, Averbach, et al., 1997; Shrikhande, Nolan, Lorch, & Rosenberg, 2000). Dopamine antagonists can also be very helpful in alleviating symptoms of Tourette's syndrome, which is often associated with OCD symptoms (Shapiro et al., 1989). Similar brain regions, for example, fronto-striatal circuits have been implicated in both OCD and Tourette's syndrome (Schultz et al., 2002). Finally, Rosenberg and Keshavan (1998) proposed that there might be a serotonin-dopamine interaction with increased dopamine: serotonin ratios as developmentally changing variables (see Fig. 6.11).

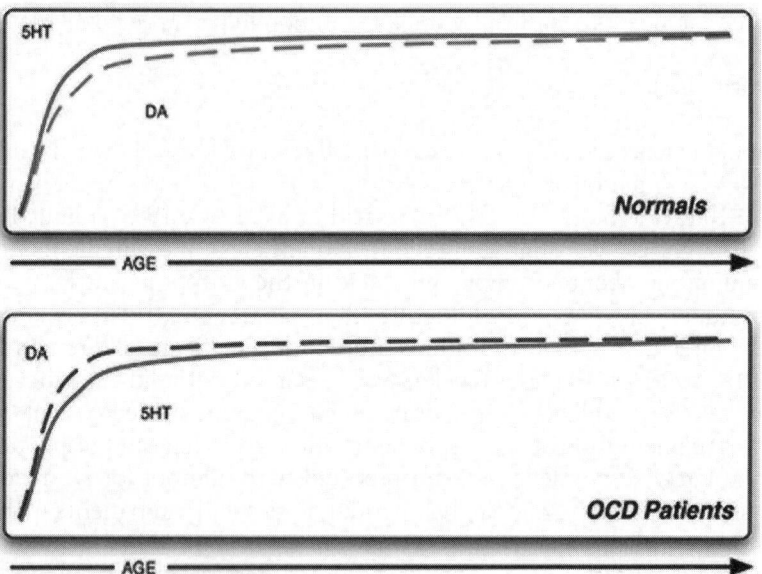

Figure 6.11. Dopamine-serotonin ratios as developmentally changing variables. High dopamine-serotonin ratio in pediatric obsessive-compulsive disorder patients may result in superior delayed response abilities. *Solid line* indicates 5-Hydroxytryptophan serotonin (5-HT); *shaded line* indicates dopamine (DA). Adapted from "Toward a Neurodevelopmental Model of Obsessive-Compulsive Disorder," by D. R. Rosenberg & M. S. Keshavan, 1998, *Biological Psychiatry, 43,* pp. 623–640. Reprinted with permission of the author.

N-Acetyl-Aspartate

The neuronal marker, N-acetyl-aspartate (NAA) has been implicated in the pathogenesis of OCD. Proton magnetic resonance spectroscopy (1H MRS) can measure NAA without the putative radiation risks associated with PET. Ebert et al. (1997) used 1H MRS and demonstrated reduced levels of the neuronal marker, NAA, in anterior cingulate cortex and the striatum. Decreased anterior cingulate NAA levels were correlated with increased OCD symptom severity. In contrast, no differences between OCD patients and controls were observed in parietal cortex, a region less implicated in the pathogenesis of OCD. Bartha et al. (1998) also found reduced NAA in the striatum of OCD patients versus healthy controls. They did not identify volumetric changes in the striatum between OCD patients and controls. They suggested that 1H MRS might be a more sensitive MR technique than conventional structural neuroimaging in identifying alterations, such as reduced neuronal viability in OCD patients. More recently, Fitzgerald, Moore, Paulson, Stewart, and Rosenberg (2000) found reduced NAA levels in medial but not lateral thalamus of treatment-naïve pediatric patients with OCD versus age- and sex-matched healthy controls. Neuronal dysfunction in anterior cingulate cortex, the striatum and thalamus could underlie the functional hyperactivity observed in these regions and be due to increased glutamate projection to these regions (Bartha et al., 1998; Ebert et al., 1997).

Choline

Increased medial but not lateral thalamic choline (Cho) has been observed in treatment-naïve pediatric patients with OCD compared to both healthy pediatric controls and treatment-naïve pediatric patients with major depressive disorder (MDD; Rosenberg, Amponsah, Sullivan, MacMillan, & Moore, 2001; Smith et al., 2003; see Fig. 6.12). In contrast, no alterations in Cho have been observed in the striatum or prefrontal cortex (Rosenberg, MacMaster et al., 2000; Russell et al., 2003). Medial thalamic Cho alterations in pediatric patients with OCD are intriguing in that choline spectra measured by 1H MRS principally arises from glycerophosphocholine and phosphocholine metabolites of the membrane lipid, phosphotidylcholine (Barker et al., 1994; Miller et al., 1996). These findings may be consistent with prior findings of increased thalamic volume in pediatric patients with OCD (Gilbert et al., 2000) and functional imaging studies showing increased metabolic activity in the thalamus of OCD patients (Baxter et al., 1992).

Phosphotidylcholine is known to play an important role in intracellular signal transduction (Exton, 1990, 1994; Loffelhoz, 1989; Ziesel, 1993) so that abnormalities in signal transduction may be involved in the pathogenesis of OCD. Cytosolic choline is also incorporated into two key neuronal

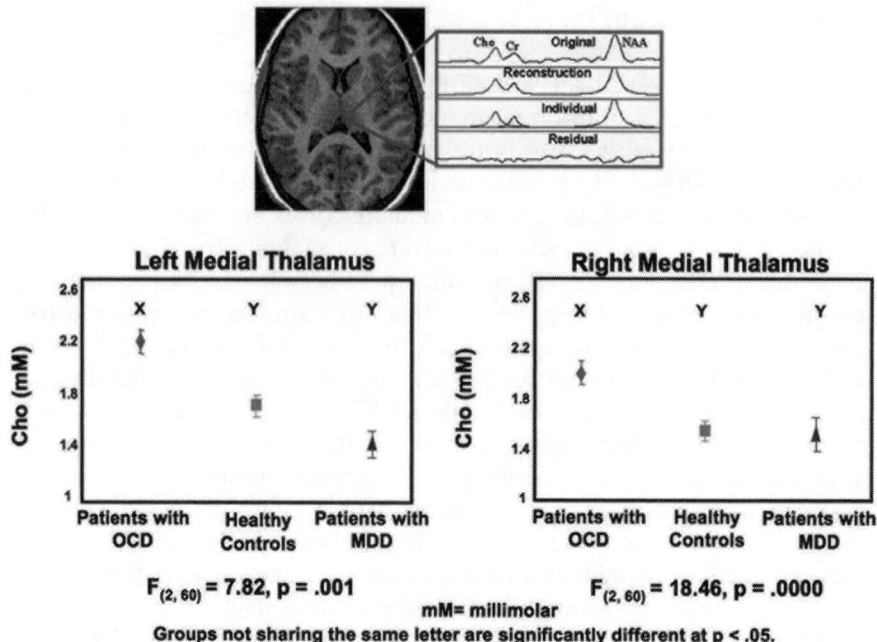

Figure 6.12.   Graphs of left and right medial thalamic choline (Cho) concentrations in 27 pediatric patients with obsessive-compulsive disorder (OCD), 18 healthy control subjects, and 18 pediatric patients with major depressive disorder (MDD). Groups not sharing the same letter are significantly different at $p < 0.05$. Lines indicate means. mmol/L, millimolar absolute metabolite concentrations. Adapted from "Increased Medial Thalamic Choline Found in Pediatric Patients With Obsessive-Compulsive Disorder Versus Major Depression or Healthy Control Subjects: a Magnetic Resonance Spectroscopy Study," by E. A. Smith et al., 2003, *Biological Psychiatry, 15,* pp. 1399–1405. Reprinted with permission of the author.

membrane phospholipids, phosphotidylcholine and sphingomyelin (Blusztajn & Wurtman, 1983; Loffelhoz) that may be consistent with the choline signal being altered in conditions involving membrane metabolism, such as areas of acute demyelination in multiple sclerosis (Ross & Michaelis, 1994; Vion-Dury, Meyerhoff, Cozzone, & Weiner, 1994) and in the neurodegenerative disorder, Alzheimer's disease (Kato, Inubushi, & Kato, 1998).

Altered medial thalamic Cho could also result from neuroendocrine abnormalities of the LHPA axis previously reported in OCD (Alsobrook & Pauls, 1998; Bodkin & White, 1989; Gehris, Kathol, Black, & Noyes 1990; Leckman, Goodman, North, et al., 1994; Monteleone et al., 1994, 1995, 1997; Swedo, Leonard, et al., 1992). Frontal and thalamic Cho abnormalities as measured by 1H MRS have been reported in patients with Cushing's syndrome (Khiat, Bard, Lacroix, Rousseau, & Boulanger, 1999). Increased

Cho has also been found in patients with congenital hypothyroidism with Cho levels normalizing after effective treatment (Gupta, Bhatia, Poptani, & Gujral, 1995). Cho abnormalities in patients with Grave's disease have also been reported to normalize after treatment (Bhatara, Tripathi, Sankar, Gupta, & Khushu, 1998).

Creatine/Phosphocreatine

The creatine, phosphocreatine peak measured by 1H MRS consists of creatine and the high-energy phosphate, phosphocreatine. Phosphocreatine has very high concentrations in the brain. Increased Cr concentrations have been reported in the caudate and medial thalamus of pediatric patients with OCD versus healthy controls (Mirza et al., 2006; Rosenberg, MacMaster, et al., 2000). Increased medial thalamic Cr levels distinguish not only pediatric patients with OCD from healthy controls but also from psychotropic-naïve pediatric patients with major depressive disorder (Fig. 6.13). No alterations in lateral thalamic or occipital cortex Cr were observed between OCD patients and controls. Increased caudate and medial thalamic Cr concentrations in psychotropic-naïve pediatric patients with OCD could reflect increased energy utilization in these regions. 31-Phosphorous spectroscopy, which allows for measurement of the individual constituents of the Cr resonance, may further delineate the role of Cr in the pathogenesis of OCD.

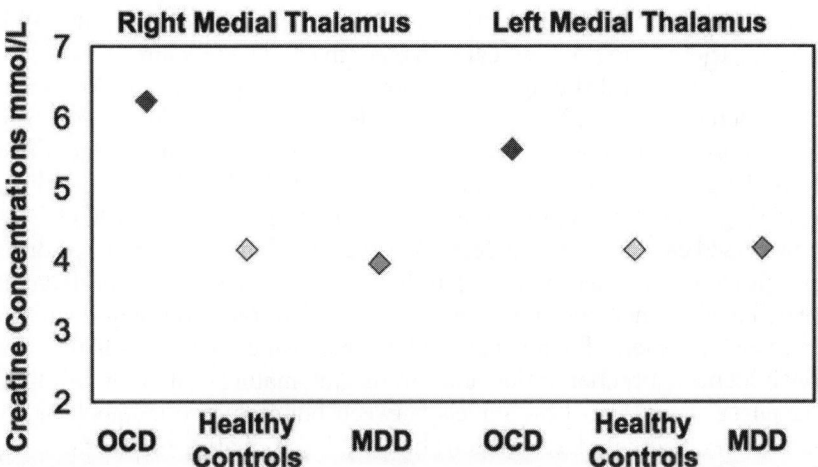

Figure 6.13.   Creatine concentrations in the left and right medial thalamus of pediatric patients with OCD, healthy controls, and MDD patients. Adapted from "Increased Medial Thalamic Creatine/Phosphocreatine Found by Proton Magnetic Resonance Spectroscopy in Children With OCD Versus Major Depression and Healthy Controls," by Y. Mirza, et al., 2006, *Journal of Child Neurology*.

Glutamate

Prior investigation had suggested possible alterations in glutamatergic-serotonin interactions in ventral prefrontal-striatal-thalamic circuitry in pediatric OCD. The caudate nucleus, which is a primary site of metabolic abnormality in OCD (Baxter et al., 1992), gets a dense glutamatergic innervation from the cortex (Becquet, Faudon, & Hery, 1990) so that the majority of axon terminals in the caudate are, in fact, comprised of glutamatergic afferents (Parent, Cote, & Lavoie, 1995; Parent & Hazrati, 1995). Ablation of frontal cortex results in a marked decrease in striatal glutamate (Calabresi, Pisani, Mercuri, & Bernardi, 1996; Kim, Hassler, Haug, & Paik, 1977). Glutamate inhibits presynaptic serotonin release in the caudate (Becquet et al., 1990; Reisine, Soubrie, Artaud, & Glowinski, 1982), while the caudate is densely innervated by cell bodies from the dorsal raphe nucleus (Greybiel & Ragsdale, 1983; Smith & Parent, 1986). Thus, serotonergic neurons can also influence glutamate neurotransmission (Edwards, Hampton, Ashby, Zhang, & Wang, 1996).

Rosenberg, MacMaster, et al. (2000) used 1H MRS to measure caudate and occipital glutamate and glutamine (Glx) concentrations in pediatric patients with OCD. They found significantly increased caudate Glx in treatment-naïve pediatric patients with OCD versus age- and sex-matched controls.

Increased caudate Glx concentrations decreased to levels not significantly different from controls after pharmacotherapy with the SSRI, paroxetine (Fig. 6.14). Reduction in caudate Glx after paroxetine treatment was positively correlated with reduction in OCD symptom severity (Fig. 6.15). In contrast, there were no significant changes in caudate Glx after 12 weeks of cognitive-behavioral therapy in psychotropic-naïve pediatric patients with OCD (Benazon et al., 2003). There were also no significant differences in occipital cortex Glx concentrations between OCD patients and controls (Rosenberg, MacMaster, et al., 2000). Arnold et al. (2004) also recently reported a glutamate receptor gene abnormality in patients with OCD.

Increased caudate Glx that decreased after SSRI treatment may be consistent with functional neuroimaging studies in OCD patients that found that increased glucose metabolism in the caudate nucleus pre-treatment decreased after SSRI treatment (Baxter et al., 1992). Glucose metabolic rates in the brain are influenced by energy demands from glutamatergic afferent terminals (Baxter et al., 2000) with parallels between brain glucose metabolism and glutamatergic activity having been shown (Sibson et al., 1997). Grome and Harper (1986) also found that serotonin agonists could decrease brain glucose metabolism. Chronic administration of SSRI's increases serotonin release by desensitizing serotonin autoreceptors (El Mansari, Bouchard, & Blier, 1995). Thus, SSRI treatment in OCD patients may alter serotonergic release in ventral prefrontal cortex that may lead to changes in prefrontal-striatal glutamate

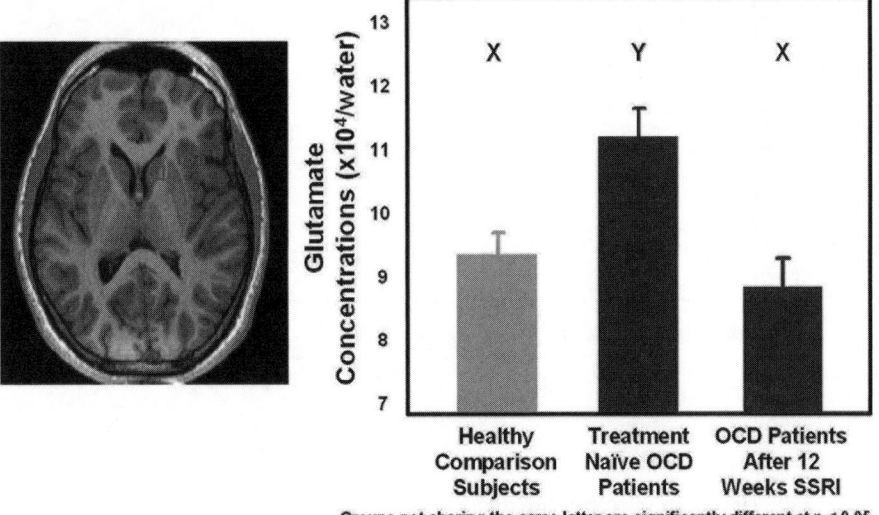

Figure 6.14.   Caudate glutamatergic concentrations by diagnostic and treatment condition. OCD = obsessive-compulsive disorder. Groups not sharing the same letter are significantly different at p < 0.05. Adapted from "Decrease in Caudate Glutamatergic Concentrations in Pediatric Obsessive-Compulsive Disorder Patients Taking Paroxetine," by D. R. Rosenberg, F. P. MacMaster, et al., 2000, *Journal of the American Academy of Child and Adolescent Psychiatry*, 39, pp. 1096–1103. Reprinted with permission of the author.

efferent projections as measured by increased caudate glutamatergic concentrations in pediatric patients with OCD (Rosenberg, MacMaster, et al., 2000).

CONCLUSIONS AND FUTURE DIRECTIONS

Over the course of the past decade, efforts have been made to delineate the core neurobiology of pediatric OCD. Alterations in the thalamus (Gilbert et al., 2000; Rosenberg, Amponsah, et al., 2001), striatum (Rosenberg, Keshavan, O'Hearn, et al., 1997; Rosenberg, MacMaster, et al., 2000), globus pallidus (Szeszko, MacMillan, McMeniman, Chen, et al., 2004), dorsolateral prefrontal cortex (Russell et al., 2003), anterior cingulate (Rosenberg & Keshavan, 1998; Rosenberg et al., 2004), pituitary gland (MacMaster et al., 2005), and corpus callosum (Farchione, Lorch, & Rosenberg, 2002; MacMaster et al., 1999; Rosenberg, Keshavan, Dick, et al., 1997) have been noted in pediatric OCD. Initial efforts to explore the effect of psychotropic treatment has noted changes in thalamic volume (Gilbert et al., 2000), amygdala volume (Szeszko, MacMillan, McMeniman, Lorch, et al., 2004) and striatal glutamate (Rosenberg, MacMaster, et al., 2000). Interestingly,

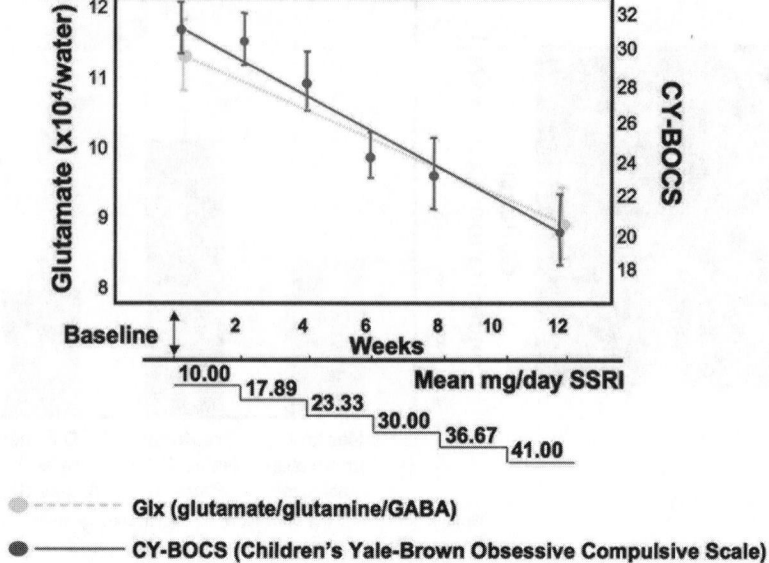

Figure 6.15.   Decreases in left caudate glutamatergic concentrations associated with reduction in Obsessive-Compulsive score of the Children's Yale-Brown Obsessive-Compulsive Scales (●————). Glx (glutamate/glutamine/GABA) (O ······). Adapted from "Genetic and Imaging Strategies in Obsessive-Compulsive Disorder: Potential Implications for Treatment Development," by D. R. Rosenberg & G. L. Hanna, 2000, *Biological Psychiatry, 48*, pp. 1210–1222.

with cognitive-behavioral therapy, no change in caudate neurochemistry (Benazon et al., 2003) or thalamic volume (Rosenberg, MacMillan, & Moore, 2001) was noted. This indicates that the mechanism of treatment has a differential effect on the neurobiology. Studies of OCD, as compared to other common psychiatric illness, such as major depression, have also established points of convergence (anterior cingulate glutamate, see Rosenberg et al., 2004) and divergence (medial thalamic choline, see Smith et al., 2003). This would indicate that there is a specific neurobiology for the disorder.

The next generation of neurobiological investigations into pediatric OCD will arise from the compelling clinical questions that exist. There are etiologic questions, such as: Do the neurobiological differences exist prior to illness onset? Studies of children at risk for developing OCD will help elucidate this. There are pathophysiology questions, such as: Are the brain changes the result of the course of illness? Longitudinal studies will describe the effect of course of illness on the neurobiology. Does adult OCD differ from pediatric OCD? To do this we can compare adult onset and pediatric onset adults as well as children with OCD versus adult onset OCD. The interplay of comorbidity and the biology of illness also needs to be explored.

From a technical perspective, multimodal studies that truly exploit the potential of neuroimaging by looking at structure, function, and chemistry concurrently will also offer insight into the neurobiology of the disorder.

ACKNOWLEDGMENTS

This work was supported in part by the State of Michigan Joe F. Young Sr. Psychiatric Research and Training Program, the Miriam L. Hamburger Endowed Chair of Child Psychiatry at Children's Hospital of Michigan and Wayne State University, Detroit, Michigan and grants from the National Institute of Mental Health (R01MH59299, R01MH65122, K24MH02037) and the Mental Illness Research Association.

REFERENCES

Alexander, G. E., Crutcher, M. D., & DeLong, M. R. (1990). Basal ganglia-thalamo-cortical circuits: Parallel substrates for motor, oculomotor, "prefrontal" and "limbic" functions. *Progress in Brain Research, 85,* 119–146.

Allen, A. J., Leonard, H. L., & Swedo, S. E. (1995). Case study: A new infection-triggered, autoimmune subtype of pediatric OCD and Tourette's syndrome. *Journal of the American Academy of Child and Adolescent Psychiatry, 34,* 307–311.

Alsobrook, J. P., & Pauls, D. L. (1998). Molecular approaches to child psychopathology. *Human Biology, 70,* 413–432.

Altemus, M., Pigott, T., Kalogeras, K. T., Demitrack, M., Dubbert, B., Murphy, D. L., et al. (1992). Abnormalities in the regulation of vasopressin and corticotropin releasing factor secretion in obsessive-compulsive disorder. *Archives of General Psychiatry, 49,* 9–20.

Arnold, P. D., Rosenberg, D. R., Mundo, E., Tharmalingam, S., Kennedy, J. L., & Richter, M. A. (2004). Association of a glutamate (NMDA) subunit receptor gene (GRIN2B) with obsessive-compulsive disorder. *Psychopharmacology, 174,* 530–538.

Asberg, M., Thoren, P., & Bertilsson, L. (1982). Clomipramine treatment of obsessive disorder: Biochemical and clinical aspects. *Psychopharmacological Bulletin, 18,* 13.

Barker, P. B., Breiter, S. N., Soher, B. J., Chatham, J. C., Forder, J. R., Samphilipo, M. A., et al. (1994). Quantitative proton spectroscopy of canine brain: In vivo and in vitro correlations. *Magnetic Resonance in Medicine, 32,* 157–163.

Bartha, R., Stein, M. B., Williamson, P. C., Drost, D. J., Neufeld, R. W., Carr, T. J., et al. (1998). A short echo 1H spectroscopy and volumetric MRI study of the corpus striatum in patients with obsessive-compulsive disorder and comparison subjects. *American Journal of Psychiatry, 155,* 1584–1591.

Bastani, B., Arora, R. C., & Meltzer, H. Y. (1991). Serotonin uptake and imipramine binding in the blood platelets of obsessive-compulsive disorder patients. *Biological Psychiatry, 30,* 131–139.

Baxter, L. R. (1994). Positron emission tomography studies of cerebral glucose metabolism in obsessive compulsive disorder. *Journal of Clinical Psychiatry, 55* (Suppl.), 54–59.

Baxter, L. R., Ackermann, R. F., Swedlow, N. R., Brody, A., Saxena, S., Schwartz, J. M., et al. (2000). Specific brain system mediation of obsessive-compulsive disorder responsive to either medication or behavior therapy. In W. K. Goodman, M. C. Rudorfer, & J.

D. Maser (Eds.), *Obsessive-compulsive disorder: Contemporary issues in treatment* (pp. 573–609). Mahwah, NJ: Lawrence Erlbaum Associates.

Baxter, L. R., Saxena, S., Brody, A. L., Ackermann, R. F., Colgan, M., Schwartz, J. M., et al. (1996). Brain mediation of obsessive-compulsive disorder symptoms: Evidence from functional brain imaging studies in the human and nonhuman primate. *Seminars in Clinical Neuropsychiatry, 1,* 32–47.

Baxter, L. R., Schwartz, J. M., Bergman, K. S., Szuba, M. P., Guze, B. H., Mazziotta, J. C., et al. (1992). Caudate glucose metabolic rate changes with both drug and behaviour therapy for obsessive-compulsive disorder. *Archives of General Psychiatry, 49,* 681–689.

Becquet, D., Faudon, M., & Hery, F. (1990). In vivo evidence for an inhibitory glutamatergic control of serotonin release in the cat caudate nucleus: Involvement of GABA neurons. *Brain Research, 519,* 82–88.

Behar, D., Rapoport, J. L., Berg, C. J., Denckla, M. B., Mann, L., Cox, C., et al. (1984). Computerized tomography and neuropsychological test measures in adolescents with obsessive-compulsive disorder. *American Journal of Psychiatry, 141,* 363–369.

Benazon, N. R., Moore, G. J., & Rosenberg, D. R. (2003). Neurochemical analyses in pediatric obsessive-compulsive disorder in patients treated with cognitive-behavioral therapy. *Journal of the American Academy of Child and Adolescent Psychiatry, 42,* 1279–1285.

Bhatara, V. S., Tripathi, R. P., Sankar, R., Gupta, A., & Khushu, S. (1998). Frontal lobe proton magnetic-resonance spectroscopy in Graves' disease: A pilot study. *Pyschoneuroendocrinology, 23,* 605–612.

Blusztajn, J. K., & Wurtman, R. J. (1983). Choline and cholinergic neurons. *Science, 221,* 614–620.

Bodkin, J. A., & White, K. (1989). Clonazepam in the treatment of obsessive compulsive disorder associated with panic disorder in one patient. *Journal of Clinical Psychiatry, 50,* 265–266.

Breiter, H. C., & Rauch, S. L. (1996). Functional MRI and the study of OCD: From symptom provocation to cognitive-behavioral probes of cortico-striatal systems and the amygdala. *Neuroimage, 4,* S127–138.

Breiter, H. C., Rauch, S. L., Kwong, K. K., Baker, J. R., Weisskoff, R. M., Kennedy, D. N., et al. (1996). Functional magnetic resonance imaging of symptom provocation in obsessive-compulsive disorder. *Archives of General Psychiatry, 53,* 595–606.

Butler, P. R., Anderson, R. J., & Venton, D. L. (1983). Human platelet phenol sulfotransferase: Partial purification and detection of two forms of the enzyme. *Journal of Neurochemistry, 41,* 630–639.

Calabresi, P., Pisani, A., Mercuri, N. B., & Bernardi, G. (1996). The corticostriatal projection: From synaptic plasticity to dysfunction of the basal ganglia. *Trends in Neuroscience, 19,* 279–280.

Catapano, F., Monteleone, P., Fuschino, A., Maj, M., & Kemali, D. (1992). Melatonin and cortisol secretion in patients with primary obsessive-compulsive disorder. *Psychiatry Research, 44,* 217–252.

Creese, I., & Iversen, S. D. (1974). The role of forebrain dopamine systems in amphetamine induced stereotyped behavior in the rat. *Psychopharmacologia, 39,* 345–357.

Cummings, J. L. (1993). Frontal-subcortical circuits and human behavior. *Archives of Neurology, 50,* 873–880.

Daniel, D. G., Weinberger, D. R., Jones, D. W., Zigun, J. R., Coppola, R., Handel, S., et al. (1991). The effect of ampthetamine on regional cerebral blood flow during cognitive activation in schizophrenia. *Journal of Neuroscience, 11,* 1907–1917.

de Lacoste, M. C., Kirkpatrick, J. B., & Ross, E. D. (1985). Topography of the human corpus callosum. *Journal of Neuropathology and Experimental Neurology, 44*, 578–591.

Ebert, D., Speck, O., Konig, A., Berger, M., Hennig, J., & Hohagen, F. (1997). 1H-magnetic resonance spectroscopy in obsessive-compulsive disorder: Evidence for neuronal loss in the cingulated gyrus and the right striatum. *Psychiatry Research, 74*, 173–176.

Edwards, E., Hampton, E., Ashby, C. R., Zhang, J., & Wang, R. Y. (1996). 5-HT3-like receptors in the rat medial prefrontal cortex: Further pharmacological characterization. *Brain Research, 733*, 21–30.

Eilam, D., Golani, I., & Szechtman, H. (1989). D2-agonist quinpirole induces perseveration of routes and hyperactivity but no perseveration of movements. *Brain Research, 26*, 255–267.

El Mansari, M., Bouchard, C., & Blier, P. (1995). Alteration of serotonin release in the guinea pig orbito-frontal cortex by selective serotonin reuptake inhibitors: Relevance to treatment of obsessive-compulsive disorder. *Neuropsychopharmacology, 13*, 117–127.

Ellinwood, E. H., Jr. (1969). Perception of faces: Disorders in organic and psychopathological states. *Psychiatric Quarterly, 43*, 622–646.

Ernst, M. (1999). PET in child psychiatry: The risks and benefits of studying normal healthy children. *Progress in Neuropsychopharmacoly and Biological Psychiatry, 23*, 561–570.

Exton, J. H. (1990). Hormonal regulation of phosphatidylcholine breakdown. *Advances in Second Messenger and Phosphoprotein Research, 24*, 152–157.

Exton, J. H. (1994). Phosphatidylcholine breakdown and signal transduction. *Biochimica et Biophysica Acta, 1212*, 26–42.

Farchione, T. R., Lorch, E., & Rosenberg, D. R. (2002). Dysfunction of the corpus callosum and obsessive-compulsive symptoms. *Journal of Child Neurology, 17*, 535–537.

Fitzgerald, K. D., MacMaster, F. P., Paulson, L. D., & Rosenberg, D. R. (1999). Neurobiology of childhood obsessive-compulsive disorder. *Child and Adolescent Psychiatric Clinics of North America, 8*, 533–575.

Fitzgerald, K. D., Moore, G. J., Paulson, L. A., Stewart, C. M., & Rosenberg, D. R. (2000). Proton spectroscopic imaging of the thalamus in treatment naïve pediatric obsessive-compulsive disorder. *Biological Psychiatry, 47*, 174–182.

Fitzgerald, K. D., Stewart, C. M., Tawile, V., & Rosenberg, D. R. (1999). Risperidone augmentation of serotonin reuptake inhibitor treatment of pediatric obsessive compulsive disorder. *Journal of Child and Adolescent Psychopharmacology, 9*, 115–123.

Fitzgerald, K. D., Welsh, R. C., Gehring, W. J., Abelson, J. L., Himle, J. A., Liberzon, I., et al. (2005). Error-related hyperactivity of the anterior cingulate cortex in obsessive-compulsive disorder. *Biological Psychiatry, 57*, 287–94.

Flament, M. F., Rapoport, J. L., Murphy, D. L., Berg, C. J., & Lake, C. R. (1987). Biochemical changes during clomipramine treatment of childhood obsessive-compulsive disorder. *Archives of General Psychiatry, 44*, 219–225.

Frye, P. E., & Arnold, L. E. (1981). Persistent amphetamine-induced compulsive rituals: Response to pyridoxine (B6). *Biological Psychiatry, 16*, 583–587.

Fuster, J. M. (1989). *The prefrontal cortex: Anatomy, physiology, and neuropsychology of the frontal lobe.* New York, NY: Raven Press.

Gehris, T. L., Kathol, R. G., Black, D. W., & Noyes, R., Jr. (1990). Urinary free cortisol levels in obsessive-compulsive disorder. *Psychiatry Research, 32*, 151–158.

Giedd, J. N., Rapoport, J. L., Garvey, M. A., Perlmutter, S., & Swedo, S. E. (2000). MRI assessment of children with obsessive-compulsive disorder or tics associated with streptococcal infection. *American Journal of Psychiatry, 157*, 281–283.

Giedd, J. N., Rapoport, J. L., Kruesi, M. J., Parker, C., Schapiro, M. B., Allen, A. J., et al. (1995). Sydenham's chorea: Magnetic resonance imaging of the basal ganglia. *Neurology, 45,* 2199–2202.

Giedd, J. N., Rapoport, J. L., Leonard, H. L., Richter, D., & Swedo, S. E. (1996). Case study: Acute basal ganglia enlargement and obsessive-compulsive symptoms in an adolescent boy. *Journal of the American Academy of Child and Adolescent Psychiatry, 35,* 913–915.

Gilbert, A. R., Moore, G. J., Keshavan, M. S., Paulson, L. A., Narula, V., MacMaster, F. P., et al. (2000). Decrease in thalamic volumes of pediatric patients with obsessive-compulsive disorder who are taking paroxetine. *Archives of General Psychiatry, 57,* 449–456.

Gonzalez, J. G., Elizondo, G., Saldivar, D., Nanez, H., Todd, L. E., & Villarreal, J. Z. (1988). Pituitary gland growth during normal pregnancy: An in vivo study using magnetic resonance imaging. *American Journal of Medicine, 85,* 217–220.

Graybiel, A. M., & Ragsdale, C. W. (1983). Biochemical anatomy of the striatum. In P. C. Emson, (Ed.), *Chemical neuroanatomy* (pp. 427–504). New York: Raven Press.

Grome, J. J., & Harper, A. M. (1986). Local cerebral glucose utilization following indoleamine- and piperazine-containing 5-hydroxytryptamine agonists. *Journal of Neurochemistry, 46,* 117–124.

Gupta, R. K., Bhatia, V., Poptani, H., & Gujral, R. B. (1995). Brain metabolic changes on in vivo proton magnetic resonance spectroscopy in children with congenital hypothyroidism. *Journal of Pediatrics, 126,* 389–392.

Insel, T. R. (1990). Serotonin in obsessive compulsive disorder. *Psychiatric Annals, 20,* 560.

Insel, T. R. (1992). Toward a neuroanatomy of obsessive-compulsive disorder. *Archives of General Psychiatry, 49,* 739–744.

Insel, T. R., Mueller, E. A., Alterman, I., Linnoila, M., & Murphy, D. L. (1985). Obsessive-compulsive disorder and serotonin: Is there a connection? *Biological Psychiatry, 20,* 1174–1188.

Insel, T. R., & Winslow, J. T. (1992). Neurobiology of obsessive compulsive disorder. *Psychiatric Clinics of North America, 15,* 813–824.

Karayiorgou, M., Altemus, M., Galke, B. L., Goldman, D., Murphy, D. L., Ott, J., et al. (1997).Genotype determining low catechol-O-methyltransferase activity as a risk factor for obsessive-compulsive disorder. *Proceedings of the National Academy of Sciences USA, 94,* 4572–2575.

Kato, T., Inubushi, T., & Kato, N. (1998). Magnetic resonance spectroscopy in affective disorders. *Journal of Neuropsychiatry and Clinical Neurosciences, 10,* 133–147.

Keshavan, M. S. (1997). Neurodevelopment and schizophrenia: Quo vadis?. In M. S. Keshavan & R. Murray (Eds.), *Neurodevelopmental models of psychopathology* (pp. 267–277). London: Cambridge University Press.

Khiat, A., Bard, C., Lacroix, A., Rousseau, J., & Boulanger, Y. (1999). Brain metabolic alterations in Cushing's syndrome as monitored by proton magnetic resonance spectroscopy. *NMR in Biomedicine, 12,* 357–363.

Kim, J. S., Hassler, R., Haug, P., & Paik, K. S. (1977). Effect of frontal cortex ablation on striatal glutamic acid level in rats. *Brain Research, 132,* 370–374.

Koizumi, H. M. (1985). Obsessive-compulsive symptoms following stimulants. *Biological Psychiatry, 20,* 1332–1333.

Leckman, J. F., Goodman, W. K., Anderson, G. M., Riddle, M. A., Chappell, P. B., McSwiggin-Hardin, M. T., et al. (1995). Cerebrospinal fluid biogenic amines in obsessive compulsive disorder, Tourette's syndrome, and healthy controls. *Neuropsychopharmacology, 12,* 73–86.

Leckman, J. F., Goodman, W. K., North, W. G., Chappell, P. B., Price, L. H., Pauls, D. L., Anderson, G. M., Riddle, M. A., McDougle, C. J., et al. (1994). The role of central oxytocin in obsessive compulsive disorder and related normal behavior. *Psychoneuroendocrinology, 19,* 723–749.

Leckman, J. F., Goodman, W. K., North, W. G., Chappell, P. B., Price, L. H., Pauls, D. L., Anderson, G. M., Riddle, M. A., McSwiggan-Hardin, M., et al. (1994). Elevated cerebrospinal fluid levels of oxytocin in obsessive-compulsive disorder. Comparison with Tourette's syndrome and healthy controls. *Archives of General Psychiatry, 51,* 782–792.

Loffelholz, K. (1989). Receptor regulation of choline phospholipid hydroloysis. A novel source of diaglycerol and phosphatidic acid. *Biochemical Pharmacology, 38,* 1543–1549.

Luxenberg, J. S., Swedo, S. E., Flament, M. F., Friedland, R. P., Rapoport, J., & Rapoport, S. I. (1988). Neuroanatomical abnormalities in obsessive-compulsive disorder detected with quantitative X-ray computed tomography. *American Journal of Psychiatry, 145,* 1089–1093.

MacMaster, F. P., Keshavan, M. S., Dick, E. L., & Rosenberg, D. R. (1999). Corpus callosal signal intensity in treatment-naïve pediatric obsessive compulsive disorders. *Progress in Neuropsychopharmacology and Biological Psychiatry, 23,* 601–612.

MacMaster, F. P., Russell, A., Mirza, Y., Keshavan, M. S., Banerjee, S. P., Bhandari, R., et al. (2006). Pituitary volume in pediatric obsessive-compulsive disorder. *Biological Psychiatry, 59,* 252–257.

Maltby, N., Tolin, D. F., Worhunsky, P., O'Keefe, T. M., & Kiehl, K. A. (2005). Dysfunctional action monitoring hyperactivates frontal-striatal circuits in obsessive-compulsive disorder: An event-related fMRI study. *Neuroimage, 24,* 495–503.

Marazziti, D., Hollander, E., Lensi, P., Ravagli, S., & Cassano, G. B. (1992). Peripheral markers of serotonin and dopamine function in obsessive-compulsive disorder. *Psychiatry Research, 42,* 41–51.

Marazziti, D., Pfanner, C., Palego, L., Gemignani, A., Milanfranchi, A., Ravagli, S., et al. (1997). Changes in platelet marker of obsessive-compulsive patients during a double-blind trial of fluvoxamine versus clomipramine. *Pharmacopsychiatry, 30,* 245–249.

March, J., Biederman, J., Wolkow, R., Safferman, A., Mardekian, J., Cook, E. H., et al. (1998). Sertraline in children and adolescents with obsessive-compulsive disorder: A multicenter randomized controlled trial. *Journal of the American Medical Association, 280,* 1752–1756.

March, J. S., & Leonard, H. L. (1996). Obsessive-compulsive disorder in children and adolescents: A review of the past 10 years. *Journal of the American Academy of Child and Adolescent Psychiatry, 35,* 1265–1273.

McDougle, C. J., Epperson, C. N., Pelton, G. H., Wasylink, S., & Price, L. H. (2000). A double-blind, placebo-controlled study of risperidone addition in serotonin reuptake inhibitor-refractory obsessive-compulsive disorder. *Archives of General Psychiatry, 57,* 794–801.

McDougle, C. J., Goodman, W. K., Leckman, J. F., Lee, N. C., Heninger, G. R., & Price, L. H. (1994). Haloperidol addition in fluvoxamine-refractory obsessive-compulsive disorder. A double blind, placebo-controlled study in patients with and without tics. *Archives of General Psychiatry, 51,* 302–308.

Mega, M. S., & Cummings, J. L. (1994). Frontal-subcortical circuits and neuropsychiatric disorders. *Journal of Neuropsychiatry and Clinical Neurosciences, 6,* 358–370.

Miller, B. L., Chang, L., Booth, R., Ernst, T., Cornford, M., Nikas, D., et al. (1996). In vivo 1H MRS choline: Correlation with in vitro chemistry/histology. *Life Science, 58,* 1929–1935.

Mirza, Y., O'Neill, J., Smith, E. A., Russell, A., Smith, J. M., Banerjee, S. P., et al. (2006). Increased medial thalamic creatine/phosphocreatine found by proton magnetic resonance spectroscopy in children with OCD versus major depression and healthy controls. *Journal of Child Neurology, 21*, 106–111.

Modell, J. G., Mountz, J. M., Curtis, C. G., & Greden, J. F. (1989). Neurophysiologic dysfunction in basal ganglia/limbic striatal and thalamocortical circuits as a pathogenetic mechanism of obsessive-compulsive disorder. *Journal of Neuropsychiatry and Clinical Neurosciences, 1*, 27–36.

Monteleone, P., Catapano, F., Del Buono, G., & Maj, M. (1994). Circadian rhythms of melatonin, cortisol, and prolactin in patients with obsessive-compulsive disorder. *Acta Psychiatrica Scandinavica, 89*, 411–415.

Monteleone, P., Catapano, F., Tortorella, A., Di Martino, S., & Maj, M. (1995). Plasma melatonin and cortisol circadian patterns in patients with obsessive-compulsive disorder before and after fluoxetine treatment. *Psychoneuroendocrinology, 20*, 763–70.

Monteleone, P., Catapano, F., Tortorella, A., & Maj, M. (1997). Cortisol response to d-fenfluramine in patients with obsessive-compulsive disorder and in healthy subjects: Evidence for a gender-related effect. *Neuropsychobiology, 36*, 8–12.

Neale, J. M., & Oltmanns, T. F. (1988). *Schizophrenia*. New York: Wiley.

Oades, R. D., Ropcke, B., & Eggers, C. (1994). Monoamine activity reflected in urine of young patients with obsessive compulsive disorder, psychosis with and without reality distortion and healthy subjects: An explorative analysis. *Journal of Neural Transmission. General Selection, 96*, 143–159.

Parent, A., Cote, P. Y., & Lavoie, B. (1995). Chemical anatomy of primate basal ganglia. *Progress in Neurobiology, 46*, 131–197.

Parent, A., & Hazrati, L. N. (1995). Functional anatomy of the basal ganglia. I. The cortico-basal ganglia-thalamo-cortical loop. *Brain Research, 20*, 91–127.

Pauls, D. L., Alsobrook, J. P., II, Phil, M., Goodman, W., Rasmussen, S., & Leckman, J. F. (1995). A family study of obsessive-compulsive disorder. *American Journal of Psychiatry, 152*, 76–84.

Pediatric OCD Treatment Study (POTS) Team. (2004). Cognitive-behavior therapy, sertraline, and their combination for children and adolescents with obsessive-compulsive disorder. *Journal of the American Medical Association, 292*, 1969–1976.

Peterson, B. S., Leckman, J. F., Tucker, D., Scahill, L., Staib, L., Zhang, H., et al. (2000). Preliminary findings of antistreptococcal antibody titers and basal ganglia volumes in tic, obsessive-compulsive, and attention deficit/hyperactivity disorders. *Archives of General Psychiatry, 57*, 364–372.

Rapoport, J. L., Leonard, H. L., Swedo, S. E., & Lenane, M. C. (1993). Obsessive-compulsive disorder in children and adolescents: Issues in management. *Journal of Clinical Psychiatry, 54* (Suppl.), S27–29.

Rasmussen, S. A., & Eisen, J. L. (1994). The epidemiology and differential diagnosis of obsessive compulsive disorder. *Journal of Clinical Psychiatry, 55* (Suppl.), 5–14.

Rauch, S. L., Jenike, M. A., Alpert, N. M., Baer, L., Breiter, H. C., Savage, C. R., et al. (1994). Regional cerebral blood flow measured during symptom provocation in obsessive-compulsive disorder using oxygen 15-labeled carbon dioxide and positron emission tomography. *Archives of General Psychiatry, 51*, 62–70.

Rauch, S. L., Whalen, P. J., Dougherty, D. D., & Jenike, M. A. (1998). Neurobiological models of obsessive compulsive disorders. In Anonymous (Ed.), *Obsessive Compulsive Disorders: Practical Management* (pp. 222–253). Boston: Mosby.

Reisine, T., Soubrie, P., Artaud, F., & Glowinski, J. (1982). Application of L-glutamic acid and substance P to the substantia nigra modulates in vivo [3H] serotonin release in the basal ganglia of the cat. *Brain Research, 236*, 317–327.

Rosenberg, D. R., Amponsah, A., Sullivan, A., MacMillan, S., & Moore, G. J. (2001). Increased medial thalamic choline in pediatric obsessive-compulsive disorder as detected by quantitative in vivo spectroscopic imaging. *Journal of Child Neurology, 16,* 636–641.

Rosenberg, D. R., Averbach, D. H., O'Hearn, K. M., Seymour, A. B., Birmaher, B., & Sweeney, J. A. (1997). Oculomotor response inhibition abnormalities in pediatric obsessive-compulsive disorder. *Archives of General Psychiatry, 54,* 831–838.

Rosenberg, D. R., Benazon, N. R., Gilbert, A., Sullivan, A., & Moore, G. J. (2000). Thalamic volume in pediatric obsessive-compulsive disorder patients before and after cognitive-behavioral therapy. *Biological Psychiatry, 48,* 294–300.

Rosenberg, D. R., & Hanna, G. L. (2000). Genetic and imaging strategies in obsessive-compulsive disorder: Potential implications for treatment development. *Biological Psychiatry, 48,* 1210–1222

Rosenberg, D. R., & Keshavan, M. S. (1998). Toward a neurodevelopmental model of obsessive compulsive disorder. *Biological Psychiatry, 43,* 623–640.

Rosenberg, D. R., Keshavan, M. S., Dick, E. L., Bagwell, W. W., MacMaster, F. P., & Birmaher, B. (1997). Corpus callosal morphology in treatment-naïve pediatric obsessive compulsive disorder. *Progress in Neuropsychopharmacology and Biological Psychiatry, 21,* 1269–1283.

Rosenberg, D. R., Keshavan, M. S., O'Hearn, K. M., Dick, E. L., Bagwell, W. W., Seymour, A. B., et al. (1997). Frontostriatal measurement in treatment naïve children with pediatric obsessive-compulsive disorder. *Archives of General Psychiatry, 54,* 824–830.

Rosenberg, D. R., MacMaster, F. P., Keshavan, M. S., Fitzgerald, K. D., Stewart, C. M., & Moore, G. J. (2000). Decrease in caudate glutamatergic concentrations in pediatric obsessive compulsive disorder patients taking paroxetine. *Journal of the American Academy of Child and Adolescent Psychiatry, 39,* 1096–1103.

Rosenberg, D. R., & MacMillan, S. (2002). Imaging and neurocircuitry of OCD. In K. L. Davis, C. B. Nemeroff, J. Coyle, & D. Charney (Eds.), *Neuropsychopharmacology. The 5th generation of progress* (pp. 1621–1646). Baltimore, MD: Lippincott Williams & Wilkins.

Rosenberg, D. R., MacMillan, S. N., & Moore, G. J. (2001). Brain anatomy and chemistry may predict treatment response in paediatric obsessive-compulsive disorder. *International Journal of Neuropsychopharmacology, 4,* 179–190.

Rosenberg, D. R., Mirza, Y. Russell, A., Tang, J., Smith, J. M., Banerjee, S. P., et al. (2004). Reduced anterior cingulate glutamatergic concentrations in childhood OCD and major depression versus healthy controls. *Journal of the American Academy of Child and Adolescent Psychiatry, 43,* 1146–1153.

Rosenberg, D. R., Russell, A., & Fougere, A. (2005). Neuropsychiatric models of obsessive-compulsive disorder. In J. S. Abramowitz & A. C. Houts (Eds.), *Handbook of obsessive compulsive spectrum disorders* (pp. 209–228). New York: Springer.

Rosenkilde, C. E. (1979). Functional heterogeneity of the prefrontal cortexin the monkey: A review. *Behavioral and Neural Biology, 25,* 301–345.

Ross, B., & Michaelis, T. (1994). Clinical applications of magnetic resonance spectroscopy. *Magnetic Resonance Quarterly, 10,* 191–247.

Russell, A., Cortese, B., Lorch, E., Ivey, J., Banerjee, S. P., Moore, G. J., et al. (2003). Localized functional neurochemical marker abnormalities in dorsolateral prefrontal cortex in pediatric obsessive-compulsive disorder. *Journal of Child and Adolescent Psychopharmacology, 13* (Suppl.), S31–38.

Sah, P., Faber, E. S., Lopez De Armentia, M., & Power, J. (2003). The amygdaloid complex: Anatomy and physiology. *Physiological Reviews, 83,* 803–834.

Sallee, F. R., Richman, H., Beach, K., Sethuraman, G., & Nesbitt, L. (1996). Platelet serotonin transporter in children and adolescents with obsessive-compulsive disorder or Tourette's syndrome. *Journal of the American Academy of Child and Adolescent Psychiatry, 35*, 1647–1656.

Sawaguchi, T., & Goldman-Rakic, P. S. (1991). D1 dopamine receptors in prefrontal cortex: Involvement in working memory. *Science, 251*, 947–950.

Schilder, P. (1938). The organic background of obsessions and compulsions. *American Journal of Psychiatry, 94*, 1397.

Schiorring, E. (1975). Changes in individual and social behavior induced by amphetamine and related compounds in monkeys and man. In E. H. Ellinwood Jr. & M. M. Kilbey (Eds.), *Cocaine and other Stimulants* (pp. 481–522). New York, NY: Plenum.

Schultz, R., Rosenberg, D. R., Pugh, K., Pine, D., Peterson, B., Kaufman, J., et al. (2002). Pediatric neuroimaging. In M. Lewis (Ed.) *Textbook of child & adolescent psychiatry: A comprehensive textbook* (pp. 132–154). Baltimore, MD: Lippincott Williams & Wilkins.

Seltzer, B., & Pandya, D. N. (1986). The topography of commissural fibers. In H. H. Jasper, F. Lepore, & M. Ptito (Eds.), *Two hemispheres, one brain. Functions of the corpus callosum* (pp. 47–73). New York: Liss.

Shapiro, E., Shapiro, A. K., Fulop, G., Hubbard, M., Mandeli, J., Nordlie, J., et al. (1989). Controlled study of haloperidol, pimozide and placebo for the treatment of Gilles de la Tourette's syndrome. *Archives of General Psychiatry, 46*, 722–730.

Shrikhande, A., Nolan, C., Lorch, E., & Rosenberg, D. R. (2000): Sexual dimorphism in delayed response performance in pediatric obsessive compulsive disorder. *Scientific Proceedings for the 49th Annual Meeting of the American Academy of Child and Adolescent Psychiatry, 110*, 7.

Sibson, N. R., Dhankhar, A., Mason, G. F., Behar, K. L., Rothman, D. L., & Shulman, R. G. (1997). In vivo 13C NMR measurements of cerebral glutamine synthesis as evidence for glutamate-glutamine cycling. *Proceedings of the National Academy of Sciences USA, 94*, 2699–2704.

Smith, E. A., Russell, A., Lorch, E., Banerjee, S. P., Rose, M., Ivey, J., et al. (2003). Increased medial thalamic choline found in pediatric patients with obsessive-compulsive disorder versus major depression or healthy control subjects: A magnetic resonance spectroscopy study. *Biological Psychiatry, 15*, 1399–1405.

Smith, Y., & Parent, A. (1986). Differential connections of caudate nucleus and putamen in the squirrel monkey (*Saimiri sciureus*). *Neuroscience, 18*, 347–371.

Swedo, S. E., Leonard, H. L., Kruesi, M. J., Rettew, D. C., Listwak, S. J., Berrettini, W., et al. (1992). Cerebrospinal fluid neurochemistry in children and adolescents with obsessive-compulsive disorder. *Archives of General Psychiatry, 49*, 29–36.

Swedo, S. E., Pietrini, P., Leonard, H. L., Schapiro, M. B., Rettew, D. C., Goldberger, E. L., Rapoport, S. I., et al. (1992). Cerebral glucose metabolism in childhood-onset obsessive-compulsive disorder. Revisualization during pharmacotherapy. *Archives of General Psychiatry, 49*, 690–694.

Swedo, S. E., Rapoport, J. L., Leonard, H., Lenane, M., & Cheslow D. (1989). Obsessive-compulsive disorder in children and adolescents. Clinical phenomenology of 70 consecutive cases. *Archives of General Psychiatry, 46*, 335–341.

Sweeney, J. A., Mintun, M. A., Kwee, S., Wiseman, M. B., Brown, D. L., Rosenberg, D. R., et al. (1996). A positron emission tomography study of voluntary saccadic eye movements and spatial working memory. *Journal of Neurophysiology, 75*, 454–468.

Szeszko, P. R., MacMillan, S., McMeniman, M., Chen, S., Baribault, K., Lim, K. O., et al. (2004). Brain structural abnormalities in psychotropic drug-naïve pediatric patients with obsessive-compulsive disorder. *American Journal of Psychiatry, 161*, 1049–1056.

Szeszko, P. R., MacMillan, S., McMeniman, M., Lorch, E., Madden, R., Ivey, J., et al. (2004). Amygdala volume reductions in pediatric patients with obsessive-compulsive disorder treated with paroxetine: Preliminary findings. *Neuropsychopharmacology, 29,* 826–832.

Thoren, P., Asberg, M., Bertilsson, L., Mellstrom, B., Sjoqvist, F., & Traskman, L. (1980). Clomipramine treatment of obsessive-compulsive disorder. II. Biochemical aspects. *Archives of General Psychiatry, 37,* 1289–1294.

Vion-Dury, J., Meyerhoff, D. J., Cozzone, P. J., & Weiner, M. W. (1994). What might be the impact on neurology of the analysis of brain metabolism by in vivo magnetic resonance spectroscopy. *Journal of Neurology, 241,* 354–371.

Vitiello, B., Shimon, H., Behar, D., Stoff, D., Bridger, W. H., & Friedman, E. (1991). Platelet imipramine binding and serotonin uptake in obsessive-compulsive patients. *Acta Psychiatrica Scandinavica, 84,* 29–32.

Wallach, M. B. (1974). Proceedings: Drug-induced stereotyped behavior: Similarities and differences. *Psychopharmacology Bulletin, 10,* 12–13.

Weizman, A., Carmi, M., Hermesh, H., Shahar, H., Apter, A., Tyano, S., et al. (1986). High-affinity imipramine binding and serotonin uptake in platelets of eight adolescent and ten adult obsessive-compulsive patients. *American Journal of Psychiatry, 143,* 335–339

Young, W. F., Jr., Laws, E. R., Jr., Sharbrough, F. W., & Weinshilboum, R. M. (1985). Human phenl sulfotransferase: Correlation of brain and platelet activities. *Journal of Neurochemistry, 44,* 1131–1137.

Ziesel, S. H. (1993). Choline phospholipids: Signal transduction and carcinogenesis. *The FASEB Journal, 7,* 551–557.

7

Pediatric Autoimmune Neuropsychiatric Disorders Associated With Streptococcal Infections

Michael J. Larson
Eric A. Storch
Tanya K. Murphy
University of Florida, Gainesville

Clinicians and researchers have recently encountered conflicting views and increasing publicity regarding the diagnosis and treatment of a subset of children that present with symptoms of obsessive-compulsive disorder (OCD) and/or tic disorders as an immune response to a Group A Streptococcus (GAS) infection. Known as Pediatric Autoimmune Neuropsychiatric Disorders Associated with Streptococcus (PANDAS), symptoms include an abrupt onset following a GAS infection (e.g., strep throat or scarlet fever), a relapsing-remitting course of illness, and include new onset psychiatric symptoms (e.g., irritability, sudden mood changes, and separation anxiety) in addition to motor/vocal tics and/or obsessions/compulsions (Swedo et al., 1998). The prevalence of PANDAS is currently unknown although some estimates suggest that 11% to 33% of patients with OCD/tics report onset associated with an infection (Giuliano et al., 2002; Singer, Giuliano, Zimmerman, & Walkup, 2000). Difficulties in identification of base-rates and probabilities for encountering the disorder will persist until definitive criteria are established and the validation of PANDAS occurs. This chapter reviews the history, potential etiology, clinical features and the currently accepted treatments for PANDAS. Controversies regarding this disorder are discussed in an effort to encourage critical thought and discussion regarding the potential of infection-triggered OCD.

HISTORY AND ETIOLOGY

The concept of PANDAS was developed by NIMH investigators subsequent to their research on Sydenham's chorea (SC) that was associated with an unexpected resurgence of RF in the United States (Hosier, Craenen, Teske, & Wheller, 1987). During these NIMH studies on SC (Swedo et al., 1993), classic OCD symptoms were found among the children. As an extension of these findings, sudden-onset OCD following streptococcal infection was reported in a case series of children that did not have the neurological findings of SC (Swedo et al., 1993). These children also presented with symptoms of separation anxiety, nightmares, personality change, oppositional behaviors, and deterioration in math skills and handwriting in addition to OCD and tic-like behaviors. The PANDAS title, therefore, describes cases of childhood-onset OCD or tics whose onset and/or exacerbation appear to be linked to GAS. Similar to SC, the current hypothesis for the pathophysiology of PANDAS is that it begins with a GAS infection that triggers the production of antibodies to GAS that cross-react with the cellular components of the basal ganglia, particularly in the caudate nucleus (Barsottini, Ferraz, Seviliano, & Barbieri, 2002; Singer, 2004; Snider & Swedo, 2004).

Potential mechanisms by which autoantibodies cause clinical manifestations in CNS diseases such as SC and PANDAS remain under debate, but likely include direct stimulation or blockade of receptors in the basal ganglia, or the formation of immune complexes promoting inflammation of these brain regions. For example, recent research implicates antibody-mediated neuronal cell signaling in the pathogenesis of SC. Monoclonal antibodies in SC patients that were targeted to N-acetyl-beta-D-glucosamine—the dominant epitope of GAS—were noted to show specificity to mammalian lysoganglioside GM1, a CNS ganglioside that influences neuronal signal transduction (Kirvan, Swedo, Heuser, & Cunningham, 2003). Serum samples from SC patients further contained antibodies that targeted human neuronal cells and specifically induced calcium/calmodulin-dependent protein (CaM) kinase II activity, whereas serum samples from patients convalescing or from patients with other streptococcal-related diseases lacked activation of this kinase. The binding of autoantibodies to these neuronal cell surface antigens may promote signal transduction, leading to the release of excitatory neurotransmitters (Kirvan et al., 2006). The potential mechanism by which symptoms occur in SC may also explain the pathogenesis of PANDAS.

Autoantibodies would need to traverse the blood–brain barrier (BBB) and gain access to the CNS. The exact mechanism of this transport is currently unknown; however, current hypotheses indicate inflammatory cytokines can cross the BBB via the circumventricular organs and, when infused peripherally, activate inflammatory cells on the CNS side of the BBB. Peripheral B cells that are cross-reactive to a CNS epitope have also been shown to induce intrathecal production of antibody (Knopf et al., 1998). Therefore, the induction of intrathecal antibodies by peripheral B cells, activation of CNS inflammatory cells by peripheral cytokines, and the traversing of the BBB by peripheral B cells and antibodies are all viable explanations by which autoantibodies produced in response to a streptococcal antigen are able to react with neural structures.

Children with PANDAS, not surprisingly, have rates of OCD symptoms in first-degree relatives higher than those in the general population and similar to children previously diagnosed with an OCD-spectrum disorder (Lougee, Perlmutter, Nicolson, Garvey, & Swedo, 2000). A study comparing the rate of RF in relatives of probands with OCD to the general population should provide interesting insights as common familial risks of OCD and RF. Interestingly, 28% of our subjects have a family history of RF in the subset of those patients with very early onset OCD/tics (under 7 years) (Murphy, 2006, personal communication). Studies of genetic loci in OCD have focused primarily on neurotransmitter receptors and transporters, rather than immune-based genes. However, one study reported a significant relationship between OCD and a polymorphism of myelin oligodendrocyte glycoprotein (MOG) by Family-Based Association Test (Zai et al., 2004). MOG is a protein implicated in multiple sclerosis pathology. As a whole, a child's risk of developing PANDAS is likely due to both genetic predisposition and to pathogen/environmental factors. Further exploration into this line of research should prove intriguing and fruitful; however, definitive statements about genetic links are premature at this point in time.

CLINICAL FEATURES OF PANDAS

Diagnostic Criteria

Current guidelines for PANDAS are: (1) the presence of OCD and/or a tic disorder, (2) childhood onset of symptoms (age 3 years to puberty), (3) an episodic or sawtooth course of symptom severity, (4) an association with GAS infection (a positive throat culture for strep or history of Scarlet Fever), and (5) evidence of concurrent neurological abnormalities (motoric hyperactivity or adventitious movements, such as choreiform movements). The period between GAS infection and symptom onset is variable; however, it is accepted that most poststreptococcal diseases occur after a latent period of 1–4 weeks following a GAS infection (Kim et al, 2004). This variable latency, coupled with difficulty in determining exact history of previous GAS infection and the differentiation between the PANDAS phenotype and

OCD and tic disorders make retrospective assessment difficult (Garvey, Giedd, & Swedo, 1998; March, 2004).

PANDAS Presentation

The symptoms and typical course of PANDAS are often similar to that of pediatric OCD and tic disorders early in the illness (Murphy, Herbstman, & Edge, 2005). The symptom dimensions are the same, for example, germ-related behaviors such as hand-washing, hoarding, and excessive toilet hygiene rituals are compulsions reported in PANDAS patients (Murphy & Pichichero, 2002, Snider & Swedo, 2003). Compulsive daytime urinary urgency and frequency have also been reported in PANDAS patients (Garvey, Giedd, & Swedo, 1998; Murphy & Pichichero, 2002).

There are several notable differences between PANDAS and traditional OCD. First, unlike typical patients with OCD who demonstrate an insidious course of illness lasting weeks to years before diagnosis, children with PANDAS have a sudden onset of OCD or tic behaviors shortly after GAS infection. Second, PANDAS, by definition, is prepubertal with an average illness onset of 7 years (Swedo et al., 1998). This is consistent with Tourette's Syndrome, but earlier than the age of onset of traditional childhood OCD (about 10 years; Murphy et al., 2005). Other psychiatric symptoms frequently reported in PANDAS patients include separation anxiety, hyperactivity, inattention, and emotional lability.

Children with PANDAS display an episodic/sawtooth course; the frequency of symptom recurrences is not definitively known. In the 12 subjects identified as PANDAS by Murphy and Pichichero (2002) 50% experienced 1–6 symptom recurrences. In another study, 14 subjects with an episodic/sawtooth course had 23 significant OCD exacerbations (i.e., greater than 9-point change on the CY-BOCS) over a 9–22 month period indicating a much higher recurrence rate (Murphy et al., 2004). Further research is required to determine whether the course of PANDAS remits completely, continues to have an erratic course, or steadily progresses to a more chronic illness (Murphy, Husted, & Edge, 2006).

The Boundaries of PANDAS

Some authors contend that the reported link between GAS and OCD lacks necessary research support (Kurlan & Kaplan, 2004; Shulman, 1999). Specifically, these authors argue that the published diagnostic criteria for PANDAS is too broad and overlaps with the presentation of typical OCD/TS, that the data suggesting a correlation between GAS and OCD/TS symptoms are tenuous, and that the published evidence of autoantibodies in PANDAS is complicated by differing methodology. These opinions led some to conclude that there is currently inadequate support for association of GAS and

TABLE 7.1
Hierarchy of GAS Association With OCD/Tic Onset/Exacerbation
(Low to High)

High titers (one point in OCD/tic course)

Exposure to GAS

Sore throat, no treatment

Sore throat, clinical diagnosis, antibiotics started

Sore throat, positive culture, antibiotic treatment

At OCD/tic onset, rise in titers from baseline assessment to 4–6 weeks later

Positive culture, associated with rise in titers from acute to ~ 6 weeks later

---

OCD/TS and therefore, routine microbiological or serological testing for GAS in children with acute onset OCD or tic symptoms and the routine use of antimicrobial or immune-based therapies is premature.

As a counterpoint, support for the association of GAS infections to the onset of tics or OCD continues to accumulate. Murphy and Pichichero examined all children who presented to a pediatric practice with a sudden onset of a neuropsychiatric problem, (such as OCD, a tic disorder, or late age-onset ADHD), for GAS—finding 12 over a 3-year period, all with obsessive-compulsive symptoms (Murphy & Pichichero, 2002). A retrospective survey of 80 children (5–17 years of age) found that 42 patients (53%) described a sudden onset or worsening of tic symptoms; 15 of these 42 had their exacerbation historically associated with an infection, with nine of the 15 specifically reporting that their abrupt changes occurred within 6 weeks of a preceding streptococcal infection. An Italian study adds further support to possible temporal relation of GAS to recent onset of tic disorders finding antistreptolysin O (ASO) titer elevations in 38% (ASO > 500 I.U./ml) of 150 patients compared with only 2% of the 150 healthy control participants (Cardona & Orefici, 2001). At the University of Florida, Murphy et al. (2004) followed a group of 25 children with OCD and/or TS at 6-week intervals for a minimum of 6 consecutive visits, evaluating them for neuropsychiatric severity and GAS antibody titers. In subjects with large symptom changes, positive correlations were found between streptococcal titers and obsessive-compulsive severity rating changes. In addition, these subjects were also more likely to have elevated GAS titers during the majority of the observations (Murphy et al., 2004). Perhaps one of the strongest studies to support the GAS association was a recent epidemiologic study that used population-based data from a large health maintenance organization and assessed whether GAS infection was associated with increased risk for OCD or

TS (Mell, Davis, & Owens, 2005). They found that patients with OCD or TS were more likely than controls to have had prior streptococcal infection in the 3 months before onset date and that having multiple GAS infections within a 12-month period was associated with a markedly increased risk for TS (OR = 13.6; Mell et al., 2005).

Pandas Criteria—Too Stringent?

NIMH guidelines require a prospectively established link of GAS infection with two separate OCD/tic symptom episodes. This requirement likely eliminates those that have had subclinical GAS-triggered symptoms and those that have prolonged symptoms following one episode of GAS. Similar presentations (i.e., prolonged symptoms with subclinical pharyngitis-trigger) are found in RF/SC literature (Veasy et al., 1987).

The high rates of comorbidity between OCD/tics and symptoms such as inattention, hyperactivity, and separation anxiety have led some researchers to suggest that the PANDAS syndrome should be expanded to include primary diagnosis of late-onset ADHD and age-inappropriate separation anxiety disorders, as well as OCD and tic disorders. Indeed, inattention and hyperactivity have been commonly reported among PANDAS patients. The clinical spectrum of PANDAS has also been proposed to include additional neuropsychiatric manifestations such as anorexia nervosa, acute disseminated encephalomyelitis, myoclonus, dystonia, and paroxysmal dyskinesias (Murphy et al., 2006). Another author suggests that researchers shift their perspective from defining the clinical phenotype to defining biological markers, specifically ABGA (Giovannoni, 2006).

A confirmed diagnosis of GAS infection is primary to a PANDAS diagnosis. Indeed, the approximately 79% of physicians who reported they would prescribe antibiotics for pharyngitis without obtaining a throat culture is too high when the question of PANDAS is present (Paluck et al., 2001). To make a definitive diagnosis of a new onset GAS infection, a positive 24-hour culture of a subtype that was not previously cultured in that child, along with acute and convalescent streptococcal titers showing a rise of 0.2 log or higher (Shet & Kaplan, 2002). This level of rigor is *not* observed in clinical practice as serotype determinations and serial titers are neither practical nor standard practice for documenting acute GAS in the office of the child's primary care provider; however, in cases of PANDAS, an exacting level of documentation is expected.

Protocols for diagnosis and treatment are based on the contingency that GAS leads to exacerbation or onset of OCD/tic behaviors. Acute/sudden onset of OCD symptoms and tic behaviors is often an initial indication for assessment of PANDAS and part of the history gathering should include risk factors associated with GAS infection such as exposure to GAS and/or recent sore throat. Also, careful attention should be given to history of unexplained abdominal pain accompanied by fever, history of scarlet fever, brief episodes of tics, OCD or compulsive urination that remitted, remission of OCD/tics during an unrelated antibiotic course, and any illness accompanied by sudden onset of OCD or tic-like behaviors (Larson, Storch, & Murphy, 2005). In patients with new onset OCD or tics, or recent symptom exacerbation, a throat culture will help rule out the possibility of symptoms being triggered by a subclinical GAS infection. Although a positive throat culture lends support that the symptoms were triggered by a subclinical GAS infection, this evidence alone will not rule out the possibility that the child is a GAS carrier.

To further complicate making the association to GAS, elevated streptococcal titers are common in the community population (Kaplan, Rothermel, & Johnson, 1998) and are not necessarily diagnostic of PANDAS. After streptococcal infections, titers may remain elevated for 6 months to a year. One study found persistent elevations in one or more strep titers in patients with dramatically fluctuating neuropsychiatric symptoms compared to those that had a course inconsistent with PANDAS (Murphy et al., 2004). Many clinicians and parents mistakenly believe that finding high titers in a child with OCD or tics proves the existence of PANDAS. However, by current standards for proof of GAS association, streptococcal titers obtained at symptom onset should be repeated to assess a rise in titers 4 to 6 weeks later. See Table 7.1 for a hierarchy of evidence for a GAS association.

TREATMENT

Current Standard of Care

The current standard of care for PANDAS is the same as that for OCD and tic disorders; namely, treat with SSRI and/or cognitive behavioral therapy (CBT) and follow the course of illness. Although novel treatments are being researched (i.e., prophylactic antibiotics, intravenous immunoglobulin, plasma exchange) it is imperative that the primary care physicians and parents continue the current standard of care and wait for results from large, well-controlled clinical trials before rushing into higher risk therapies.

Antibiotic Treatment

Antibiotic treatment of GAS infection has not received adequate attention in the PANDAS literature; however, such treatment has been thoroughly studied among patients with rheumatic fever. American Heart Association guidelines for the prevention of rheumatic fever following GAS recommend the use of oral penicillin at 250 mg taken twice daily (Dajani, Taubert, Ferrieri, Peter, & Shulman, 1995). Recent studies also indicate an antibiotic from the macrolide class, azithromycin, at a dose of 500mg taken once weekly, is effective in prophylaxis against GAS, but has the drawback of increased prevalence of GAS resistance to macrolides (Gray et al., 1998).

Given the effectiveness of antibiotic prophylaxis for treatment of rheumatic fever, several researchers have hypothesized that PANDAS patients would exhibit decreased neuropsychiatric symptoms while maintained on antibiotic prophylaxis for GAS infection.

An initial clinical trial utilizing penicillin in treating apparent PANDAS episodes showed no conclusive evidence of reduced clinical exacerbations (Garvey et al., 1999); however, these findings may have been due to the failure of the antibiotic to eliminate streptococcal colonization. Subsequent studies have documented rapid resolution of primary OCD, tic, and anxiety symptoms following appropriate antibiotic treatment in PANDAS (Leonard & Swedo, 2001; Murphy & Pichichero, 2002) however, nearly 50% of patients studied had at least one recurrence of OCD, with all recurrent cases having a documented throat culture or rapid antigen-detection assay positive for GAS, leading to some question regarding the long-term efficacy of antibiotic treatment. Longer term studies, however, have demonstrated consistent improvement in PANDAS symptoms following antibiotic treatments, with prophylactic administration of antibiotics inhibiting the recurrence of streptococcal infections (Leonard & Swedo, 2001). Nonetheless, evidence that symptoms remit following antibiotic treatment remains tenuous in the absence of well-controlled clinical trials. Importantly, antibiotic treatment of obsessive-compulsive symptoms is appropriate only in very select cases when a documented case of PANDAS exists and the recurrent neuropsychiatric symptoms lead to considerable impairment (Leonard & Swedo, 2001). Judicious use of antibiotics in children is strongly encouraged due to the possibility of the development of antibiotic-resistant organisms and potential for adverse effects. Consultation and collaborative treatment with the child's pediatrician is recommended to ensure appropriate monitoring and treatment of streptococcal infections.

Immunomodulatory Therapies

Therapies that modulate the immune system (i.e., those that interrupt the action of autoantibodies on the CNS) would also seem a reasonable course of treatment for severe cases given PANDAS proposed pathophysiology. Administration of intravenous immunoglobulin (IVIG) or plasma exchange has led to moderate reduction in the current (40% to 55%) and long-term (more the 1 year) resolution of symptoms, with plasma exchange being better tolerated and providing greater relief in symptoms (Perlmutter et al, 1999). Both IVIG and plasma exchange are invasive treatments associated with adverse side effects (e.g., dizziness, nausea, and perioral tingling for plasma exchange; nausea, vomiting, and headache for IVIG). Due to this side-effect profile, these invasive therapies should be reserved for the severe, clearly established PANDAS cases only when less invasive treatments (antibiotics, standard OCD therapies) have proven ineffective and then only under research protocols and by those physicians experienced in administering these therapies.

Cognitive-Behavioral Therapy

Recent evidence suggests that CBT, the front-line approach for mild to moderate pediatric OCD (March et al., 2004), may also have utility in cases of PANDAS (Storch et al., 2004). Storch et al. (2004) presented a case example of the effectiveness of intensive behavioral treatment of rapid-onset pediatric OCD of the PANDAS phenotype, with the patient showing a nearly 76% reduction in symptoms following five treatment sessions spanning 1 week with symptoms remaining in remission for more than 6 months. Subsequently, Storch et al. (2006) described the treatment of children with OCD of the PANDAS subtype who were treated in a 3-week intensive CBT program. Overall, the majority of participants were treatment responders at post-treatment, and half of those remained responders at follow-up. To the best of our knowledge, these data represent the only published administration of CBT to patients with PANDAS. Therefore, based on our clinical experience with properly trained clinicians, CBT provides an appropriate treatment option for PANDAS. Results, however, should be interpreted with caution as they represent only a handful of cases and given the fluctuating course of individuals with the PANDAS phenotype, the authors did not rule out the possibility of spontaneous remission of symptoms. It is also plausible that CBT buffers against future symptom exacerbations. Future adequately controlled trials of CBT are required to establish the efficacy of CBT for documented PANDAS cases.

Selective Serotonin Reuptake Inhibitors

Selective serotonin reuptake inhibitors (SSRIs) are indicated for pharmacological management of PANDAS symptoms. Although no published reports of SSRI use in the literature are specific to PANDAS, there is a wealth of literature supporting SSRI use in pediatric OCD. As with any SSRI administration in the pediatric population, clinicians should be aware of the possibility of increased suicidal ideations in children taking SSRI medications and use SSRIs judiciously, as well as monitor patient SSRI intake and suicidal ideation closely. Some recent data suggest that children of the PANDAS subtype may be at elevated risk for behavioral activation relative to non-PANDAS OCD (Murphy, Storch, & Strawser, 2006). Even with activation, OCD can be successfully treated with low doses of SSRIs; the keys are conservative dosing and close monitoring.

SUMMARY

PANDAS is diagnostically characterized by abrupt onset and/or exacerbation of neuropsychiatric symptoms following GAS infection. The validity of the association between GAS and these symptoms, however, is questioned because GAS infections are common and the role GAS plays in the pathophysiology of OCD and other childhood-onset neuropsychiatric disorders remains largely unknown. PANDAS may provide an excellent framework to examine the possible association of immune and infectious triggers to neuropsychiatric symptom onset and/or exacerbations. Continued research into possible immune markers and correspondence with clinical symptoms is imperative to obtain the necessary understanding of the proposed relationship.

Research on antibiotic treatment of GAS leading to remission of symptoms remains tenuous in the absence of well-controlled clinical trials. Front-line treatment of PANDAS symptoms is the same as that for pediatric OCD or other tic disorders, namely cognitive-behavioral therapy and SSRIs with added surveillance for GAS infections at times of symptom onset or worsening.

REFERENCES

Barsottini, O. G., Ferraz, H. B., Seviliano, M. M., & Barbieri, A. (2002). Brain SPECT imaging in Sydenham's chorea. *Brazilian Journal of Medical and Biological Research, 35,* 431–432.

Cardona, F., & Orefici, G. (2001). Group A streptococcal infections and tic disorders in an Italian pediatric population. *Journal of Pediatrics, 138,* 71–75.

Dajani, A., Taubert, K., Ferrieri, P., Peter, G., & Shulman, S. (1995). Treatment of acute streptococcal pharyngitis and prevention of rheumatic fever: A statement for health professionals. Committee on Rheumatic Fever, Endocarditis, and Kawasaki Disease of the Council on Cardiovascular Disease in the Young, the American Heart Association. *Pediatrics, 94*(4 Pt. 1), 758–764.

Garvey, M. A., Giedd, J., & Swedo, S. E. (1998). PANDAS: The Search for environmental triggers of pediatric disorders. Lessons from rheumatic fever. *Journal of Child Neurology, 13,* 413–423.

Garvey, M. A., Perlmutter, S. J., Allen, A. J., Hamburger, S., Lougee, L., Leonard, H. L., et al. (1999). A pilot study of penicillin prophylaxis for neuropsychiatric exacerbations triggered by streptococcal infections. *Biological Psychiatry, 45,* 1564–1571.

Giovannoni, G. (2006). PANDAS: Overview of the hypothesis. In J. T. Walkup, J. W. Mink, & P. J. Hollenback (Eds.), *Advances in neurology: Tourette Syndrome* (Vol. 99; pp. 159–165). Philadelphia: Lippincott, Williams, & Wilkins.

Giuliano, L., Gammon, P., Sullivan, K., Franklin, M., Foa, E., Maid, R., et al. (2002). Is parental report of upper respiratory infection at the onset of obsessive-compulsive disorder suggestive of pediatric autoimmune neuropsychiatric disorder associated with streptococcal infection? *Journal of Child and Adolescent Psychopharmacology, 12,* 157–164.

Gray, G. C., McPhate, D. C., Leinonen, M., Cassell, G. H., Deperalta, E. P., Putnam, S. D., et al. (1998). Weekly oral azithromycin as prophylaxis for agents causing acute respiratory disease. *Clinical Infectious Disorders, 26,* 103–110.

Hosier, D. M., Craenen, J. M., Teske, D. W., & Wheller, J. J. (1987). Resurgence of acute rheumatic fever. *American Journal of Disorders in Childhood, 141,* 730–733.

Kaplan, E. L., Rothermel, C. D., & Johnson, D. R. (1998). Antistreptolysin O and Anti-Deoxyribonuclease B Titers: Normal values for children ages 2 to 12 in the United States. *Pediatrics, 101,* 86–88.

Kim, S. W., Grant, J. E., Kim, S. I., Swanson, T. A., Bernstein, G. A., Jaszcz, W. B., et al. (2004). A possible association of recurrent streptococcal infections and acute onset of obsessive-compulsive disorder. *Journal of Neuropsychiatry and Clinical Neuroscience, 16,* 252–260.

Kirvan, C. A., Swedo, S. E., Heuser, J. S., & Cunningham, M. W., (2003). Mimicry and autoantibody-mediated neuronal cell signing in Sydenham chorea. *Nature Medicine, 9,* 914–920.

Kirvan, C. A., Swedo, S. E., Kurahara, D., & Cunningham, M. W. (2006). Streptococcal mimicry and antibody-mediated cell signaling in the pathogenesis of Sydenham's chorea. *Autoimmunity, 39*(1), 21–29.

Knopf, P. M., Harling-Berg, C. J., Cserr, H. F., Basu, D., Sirulnick, E. J., Nolan, S. C., et al. (1998). Antigen-dependent intraethical antibody synthesis in the normal rat brain: Tissue entry and local retention of antigen-specific B cells. *Journal of Immunology, 161,* 692–701.

Kurlan, R., & Kaplan, E. L. (2004). The pediatric autoimmune neuropsychiatric disorders associated with streptococcal infections (PANDAS) etiology for tics and obsessive-compulsive symptoms: Hypothesis or entity? Practical considerations for the clinician. *Pediatrics, 11,* 883–886.

Larson, M. J., Storch, E. A., & Murphy, T. K. (2005). Is it PANDAS? How to confirm the sore throat/OCD connection. *Current Psychiatry, 4,* 33–34, 39–48.

Leonard, H. L., & Swedo, S. E. (2001). Paediatric autoimmune neuropsychiatric disorders associated with streptococcal infection (PANDAS). *International Journal of Neuropsychopharmacology, 4,* 191–198.

Lougee, L. Perlmutter, S. J., Nicolson, R., Garvey, M. A., & Swedo, S. E. (2000). Psychiatric disorders in first-degree relatives of children with pediatric autoimmune neuropsychiatric disorders associated with streptococcal infections (PANDAS). *Journal of the American Academy of Child and Adolescent Psychiatry, 39,* 1120–1126.

March, J. S. (2004). Pediatric autoimmune neuropsychiatric disorders associated with streptococcal infection (PANDAS): Implications for clinical practice. *Archives of Pediatric and Adolescent Medicine, 158,* 927–929.

March, J. S., Foa, E., Gammon, P., Chrisman, A., Curry, J., Fitzgerald, D. H., et al. (2004). Cognitive-behavior therapy, sertraline, and their combination for children and adolescents with obsessive-compulsive disorder: The Pediatric OCD Treatment Study (POTS) randomized controlled trial. *Journal of the American Medical Association, 292,* 1969–1976.

Mell, L. K., Davis, R. L., & Owens, D. (2005). Association between streptococcal infection and obsessive-compulsive disorder, Tourette's syndrome, and tic disorder. *Pediatrics, 116,* 56–60.

Murphy, M. L., & Pichichero, M. E. (2002). Prospective identification and treatment of children with pediatric autoimmune neuropsychiatric disorder associated with group A streptococcal infection (PANDAS). *Archives of Pediatric and Adolescent Medicine, 156,* 356–361.

Murphy, M. L., Sajid, M., Soto, O., Shapira, N., Edge, P., Yang, M., et al. (2004). Detecting pediatric autoimmune disorders associated with streptococcus in children with obsessive-compulsive disorder and tics. *Biological Psychiatry, 55,* 61–68.

Murphy, T. K., Herbstman, D. M., & Edge, P. J. (2005). Infectious trigger in obsessive compulsive and tic disorders. In S. H. Fatemi (Ed.), *Neuropsychiatric disorders and infection* (pp. 135–153). London & New York: Taylor and Francis.

Murphy, T. K., Husted, D. S., & Edge, P. J. (2006). Preclinical/clinical evidence of central nervous system etiology in PANDAS. In J. T. Walkup, J. W. Mink, & P. J. Hollenbeck (Eds.), *Advances in neurology: Tourette Syndrome* (Vol. 99, pp. 148–149). Philadelphia: Lippincott, Williams, & Wilkins.

Murphy, T. K., Storch, E. A., & Strawser, M. S. (2006). Selective serotonin reuptake inhibitor-induced behavioral activation in the PANDAS subtype. *Primary Psychiatry, 13*(8), 87–89.

Paluck, E. Katzenstein, D., Frankish, C. J., Herbert, C. P., Milner, R., Speert, D., et al. (2001). Prescribing practices and attitudes towards giving children antibiotics. *Canadian Family Physician, 47*, 521–527.

Perlmutter, S. J., Leitman, S. F., Garvey, M. A., Hamburger, S., Feldman, E., Leonard, H. L., et al. (1999). Therapeutic plasma exchange and intravenous immunoglobin for obsessive-compulsive disorder and tic disorders in childhood. *Lancet, 54*, 1153–1158.

Shet, A., & Kaplan, E. L. (2002). Clinical use and interpretation of the group A streptococcal antibody tests: A practical approach for the pediatrician or primary care physician. *Pediatric Infectious Disease Journal, 21*, 420–430.

Shulman, S. T. (1999). Pediatric autoimmune neuropsychiatric disorders associated with streptococci (PANDAS). *Pediatric Infectious Disease Journal, 18*, 281–282.

Singer, H. S. (2004). PANDAS—Pediatric autoimmune neuropsychiatric disorders associated with streptococcal infection. Is it a specific clinical disorder? *Revista Brasileira de Psiquiatria, 26*, 220–221.

Singer, H. S., Giuliano, J. D., Zimmerman, A. M., & Walkup, J. T. (2000). Infection: A stimulus for tic disorders. *Pediatric Neurology, 22*, 380–383.

Snider, L. A., & Swedo, S. E. (2003). Childhood-onset obsessive-compulsive disorder and tic disorders: Case report and literature review. *Journal of Child and Adolescent Psychopharmacology, 13*(S1). S81–88

Snider, L. A., & Swedo, S. E. (2004). PANDAS: Current status and directions for research. *Molecular Psychiatry, 9*, 900–907.

Storch, E. A., Gerdes, A. C., Adkins, J. W., Geffken, G. R., Star, J., & Murphy, T. (2004). Behavioral treatment of a child with PANDAS. *Journal of the American Academy of Child and Adolescent Psychiatry, 43*, 510–511.

Storch, E. A., Murphy, T. K., Geffken, G. R., Mann, G., Adkins, J., Merlo, L. J., Duke, D., Munson, M., Swaine, Z., & Goodman, W. K. (2006). Cognitive-behavioral therapy for PANDAS related obsessive-compulsive disorder: Findings from a preliminary wait-list controlled open trial. *American Academy of Child and Adolescent Psychiatry, 45*, 1171–1178.

Swedo, S. E., Leonard, H. L., Garvey, M., Mittleman, B., Allen, A. J., Perlmutter, S., et al. (1998). Pediatric autoimmune neuropsychiatric disorders associated with streptococcal infections: Clinical description of the first 50 cases. *American Journal of Psychiatry, 155*, 264–271.

Swedo, S. E., Leonard, H. L., Schapiro, M. B., Casey, B. J., Mannheim, G. B., Lenane, M. C., et al. (1993). Syndenham's chorea: Physical and psychological symptoms of St. Vitus dance. *Pediatrics, 91*, 706–713.

Veasy, L. G., Wiedmeier, S. E., Orsmond, G. S., Ruttenburg, H. D., Boucek, M. M., Roth, S. J., et al. (1987). Resurgence of acute rheumatic fever in the intermountain area of the United States. *New England Journal of Medicine, 316*, 421–427.

Zai, G., Bezchlibnyk, Y. B., Richter, M. A., Arnold, P., Burroughs, E., Barr, C. L., et al. (2004). Myelin oligodendrocyte glycoprotein (MOG) gene is associated with obsessive-compulsive disorder. *American Journal of Medical Genetics, Part B: Neuropsychiatric Genetics, 129*, 64–68.

8

Genetics of Obsessive-Compulsive Disorder: Evidence From Pediatric and Adult Studies

Paul Daniel Arnold
Margaret A. Richter
University of Toronto

Since the earliest descriptions of OCD, it has been observed that there appears to be a familial pattern to this disorder. However, finding a genetic "cause" for OCD remains elusive. In contrast to simple Mendelian disorders (e.g., Huntington's disease, cystic fibrosis), in which a single genetic variant is necessary and sufficient to cause the disorder, neuropsychiatric disorders such as OCD are classified as "complex" genetic disorders or traits in which segregation at more than one genetic locus is likely involved (Elston, 2000). Such phenomena as pleiotropy (the same gene produces more than one possible phenotype), genetic heterogeneity (more than one gene may produce a given trait), epistasis (genes interact in a non-additive fashion to produce a trait), and gene–environment interaction may all be involved in causation of a complex trait. For such multifactorial conditions, genetic causes are best conceptualized as "probabilistic" (the cause increased the probability of a condition occurring) or "counterfactual" (the cause makes a difference in the outcome when it is present compared with when it is absent; Page, George, Go, Page, & Allison, 2003; Parascandola & Weed, 2001). This definition of causation provides a necessary antidote to claims of genetic determinism, in an era when a gene "for" a disorder is reported in the media on a regular basis.

In this chapter, we provide a comprehensive and critical review of the current state of knowledge regarding the probabilistic genetic determinants of OCD. We begin with a review of family, segregation and twin studies that are designed to answer a series of questions including: (1) Does OCD aggregate in families? (2) What is the familial relationship between OCD and other psychiatric disorders? (3) Is OCD due to one gene or many? (4) What is the mode of inheritance for OCD? and (5) Is OCD due to genetic or environmental causes? We then describe the current state of knowledge regarding the molecular genetics of OCD. Finally, we conclude with a discussion of novel approaches to "dissecting" the OCD phenotype and the impact of rapid technological advances on genetic studies of OCD.

DOES OCD AGGREGATE IN FAMILIES?
EVIDENCE FROM FAMILY STUDIES

Family studies generally constitute the first step in establishing that genetic determinants are important in the etiology of a disorder. Although such studies are not sufficient to establish the role of genetic factors as there are alternative explanations for familial aggregation (e.g., common environment), they are a necessary prerequisite to further studies as genetic transmission is unlikely to be present if no familial transmission of a trait or disorder is seen. Typically, family studies are modeled after case-control studies in epidemiology, with the risk factor defined as the presence or absence of a trait in a family member. "Probands" (individuals ascertained due to having a diagnosis or trait of interest such as OCD) are collected and information obtained regarding their relatives in order to determine if OCD is more likely in the first-degree relatives of probands compared with the relatives of control individuals.

The idea that OCD may aggregate in families is not new, with the first family study dating back to 1936 (Lewis, 1936). However, early studies are difficult to interpret as they did not use consistent diagnostic criteria. A meta- analysis of five controlled family studies ascertained through adult subjects with OCD resulted in an aggregate risk of 8.3% in first-degree relatives of OCD probands ($n = 1,209$) compared with 2% in first-degree relatives of control probands ($n = 746$), and a Mantel-Haenzel summary odds ratio of 4.0 (Hettema, Neale, & Kendler, 2001). The largest controlled family studies included in this meta-analysis indicated that first-degree relatives of OCD probands were approximately six times more likely to have, OCD compared to control relatives, and that OCD was more common in relatives of child onset compared with adult onset probands (Nestadt, Samuels, et al., 2000; Pauls, Alsobrook, Goodman, Rasmussen, & Leckman, 1995). For example, Nestadt et al. detected no cases of OCD in relatives of probands with an age of onset greater than 18 years (Nestadt,

Samuels, et al., 2000). These studies and other observations led some researchers to propose that pediatric onset OCD has a stronger genetic contribution compared with OCD beginning later in life.

In recent years, three controlled family studies have been published comparing pediatric OCD probands to children with no psychiatric illness, based on systematic assessment of probands and relatives using operationalized diagnostic criteria (do Rosario-Campos et al., 2005; Hanna, Himle, Curtis, & Gillespie, 2005; Reddy et al., 2001). In a sample derived from India, the age-corrected risk of OCD in both groups was low compared to other family studies of pediatric OCD, with only 5% of case relatives and none of the control relatives exhibiting either OCD or subclinical OCD. Methodological limitations of the study included: (1) 50% of control relatives were not directly interviewed, and (2) interviewers of relatives were not blind to proband diagnosis (Reddy et al., 2001).

The other two controlled studies were both published in 2005 and based on North American samples. Both studies included direct interviews of probands, as well as the majority of both case and control relatives. Information on relatives not directly interviewed was obtained through family history interviews of other family members. In a large study, 325 first-degree relatives of 106 child and adolescent probands (mean age at interview 11.9, mean age of onset 6.7) were compared with 140 relatives of 44 community controls (mean age 11.2; do Rosario-Campos et al., 2005). Odds ratios were calculated using logistic regression with generalized estimating equations (GEE), a method that accounts for within-family correlations among relatives (Liang & Pulver, 1996). Their major finding was a significantly increased age-corrected rate of OCD in case relatives (22.7%) compared with control relatives (0.9%), resulting in an odds ratio (OR) of 32.5. Inclusion of both OCD and subclinical OCD in the definition of affected status also resulted in a significantly increased risk to case compared with control relatives but a lower OR compared to considering OCD alone (OR = 15.4).

In a smaller but similarly well-designed study, Hanna, Himle, et al. (2005) compared 102 first-degree relatives of 35 pediatric OCD probands (mean age at interview = 13.7 years, median age of onset = 9 years) with 39 first-degree relatives of 17 probands (mean age = 12.4 years). Using a GEE method, these investigators discovered a rate of OCD in first-degree relatives virtually identical to that of the rate in the do Rosario-Campos (2005) study at 22.5% compared with 2.6% in control relatives, resulting in an OR of 11.06. Inclusion of subthreshold OCD in the definition of affected increased the odds ratio slightly to 14.38. Although these reported odds ratios are not age-corrected, comparison of age-corrected rates using Cox proportional hazards regression produced similar results (e.g., hazard ratio of 12.4 for OCD plus subthreshold OCD).

An earlier study (Thomsen, 1995) included a comparison group ascertained through children with a variety of psychiatric conditions. OCD was found in 3 of 20 fathers and none of the 20 mothers of OCD probands in contrast to no OCD amongst the control parents. No inferential testing was performed to test differences in the rate of OCD in case versus control relatives. Another family study (Toro, Cervera, Osejo, & Salamero, 1992) relied on chart review for diagnostic information, and so is not considered further herein. Uncontrolled family studies based on pediatric probands have revealed rates of 11% to 17% for OCD in first-degree relatives (Chabane et al., 2005; Lenane et al., 1990; Leonard et al., 1992; Riddle et al., 1990).

A complementary design to the family study is a prospective study of "high-risk" individuals ascertained due to being the offspring of an individual with a disorder. There is only one published study to our knowledge that has used this approach following children of OCD individuals over time (Black, Gaffney, Schlosser, & Gabel, 2003). A total of 43 children of OCD probands (mean age 12.3 years at baseline) and 35 children of control subjects (mean age 11.5 years at baseline) were assessed at baseline and approximately 2 years later. At follow-up, 23% of the high-risk offspring met criteria for OCD, a proportion significantly higher than that for control offspring and remarkably congruent with the 23% of first-degree relatives meeting criteria for OCD in the family studies of pediatric probands just noted (do Rosario-Campos et al., 2005; Hanna, Himle, et al., 2005). High-risk offspring were more likely to meet criteria for an anxiety disorder generally (particularly overanxious disorder or separation anxiety disorder) and scored higher on dimensional measures of anxiety/depression and somatic complaints. A logistic regression analysis revealed the following significant predictors of the development of OCD or OCD symptoms at 2-year follow-up: high symptom levels as measured by the Child Behavior Checklist (Achenbach, 1991), female gender of OCD parent, and certain aspects of family dysfunction.

Taken together, family studies of child probands or adult probands with early onset indicate that childhood onset OCD has a particularly large genetic contribution, with rates of OCD in first-degree relatives typically ranging from 11% to 23% compared with the 8.3% risk determined in a meta-analysis of families of adult probands. Childhood onset OCD is also characterized by distinct clinical features that have independently been demonstrated to correlate with increased genetic loading, including an increased likelihood of comorbid tics and symptoms related to symmetry/ordering (Alsobrook, Leckman, Goodman, Rasmussen, & Pauls, 1999; Lensi et al., 1996). Some investigators have argued that the increased aggregation of OCD seen in families of child probands, combined with its distinct clinical features, indicate that childhood onset OCD represents a distinct subtype that may be particularly useful for genetic studies (Miguel et al., 2005).

WHAT IS THE FAMILIAL RELATIONSHIP BETWEEN OCD AND OTHER PSYCHIATRIC DISORDERS? EVIDENCE FROM FAMILY STUDIES

A number of psychiatric disorders that are highly comorbid with OCD have also been shown to co-aggregate in families of adult OCD probands. Disorders most commonly classified as "obsessive-compulsive spectrum disorders" (Phillips, 2002) include tic disorders, body dysmorphic disorder, and trichotillomania. Tic disorders have been found at increased rates in relatives of adult (Grados et al., 2001; Pauls et al., 1995) and pediatric (do Rosario-Campos et al., 2005) probands in three large controlled family studies. For example, do Rosario-Campos et al. found that chronic tics were significantly more common in case compared with control relatives with an OR of 7.9. In contrast, Hanna, Himle, and colleagues (2005), did not find significantly elevated rates of chronic tics in first-degree relatives of pediatric probands, a finding that the authors attributed to relatively high base-rates of tics in the control relatives and a small sample size limiting their power to detect differences. In another small controlled family study including 35 pediatric probands, only 1% of case relatives of OCD probands had a chronic tic disorder compared with no control relatives, consistent with the low rates of OCD noted in both groups in the same study (Reddy et al., 2001).

In contrast with tics, comparatively little is known regarding the familial relationship between OCD and other putative OCD spectrum disorders. A well-designed family study from the Johns Hopkins group revealed increased rates of body dysmorphic disorder (OR = 5.4) and grooming disorders (including trichotillomania, pathological skin-picking, and pathological nail-biting, overall OR = 1.8) in relatives of adult OCD probands compared with control relatives (Bienvenu et al., 2000). These findings are consistent with findings from studies of probands with BDD (Phillips, Menard, Fay, & Weisberg, 2005) and trichotillomania (Lenane et al., 1992) in which OCD was more common in relative of case compared with control probands. In contrast, no significant increased risk to first-degree relatives was found for impulse control disorders such as pathological gambling (Bienvenu et al., 2000). Despite a hypothesized link between OCD and eating disorders, the Hopkins group similarly failed to find a familial association between these disorders (Bienvenu et al., 2000). However, family studies of eating disorders (ED) have suggested that there may be a link in a subgroup of patients, given that an elevated rate of OCD has been reported in the first-degree relatives of ED probands (Bellodi et al., 2001). Interestingly, some investigators have suggested a possible link between eating disorder, anorexia, and perfectionism, with perfectionism being the factor that is common to the other two disorders and perhaps representing a heritable trait (Serpell, Livingstone, Neiderman, & Lask, 2002). Perfectionism is a prominent feature of obsessive-compulsive personality disorder, which has also been reported to be more prevalent in relatives of OCD compared with case relatives (Samuels et al., 2000).

Although obsessive-compulsive behaviors are common in individuals with pervasive developmental disorders (PDD, also referred to as autism spectrum disorders), to our knowledge, no studies have systematically investigated the prevalence of PDD symptoms in relatives of OCD probands. However, family studies of adults with PDD indicate that obsessive-compulsive symptoms (Kano, Ohta, Nagai, Pauls, & Leckman, 2004) and OCD (Bolton, Pickles, Murphy, & Rutter, 1998; Wilcox, Tsuang, Schnurr, & Baida-Fragoso, 2003) are more common in relatives compared with control relatives. Furthermore, it has been reported that autistic children with high rates of repetitive behaviors, particularly those with high scores on a measure of narrow restricted interests and rituals, are more likely than autistic individuals without these features to have one or more parents with OCD or obsessive-compulsive symptoms (Hollander, King, Delaney, Smith, & Silverman, 2003).

Taken together, the family studies just described suggest that there may be common genetic determinants underlying these OCD spectrum disorders. Some authors have proposed a broader "affective spectrum" in which a variety of mood and anxiety disorders, including OCD, are influenced by a common underlying genetic etiology (Hudson et al., 2003). Consistent with this hypothesis is the finding that neuroticism, a dimensionally measured trait believed to influence a broad range of mood and anxiety disorders, is elevated in relatives of OCD probands compared with case relatives (Samuels et al., 2000). Generalized anxiety disorder (GAD) has also been found to be more common in relatives of OCD adult probands compared with control relatives in two controlled family studies (Black, Noyes, Goldstein, & Blum, 1992; Nestadt et al., 2001), and in the relatives of early onset (but not late onset) OCD probands in another controlled study (Carter, Pollock, Suvak, & Pauls, 2004). In order to rule out the possibility that the co-aggregation of OCD results from secondary development of anxiety or depression in OCD-affected relatives rather than common underlying risk factors, it is important to analyze whether the increased rates of other disorders in relatives occurs *independent* of the relative's diagnosis. In the Hopkins family study, the co-aggregation of GAD and OCD was found to be independent of the relative's OCD status, whereas in the study by Carter et al. the increased risk for GAD (and panic disorder and major depressive disorder) was only present in OCD-affected relatives. Therefore, further research is needed to clarify the familial relationship between OCD and GAD and whether these disorders are likely to result from common genetic risk factors.

IS OCD DUE TO ONE GENE OR MANY?
WHAT IS THE MODE OF INHERITANCE FOR OCD?
SEGREGATION STUDIES

Once family studies have indicated that a disorder aggregates in families, the next step is to conduct segregation studies to determine the mode of inheritance. Segregation analyses may be less informative in complex disorders like OCD, in which multiple loci are likely involved, as compared to disorders in which variance of a trait is primarily due to a single inherited locus (Elston, 2000). An early "classical" segregation analysis (Nicolini et al., 1991) of families of child OCD probands suggesting a dominant model of inheritance was limited by the assumption of single-locus Mendelian inheritance. Segregation analyses of OCD published since then have used "complex" segregation analysis that enables testing of a variety of alternative modes of genetic and nongenetic transmission in addition to simple Mendelian models. Four complex segregation analyses of OCD have been reported: three based on families of adult OCD probands (Alsobrook et al., 1999; Cavallini, Pasquale, Bellodi, & Smeraldi, 1999; Nestadt, Lan et al., 2000), and one based on families of pediatric OCD probands (Hanna, Fingerlin, Himle, & Boehnke, 2005). Cavallini et al. reported results consistent with a gene of major effect when using a narrow OCD phenotype, but not when broadening the phenotype to include tic disorders, and the specific mode of inheritance could not be determined at the level of statistical significance. A limitation of this study was that only 35% of first-degree relatives were assessed directly, and the authors also did not state whether the analysis was adjusted for the age of the relatives. Using similar analytic methods to Cavallini et al., Nestadt and colleagues found strong evidence for a major gene combined with significant residual familial effects (possibly due to additional polygenic influences) and either dominant or codominant inheritance. Families of female probands exhibited a pattern of inheritance consistent with either a dominant or codominant model (similar to the total sample), whereas in the families of male probands there was no evidence to support one of the Mendelian models over the others. Alsobrook et al. were only able to reject the "no transmission" model in their complex segregation analysis of OCD diagnosis, consistent with genetic transmission but not consistent with a specific model of inheritance. However, they did demonstrate involvement of a major locus in families ascertained according to high symptom-based factor scores for symmetry/ordering.

A complex segregation analysis of pediatric subjects (10 to 17 years of age) based on a sample of 35 families of child OCD probands and 17 families of control probands has recently been reported by Hanna, Fingerlin, et al. (2005), using similar analytic methods to Nestadt, Lan et al. (2000) and Cavallini et al. (1999). However, unlike previous segregation analyses their model explicitly incorporated age at onset. Like Nestadt, Lan et al., their results were most consistent with a major locus in addition to residual familial effects and either a dominant or codominant model of inheritance. Age of onset did not vary depending on whether OCD probands had an affected parent, in contrast with a report of earlier age of onset in the younger generation in multiply affected families of OCD individuals (Cavallini, Albertazzi, Bianchi, & Bellodi, 2002). This latter observation of decreased age of onset with succeeding generations suggests "anticipation," a phenomenon that merits further investigation as it has been found in other genetic disorders (e.g., Huntington's Disease) and suggests specific genetic mechanisms.

Taken together, the segregation analyses suggest that transmission of OCD is influenced by genes of major effect, likely occurring on a background of additional polygenic effects. The mode of inheritance is less clear, although two studies have suggested an additive (codominant) or dominant model of inheritance.

IS OCD DUE TO GENETIC OR ENVIRONMENTAL CAUSES? EVIDENCE FROM TWIN STUDIES

For a comprehensive recent review of twin studies in OCD, please refer to Van Grootheest et al. (2006). Most of the studies in which one twin met criteria for OCD had significant methodological limitations including small sample sizes, lack of standardized diagnostic criteria and uncertain determination of monozygotic/dizygotic twin status. An early Japanese twin study (Inouye, 1965) reported on a sample of 14 Japanese twin pairs (10 monozygotic, 4 dizygotic) in which one twin was characterized by "obsessive-compulsive reaction." Concordance in this study was increased in monozygotic twins (80%) compared with dizygotic twins (33%). The largest twin study (Carey & Gottesman, 1981) consisted of 15 monozygotic and 15 dizygotic twin pairs from the Maudsley Twin Registry. Concordance rates were again increased in the monozygotic twins (87%) compared with the dizygotic twins (47%) for the phenotype of "obsessive-compulsive neurosis with or without treatment."

Another approach has been the study of large samples of nonclinical twins in which obsessive-compulsive symptoms have been assessed through self-report measures. Such studies enable estimates of heritability, the proportion of variance in a trait that is attributable to additive genetic effects. In a sample of 419 MZ and DZ twins (mixed gender), heritability of 47% was reported for obsessive-compulsive symptoms measured using the Leyton Obsessional Inventory (Clifford, Murray, & Fulker, 1984). A larger study of 1054 unselected adult female twin pairs indicated a heritability of 33% for obsessions and 26% for compulsions based on 20 items from the Padua Inventory (Jonnal, Gardner, Prescott, & Kendler, 2000). One of the limitations of this study is the use of the Padua Inventory (Burns, Keortge, Formea, & Sternberger, 1996), which did not contain many common symptoms of OCD such as symmetry, ordering, counting and ritual obsessions and compulsions.

Recently, two large twin studies using data from parent reports of child symptoms have shed light on the heritability of childhood obsessive-compulsive symptoms. A twin study of anxiety-related behaviors involved mothers of 4,564 pairs of 4-year-old twins (1,541 MZ, 3,032 DZ) who had completed a 16-item questionnaire including anxiety-related items gleaned from various measures with well-established reliability and validity in child psychiatric populations. Confirmatory factor analysis of this questionnaire produced five factors including an obsessive-compulsive behaviors (OCB) factor with 4 items. The OCB factor had a heritability of 65% in univariate analyses, and the genetic variance for OCB had very little correlation with other anxiety-related behaviors. This data suggested that the genetic influences on OCB in preschool children are substantial and are distinct from genetic factors influencing other anxiety-related behaviors (Eley et al., 2003).

A second pediatric twin study involved a total of 10,110 twin pairs (3,830 MZ, 6,280 DZ) with ages ranging from 7 to 12 years of age ascertained in the United States and the Netherlands. The measure used in this study was based on eight OCD-related items contained within the parent-completed Child Behavior Checklist (CBCL-OCS; Achenbach, 1991). The authors had previously established this scale as predictive of a DSM–IV diagnosis of OCD. The authors found that OCB in children 10 years old or younger was substantially influenced by genetic factors (heritability 55%) with the remainder of the variance being accounted for by nonshared environmental influences. In the older (12-year-old) twins shared environmental factors also play a significant role (Hudziak et al., 2004). This study suggests that pediatric OCD has a high genetic contribution, which appears to be higher than that demonstrated in studies of adult OCD twin pairs. However, direct comparison of twin studies based on self-report measures is difficult, there has been inconsistancy between studies with regard to instruments used to assess OCB.

In summary, family and segregation studies support a substantial genetic contribution to obsessive-compulsive behaviors. Genetic loading appears elevated in pediatric OCD as demonstrated by increased odds ratios in relatives of child onset probands. The twin studies resulted in highly variable heritability estimates ranging from 26% to 65%, with the higher estimates derived from studies of children. These studies provide an essential foundation for the molecular genetic studies described in the next section.

MOLECULAR GENETIC APPROACHES TO OCD

Genome Scans in OCD

Two complementary approaches used in molecular genetic studies of complex disorders are linkage studies and association studies of candidate genes. The linkage approach typically involves the collection of large pedigrees or affected relative pairs (usually siblings). The entire genome is scanned using evenly spaced, anonymous DNA markers in order to determine chromosomal segments shared by affected individuals within families, thereby indicating the approximate chromosomal location of the susceptibility gene(s). The strength of linkage is summarized in various ways, the most widely used method being the "Logarithm of the Odds" (LOD) score, with the odds reflecting the likelihood of linkage being present divided by the likelihood of no linkage. Sometimes the linkage approach will be used on a selected region of the genome identified in a previous whole genome scan. Although linkage studies have the advantage of not requiring *a priori* hypotheses regarding which genes are involved, as compared with candidate gene studies they have limited power to detect genes of small or modest effect (i.e., a relative risk of less than two; Risch & Merikangas, 1996).

Two genome scans for OCD have been conducted to date (Hanna et al., 2002; Shugart et al., 2006). In the first genome scan, a region of suggestive linkage was found in chromosome 9p24 based on seven multigenerational large pedigrees in which there was a pediatric proband with OCD and at least two affected relatives. In this study, initial genotyping performed on 56 subjects resulted in a dominant parametric LOD score of 2.25 peaking in 9p24. Fine mapping of 9p using 13 microsatellites at a higher average density in the original sample plus 10 additional subjects led to a slightly reduced LOD score of 1.97 in 9p24. The 9p24 finding was subsequently replicated through linkage analysis on 38 small nuclear pedigrees using the same set of 13 microsatellites (Willour et al., 2004). Willour et al. noted substantial heterogeneity within their sample, with only 59% of their families showing evidence for linkage with 9p24. Interestingly, it was previously reported that a patient with Tourette's Disorder and OCD had only one rather than the usual two copies of 9p (monosomy; Taylor et al., 1991).

A second genome scan was based on a large sample of over 219 families recruited from the multi-site OCD Collaborative Genetics Study led by investigators at Johns Hopkins University. Using multi-point nonparametric linkage analysis, the strongest linkage signal was identified at 3q27~28 (LOD = 2.67, suggestive linkage), with weaker but still suggestive signals at 1q, 7p and 15p. The investigators noted that 3q27~28 contains the gene encoding the serotonin 3C receptor, suggesting a strong candidate gene not previously investigated in OCD (Shugart et al., 2006).

Candidate Gene Studies in OCD

Using the candidate gene approach, individuals are analyzed for variation in genes hypothesized *a priori* to be implicated in the disorder. The simplest design for a candidate gene study compares affected subjects and matched population-based controls. However, a significant disadvantage of traditional case-control methods is the problem of population stratification (Ewens & Spielman, 2001), in which false positive results occur due to detection of genetic differences between cases and control populations that are unrelated to the illness. Recently, a variation of the case-control design known as genomic control (GC) has been developed in which the problem of population stratification is controlled by adjusting results for baseline differences between cases and controls for multiple random markers (Devlin, Roeder, & Wasserman, 2001). This method has only become feasible with the advent of relatively high-throughput automated genotyping techniques and has not yet been applied to OCD. A more established alternative to the case-control design is the use of family-based methods. The prototypical family-based association method is the transmission disequilibrium test (TDT; Spielman, McGinnis, & Ewens, 1993). In its most basic form, the TDT is based on a comparison of the number of times a risk allele (variant) is transmitted from parents to an affected offspring compared to the number of times it is not transmitted, with increased transmission of the risk allele (above the 50% expected) constituting an association between the allele and the disorder (Ewens & Spielman, 2001). The TDT has been shown to have increased power to detect genes of small or modest effect compared with linkage methods (RR < 2; Risch & Merikangas, 1996). The need for DNA from family members can limit the feasibility of this method, however this is less of a problem with childhood OCD because parents and siblings are typically available and often willing to participate.

In the following section, the results of candidate gene studies are described, including a small number of studies focusing on child and adolescent subjects (Dickel et al., 2006; Mossner et al., 2005; Veenstra-VanderWeele et al., 2001; Walitza et al., 2004; Walitza et al., 2002), and the majority based on adult OCD probands.

Candidate Genes Affecting Serotonin Neurotransmission

The majority of studies to date have focused on candidates in the serotonin system. The "serotonergic hypothesis" of OCD, is based primarily on the selective efficacy of serotonin reuptake inhibitor (SRI) medications in the treatment of OCD (Pigott & Sheay, 2000), in addition to other less consistent evidence from studies measuring peripheral markers of serotonin (5-HT) and biological challenges with serotonergic agents (reviewed in Fitzgerald, McMaster, Paulson, & Rosenberg, 1999). Although most of these studies have used population-based controls, and are therefore susceptible to population stratification, an increasing number of studies have recently been published using family-based designs. Association studies have been conducted for the following serotonin genes: serotonin transporter, serotonin 1B, serotonin 2A, serotonin 2C, and tryptophan hydroxylase 1 and 2, with mixed findings overall but more negative than positive reports.

The gene encoding the serotonin transporter (5-HTT) is regarded as a prime candidate gene for OCD given that this presynaptic transporter protein is the primary target of SSRI's. Functional neuroimaging studies of the serotonin transporter in adult OCD patients have produced variable findings, with reports of elevated (Pogarell et al., 2003), reduced (Stengler-Wenzke, Muller, Angermeyer, Sabri, & Hesse, 2004) and unaltered 5-HTT availability (Simpson et al., 2003). A functional variant known as the serotonin transporter-linked polymorphic region (5HTLLPR), located in the promoter region of the gene, consists of an insertion (long allele, L) or deletion (short allele, S) of a 44 base pair sequence. Expression of the 5-HTT protein is decreased in individuals with one or two copies of the S allele compared with individuals with two copies of the L allele, consistent with a dominant effect of the S allele (Lesch et al., 1996).

Investigations of the 5HTTLPR in OCD have been mixed. A case-control study (Bengel, Greenberg et al., 1999) and a small family-based study (McDougle, Epperson, Price, & Gelernter, 1998), both suggested that the long allele of 5HTTLPR confers susceptibility to OCD. Similarly, a recent study reported a lower frequency of the s allele in 24 female patients with OCD compared with controls (Baca-Garcia et al., 2005). However, there have been eight negative reports: five relied on case-control methods (Billett et al., 1997; Cavallini, Di Bella, Siliprandi, Malchiodi, & Bellodi, 2002; Frisch et al., 2000; Kinnear et al., 2000; Meira-Lima et al., 2004), two included both case-control and family-based samples (Camarena, Rinetti, Cruz, Hernandez et al., 2001; Chabane et al., 2004), and one involved TDT analysis of child OCD probands and their parents (Walitza et al., 2004).

Recently, a new single nucleotide polymorphism (SNP) within the 5HTTLPR L allele has been described that alters transcriptional activity. The discovery of this variant effectively makes the 5HTTLPR a "tri-allelic" system and forces a reexamination of previously published association studies involving this polymorphism. The high activity L_A allele (frequency 50% in U.S. Caucasians) is associated with increased transcription, whereas the L_G allele (frequency 15%) and S alleles are both associated with decreased transcription. A collaborative study between David Goldman's group at NIH/NIAA and our group recently discovered a positive association between the L_A allele and OCD in a case-control as well as an independent family-based sample (Hu et al., 2006).

In addition to the study of the L_A/L_G variant just described, there is currently intense interest in 5-HTT polymorphisms outside of 5HTTLPR that may be associated with OCD. A variable number of tandem repeats (VNTR) polymorphism in the second intron of 5-HTT has not been systematically studied in OCD to our knowledge, although preliminary data from our own sample suggests that no association is present. Recently, a rare A/G transversion in transmembrane domain 8 has been discovered that produces an isoleucine-valine substitution (I425V). The rare G (valine) variant was identified in two OCD probands and their families and co-segregated with a rather severe, atypical phenotype including multiple comorbid disorders (Ozaki et al., 2003). Expression studies indicate that this is a "gain of function" mutation, which produces an approximately twofold increase in serotonin uptake activity (Kilic, Murphy, & Rudnick, 2003). Recently, an independent group has reported the 425V variant to be present in three OCD patients and one control subject (Delorme, Betancur, Wagner et al., 2005) Cumulative data from the 457 OCD patients and 884 control subjects screened in these two studies suggest that the 425V variant is rare (frequency approximately 1.1% in Caucasians) but significantly more common in OCD patients compared with controls.

A recent association study in families of autistic individuals (Sutcliffe et al., 2005) may have important implications for the role of 5-HTT in OCD, and also suggests that investigators need to shift their focus from studying any single variant such as 5HTTLPR and test for multiple functional variants that are now being discovered in this intensively studied gene (Kraft, Slager, McGrath, & Hamilton, 2005; Prasad et al., 2005). Specifically, preferential transmission of *multiple* variants was associated with autism. In addition, the variants were associated with rigid-compulsive behaviors in autism, providing further evidence that this gene may be involved in the obsessive-compulsive spectrum (Sutcliffe et al., 2005).

A second serotonergic candidate susceptibility gene for OCD is the gene encoding the serotonin 1B receptor (5HT1B, formerly known as 5HT1Dbeta), a presynaptic autoreceptor that regulates serotonin release. A number of association studies in OCD have examined the common G861C polymorphism in 5HT1B, a "silent" variant that occurs within the coding region but does not cause changes in the amino acid sequence (Lappalainen et al., 1995). Our group was the first to reported increased transmission of the more common G allele of 5HT1B-G861C in a family-based study (Mundo, Richter, Sam, Macciardi, & Kennedy, 2000), a finding that was replicated in a larger sample (Mundo et al., 2002). Two other groups have reported positive findings in male probands—a Mexican family-based study (Camarena, Aguilar, Loyzaga, & Nicolini, 2004) and an Afrikaner case-control study (Lochner et al., 2004). However, two negative family-based studies have been published (Di Bella, Cavallini, & Bellodi, 2002; Walitza et al., 2004). Possible reasons for this inconsistency include genetic heterogeneity, low power due to small sample sizes, or the possibility that a variant other than G861C is associated with OCD. Our group is currently genotyping additional 5HT1B polymorphisms (Sicard et al., 2004), including variants that have been shown to influence transcriptional activity (Duan et al., 2003).

A number of candidate gene studies have focused on the gene encoding the serotonin 2A receptor (5HT2A), utilizing the closely linked markers -1438G/A and T102C. The -1438G/A variant may affect gene expression due to its location in the promoter region, though its actual functional effects have not been established; the T102C variant is located in the coding region but does not change amino acid sequence and has no known functional effect. Positive associations between OCD and either the -1438G/A or T102C variant have been reported in case-control studies of adult (Enoch, Greenberg, Murphy, & Goldman, 2001; Enoch et al., 1998; Hemmings et al., 2003) and child (Walitza et al., 2002) populations. A sex-specific finding of association between the -1438A allele and OCD in females only was reported in a population consisting largely of subjects with early onset OCD (Enoch et al., 2001). A recent Turkish case-control study revealed no association between -1438 G/A or T102C and OCD diagnosis, although these variants were associated with symptom severity within the OCD group (Tot, Erdal, Yazici, Yazici, & Metin, 2003). Three other case-control samples found no association with the T102C variant (Frisch et al., 2000; Meira-Lima et al., 2004; Nicolini et al., 1996). Although their study did not implicate the T102C polymorphism, a Brazilian group found an association with the C516T variant, an example of the importance of examining more than one polymorphism in a gene (Meira-Lima et al., 2004). There have been no published family-based association studies examining 5HT2A in OCD.

No association with OCD diagnosis was demonstrated in two case-control studies examining the Cys23Ser variant of the gene encoding the serotonin 2C (5HT2C) receptor (Cavallini, Di Bella, Pasquale, Henin, & Bellodi, 1998; Frisch et al., 2000). Two studies examining tryptophan hydroxylase 1 (TPH1) in OCD produced negative findings (Frisch et al., 2000; Walitza et al., 2004), which is not surprising given more recent data revealing that TPH1 is not expressed in most brain tissues (Walther et al., 2003). It is now known that TPH2 is the enzyme responsible for serotonin synthesis in the brain, and two variants within the gene for TPH2 were therefore studied in a sample of 71 parent-offspring trios ascertained through probands with onset of symptoms in childhood or adolescence. These investigators found that a G-C haplotype of these two variants (one of which is located in the putative promoter region) was significantly associated with OCD (Mossner, Walitza, Geller et al., 2005). Further study of these and other TPH2 variants in OCD is clearly warranted.

As evident from the preceding paragraphs, only a limited number of serotonin genes and variants have been examined in OCD. In order to discover new markers that impact on serotonin neurotransmission that might be useful for genetic association studies of OCD, a group of investigators at the University of Chicago has published two studies involving screening for novel gene candidates in samples including patients with OCD. In one study, mutation screening of the serotonin 2B receptor revealed one SNP in intron 1 (Kim, Veenstra-VanderWeele et al., 2000). In a second study, the gene encoding NESP55, which is believed to be a precursor of a peptide with 5HT1B receptor antagonist activity, was screened and six novel SNP's identified. In addition, the investigators identified a deletion coding region polymorphism in one OCD proband, which was inherited in a Mendelian fashion in the family of this individual, always through maternal inheritance (Kim, Gonen, Hanna, Leventhal, & Cook, 2000). The variants identified in these two studies have yet to be tested for association with OCD.

Candidate Genes Affecting Dopamine Neurotransmission

Dopamine genes have also been investigated in candidate gene studies, based on a number of lines of evidence including: the putative role of dopamine in tic disorders (hypothesized to be genetically linked to OCD), the well-established efficacy of dopamine antagonists as augmenting agents for OCD patients refractory to SRI treatment (Bloch et al., 2006), and the fact that stereotypic behaviors resembling compulsions or complex tics have been induced in humans or animals with various dopaminergic agents such as amphetamine and L-Dopa (Berridge, Aldridge, Houchard, & Zhuang, 2005; Joel & Doljansky, 2003). A functional 48 bp VNTR polymorphism located in the third exon of the dopamine D4 receptor (DRD4) gene has attracted a lot of interest in psychiatric genetics (Tarazi, Zhang, & Baldessarini, 2004). An association has been demonstrated between decreased transmission of the 2-repeat allele of the DRD4-VNTR using overlapping family-based ($p = .005$) and case-control ($p = .02$) samples drawn from the same French population. There were no significant differences between patients with and without tics although given the modest sample size (55 trios) the power to conduct such a sub-analysis was low (Millet et al., 2003). Our group reported reduced frequency of the 2/4 genotype and a trend towards decreased frequency of the 2-repeat allele of the DRD4-VNTR in OCD cases compared with controls (Billett et al., 1998), however we have since failed to replicate this finding using the family-based association test (unpublished results). In an Israeli Jewish population, no association was found in the total sample, although the 7-repeat allele was found to be significantly less frequent in OCD patients compared with controls when considering only the non-Ashkenazi Jewish subjects ($p = .04$). However, as pointed out by the authors, these results would fail to achieve significance when corrected for the multiple polymorphisms tested in this study (Frisch et al., 2000). Similarly, another case-control study reported a trend towards a lower frequency of the 7-repeat allele of DRD4 in an Afrikaner OCD sample (Hemmings et al., 2003), and the same group later reported that the 7-repeat allele was significantly less frequent in early-onset compared with late onset OCD probands (Hemmings et al., 2004). An earlier case-control study demonstrated an increase in frequency of the 7-repeat allele in patients with OCD with tics compared to those without (Cruz et al., 1997), consistent with two family-based association studies of Tourette Syndrome patients suggesting an association between TS and the 7-repeat allele

(Diaz-Anzaldua et al., 2004; Grice et al., 1996). Overall, methodological limitations in most of the studies described preclude making any conclusions regarding the association between the DRD4-VNTR and OCD, however the preliminary positive findings and functional importance of this variant should provide impetus for further study.

One early study of 157 OCD subjects and 162 controls of Italian descent examined another null mutation in exon 1 of the DRD4 gene, which is characterized by a 13 bp deletion that is believed to result in a truncated, nonfunctional D4 receptor. No differences were found between cases and controls for this variant (Di Bella, Catalano, Cichon, & Nothen, 1996). Studies of DRD2, DRD3, and the dopamine transporter using case-control methods have been negative to date (Billett et al., 1998; Catalano et al., 1994; Frisch et al., 2000; Hemmings et al., 2003; Nicolini et al., 1996). An early study that screened the DRD2 gene for mutations in a group of OCD patients found a single variant in exon 6 that did not differ between subjects with and without tics (Novelli, Nobile, Diaferia, Sciuto, & Catalano, 1994).

Candidate Genes for Enzymes That Metabolize Monoamine Neurotransmitters

Other investigators have reported that variants for genes encoding catechol-o-methyltransferase (COMT) and monoamine oxidase A (MAOA), enzymes that metabolize monoamine neurotransmitters, are associated with OCD in a sex-specific fashion. COMT is located on Chromosome 22q11, a region that is deleted in velo-cardio-facial syndrome. This syndrome has been associated with obsessive-compulsive symptoms in adults (Gothelf et al., 2004) and children (Arnold, Siegel-Bartelt, Cytrynbaum, Teshima, & Schachar, 2001). A functional variant involving a valine/methionine substitution at codon 158 has been identified that leads to a 3- to 4-fold difference in the activity of COMT. Given that dopamine and noradrenaline are the normal substrate of this enzyme, alterations in COMT activity have potential functional relevance for OCD. One group of investigators initially reported that the Met/Met (low/low with respect to enzyme activity) genotype was associated with OCD in a case-control sample in males only (Karayiorgou et al., 1997), and later went on to demonstrate that the Met allele was preferentially transmitted to male but not female probands in a family-based association study (Karayiorgou et al., 1999). However, the opposite gender association between transmission of the low activity allele to *female* rather than male probands has also been reported (Alsobrook, et al., 2002). Our group, in collaboration with the University of Buffalo, found no gender-specific association but did demonstrate an association with homozygosity of either allele (i.e., met/met or val/val genotype) in families of OCD probands (Schindler, Richter, Kennedy, Pato, & Pato, 2000). A small case-control analysis of an Afrikaner population revealed a positive association with the heterozygous genotype of the COMT-Val158Met variant (Niehaus et al., 2001). Meta-analyses based on published case-control (Karayiorgou et al., 1997; Niehaus et al., 2001; Ohara, Nagai, Suzuki, & Ochiai, 1998) and family-based (Alsobrook, et al., 2002; Karayiorgou et al., 1999; Schindler et al., 2000) studies indicated that there was insufficient evidence to support an association between COMT and OCD whether or not the data were stratified by gender (Azzam & Mathews, 2003). Two more recent case-control studies (Erdal et al., 2003; Meira-Lima et al., 2004) have not demonstrated an association between COMT and OCD, although one of these studies reported that patients with the Met allele exhibited poorer insight compared with OCD patients without this allele (Erdal., 2003). In the only study to examine a COMT variant other than Val158Met, no association was found between OCD and a promoter variant lying next to an estrogen-response element (Kinnear et al., 2001). Overall, these findings do not provide strong support for a role for COMT in conferring susceptibility to OCD, whether or not the effect of gender is considered. However, it should be noted that even considered in aggregate the number of subjects assessed (282 cases in the case-control and 269 affected individuals in family-based studies) may not be large enough to detect a gene of small effect, particularly one that is active only in a subgroup of OCD individuals or in a particular environmental context.

More consistent gender-specific effects have been reported for the gene encoding Monoamine oxidase A (MAOA), an enzyme that metabolizes dopamine and serotonin. Such sex-specific inheritance is not surprising given that MAOA is located on the X chromosome. Two polymorphisms in linkage disequilibrium with one another, identified by the restriction enzymes *Fnu4H1* and *EcoRV* respectively, have been studied in OCD. Both variants do not change the amino acid sequence but have been demonstrated to produce changes in enzyme activity (Hotamisligil & Breakefield, 1991). In an early case-control study, the low-activity allele of the MAOA/*EcoRV* polymorphism was found to be significantly more frequent in OCD females (0.86) compared with controls (0.6), whereas the allele frequencies were not significantly different in the total OCD sample or in OCD males compared with controls. They did not replicate this finding in an expanded case-control sample (Camarena, Cruz, de la Fuente, & Nicolini, 1998). However, in 51 trios (32 with female probands, 19 male probands drawn from the case-control sample), they were able to demonstrate a sex-specific association between the low-activity allele of the MAOA/*EcoRV* polymorphism consistent with their original findings (Camarena, Rinetti, Cruz, Gomez et al., 2001). This finding should be interpreted with caution given the small size of the subdivided sample of trios. However, the finding has been replicated in a study demonstrating increased transmission of the high activity allele of MAOA/*EcoRV* to male OCD cases and increased transmission of the low activity allele to female probands (Lochner et al., 2004). Similarly, another group of investigators has reported preferential transmission of the high-activity allele of the Fnu4H1 variant to male OCD probands. This association was more pronounced in the presence of comorbid major depressive disorder (Karayiorgou et al., 1999). These intriguing findings of sex-specific association with MAOA require further replication and explication, including genotyping of additional polymorphisms, such as a VNTR promoter polymorphism for which the high activity allele has been associated with Tourette's Syndrome in a family-based association study (Diaz-Anzaldua et al., 2004).

Candidate Genes Affecting Glutamate Neurotransmission

A few investigators have begun testing genes in the glutamate system, based on mounting evidence for a role of altered glutamate neurotransmission within cortico-striatal-thalamic circuits in the pathogenesis of OCD (Rosenberg & Keshavan, 1998). Indirect support for this hypothesis is provided by an animal model in which transgenic mice with increased cortico-striatal glutamate output exhibit a phenotype reminiscent of OCD and OCD spectrum disorders including generalized behavioral perseveration, compulsive leaping, grooming-associated pulling and biting of skin and hair (similar to trichotillomania), and tics (Nordstrom & Burton, 2002). More direct support for the role of glutamate in OCD is provided by recent investigation using proton magnetic resonance spectroscopy (1-H MRS) suggesting a pharmacologically reversible glutamatergically mediated thalamo- cortical-striatal dysfunction in OCD (Rosenberg et al., 2000; Rosenberg et al., 2004). Two candidate gene studies of glutamate receptor genes have been published. Our group initially tested the glutamate receptor, ionotropic, NMDA subunit 2B gene (GRIN2B). Focusing on the 3'-untranslated region of GRIN2B, three informative markers were genotyped (5072T/G, 5806A/C, and 5988T/C). Positive associations were identified between OCD diagnosis and the GRIN2B-5072G allele ($p = 0.014$) and the 5072G – 5988T haplotype ($p = 0.002$; Arnold et al., 2004). Associations between OCD diagnosis and variants tightly linked to the GRIN2B 5072G – 5988T haplotype have since been replicated in two independent family-based samples (Arnold, Sicard, Hanna et al., 2005). In a study of two genes encoding kainate glutamate receptors (GRIK2 and GRIK3), nominally significant undertransmission of a single variant of GRIK2 (867Ile) was demonstrated, a finding that should be cautiously interpreted given the low number of informative transmissions for this marker (Delorme et al., 2004).

The glutamate transporter gene SLC1A1 is located within the 9p24 region, the strongest linkage peak identified in the genome scan of Hanna and colleagues (2005) just described. Therefore, it represents an excellent positional candidate for OCD as well as having possible functional relevance given the putative role of glutamate in OCD pathogenesis. Two groups have recently reported an association between SLC1A1 and OCD. Our group genotyped nine single nucleotide polymorphisms (SNPs) spanning SLC1A1 in families of 157 Caucasian OCD probands (mostly adults). After correction for permutation testing, positive associations were found with variants rs301434 ($p = 0.006$) and rs301435 ($p = 0.03$) lying in a single haplotype block. Furthermore, a specific two marker haplotype within this block was significantly associated with OCD ($p = 0.005$). Interestingly, these single-locus and haplotype associations were statistically significant in transmissions to male but not female offspring (Arnold, Sicard, Burroughs, Richter, & Kennedy, 2006).

Dickel and colleagues (2006) independently identified an association with SLC1A1 in a sample of 71 children and adolescents with OCD and their parents. Interestingly, the haplotype they identified was located towards the 3' end of the gene adjacent to our association signal, and as with our sample this finding was specific to male probands. This group of investigators also detected a deletion in the 3' flanking region of SLC1A1 in a single large multigenerational pedigree containing multiple affected individuals (Dickel et al., 2006). An earlier study by the same group reported negative findings for SLC1A1 based on analysis of only two variants in a smaller sample (Veenstra-VanderWeele et al., 2001). Modest association with OCD was also reported for two microsatellite markers flanking SLC1A1, GATA62F03 ($p = 0.02$) and D9S288 ($p = 0.05$) in a third independent sample using family-based methods (Willour et al., 2004). Taken together, three studies combined with the replicated linkage to 9p24 all strongly suggest a role for SLC1A1 in OCD, particularly in males. However, further research, including genotyping of additional known variants and possibly sequencing of the 3' region of SLC1A1 is needed to locate the actual functional variant(s) contributing to the OCD phenotype.

Other Candidate Genes

Brain-derived neurotrophic factor (BDNF) is a growth factor that has a variety of actions that may be relevant to OCD, including modulatory effects on serotonergic transmission (Mossner et al., 2000), effects on the differentiation of dopaminergic and serotonergic neurons (Eaton, Staley, Globus, & Whittemore, 1995; Studer et al., 1995; Zhou, Bradford, & Stern, 1994) and enhanced phosphorylation of the postsynaptic NMDA receptor subunit 1 (Suen et al., 1997). In a recent report of a large sample of 164 OCD trios, five variants (in significant linkage disequilibrium with one another) of the gene encoding BDNF were reported to be associated with OCD, including Val66Met, a functional variant that affects the amino acid sequence of the proBDNF protein (Hall, Dhilla, Charalambous, Gogos, & Karayiorgou, 2003). Haplotype analysis produced similarly positive results, and indicated that there may be a distinct BDNF haplotype, including the less frequent Met allele of Val66Met, which is undertransmitted to OCD probands and may therefore confer protection against the disorder. Undertransmission of a haplotype containing the Met allele has also been shown in two other studies examining BDNF in bipolar disorder (Neves-Pereira et al., 2002; Sklar et al., 2002), indicating that this haplotype may confer a general protective effect in other neuropsychiatric disorders as well as OCD. Given the known association of BDNF with mood disorders, the authors also repeated their analyses on families with probands with comorbid major depressive disorder, and did not find their results strengthened by the presence of comorbid MDD. Another interesting aspect to the study was that when the authors stratified their sample by age of onset, their results only remained positive in families of probands with OCD onset before 18 years of age, consistent with the family studies outlined above that have suggested increased genetic effects in families of younger probands. However, a recent analysis of BDNF-Val66Met in 67 parent–offspring trios ascertained through a child or adolescent with OCD produced negative findings (Mossner, Walitza, Lesch et al., 2005) as did our study of two BDNF variants in a family-based, mostly adult sample of 127 families (Zai, Arnold, Strauss et al., 2005).

With the identification of a subgroup of children with onset or exacerbation of symptoms following streptococcal infections, there has been increasing interest in the possible role of autoimmune processes in OCD (Arnold & Richter, 2001; Swedo, Leonard, & Rapoport, 2004). Based on this rationale, our group has examined the gene encoding myelin oligodendrocyte glycoprotein (MOG), a protein involved in mediation of interactions between myelin and the immune system, particularly as an activator of the complement cascade (Johns & Bernard, 1997). Using a family-based association strategy, we have demonstrated an association with OCD diagnosis and severity for the 459bp allele of a tetranucleotide repeat variant of MOG (MOG4) and an association with OCD diagnosis for a specific two-locus haplotype containing the same MOG4 variant (Zai et al., 2004). More recently, we conducted a family-based analysis of a single functional variant within the gene encoding the cytokine tumour necrosis-alpha (TNF-alpha) and did not demonstrate an association with OCD (Zai, Arnold, Burroughs, Richter, & Kennedy, 2006).

Interestingly, recent evidence of white matter abnormalities in OCD (Szeszko et al., 2005) suggest an additional rationale for studying MOG, namely its role in myelination. Based on a myelination hypothesis, a group based at Harvard recently reported an association between variation in oligodendrocyte lineage transcription factor 2 (Olig2) and OCD. Interestingly, the association was specific to the subgroup of 47 families in which the proband did not have comorbid Tourette's Disorder (Stewart et al., 2005). Associations with MOG and Olig2 suggest further research should be performed based on candidate genes influencing myelination.

Preliminary analyses of genes encoding receptors for GABA, the primary inhibitory neurotransmitter within cortico-striatal circuits, have been conducted by our group. A particularly intriguing GABA candidate is the gene encoding the $GABA_B$-beta1 receptor (GABBR1), which is of interest due both to its possible functional role in OCD and its genomic location close to the HLA region in 6p21.3, a region associated with a weak linkage signal (LOD score = 1.4) in the genome scan of Hanna and colleagues (2002). In a recent analysis of five variants spanning GABBR1 in a sample of 159 families, we identified trends towards biased transmission of one of the variants and OCD diagnosis and severity, as well as a trend towards biased transmission of a five-marker haplotype (Zai, Arnold, Burroughs et al., 2005). Analysis of a single variant of the $GABA_A$-gamma2 gene was negative in our sample of OCD families (Richter, Mundo, Sam, Swinson, & Kennedy, 2001). However, in a preliminary case-control analysis of 47 probands with body dysmorphic disorder (25 with primary diagnoses of BDD, 22 with primary diagnoses of OCD), our group found a positive association with this same variant of $GABA_A$-gamma2 (Tharmalingam et al., 2003). Though these latter results are preliminary and subject to confounding due to population stratification, they are interesting given the paucity of genetic studies in BDD.

Finally, the μ-opioid receptor was genotyped in families of OCD probands based on the rationale that OCD symptoms are exacerbated by opioid antagonists and alleviated by opioid agonists. This study revealed a nonsignificant trend for biased transmission of one marker, but no statistically significant association (Urraca, Camarena, Gomez-Caudillo, Esmer, & Nicolini, 2004).

In summary, although no susceptibility genes have been conclusively identified a small number of candidates appear relatively promising based on positive findings with at least one replication, including: 5HT1B, MAOA, GRIN2B and SLC1A1. Despite earlier conflicting findings, the 5-HTT gene remains of high interest, given the recent descriptions of previously unrecognized functional variants that may be associated with OCD. A number of other candidate gene associations just described have yet to be replicated but merit further study due to preliminary positive findings coupled with a good rationale for studying the gene.

NOVEL APPROACHES TO THE OCD PHENOTYPE: SYMPTOM DIMENSIONS, PHARMACOGENETICS, AND ENDOPHENOTYPES

The clinical heterogeneity of OCD greatly complicates the search for susceptibility genes. Phenotypic heterogeneity has begun to be addressed through examination of specific factors generated by analyses of the Yale-Brown Obsessive-compulsive Scale (Goodman et al., 1989a, 1989b). Although there have been minor differences with regard to the symptoms contained in each factor, multiple factor analyses of adult samples have consistently identified three to five symptom dimensions, which have been associated with distinct neurobiological profiles and differential treatment response (reviewed in Mataix-Cols, do Rosario-Campos, & Leckman, 2005). There is also evidence that symptom dimensions are quite temporally stable, with changes in symptoms typically occurring within rather than between dimensions (Rufer, Grothusen, Mass, Peter, & Hand, 2005). It has recently been demonstrated that the factor structure of children with OCD based on the Children's Yale-Brown Obsessive-compulsive Scale (CY-BOCS; Scahill et al., 1997) scale is remarkably similar to that in adults (Stewart, 2005). The evidence supporting hoarding as a distinct symptom dimension is particularly robust (Mataix-Cols et al., 2005).

There is evidence from family and segregation analyses, as well as a small number of candidate gene studies, that OCD symptom dimensions may have distinct genetic correlates. Interestingly, there has been converging evidence that the symmetry/ordering dimension may have a particularly strong genetic component. Three independent groups (including our own) have identified an increased rate of OCD in first-degree relatives of OCD probands with predominant symmetry/ordering symptoms (Alsobrook et al., 1999; Denys, de Geus, van Megen, & Westenberg, 2004; Richter, Summerfeldt, Swinson, & Kennedy, 2000). Furthermore, a segregation analysis based on symptom factor scores revealed a pattern of inheritance consistent with a major locus in families ascertained through high symmetry/ordering scores (symmetry obsessions, ordering, counting and repeating rituals), whereas such a pattern was not found for other symptom dimensions (Alsobrook et al., 1999). Ordering compulsions have also been found to be more prevalent in OCD probands if they have a positive family history of OCD (Hanna, Fischer, Chadha, Himle, & Van Etten, 2005). Preliminary results from candidate gene studies suggest that symmetry/ordering may be more strongly associated with serotonin system genes than other symptom dimensions. One study found a trend for association between repeating rituals and counting (similar to symmetry/ordering) and the L/L genotype of the 5HTTLPR, an association that became significant if one considered only patients with comorbid Tourette's Disorder (Cavallini, Di Bella et al., 2002). Similarly, our group reported that the 5HT1B-861G and 5HTTLPR-L$_A$ alleles are more strongly associated with symmetry/ordering compared with other symptoms (Arnold, Summerfeldt et al., 2004). However, in another study the 5HTTLPR-L allele was most strongly associated with religious/somatic symptoms (Kim, Lee, & Kim, 2005).

In contrast to the preceding evidence supporting symmetry/ordering as the symptom dimension with the strongest genetic "loading," a complex segregation analysis of sibling pairs concordant for Tourette's Disorder and their parents suggests that all symptom factors may have significant genetic determinants but that their pattern of inheritance might vary (Leckman et al., 2003). Factor scores for obsessions/checking and symmetry/ordering were significantly correlated in sibling and mother–child pairs (but not father–child pairs). These symptom factors also segregated in a pattern consistent with a major gene effect combined with polygenic loci, and a dominant pattern of inheritance. Segregation of contamination/cleaning and hoarding also appeared to be consistent with a major locus effect, but with a recessive inheritance pattern. Although scores for these dimensions were not correlated between affected relatives, the authors pointed out that significant correlation between parent-child and sibling pairs would not be expected under a recessive model of inheritance.

In a study that used a different approach to subtyping OCD patients by classifying them as either "washers" or "checkers" (which would not allow for other phenotypes such as symmetry/ordering or hoarding), relatives of checkers were found to have a significantly higher risk of OCD or subclinical OCD compared with relatives of washers, and the majority of relatives exhibited the same symptom type as the proband (Bhattacharyya, Prasanna, Khanna, Janardhan Reddy, & Sheshadri, 2005).

Based on clinical and neurobiological evidence supporting hoarding as a distinct subtype of OCD, a number of genetic studies have been conducted to examine the hoarding phenotype. A recent study comparing OCD individuals with and without hoarding (Bienvenu et al., 2000) found that the hoarders were significantly more likely to have relatives with hoarding themselves (OR = 4.1). In a genome scan of 77 sib pairs affected with Tourette's Syndrome (TS), the phenotype of hoarding was linked with the chromosomal regions 4q (in close proximity to a region previously linked to TS), 15q, and 17q (Zhang et al., 2002). Using recursive partitioning, a statistical technique that enables examination of multiple markers simultaneously, the investigators also reported significant joint effects of specific loci on 4q and 5q. In an Afrikaner sample, genotype and allele frequencies of the COMT-Val158Met polymorphism were found to differ significantly between OCD patients with current hoarding symptoms, nonhoarding OCD patients, and controls, with the Met (low activity) allele over-represented in the hoarding group (Lochner et al., 2005). Although based on a small sample, these results should provide the impetus for a second look at the COMT gene with respect to hoarding and other OCD subtypes.

In addition to symptom dimensions or subtypes, a variety of other methods have been suggested for refining the OCD phenotype for genetic studies based on clinical characteristics of the proband (reviewed in Miguel et al., 2005). As just discussed, most genetic studies now examine the influence of age of onset, gender, and comorbid tics. Given evidence from family studies that only 50 to 60% of OCD probands have first-degree relatives with the disorder (do Rosario-Campos et al., 2005; Hanna, Himle et al., 2005; Pauls et al., 1995), subtyping based on family history of OCD may be a useful approach. In an exploratory study, individuals with a positive family history were found to differ from nonfamilial counterparts only with respect to an increased likelihood of life events prior to symptom onset. However, the power to detect differences based on familiality was limited in this study given that only eight probands were included in the familial group (Albert et al., 2002). Hanna and colleagues compared 17 pediatric OCD probands with a positive family history to 33 "sporadic" cases. The major findings in this study were increased prevalence of ordering compulsions (just noted), pathological grooming behaviors (particularly skin-picking), and other anxiety disorders in the familial group (Hanna, Fischer et al., 2005).

Pharmacogenetics

Pharmacogenetics is a rapidly emerging field defined as the study of the effects of genotypic variation on drug response. Our group (Billett et al., 1997) found no relationship between 5HTTLPR genotype and retrospective ratings of SSRI response. A study examining the effect of the 5HTTLPR on fluvoxamine suggested that individuals with the heterozygous L/S genotype were more likely to improve compared with other genotype groups, particularly in individuals without a comorbid tic disorder. The rare V allele of the I425V variant of 5-HTT has been associated SSRI resistance in two studies (Delorme et al., 2005; Ozaki et al., 2003). Further study of the effect of 5-HTT variants on SSRI response appears warranted given that the serotonin transporter is the primary target of the drug.

The genetic variants involved in drug response are not necessarily the same as those involved in pathogenesis of OCD. For example, our group has begun studying the relationship between genes in the Cytochrome P450 system that influence drug metabolism and OCD. To date, we have analyzed 2C19 and 3A4 in a sample of 95 individuals with OCD and found no statistically significant associations with SSRI response (Richter, Sicard, Arnold, Burroughs, & Kennedy, 2005). Further pharmacogenetic studies are clearly needed given the potential clinical benefits of identifying gene variants that influence treatment response.

Endophenotypes

Endophenotypes are biologically salient, intermediate phenotypes that are presumed to be more etiologically homogeneous and closely linked to the action of genes compared with more complex behavioral phenomena (Gottesman & Gould, 2003). In future, brain imaging profiles will likely prove useful as endophenotypes (Rosenberg & Hanna, 2000) given the extensive literature on the role of cortico-striatal-thalamic circuits in OCD (Friedlander & Desrocher, 2005). In a pioneering study of anxiety responses in normal subjects, individuals with either one or two copies of the 5HTTLPR-S allele exhibited heightened amygdala response during an emotional task as measured by functional magnetic resonance imaging compared with their L/L counterparts. The genotype difference was associated with a large effect size, accounting for 20% of the variance (Hariri et al., 2002). Although there are no published genetic studies of OCD utilizing neuroimaging phenotypes, we recently presented a preliminary report of a significant association between GRIN2B and putamen volume, and GRIN2A and anterior cingulate volume (Arnold, Sicard, Burroughs, et al., 2005) based on a collaboration with Dr. Rosenberg of Wayne State University.

Other measures and biological markers have also been suggested as candidate endophenotypes that may mediate the influence of genetic variants on OCD. Neuropsychological tests have been suggested as endophenotypes for OCD in a recent review (Chamberlain, Blackwell, Fineberg, Robbins, & Sahakian, 2005). To our knowledge there are no genetic studies that have examined neuropsychological measures as intermediate phenotypes for OCD. Future candidate gene studies may be informed by growing evidence that OCD individuals exhibit deficits in various aspects of executive functioning (Kuelz, Hohagen, & Voderholzer, 2004), procedural or implicit learning (Joel et al., 2005), or visual memory encoding (Penades, Catalan, Andres, Salamero, & Gasto, 2005). Abnormalities in the neural processing of disgust, a basic emotion mediated by distinct cortico-striatal circuits, may be particularly relevant as an endophenotype for contamination/cleaning symptoms (reviewed in Husted, Shapira, & Goodman, 2006). Measurement of event-related potential (ERP) may also provide useful endophenotypes, particularly error-related negativity that has been shown to be enhanced in OCD patients compared with controls during the process of monitoring action and detecting errors (Hacjak & Simons, 2002). Finally, blood indices such as platelet serotonergic markers have been proposed as useful endophenotypes (Delorme, Betancur, Callebert et al., 2005). These proposed phenotypic markers are only intended as examples, as improved understanding of the pathogenesis of OCD will no doubt provide future genetic researchers with many more potential endophenotypes.

CONCLUSION AND FUTURE DIRECTIONS

The rapid pace of technological advances is expected to revolutionize molecular genetic studies in the near future. For example, genome-wide association studies based on genotyping thousands of candidate gene variants on a single microarray ("gene chip") are now becoming feasible. New automated genotyping techniques combined with an international effort to catalogue human genetic variation (the HapMap project) is now enabling increasingly efficient investigation of multiple variants within a gene and more informative haplotype analyses compared with older approaches focusing on single gene variants. Moreover the functional effects of genetic differences on OCD are largely not understood but will be investigated through studies of gene expression in the years ahead.

Future studies will also benefit from increasingly sophisticated approaches to modelling gene-gene and gene-environment interaction. Methods of analyzing gene–gene interaction are in their infancy, and will require large sample sizes compared with methods to detect single gene effects. An example of the importance of gene-environment interaction comes from a study demonstrating that individuals with the 5HTTLPR-SS genotype were only at increased risk of developing depression in the presence of salient environmental factors, such as stressful life events or childhood maltreatment (Caspi et al., 2003).

In summary, there are now numerous convergent and exciting findings emerging, and the future holds even greater promise due to rapid advances in our understanding of the pathogenesis of OCD and knowledge of the human genome. Most importantly, a more definitive understanding of the genetic roots of OCD is expected to provide the basis for improved identification and treatment of this common and debilitating disorder.

ACKNOWLEDGMENT

We are grateful to Ms. Eliza Burroughs for her invaluable editorial assistance and help in finding references.

REFERENCES

Achenbach, T. M. (1991). *Manual for the child behavior checklist/4–18 and 1991 Profile.* Burlington, VT: University of Vermont.

Albert, U., Maina, G., Ravizza, L., & Bogetto, F. (2002). An exploratory study on obsessive-compulsive disorder with and without a familial component: Are there any phenomenological differences? *Psychopathology, 35,* 8–16.

Alsobrook, II, J. P., Leckman, J., Goodman, W., Rasmussen, S., & Pauls, D. (1999). Segregation analysis of obsessive-compulsive disorder using symptom-based factor scores. *American Journal of Medical Genetics, (Neuropsychiatric Genetics), 88,* 669–675.

Alsobrook, II, J. P., Zohar, A. H., Leboyer, M., Chabane, N., Ebstein, R. P., & Pauls, D. L. (2002). Association between the COMT locus and obsessive-compulsive disorder in females but not males. *American Journal of Medical Genetics (Neuropsychiatric Genetics), 114,* 116–120.

Arnold, P. D., Hu, X., Trakalo, J., Richter, M. A., Goldman, D., & Kennedy, J. L. (2004, October). *Association of a novel serotonin transporter polymorphism with obsessive-compulsive disorder based on qualitative and quantitative traits* [Abstract]. Poster session presented at the annual meeting of the American Society of Human Genetics, Toronto, ON.

Arnold, P. D., & Richter, M. A. (2001). Is obsessive-compulsive disorder an autoimmune disease? *Canadian Medical Association Journal, 165,* 1353–1358.

Arnold, P. D., Rosenberg, D. R., Mundo, E., Tharmalingam, S., Kennedy, J. L., & Richter, M. A. (2004). Association of a glutamate (NMDA) subunit receptor gene (GRIN2B) with obsessive-compulsive disorder: A preliminary study. *Psychopharmacology (Berlin), 174,* 530–538.

Arnold, P. D., Sicard, T., Burroughs, E., MacMaster, F., Mirza, Y., Smith, J., et al. (2005, October). *NMDA genes and neuroimaging phenotypes in pediatric obsessive-compulsive disorder.* Poster session presented at the annual meeting of the American Academy of Child and Adolescent Psychiatry (AACAP), Toronto, ON.

Arnold, P. D., Sicard, T., Burroughs, E., Richter, M. A., & Kennedy, J. L. (2006). Glutamate transporter gene (SLC1A1) associated with obsessive-compulsive disorder. *Archives of General Psychiatry, 63*(7), 769–776.

Arnold, P. D., Sicard, T., Hanna, G., Pato, M., Tharmalingam, S., Burroughs, E., et al. (2005, March). *Glutamate (NMDA) receptor genes in families of children and adults with obsessive-compulsive disorder: Findings in Three Independent Samples.* Poster session presented at the annual meeting of the Anxiety Disorders Association of America (ADAA), Seattle WA.

Arnold, P. D., Siegel-Bartelt, J., Cytrynbaum, C., Teshima, I., & Schachar, R. (2001). Velo-cardio-facial syndrome: Implications of microdeletion 22q11 for schizophrenia and mood disorders. *American Journal of Medical Genetics (Neuropsychiatric Genetics), 105,* 354–362.

Arnold, P. D., Summerfeldt, L. J., Sicard, T., Geronimo, J., Trakalo, J., Zai, G., et al. (2004). A family-based association study of novel serotonin polymorphisms in OCD and OCD symptom subgroups [abstract]. *American Journal of Medical Genetics (Part B: Neuropsychiatric Genetics), 130B,* 69.

Azzam, A., & Mathews, C. A. (2003). Meta-analysis of the association between the catecholamine-O-methyl-transferase gene and obsessive-compulsive disorder. *American Journal of Medical Genetics (Part B: Neuropsychiatric Genetics), 123B,* 64–69.

Baca-Garcia, E., Salgado, B. R., Segal, H. D., Lorenzo, C. V., Acosta, M. N., Romero, M. A., et al. (2005). A pilot genetic study of the continuum between compulsivity and impulsivity in females: The serotonin transporter promoter polymorphism. *Progress in Neuropsychopharmacology and Biological Psychiatry, 29,* 713–717.

Bellodi, L., Cavallini, M. C., Bertelli, S., Chiapparino, D., Riboldi, C., & Smeraldi, E. (2001). Morbidity risk for obsessive-compulsive spectrum disorders in first-degree relatives of patients with eating disorders. *American Journal of Psychiatry, 158,* 563–569.

Bengel, D., Greenberg, B. D., Cora-Locatelli, G., Altemus, M., Heils, A., Li, Q., et al. (1999). Association of the serotonin transporter promoter regulatory region polymorphism and obsessive-compulsive disorder. *Molecular Psychiatry, 4,* 463–466.

Berridge, K. C., Aldridge, J. W., Houchard, K. R., & Zhuang, X. (2005). Sequential super-stereotypy of an instinctive fixed action pattern in hyper-dopaminergic mutant mice: A model of obsessive compulsive disorder and Tourette's. *BMC Biology, 3,* 4.

Bhattacharyya, S., Prasanna, C. L., Khanna, S., Janardhan Reddy, Y. C., & Sheshadri, S. (2005). A family genetic study of clinical subtypes of obsessive-compulsive disorder. *Psychiatric Genetics, 15,* 175–180.

Bienvenu, O. J., Samuels, J. F., Riddle, M. A., Hoehn-Saric, R., Liang, K. Y., Cullen, B. A., et al. (2000). The relationship of obsessive-compulsive disorder to possible spectrum disorders: Results from a family study. *Biological Psychiatry, 48,* 287–293.

Billett, E. A., Richter, M. A., King, N., Heils, A., Lesch, K. P., & Kennedy, J. L. (1997). Obsessive compulsive disorder, response to serotonin reuptake inhibitors and the serotonin transporter gene. *Molecular Psychiatry, 2,* 403–406.

Billett, E. A., Richter, M. A., Sam, F., Swinson, R. P., Dai, X. Y., King, N., et al. (1998). Investigation of dopamine system genes in obsessive-compulsive disorder. *Psychiatric Genetics, 8,* 163–169.

Black, D. W., Gaffney, G. R., Schlosser, S., & Gabel, J. (2003). Children of parents with obsessive-compulsive disorder—A 2-year follow-up study. *Acta Psychiatrica Scandinavica, 107,* 305–313.

Bloch, M. H., Landeros-Wisenberger, A., Kelmendi, B., Coric, V., Bracken, M. B., & Leckman, J. F. (2006). A systematic review: Antipsychotic augmentation with treatment refractory obsessive-compulsive disorder. *Mol Psychiatry, 11*(8), 795.

Black, D. W., Noyes, R., Jr., Goldstein, R. B., & Blum, N. (1992). A family study of obsessive-compulsive disorder. *Archives of General Psychiatry, 49*, 362–368.

Bolton, P. F., Pickles, A., Murphy, M., & Rutter, M. (1998). Autism, affective and other psychiatric disorders: Patterns of familial aggregation. *Psychological Medicine, 28*, 385–395.

Burns, G. L., Keortge, S. G., Formea, G. M., & Sternberger, L. G. (1996). Revision of the Padua Inventory of Obsessive Compulsive Disorder Symptoms: Distinctions between worry, obsessions and compulsions. *Behavior, Research and Therapy, 34*, 163–173.

Camarena, B., Aguilar, A., Loyzaga, C., & Nicolini, H. (2004). A family-based association study of the 5-HT-1D receptor gene in obsessive compulsive disorder. *International Journal of Neuropsychopharmacology*, 49–53.

Camarena, B., Cruz, C., de la Fuente, J. R., & Nicolini, H. (1998). A higher frequency of a low activity-related allele of the MAO-A gene in females with obsessive-compulsive disorder. *Psychiatric Genetics, 8*, 255–257.

Camarena, B., Rinetti, G., Cruz, C., Gomez, A., de La Fuente, J. R., & Nicolini, H. (2001). Additional evidence that genetic variation of MAO-A gene supports a gender subtype in obsessive-compulsive disorder. *American Journal of Medical Genetics (Neuropsychiatric Genetics), 105*, 279–282.

Camarena, B., Rinetti, G., Cruz, C., Hernandez, S., de la Fuente, J. R., & Nicolini, H. (2001). Association study of the serotonin transporter gene polymorphism in obsessive-compulsive disorder. *International Journal of Neuropsychopharmacology, 4*, 269–272.

Carey, G., & Gottesman, I. (1981). Twin and family studies of anxiety, phobic and obsessive disorders. In D. Klein & J. Rabkin (Eds.), *Anxiety: New research and changing concepts* (pp. 117–135). New York: Raven Press.

Carter, A. S., Pollock, R. A., Suvak, M. K., & Pauls, D. L. (2004). Anxiety and major depression comorbidity in a family study of obsessive-compulsive disorder. *Depression and Anxiety, 20*, 165–174.

Caspi, A., Sugden, K., Moffitt, T. E., Taylor, A., Craig, I. W., Harrington, H., et al. (2003). Influence of life stress on depression: Moderation by a polymorphism in the 5-HTT gene. *Science, 301*, 386–389.

Catalano, M., Sciuto, G., Di Bella, D., Novelli, E., Nobile, M., & Bellodi, L. (1994). Lack of association between obsessive-compulsive disorder and the dopamine D3 receptor gene: Some preliminary considerations. *American Journal of Medical Genetics (Neuropsychiatric Genetics), 54*, 253–255.

Cavallini, M. C., Albertazzi, M., Bianchi, L., & Bellodi, L. (2002). Anticipation of age at onset of obsessive-compulsive spectrum disorders in patients with obsessive-compulsive disorder. *Psychiatry Research, 111*, 1–9.

Cavallini, M. C., Di Bella, D., Pasquale, L., Henin, M., & Bellodi, L. (1998). 5HT2C CYS23/SER23 polymorphism is not associated with obsessive-compulsive disorder. *Psychiatry Research, 77*, 97–104.

Cavallini, M. C., Di Bella, D., Siliprandi, F., Malchiodi, F., & Bellodi, L. (2002). Exploratory factor analysis of obsessive-compulsive patients and association with 5-HTTLPR polymorphism. *American Journal of Medical Genetics (Neuropsychiatric Genetics), 114*, 347–353.

Cavallini, M. C., Pasquale, L., Bellodi, L., & Smeraldi, E. (1999). Complex segregation analysis for obsessive compulsive disorder and related disorders. *American Journal of Medical Genetics (Neuropsychiatric Genetics), 88*, 38–43.

Chabane, N., Delorme, R., Millet, B., Mouren, M. C., Leboyer, M., & Pauls, D. (2005). Early-onset obsessive-compulsive disorder: A subgroup with a specific clinical and familial pattern? *Journal of Child Psychology and Psychiatry, 46*, 881–887.

Chabane, N., Millet, B., Delorme, R., Lichtermann, D., Mathieu, F., Laplanche, J. L., et al. (2004). Lack of evidence for association between serotonin transporter gene (5-HTTLPR) and obsessive-compulsive disorder by case control and family association study in humans. *Neuroscience Letters, 363,* 154–156.

Chamberlain, S. R., Blackwell, A. D., Fineberg, N. A., Robbins, T. W., & Sahakian, B. J. (2005). The neuropsychology of obsessive compulsive disorder: The importance of failures in cognitive and behavioural inhibition as candidate endophenotypic markers. *Neuroscience and Biobehavioral Reviews, 29,* 399–419.

Clifford, C. A., Murray, R. M., & Fulker, D. W. (1984). Genetic and environmental influences on obsessional traits and symptoms. *Psychological Medicine, 14,* 791–800.

Cruz, C., Camarena, B., King, N., Paez, F., Sidenberg, D., de la Fuente, J. R., et al. (1997). Increased prevalence of the seven-repeat variant of the dopamine D4 receptor gene in patients with obsessive-compulsive disorder with tics. *Neuroscience Letters, 231,* 1–4.

Delorme, R., Betancur, C., Callebert, J., Chabane, N., Laplanche, J. L., Mouren-Simeoni, M. C., et al. (2005). Platelet serotonergic markers as endophenotypes for obsessive-compulsive disorder. *Neuropsychopharmacology, 30,* 1539–1547.

Delorme, R., Betancur, C., Wagner, M., Krebs, M. O., Gorwood, P., Pearl, P., et al. (2005). Support for the association between the rare functional variant I425V of the serotonin transporter gene and susceptibility to obsessive compulsive disorder. *Molecular Psychiatry, 10,* 1059–1061.

Delorme, R., Krebs, M. O., Chabane, N., Roy, I., Millet, B., Mouren-Simeoni, M. C., et al. (2004). Frequency and transmission of glutamate receptors GRIK2 and GRIK3 polymorphisms in patients with obsessive compulsive disorder. *Neuroreport, 15,* 699–702.

Denys, D., de Geus, F., van Megen, H. J., & Westenberg, H. G. (2004). Use of factor analysis to detect potential phenotypes in obsessive-compulsive disorder. *Psychiatry Research, 128,* 273–280.

Devlin, B., Roeder, K., & Wasserman, L. (2001). Genomic control, a new approach to genetic-based association studies. *Theoretical Population Biology, 60,* 155–166.

Di Bella, D., Catalano, M., Cichon, S., & Nothen, M. M. (1996). Association study of a null mutation in the dopamine D4 receptor gene in Italian patients with obsessive-compulsive disorder, bipolar mood disorder and schizophrenia. *Psychiatric Genetics, 6,* 119–121.

Di Bella, D., Cavallini, M. C., & Bellodi, L. (2002). No association between obsessive-compulsive disorder and the 5-HT1D{beta} receptor gene. *American Journal of Psychiatry, 159,* 1783–1785.

Diaz-Anzaldua, A., Joober, R., Riviere, J. B., Dion, Y., Lesperance, P., Richer, F., et al. (2004). Tourette syndrome and dopaminergic genes: A family-based association study in the French Canadian founder population. *Molecular Psychiatry, 9,* 272–277.

Dickel, D., Veenstra-Vanderweele, J., Cox, N., Wu, X., Fischer, D., Etten-Lee, M. V., et al. (2006). Association testing of the positional and functional candidate gene SLC1A1 in early-onset obsessive-compulsive disorder. *Archives of General Psychiatry, 63*(7), 778–785.

Do Rosario-Campos, M. C., Leckman, J. F., Curi, M., Quatrano, S., Katsovitch, L., Miguel, E. C., et al. (2005). A family study of early-onset obsessive-compulsive disorder. *American Journal of Medical Genetics (Part B: Neuropsychiatric Genetics), 136B,* 92–97.

Duan, J., Sanders, A. R., Molen, J. E., Martinolich, L., Mowry, B. J., Levinson, D. F., et al. (2003). Polymorphisms in the 5'-untranslated region of the human serotonin receptor 1B (HTR1B) gene affect gene expression. *Molecular Psychiatry, 8,* 901–910.

Eaton, M. J., Staley, J. K., Globus, M. Y., & Whittemore, S. R. (1995). Developmental regulation of early serotonergic neuronal differentiation: The role of brain-derived neurotrophic factor and membrane depolarization. *Developmental Biology, 170,* 169–182.

Eley, T. C., Bolton, D., O'Connor, T. G., Perrin, S., Smith, P., & Plomin, R. (2003). A twin study of anxiety-related behaviours in pre-school children. *Journal of Child Psychology and Psychiatry, 44*, 945–960.

Elston, R. C. (2000). Introduction and overview. Statistical methods in genetic epidemiology. *Statistical Methods in Medical Research, 9*, 527–541.

Enoch, M. A., Greenberg, B. D., Murphy, D. L., & Goldman, D. (2001). Sexually dimorphic relationship of a 5-HT2A promoter polymorphism with obsessive-compulsive disorder. *Biological Psychiatry, 49*, 385–388.

Enoch, M. A., Kaye, W. H., Rotondo, A., Greenberg, B. D., Murphy, D. L., & Goldman, D. (1998). 5-HT2A promoter polymorphism -1438G/A, anorexia nervosa, and obsessive-compulsive disorder. *Lancet, 351*, 1785–1786.

Erdal, M. E., Tot, S., Yazici, K., Yazici, A., Herken, H., Erdem, P., et al. (2003). Lack of association of catechol-O-methyltransferase gene polymorphism in obsessive-compulsive disorder. *Depression and Anxiety, 18*, 41–45.

Ewens, W. J., & Spielman, R. S. (2001). Locating genes by linkage and association. *Theoretical Population Biology, 60*, 135–139.

Fitzgerald, K., McMaster, F., Paulson, L., & Rosenberg, D. (1999). Neurobiology of childhood OCD. *Child and Adolescent Psychiatric Clinics of North America, 8*, 533–575.

Friedlander, L., & Desrocher, M. (2005). Neuroimaging studies of obsessive-compulsive disorder in adults and children. *Clinical Psychology Review, 26*, 32–49.

Frisch, A., Michaelovsky, E., Rockah, R., Amir, I., Hermesh, H., Laor, N., et al. (2000). Association between obsessive-compulsive disorder and polymorphisms of genes encoding components of the serotonergic and dopaminergic pathways. *European Neuropsychopharmacology, 10*, 205–209.

Goodman, W. K., Price, L. H., Rasmussen, S. A., Mazure, C., Fleischmann, R. L., Hill, C. L., et al. (1989a). The Yale-Brown Obsessive Compulsive Scale: I. Development, use, and reliability. *Archives of General Psychiatry, 46*, 1006–1011.

Goodman, W. K., Price, L. H., Rasmussen, S. A., Mazure, C., Delgado, P., Heninger, G. R., et al. (1989b). The Yale-Brown Obsessive Compulsive Scale: II. Validity. *Archives of General Psychiatry, 46*, 1012–1016.

Gothelf, D., Presburger, G., Zohar, A. H., Burg, M., Nahmani, A., Frydman, M., et al. (2004). Obsessive-compulsive disorder in patients with velocardiofacial (22q11 deletion) syndrome. *American Journal of Medical Genetics (Part B: Neuropsychiatric Genetics), 126B*, 99–105.

Gottesman, I. I., & Gould, T. D. (2003). The endophenotype concept in psychiatry: Etymology and strategic intentions. *American Journal of Psychiatry, 160*, 636–645.

Grados, M. A., Riddle, M. A., Samuels, J. F., Liang, K. Y., Hoehn-Saric, R., Bienvenu, O. J., et al. (2001). The familial phenotype of obsessive-compulsive disorder in relation to tic disorders: The Hopkins OCD family study. *Biological Psychiatry, 50*, 559–565.

Grice, D. E., Leckman, J. F., Pauls, D. L., Kurlan, R., Kidd, K. K., Pakstis, A. J., et al. (1996). Linkage disequilibrium between an allele at the dopamine D4 receptor locus and Tourette syndrome, by the transmission-disequilibrium test. *American Journal of Human Genetics, 59*, 644–652.

Hacjak, G., & Simons, R. (2002). Error-related brain activity in obsessive-compulsive undergraduates. *Psychiatry Research, 110*, 63–72.

Hall, D., Dhilla, A., Charalambous, A., Gogos, J. A., & Karayiorgou, M. (2003). Sequence variants of the brain-derived neurotrophic factor (BDNF) gene are strongly associated with obsessive-compulsive disorder. *American Journal of Human Genetics, 73*, 370–376.

Hanna, G., Veenstra-VanderWeele, J., Cox, N., Boehnke, M., Himle, J., Curtis., G., et al. (2002). Genome-wide linkage analysis of families with obsessive-compulsive disorder ascertained through pediatric probands. *American Journal of Medical Genetics (Neuropsychiatric Genetics)*, *114*, 541–552.

Hanna, G. L., Fingerlin, T. E., Himle, J. A., & Boehnke, M. (2005). Complex segregation analysis of obsessive-compulsive disorder in families with pediatric probands. *Human Heredity*, *60*, 1–9.

Hanna, G. L., Fischer, D. J., Chadha, K. R., Himle, J. A., & Van Etten, M. (2005). Familial and sporadic subtypes of early-onset obsessive-compulsive disorder. *Biolocial Psychiatry*, *57*, 895–900.

Hanna, G. L., Himle, J. A., Curtis, G. C., & Gillespie, B. W. (2005). A family study of obsessive-compulsive disorder with pediatric probands. *American Journal of Medical Genetics (Part B: Neuropsychiatric Genetics)*, *134B*, 13–19.

Hariri, A. R., Mattay, V. S., Tessitore, A., Kolachana, B., Fera, F., Goldman, D., et al. (2002). Serotonin transporter genetic variation and the response of the human amygdala. *Science*, *297*, 400–403.

Hemmings, S. M., Kinnear, C. J., Lochner, C., Niehaus, D. J., Knowles, J. A., Moolman-Smook, J. C., et al. (2004). Early- versus late-onset obsessive-compulsive disorder: Investigating genetic and clinical correlates. *Psychiatry Research*, *128*, 175–182.

Hemmings, S. M., Kinnear, C. J., Niehaus, D. J., Moolman-Smook, J. C., Lochner, C., Knowles, J. A., et al. (2003). Investigating the role of dopaminergic and serotonergic candidate genes in obsessive-compulsive disorder. *European Neuropsychopharmacology*, *13*, 93–98.

Hettema, J. M., Neale, M. C., & Kendler, K. S. (2001). A review and meta-analysis of the genetic epidemiology of anxiety disorders. *American Journal of Psychiatry*, *158*, 1568–1578.

Hollander, E., King, A., Delaney, K., Smith, C. J., & Silverman, J. M. (2003). Obsessive-compulsive behaviors in parents of multiplex autism families. *Psychiatry Research*, *117*, 11–16.

Hotamisligil, G. S., & Breakefield, X. O. (1991). Human monoamine oxidase A gene determines levels of enzyme activity. *American Journal of Human Genetics*, *49*, 383–392.

Hu, X.-Z., Lipsky, R., Zhu, G., Akhtar, L., Taubman, J., Greenberg, B., et al. (2006). Serotonin transporter gain-of-function polymorphisms are linked to obsessive-compulsive disorder. *American Journal of Human Genetics*, *78*(5), 815–826.

Hudson, J. I., Mangweth, B., Pope, H. G., Jr., De Col, C., Hausmann, A., Gutweniger, S., et al. (2003). Family study of affective spectrum disorder. *Archives of General Psychiatry*, *60*, 170–177.

Hudziak, J. J., Van Beijsterveldt, C. E., Althoff, R. R., Stanger, C., Rettew, D. C., Nelson, E. C., et al. (2004). Genetic and environmental contributions to the Child Behavior Checklist Obsessive-Compulsive Scale: A cross-cultural twin study. *Archives of General Psychiatry*, *61*, 608–616.

Husted, D. S., Shapira, N. A., & Goodman, W. K. (2006). The neurocircuitry of obsessive-compulsive disorder and disgust. *Progress in Neuropsychopharmacology and Biological Psychiatry* [Electronic version]. Retrieved January 26, 2006, from http://dx.doi.org/10.1016/j.pnpbp.2005.11.024

Inouye, E. (1965). Similar and dissimilar manifestations of obsessive-compulsive neurosis in monozygotic twins. *American Journal of Psychiatry*, *121*, 1171–1175.

Joel, D., & Doljansky, J. (2003). Selective alleviation of compulsive lever-pressing in rats by d(1), but not d(2), blockade: Possible implications for the involvement of d(1) receptors in obsessive-compulsive disorder. *Neuropsychopharmacology*, *28*, 77–85.

Joel, D., Zohar, O., Afek, M., Hermesh, H., Lerner, L., Kuperman, R., et al. (2005). Impaired procedural learning in obsessive-compulsive disorder and Parkinson's disease, but not in major depressive disorder. *Behavioral Brain Research*, *157*, 253–263.

Johns, T. G., & Bernard, C. C. (1997). Binding of complement component C1q to myelin oligodendrocyte glycoprotein: A novel mechanism for regulating CNS inflammation. *Molecular Immunology, 34*, 33–38.

Jonnal, A. H., Gardner, C. O., Prescott, C. A., & Kendler, K. S. (2000). Obsessive and compulsive symptoms in a general population sample of female twins. *American Journal of Medical Genetics (Neuropsychiatric Genetics), 96*, 791–796.

Kano, Y., Ohta, M., Nagai, Y., Pauls, D. L., & Leckman, J. F. (2004). Obsessive-compulsive symptoms in parents of Tourette syndrome probands and autism spectrum disorder probands. *Psychiatry and Clinical Neurosciences, 58*, 348–352.

Karayiorgou, M., Altemus, M., Galke, B. L., Goldman, D., Murphy, D. L., Ott, J., et al. (1997). Genotype determining low catechol-O-methyltransferase activity as a risk factor for obsessive-compulsive disorder. *Proceedings of the National Academy of Sciences of the United States of America, 94*, 4572–4575.

Karayiorgou, M., Sobin, C., Blundell, M. L., Galke, B. L., Malinova, L., Goldberg, P., et al. (1999). Family-based association studies support a sexually dimorphic effect of COMT and MAOA on genetic susceptibility to obsessive-compulsive disorder. *Biological Psychiatry, 45*, 1178–1189.

Kilic, F., Murphy, D. L., & Rudnick, G. (2003). A human serotonin transporter mutation causes constitutive activation of transport activity. *Molecular Pharmacology, 64*, 440–446.

Kim, S. J., Gonen, D., Hanna, G. L., Leventhal, B. L., & Cook, E. H., Jr. (2000). Deletion polymorphism in the coding region of the human NESP55 alternative transcript of GNAS1. *Molecular and Cellular Probes, 14*, 191–194.

Kim, S. J., Lee, H. S., & Kim, C. H. (2005). Obsessive-compulsive disorder, factor-analyzed symptom dimensions and serotonin transporter polymorphism. *Neuropsychobiology, 52*, 176–182.

Kim, S. J., Veenstra-VanderWeele, J., Hanna, G. L., Gonen, D., Leventhal, B. L., & Cook, E. H., Jr. (2000). Mutation screening of human 5-HT(2B) receptor gene in early-onset obsessive-compulsive disorder. *Molecular and Cellular Probes, 14*, 47–52.

Kinnear, C., Niehaus, D. J., Seedat, S., Moolman-Smook, J. C., Corfield, V. A., Malherbe, G., et al. (2001). Obsessive-compulsive disorder and a novel polymorphism adjacent to the oestrogen response element (ERE 6) upstream from the COMT gene. *Psychiatric Genetics, 11*, 85–87.

Kinnear, C. J., Niehaus, D. J., Moolman-Smook, J. C., du Toit, P. L., van Kradenberg, J., Weyers, J. B., et al. (2000). Obsessive-compulsive disorder and the promoter region polymorphism (5-HTTLPR) in the serotonin transporter gene (SLC6A4): A negative association study in the Afrikaner population. *International Journal of Neuropsychopharmacology, 3*, 327–331.

Kraft, J. B., Slager, S. L., McGrath, P. J., & Hamilton, S. P. (2005). Sequence analysis of the serotonin transporter and associations with antidepressant response. *Biological Psychiatry, 58*, 374–381.

Kuelz, A. K., Hohagen, F., & Voderholzer, U. (2004). Neuropsychological performance in obsessive-compulsive disorder: A critical review. *Biological Psychology, 65*, 185–236.

Lappalainen, J., Dean, M., Charbonneau, L., Virkkunen, M., Linnoila, M., & Goldman, D. (1995). Mapping of the serotonin 5-HT1D beta autoreceptor gene on chromosome 6 and direct analysis for sequence variants. *American Journal of Medical Genetics (Neuropsychiatric Genetics), 60*, 157–161.

Leckman, J. F., Pauls, D. L., Zhang, H., Rosario-Campos, M. C., Katsovich, L., Kidd, K. K., et al. (2003). Obsessive-compulsive symptom dimensions in affected sibling pairs diagnosed with Gilles de la Tourette syndrome. *American Journal of Medical Genetics (Part B: Neuropsychiatric Genetics), 116B*, 60–68.

Lenane, M. C., Swedo, S. E., Leonard, H., Pauls, D. L., Sceery, W., & Rapoport, J. L. (1990). Psychiatric disorders in first-degree relatives of children and adolescents with obsessive compulsive disorder. *Journal of the American Academy of Child and Adolescent Psychiatry, 29,* 407–412.

Lenane, M. C., Swedo, S. E., Rapoport, J. L., Leonard, H., Sceery, W., & Guroff, J. J. (1992). Rates of Obsessive Compulsive Disorder in first-degree relatives of patients with trichotillomania: A research note. *Journal of Child Psychology and Psychiatry, 33,* 925–933.

Lensi, P., Cassano, G. B., Correddu, G., Ravagli, S., Kunovac, J. L., & Akiskal, H. S. (1996). Obsessive-compulsive disorder. Familial-developmental history, symptomatology, comorbidity and course with special reference to gender-related differences. *British Journal of Psychiatry, 169,* 101–107.

Leonard, H. L., Lenane, M. C., Swedo, S. E., Rettew, D. C., Gershon, E. S., & Rapoport, J. L. (1992). Tics and Tourette's disorder: A 2- to 7-year follow-up of 54 obsessive-compulsive children. *American Journal of Psychiatry, 149,* 1244–1251.

Lesch, K.-P., Bengel, D., Heils, A., Sabol, S. Z., Greenberg, B. D., Petri, S., et al. (1996). Association of anxiety-related traits with a polymorphism in the serotonin transporter gene regulatory region. *Science, 274,* 1527–1531.

Lewis, A. (1936). Problems of obsessional illness. *Proceedings of the Royal Society of Medicine, 29,* 325–336.

Liang, K. Y., & Pulver, A. E. (1996). Analysis of case-control/family sampling design. *Genetic Epidemiology, 13,* 253–270.

Lochner, C., Hemmings, S. M., Kinnear, C. J., Moolman-Smook, J. C., Corfield, V. A., Knowles, J. A., et al. (2004). Gender in obsessive-compulsive disorder: Clinical and genetic findings. *European Neuropsychopharmacology, 14,* 105–113.

Lochner, C., Kinnear, C. J., Hemmings, S. M., Seller, C., Niehaus, D. J., Knowles, J. A., et al. (2005). Hoarding in obsessive-compulsive disorder: Clinical and genetic correlates. *Journal of Clinical Psychiatry, 66,* 1155–1160.

Mataix-Cols, D., Rosario-Campos, M. C., & Leckman, J. F. (2005). A multidimensional model of obsessive-compulsive disorder. *American Journal of Psychiatry, 162,* 228–238.

McDougle, C. J., Epperson, C. N., Pelton, G. H., Wasylink, S., & Price, L. H. (2000). A double-blind, placebo-controlled study of risperidone addition in serotonin reuptake inhibitor-refractory obsessive-compulsive disorder. *Archives of General Psychiatry, 57,* 794–801.

McDougle, C. J., Epperson, C. N., Price, L. H., & Gelernter, J. (1998). Evidence for linkage disequilibrium between serotonin transporter protein gene (SLC6A4) and obsessive compulsive disorder. *Molecular Psychiatry, 3,* 270–273.

Meira-Lima, I., Shavitt, R. G., Miguita, K., Ikenaga, E., Miguel, E. C., & Vallada, H. (2004). Association analysis of the catechol-o-methyltransferase (COMT), serotonin transporter (5-HTT) and serotonin 2A receptor (5HT2A) gene polymorphisms with obsessive-compulsive disorder. *Genes Brain and Behavior, 3,* 75–79.

Miguel, E. C., Leckman, J. F., Rauch, S., do Rosario-Campos, M. C., Hounie, A. G., Mercadante, M. T., et al. (2005). Obsessive-compulsive disorder phenotypes: Implications for genetic studies. *Molecular Psychiatry, 10,* 258–275.

Millet, B., Chabane, N., Delorme, R., Leboyer, M., Leroy, S., Poirier, M. F., et al. (2003). Association between the dopamine receptor D4 (DRD4) gene and obsessive-compulsive disorder. *American Journal of Medical Genetics (Neuropsychiatric Genetics), 116*(Suppl. 1), 55–59.

Mossner, R., Daniel, S., Albert, D., Heils, A., Okladnova, O., Schmitt, A., et al. (2000). Serotonin transporter function is modulated by brain-derived neurotrophic factor (BDNF) but not nerve growth factor (NGF). *Neurochemistry International, 36,* 197–202.

Mossner, R., Walitza, S., Geller, F., Scherag, A., Gutknecht, L., Jacob, C., et al. (2005). Transmission disequilibrium of polymorphic variants in the tryptophan hydroxylase-2 gene in children and adolescents with obsessive-compulsive disorder. *International Journal of Neuropsychopharmacology, 9,* 1–6.

Mossner, R., Walitza, S., Lesch, K. P., Geller, F., Barth, N., Remschmidt, H., et al. (2005). Brain-derived neurotrophic factor V66M polymorphism in childhood-onset obsessive-compulsive disorder. *International Journal of Neuropsychopharmacology, 8,* 133–136.

Mundo, E., Richter, M. A., Sam, F., Macciardi, F., & Kennedy, J. L. (2000). Is the 5-HT(1Dbeta) receptor gene implicated in the pathogenesis of obsessive-compulsive disorder? *American Journal of Psychiatry, 157,* 1160–1161.

Mundo, E., Richter, M. A., Zai, G., Sam, F., McBride, J., Macciardi, F., et al. (2002). 5HT1Dbeta Receptor gene implicated in the pathogenesis of obsessive-compulsive disorder: Further evidence from a family-based association study. *Molecular Psychiatry, 7,* 805–809.

Nestadt, G., Lan, T., Samuels, J., Riddle, M., Bienvenu, O. J., III, Liang, K. Y., et al. (2000). Complex segregation analysis provides compelling evidence for a major gene underlying obsessive-compulsive disorder and for heterogeneity by sex. *American Journal of Human Genetics, 67,* 1611–1616.

Nestadt, G., Samuels, J., Riddle, M., Bienvenu, O. J., III, Liang, K. Y., LaBuda, M., et al. (2000). A family study of obsessive-compulsive disorder. *Archives of General Psychiatry, 57,* 358–363.

Nestadt, G., Samuels, J., Riddle, M.A., Liang, K. Y., Bienvenu, O. J., Hoehn-Saric, R., et al. (2001). The relationship between obsessive-compulsive disorder and anxiety and affective disorders: Results from the Johns Hopkins OCD Family Study. *Psychological Medicine, 31,* 481–487.

Neves-Pereira, M., Mundo, E., Muglia, P., King, N., Macciardi, F., & Kennedy, J. L. (2002). The brain-derived neurotrophic factor gene confers susceptibility to bipolar disorder: Evidence from a family-based association study. *American Journal of Human Genetics, 71,* 651–655.

Nicolini, H., Cruz, C., Camarena, B., Orozco, B., Kennedy, J. L., King, N., et al. (1996). DRD2, DRD3 and 5HT2A receptor genes polymorphisms in obsessive-compulsive disorder. *Molecular Psychiatry, 1,* 461–465.

Nicolini, H., Hanna, G., Baxter, L., Schwartz, J., Weissbacker, K., & Spence, M. (1991). Segregation analysis of obsessive compulsive and associated disorders. *Ursus Medicus, 1,* 25–28.

Niehaus, D. J., Kinnear, C. J., Corfield, V.A., du Toit, P.L., van Kradenburg, J., Moolman-Smook, J. C., et al. (2001). Association between a catechol-o-methyltransferase polymorphism and obsessive-compulsive disorder in the Afrikaner population. *Journal of Affective Disorders, 65,* 61–65.

Nordstrom, E. J., & Burton, F. H. (2002). A transgenic model of comorbid Tourette's syndrome and obsessive-compulsive disorder circuitry. *Molecular Psychiatry, 7,* 524, 617–625.

Novelli, E., Nobile, M., Diaferia, G., Sciuto, G., & Catalano, M. (1994). A molecular investigation suggests no relationship between obsessive-compulsive disorder and the dopamine D2 receptor. *Neuropsychobiology, 29,* 61–63.

Ohara, K., Nagai, M., Suzuki, Y., & Ochiai, M. (1998). No association between anxiety disorders and catechol-O-methyltransferase polymorphism. *Psychiatry Research, 80,* 145–148.

Ozaki, N., Goldman, D., Kaye, W. H., Plotnicov, K., Greenberg, B. D., Lappalainen, J., et al. (2003). Serotonin transporter missense mutation associated with a complex neuropsychiatric phenotype. *Molecular Psychiatry, 8,* 895, 933–896.

Page, G. P., George, V., Go, R. C., Page, P. Z., & Allison, D. B. (2003). "Are we there yet?": Deciding when one has demonstrated specific genetic causation in complex diseases and quantitative traits. *American Journal of Human Genetics, 73,* 711–719.

Parascandola, M., & Weed, D. L. (2001). Causation in epidemiology. *Journal of Epidemiology and Community Health, 55,* 905–912.

Pauls, D., Alsobrook, J. P., Goodman, W., Rasmussen, S., & Leckman, J. (1995). A family study of obsessive-compulsive disorder. *American Journal of Psychiatry, 152,* 76–84.

Penades, R., Catalan, R., Andres, S., Salamero, M., & Gasto, C. (2005). Executive function and nonverbal memory in obsessive-compulsive disorder. *Psychiatry Research, 133,* 81–90.

Phillips, K. A. (2002). The obsessive-compulsive spectrums. *Psychiatric Clinics of North America, 25,* 791–809.

Phillips, K. A., Menard, W., Fay, C., & Weisberg, R. (2005). Demographic characteristics, phenomenology, comorbidity, and family history in 200 individuals with body dysmorphic disorder. *Psychosomatics, 46,* 317–325.

Pigott, T., & Sheay, S. (2000). Pharmacotherapy of obsessive-compulsive disorder: Overview and treatment-refractory strategies. In W. Goodman, M. Rudorfer, & J. Maser (Eds.), *Obsessive-compulsive disorder: Contemporary issues in treatment* (pp. 277–302). Mahwah, NJ: Lawrence Erlbaum Associates.

Pogarell, O., Hamann, C., Popperl, G., Juckel, G., Chouker, M., Zaudig, M., et al. (2003). Elevated brain serotonin transporter availability in patients with obsessive-compulsive disorder. *Biological Psychiatry, 54,* 1406–1413.

Prasad, H. C., Zhu, C. B., McCauley, J. L., Samuvel, D. J., Ramamoorthy, S., Shelton, R. C., et al. (2005). Human serotonin transporter variants display altered sensitivity to protein kinase G and p38 mitogen-activated protein kinase. *Proceedings of the National Academy of Science of the United States of America, 102,* 11545–11550.

Reddy, P. S., Reddy, Y. C., Srinath, S., Khanna, S., Sheshadri, S. P., & Girimaji, S. R. (2001). A family study of juvenile obsessive-compulsive disorder. *Canadian Journal of Psychiatry, 46,* 346–351.

Richter, M. A., Mundo, E., Sam, F., Swinson, R. P., & Kennedy, J. L. (2001, May). *The GABA$_A$–2 (Gamma2) receptor gene in OCD.* Annual meeting of the American Psychiatric Association, New Orleans.

Richter, M. A., Sicard, T., Arnold, P. D., Burroughs, E., & Kennedy, J. L. (2005, April). *Medication response in obsessive-compulsive disorder and the genetics of hepatic enzyme Cyp2C19 metabolism.* Paper presented at the Pharmacogenetics in Psychiatry Meeting, New York.

Richter, M. A., Summerfeldt, L. J., Swinson, R. P., & Kennedy, J. L. (2000, May). Symptom subtypes and family history in OCD. In M. Pato (Chair), *Models for subtyping OCD.* Symposium conducted at the annual meeting of the American Psychiatric Association, Chicago, IL.

Riddle, M. A., Scahill, L., King, R., Hardin, M. T., Towbin, K. E., Ort, S. I., et al. (1990). Obsessive compulsive disorder in children and adolescents: Phenomenology and family history. *Journal of the American Academy of Child and Adolescent Psychiatry, 29,* 766–772.

Risch, N., & Merikangas, K. (1996). The future of genetic studies of complex human diseases. *Science, 273*(5281), 1516–1517.

Rosenberg, D., & Hanna, G. (2000). Genetic and imaging strategies in obsessive-compulsive disorder: Potential implications for treatment development. *Biological Psychiatry, 48,* 1210–1222.

Rosenberg, D., & Keshavan, M. (1998). Toward a neurodevelopmental model of obsessive-compulsive disorder. *Biological Psychiatry, 43,* 623–640.

Rosenberg, D., MacMaster, F., Keshavan, M., Fitzgerald, K., Stewart, C., & Moore, G. (2000). Decrease in caudate glutamatergic concentrations in pediatric obsessive-compulsive disorder patients taking paroxetine. *Journal of the American Academy of Child and Adolescent Psychiatry, 39,* 1096–1103.

Rosenberg, D. R., Mirza, Y., Russell, A., Tang, J., Smith, J. M., Banerjee, S. P., et al. (2004). Reduced anterior cingulate glutamatergic concentrations in childhood OCD and major depression versus healthy controls. *Journal of the American Academy of Child and Adolescent Psychiatry, 43,* 1146–1153.

Rufer, M., Grothusen, A., Mass, R., Peter, H., & Hand, I. (2005). Temporal stability of symptom dimensions in adult patients with obsessive-compulsive disorder. *Journal of Affective Disorders, 88,* 99–102.

Samuels, J., Nestadt, G., Bienvenu, O. J., Costa, P. T., Jr., Riddle, M. A., Liang, K. Y., et al. (2000). Personality disorders and normal personality dimensions in obsessive-compulsive disorder. *British Journal of Psychiatry, 177,* 457–462.

Scahill, L., Riddle, M. A., McSwiggin-Hardin, M. T., Ort, S. I., King, R. A., Goodman, W. K., et al. (1997). Children's Yale-Brown Obsessive Compulsive Scale: Reliability and validity. *Journal of the American Academy of Child and Adolescent Psychiatry, 36,* 844–852.

Schindler, K. M., Richter, M. A., Kennedy, J. L., Pato, M. T., & Pato, C. N. (2000). Association between homozygosity at the COMT gene locus and obsessive compulsive disorder. *American Journal of Medical Genetics (Neuropsychiatric Genetics), 96,* 721–724.

Serpell, L., Livingstone, A., Neiderman, M., & Lask, B. (2002). Anorexia nervosa: Obsessive-compulsive disorder, obsessive-compulsive personality disorder, or neither? *Clinical Psychology Review, 22,* 647–669.

Shugart, Y. Y., Samuels, J., Willour, V. L., Grados, M. A., Greenberg, B. D., Knowles, J. A. et al. (2006). Genomewide linkage scan for obsessive-compulsive disorder: Evidence for susceptibility loci on chromosomes 3q, 7p, 1q, 15q, and 6q. *Molecular Psychiatry, 11*(8), 763–770.

Sicard, T. L., Arnold, P. D., Geronimo, J. M., Hanna, G. L., Pato, M., Richter, M. A., & Kennedy, J. L. (2004, October). *Haplotype analysis of four HTR1B polymorphisms in obsessive-compulsive disorder* (Abstract 2259, p. 410). American Society of Human Genetics, Toronto, ON.

Simpson, H. B., Lombardo, I., Slifstein, M., Huang, H. Y., Hwang, D. R., Abi-Dargham, A., et al. (2003). Serotonin transporters in obsessive-compulsive disorder: A positron emission tomography study with [(11)C]McN 5652. *Biological Psychiatry, 54,* 1414–1421.

Sklar, P., Gabriel, S. B., McInnis, M. G., Bennett, P., Lim, Y. M., Tsan, G., et al. (2002). Family-based association study of 76 candidate genes in bipolar disorder: BDNF is a potential risk locus. Brain-derived neutrophic factor. *Molecular Psychiatry, 7,* 579–593.

Spielman, R. S., McGinnis, R. E., & Ewens, W. J. (1993). Transmission test for linkage disequilibrium: The insulin gene region and insulin-dependent diabetes mellitus (IDDM). *American Journal of Human Genetics, 52,* 506–516.

Stengler-Wenzke, K., Muller, U., Angermeyer, M. C., Sabri, O., & Hesse, S. (2004). Reduced serotonin transporter-availability in obsessive-compulsive disorder (OCD). *European Archives of Psychiatry and Clinical Neuroscience, 254,* 252–255.

Stewart, S. (2005, October). *Obsessive compulsive disorder (OCD) phenotypes in pediatric OCD.* Paper presented at the American Academy of Child and Adolescent Psychiatry/Canadian Academy of Child and Adolescent Psychiatry Joint Annual Meeting, Toronto, ON, Canada.

Stewart, S., Platko, J., Fagerness, J., Birns, J., Jenike, M., Rauch, S., et al. (2005, October). *Family-based association study of OLIG2 in obsessive-compulsive disorder.* Poster presented at the World Congress of Psychiatric Genetics, Boston, MA.

Studer, L., Spenger, C., Seiler, R. W., Altar, C. A., Lindsay, R. M., & Hyman, C. (1995). Comparison of the effects of the neurotrophins on the morphological structure of dopaminergic neurons in cultures of rat substantia nigra. *European Journal of Neuroscience, 7*, 223–233.

Suen, P. C., Wu, K., Levine, E. S., Mount, H. T., Xu, J. L., Lin, S. Y., et al. (1997). Brain-derived neurotrophic factor rapidly enhances phosphorylation of the postsynaptic N-methyl-D-aspartate receptor subunit 1. *Proceedings of the National Academy of Science of the United States of America, 94*, 8191–8195.

Sutcliffe, J. S., Delahanty, R. J., Prasad, H. C., McCauley, J. L., Han, Q., Jiang, L., et al. (2005). Allelic heterogeneity at the serotonin transporter locus (SLC6A4) confers susceptibility to autism and rigid-compulsive behaviors. *American Journal of Human Genetics, 77*, 265–279.

Swedo, S. E., Leonard, H. L., & Rapoport, J. L. (2004). The pediatric autoimmune neuropsychiatric disorders associated with streptococcal infection (PANDAS) subgroup: Separating fact from fiction. *Pediatrics, 113*, 907–911.

Szeszko, P. R., Ardekani, B. A., Ashtari, M., Malhotra, A. K., Robinson, D. G., Bilder, R. M., et al. (2005). White matter abnormalities in obsessive-compulsive disorder: A diffusion tensor imaging study. *Archives of General Psychiatry, 62*, 782–790.

Tarazi, F. I., Zhang, K., & Baldessarini, R. J. (2004). Dopamine D4 receptors: Beyond schizophrenia. *Journal of Receptor and Signal Transduction Research, 24*, 131–147.

Taylor, L., Krizman, D., Jankovic, J., Hayani, A., Steuber, P., Greenberg, F., et al. (1991). 9p monosomy in a patient with Gilles de la Tourette's syndrome. *Neurology, 41*, 1513–1515.

Tharmalingam, S., Richter, M. A., Phillips, K. A., King, N. A., Jeffers, J. C., & Kennedy, J. L. (2003, June). *A Preliminary Candidate Gene Study of Body Dysmorphic Disorder*. Poster session presented at the 29th Annual Harvey Stancer Research Day, University of Toronto. Toronto, ON.

Thomsen, P. H. (1995). Obsessive-compulsive disorder in children and adolescents: A study of parental psychopathology and precipitating events in 20 consecutive Danish cases. *Psychopathology, 28*, 161–167.

Toro, J., Cervera, M., Osejo, E., & Salamero, M. (1992). Obsessive-compulsive disorder in childhood and adolescence: A clinical study. *Journal of Child Psychology and Psychiatry, 33*, 1025–1037.

Tot, S., Erdal, M. E., Yazici, K., Yazici, A. E., & Metin, O. (2003). T102C and -1438 G/A polymorphisms of the 5-HT2A receptor gene in Turkish patients with obsessive-compulsive disorder. *European Psychiatry, 18*, 249–254.

Urraca, N., Camarena, B., Gomez-Caudillo, L., Esmer, M. C., & Nicolini, H. (2004). Mu opioid receptor gene as a candidate for the study of obsessive compulsive disorder with and without tics. *American Journal of Medical Genetics (Part B: Neuropsychiatric Genetics, 127B*, 94–96.

Van Grootheest, D. S., Cath, D. C., Beekman, A. T., & Boomsma, D. I. (2005). Twin studies on obsessive-compulsive disorder: A review. *Twin Research and Human Genetics, 8*(5), 450–458.

Veenstra-VanderWeele, J., Kim, S. J., Gonen, D., Hanna, G. L., Leventhal, B. L., & Cook, E. H., Jr. (2001). Genomic organization of the SLC1A1/EAAC1 gene and mutation screening in early-onset obsessive-compulsive disorder. *Molecular Psychiatry, 6*, 160–167.

Walitza, S., Wewetzer, C., Gerlach, M., Klampfl, K., Geller, F., Barth, N., et al. (2004). Transmission disequilibrium studies in children and adolescents with obsessive-compulsive disorders pertaining to polymorphisms of genes of the serotonergic pathway. *Journal of Neural Transmission, 111*, 817–825.

Walitza, S., Wewetzer, C., Warnke, A., Gerlach, M., Geller, F., Gerber, G., et al. (2002). 5-HT2A promoter polymorphism -1438G/A in children and adolescents with obsessive-compulsive disorders. *Molecular Psychiatry, 7*, 1054–1057.

Walther, D. J., Peter, J. U., Bashammakh, S., Hortnagl, H., Voits, M., Fink, H., et al. (2003). Synthesis of serotonin by a second tryptophan hydroxylase isoform. *Science, 299*, 76.

Wilcox, J. A., Tsuang, M. T., Schnurr, T., & Baida-Fragoso, N. (2003). Case-control family study of lesser variant traits in autism. *Neuropsychobiology, 47*, 171–177.

Willour, V. L., Yao Shugart, Y., Samuels, J., Grados, M., Cullen, B., Bienvenu, O. J., 3rd, et al. (2004). Replication study supports evidence for linkage to 9p24 in obsessive-compulsive disorder. *American Journal of Human Genetics, 75*, 508–513.

Zai, G., Arnold, P. D., Burroughs, E., Barr, C. L., Richter, M. A., & Kennedy, J. L. (2005). Evidence for the gamma-amino-butyric acid type B receptor 1 (GABBR1) gene as a susceptibility factor in obsessive-compulsive disorder. *American Journal of Medical Genetics (Part B: Neuropsychiatric Genetics), 134B*, 25–29.

Zai, G., Arnold, P. D., Strauss, J., King, N., Burroughs, E., Richter, M. A., et al. (2005). No association between brain-derived neurotrophic factor gene and obsessive-compulsive disorder. *Psychiatric Genetics, 15*, 235.

Zai, G., Arnold, P. D., Burroughs, E., Richter, M. A., & Kennedy, J. L. (2006). Tumor necrosis factor-alpha gene is not associated with obsessive-compulsive disorder. *Psychiatric Genetics, 16*, 43–45.

Zai, G., Bezchlibnyk, Y. B., Richter, M. A., Arnold, P. D, Burroughs, E., Barr, C. L., et al. (2004). Myelin oligodendrocyte glycoprotein (MOG) gene is associated with obsessive-compulsive disorder. *American Journal of Medical Genetics (Part B: Neuropsychiatric Genetics), 129B*, 64–68.

Zhang, H., Leckman, J. F., Pauls, D. L., Tsai, C. P., Kidd, K. K., & Campos, M. R. (2002). Genomewide scan of hoarding in sib pairs in which both sibs have Gilles de la Tourette syndrome. *American Journal of Human Genetics, 70*, 896–904.

Zhou, J., Bradford, H. F., & Stern, G. M. (1994). The stimulatory effect of brain-derived neurotrophic factor on dopaminergic phenotype expression of embryonic rat cortical neurons in vitro. *Brain Research: Developmental Brain Research, 81*, 318–324.

9

Cognitive-Behavioral Treatment of Pediatric Obsessive-Compulsive Disorder

Eric A. Storch
Kelly O'Brien
Jennifer Adkins
Lisa J. Merlo
Tanya K. Murphy
Gary R. Geffken
University of Florida

Obsessive-compulsive disorder (OCD) was once perceived as being resistant to psychological treatment, because no known treatment (e.g., insight-oriented therapy, client-centered therapy, family therapy, or play therapy) had demonstrated efficacy in decreasing symptoms. However, Meyer's (1966) pioneering work involving the use of exposure with response prevention (E/RP) led to the development of a successful behavioral treatment for OCD. Foa and Kozak (1986) continued to build on the model and began to disseminate E/RP more widely. E/RP is based on the premise that there are functional relationships between OCD symptoms and anxiety. Specifically, obsessions are associated with increases in anxiety, which motivate compulsions in efforts to reduce anxiety. Proponents of E/RP believed that these associations could be weakened through extinction processes, and research has consistently supported the effectiveness of this approach (see Abramowitz, Whiteside, & Deacon, 2005;

Storch & Merlo, 2006; Van Balkom et al., 1994). In fact, E/RP has been recognized as a powerful empirically supported treatment for OCD (Expert Consensus Panel for Obsessive-Compulsive Disorder, 1997). However, not all patients show a clinically significant decrease in OCD symptoms following E/RP (Baer & Minichiello, 1998), and some individuals refuse E/RP treatment or drop-out due to its anxiety-provoking nature (Stanley & Turner, 1995). Others are poor candidates for various reasons (e.g., Axis II pathology, poor insight).

Cognitive therapy thus emerged as both an alternative treatment for OCD as well as an adjunct to traditional E/RP, based mainly on the work of Salkovskis (1985). Cognitive treatment for OCD involves targeting distorted and intrusive thoughts; Salkovskis (1985, 1996) hypothesized that these faulty cognitions lead to increased anxiety and the urge to neutralize anxious feelings (through compulsions). The Obsessive-Compulsive Cognitions Working Group (OCCWG, 1997) identified several examples of faulty cognitions that are common in patients with OCD (e.g., inflated responsibility, overestimations of threat, overimportance of thoughts, and need to control thoughts). In general, cognitive interventions have been implemented successfully as an additive component to E/RP (Abramowitz, 1997), and the combined treatment is typically referred to as *cognitive-behavioral therapy* (CBT) for OCD. However, it should be noted that E/RP by itself has been referred to as CBT as the frequent result of behavioral exposure is correcting faulty OCD related cognitions.[1]

Following the successful application of CBT to adult OCD patients, researchers and clinicians began to adapt the intervention for use with children and adolescents with OCD (see Wolff & Rapoport, 1988). Since then, significant advances have been made in the cognitive-behavioral treatment of pediatric OCD (for reviews, see Lewin et al., 2005, and March & Leonard, 1996), and several distinct groups have continued to make adaptations to the intervention to facilitate its implementation with pediatric patients (e.g., Barrett, Healy-Farrell, & March, 2004; March & Mulle, 1998; Piacentini et al., 2002; POTS, 2004; Storch et al., 2005). Perhaps most significantly, March and Mulle (1998) developed a manualized treatment that outlined a child-friendly CBT intervention for OCD. This publication provided the foundation on which CBT for pediatric OCD was developed.

Generally speaking, CBT for pediatric OCD is a time-limited, present-oriented approach to psychotherapy that teaches children and family members the cognitive and behavioral competencies needed to adaptively respond to obsessions and compulsions. CBT represents a joint effort of therapist and patient (which includes the child and significant others), who form a collaborative team to address symptoms. CBT embraces an evidence-based orientation, in which empirical data informs clinical practice. The present chapter

---

[1]CBT with E/RP will hereby be referred to as CBT.

provides a pragmatic discussion of CBT for pediatric OCD, presenting behavioral and cognitive characteristics of treatment, and reviewing the outcome literature, and treatment options. A case illustration is provided to highlight treatment in its natural course. Finally, reproducible patient forms are included to facilitate treatment with your own patients.

BEHAVIORAL COMPONENTS

The Pavlovian or classical conditioning model posits that fears and anxiety emerge when associations develop between neutral and aversive stimuli. This results in the neutral, or conditioned, stimulus taking on the aversive and threatening qualities of the original aversive, or unconditioned, stimulus. In response to anxiety associated with the negative stimuli, individuals with OCD engage in compulsions or avoidance (conditioned responses) aimed at neutralizing the threat, thereby artificially reducing their anxiety. The combination of delaying and reducing anxiety with rituals or avoidance strengthens the conditioned fear through negative reinforcement. This increases the likelihood of continued avoidant and ritualistic behavior due to the distress-reducing properties of the ritual (see Fig. 9.1; see chap. 5 for a more detailed review).

Given this theoretical framework, E/RP exercises aid the patient in confronting stimuli that provoke fears and compensatory rituals. E/RP is a central component to effective CBT, with the key component involving the patient enduring initial anxiety so that the natural conditioning processes involved in fear reduction (habituation and extinction) can occur. As an initial step, the patient, his or her parent(s), and therapist develop a rank-

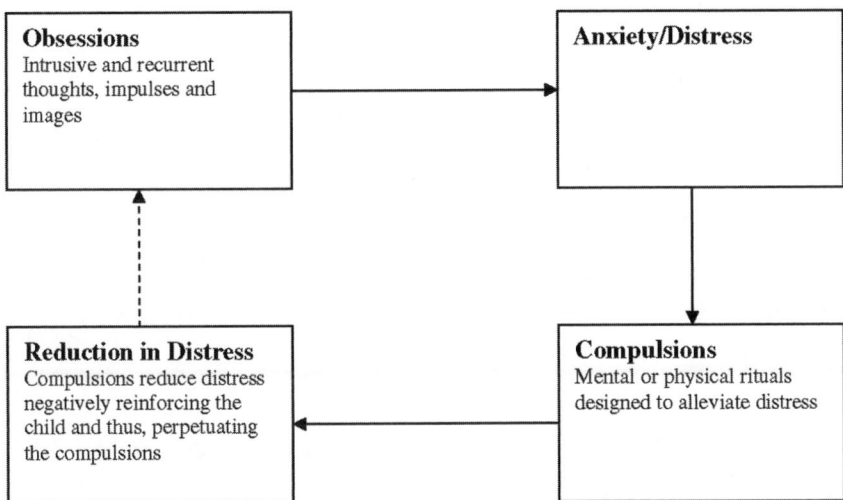

Figure 9.1.   The obsessive-compulsive cycle.

ordered list of anxiety-provoking situations (termed a *fear hierarchy*) in which the youngster refrains from performing anxiety reducing rituals (see Table 9.1 for an example, and Table 9.2 for a reproducible fear hierarchy). It is important that situations listed on the hierarchy have the ability to be recreated and controlled. For example, for a child with contamination-re-

TABLE 9.1
Example Ritual Hierarchy Form

Ritual	SUDS (0–100)	Date Assigned
Not counting steps/timing/breathing while *running*	95	
Watching TV without counting faces	92	
Not counting steps/timing/breathing while *walking*	90	
Not counting lines while reading	85	
Not counting beats when listening to the radio	85	
Riding in car without counting headlights/car lights	82	
Not counting while swallowing water/liquid	80	
Walking on sidewalk without counting sidewalk cracks	75	
Walking on tile floor without counting tiles	73	
Vacuuming without counting	70	
Dusting without counting	67	
Not counting while scrubbing	65	
Having entire hands sticky without washing	63	
Clicking pencil without counting	61	
Not counting squares on floor (or elsewhere)	60	
Looking at bookshelf without counting books	50	
Not washing hands when hands 'stink'	45	
Not washing hands while syrup is on them	43	
Brushing teeth without counting	40	
Eating after playing basketball, without washing hands first	35	
Not washing hands for 30 minutes after playing basketball	25	
Not counting pictures or things on walls	20	
Chewing without counting	10	

TABLE 9.2
Reproducible Fear Hierarchy Form

Ritual	Distress(0–100)	Date Assigned

lated symptoms of OCD, one exposure that can easily be conducted would be to touch a public bathroom sink without washing. This is in contrast to that same child being exposed to toxic waste without washing (which, of course, is not safe). The patient begins by working on the less-feared situations and approaches increasingly more difficult steps as a sense of mastery over the lesser situations is achieved. Although in vivo exposures are preferable, some situations may require imaginal exposures in which a script is created and read by the therapist or parent while the child imagines the event. With the help of the therapist, a script can be created of the child's distressing obsessions, which is then audiotaped. The resulting exposure consists of listening to the tape repeatedly while letting anxiety naturally habituate.

Regardless of the type of exposure, we recommend that the exposure continue until the child's anxiety has substantially decreased (to a maximum distress rating of 20 out of 100, on a scale of 0–100, with 0 corresponding to "no anxiety"). Discontinuing the exposure while the child's anxiety remains elevated would not demonstrate that anxiety naturally habituates and that feared outcomes do not take place. Rather, for exposures to have maximal therapeutic benefit, patients must allow themselves to be engaged in the feared situation. It is important to pay full attention to the situation and to allow anxiety and arousal to occur. Because this is difficult for many anxious youth, they may engage in "safety" behaviors (e.g., performing covert rituals, performing compensatory rituals at a later time) counter to the exposure or provide inaccurate reports of distress(see Fig. 9.2).

CBT may be described as an intervention that develops and/or enhances skills. In addition to tasks conducted within session, homework plays a significant role in facilitating and generalizing gains. Patients and parents are expected to complete between-session assignments that are agreed on by both the patient and therapist. Common assignments include independently en-

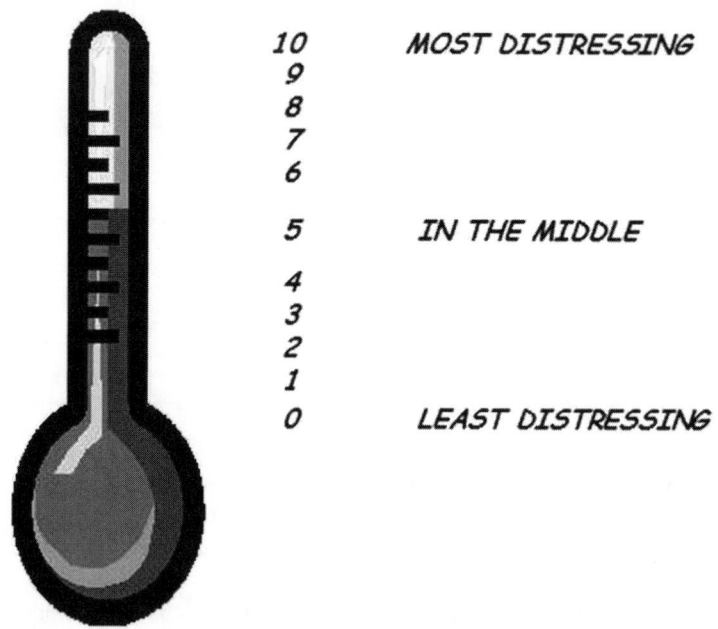

Figure 9.2.   Fear thermometer for pediatric OCD treatment.

gaging in E/RP exercises (particularly when symptoms are home-specific), conducting behavioral experiments (e.g., "If I do not touch this rock, will my mom really die?"), completing thought records (see the following section), and engaging in pleasurable activities (e.g., inviting a friend over to play).

Cognitive Components

The findings of psychopathology research highlight the importance of examining the obsessions and the beliefs that may underlie them. In fact, recent cognitive-behavioral models of OCD suggest that symptoms arise from inaccurate beliefs about the potential dangers posed by stimuli, negative predictions about the outcomes of these situations, and doubt or uncertainty about one's actions (Salkovskis, 1996, 1999). For example, a youth with contamination-related symptoms may overexaggerate the probability of contracting a disease, as well as the severity of the disease, if she or he did not compulsively wash after using a public toilet. Table 9.3 lists common cognitive distortions in children with OCD.

Given this, cognitive restructuring aims to correct anxiety-provoking thoughts in an explicit manner. Individuals are taught to (1) identify negative thoughts that occur before, during, or after anxiety-provoking situations; (2) evaluate the accuracy of their thoughts in light of data derived from Socratic questioning or as a result of behavioral experiments (e.g., testing to see if something terrible really happens if a patient does not engage in a perceived harm-reducing ritual, such as checking); and (3) derive rational alternative thoughts based on the acquired information. Cognitive restructuring techniques contain a substantive exposure component; however, the focus of exposure in this context is on the collection of information that will allow patients to revise their judgments about the degree of risk to which they are exposed in feared situations. By "talking back" to anxious thoughts with more objective, data-based information, reductions in anxiety occur (see

TABLE 9.3
Common Cognitive Distortions in Children With OCD

Cognitive Distortion	Example
Doubt or uncertainty	"I cannot remember if I turned off my video game consol."
Thought-action fusion	"If I think about killing mom with a knife, then I must want to do it."
Over-catastrophizing	"If I sit on a toilet seat, I'll probably get HIV."
Over-estimating	"The chances of catching HIV if I sit on the toilet is at least 10%."
Inflated responsibility	"If I don't touch this rock, my mom will get cancer."

Tables 9.4 and 9.5 for reproducible forms to assist with "talking back." The following is an example of in-session dialogue in which a child's contamination obsessions are challenged.

Therapist: It is actually really common for kids and even grown-ups to have thoughts that seem to pop up out of nowhere. Sometimes these thoughts don't really even make sense, but they can still bother you or make you worry. Most people don't get as bothered by these thoughts because they don't pay much attention to them. But people with OCD have a very hard time forgetting the worry thoughts. They usually keep thinking about it and then the worrying gets worse and

TABLE 9.4

Reproducible Thought Record (Form 1)

Day	What Happened?	What Did I Think?	How Did I Feel? (0–100)

TABLE 9.5

Reproducible Thought Record (Form 2)

What Happened?	What Did I Think?	How Did I Feel? (0–100)	Talk Back	How Did I Feel? (0–100)	What Happened in the End?
			—Evidence for and against the thought —So what? What's the worst that will happen? —What's happened in the past —What's the probability —What do you know about OCD thoughts?		

they feel like it won't go away unless they do something to make it go away. Can you think of any thoughts you have that are like this?

Child: That there are germs on doors?

Therapist: Exactly! Just like a lot of other kids, you sometimes worry that there are germs on doorknobs you have to touch. Can you remember what it was like the first time you had that worry?

Child: I think so. I think I had that thought about the door to Mrs. Smith's class.

Therapist: Okay, can you remember what that was like? How did you feel?

Child: I felt scared.

Therapist: So you were going up to the door and it made you feel scared. What did you do next?

Child: I waited for another kid to open the door so I didn't have to touch the handle.

Therapist: So that time another kid opened that door and you didn't have to worry about it anymore. What about now?

Child: It's a lot worse now. I can't stop worrying about doors everywhere.

Therapist: Yeah, that's the problem with doing things to make the worry go away so quickly. At first it seems like a good idea because your worry disappears, but then your body doesn't get a chance to learn that the door was safe, because you never tried touching it. So then, every time you avoid touching or going through doors after that, it makes the worry stronger. It sounds like that's what's going on with you now. It isn't just your teacher's door that worries you, but now you also about doors at home and at stores. Plus, it sounds like now you worry about the doors almost all the time and not just when you are near them.

Parent: He doesn't even go in his bedroom or the upstairs bathrooms. We had to remove the guest bathroom door so he could use that bathroom and he sleeps in the living room so he doesn't have to go through a door before going to bed. If he has to walk through a door at home, he washes his hands and forearms with hand sanitizer and alcohol.

Therapist: (to child) That sounds really hard. What do you think when you walk through a doorway or when you touch a door handle?

Child: That I'll get sick and die.

Therapist: Wow, that does sound scary and I bet you don't like having those thoughts. But the good news is that we can work on it to make it better for you. One way to start feeling better is to argue with the thoughts that make you worry. Right now it sounds like your OCD is trying to boss you around, but we can practice "talking back" to your OCD so that you don't have to listen anymore. Actually, there are a few different ways to do it. One way is to just say the opposite of the worry thought. What would be the opposite of your worry thought?

Child: I don't know.

Therapist: Maybe your mom would have an idea? (to mother) Can you tell him the opposite of his worry thought?

Parent: That he will not get sick or die just from touching a door.

Therapist:	That's right! How do you know that?
Parent:	Well lots of people touch those doors and don't get sick.
Therapist:	That's right! Let's try another way of talking back. Before you had OCD, did you touch doors and doorknobs?
Child:	Sure, lots of them.
Therapist:	How many do you think?
Child:	I don't know, probably about 100,000 times.
Therapist:	(to child and mother): How many times did you get sick during this time?
Parent:	Actually, he was really a healthy child – I'd say about 5 times.
Therapist:	Ok, first let's do the math. Five divided by 100,000 equals 0.005% chance of getting sick after you've touched a door. Pretty good odds, huh?
Therapist:	But wait – were each of those five times you got sick related to touching a door? Or maybe they were related to other things.
Parent:	That's right – on at least two of those times your sister was also sick. Or colds were going around the school.
Therapist:	Good point. So, when we practice walking through doors I want you to try this way of arguing with your worry thoughts. Then we'll see how it works.

Behavioral experiments are assignments for patients to engage in activities that will undermine their belief(s) about the predicted outcome of situations, and the need to engage in compulsions. For example, a patient who believed that he would contract the flu from not excessively washing after using a public toilet would record the incidence of sickness after not washing. The following example illustrates how to implement a behavioral experiment during the session:

Therapist:	So we need to pick an experiment to do that will challenge your worry thoughts, but before we do that, I need to explain the rules for these experiments. First, we choose something that's going to make you worry. At first we'll only choose things that make you worry a little bit. Then we'll try harder ones. The second rule is that you keep doing the experiment until you aren't really worrying too much anymore. We call that "sitting with it" because we're just going to sit here, not talking much and we're going to quietly wait until your worry goes down. The third rule is that you don't do any behaviors that will make your worry go away before your body has time to calm down on its own. That means no cleaning and no asking me or mom if "everything is going to be ok." When you are at home practicing, this even means no talking, reading, eating, drinking, watching TV or playing games. That's because those things might distract you and your body wouldn't learn as much from the experiment. So lets choose a behavior from the list we made. "Touching therapist's door with bare hand" is an 80 out of 100, that's too high for now. Lets start with an easier one. "Walking through and touching the reception door by myself" is a 50 out of 100. That's a good place to start. So I'll walk you over to

Child: the waiting room and have you walk through that door and back on your own. Ok?

Child: (Shakes his head yes, engages in the exposure, comes back into the therapist office and sits down)

Therapist: How are you feeling? Rate how nervous or scared you are on the 0 to 100 scale.

Child: Seventy or so.

Therapist: What are you thinking?

Child: That I might have brushed up against the door when I walked through it and got something on me that will make me sick.

Therapist: How can you challenge that?

Child: (Shrugs)

Therapist: What is the opposite?

Child: That I didn't touch anything?

Therapist: AND that if you did it wouldn't make you sick. Try telling yourself that once or twice every couple minutes to see if that helps your worry. Also, remind yourself what has happened to you and to others in the past when they have touched a door. Now we'll just sit quietly for a few minutes and see what happens with the worry.

Therapist: (after 5 minutes) How is your worry now on that 0 to 100 scale?

Child: About a 30.

Therapist: Great job! Let's keep going until it is almost gone.

Therapist: (15 minutes later) How about now?

Child: Not much at all – maybe a 5 or 10.

Therapist: Great!! Let's try it again then.

DEVELOPMENTAL ADAPTATIONS

As with any pediatric psychosocial interventions, a variety of developmental issues must be considered in conducting treatment. Frequently, adaptations to standard CBT for OCD must be made to address these issues. Of particular importance are adaptations to initial assessment, psychoeducation, and motivational procedures. In the assessment phase, it may be difficult to gain a full understanding of a child's OCD presentation based solely on self-reports. In particular, some younger children have difficulty recognizing obsessions and the relationship between obsessions and compulsive behaviors. Thus, therapists may use treatment exercises as an opportunity to gain further information and to teach the child about obsessions. Specifically, a therapist may get a child started with an exposure exercise to something the child avoids then ask the child during a state of clear distress "What are you thinking?" In children who do not acknowledge presence of specific cognitive components, therapists can defer to a sense of discomfort as the trigger for ritual engagement. Additionally, psychoeducation and metaphors used in therapy must be adjusted to meet the cognitive development of the child, while adequately conveying the conceptual basis of the therapy. Finally, younger children tend to focus on the present. Thus, the temporary distress associated with E/RP may have a stronger effect on their motivation to engage in therapy than the abstract future positive gains. This is particularly difficult in children who do not find their obsessions or ritual engagement distressing. To address this, contingency management techniques may be used to motivate a child to engage in therapy exercises.

ACCOMMODATION

The importance of family involvement in treatment of pediatric OCD is generally accepted as a central component of treatment (Calvocoressi, Lewis, Harris, & Trufan, 1995; Calvocoressi et al., 1999; Piacentini & Langley, 2004). Of particular importance is addressing accommodating behaviors that contribute to the maintenance of their child's OCD. Systematically identifying and reducing family accommodation of rituals can make if difficult for a child to engage in these behaviors and, thus, increases the likelihood that a child will make efforts to engage in alternate behaviors when faced with distressing obsessions. The following is an example of a therapist discussing the accommodation with a parent of the child in the earlier example involving contamination obsessions. These discussions typically take place with the child in the room, but at times this will happen without the child present should it not be appropriate for the child to witness the discussion.

Therapist: From what you have mentioned about Johnny's OCD, it sounds like this disorder has resulted in a lot of changes for your family. For example, you mentioned simple things like your son having to frequently wash his hands, and even changes to your house like removing doors and him sleeping in the living room. Are there any other changes that have been necessary to calm your son down?

Parent: Well there are times he keeps us from going through doors, or has us wash our hands. He also makes us tell him we're clean multiple times before he will let us cook his dinner or come into a room he is in.

Therapist: That happens a lot with OCD, even with adults who have OCD. What we've been talking about doing for treatment of OCD might seem kind of mean. What your family has done to calm your son down is natural. It comes from a very nurturing instinct. Unfortunately, it also makes it easier for your son to live with his OCD, which means he may not be motivated to challenge it. And that doesn't even include the burden it must place on you and your husband. As we progress in therapy, we will ask that you slowly remove some of the accommodating behaviors you have made in the past. We'll discuss this with your son and we'll remove accommodation just like we do with the exposures. We'll start with things that will only make him slightly uncomfortable. Maybe we'll have you stop carrying around hand sanitizers so he has to wash his hands with plain soap and water.

THERAPY INTENSITY

Traditionally, CBT for pediatric OCD takes place in the context of a 1-hour, in-office therapy session once a week; however, a variety of factors may be adjusted to best suit the needs of the child. For example, exposure sessions can be (and very often are) moved outside of the therapy office into more relevant environments (e.g., public bathrooms, school, home, public places). The duration of the sessions may also be increased to accommodate multiple in-session exposure exercises or the frequency of the sessions may be increased to multiple times per week. Although the comparative efficacy of these methods of intervention has not been well established, some data suggests increased frequency of sessions may increase the effectiveness for children who do not respond to once-weekly sessions (Storch et al., 2005).

OUTCOME STUDIES

CBT and pharmacotherapy, particularly selective serotonin reuptake inhibitors (SSRIs), are empirically supported treatment modalities for OCD in the pediatric population. Unfortunately, implementation of such treatments, particularly CBT, in the clinical setting has lagged behind the supporting empirical literature. For example, only 28%–35% of OCD sufferers actually seek medical treatment and only half of those who did actually visited a mental health specialist (Goodwin, Koenen, Hellman, Guardino, & Struening, 2002).

COGNITIVE-BEHAVIORAL THERAPY

The efficacy of CBT in children has been demonstrated in four controlled trials (Barrett, Healy-Farrell, & March, 2004) and numerous open trials (Benazon, Ager, & Rosenberg, 2002; Fischer, Himle, & Hanna, 1998; Franklin et al., 1998; March, Mulle, & Herbel, 1994; Piancentini, Bergman, Jacobs, McCracken, & Kretchman, 2002; Piancentini, Gitow, Jaffer, Graae, & Whitaker, 1994; Thienemann, Martin, Cregger, Thompson, & Dyer-Friedman, 2001; Waters, Barrett, & March, 2001; Wever & Ray, 1997). Table 9.6 provides a brief summary of these trials and includes information on the nature of each trial (e.g., control conditions, sample size), outcome measures utilized, and a synopsis of pertinent results.

Among the controlled trials, the Pediatric OCD Treatment Study (POTS) randomized controlled trial found that CBT alone, sertraline alone, or a combination of the treatments was more effective than placebo. Using the Children's Yale-Brown Obsessive-Compulsive Scale (CY-BOCS; Scahill et al., 1997) as the primary outcome measure, combined treatment was superior to CBT alone, sertraline alone, and placebo. CBT alone did not differ from sertraline, and both were superior to placebo. Approximately 54% of

TABLE 9.6

Controlled and open trials of cognitive-behavioral therapy for pediatric OCD

Study Authors	Trial Information	Outcome Measures	Study Results
Controlled Trials			
de Haan et al., 1998	E/RP vs. clomipramine 12 weekly meetings for both treatments Total N = 22 Ages 8–18 yrs.	CY-BOCS LOI-C CDS CBCL	• 59.9% CY-BOCS reduction in E/RP condition • 33.4% CY-BOCS reduction in clomipramine • E/RP significantly greater change on CY-BOCS than clomipramine • No differences between treatment groups on LOI-CVCDS and CBCL scores significantly decreased in both groups • No between groups differences on CDS or CBCL
Barrett et al., 2004	Individual family-based CBT (CBFT); Group family-based CBT; Waitlist control 14 weekly sessions 2 booster sessions Total N = 77 Ages 7–17 yrs.	ADIS-P CY-BOCS NIMH GOCS MASC CDI FAD DASS-21 SAS	• 88% in individual CBFT condition without ADIS-based OCD diagnosis post-treatment • 76% of group-based CBFT without diagnosis • All in wait-list group remained with diagnosis • NIMH-GOCS and CY-BOCS ratings indicate significant reductions in OCD symptoms for group and individual CBFT groups compared to waitlist • 65% reduction in CY-BOCS score for individual CBFT • 61% reduction in CY-BOCS for group-CBFT • No differences on NIMH-GOCS and CY-BOCS for individual and group CBFT • All groups showed significant reduction in MASC and CDI scores, but no significant treatment group effects • No time, group, or time × group effects for FAD, DASS-21, and SAS measures

(continued)

TABLE 9.6 (continued)

Study Authors	Trial Information	Outcome Measures	Study Results

Pediatric OCD Treatment Study (POTS) 2004	Four Conditions
	CBT alone
	Sertraline
	CBT & Sertraline
	Pill Placebo
	
	12-weeks for all treatments
	
	Total N = 97
	Ages 7–17 yrs.
		CY-BOCS	• CBT alone, sertraline alone, and combined CBT and sertraline showed lower CY-BOCS scores than placebo
			• Combined CBT and sertraline lower CY-BOCS score than CBT alone and sertraline alone
			• CY-BOCS score following CBT alone and sertraline alone did not differ
			• Clinical remission (CY-BOCS < 10):
			  • 53.6% for CBT and sertraline combined
			  • 39.3% for CBT alone
			  • 21.4% for sertraline alone
			  • 3.6% for placebo
			• Remission rate for combined CBT and sertraline did not differ from CBT alone, but did differ from sertraline alone and placebo

Storch et al., 2005	Intensive vs. Weekly Family-based CBT Total N = 32 Ages 7–17 yrs	ADIS-P CY-BOCS CGI Scale	• Greater improvement rates in Intensive CBT (94%) than Weekly CBT (67%) • No difference in final CY-BOCS scores • Greater attrition in Weekly CBT (3 drop-outs versus 0) than Intensive CBT
Open Trials			
March et al., 1994	CBT, most with concurrent pharmacological treatment Approximately 10 sessions Total N = 15 Ages 8–18 yrs.	Y-BOCS NIMH GOCS CGI Scale	• 50% Y-BOCS score reduction • 40% asymptomatic by NIMH-GOCS scale criteria • Gains maintained at 18 month follow-up

Study	Treatment	Measures	Results
Piacentini et al., 1994	CBT with family component 10 sessions Total N = 3 Ages 9–13 yrs.	CY-BOCS NIMH GOCS CGI Scale	• 56% CY-BOCS score reduction • 51% NIMH GOCS score reduction • Gains maintained at 12 month follow-up
Wever & Rey, 1997	Results reported for only CBT and pharmacological combination 2 Weekly session 12 daily sessions Total N = 57	CY-BOCS CBCL GFES	• 60% CY-BOCS score reduction • 68% remission at post-treatment follow-up • Gains maintained at 24-month follow-up • 39% of patients weaned off drug

Franklin et al., 1998	CBT —57% with concurrent pharmacological
	  Intensive (18 sessions)
	  Weekly (16 sessions)
	
	N = 4
	Ages 10–17 yrs.
		Y-BOCS
		HAM-D
			• 67% mean Y-BOCS reduction • Gains maintained at 9-month follow-up
			• No difference between intensive and weekly CBT sessions
			• CBT effectiveness not different with or without pharmacoptherapy
			• No change in depression ratings over time

Fischer et al., 1998	CBT with and without concurrent pharmacological 7 weekly sessions Total N = 15 Ages 12–17 yrs.	CY-BOCS	• 32% CY-BOCS reduction • 50% CY=BOCS reduction at 6-month follow-up

(continued)

TABLE 9.6   (continued)

Study Authors	Trial Information	Outcome Measures	Study Results
Thienemann et al., 2001	Group-based CBT with and without concurrent pharmacological and other treatments 14 weekly sessions Total N = 18 Ages 13–17 yrs.	CY-BOCS CGI Scale CDI MASC CBCL PSI	• Significant reductions in CY-BOCS, CGI Scale, CDI, MASC, and CBCL post-treatment • 25% CY-BOCS reduction • No change on PSI pre- to post-treatment
Waters et al., 2001	CBT with family component 14 weekly sessions Total N = 7 Ages 10–14 yrs.	ADIS-C/P CY-BOCS NIMH GOCS CGAS MA OC CDI FAD FAS	• 86% ADIS diagnosis-free post-treatment • 60% NIMH-GOCS and CY-BOCS reductions • Gains maintained at 3-month follow-up • No change in family functioning

| Benazon et al., 2002 | CBT
12 weekly sessions

Total N = 16
Ages 8–17 yrs. | CY-BOCS
NIMH
GOCS
CGI Scale
HAM-A | • 44% asymptomatic on NIMH-GOCS50% CY-BOCS reduction |
| Piacentini et al., 2002 | CBT with and without concurrent pharmacological

Average 12.5 sessions

Total N = 42
Ages 5–17 yrs. | ADIS-C/P
CY-BOCS
NIMH GOCS
CGI Scale
COIS
CDI
MASC
CBCL | • 79% treatment response rate45% mean reduction in NIMH GOCS score
• No differences between CBT alone and CBT with pharmacological treatment |

patients in the combined treatment condition experienced symptom remission as defined by the *DSM–IV–TR*, compared to 39% for CBT alone and 21% for sertraline alone, leading to the conclusion that children and adolescents diagnosed with OCD should be treated with the combination of CBT plus SSRI or CBT alone.

Other controlled findings have produced relatively more robust findings. For example, de Haan et al. (1998) found a nearly 60% reduction in OCD symptoms as measured by the CY-BOCS in children treated with E/RP, whereas patients treated with clomipramine demonstrated a 33% reduction in OCD symptoms. Barrett et al. (2004) demonstrated a 65% reduction in CY-BOCS scores for individual CBT and a 61% reduction for group CBT. At 6-month follow-up, 65% of children receiving individual CBT and 87% of those receiving group CBT were OCD diagnosis-free. At 18-month follow-up, 70% of those who received individual CBT and 84% of those who received group CBT remained OCD diagnosis-free (Barrett, Farrell, Dadds, & Boulter, 2005).

Finally, our laboratory (PI: Storch) is completing a randomized controlled trial of Intensive CBT (14 sessions over 3 weeks) versus Weekly CBT (14 sessions over 12 weeks; Storch et al., 2005). Preliminary analyses indicated that greater improvement rates were found for Intensive CBT (94%) relative to Weekly CBT (67%). However, no differences in final CY-BOCS scores at post-treatment were found. Intensive treatment had certain advantages over weekly treatment, including relatively less attrition and faster symptom remission. A full report of this study is forthcoming.

In sum, these trials correspond with adult findings (e.g., Foa et al., 2005) and suggest that CBT alone or with concurrent pharmacotherapy is the front-line treatment for OCD (Abramowitz, 1997; March, Franklin, Nelson, & Foa, 2001; POTS, 2004). A recent meta-analysis by Abramowitz, Whiteside, and Deacon (2005) further supports this notion, finding greater effect sizes of CBT (ES = 1.98) versus SRI medication (1.13), and greater CY-BOCS reductions for CBT ($M_{pre-treatment} = 23.9$; $M_{post-treatment} = 11.1$) than SRI medication $M_{pre-treatment} = 24.5$; $M_{post-treatment} = 17.1$).

ALTERNATIVE CBT APPROACHES

Group Treatment

CBT for pediatric OCD has also been shown effective in the group setting. A controlled trial of CBT that utilized an active family component in a group setting found marked reductions in OCD symptoms in both individual and group conditions relative to wait-list controls (Barrett et al., 2004). Eighty-eight percent of children who enrolled in individual CBT and 76% of those who enrolled in group CBT were without an OCD diagnosis following treatment, while all children in the wait-list condition continued to meet diagnostic criteria following a 6–8 week wait-list. Gains were maintained over an 18-month follow-up period (Barrett et al., 2005). Further support comes from open trials (Fischer et al., 1998, Martin & Thienemann, 2005, Thienemann et al., 2001). Overall, it is relevant to note that improvements found in group treatment are slightly less robust than those in individual therapy (Barrett et al., 2005).

Intensive Treatment

Despite the high rates of treatment success, not all patients respond to traditional therapeutic approaches. An alternative for such cases of intractable OCD is intensive CBT. Intensive treatment incorporates identical principles to standard weekly CBT; however, children undergo a concentrated course of therapy over 2 to 4 weeks, which is characterized by an aggressive targeting of symptoms. There are also additional benefits to intensive treatment, such as reduced geographical barriers and increased access to skilled CBT practitioners, as well as the possibility of facilitating a more rapid return to premorbid functioning (Lewin et al., 2005; Storch, Gelfand, Geffken, & Goodman, 2003).

To date, four published reports have supported this approach. In the most comprehensive trial to date, Storch et al. (2005) compared the relative efficacy of intensive CBT over 3 weeks (14 sessions in total) to 14 weekly CBT sessions. A more detailed description of findings is presented in the previous section. Other open trials (e.g., Franklin et al., 1998; Storch et al., 2004, 2005) have supported intensive treatment in both treatment-naïve and refractory populations.

SUMMARY OF EVIDENCE BASE FOR CBT

Overall, obsessive-compulsive symptoms are more likely to diminish in patients receiving CBT alone or in combination with pharmacotherapy, strongly suggesting that the "gold standard" for pediatric OCD treatment is CBT alone or CBT in combination with an SSRI (POTS, 2004). In light of concerns about suicidality secondary to SSRI use (e.g., Whittington et al., 2004), many are suggesting that CBT be employed alone as a first-line approach, only adding SSRIs when there is an incomplete treatment response (POTS, 2004; Storch et al., 2005). These results stand in contrast with play-based, supportive, insight-oriented, psychoanalytic, and psychodynamic therapies, which lack evidence showing effectiveness in the treatment of pediatric OCD (Franklin & Foa, 2002; March et al., 2001; March & Mulle, 1998; Practice Parameters, 1998).

TREATMENT RESPONSE PREDICTORS

The literature on pediatric predictors of CBT response is relatively small, lagging behind the modest data on adult predictors. The extant literature has, for the most part, been derived from pharmacological trials. A detailed account of treatment response predictors is contained in chapter 11 of this text.

Case Description

Jason was a 12-year-old Caucasian male who presented with obsessions related to saying, writing, reading, and thinking about phrases "perfectly." His related compulsions included repeating phrases, re-reading, and re-writing until he felt "just right." He also exhibited checking behaviors (e.g., repeatedly checking doors and cabinets to ensure they were shut completely), counting, and sequencing compulsions. Jason's parents reported a 10-month history of OCD symptoms, with significant distress and impairment from symptoms observed for 3 months prior to seeking treatment. The family reported that they were interested in trying behavioral interventions before considering pharmacological treatment; Jason had received no treatment prior to presenting to clinic.

At his baseline assessment, Jason's score on the CY-BOCS was a 27, indicating moderate-to-severe OCD symptoms. He was also given a diagnosis of Depressive Disorder NOS due to his endorsement of depressed mood, feelings of hopelessness, decreased sleep, and difficulty concentrating (Children's Depression Inventory t-score $= 67$).

CURRENT SYMPTOMS AND SYMPTOM DEVELOPMENT

Jason's parents reported that he began having difficulties at the beginning of his seventh-grade school year as a result of spending significant time re-reading and re-writing assignments. Jason noted that he would sometimes spend all of his time writing his name because he had to have all of the letters "perfect" before moving on. Jason's parents also reported extreme difficulty communicating with Jason because of his need to repeat phrases over and over again until he said them "just right." For example, whenever saying "uh-huh," Jason would repeat the phrase up to one dozen times using differing inflections. Jason was extremely motivated to participate in treatment and demonstrated good insight into the irrationality of his OCD.

ACADEMIC AND SOCIAL FUNCTIONING/IMPAIRMENT

Jason was described as a dedicated student who had received all A's throughout his schooling. When he presented for treatment, he was no longer attending public school because of his distress from OCD symptoms and his parents were pursuing homebound school services. Jason's parents reported that he had previously managed to "keep himself together at school," which would result in major episodes of "losing it" and significant distress related to OCD symptoms when he returned home from school.

Jason had played football for several years; however, he quit the team due to his difficulty concentrating and performing during games. He described standing on the sideline worrying about having a "perfect" thought as opposed to paying attention to what was happening on the field. Jason's parents noted that Jason had withdrawn from all social activities and avoided his friends after he stopped attending school. In addition, Jason frequently resisted going to restaurants, malls, family gatherings, and church services due to his worry about handling OCD thoughts in front of others.

FAMILY FUNCTIONING/ACCOMMODATION

Jason lived with his mother, father, and 3-year old sister. His family expressed frustration with not knowing how to help Jason when he displayed significant distress about obsessions or engaged in compulsions. They would try to comfort him when he was in an "OCD episode" and he would become angry with them when they interrupted his mental rituals. Jason's family accommodated his symptoms in multiple ways, including making sure that doors and cabinets remained closed, putting off activities so they would not interrupt his rituals, and not requiring him to join the family in social settings like restaurants and malls.

CASE CONCEPTUALIZATION

As noted previously, CBT for OCD is based on the premise that obsessions and compulsions are functionally related (compulsions are performed to reduce/avoid anxiety related to obsessions); therefore, exposure to feared stimuli and refraining from compulsions (i.e., response prevention) are critical components of OCD symptom reduction. In addition, teaching cognitive strategies helps the child to make more objective appraisals of their obsessions as a way to reduce anxiety. Cognitive strategies include teaching the child to identify thoughts as part of the OCD and subsequently modify their interpretations of anxiety-provoking thoughts.

Given the severity of his symptoms (e.g., his withdrawal from school and avoidance of most social situations) and high motivation for treatment, Jason's family decided to participate in the intensive CBT protocol. The intensive treatment program consisted of five 90-minute daily sessions per week for the course of 3 weeks. This treatment option allowed the family to predominantly focus on treatment for a relatively short amount of time (compared to weekly sessions over a period of months) in order to increase functioning quickly and efficiently. Given the direct link between his OCD and depressive symptoms, we also believed that Jason's depressive symptoms would decrease as his distress and impairment related to OCD symptoms improved during treatment. For example, Jason's avoidance of activities he had previously enjoyed and withdrawal from social settings due to embarrassment from OCD symptoms were seen as contributing to his feelings of hopelessness and depressed mood.

COURSE OF TREATMENT

Jason and his family were first provided with psychoeducation about OCD and the function of anxiety in maintaining OCD symptoms. Jason's symptoms of wanting to feel "just right," repeating, and checking were normalized for the family as common problems for people with OCD that can be greatly reduced or eliminated with treatment. Throughout treatment, concepts and skills were presented in a way that would be understood by Jason given his developmental level. For example, his OCD was externalized as a character so that he could imagine "talking back to OCD" and to help him distinguish "OCD thoughts" from normal thoughts given that they were both "in his brain." It was also conveyed that Jason and his family would be learning a set of skills together that would be used in their everyday lives to decrease impairment and distress from Jason's OCD symptoms.

EXPOSURE AND RESPONSE PREVENTION

Exposure to feared stimuli was explained as a way to habituate to anxious feelings without engaging in compulsions, and Jason was assured that his anxiety would naturally decrease if he refrained from compulsions. Anxiety ratings for each of his symptoms were obtained with the use of a "fear thermometer" (see Fig. 9.2) so that items could be ordered on from least to greatest distress and anxiety. A "fear ladder" was constructed with the least anxiety-provoking stimuli on the bottom rungs and most anxiety-provoking stimuli at the top. For example, Jason reported that closing a door once and not checking would be a "3" out of 10 on the fear thermometer, while writing his name purposefully wrong was rated an "8" out of 10. Jason was told that he would begin practicing the skills for the easier situations and then he would slowly move his way up the ladder as he mastered the items. The first in-session exposure involved Jason closing all open doors in the clinic once and moving on without checking. His first homework assignment extended this exposure to quickly closing doors and cabinets only once at home. Jason's anxiety related to making sure that doors were closed "just right" quickly decreased and his success with the initial exposure motivated him to continue climbing the ladder to harder exposures. Other in-session exposures and homework assignments included writing letters and phrases purposefully wrong without correction, reading aloud without going back and repeating words, and remaining silent after phrases that he would usually repeat to feel "just right."

"TALKING BACK" TO OBSESSIONS

Although Jason's overt compulsions of checking, repeating, and sequencing quickly reduced with E/RP exercises, Jason had significant difficulties with his frequent obsessions of "getting a perfect thought." Therefore, the focus of treatment for Jason's mental rituals was developing his use of cognitive coping strategies to help manage his extreme anxiety during obsessions and response prevention. Jason was taught cognitive restructuring techniques to help examine his obsessive thoughts and feelings in a more realistic way. For example, Jason was taught to "talk back" to OCD with challenges such as, "So what if it is not perfect?" "What is the worst that could happen?" and "What is perfect anyway?"

Jason was taught to record his obsessive thoughts so they could be discussed in sessions. Guided self-talk was role-played in session to help Jason become able to use challenging statements, as well as coping self-statements after identifying an OCD thought (e.g., "This feeling will pass"). Jason was also assisted with forming a list of pleasurable activities that he could engage in following his use of guided self-talk after an obsession (e.g., play basketball, play with his sister, look at pictures) to prevent him from concentrating on obsessions. Jason and his family were coached in the procedure of identifying an OCD thought, using challenging and coping self-statements to reduce anxiety, and quickly moving on to another activity.

EXPOSURE TO SOCIAL SITUATIONS

Another important component of treatment was increasing Jason's involvement in social activities that he had begun to avoid due to embarrassment of his OCD symptoms. We discussed examining his fears of what others would think of him in a more objective and realistic manner (e.g., "Others probably won't notice," "There will be more to distract me from my obsessions," and "What's the worst that could happen?"). Another "fear ladder" was constructed that listed situations that Jason was avoiding in terms of least to most anxiety-provoking. For example, Jason noted that he would feel more comfortable having a friend over to his house than going to the mall where he may see a variety of classmates. Jason was encouraged to begin going in restaurants with his family rather than sitting in the car and to resume attending family gatherings (the family had accommodated these avoidance behaviors). He reported that his anxiety greatly decreased after remaining in the situations, and his mood began to improve as he became more involved socially with others and became more confident in his use of the cognitive restructuring skills.

FAMILY INVOLVEMENT

Jason's family was engaged in his treatment to reduce their involvement in Jason's symptoms (which may have contributed to the maintenance of these behaviors), as well as to improve family communication and problem-solving related to managing Jason's OCD. First, his parents were instructed in Jason's use of response-prevention and cognitive restructuring techniques so that they could guide exposures in the home environment when appropriate. Given Jason's conflict with his parents when he was distressed by an obsession, the family was instructed in how to disengage from Jason's OCD behaviors. Instead of tolerating his delays due to mental obsessions or avoidance, the family practiced providing brief support and then encouraging Jason to use the skills he had learned (e.g., prompting Jason to "talk back" to OCD). In addition, the therapist worked with the family to help attribute their frustration and anger to OCD itself rather than to Jason or to each other. The family's reinforcement of Jason's engagement in pleasurable activities following mental obsessions was also helpful to increase this behavior. The family's facilitation of social exposures and not accommodating his mental rituals or avoidance were viewed as critical aspects of Jason's treatment success.

TREATMENT OUTCOME

After 3 weeks of intensive CBT, Jason reported little to no difficulty resisting checking, repeating, and sequencing compulsions. He still reportedly experienced some distress related to obsessing about "perfect thoughts," but by the end of treatment he was able to move on much more quickly following obsessions. His family also reported decreased frustration and improved family functioning following OCD treatment.

Jason's score on the CY-BOCS decreased from 27 at pre-treatment to an 8 at post-treatment and 0 at 3-month follow-up, indicating no OCD symptoms. His depressive symptoms also decreased significantly (t-score $= 46$). Numerous qualitative improvements were also noted. By the end of treatment, for example, Jason was attending church services, visiting with friends and family, and attending other social activities.

CONCLUSIONS AND FUTURE DIRECTIONS

Cognitive-behavioral treatment of pediatric OCD has grown extensively in the past decade. As it is with the general state of health care, the study of the treatment of pediatric OCD lagged behind the treatment of adult OCD, and clinical care has lagged behind research. It was in 1998 that March and Mulle published the first CBT manual for pediatric OCD. It is widely recognized that there is a major impact of pediatric OCD on the family, and that guided parental involvement in CBT for pediatric OCD is essential. Similarly, there must be consideration of and adaptation to the developmental level of the youth for CBT. Rates of remission of symptoms in controlled studies of CBT for pediatric OCD are notable (POTS [2004] = 39% for CBT alone and 54% for CBT plus SSRI; Barrett et al. [2004] = 70% for family CBT; and Storch et al. [2005] = 94% for intensive family CBT); yet all controlled studies lead to the conclusion that family CBT alone or in combination with SSRI is the gold standard for treatment of pediatric OCD. There is no evidence base for the mental health treatment of pediatric OCD with play-based therapy, supportive therapy, insight-oriented therapy, psychoanalytic therapy, or psychodynamic therapy (Franklin & Foa, 2002; March et al., 2001; Practice Parameters, 1998). Thus, it is extremely important that recognition of this treatment information on pediatric OCD become more widespread among medical practitioners, school personnel, and mental health professionals, as well as health care professionals in general. More widespread dissemination of CBT training is indicated for appropriate professional mental and behavioral health training programs.

Continuing research is of the utmost importance an answer questions about refractory or unresponsive patients. Augmentation strategies for CBT and SSRIs are essential, yet there is very little data on augmentations strategies to date. As just noted, delivery of CBT in an intensive mode for pediatric OCD is one option. Chapter 10 discusses psychopharmacological options. However, augmentation of CBT or medications has not been systematically studied. This is an important area for future study.

Finally, additional research is needed to understand individual patient differences in response to treatment. Research on mediators and moderators of treatment response is needed. Clinical experience, hypotheses of clinical researchers, and research on other psychiatric disorders suggest that factors influencing treatment outcome might include comorbidity, motivation, family factors such as accommodation or expressed emotion, symptom typology or features of clinical presentation, and degree of insight into OCD symptoms. However, systematic research is needed to understand how patient and family characteristics might affect response to treatment (Geffken et al., 2006). This much needed research can help in developing evidence-based models of what treatments or treatment augmentations are likely to have efficacy with pediatric OCD patients, and particularly those with characteristics that have been empirically demonstrated to show differential responses. It is our hope and expectation that this chapter will stimulate future research for evidence-based practice in the care of pediatric OCD.

REFERENCES

Abramowitz, J. S. (1997). Effectiveness of psychological and pharmacological treatments for obsessive-compulsive disorder: A quantitative review. *Journal of Consulting and Clinical Psychology, 65*, 44–52.

Abramowitz, J., Whiteside, S. P., & Deacon, B. J. (2005). The effectiveness of treatment for pediatric Obsessive-compulsive disorder: A meta-analysis. *Behavior Therapy, 36*, 55–63.

Baer, L., & Minichiello, W. E. (1998). Behavior therapy for obsessive-compulsive disorder. In M. A. Jenike, L. Baer, & W. E. Minichiello (Eds.), *Obsessive-compulsive disorder: Practical management* (pp. 44–64). St. Louis, MO: Mosby.

Barrett, P., Farrell, L., Dadds, M., & Boulter, N. (2005). Cognitive-behavioral family treatment of childhood obsessive-compulsive disorder: Long-term follow-up and predictors of outcome. *Journal of the American Academy of Child and Adolescent Psychiatry, 44,* 1005–1014.

Barrett, P., Healy-Farrell, L., & March, J. S. (2004). Cognitive-behavioral family treatment of childhood obsessive-compulsive disorder: A controlled trial. *Journal of the American Academy of Child and Adolescent Psychiatry, 43,* 46–62.

Benazon, N. R., Ager, J., & Rosenberg, D. R. (2002). Cognitive behavior therapy in treatment-naive children and adolescents with obsessive-compulsive disorder: An open trial. *Behavior Research and Therapy, 40,* 529–539.

Calvocoressi, L., Lewis, B., Harris, M., & Trufan, S. J. (1995). Family accommodation in obsessive-compulsive disorder. *American Journal of Psychiatry, 152,* 441–443.

Calvocoressi, L., Mazure, C. M., Kasl, S. V., Skolnick, J., Fisk, D., Vegso, S. J., et al. (1999). Family accommodation of obsessive-compulsive symptoms: Instrument development and assessment of family behavior. *Journal of Nervous and Mental Disease, 187,* 636–642.

de Haan, E., Hoogduin, K. A. L., Buitelaar, J. K., & Keijsers, G. P. J. (1998). Behavior therapy versus clomipramine for the treatment of obsessive-compulsive disorder in children and adolescents. *Journal of the American Academy of Child and Adolescent Psychiatry, 37,* 1022–1029.

Expert Consensus Panel for Obsessive-Compulsive Disorder. (1997). Treatment of obsessive compulsive disorder. *Journal of Clinical Psychiatry, 58,* 3–28.

Fischer, D., Himle, J. A., & Hanna, G. L. (1998). Group behavioral therapy for adolescents with obsessive-compulsive disorder: Preliminary outcomes. *Research in Social Work, 8,* 629–636.

Foa, E. B., & Kozak, M. J. (1986). Emotional processing of fear: Exposure to corrective information. *Psychological Bulletin, 99,* 20–35.

Foa, E. B., Liebowitz, M. R., Kozak, M. J., Davies, S., Campeas, R., Franklin, M. E., et al. (2005). Randomized, placebo-controlled trial of exposure and ritual prevention, clomipramine, and their combination in the treatment of obsessive-compulsive disorder. *American Journal of Psychiatry, 162,* 151–161.

Franklin, M. E., & Foa, E. B. (2002). Cognitive behavioral treatments for obsessive-compulsive disorder. In P. Nathan & J. Gorman (Eds.), *A guide to treatments that work* (pp. 367–386). New York: Oxford University Press.

Franklin, M. E., Kozak, M. J., Cashman, L. A., Coles, M. E., Rheingold, A. A., & Foa, E. (1998). Cognitive-behavioral treatment of pediatric obsessive-compulsive disorder: An open clinical trial. *Journal of the American Academy of Child and Adolescent Psychiatry, 37,* 412–419.

Geffken, G. R., Storch, E. A., Duke, D., Lewin, A., Monaco, L., & Goodman, W. K. (2006). Hope and coping in family members of patients with obsessive compulsive disorder. *Journal of Anxiety Disorders, 20,* 58–70.

Goodwin, R., Koenen, K. C., Hellman, F., Guardino, M., & Struening, E. (2002). Help-seeking and access to mental health treatment for obsessive-compulsive disorder. *Acta Psychiatrica Scandinavica, 106,* 143–149.

Lewin, A. B., Storch, E. A., Merlo, L. J., Adkins, J. W., Murphy, T. K., & Geffken, G. R. (2005). Intensive cognitive behavioral therapy for pediatric obsessive compulsive disorder: A treatment protocol for mental health providers. *Psychological Services, 2,* 91–104.

March, J. S., & Leonard, H. (1996). Obsessive-compulsive disorder in children and adolescents: A review of the past 10 years. *Journal of the American Academy of Child and Adolescent Psychiatry, 35,* 1265–1273.

March, J. S., & Mulle, K. (1998). OCD in children and adolescents: A cognitive-behavioral treatment manual. New York: Guilford.

March, J. S., Franklin, M. E., Nelson, A., & Foa, E. (2001). Cognitive-behavioral psychotherapy for pediatric obsessive-compulsive disorder. Journal of Clinical Child Psychology, 30, 8–18.

March, J. S., Mulle, K., & Herbel, B. (1994). Behavioral psychotherapy for children and adolescents with obsessive-compulsive disorder: An open trial of a new protocol-driven treatment package. Journal of the American Academy of Child and Adolescent Psychiatry, 33, 333–341.

Martin, J., & Thienemann, M. (2005). Group cognitive-behavior therapy with family involvement for middle-school-age children with obsessive-compulsive disorder: A pilot study. Child Psychiatry and Human Development, 36, 113–127.

Meyer, V. (1966). Modification of expectations in cases with obsessional rituals. Behaviour Research and Therapy, 4, 273–280.

Obsessive-Compulsive Cognitions Working Group. (1997). Cognitive assessment of obsessive-compulsive disorder. Behaviour Research and Therapy, 35, 667–682.

Pediatric OCD Treatment Study Team. (2004). Cognitive-behavior therapy, sertraline, and their combination for children and adolescents with obsessive-compulsive disorder. Journal of the American Medical Association, 292, 1969–1976.

Piacentini, J., & Langley, A. K. (2004). Cognitive-behavioral therapy for children who have obsessive-compulsive disorder. Journal of Clinical Psychology, 60, 1181–1194.

Piacentini, J., Bergman, R. L., Jacobs, C., McCracken, J., & Kretchman, J. (2002). Open trial of cognitive-behavioral therapy for childhood obsessive-compulsive disorder. Journal of Anxiety Disorders, 16, 207–219.

Piacentini, J., Gitow, A., Jaffer, M., Graae, F., & Whitaker, A. (1994). Outpatient behavioral treatment of child and adolescent obsessive-compulsive disorder. Journal of Anxiety Disorders, 8, 277–289.

Practice Parameters. (1998). Practice parameters for the assessment and treatment of children and adolescents with obsessive-compulsive disorder. Journal of the American Academy of Child and Adolescent Psychiatry, 37S, 27S–45S.

Salkovskis, P. (1996). Cognitive-behavioral approaches to the understanding of obsessional problems. In R. Rapee (Ed.), Current controversies in the anxiety disorders (pp. 103–133). New York: Guilford.

Salkovskis, P. M. (1985). Obsessional-compulsive problems: A cognitive-behavioural analysis. Behaviour Research Therapy, 23, 571–583.

Salkovskis, P. M. (1999). Understanding and treating obsessive-compulsive disorder. Behavior Research and Therapy, 37S1, S29–S52.

Scahill, L., Riddle, M. A., McSwiggin-Hardin, M., Ort, S. I., King, R. A., Goodman, W. K., et al. (1997). Children's Yale-Brown Obsessive Compulsive Scale: Reliability and validity. Journal of the American Academy of Child and Adolescent Psychiatry, 36, 844–852.

Stanley, M. A., & Turner, S. M. (1995). Current status of pharmacological and behavioral treatment of obsessive-compulsive disorder. Behavior Therapy, 26, 163–186.

Storch, E. A., & Merlo, L. J. (in press). Evaluation and treatment of the patient with obsessive-compulsive disorder. Journal of Family Practice.

Storch, E. A., Geffken, G. R., Duke, D., Munson, M., Merlo, L., Adkins, J., et al. (2005). Cognitive-behavioral therapy for pediatric obsessive-compulsive disorder: Comparison between weekly and intensive approaches. Unpublished manuscript.

Storch, E. A., Gelfand, K. M., Geffken, G. R., & Goodman, W. K. (2003). An intensive outpatient approach to the treatment of obsessive-compulsive disorder: Case exemplars. Annals of the American Psychotherapy Association, 4(6), 14–19.

Storch, E. A., Gerdes, A., Atkins, J., Geffken, G. R., Star, J., & Murphy, T. (2004). Behavioral treatment of child with pediatric autoimmune neuropsychiatric disorder associated with Group A streptococcal infection. *Journal of the American Academy of Child and Adolescent Psychiatry, 43,* 510–511.

Thienemann, M., Martin, J., Cregger, B., Thompson, H. B., & Dyer-Friedman, J. (2001). Manual-driven group cognitive-behavioral therapy of adolescents with obsessive-compulsive disorder: A pilot study. *Journal of the American Academy of Child and Adolescent Psychiatry, 40,* 1254–1260.

Van Balkom, A. J. L. M., van Oppen, P., Vermeulen, A. W. A., van Dyck, R., Nauta, M. C. E., & Vorst, H. C. M. (1994). A meta-analysis on the treatment of obsessive compulsive disorder: A comparison of anti-depressants, behavior, and cognitive therapy. *Clinical Psychology Review, 14,* 359–381.

Waters, T., & Barrett, P. (2000). The role of the family in childhood obsessive-compulsive disorder. *Clinical Child & Family Psychology Review, 3,* 173–184.

Waters, T., Barrett, P., & March, J. S. (2001). Cognitive-behavioral family treatment of childhood obsessive-compulsive disorder: An open clinical trial. *American Journal of Psychotherapy, 55,* 372–387.

Wever, C., & Rey, J. (1997). Juvenile obsessive-compulsive disorder. *Australia New Zealand Journal of Psychiatry, 31,* 105–113.

Whittington, C. J., Kendall, T., Fonagy, P., Cottrell, D., Cotgrove, A., & Boddington, E. (2004). Selective serotonin reuptake inhibitors in childhood depression: systematic review of published versus unpublished data. *Lancet, 363,* 1341–1345.

Wolff, R., & Rapoport, J. L. (1988). Behavioral treatment of childhood obsessive-compulsive disorder. *Behavior Modification, 12,* 252–256.

10

Psychopharmacology of Pediatric Obsessive-Compulsive Disorder

Daniel A. Geller
Harvard Medical School

Cognitive neuroscience approaches, including neuroimaging and neuropsychological assessment, have demonstrated utility as paradigms for understanding neuropsychiatric disorders, particularly obsessive-compulsive disorder (OCD; Rauch & Savage, 1997; Savage, 1998). Until recently, there has been limited application of these models to pediatric OCD. However, recent studies on the developmental progression of neuronal maturation and reorganization, and the literature on age-related progress in neuropsychological performance, suggest that neuropsychiatric models of pediatric OCD must consider the developmental context in which abnormal neuropsychological findings are expressed.

ANATOMY OF FRONTOSTRIATAL SYSTEMS

Several cortico-striatal-thalamic circuits have been implicated in the pathophysiology of OCD: areas of frontal and prefrontal cortices, including the orbitofrontal cortex and anterior cingulate cortex send numerous excitatory projections to the striatum (Goldman-Rakic, 1987). In turn, regions of the striatum send efferents directly and indirectly (through other basal ganglia structures) to dorso-medial thalamic nuclei, which in turn project back to the prefrontal cortex, stimulating cortical output and completing this feedback loop (Fitzgerald, McMaster et al., 1999; Rauch & Savage, 1997). Several parallel, though functionally distinct cortico-striatal circuits have been identified (Rauch, Bates, & Grachev, 1997). Two of these have been consistently implicated in OCD: The "ventral cognitive circuit" has been specifically associated with obsessive symptomatology, whereas the "affective circuit" may mediate nonspecific anxiety states, including that experienced in OCD (Rauch & Savage, 1997).

Several neurotransmitter systems modulate this feedback loop. The excitatory amine glutamate is involved in output from the ventral prefrontal cortex (VPFC), projecting to the anterior striatum, nucleus accumbens, and substantia nigra (Baxter et al., 1996). Dopamine and serotonin-containing neurons affect other brain areas implicated in OCD by modulating efferents from the basal ganglia (Rosenberg & Keshavan, 1998). For example, D2 receptors are found in dorsal striatal caudate areas (Baxter et al., 1996), and serotonin receptors are densely located in ventromedial caudate and nucleus accumbens regions (Rosenberg & Keshavan, 1998). Dopaminergic stimulation of the prefrontal cortex may act by inhibiting pyramidal cells, which in turn reduces glutamatergic excitatory output from these cortical cells to basal ganglia and other brain regions (Spear, 2000).

Some of the earliest evidence for the role of the prefrontal cortex and basal ganglia comes from studies of patients with brain lesions or other cerebral insult. OCD symptom onset has been observed following cingulate epilepsy (Levin & Duchowny, 1991), as well as traumatic brain lesions, either more globally or to focal areas such as the basal ganglia (Chacko et al., 2000) or frontal lobe (Max et al., 1995). The high incidence of OCD among patients with basal ganglia disorders, including Sydenham's chorea has also been described in multiple case studies (Asbahr et al., 1999; Mercadante et al., 2000; Swedo et al., 1997) prompting the search for streptococcal triggered OCD (Swedo et al., 1998; see chap. 7).

A NEUROBIOLOGICAL MODEL OF OCD

OCD may be associated with an imbalance in tone between the direct and indirect striatopallidal pathways that in turn leads to increased activity in orbitofrontal-subcortical circuits (Saxena et al., 1998; Saxena & Rauch, 2000). Involuntary thoughts, sensations, and actions are normally suppressed with little conscious effort, partly through the action of the indirect basal ganglia pathway that in turn inhibits thalamic activity (Baxter, 1990; Baxter et al., 1996). Dysfunction in striatopallidal circuits, and insufficient inhibition of thalamocortical pathways may result in the sustained activity of a "worry" circuit involving the orbital cortex, caudate, and thalamus. This may lead to deficient gating of cortical function, and the experience of intrusive thoughts and sensations (Baxter et al., 1996). The orbitofrontal cortex may also be involved in fear conditioning and anticipatory anxiety (Zald &

Kim, 1996b). Abnormalities in orbitofrontal and cingulate cortices may therefore be linked to the persistent feeling in OCD that "things are not what they should be" and the intrusive quality of OCD symptoms. Both orbitofrontal and anterior cingulate gyri send dense glutamatergic projections into the head of the caudate nucleus, which then processes this information in initiation of behavioral responses (Schwartz, 1998). The caudate and other striatal regions have been implicated in numerous affective, learning, and memory processes, including conditioned behavioral responses that occur rapidly without allocation of conscious thought or awareness (Schwartz, 1998). The temporal lobe and amygdala also play a role in the emotional appraisal of stimuli characteristic of OCD (perception of danger or risk; Davis, 1997; Whalen et al., 1998).

Taken together, findings from structural and functional imaging studies suggest that abnormalities in VPFC-striatal-thalamic pathways play a central role in the clinical presentation of both adult and pediatric OCD (Rosenberg et al., 2001; Rosenberg & Hanna, 2000). Significantly elevated concentrations of caudate nucleus glutamate were reversed by successful SSRI treatment (paroxetine) to normal levels, with clinical response occurring in parallel with glutamate decrease (Rosenberg, McMaster, et al., 2000). Successful paroxetine treatment may be mediated by reductions in serotonergically modulated levels of glutamate in the caudate (Rosenberg et al., 2001; Rosenberg, Benazon, et al., 2000). Volumetric decrease in medial dorsal thalamus showed a similar pattern with paroxetine treatment (Gilbert et al., 2000). The consistent lack of association between illness duration, age of onset, and morphological findings for both adults and children, argues against a neurodegenerative process in OCD. However, differences in the neuroanatomical findings in youth and adults with OCD point to the importance of developmental factors in the pathogenesis and maintenance of this disorder. Finally, pediatric OCD may represent a neurodevelopmentally distinct disorder from adult OCD, characterized by specific anatomic and metabolic features attributable to developmental factors, including neuronal pruning and myelinization. In summary, child-onset OCD may be distinguished from adult-onset disorder by increased white matter, and enlargements of the basal ganglia, frontal lobes, and thalamus.

THE SEROTONERGIC HYPOTHESIS OF OCD

Evidence of a serotonin role derives primarily from the highly selective drug response to SSRIs and has led to the so-called "serotonergic hypothesis" of OCD. The anti-obsessional effects of SSRIs are independent of their antidepressant action. Long-term treatment leads to reduced responsiveness of postsynaptic receptors to endogenous serotonin probably mediated by down regulating 5HTID autoreceptors.

Acute treatment leads to higher serotonin metabolites (5HIAA) in the CSF (Zahn, Insel, & Murphy, 1984) whereas more chronic treatment (> 3 weeks) causes reduced 5HIAA in the CSF as well as reduced platelet serotonin parallel to the anti-obsessional effect. Challenge tests using MCPP (a 5HTIC agonist and 5HTID antagonist) causes increase in OCD symptoms but pre-treatment with clomipramine protects against this increase. Unfortunately, the efficacy of SSRIs does not establish that serotonin is dysfunctional in OCD and the "serotoninergic hypothesis" remains unproven. In fact, short- and long-term clomipramine treatment produces many CSF changes and serotonin anatomy and physiology are quite complex. Midline brainstem (raphe) serotonin neurons project widely: nucleus raphe magnus projects caudally to spinal cord and modulates pain; dorsal raphe neurons project to cortex, striatum, substantia nigra and amygdala while median raphe serotonin neurons project to the limbic system including hippocampus. A plethora of serotonin receptors (5HTIA, 5HTID, 5HT2A, 5HT2C, 5HT3, 5HT4) are involved in a wide range of physiological functions including sleep, body temperature regulation, food satiation, libido and sexual function, release of prolactin and ACTH, harm avoidance and frustration tolerance (high 5HT), and aggression, impulsivity and suicide (low 5HT). It is this broad array of physiological activity that accounts for the wide range of potential adverse effects seen with SRI treatment. Research using direct probes of the serotonergic system is needed and functional imaging using radioligands for selective receptor subtypes is now possible.

CLINICAL FEATURES OF OCD IN CHILDREN
AND ADOLESCENTS

Despite continuity in the phenotypic presentation of children and adults, issues such as limited insight and evolution of symptom profiles that follow developmental themes over time may differentiate children from adults with OCD (Geller, Biederman, Agranat, et al., 2001; Hanna, 1995; Sobin, Blundell, & Karayiorgou, 2000; Thomsen & Jensen, 1994). In addition, children with early-onset OCD frequently display compulsions without well-defined obsessions, and symptoms other than typical washing or checking rituals (e.g., blinking and breathing rituals; Rettew et al., 1992). Early-onset OCD may also be characterized by male predominance (Fireman et al., 2001), higher familial aggregation (Nestadt et al., 2000; Pauls et al., 1995), increased association with tics and Tourette's (Eichstedt & Arnold, 2001; Rapoport et al., 1992) higher frequency of learning disabilities (Sobin et al., 2000) and frequent comorbidity with disruptive behavior disorders (Geller et al., 1996; Geller, Biederman, Jones, Shapiro, et al., 1998).

In one review of 43 original articles on juvenile OCD, 11 studies reported on the clinical characteristics of children and adolescents with OCD (Geller, Biederman, Jones, Park, et al., 1998). These studies reported data on a total of 419 pediatric OCD patients (range 5–70). All but one study reported a male predominance with an average of a 3:2 male to female ratio. The mean age of onset of OCD in these studies ranged from 7.5 to 12.5 years (mean: 10.3 years) and the mean age at assessment ranged from 12 to 15.2 years (mean: 13.2 years). Ten studies documented that, on average, age at assessment was 2.5 years after age at onset. Two reports found that boys had an earlier age of onset of OCD than girls. Precipitating psychosocial events were described in five reports that suggested that these may be associated with the onset of OCD in 38%–54% of juvenile OCD cases.

Phenotypic characteristics of juvenile OCD were described in 10 studies. These indicated that although the majority of children exhibit both multiple obsessions and compulsions (mean number over lifetime was 4.0 and 4.8 respectively; Hanna, 1995), compulsions only without obsessions were more common in children than adolescents. Neither gender nor age-at-onset were reported to determine the type, number or severity of OCD symptoms. In eight studies children's obsessions centered on fear of a catastrophic family event (e.g., death of a parent). Contamination, sexual, somatic obsessions, and scruples were the most commonly reported obsessions and washing, repeating, checking and ordering were the most commonly reported compulsions. These studies also reported that although OCD symptoms tended to wax and wane, they were persistent in the majority of patients and frequently changed over time so that the presenting symptom constellation was not maintained (Rettew et al., 1992). In six reports, parents were noted to be intimately involved in their child's rituals, especially in reassurance seeking, a form of verbal checking.

Although pediatric OCD is increasingly recognized as a putative developmental subtype of the disorder, it remains uncertain as to whether additional subtyping by age at onset in childhood or adolescence is warranted.

PSYCHIATRIC COMORBIDITY AND ITS IMPACT ON CHILDREN AND ADOLESCENTS WITH OCD

The rates of comorbidity varied widely in these studies. Six of the 11 clinical studies did not use structured clinical interviews but rather clinical assessments to arrive at diagnoses and five used numerous exclusion criteria to characterize their sample. Despite these limitations, these studies consistently reported not only high rates of tic disorders, but also mood, anxiety, disruptive behavior, and specific developmental disorders and enuresis in youth with OCD (Fig. 10.1).

In a study aimed at disentangling chronological age from age at onset, Geller et al. (Geller, Biederman, Faraone, et al., 2001) included children and adolescents meeting *DSM–III–R* and *DSM–IV* criteria for OCD referred to a specialized OCD clinic. Irrespective of current age, an earlier age at onset predicted increased risk for Attention Deficit Hyperactivity Disorder, Simple

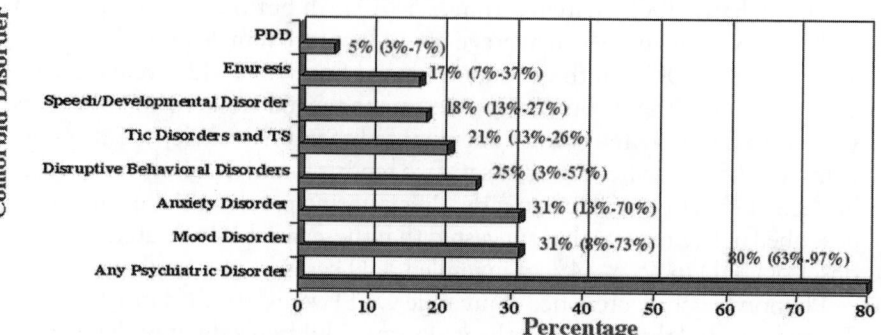

Figure 10.1.　Comorbidity in pediatric OCD: Review of clinical studies. Adapted from Geller et al. (1998). *Journal of the American Academy of Child and Adolescent Psychiatry.*

Phobia, Agoraphobia and multiple anxiety disorders. In contrast, mood and psychotic disorders were associated with chronological age and were more prevalent in older subjects. Tourette's Disorder showed associations with both chronological age and age at onset. Chronological age and age at onset predicted different patterns of comorbidity and dysfunction in children and adolescents with OCD.

In another study that examined the effect of referral bias in children with OCD referred to a specialized clinic and a general child psychiatry clinic (Geller et al., 2000), the rate of comorbid psychopathology was equally high in both samples (Table 10.1).

The presence of disruptive behavior disorders in particular may represent a therapeutic challenge for clinicians, especially cognitive-behavioral clinicians. Phenotypic features and functional correlates of ADHD-like symptoms in youth with and without OCD from a large sample of consecutively referred pediatric psychiatry patients showed that the number, frequency, and types of core ADHD symptoms as well as ADHD-associated functional indices were identical irrespective of the presence or absence of comorbid OCD (Geller, Biederman, Wagner, et al., 2001). In addition the OCD phenotype is independent of the presence or absence of ADHD either in symptoms, patterns of comorbid disorders, or OCD-specific functional impairment (Geller, Coffey, et al., 2003). These findings suggest that when ADHD-like symptoms are seen in OCD youth, they reflect a true comorbid state of OCD plus ADHD. Thus, careful consideration of the presence of ADHD symptoms should be given in both the assessment and management of OCD subjects at all ages in both clinical and research settings.

The consideration of comorbid disorders in youth with OCD is not simply an academic matter. We examined the influence of psychiatric

TABLE 10.1

Comorbidity of Pediatric OCD by Ascertainment Source

Diagnosis	OCD Specialty Clinic (N=81)		General Psychiatry Clinic (N=106)		Significance (one-way ANOVA)
	N	%	N	%	p
Tic Disorders					
Tourette's Disorder	14	17	20	20	0.69
Chronic Tic Disorder	18	22	29	28	0.36
Anxiety Disorders					
Panic Disorder	16	20	18	17	0.62
Agoraphobia	22	27	34	32	0.47
Social Phobia	8	10	29	28	0.003
Simple Phobia	22	27	32	31	0.62
Overanxious Disorder	29	36	51	48	0.11
Separation Anxiety	35	43	43	41	0.72
Multiple Anxiety Disorders*	39	48	62	59	0.16
Mood Disorders					
Major Depression	55	68	70	66	0.79
Bipolar Disorder	14	17	29	27	0.11
Dysthymia	6	8	14	13	0.21
Disruptive Behavior Disorders					
ADHD	36	44	63	59	0.042
Conduct Disorder	5	6	15	14	0.08
Oppositional Defiant Disorder	35	43	56	53	0.19
Developmental Disorders					
Speech & Language Disorder	24	30	32	31	0.90
Stuttering	8	10	6	6	0.31
Enuresis	27	33	35	34	0.89
Encopresis	5	6	10	10	0.37
Other					
Psychosis	11	14	16	15	0.62
Anorexia	0	0	1	1	0.38
Bulimia	0	0	0	0	NA

*two or more non-OCD Anxiety Disorders

Adapted from Geller et al., 2000

comorbidity on response and relapse rates in children and adolescents treated with paroxetine for obsessive-compulsive disorder (OCD; Geller Biederman, Stewart, Mullin, Farrell, et al., 2003). At entry, 193/335 (57.6%) patients had at least one (1) psychiatric disorder in addition to OCD and 102/335 (30.4%) had multiple other disorders (> 2). Although the response rate to paroxetine in the overall population was high (71%), the response rates in patients with comorbid ADHD, tic disorder, or ODD (56%, 53%, and 39%, respectively) were significantly less than in patients with OCD only (75%; ITT LOCF; $p < 0.05$).

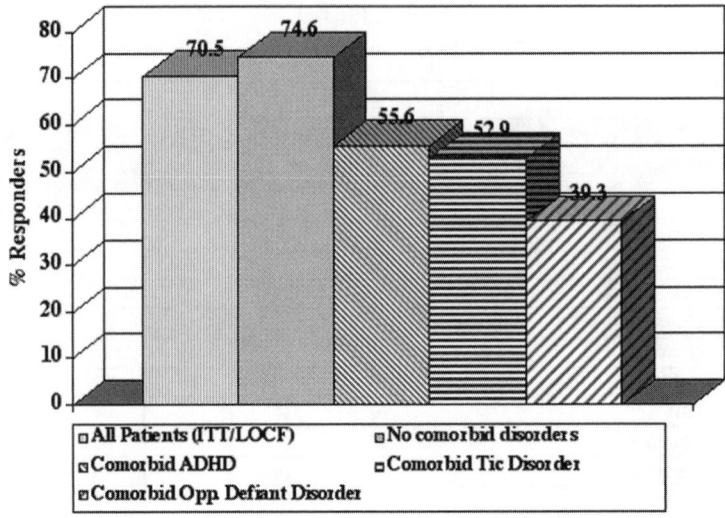

Figure 10.2.   Proportion of responders (5) to paroxetine treatment by psychiatric comorbidity. Adapted from Geller et al., 2003, *Journal of Child and Adolescent Psychopharmacology.*

Psychiatric comorbidity was associated with a greater rate of relapse in the total patient population (46% for 1 comorbid disorder [$p = 0.04$] and 56% for 2 comorbid disorders [$p < 0.05$] vs. 32% for no comorbidity).

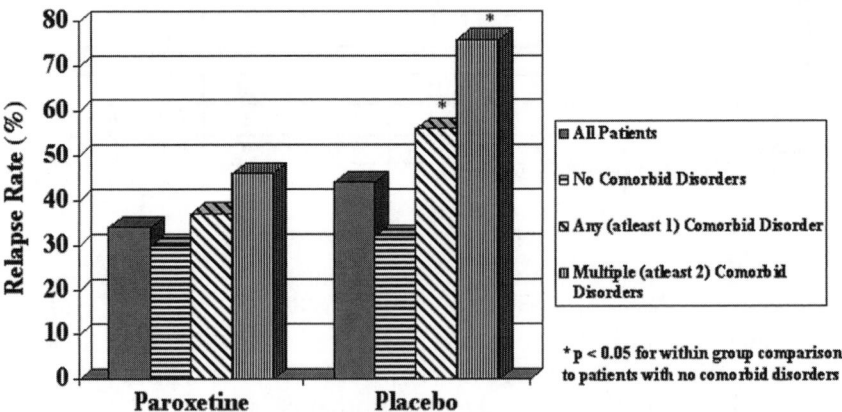

Figure 10.3.   Relapse rate (%) by presence of comorbid psychiatric disorders following discontinuation of paroxetine in children and adults treated for OCD. Adapted from Geller et al., 2003, *Journal of Child and Adolescent Psychopharmacology.*

Thus, comorbid illness adversely impacted response to pharmacotherapy with paroxetine in pediatric OCD and significantly increased risk of relapse following withdrawal from treatment.

TREATMENT—GENERAL PRINCIPLES

Although this chapter focuses on pharmacological treatment, the reader should be aware of the important role of cognitive-behavior therapy (CBT) and family involvement in the management of the child and adolescent patient with OCD. Cognitive-behavioral therapy is discussed in more detail elsewhere in this book. Although the extant literature regarding CBT in young OCD patients does not achieve the scientific rigor of drug trials because of methodological difficulties and small numbers, there is little doubt that CBT is an effective treatment for some children. This is reflected in the Expert Consensus Guidelines for treatment of OCD and the American Academy of Child and Adolescent Psychiatry Practice Parameters for OCD that recommend CBT, with or without medication, as a first-line intervention in youth (Action, 1998).

Unfortunately we cannot predict that subjects will benefit most from CBT. Experience indicates that absence of comorbid disorders and good insight will increase chances for successful CBT, the latter permitting a subject to tolerate anxiety-provoking stimuli without ritualizing based on intact reality testing. However, in very young children, insight may not be necessary for a good outcome because parents control so many of the contingencies of the CBT. In contrast, the presence of a concurrent major depressive disorder, other (multiple) anxiety disorders, or disruptive behavior disorders could severely limit the response to CBT in some children.

Severe functional impairment, CY-BOCS scores in the severe range (28), poor insight, and lack of family resources or skilled therapists for adequate CBT should influence a clinician toward earlier introduction of medication. Failure to respond to a well-delivered trial of CBT in a compliant patient after about 4–6 weeks is an indication for SSRI medication. An important message for clinicians is that a decision to treat with medication without prior discussion of CBT with parent or guardian is probably not true "informed consent."

ASSESSING RESPONSE

In most randomized controlled studies, response was defined as at least a 25% reduction in CY-BOCS scores at end point. In general, rates are quite modest ranging from 42% for fluvoxamine to 49% for fluoxetine and 53% for sertraline. Clinician- and subject-rated global improvement ratings find a somewhat higher proportion of those deemed much or very much improved (e.g., 60% for clomipramine). Translated into quantitative measures, analyses of RCTs using an intent-to-treat model typically showed an absolute decrease in CY-BOCS scores, of about 4–6 points, or a 30%–38% decrement from baseline CY-BOCS scores (Geller, Biederman, Stewart, Mullin, et al., 2003). This apparently limited effect size may actually reflect a dramatic clinical response due to the nonlinear properties of the CY-BOCS scale, its lack of sensitivity in the severe/extreme range is similar to that observed in treatment studies of adults with OCD. Therefore, even in the presence of a positive response, residual OCD symptoms frequently remain, because post-treatment scores of 15 to 20 indicate mild to moderate OCD. Thus, for many children and adolescents with OCD, even when treated, persistent low-grade symptoms and impairment are the norm.

PHARMACOTHERAPY OF OCD IN CHILDREN AND ADOLESCENTS

In the first meta-analysis of randomized controlled pharmacological trials of OCD or SRIs in children and adolescents, Geller et al. (Geller, Biederman, Stewart, Mullin, et al., 2003) found highly significant pooled effects of medication versus placebo, as well as important similarities and differences between individual drugs and differential sensitivity of quantitative measures of severity to change. An overall effect size of 0.46 equaling a CY-BOCS score difference of about 4–6 points between active and placebo treatments was found in the pooled studies, while each drug examined individually was significantly better than placebo or comparator treatments (see Table 10.2).

SSRIs currently available in the United States include citalopram (Celexa©), escitalopram (Lexapro©), fluoxetine (Prozac©), fluvoxamine (Luvox©), paroxetine (Paxil©) and sertraline (Zoloft©). At this time only fluoxetine (depression and OCD), fluvoxamine (OCD) and sertraline (OCD) are FDA-approved for use in children. The meta-analytic findings should confirm support for the role of SRI pharmacotherapy in pediatric OCD patients, including pre-adolescent children. Varying study designs with differing diagnostic classification, diagnostic method and type of outcome measure used, reliably and comparably separated active from placebo treatment conditions (see Fig. 10.4).

Most of the RCTs examined used numerous exclusion criteria to select their samples in order to achieve homogenous cohorts not confounded by comorbid disorders. For example, all the above studies excluded subjects with a primary diagnosis of major depressive disorder, bipolar disorder, psychosis, Tourette's disorder (TD), autism, eating disorders, and substance abuse disorders. Most studies also excluded subjects with Attention Deficit Hyperactivity Disorder (ADHD), and no studies permitted concurrent cognitive-behavioral therapy or other medications (Table 10.3).

Although these exclusions may be reasonable given the purpose of these studies, whether the results obtained from these randomized controlled

TABLE 10.2

Characteristics of 12 Randomized, Controlled Trials for Pediatric Obsessive-Compulsive Disorder

Study	Group	Type	N	% Male	Classification System	Diagnostic Method	Length of Tx (wks)	% Completers	Dose Range mg/day (mean)	Mean Age (yrs)	Age Range in yrs (N: 6-11/12-18)
Liebowitz (2002)	Fluoxetine Placebo	P	21 22	52 64	DSM III-R or DSM IV	DISC	16	52 32	20-80 (65.5) 20-80 (56.7)	13.0 12.3	6-18 (17/26)
Geller (2002)	Paroxetine Placebo	P	98 105	54 61	DSM IV	K-SADS Clinical	10	65 75	10-50 (23.0)	11.3 11.3	7-17 (115/88)
Geller (2001a)	Paroxetine Placebo	W	95 98	50 59	DSM IV	K-SADS Clinical	16	44 34	10-60 (32.2)	11.8 11.6	8-17 (167/168)*
Geller (2001b)	Fluoxetine Placebo	P	71 32	48 47	DSM IV	K-SADS Clinical	13	69 63	20-60 (24.6)	11.4 11.4	7-17 (75/28)
Riddle (2001)	Fluvoxamine Placebo	P	57 63	51 56	DSM III-R	Clinical	10	67 57	50-200 (166)	13.4 12.7	8-17 (59/61)
March (1998)	Sertraline Placebo	P	92 95	NR NR	DSM III-R	Clinical	12	80 86	25-200 (167)	12.6[1] 12.6[1]	6-17 (NR)
Riddle (1992)	Fluoxetine Placebo	C	7 6	29 50	DSM III-R	Clinical	8	86 83	20 (20)*	11.8[1] 11.8[1]	8-15 (7/7)
DeVeaugh-Geiss (1992)	Clomipramine Placebo	P	31 29	74 55	DSM III	Clinical	8	87 93	75-200 (NR)	14.5 14.0	16-17 (NR)
Leonard (1991)[1]	Clomipramine Desipramine	S	11 9	NR NR	DSM III	DICA	8	100 90	50-225 (143) 50-250 (123)	14.7[1] 14.7[1]	8-19 (NR)
March (1990)	Clomipramine Placebo	P	8 8	69[1] 69[1]	DSM III-R	Clinical	10	75 100	50-200 (190)	15.0[1] 15.0[1]	16-18 (NR)
Leonard (1989)	Clomipramine Desipramine	C	23 25	63[1] 63[1]	DSM III	DICA	10	92[1] 92[1]	25-250 (150) 25-250 (153)	13.9[1] 13.9[1]	7-19 (NR)
Flament (1985)	Clomipramine Placebo	C	19 19	73.7[1] 73.7[1]	DSM III	DICA	10	91[1] 91[1]	50-200 (141)	14.5[1] 14.5[1]	16-18 (NR)

Adapted from Geller et al., 2003, *Journal of Child and Adolescent Psychopharmacology*.

[1]Pooled data provided for drug and placebo; [2]Used as comparator; *fixed dose.

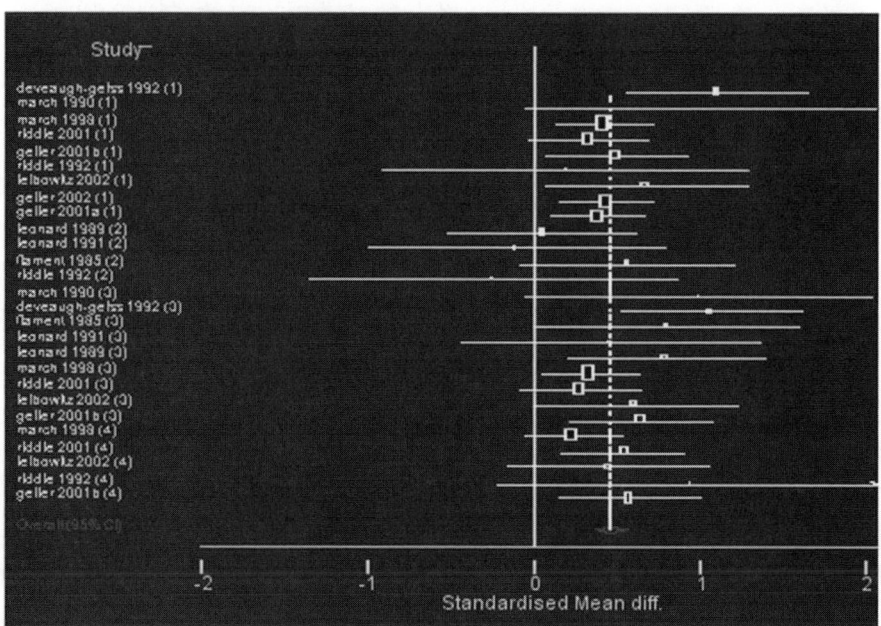

Figure 10.4. Effect size of change in outcome measures in 12 randomized, controlled trials of pharmacotherapy for pediatric obsessive-compulsive disorder. Adapted from Geller et al., 2003, *Journal of Child and Adolescent Psychopharmacology*.

TABLE 10.3

Exclusion Criteria Used in Pediatric OCD Medication Trials

Study	Drug	MDD	Psychosis	Organic Mental Disorder	TD	Alcohol Substance < Abuse	BAD	Agor	ADBD	Eating Disorder	Panic	Autism / PDD	MR	CBT	Previous Tx w/ Study Drug
Geller 2002	Paroxetine	+[1]	+	+	+[1]	+	+	+[1]	+[1]	+[1]	+[1]	+	+	+	
Geller 2001·	Paroxetine	+[1]	+	+	+[1]	+	+	+[1]	+[1]	+[1]	+[1]	+	+	+	[3]
Geller 2001	Fluoxetine	+[1]	+	+	+		+		+			+		+	
Riddle 2001	Fluvoxamine	+	+	+	+		+			+			+	[2]	[3]
March 1998	Sertraline	+[1]	+[1]	+[1]	+[1]	+[1]	+[1]	+[1]	+[1]	+[1]	+[1]	+[1]		+[1]	+
Riddle 1992	Fluoxetine	+	+	+	+	+						+	+		+
DeVeaugh-Geiss 1992	Clomipramine	+[1]	+	+	+	+	+	+	+	+	+	+	+	+	+
Leonard 1991	Clomipramine	+[1]	+	+	+				+[1]			+	+		
March 1990	Clomipramine	+[1]	+	+	+		+	+		+	+	+	+	+	
Leonard 1989	Clomipramine	+[1]	+	+	+				+[1]			+	+		
Flament 1985	Clomipramine	+[1]	+	+	+								+		

* Study of focus
[1] Cannot be primary diagnosis
[2] History of non-response to SSRIs
[3] CBT allowed, not ERP (Exposure Response Prevention)

MDD - major depressive disorder
TD - motor tic's disorder
BAD - bipolar disorder
Agor - agoraphobia

ADBD - attention deficit hyperactivity disorder
PDD - pervasive developmental disorder
MR - mental retardation
CBT - cognitive behavioral therapy

Adapted from Geller et al., 2003, *Journal of Child and Adolescent Psychopharmacology.*

medication trials apply equally to naturalistic clinical samples remains un-known. For example, several studies have suggested that treatment outcome in OCD patients may be poorer in those with comorbid tic disorders (Geller, Biedermann, Wagner, et al., 2001; Geller, Coffey, et al., 2003). As such, well-designed treatment trials that take into account the common comorbid disorders that are prevalent in children with OCD are very much needed (Geller et al., 2004).

CHOOSING AN INITIAL MEDICATION

Because the other SSRIs were statistically indistinguishable from each other with respect to overall effect (Table 10.4), a decision to use any one may de-pend more on adverse event profiles and individual pharmacokinetic prop-erties than on efficacy. Relevant factors to consider in the choice of a specific agent include half-life of the compound, presence of active metabolites, the linear or nonlinear nature of its clearance, and its capacity to inhibit various cytochrome P-450 (CYP-450) enzymatic pathways in the liver and so pro-duce drug interactions.

Several important pharmacokinetic variables include the half-life of the compound, presence of active metabolites, the linear or nonlinear nature of its clearance, and its capacity to inhibit various cytochrome P450 (CYP) en-zymatic pathways in the liver. Paroxetine and fluvoxamine have nonlinear

TABLE 10.4

Pairwise Comparison of Pooled Drug and Placebo in Randomized, Controlled Trials in Pediatric OCD

	Clomipramine	Sertraline	Fluvoxamine	Fluoxetine	Paroxetine
Placebo	$z=6.23$ $p<.001$ SMD=.693	$z=3.84$ $p<.001$ SMD=.327	$z=3.52$ $p<.001$ SMD=.375	$z=5.56$ $p<.001$ SMD=.546	$z=3.95$ $p<.001$ SMD=.405
Paroxetine	$z=2.99$ $p=.003$	$z=-0.36$ $p=0.72$	$z=-0.04$ $p=0.97$	$z=1.17$ $p=0.24$	
Fluoxetine	$z=2.24$ $p=.025$	$z=-1.86$ $p=0.06$	$z=-1.33$ $p=0.18$		
Fluvoxamine	$z=3.24$ $p=.001$	$z=-0.36$ $p=0.72$			
Sertraline	$z=3.78$ $p<.001$				

Adapted from Geller et al., 2003, *American Journal of Psychiatry.*

kinetics and interfere with (autoinhibit) their own metabolism. Thus, the half-life of a single dose of paroxetine (10 hours) becomes twice as long with multiple dosing (Lane & Baldwin, 1997). This quality may be more important when decreasing rather than increasing medication, because rapidly falling levels are more common with nonlinear kinetics and may predispose to the SSRI discontinuation syndrome that is seen most commonly with clomipramine (31%), paroxetine (20%) and fluvoxamine (14%; Coupland, Bell, & Potokar, 1996). Fluoxetine has an active metabolite, norfluoxetine, with a very long half-life (4–7 days) that delays the achievement of steady state plasma levels.

Despite the finding that clomipramine showed superiority over the other SSRIs, it does not follow that clomipramine should be recommended as a treatment of first choice in pediatric OCD patients, due to frequent adverse events (DeVeaugh-Geiss et al., 1992) and concerns around monitoring potential arrythmogenic effects (Biederman, 1991; Puig-Antich et al., 1979; Puig-Antich et al., 1987). Clomipramine is less user-friendly for children than the other SSRIs, where EKG and blood level monitoring are not routinely required, and is usually not employed as a first line agent in uncomplicated cases. However, clomipramine is an important drug in the armamentarium of anti-obsessional medications.

By virtue of the fact that clomipramine was the first serotonergic agent approved for pediatric OCD, earlier subjects were essentially "medication-naïve" for such compounds and may have represented a different population of patients than those enrolled in later trials. However, the effect of the drug remained significant when "year of study" was included as a covariate in the analysis, and there was not a statistically significant association between year of study and percent improvement in placebo groups, nor were there differences in drop-out rates between active and placebo conditions in studies either individually or collectively (Geller, Stewart, Mullin, Martin, et al., 2003). In adult studies, clomipramine has never shown significant superiority in direct comparison with other agents but there are no such head-to-head studies in the pediatric age group.

Nonetheless, clomipramine has unique pharmacodynamic properties among the serotonergic agents because it is metabolized to desmethylclomipramine, a secondary amine tricyclic antidepressant that is identical to desipramine with a chloride atom substitution. This agent has noradrenergic properties that have been reported to be useful in the treatment of both ADHD (Biederman et al., 1989) and tic disorders (Spencer et al., 1993) so that clomipramine may offer the potential advantage of targeting symptoms that are often comorbid in these children. Its wider spectrum of action as a nonselective drug with both serotonergic and noradrenergic action may be associated with its observed superiority. Although the decision to use a specific agent is a complex clinical decision based on many factors, these findings suggest that clomipramine should be considered for treatment or augmentation in more severe or treatment resistant cases of pediatric OCD (see Table 10.5).

Duration of Treatment in Pediatric OCD

Optimal duration of treatment for OCD children is unknown. Most authors (March, Frances, Carpenter, & Kahn, 1997) recommend 9 to 18 months of treatment after symptom resolution or stabilization, followed by very gradual taper (25% per 1–2 months). Relapse on discontinuation is common (Flament et al., 1990; Leonard et al., 1993). Long-term maintenance after three to four mild relapses or two to three severe relapses is recommended.

Combined CBT and Medication Treatment in Pediatric OCD

The combination of medication treatment with CBT may be more efficient than either one alone. CBT may also reduce relapse rate in patients withdrawn from medication. CBT appears to be a more durable form of intervention. The Pediatric OCD Treatment Study (POTS I; March et al., 2004) was a 5-year treatment, three sites-outcome study that used a balanced 1 × 4 design to compare placebo, sertraline, CBT, and combined CBT with sertraline and the CYBOCS as the dependent measure.

TABLE 10.5

Dose Ranges for SRIs in Pre-Adolescents and Adolescents With
Obsessive-Compulsive Disorder

Drug	Starting Dose (mg)		Typical Dose Range (mg) (Mean Dose)*
	Pre-Adolescent	Adolescent	
Clomipramine **	6.25-25	25	50-200
Fluoxetine ***	2.5-10	10-20	10-80 (25)
Sertraline ***	12.5-25	25-50	50-200 (178)
Fluvoxamine**	12.5-25	25-50	50-300 (165)
Paroxetine ****	2.5-10	10	10-60 (32)
Citalopram ***	2.5-10	10-20	10-60

*Mean daily doses used in controlled trials
**Doses < 25 mg/day may be administered by compounding 25mg into 5ml suspension.
***Oral concentrate commercially available
****Oral suspension commercially available

The POTS sample reflected a community clinical practice in that 80% of children had at least one comorbid disorder including an internalizing disorder (63%), or an externalizing disorder (27%). The magnitude of the effect for each treatment condition for combined treatment, CBT alone, and sertraline were 1.4, 0.97, and 0.67, respectively. Clinical remission rates (defined as CYBOCS < 10) for combined treatment was 53.6% (95% confidence interval [CI], 36%–70%); for CBT alone, 39.3% (95% CI, 24%–58%); for sertraline alone, 21.4% (95% CI, 10%–40%); and for placebo, 3.6% (95% CI, 0%–19%). The remission rate for combined treatment did not differ from that for CBT alone ($P = .42$) but did differ from sertraline alone ($P = .03$) and from placebo ($P = .002$).

In summary, POTS found that combined treatment had an additive effect on outcome with the greatest overall effect size (March, 2003). In general therefore, children and adolescents with OCD should start with either CBT or the combination of CBT and medication

TREATING THE CHILD WITH OCD AND COMORBID DISORDERS

Tics in Pediatric OCD

For children and adolescents with OCD and comorbid tic disorder, SSRIs alone may have less anti-obsessional effect (Geller, Hoog, et al., 2001; Kurlan et al., 1993). In addition, there are case reports suggesting that SSRIs, especially at higher doses, may exacerbate or even induce tics in some patients (Delgado et al., 1990; Fennig et al., 1994; Riddle et al., 1992). Strategies for managing the child with comorbid OCD and Tourette's syndrome include using an SSRI alone, clomipramine alone, combined SSRI and clomipramine, an SSRI or clomipramine plus a typical or atypical neuroleptic (with vigilance for the cardiac cycle QTc) or an SSRI or clomipramine plus an alpha 2 agonist such as clonidine or guanfacine (Geller & Spencer, 2003).

OCD with Comorbid Major Depressive Disorder

Major depression may be more impairing than OCD symptoms in some children and may impact response to OCD treatments, whether pharmacological or behavioral. Some children will require hospitalization for severe depressive episodes, especially if suicidal ideation or behavior is present. Therefore mood symptoms should be treated aggressively with antidepressant augmentation and/or mood stabilizers as needed.

OCD and Comorbid Bipolar Disorder

In adults, evidence of a higher-than-expected overlap between obsessive-compulsive disorder (OCD) and bipolar disorder (BPD) first came from the Epidemiological Catchment Area (ECA) study, where 23% of those with BPD also met criteria for OCD (Robins & Price, 1991). Subsequent studies have consistently found that OCD as well as other anxiety disorders are found in adults with BPD at rates as high as 20–30% (Chen & Dilsaver, 1995; Perugi et al., 1997). The concurrence of these two challenging disorders may have far ranging clinical and therapeutic implications, for example, more frequent hospitalizations and more complex pharmacological interventions than those without BPD (Perugi et al., 1997; Perugi et al., 2002). Recently, several separate studies have reported a bidirectional overlap between BPD and OCD in children at rates greater than expected. Masi et al. (2001) reported that fully 44% of their pediatric BPD patients had a lifetime diagnosis of OCD, which usually preceded the onset of mood symptoms. Similarly, Faedda et al. (2004) found that 27% of children diagnosed with BPD also had comorbid OCD. We have also identified higher than expected rates of comorbid BPD in our youth with OCD (approximately 5–10%; Joshi et al., 2005). On the other hand, Reddy et al. (2000) reported a much lower rate of BPD (1.9%) in their pediatric OCD population who were largely treatment naïve and of only moderate severity. Although this inconsistency in the rate of co-occurrence of the two disorders could be attributed to selection and/or referral bias, it nevertheless suggests that a true comorbidity risk may have been overlooked in these patients.

OCD with comorbid bipolar disorder clearly presents a therapeutic dilemma. Specifically, all agents (including SSRIs) documented to be helpful in treating OCD also have the risk of exacerbating mood symptoms and precipitating mania. Several reports have described the high risk of (hypo)manic switches in OCD children and adolescents treated with tricyclics or SSRIs (Go, Malley, Birmaher, & Rosenberg, 1998; King et al., 1991). Further, anti-manic agents, although effective in controlling manic symptoms, do not show any efficacy in treating OCD symptoms. Mood stabilizers or atypical neuroleptics may therefore be needed to counteract activating effects of SRIs, because these are required in order to treat OCD symptoms.

OCD with Disruptive Behavior Disorders (DBD)

The presence of comorbid disruptive behavior can limit efficacy of behavioral and medication treatment for OCD (Geller, Biederman, Wagner, et al., 2001) and lead to more severe impairment than OCD without DBD. For example, OCD+DBD youth had higher Internalizing, Externalizing, and Total Problem scores on the Child Behavior Checklist (CBCL; Geller Biederman, Wagner, et al., 2001; Hanna, Yuwiler, & Coates, 1995) suggest cumulative morbidity from each diagnosis.

Stimulants have been the mainstay of treatment for ADHD with OCD but may increase primary obsessions and rituals and/or anxiety and there is a lack of agreement on their benefits in anxiety disorders (Diamond, Tannock, & Schacher, 1999; Tannock, Icowicz, & Schacher, 1995), where they are relatively contraindicated (see package labels). Most, but not all, extant studies support the labeling contraindication for stimulants when anxiety is present. For example, increases in heart rate (Tannock et al., 1995), and diastolic blood pressure (Urman, Ickowicz, Fulford, & Tannock, 1995) have been reported to occur more frequently during stimulant treatment of ADHD children with comorbid anxiety compared to those without anxiety. Moreover, children with ADHD and comorbid anxiety may experience less benefit (Pliszka, 1989; Tannock et al., 1995; Taylor et al., 1987) and more adverse cognitive (Swanson et al., 1978) or behavioral responses (DuPaul et al., 1994) from stimulant treatment as compared with their noncomorbid counterparts.

In this situation, empirical wisdom asserts that the clinician should treat OCD first and address residual ADHD symptoms when the OCD is stabilized. Thus stimulants may be very useful when anxiety is controlled and are not absolutely contraindicated. Alternatives include consideration of clomipramine used alone or in augmentation with SSRIs due to its noradrenergic properties or even augmentation with bupropion. For motoric overactivity, impulsivity or aggression consider SSRI augmentation with the alpha-agonist agents clonidine or guanfacine. A newer medication, atomoxetine, a selective norepinephrine uptake inhibitor, has recently shown promise in that it has efficacy for treatment of ADHD while not exacerbating anxiety symptoms.

OCD With Pervasive Developmental Disorders (PDD)

OC symptoms in children with PDD present diagnostic and nosological dilemmas and a small number of children may actually meet criteria for both diagnoses, for example, with typical contamination concerns and cleaning behavior. Fortunately, SSRIs are effective in symptomatic management of both disorders, and good insight is not necessarily required for a drug response. Drug treatment of PDD is similar to that for OCD but low doses of SSRIs are advised due to the great sensitivity of such children to these agents.

OCD With Psychotic Symptoms

It may be difficult to distinguish obsessions from overvalued ideas or delusions, especially as insight diminishes at younger age. Flags for emerging psychosis include symptoms that are atypical for OCD, other positive and negative psychotic symptoms, and a poor response to treatment or deteriorating course. Psychosis may be associated with a mood disorder, especially bipolar and if there is suspicion that psychotic symptoms are affectively driven, then aggressive mood stabilization is warranted. In our (unpublished) sample of children and adolescents with OCD acquired during a family genetic study, the rate of psychotic symptoms was 6% (Total $N = 130$).

STRATEGIES IN TREATMENT RESISTANCE

If there is no clinical response after 10 to 12 weeks of the first SSRI, switch to another SSRI. Clinicians may rotate through the SSRIs attempting to deliver an adequate dose (Table 10. 5) and duration (8 weeks) with each if tolerated. After two successive SSRIs, consider using clomipramine alone or in combination with an SSRI. Increase the intensity and frequency of CBT using exposure and response prevention (ERP)

For patients with only partial therapeutic response after several successive trials, augmentation strategies may be useful. Studies in adults showed both haloperidol (McDougle et al., 1994) and clonazepam (Hewlett, 1993) were effective to treat OCD and clonazepam has also been shown to be useful in children (Leonard et al., 1994). Antipsychotics may be especially helpful for delusional thinking or unresponsive comorbid tic disorder (McDougle et al., 1994). Adjunctive atypical neuroleptics have increasingly been shown in controlled trials and case reports to be helpful in adults with treatment refractory OCD (Giakas, 1995; Jacobsen, 1995; Koran, Quirk, Lorberman, & Elliott, 2001; Lombroso, Scahill, King, & Lynch, 1995; McDougle et al., 1995; Ravizza, Barzega, Bellino, Bogetto, & Maina, 1996; Remington & Adams, 1994) but systematic data in children are lacking.

In fact, there are anecdotal reports of increased obsessions and anxiety with atypical neuroleptics (Lykovras et al., 2003; Diler, Yolga, Avci, &

Scahill, 2003; Lykouras, Alevizos, Michalpoulou, & Rabavilas, 2003) that may be dose dependent (Khullar, Chue, & Tibbo, 2001). However, there are case reports of benefit for tics occurring with OCD (Bruggeman et al., 2001; Fitzgerald, Moore, et al., 2000; Parraga, Parraga, Woodward, & Fenning, 2001; Sallee et al., 2000).

Other approaches for treatment resistance in pediatric OCD that are not supported by randomized controlled evidence but derive from expert opinion include use of venlafaxine or augmentation with gabapentin, a gaba-ergic agent, and use of the beta-blocker pindolol. In adults there are reports of beneficial response to narcotics such as morphine sulphate or narcotic derivatives such as tramadol but their use in children is not appropriate.

ADVERSE EVENTS

Adverse events are relatively common with clomipramine (dry mouth 63%, sedation 46%, dizziness 41%, tremor 33%, as well as constipation, flushing, sweating, and memory impairment; DeVeaugh-Geiss et al., 1992). Adverse events, though less frequent, are also quite common with the SSRIs and involve mainly the central nervous system (insomnia, agitation, hyperkinesia, loss of energy, fatigue, somnolence, tremor) and gastrointestinal system (nausea, dyspepsia, diarrhea). One should also remember to discuss sexual dysfunction as a potential side effect of the SSRIs in teenagers. Behavioral activation (behavioral side effects, disinhibition) deserves special mention, because it is relatively frequent (Riddle et al., 1991) and may limit the usefulness of these medications. It may have a delayed onset that parallels the reduction in anxiety and may follow a honeymoon period of rapid improvement. Like other adverse events, it appears to be dose-dependent and in our experience, it is more frequent in preadolescent patients. All the SSRIs have the potential to produce this reaction and it is unclear whether it is more common with any particular agent. Recently, Martin et al. (Martin et al., 2004) examined a national database (1997–2000) of 7 million mental health users aged 5 to 29 years old to assess the risk of mood switching (manic conversion) by age and antidepressant class. The authors found manic conversion in 4,786 patients (5%), with the lowest risk in the SSRI class (hazard ratio 2.1) versus other antidepressant classes (hazard ratio 3.8–3.9). In this review, peripubertal children (10–14 yrs old) were at highest risk of conversion. If dose reduction is not possible, addition of a mood stabilizer may be required to permit anti-obsessional treatment (see the previous section). Significant weight gain may occasionally occur with SSRI treatment. There are no known long-term adverse effects of the use of SSRI medications in pediatric populations.

Other serious adverse effects, including the serotonin syndrome, have been described in children taking SSRIs (Pao & Tipnis, 1997). Numerous case reports also document the emergence of extrapyramidal symptoms

(EPS) as well as tics and myoclonus over the last several years in children and adolescents treated with SSRI medications (Diler, Yolga, & Avci, 2002; Ghaziuddin, Iqbal, & Khetarpal, 2001; Jones-Fearing, 1996) as well as in adults (Baldassano et al., 1996). Hyper-reflexic tendon reflexes are common on neurological exam. Animal studies have suggested that SSRIs possess tonic inhibitory properties within the central dopamine system, but it is unknown if this is the cause for motoric adverse effects because their dopaminergic effects are clinically insignificant (Tollefson & Rosenbaum, 2001). The amotivational syndrome, previously described in adults taking SSRIs, has been described in several children and adolescents and could reflect dopamine inhibition (Garland & Baerg, 2001).

Recently, concerns have been expressed regarding increased bleeding rates (Calhoun & Calhoun, 1996; Lake, Birmaher, Wassick, Mathos, & Yelovich, 2000) in SSRI-treated patients. In a population-based cohort study in Denmark and the Netherlands, serotonergic antidepressants increased the risk of gastrointestinal adverse effects in adults, including upper GI bleeding, which was increased in turn by nonsteroidal anti-inflammatory drugs (NSAIDS) and low-dose aspirin (Dalton et al., 2003). Disruption in sleep architecture along with sleep disturbance and subjective accounts of vivid dreaming have also been described with SSRIs, although infrequently in children (Armitage, Emslie, & Rintelmann, 1997).

SAFETY

Perhaps the most important characteristic of the anti-obsessional medications is their degradation by and inhibition of the hepatic CYP subsystems. Clinically significant drug–drug interactions are possible in a number of common situations in which combined pharmacotherapy is employed. For example, the combination of an SSRI that potently inhibits the CYP 2D6 (fluoxetine and paroxetine) system may cause markedly elevated, even dangerous, serum levels of clomipramine that utilizes this same metabolic pathway as a substrate. Fluvoxamine as an inhibitor of CYP1A2 and CYP2C19 may also increase clomipramine levels. Many other medications are removed by the CYP2D6 (tricyclics, haloperidol, codeine, beta-blockers, risperidone, thioridazine, perphenazine, nefazadone), CYP1A2 (chlorprozamine, clozapine, tricyclics, cisapride, verapamil), and CYP3A4 (carbemazepine, alprazolam, steroids, nifedipine, erythromycin) enzymes creating other potential drug–drug interactions.

MAOIs should not be given within 5 weeks after discontinuation of fluoxetine, or within 2 weeks after other SSRIs. Conversely, SSRIs should not be administered within 2 weeks after discontinuing MAOI treatment. Inappropriate combination with MAOI may induce potentially serious adverse effects, including serotonin syndrome.

Because of the potential arrythmogenic properties of clomipramine, it is usually not employed as a first-line agent in uncomplicated OCD. Its use mandates an evaluation of the pediatric patient's medical condition and cardiac status in particular. Baseline evaluation should include a systems review and inquiry regarding a personal or family history of heart disease. A history of nonfebrile seizures should also be noted but is not an absolute contraindication to clomipramine. If in doubt, a general pediatric examination to include auscultation of the heart and measurement of pulse and blood pressure is indicated. A baseline (pretreatment) electrocardiogram (EKG) should be requested. Although changes in conduction intervals and heart rate may occur, these are rarely of clinical significance. The prudent practitioner will evaluate and document EKG parameters.

Guidelines regarding unacceptable EKG indices for the use (or increase) of clomipramine have been recommended by the Federal Drug Administration (FDA) as follows: (1) PR interval > 200 ms; (2) QRS interval > 30% increased over baseline or > 120 ms; (3) blood pressure > 140 systolic or 90 diastolic; and (4) heart rate > 130 bpm at rest (Biederman, 1991; Puig-Antich et al., 1979). Finally a prolonged QTc (corrected QT interval = 450 ms) is associated with an increased risk of ventricular tachyarrythmias and is a contraindication for clomipramine use (or further increase). Despite these concerns, clomipramine remains an important and perhaps unique drug in the armamentarium of antiobsessional medications.

SUICIDALITY

"After the U.K. Department of Health statement in the summer of 2003 alerting the public of a 1.5- to 3-fold increased risk of self-harm or suicidal thinking in youth taking paroxetine, the FDA and expert panels conducted extensive review of SSRI medications in all short-term pediatric clinical trials" (Geller et al., 2006, pp. 589–668). In weighing the benefit observed in SSRI studies against the current risks regarding safety of SSRIs in youth, one should note the Food and Drug Administration's (FDA) recent black-box warning regarding increased risk of suicidal thinking and behavior (suicidality) in short-term studies in children and adolescents treated with these agents (http://www.fda.gov/cder/drug/antidepressants/default.htm; see the following section). In addition, Web sites and reports including the American Academy of Child and Adolescent Psychiatry (AACAP), the American Psychiatric Association (APA), the American College of Neuropsychopharmacology (ACNP), the Food and Drug Administration (FDA) Center for Drug Evaluation and Research (CDER) and Office of Drug Safety (ODS), the UK Committee on Safety of Medicines (CSM), and the Agency for Healthcare Research and Quality (AHRQ) provide the latest bulletins and advisories on safety and efficacy in pediatric populations. Pharmaceutical company Web sites that have posted data and analysis of unpublished studies as well as the meta-analysis of the FDA Division of Neuropharmacological Drug Products, the FDA Division of Pediatric Drug Development Report of the Audit of the Columbia Suicidality Classification Methodology and the Follow-up Consult from the FDA Division of Drug Risk Analysis on the comparison between previous analyses and Columbia University classification (August, 2004) may also be surveyed.

Based on these analyses of 24 pediatric antidepressant trials involving more than 4,400 patients, in October 2004, the FDA issued a black-box warning on all pediatric antidepressants (http://www.fda.gov/cder/drug/antidepressants/SSRIlabelChange.htm), as well as a public health advisory (http://www.fda.gov/cder/drug/antidepressants/SSRIPHA200410.htm). A greater risk of suicidality during the first few months of treatment in those receiving antidepressants was concluded; 4% average risk of such events on drug, twice the placebo risk of 2%. No completed suicides occurred in any of these trials. Although there was a 4% average risk of spontaneously reported (parent or youth) suicidal thinking or suicidality on drug versus 2% on placebo, in 17 of these 23 trials, a direct assessment (standardized youth self-assessment) of suicidality demonstrated a slight reduction in suicidality. In addition, treatment with antidepressants for at least 6 months reduced the likelihood of suicide attempt compared with antidepressant treatment for just 8 weeks (Hazard Ratio = 0.34; CI 0.21, 0.55).

SAFETY: CONCLUSIONS

While monitoring agencies, such as the FDA and the mental health field, continue to examine critically the evidence supporting the use of SSRIs, as well as serious adverse events such as suicidal behavior, practitioners are warned against withholding treatment with SSRIs from youth with well-defined OCD. Although other treatment options such as cognitive-behavioral therapy (CBT) should be encouraged, controlled studies in MDD and OCD suggest that the most efficacious treatment is likely the combined CBT and treatment with SSRIs (March, 2003), and that therapy alone is not superior to medication. Thus, we continue to recommend use of the SSRIs for youth with OCD.

NOVEL APPROACHES

Pediatric Autoimmune Neuropsychiatric Disorders Associated with Streptococcus (PANDAS; Garvey et al., 1999; Kurlan & Kaplan, 2004; Murphy et al., 2004; Snider, Lougee, Slatter, Grant, & Swedo, 2005; Swedo et al., 1998; Swedo et al., 2004) are discussed elsewhere in this book but are relevant here for the notion that some antibiotics may be effective treatments for some types of OCD with early onset.

Antiglutamatergic agents such as riluzole and N-methyl D-aspartase (NMDA) receptor antagonists such as memantine may prove to be useful future treatments of OCD as the glutamatergic system has been increasingly implicated in pathophysiology of the disorder but controlled studies are needed.

SUMMARY

Both pharmacological and nonpharmacological treatments have advanced rapidly in the last decade and a half and improved the outlook for the many children affected with OCD. However treatment effects are only modest to good and are greatest when modalities are combined. Better understanding of genetic and nongenetic risk factors and early intervention can be expected to improve outcomes over the longer term.

REFERENCES

Action, A. O. (1998). Practice parameters for the assessment of treatment of children and adolescents with obsessive-compulsive disorder. *Journal of the American Academy of Child and Adolescent Psychiatry, 37S*, S27–S45.

Armitage, R., Emslie, G., & Rintelmann, J. (1997). The effect of fluoxetine on sleep EEG in childhood depression: A preliminary report. *Neuropsychopharmacology, 17*, 241–245.

Asbahr, F. R., Ramos, R. T., Negrao, A. B., & Gentil, V. (1999). Case series: Increased vulnerability to obsessive-compulsive symptoms with repeated episodes of Sydenham chorea. *Journal of the American Academy of Child and Adolescent Psychiatry, 38*, 1522–1525.

Baldassano, C. F., Truman, C. J., Nierenberg, A., Ghaemi, S. N., & Sachs, G. S. (1996). Akathisia: A review and case report following paroxetine treatment. *Comprehensive Psychiatry, 37*, 122–124.

Baxter, L. R. (1990). Brain imaging as a tool in establishing a theory of brain pathology in obsessive compulsive disorder. *Journal of Clinical Psychiatry, 51S*, 22–26.

Baxter, L. R., Jr., Saxena, S., Brody, A. L., Ackermann, R. F., Colgan, M., Schwartz, J. M., et al. (1996). Brain Mediation of obsessive-compulsive disorder symptoms: Evidence from functional brain imaging studies in the human and nonhuman primate. *Seminars in Clinical Neuropsychiatry, 1*, 32–47.

Biederman, J. (1991). Sudden death in children treated with a tricyclic antidepressant: A commentary. *Journal of the American Academy of Child and Adolescent Psychiatry, 30*, 495–497.

Biederman, J., Baldessarini, R., Wright, V., Knee, D., & Harmatz, J. (1989). A double-blind placebo controlled study of desipramine in the treatment of attention deficit disorder: I. Efficacy. *Journal of the American Academy of Child and Adolescent Psychiatry, 28*, 777–784.

Bruggeman, R., van der Linden, C., Buitelaar, J. K., Gericke, G. S., Hawkridge, S. M., & Temlett, J. A. (2001). Risperidone versus pimozide in Tourette's disorder: A comparative double-blind parallel-group study. *Journal of Clinical Psychiatry, 62*, 50–56.

Calhoun, J. W., & Calhoun, D. D. (1996). Prolonged bleeding time in a patient treated with sertraline. *American Journal of Psychiatry, 153*, 443.

Chacko, R. C., Corbin, M. A., & Harper, R. G. (2000). Acquired obsessive-compulsive disorder associated with basal ganglia lesions. *Journal of Neuropsychiatry and Clinical Neuroscience, 12,* 269–272.

Chen, Y. W., & Dilsaver, S. C. (1995). Comorbidity for obsessive-compulsive disorder in bipolar and unipolar disorders. *Psychiatry Research, 59,* 57–64.

Coupland, N. J., Bell, C. J., & Potokar, J. P. (1996). Serotonin reuptake inhibitor withdrawal. *Journal of Clinical Psychopharmacology, 16,* 356–362.

Dalton, S., Johansen, C., Mellemkjaer, L., Norgard, B., Sorensen, H., & Olsen, J. (2003). Use of selective serotonin reuptake inhibitors and risk of upper gastrointestinal tract bleeding: A population-based cohort study. *Archives of Internal Medicine, 163,* 59–64.

Davis, M. (1997). Neurobiology of fear responses: The role of the amygdala. *Journal of Neuropsychiatry and Clinical Neuroscience, 9,* 382–402.

Delgado, P., Goodman, W., Price, L., Heninger, G., & Charney, D. (1990). Fluvoxamine/pimozide treatment of concurrent Tourette's and obsessive-compulsive disorder. *British Journal of Psychiatry, 157,* 762–765.

DeVeaugh-Geiss, J., Moroz, G., Biederman, J. B., Cantwell, D., Fontaine, R., Greist, J., et al. (1992). Clomipramine hydrochloride in childhood and adolescent obsessive-compulsive disorder: A multicenter trial. *Journal of the American Academy of Child and Adolescent Psychiatry, 31,* 45–49.

Diamond, I. R., Tannock, R., & Schachar, R. J. (1999). Response to methylphenidate in children with ADHD and comorbid anxiety. *Journal of the American Academy of Child and Adolescent Psychiatry, 38,* 402–409.

Diler, R. S., Yolga, A. Y., & Avci, A. (2002). Fluoxetine-induced extrapyramidal symptoms in an adolescent: A case report. *Swiss Medical Weekly, 132,* 125–126.

Diler, R., Yolga, A., Avci, A., & Scahill, L. (2003). Risperidone-induced obsessive-compulsive symptoms in two children. *Journal of Child and Adolescent Psychopharmacology, 13S,* S89–92.

DuPaul, G., Barkley, R., & McMurray, M. (1994). Response of children with ADHD to methylphenidate: Interaction with internalizing symptoms. *Journal of the American Academy of Child and Adolescent Psychiatry, 33,* 894–903.

Eichstedt, J. A., & Arnold, S. L. (2001). Childhood-onset obsessive-compulsive disorder: A tic-related subtype of OCD? *Clinical Psychology Review, 21,* 137–157.

Faedda, G. L., Baldessarini, R. J., Glovinsky, I. P., & Austin, N. B. (2004). Pediatric bipolar disorder: Phenomenology and course of illness. *Bipolar Disorders, 6,* 305.

Fennig, S., Fennig, S. N., Pato, M., & Weitzman, A. (1994). Emergence of symptoms of Tourette's syndrome during fluvoxamine treatment of obsessive-compulsive disorder. *British Journal of Psychiatry, 164,* 839–841.

Fireman, B., Koran, L. M., Leventhal, J. L., & Jacobson, A. (2001). The prevelance of clinically recognized obsessive-compulsive disorder in a large health maintenance organization. *American Journal of Psychiatry, 158,* 1904–1910.

Fitzgerald, K. D., MacMaster, F. P., Paulson, L. D., & Rosenberg, D. R. (1999). Neurobiology of childhood obsessive-compulsive disorder. *Child and Adolescent Psychiatric Clinics of North America, 8,* 533–575.

Fitzgerald, K. D., Moore, G. J., Paulson, L. A., Stewart, C. M., & Rosenberg, D. R. (2000). Proton spectroscopic imaging of the thalamus in treatment-naive pediatric obsessive compulsive disorder. *Biological Psychiatry, 47,* 174–182.

Fitzgerald, K. D., Stewart, C. M., Tawile, V., & Rosenberg, D. R. (1999). Case report: Risperidone augmentation of serotonin reuptake inhibitor treatment of pediatric obsessive compulsive disorder. *Journal of Child and Adolescent Psychopharmacology, 9,* 115–123.

Flament, M., Koby, E., Rapoport, J., Berg, C., Zahn, T., Cox, C., et al. (1990). Childhood obsessive-compulsive disorder: A prospective follow-up study. *Journal of Child Psychology and Psychiatry and Allied Disciplines, 31,* 363–380.

Garland, E. J., & Baerg, E. A. (2001). Amotivational syndrome associated with selective serotonin reuptake inhibitors in children and adolescents. *Journal of Child and Adolescent Psychopharmacology, 11,* 181–186.

Garvey, M., Perlmutter, S., Allen, A., Hamburger, S., Lougee, L., Leonard, H., et al. (1999). A pilot study of penicillin prophylaxis for neuropsychiatric exacerbations triggered by streptococcal infections. *Biological Psychiatry, 45,* 1564–1571.

Geller, D., Biederman, J., Agranat, A., Cradock, K., Hagermoser, L. M., Kim, G. S., et al. (2001). Developmental aspects of obsessive compulsive disorder: Findings in children, adolescents and adults. *The Journal of Nervous and Mental Disease, 189,* 471–477.

Geller, D., Biederman, J., Faraone, S. V., Bellorder, C. A., Kim, G. S., & Hagermoser, L. M. (2001). Disentangling chronological age from age of onset in children and adolescents with obsessive compulsive disorder. *International Journal of Neuropsychopharmacology, 4,* 169–178.

Geller, D., Biederman, J., Faraone, S. V., Frazier, J., Coffey, B. J., Kim, G. S., et al. (2000). Clinical correlates of obsessive compulsive disorder in children and adolescents referred to specialized and non-specialized clinical settings. *Depression and Anxiety, 11,* 163–168.

Geller, D. A., Biederman, J., Faraone, S. V., Spencer, T., Doyle, R., Mullin, B., et al. (2004). Re-examining comorbidity of obsessive compulsive and attention-deficit/hyperactivity disorder using an empirically derived taxonomy. *European Journal of Child and Adolescent Psychiatry.*

Geller, D., Biederman, J., Griffin, S., Jones, J., & Lefkowitz, T. R. (1996). Comorbidity of juvenile obsessive-compulsive disorder with disruptive behavior disorders. *Journal of the American Academy of Child and Adolescent Psychiatry, 35,* 1637–1646.

Geller, D., Biederman, J., Jones, J., Park, K., Schwartz, S., Shapiro, S., et al. (1998). Is juvenile obsessive compulsive disorder a developmental subtype of the disorder?: A review of the pediatric literature. *Journal of the American Academy of Child and Adolescent Psychiatry, 37,* 420–427.

Geller, D., Biederman, J., Jones, J., Shapiro, S., Schwartz, S., & Park, K. (1998). Obsessive compulsive disorder in children and adolescents: A review. *Harvard Review of Psychiatry, 5,* 260–273.

Geller, D. A., Biederman, J., Stewart, S. E., Mullin, B., Farrell, C. F., Wagner, K. D., et al. (2003). Impact of comorbidity on treatment response to paroxetine in pediatric obsessive compulsive disorder: Is the use of exclusion criteria empirically supported in randomized clinical trials? *Journal of Child and Adolescent Psychopharmacology, 13*(S1), S19–S29.

Geller, D. A., Biederman, J., Stewart, S. E., Mullin, B., Martin, A., Spencer, T., et al. (2003). Which SSRI? A meta-analysis of pharmacotherapy trials in pediatric obsessive compulsive disorder. *American Journal of Psychiatry, 160,* 1919–1928.

Geller, D., Biederman, J., Wagner, K., Emslie, G., Gallagher, D., Wetherhold, E., et al. (2001). Comorbid psychiatric illness and response to treatments, relapse rates, and behavioral adverse event incidents in pediatric OCD. *Journal of Child and Adolescent Psychopharmacology, 11,* 331–332.

Geller, D. A., Coffey, B. J., Faraone, S., Hagermoser, L. M., Zaman, N. K., Farrell, C. F., et al. (2003). Does comorbid attention-deficit/hyperactivity disorder impact the clinical expression of pediatric obsessive compulsive disorder. *CNS Spectrums, 8,* 259–264.

Geller, D., Hammerness, P., & Spencer, T. (2006). Pediatric psychopharmacology. In E. Coffey (Ed.), *Textbook of pediatric neuropsychiatry* (2nd. ed., pp. 589–668). Washington, DC: American Psychiatric Press.

Geller, D. A., Hoog, S. L., Heiligenstein, J. H., Ricardi, R. K., Tamura, R., Kluszynski, S., et al. (2001). Fluoxetine treatment for obsessive-compulsive disorder in children and adolescents: A placebo-controlled clinical trial. *Journal of the American Academy of Child and Adolescent Psychiatry, 40,* 773–779.

Geller, D., & Spencer, T. (2003). Obsessive-compulsive disorder. In A. Martin, L. Scahill, D. Charney, & J. Leckman (Eds.), *Pediatric psychopharmacology: Principles and practice* (pp. 511–525). New York: Oxford University Press.

Ghaziuddin, N., Iqbal, A., & Khetarpal, S. (2001). Myoclonus during prolonged treatment with sertraline in an adolescent patient. *Journal of Child and Adolescent Psychopharmacology, 11,* 199–202.

Giakas, W. J. (1995). Risperidone treatment for a Tourette's disorder patient with comorbid obsessive-compulsive disorder. *American Journal of Psychiatry, 152,* 1097–1098.

Giedd, J. N., Rapoport, J. L., Garvey, M. A., Perlmutter, S., & Swedo, S. E. (2000). MRI assessment of children with obsessive-compulsive disorder or tics associated with streptococcal infection. *American Journal of Psychiatry, 157.*

Gilbert, A. R., Moore, G. J., Keshavan, M. S., Paulson, L. A. D., Narula, V., MacMaster, F. P., et al. (2000). Decrease in thalamic volumes of pediatric patients with obsessive-compulsive disorder who are taking paroxetine. *Archives of General Psychiatry, 57,* 449–456.

Go, F. S., Malley, E. E., Birmaher, B., & Rosenberg, D. R. (1998). Manic behaviors associated with fluoxetine in three 12- to 18-year-olds with obsessive-compulsive disorder. *Journal of Child and Adolescent Psychopharmacology, 8,* 73–80.

Goldman-Rakic, P. S. (1987). Circuit basis of a cognitive function in non-human primates. In S. M. Stahl, S. D. Iversen, & E. C. Goodman (Eds.), *Cognitive neurochemistry* (pp. 90–110). New York: Oxford University Press.

Hanna, G. L. (1995). Demographic and clinical features of obsessive-compulsive disorder in children and adolescents. *Journal of the American Academy of Child and Adolescent Psychiatry, 34,* 19–27.

Hanna, G. L., Yuwiler, A., & Coates, J. K. (1995). Whole blood serotonin and disruptive behaviors in juvenile obsessive-compulsive disorder. *Journal of the American Academy of Child and Adolescent Psychiatry, 34,* 28–35.

Hewlett, W. A. (1993). The use of benzodiazepines in obsessive compulsive disorder and Tourette's Syndrome. *Psychiatric Annals, 23,* 309–316.

Jacobsen, F. M. (1995). Risperidone in the treatment of affective illness and obsessive-compulsive disorder. *Journal of Clinical Psychiatry, 56,* 423–428.

Jones-Fearing, K. B. (1996). SSRI and EPS with fluoxetine. *Journal of the American Academy of Child and Adolescent Psychiatry, 35,* 1107–1108.

Joshi, G., Geller, D., Wozniak, J., Petty, C., Vivas, F., & Biederman, J. (2005, October 2005). *Clinical characteristics of comorbid obsessive-compulsive disorder and bipolar disorder in children and adolescents.* Paper presented at the American Academy of Child and Adolescent Psychiatry 52nd Annual Meeting, Toronto.

Khullar, A., Chue, P., & Tibbo, P. (2001). Quetiapine and obsessive-compulsive symptoms (OCS): Case report and review of atypical antipsychotic-induced OCS. *Journal of Psychiatry and Neuroscience, 26,* 55–59.

King, R., Riddle, M., Chappell, P., Hardin, M., Anderson, G., et al. (1991). Emergence of self-destructive phenomena in children and adolescents during fluoxetine treatment. *Journal of American Academy of Child and Adolescent Psychiatry, 30,* 179–186.

Koran, L., Quirk, T., Lorberbaum, J., & Elliott, M. (2001). Mirtazapine treatment of obsessive-compulsive disorder. *Journal of Clinical Psychopharmacology, 21,* 537–539.

Kurlan, R., Deeley, C., McDermott, M., & McDermott, M. P. (1993). A pilot-controlled study of fluoxetine for obsessive-compulsive symptoms in children with Tourette's syndrome. *Clinical Neuropharmacology, 16,* 167–172.

Kurlan, R., & Kaplan, E. L. (2004). The pediatric autoimmune neuropsychiatric disorders associated with streptococcal infection (PANDAS) etiology for tics and obsessive-compulsive symptoms: Hypothesis or entity? Practical considerations for the clinician. *Pediatrics, 113,* 883–886.

Lake, M. B., Birmaher, B., Wassick, S., Mathos, K., & Yelovich, A. K. (2000). Bleeding and selective serotonin reuptake inhibitors in childhood and adolescence. *Journal of Child and Adolescent Psychopharmacology, 10,* 35–38.

Lane, R., & Baldwin, D. (1997). Selective serotonin reuptake inhibitor-induced serotonin syndrome: Review. *Journal of Clinical Psychopharmacology, 17,* 208–221.

Leonard, H. L., Swedo, S. E., Lenane, M. C., Rettew, D. C., Hamburger, S. D., Bartko, J. J., et al. (1993). 2- to 7-Year follow-up study of 54 obsessive-compulsive children and adolescents. *Archives of General Psychiatry, 50,* 429–439.

Leonard, H. L., Topol, D., Bukstein, O., Hindmarsh, D., Allen, A. J., & Swedo, S. E. (1994). Clonazepam as an augmenting agent in the treatment of childhood-onset obsessive-compulsive disorder. *Journal of the American Academy of Child and Adolescent Psychiatry, 33,* 792–794.

Levin, B., & Duchowny, M. (1991). Childhood obsessive-compulsive disorder and cingulate epilepsy. *Biological Psychiatry, 30,* 1049–1055.

Lombroso, P. J., Scahill, L., King, R. A., & Lynch, K. A. (1995). Risperidone treatment of children and adolescents with chronic tic disorders: A preliminary report. *Journal of the American Academy of Child and Adolescent Psychiatry, 34,* 1147–1152.

Lykouras, L., Alevizos, B., Michalopoulou, P., & Rabavilas, A. (2003). Obsessive-compulsive symptoms induced by atypical antipsychotics. A review of the reported cases. *Progress in Neuro-Psychopharmacology and Biological Psychiatry, 27,* 333–346.

MacMaster, F. P., Dick, E. L., Keshavan, M. S., & Rosenberg, D. R. (1999). Corpus callosal signal intensity in treatment-naive pediatric obsessive-compulsive disorder. *Progress in Neuro-Psychopharmaclogy and Biological Psychiatry, 23,* 601–612.

March, J., Foa, E., Gammon, P., Chrisman, A., Curry, J., Fitzgerald, D., et al. (2004). Cognitive-behavior therapy, sertraline, and their combination for children and adolescents with obsessive-compulsive disorder: The Pediatric OCD Treatment Study (POTS) Randomized controlled trial. *Journal of the American Medical Association, 292,* 1969–1976.

March, J. S. (2003). *Pediatric OCD Treatment Study (POTS).* Paper presented at the 156th annual meeting of the American Academy of Child and Adolescent Psychiatry, San Francisco.

March, J. S., Frances, A., Carpenter, D., & Kahn, D. A. (1997). The expert consensus guideline series: Treatment of obsessive-compulsive disorder. *Journal of Clinical Psychiatry, 58*(S4), 5–72.

Martin, A., Young, C., Leckman, J. F., Mukonoweshuro, C., Rosenheck, R., & Douglas, L. (2004). Age effects of antidepressant-induced manic conversion. *Archives of Pediatrics and Adolescent Medicine, 158,* 773–780.

Masi, G., Toni, C., Perugi, G., Mucci, M., Millepiedi, S., & Akiskal, H. S. (2001). Anxiety disorders in children and adolescents with bipolar disorder: A neglected comorbidity. *Canadian Journal of Psychiatry, 46,* 797–802.

Max, J., Smith, W., Lindgren, S., Robin, D., Mattheis, P., Stierwalt, J., et al. (1995). Case study: Obsessive-compulsive disorder after severe traumatic brain injury in an adolescent. *Journal of the American Academy of Child and Adolescent Psychiatry, 34,* 45–49.

McDougle, C., Goodman, W., Leckman, J., Lee, N., Heninger, G., & Price, L. (1994). Haloperidol addition in fluvoxamine-refractory obsessive compulsive disorder: A double-blind, placebo-controlled study in patients with and without tics. *Archives of General Psychiatry, 51,* 302–308.

McDougle, C. J., Barr, L. C., Goodman, W. K., Pelton, G. H., Aronson, S. C., Anand, A., et al. (1995). Lack of efficacy of clozapine monotherapy in refractory obsessive-compulsive disorder. *American Journal of Psychiatry, 152,* 1812–1814.

Mercadante, M. T., Busatto, G. F., Lombroso, P. J., Prado, L., Rosario-Campos, M. C., do Valle, R., et al. (2000). The psychiatric symptoms of rheumatic fever. *American Journal of Psychiatry, 157,* 2036–2038.

Murphy, T. K., Sajid, M., Soto, O., Shapira, N., Edge, P., Yang, M., et al. (2004). Detecting pediatric autoimmune neuropsychiatric disorders associated with streptococcus in children with obsessive-compulsive disorder and tics. *Biological Psychiatry, 55,* 61–68.

Nestadt, G., Samuels, J., Bienvenu, O. J., Grados, M., Hoehn-Saric, R., Liang, K., et al. (2000). A family study of obsessive compulsive disorder. *Archives of General Psychiatry, 57,* 358–363.

Pao, M., & Tipnis, T. (1997). Serotonin syndrome after sertraline overdose in a 5-year-old girl. *Archives of Pediatrics and Adolescent Medicine, 151,* 1064–1067.

Parraga, H. C., Parraga, M. I., Woodward, R. L., & Fenning, P. A. (2001). Quetiapine treatment of children with Tourette's Syndrome: Report of two cases. *Journal of Child and Adolescent Psychopharmacology, 11,* 187–191.

Pauls, D., Alsobrook II, J., Goodman, W., Rasmussen, S., & Leckman, J. (1995). A family study of obsessive-compulsive disorder. *American Journal of Psychiatry, 152,* 76–84.

Perugi, G., Akiskal, H. S., Pfanner, C., Presta, S., Gemignani, A., Milanfranchi, A., et al. (1997). The clinical impact of bipolar and unipolar affective comorbidity on obsessive-compulsive disorder. *Journal of Affective Disorders, 46,* 46.

Perugi, G., Toni, C., Frare, F., Travierso, M. C., Hantouche, E., & Akiskal, H. S. (2002). Obsessive-compulsive-bipolar comorbidity: A systematic exploration of clinical features and treatment outcome. *Journal of Clinical Psychiatry, 63,* 1129–1134.

Pliszka, S. R. (1989). Effect of anxiety on cognition, behavior, and stimulant response in ADHD. *Journal of the American Academy of Child and Adolescent Psychiatry, 28,* 882–887.

Puig-Antich, J., Perel, J. M., Lupatkin, W., Chambers, W. J., Shea, C., Tabrizi, M., et al. (1979). Plasma levels of imipramine (IMI) and desmethylimipramine (DMI) and clinical response in prepubertal major depressive disorder. *Journal of American Academy of Child Psychiatry, 18,* 616–627.

Puig-Antich, J., Perel, J. M., Lupatkin, W., Chambers, W. J., Tabrizi, M. A., King, J., et al. (1987). Imipramine in prepubertal major depressive disorders. *Archives of General Psychiatry, 44,* 81–89.

Rapoport, J., Swedo, S., & Leonard, H. (1992). Childhood obsessive compulsive disorder. *Journal of Clinical Psychiatry, 53,* 11–16.

Rauch, S. L., Bates, J. F., & Grachev, I. D. (1997). Obsessive-compulsive disorder. *Child and Adolescent Psychiatric Clinics of North America, 6,* 365–381.

Rauch, S. L., & Savage, C. R. (1997). Neuroimaging and neuropsychology of the striatum: Bridging basic science and clinical practice. *Psychiatric Clinics of North America, 20,* 741–768.

Ravizza, L., Barzega, G., Bellino, S., Bogetto, F., & Maina, G. (1996). Therapeutic effect and safety of adjunctive risperidone in refractory obsessive-compulsive disorder (OCD). *Psychopharmacology Bulletin, 32,* 677–682.

Reddy, Y. C., Reddy, P. S., Srinath, S., Khanna, S., Sheshadri, S., & Girimaji, S. (2000). Comorbidity in juvenile obsessive-compulsive disorder: A report from India. *Canadian Journal of Psychiatry, 45*, 274–278.

Remington, G., & Adams, M. (1994). Risperidone and obsessive-compulsive symptoms. *Journal of Clinical Psychopharmacology, 14*, 358–359.

Rettew, D. C., Swedo, S. E., Leonard, H. L., Lenane, M. C., & Rapoport, J. L. (1992). Obsessions and compulsions across time in 79 children and adolescents with obsessive-compulsive disorder. *Journal of the American Academy of Child and Adolescent Psychiatry, 31*, 1050–1056.

Riddle, M., King, R., Hardin, M., Scahill, L., Ort, S., Chappell, P., et al. (1991). Behavioral side effects of fluoxetine in children and adolescents. *Journal of Child and Adolescent Psychopharmacology, 1*, 193–198.

Riddle, M., Scahill, L., King, R., Hardin, M., Anderson, G., Ort, S., et al. (1992). Double-blind, crossover trial of fluoxetine and placebo in children and adolescents with obsessive-compulsive disorder. *Journal of the American Academy of Child and Adolescent Psychiatry, 31*, 1062–1069.

Robins, L. N., & Price, R. K. (1991). Adult disorders predicted by childhood conduct problems: Results from the NIMH epidemiological catchment area project. *Psychiatry, 54*, 116–132.

Rosenberg, D. R., Amponsah, A., Sullivan, A., MacMillan, S., & Moore, G. J. (2001). Increased medial thalamic choline in pediatric obsessive-compulsive disorder as detected by quantitative in vivo spectroscopic imaging. *Journal of Child Neurology, 16*, 636–641.

Rosenberg, D. R., Benazon, N. R., Gilbert, A., Sullivan, A., & Moore, G., J. (2000). Thalamic volume in pediatric obsessive-compulsive disorder patients before and after cognitive-behavioral therapy. *Biological Psychiatry, 48*, 294–300.

Rosenberg, D. R., & Hanna, G. L. (2000). Genetic and imaging strategies in obsessive-compulsive disorder: Potential implications for treatment development. *Biological Psychiatry, 48*, 1210–1222.

Rosenberg, D. R., & Keshavan, M. S. (1998). Toward a neurodevelopmental model of obsessive-compulsive disorder. *Biological Psychiatry, 43*, 623–640.

Rosenberg, D. R., MacMaster, F. P., Keshavan, M. S., Fitzgerald, K. D., Stewart, C. M., & Moore, G. J. (2000). Decrease in caudate glutamatergic concentrations in pediatric obsessive-compulsive disorder patients taking paroxetine. *Journal of the American Academy of Child and Adolescent Psychiatry, 39*, 1096–1103.

Sallee, F. R., Kurlan, R., Goetz, C. G., Singer, H., Scahill, L., Law, G., et al. (2000). Ziprasidone treatment of children and adolescents with Tourette's Syndrome: A pilot Study. *Journal of the American Academy of Child and Adolescent Psychiatry, 39*, 292–299.

Savage, C. R. (1998). Neuropsychology of obsessive-compulsive disorder: Research findings and treatment implications. In M. A. Jenike, L. Baer & W. E. Minichiello (Eds.), *Obsessive-compulsive disorders: Practical management* (pp. 254–275). St. Louis: Mosby.

Saxena, S., Brody, A. L., Schwartz, J. M., & Baxter, L. R. (1998). Neuroimaging and frontal-subcortical circuitry in obsessive-compulsive disorder. *British Journal of Psychiatry, Suppl*(35), 26–37.

Saxena, S., & Rauch, S. L. (2000). Functional neuroimaging and the neuroanatomy of obsessive-compulsive disorder. *Psychiatric Clinics of North America, 23*, 563–586.

Schwartz, J. M. (1998). Neuroanatomical aspects of cognitive-behavioural therapy response in obsessive-compulsive disorder. An evolving perspective on brain and behaviour. *British Journal of Psychiatry (Suppl)*, 38–44.

Snider, L. A., Lougee, L., Slattery, M., Grant, P., & Swedo, S. E. (2005). Antibiotic prophylaxis with azithromycin or penicillin for childhood-onset neuropsychiatric disorders. *Biological Psychiatry, 57*, 788–792.

Sobin, C., Blundell, M., & Karayiorgou, M. (2000). Phenotypic differences in early- and late-onset obsessive-compulsive disorder. *Comprehensive Psychiatry, 41,* 373–379.

Spear, L. P. (2000). The adolescent brain and age-related behavioral manifestations. *Neuroscience and Biobehavioral Reviews, 24,* 417–463.

Spencer, T., Biederman, J., Kerman, K., Steingard, R., & Wilens, T. (1993). Desipramine treatment of children with attention deficit hyperactivity disorder and tic disorder or Tourette's Syndrome. *Journal of the American Academy of Child and Adolescent Psychiatry, 32,* 354–360.

Swanson, J., Kinsbourne, M., Roberts, W., & Zucker, K. (1978). Time-response analysis of the effect of stimulant medication on the learning ability of children referred for hyperactivity. *Pediatrics, 61,* 21–24.

Swedo, S. E., Leonard, H. L., Garvey, M., Mittleman, B., Allen, A. J., Perlmutter, S., et al. (1998). Pediatric autoimmune neuropsychiatric disorders associated with streptococcal infections: Clinical description of the first 50 cases. *American Journal of Psychiatry, 155,* 264–271.

Swedo, S., Leonard, H., Mittleman, B., Allen, A., Rapoport, J., Dow, S., et al. (1997). Identification of children with pediatric autoimmune neuropsychiatric disorders associated with streptococcal infections by a marker associated with rheumatic fever. *American Journal of Psychiatry, 154,* 110–112.

Swedo, S. E., Leonard, H. L., & Rapoport, J. L. (2004). The pediatric autoimmune neuropsychiatric disorders associated with streptococcal infection (PANDAS) subgroup: Separating fact from fiction. *Pediatrics, 113,* 907–911.

Tannock, R., Ickowicz, A., & Schachar, R. (1995). Differential effects of methylphenidate on working memory in ADHD children with and without comorbid anxiety. *Journal of the American Academy of Child and Adolescent Psychiatry, 34,* 886–896.

Taylor, E., Schachar, R., Thorley, G., Wieselberg, H. M., Everitt, B., & Rutter, M. (1987). Which boys respond to stimulant medication? A controlled trial of methylphenidate in boys with disruptive behaviour. *Psychological Medicine, 17,* 121–143.

Thomsen, P. H., & Jensen, J. (1994). Obsessive-compulsive disorder: Admission patterns and diagnostic stability. A case-register study. *Acta Psychiatrica Scandinavica, 90,* 19–24.

Tollefson, G. D., & Rosenbaum, J. F. (2001). Selective serotonin reuptake inhibitors. In A. F. Schatzberg & C. B. Nemeroff (Eds.), *Essentials of clinical psychopharmacology* (pp. 27–41). Washington, DC: American Psychiatric Publishing.

Urman, R., Ickowicz, A., Fulford, P., & Tannock, R. (1995). An exaggerated cardiovascular response to methylphenidate in ADHD children with anxiety. *Journal of Child and Adolescent Psychopharmacology, 5,* 29–37.

Whalen, P. J., Rauch, S. L., Etcoff, N. L., McInerney, S. C., Lee, M. B., & Jenike, M. A. (1998). Masked presentations of emotional facial expressions modulate amygdala activity without explicit knowledge. *Journal of Neuroscience, 18,* 411–418.

Zahn, T., Insel, T., & Murphy, D. (1984). Psychophysiological changes during the pharmacological treatment of patients with obsessive compulsive disorder. *British Journal of Psychiatry, 145,* 39–44.

Zald, D. H., & Kim, S. W. (1996b). Anatomy and function of the orbital frontal cortex, II: Function and relevance to obsessive-compulsive disorder. *Journal of Neuropsychiatry and Clinical Neuroscience, 8,* 249–261.

11

Clinical Challenges in the Treatment of Pediatric OCD

Kimberli R. H. Treadwell
University of Connecticut

David F. Tolin
The Institute of Living and University of Connecticut School of Medicine

Readers of this book are no doubt aware of the fact that exposure and response prevention (ERP) is an effective intervention for OCD in adults (Foa et al., 2005) as well as in children (Pediatric OCD Treatment Study Team [POTS], 2004). In pediatric samples, ERP is associated with a large pre–post treatment effect size, and may result in a greater proportion of "clinically significant" treatment responders than do the serotonergic antidepressants (Abramowitz, Whiteside, & Deacon, 2005). However, as is the case with any form of treatment, the process of ERP is often slow, inconsistent, or frustrating. Consider the following scenarios from our research and clinical settings:

- A recently divorced father called the clinic and reported, in an emotional voice, that his 5-year-old son is consumed with counting his toys and adjusting household items to the extent that the slightest movement of an item sent him into lengthy tantrums. In contrast to the father's obvious distress about this behavior, the son appeared remarkably unconcerned about his symptoms (so long as nothing was disturbed in the house) and refused to change.
- An adolescent boy was referred to the clinic for intense emotional distress resulting from intrusive images that were sacrilegious or blasphe-

mous in nature. Because he spent an inordinate amount of time engaged in extensive praying rituals, he was facing the threat of expulsion from his private boarding school. Understandably, his parents demanded to know the details of their son's treatment. The adolescent refused to tell his parents anything about his symptoms or his treatment. However, his progress in treatment was slow at best, he was not adhering to his homework exercises, and his therapist wondered whether the parents should be informed.

• A teenage girl had recently begun ERP treatment for her fears of contamination. Her first session seemed to go reasonably well, although her therapist noticed that, as she touched progressively "dirtier" objects without washing her hands, her self-reported anxiety level did not decrease. When she returned for the second ERP session, she told the therapist that she had been experiencing depressed mood for the past few months, and that she did not feel like she had the energy to continue with treatment. She also indicated that over the past week, she had experienced thoughts of suicide.

Each of these cases of pediatric OCD typifies clinical challenges that commonly occur when treating this disorder. In this chapter, we discuss clinical challenges that arise in the treatment of children and adolescents with OCD, including noncompliance, comorbidity, family issues, and performance of rituals. The clinical challenges we highlight are not all unique to pediatric OCD, but encompass issues when treating OCD at any age and when conducting treatment with children and adolescents for any psychological disorder.

INITIATING OCD TREATMENT

Is ERP Right for This Child?

In general, ERP should be at least considered for all children with OCD, given the compelling evidence of its efficacy (March, Frances, Carpenter, & Kahn, 1997). Currently, the contraindications for ERP are not clear (Tolin & Steketee, in press) although some variables have been identified that may make the prognosis less favorable.

OCD Severity. Some studies have found poorer outcomes among adults with more severe OCD (de Haan et al., 1997; Keijsers, Hoogduin, & Schaap, 1994), whereas others have not (Cottraux, Messy, Marks, Mollard, & Bouvard, 1993; Steketee & Shapiro, 1995). We typically recommend ERP for the full range of OCD symptoms, including the most severe cases. Severe OCD may, however, warrant modifications to the treatment plan. For example, we would be more likely to recommend medications in addition to ERP. The therapist should remain in close contact with the prescribing physician to coordinate CBT with both the onset of and dosage changes in medication, and to assist in establishing an overall treatment plan.

Compulsive Hoarding. Although ERP appears effective for a wide range of OCD symptoms (e.g., washing, checking, repeating, etc.), adults with compulsive hoarding symptoms may show poor response to ERP (Abramowitz, Franklin, Schwartz, & Furr, 2003; Black et al., 1998; Mataix-Cols, Marks, Greist, Kobak, & Baer, 2002; Saxena et al., 2002), but may benefit from alternative forms of CBT (Steketee & Frost, 2003). Compared to ERP, CBT for compulsive hoarding places less emphasis on exposure to feared stimuli, and more emphasis on improving decision-making ability (Hartl & Frost, 1999). To date, we are aware of no research investigating cognitive-behavioral interventions for young people with compulsive hoarding, leaving questions about the efficacy of ERP for children and adolescents with those symptoms.

Psychiatric Comorbidity. Comorbid psychiatric conditions may also influence treatment decision making. In general, ERP should not be initiated when another disorder is primary (e.g., more severe or causing a greater degree of functional impairment). A referral for a psychiatric evaluation or placing OCD symptoms on the back burner until the primary problem is addressed are preferred courses of action.

Although the presence of comorbidity might predict a poor outcome for children undertaking ERP, there is currently little empirical literature as to moderators of treatment response for pediatric OCD. The Expert Consensus Guidelines for OCD (March et al., 1997) outline recommended augmentation to CBT for multiple comorbid conditions. Generally, the clinician should consider the extent to which the comorbid symptomatology negatively impacts the child's ability to engage in treatment or threatens safety. Severe depression may be associated with attenuated outcome of ERP in adults, although even those patients can show significant clinical improvement (Abramowitz, Franklin, Street, Kozak, & Foa, 2000). Concurrent pharmacotherapy may be indicated for moderate to severe depression, and expressions of suicidality by the youth must always be a primary target of treatment. Substance abuse or dependence should also be addressed prior to initiating OCD treatment, so that altered states of consciousness do not interfere with habituation. Attention-Deficit Hyperactivity Disorder (ADHD) should be managed to maximize attention to the therapeutic process of ERP. The presence of thought disorder or bipolar disorder would also suggest alternate forms of treatment for OCD, such as medication. Finally, impaired intellectual or developmental functioning that interferes with the youth's ability to be a collaborative partner in the therapeutic process and/or the ability to voluntarily refrain from rituals would not be amenable to CBT. A greater emphasis on applied behavior analysis, parent training, and medication can be evaluated for potential therapeutic use when these conditions are present.

Family Problems.   Family conflict, such as violence or parent–child conflict precluding conflict resolution, may also warrant initial intervention efforts prior to CBT. For instance, if a child's oppositional behavior is second-ary to OCD, yet many parent–child interactions involve an escalating pat-tern of hostile interchanges, the family's coercive pattern of interactions should be addressed prior to OCD. The therapist should also intervene when high levels of expressed emotion (e.g., critical, hostile, or emotionally charged patterns of interaction) are noted. Such family patterns appear to predict poor response and relapse (Chambless & Steketee, 1999; Leonard et al., 1993). The therapist may begin by providing education about the some-times harmful effects of expressed emotion, reframing the child's behavior as manifestations of an illness rather than as a personality flaw or malicious be-havior, and improving coping strategies among family members (Van Noppen & Steketee, 2003).

Motivational Problems.   Studies of adults with OCD have demon-strated that low motivation is associated with attenuated outcome of ERP (de Haan et al., 1997; Keijsers et al., 1994), most likely due to poor treatment adherence (Araujo, Ito, & Marks, 1996; O'Sullivan, Noshirvani, Marks, Monteiro, & Lelliott, 1991). Therefore, it is important that the child and family be adequately motivated to adhere to treatment. ERP is an active treatment requiring hard work on the part of the youth and family. At the outset of treatment, the requirements of ERP are reviewed with the child and family, highlighting such details as the time involved in daily practice, the courage needed to face fears and the distress they cause, the fortitude needed to refrain from rituals, and the cooperation of family members to develop new interaction patterns to combat OCD (Kozak & Foa, 1997). Initial plan-ning with the family and child regarding what is involved, how they plan to address the requirements of treatment, and how the family will support the child can help to circumvent noncompliance and early treatment with-drawal. If a child is at least willing to attempt these things, and the parents have the organization and communication skills to assist, ERP can begin. If the child or family is unwilling or have multiple excuses about their ability to address fears or time to invest in treatment, additional sessions to bolster mo-tivation may be useful prior to initiating ERP. Pilot research (Maltby & Tolin, 2005) suggests that a brief (4-session) intervention consisting of psycho-education, a videotape example of an ERP session, motivational interview-ing techniques (Miller & Rollnick, 1991), and a phone conversation with a former ERP patient significantly reduced the rate of treatment refusal and led to favorable clinical outcomes when ERP was conducted. In a small per-centage of cases, however, the child (or parent) will flatly refuse to participate in ERP. In such a case, ERP may not be the best choice. A referral for alternate treatment, such as medication, or time to weigh treatment requirements, may be recommended under these circumstances.

We have met some children whose motivation to engage in ERP decreases when they experience some symptom relief from medications. If the clinician and parents believe that CBT continues to be in the child's best interest, several strategies can be adopted to motivate the child to continue. First, the clinician can explain that exposures will be easier to master with reduced symptoms because the distress level created by the obsessions will be lessened, making the exposures more tolerable. Lower distress facilitates habituation, which will most likely reduce the total number of sessions needed to address the OCD symptoms. Other motivation strategies include focusing on the interplay of symptom relief and age appropriate functioning (e.g., can they do the things their friends are doing?) and the achievement of long-term goals (e.g., are they ready to go to prom, start college applications, or use public restrooms?). Outlining additional gains may motivate the child to continue CBT strategies to reduce OCD to a level the child envisioned. These strategies should of course be implemented in a noncoercive manner, and the clinician and family must give careful consideration to the child's wish to refuse treatment.

Limits To Confidentiality

Outlining limits to confidentiality is an issue to consider whenever working with children and adolescents. As specifically applied to OCD, the child and parents should agree on the extent to which the content of a child's obsessions and rituals will be shared with the parents prior to assessment. Children, particularly adolescents, may not be comfortable revealing certain symptoms if they fear their parents will disapprove or think they are "bad." For instance, obsessions involving satanic images, violent images of aggression towards a family member, or explicit sexual images may be concealed by the child for fear of the reaction by his or her parents and others. Prior to assessment, parameters of what information will be shared with the parents must be outlined. During the evaluation, the therapist may include private time with the child to help the child feel comfortable revealing "taboo" thoughts or images, while keeping the parents informed about the general presence of OCD and treatment progress.

CHALLENGES DURING TREATMENT

Difficulties With the Rating Scale

Rating Scale Is Too Hard to Use.   A task for children during OCD treatment is to identify and evaluate their anxious symptomatology by creating a subjective units of discomfort scale (SUDS). Children less than 9 years old may have difficulty grasping the concept of differential ratings for their various obsessions and triggers, making it a challenge to arrive at a useful and accurate scale. The pain rating scale used at many pediatrician offices depicting drawings of progressively distressed faces can be useful for younger children in rating anxious distress. With most elementary and middle school children, a rating scale from 0–10 is often sufficient to differentiate levels of anxious distress. A fear thermometer is a useful means of depicting this scale (March & Mulle, 1998), as most children easily identify with an anxiety "temperature."

To prevent challenges created by inaccurate use of the OCD thermometer, guide the child to develop descriptors for the scale that are not associated with OCD. For instance, "0" may be a relaxing day at the beach, and a "5" would be moderately distressing, such as getting in trouble for breaking a vase, or getting an "F" on a school assignment. For "10," prompt the child to choose a situation with physiological, behavioral, and cognitive components, such as seeing a bear charging at you during a hike through a state forest. The clinician can instruct the child to practice using their scale by rating some non-OCD situations first, and then proceed to rating OCD obsessions and their cues for treatment planning. If the child chooses a theme in combating OCD (e.g., emulating Superman), the thermometer could also use descriptors associated with that theme (how much Kryptonite is present as a barometer for anxiety).

If children are capable of making finer distinctions than a 10-point scale allows (e.g., ratings of 5½, 6¾, etc.), extending the scale from 0–100 may be beneficial, especially for preteens and adolescents. This makes it easier for the child to differentiate levels of anxious arousal. If the child balks at the numerical system, assist them in creating their own SUDS scale. One of our young patients created a personal rating scale ranging from "rare–medium rare–medium–medium well–well done." It served the intent of a SUDS scale and personalized the child's treatment.

Everything is a "10."   There are some clients who report that all cues are at the highest end of the SUDS scale. Several options may assist the client in constructing a hierarchy for the treatment plan. One therapeutic response is to ask the child to visualize the cues one at a time and then rank the accompanying response. In so doing, the child may note minor variations in responses among the cues to allow differentiation in the SUDS ranking. Alternatively, the clinician can assess physiological, cognitive, and behavioral responses separately for each trigger to note any differentiation. Another option is to expand the temperature scale as just outlined to allow the child more choices at the high end of the scale to prevent a ceiling effect.

Re-examining the anchor points for the OCD thermometer may also be helpful to allow differentiation. Other descriptions of the numerical scale, especially the upper half, may help eliminate a ceiling effect by describing more examples of affective arousal. Probing for other OCD triggers that are less distressing is another option. For instance, if doorknobs rank a "10," and the child cannot think of other cues that are slightly less disturbing, the therapist can ask whether other cues, such as the door to the office or thoughts of a doorknob, are less disturbing. If differentiation of cues is still not obtained, ask the child to rank order the cues in order of preferred approach, perhaps by writing each potential exposure on a separate index card and then sorting the cards. In this way, the therapist acknowledges that all cues are perceived as extremely distressing, while still creating a hierarchy based on the child's input for treatment planning.

Noncompliance to Exposure

It is the first exposure session, and the child and therapist have chosen an exposure exercise, agreed on the response prevention, and planned a reward for the end of session. The exposure begins and (contrary to the ritual prevention instructions) the child performs the compulsion. At this point, the therapist should pause the exercise, assessing what the child experienced, and why the child chose to perform the ritual. Common reasons are "forgetting," experiencing greater anxiety than anticipated, diminishing motivation to withstand anxiety, and fearing that the anxiety will not abate without the ritual. Perhaps performing the ritual was an old habit, and simple reminders to withstand the pressure to ritualize will suffice in assisting the child to be successful. If the child thinks additional coaching would be helpful, start the exposure again, adding more frequent prompts to the child about their efforts, the goal of their efforts, praise for response prevention, and encouragement to continue.

Alternatively, the child might report that the anxiety was greater than anticipated (e.g., a "7" rather than a "4"). If so, the therapist should choose an alternate cue lower on the hierarchy or an imaginal exposure to the chosen cue, then initiate the exposure again with the new cue. With less distress, the child may be able to restrain from the ritual. Experiencing anxiety is not a comfortable experience and takes courage. Reminding the child of this in the face of uncomfortable anxiety and rallying their motivation may assist in response prevention. To increase motivation, ask the child to list what about their OCD makes them angry, or things they will do when they no longer are plagued by OCD (e.g., trips to the mall, participate in sports). If reduction of anxiety is not sufficient motivation, session reinforcers may be introduced, such as small prizes drawn from a "goodie bag" (e.g., stickers, party favors, decorated pencils), a game with the therapist, or a light refreshment. This may assist in motivating the child with an immediate pay-off for ritual prevention, rather than the longer term relief from OCD.

If a child fears that his or her anxiety will never stop, an analogy of habituation may be helpful. The example of water in a bath feeling a bit too hot at first, but then gradually feeling better often resonates with children. Point out that anxiety works the same way. If the child fears consequences due to prolonged anxiety, cognitive restructuring to contradict the fear may be helpful. These strategies may serve as buffers, assisting the child in garnering their efforts to withstand increasing pressures to perform rituals as exposures become more intense.

Homework Noncompliance

Some children will refrain from compulsions within session, but fail to do so during homework assignments. Check the structure of the homework. Did the home exercise mirror the session exercise? The first homework exercise each week should replicate the session exercise as much as possible. Discuss what parameters of the in-session exposure were not present that led to the difficulty at home. It could be that the child attempted a generalization of the exposure prior to replicating a successful one, which turned out to be too big a step. Repeat the exposure in session, or have the child bring a cue from home for practice in session. For other children, the lapse of time between the session and the first at-home exposure may have been too long for the child to perform the exposure again successfully. If so, strategize with the child to structure his or her OCD homework. Ideally, the child should go home and practice an exposure on the same day as the session. Problems that arise may be a signal to the child to request help from a parent or to consult with the therapist via the telephone or email to get homework back on track for the rest of the week.

A second reason for homework noncompliance may be that response prevention was too demanding at that juncture. Although ERP typically involves immediate and total ritual prevention (e.g., Kozak & Foa, 1997), in some cases we recommend sequential removal of compulsions when working with children. Sequential removal may improve a child's ability to cope with the progressive removal of anxiety-relieving procedures as habituation takes place across multiple cues so that, over time, the negative reinforcement of rituals is removed. Smaller steps may be needed when difficulty arises with homework compliance. To assist the child in refraining from rituals, have the child identify the final goal (e.g., hand-washing after the bathroom and when dirty), then outline how many fewer hand washes will occur that day compared to current OCD practice. Limiting rituals can be performed in a variety of ways. Showers can be shortened, coupons can be given each day for the number of questions asked of a parent, the number of pages allowed for re-writes of homework can be decreased, or cleaning can be accomplished with smaller amounts of cleanser. Another strategy is to have OCD-free zones where OCD will not be present. For instance, choose one bathroom where the child will not wash their hands, choose one subject the child will not re-copy, or choose one drawer that the child will not order. Ask the child to identify how his or her parent can assist them in taking smaller steps, such as encouragement to focus on other activities, help tracking their daily progress, or limiting OCD supplies such as soap. The parent should also learn the ritual-prevention technique for the week so that if the child has a question or doesn't perform it quite right and asks for help, the parent has practiced the method. Smaller steps in response prevention may allow the child to delay or decrease the ritual to introduce the idea of choosing not to do a ritual, allowing the child to make further treatment gains.

Alternatively, anxiety management strategies (e.g., relaxation training, practicing coping self-statements) could be introduced to assist in response prevention. However, we do not recommend this as a first-line treatment for both theoretical and practical reasons (Tolin & Franklin, 2002). Theoretically, the purpose of ERP is to evoke anxiety in order to allow for habituation and cognitive change; methods that are designed to attenuate anxiety may therefore interfere with this process. Practically, the inconsistency between exposure and anxiety management may prove confusing to the child who is being advised to intentionally elicit anxiety while also being taught strategies to minimize it. As a general rule, we have found that most children are able to tolerate the distress of ERP and do not require additional anxiety management training (Franklin, Tolin, March, & Foa, 2001). Low-level exposures guided by the therapist often allow the child to develop necessary frustration tolerance to face the anxiety and experience habituation in the absence of the compulsion. For some children, though, assistance in tolerating anxiety such as deep breathing or muscle relaxation may help them remain in an exposure until habituation occurs. The goal is not to distract the child from the cue or the distress, which could prevent habituation, but to assist the child in tolerating anxious distress while habituation occurs.

It is not uncommon for parents to be part of their child's compulsions, such as reassuring the child or laundering clothes in a certain fashion (Calvocoressi et al., 1995). Failure to prevent rituals at home may involve the parent's inability to ignore/disregard their child's distress. In these situations, a family meeting to redress this issue is important. First, assist the child in developing a strategy to use during exposures that trigger their request for the parent to ritualize. Include a planned response for the parent in case the child asks for a compulsive response. For instance, the child may plan for the parent to remind them that they can "beat" OCD and to do their best to stay with the exposure. Once planned, the child can present the plan to the parent for that week's exposure exercises. Next, the therapist should gather the parent's input about the plan, their expectations for success, difficulties they experience in refraining from the child's request when distressed (e.g., it may remind them of their own distress) and motivators to help the parent coach in the identified situation. A family reinforcer is recommended for that week's practice, such as a special family dinner, watching a movie together, board games, or a local trip. In this man-

ner the entire family can experience a reinforcer acknowledging their efforts in response prevention.

Concerned siblings may also interfere with homework practice, often in
the form of unplanned exposures. For instance, one 15-year-old female had
difficulty with response prevention due to her older brother's "help." He
would throw feared items in her lap and remark "just get over it and touch
this (the feared stimulus)." His intentions were channeled into giving his sister support throughout the week, and allowing her to show him when she was
touching things again. A similar scenario can occur when siblings tease the
client with triggers that they know will get a reaction. When this occurs, a
session involving the family can focus on teasing, how it will be addressed for
all family members, and overall family expectations for behaviors. This allows the sibling to be involved in a positive manner with treatment, especially when concerns arise regarding extra attention or "prizes" involved in
OCD practice.

Finally, homework noncompliance may indicate that the reward system
for at-home exercises needs adjustment. Discuss the incentive system with
the child and parent to review its efficacy, altering it as needed to help motivate the child. This does not necessarily mean spending more money, but
perhaps rearranging the reward delivery (e.g., immediately after an exposure
rather than at the end of the day) or the form of the rewards (e.g., changing
from a check-off system to stickers or privileges each day).

The Family Undermines Treatment

Pushy Parents.   Some parents may wish to be in charge of their child's
treatment, such as choosing exercises, the length of the exposure, and practice time, in a way that exceeds their child's developmental need for structure. Discuss the parent's motivation for taking charge, the extent that they
do so in other areas of the child's life, and the child's response. Some parents
may be so desperate for the OCD to diminish that they take over exercises to
make certain their child completes homework. Comparing treatment for
OCD with learning to walk may provide a useful analogy for the parents. Just
as they could help their child learn to walk by holding their hand and encouraging them to stand, but could not take the actual step for their child, parents
need to help with treatment but not take over the child's homework. The
child ultimately must learn new methods of facing OCD fears, habituating to
the anxiety, and thinking in new ways.

The therapist should assure the parent that they still have a major role to
fulfill for their child in this step of life and that their actions greatly affect the
direction treatment takes. In this respect, we often find it helpful to ask parents to think of themselves as assistant OCD coaches (Knox, Albano, &
Barlow, 1996). They can take charge by creating a home environment that
supports and prioritizes their child's OCD efforts, as well as providing overall

family discipline, serving as an assistant OCD coach that is sensitive to their child's need for assistance, and maintaining a model of healthy functioning. Define with the parent what specific steps can be taken each week in each of these areas. The parent can take charge of the family, prioritize OCD treatment, and turn down other social commitments or usual activities that would divert time and attention away from the important work of treating their child's OCD. This may include instrument lessons, soccer practice, social groups, or chores, such as house cleaning. The parent and child should certainly be allowed social contacts and activities for personal growth and stress release, but the idea is that often families and children have so many time pressures, the parent must make OCD a priority, canceling activities that would interfere with its treatment. Parents can also provide encouragement and support to their child undergoing treatment as well as their other children, and provide a healthy family environment (e.g., good eating habits, sleep schedules). Ask the parent to focus on their general parenting style and household rules prior to the onset of OCD, which are often abandoned due to their inadequacy of effectively addressing OCD. Parents can be encouraged to return to or continue to reinforce overall discipline strategies to create a healthy family environment.

As an assistant OCD coach, discuss with the parent how best to assess the level of coaching needed by their child day by day. The clinician can develop a "Coaching Scale" with the child similar to their SUDS scale, only this time ranking the level of coaching needed by the child (ranging from "0," no help needed, to a "10," maximum assistance is needed immediately). Such a scale allows the child to calibrate parental input as well as a verbal or visual cue to parents to let them know how to titrate their directions. The parents can also take an active role in treatment by reacting to their child in new ways that support treatment goals, rather than supporting OCD.

To serve as both a family supporter and coach, the parent must have adequate personal resources. Parenting a child with OCD can be very stressful, and often parents do not have personal time when juggling the demands of a child with significant difficulties along with daily responsibilities. The clinician can review the parent's stress level and strategies to relieve stress, bolstering them as needed. Encourage the parent to take stock of personal stress levels and devise daily routines to rejuvenate him or herself, such as a hot bath, listening to music, reading a book, or taking a walk. Finally, parents can be put in charge of identifying/accessing support groups in the area, the Obsessive Compulsive Foundation, or other resources to arm themselves with knowledge and support about their child's condition. These strategies may assist in the challenge of redirecting "take charge" parental reactions into more therapeutically beneficial actions.

Misinformed Parents. Difficulties can be encountered when parents may not be matching their parenting and coaching style to their child's developmental status and needs. A general guideline for the therapist is that elementary age children from kindergarten through third grade generally require the parent to be involved in each aspect of treatment. This includes sitting in during the treatment sessions, helping to identify cues and exposure exercises, assistance and prompts to use the SUDS rating, observations at home when they note OCD, presence at almost all exposures at home to help guide the child through the exercise, and guidance in the choice of reinforcers and systems of reinforcement.

Children of intermediate school age (fourth through sixth grade) will often require active coaching, yet can be given greater input on the amount and type of assistance to be provided. Parents may either sit in during most of the session or can check in towards the end of the session. The parent should be apprised of the week's exercise choices, have the opportunity for input that could enhance the exercises, and review with the child how he or she can coach during each day's exercises. Although children of this age will usually suggest a variety of items and activities, the parent's input on the choice of reinforcers and structure of reinforcement will guide the reward system. Prepare the parents for greater variation in coaching each day, as their role may vary from providing encouragement to assisting in each aspect of the exercise. The parental role at this stage involves helping the child to notice when OCD is intruding, prompting the child to record their OCD intrusions outside of the exercises, helping organize the therapy materials (e.g., where to keep them in the house), and delivering reinforcers.

Flexibility will become increasingly important when coaching children in middle school. Devise a plan with the family for assessing the level of assistance needed at any given time of OCD treatment, such as the aforementioned "coaching SUDS." At this stage, the parent will usually check in at the end of session to receive an overview of the upcoming weekly exercises and an outline for their participation. The child may not know how much help they will need for some exercises, so the parent should plan to be available in the home, but not to intrude until asked. Reinforcers and the structure of the reward system will be guided by the preteen's ideas, with parental input suggesting both additional reinforcers and the final structure of the reward system. In homework, their help will often still be useful and needed by the preteen, but the role of supporter and motivator is more the focus at this stage.

Adolescents in high school are developing their personal identity and autonomy from their family. Coaching at this stage is often limited, as the adolescent will want to make decisions for him/herself. Parental involvement is still important, usually in support and motivation. Parents can continue to check in at the end of sessions, but may receive a summary of the upcoming week's exercises or goals rather than details of each day's plan, as well as an outline of how best to support the adolescent that week. It remains important for the parent to be at home and available to the adolescent when completing OCD exercises if they are needed, but not to offer assistance unless asked. Parents of adolescents who observe their child exhibiting anxiety or performing rituals may do well to not point it out at that time, but to instead observe how well the adolescent is managing the OCD. Some adolescents may find a weekly check-in with their parent helpful, as it allows them to get their parents' perspective on home exercises and progress. The focus should be positive and encouraging, while allowing problem solving about possible intrusions the parent saw over the week. Depending on the family's communication pattern, this may be done within or outside of session. These guidelines may assist parents in providing developmentally appropriate coaching that is sensitive to their child's specific needs, rather than preconceived notions of what children require.

Parents Who View Reinforcers as Bribes. Creating a reinforcer system for exposures at home is a critical component of treatment for children and adolescents. Parents may voice concerns such as that they are bribing their children to comply, that the child should want to get rid of OCD without an incentive, or that reinforcers are artificial. The goal then becomes helping the parent to understand that the reinforcer system is an aid in treatment. An analogy that can be helpful in making this point is to ask the parent why they work. Often they report deriving personal satisfaction, a sense of accomplishment, or benefits to society. The clinician can point out that it is also nice to have a regular reinforcer in the form of a paycheck. The point can then be made that OCD reinforcers are similar to a paycheck. Treatment is designed to assist the child in overcoming their symptoms that can lead to personal growth and satisfaction, but having a tangible incentive when facing distressing anxiety can be that "little something extra" to help the child stick with their plan. It may also be helpful to point out to parents that they and the child will work together over the following week to devise a reinforcer system that fits with their family, their values, and their wallets.

Review several systems for reinforcement and potential reinforcers to get the family discussion started. Some families choose daily rewards based on practice, some may instead choose daily tokens (e.g., stickers or checkmarks) to be traded in weekly for a bigger incentive, and still others choose weekly incentives. Daily reinforcers can include gaining privileges such as a television show, extra time with a parent, choosing a meal for dinner, skipping one chore, or staying up an extra 15 minutes before bed, or receiving tangible items such as dessert, lip gloss, or stickers. Some children might choose to have a larger reward broken down into daily rewards, such as a new colored pencil set, earning one pencil each day. Weekly reinforcers that are "purchased" with tokens, daily checks, or stickers could include social events (e.g., a trip to a park, museum, library, or mall, time with a parent or peers) or privileges (e.g., watching a movie, choosing a meal at a restaurant, extra personal time, baking cookies, or inviting a friend over). To further address parental concerns about the artificial nature of such a system, the clinician can also review with the parents that the reinforcer system is a short-term project that will give way to naturally occurring reinforcers as treatment progresses, such as improved mental functioning and greater ability to go places set off-limits by OCD.

Disengaged Parents. Some parents enter treatment wanting the clinician to "fix" their child. Careful preparation when initiating treatment will set the stage for expectations in terms of coaching and support on the part of the parent. Pointing out advantages of successful treatment, such as less time in doctors' offices and a child functioning at a higher level of health, may motivate them to participate as indicated. It can be helpful to have the parent practice coaching during sessions to reinforce their engagement with the child. A homework assignment to consider in this circumstance is 15 minutes each day spent together in a child-directed activity that does not involve OCD as a means of increasing daily interactions.

Parent–Child Conflict. If parent–child conflict exists, reviewing parenting strategies for overall discipline and conflict resolution is in order. Parenting a child exhibiting distressing obsessions and lengthy rituals can take a toll on the family, and exploring the impact on the family allows the parent to clarify current functioning, areas of conflict, and the broader context of OCD's impact. For instance, a mother and son argued on the way to an appointment regarding whether or not they should stop and eat lunch prior to the appointment. Both were angry on entering the office. The mother "contaminated" all the office chairs by touching them with her foot so that her son stood for the 3-hour evaluation (without lunch). In these situations, a private meeting with the parent allows the therapist to explore how OCD has affected the parent's life, how they have attempted to cope with the situation, what stressors they are personally experiencing, how conflict is resolved, and how they cope. The clinician can then decide whether the conflict and parental stress can be addressed within OCD sessions or addressed separately.

If conflict is addressed within the context of OCD treatment, aligning the parent with the therapist and child against OCD will be pivotal in shifting the focus away from parent–child conflicts and toward an alliance against OCD. Viewing OCD as a third party also distances the problem from the child, which may assist the parent in gaining a perspective toward therapeutic goals. It will be important not to alienate the parent for their actions and to involve them with specific coaching assignments. An additional component can outline, with the parent, general expectations they should establish and enforce in the household. These expectations can encompass safety and health (e.g., curfews, level of supervision, diet), daily and weekly routines (e.g., when homework and chores are completed), school expectations (e.g., maintaining grades), limits associated with behavioral issues (e.g., tantrums, yelling, losing control), and family interactions (e.g., respect for self, parents, and siblings).

Parents Have Limited Coping Resources. Coping with the ramifications of OCD in a child can be taxing for even a well-functioning parent. For parents with limited coping resources, several strategies may bolster their ability to function as a helpful coach. Defining a specific role as a coach and specific tasks during exposures can concretely outline ways to assist their child in the therapeutic process. Helping the parent explore community resources, such as parenting support groups or religious affiliations, can increase social support systems.

Parental Psychiatric Condition Interferes with Treatment. When a parent exhibits a mental disorder that interferes with their ability to serve as a coach against OCD, or to provide a supportive and nurturing environment for their child, it is best to refer them to another provider to address the condition. The clinician should assess the extent to which the parent is capable of appropriately contributing to the child's OCD treatment and determine whether that parent might still serve a smaller role during treatment. If the child requires assistance for exposures between sessions, most likely an alternate coach should be identified, such as another parent, relative, or even older sibling (16 years or older). The identified coach should be able to attend sessions to outline their role and demonstrate their coaching ability. Alternately, the child may be able to conduct self-administered exposures with guided structure provided during sessions to better prepare for his or her out-of-session exposures. The therapist may wish to increase the frequency or duration of sessions if the child requires coaching assistance that is not available at home or telephone the child between sessions. If the child is not able to continue with exposures at home given the parent's incapacitation, postponing OCD treatment until the parent has achieved a higher functioning level should be considered.

PARTIAL OR LACK OF RESPONSE TO TREATMENT

Habituation Does Not Occur Within the Session

Even with careful construction of a SUDS rating scale, treatment hierarchy, and exposure exercise, a child may fail to habituate. The reasons for this failure must be ascertained prior to advancing to the next step of the treatment plan. Likely sources include irrational beliefs about consequences, negative distress, subtle compulsions or avoidance, and failure to tap core features of the child's OCD. If a child believes that his or her beliefs are rational and necessary, the therapist can employ cognitive techniques to realign risk assessments. These techniques help the child develop an understanding of the actual risk that contradicts the fear, rather than persuasion that the feared situation is really safe. Focusing on the feared consequences and risks during the exposure may allow greater access to the core of the fear, allowing habituation to occur. Homework assignments can include fact-finding missions regarding rational appraisals of risks, such as consulting encyclopedias regarding germ transmission or consulting newspapers at the local library regarding actual numbers of natural disasters to assist in addressing this challenge.

Other negative feelings concomitant with OCD such as anger, frustration, and aggression, are likely to occur when the child is highly distressed. In particular, depressive features such as cognitive indecisiveness, anhedonia, and hopelessness can greatly interfere with exposure exercises and the process of habituation. Teaching the child to moderate negative emotions through techniques, including reducing negative self-talk or increasing effective coping skills, can address these other negative emotions so that the child can engage in exposure. Utilizing anxiety management techniques may also be helpful, but note that their overuse can prevent successful habituation.

Another reason the child may not habituate is if he or she engages in subtle rituals or if anxious arousal is otherwise avoided. Some children might be able to refrain from overt compulsive behaviors, but continue to engage in mental rituals such as reviewing, counting, praying, or reassuring. Although these rituals may prevent anxiety from becoming uncomfortably high, they may also block the habituation process. Other forms of subtle avoidance may take place that result in maintained anxiety. For instance, the child may avoid the arousal by daydreaming, looking away from the cue, or "chatting" with the therapist. In so doing, the child escapes the anxious arousal momentarily, but then is reminded of it when re-engaging with the cue. This usually results in limited, if any, habituation. Help the child to focus on the anxiety through encouragement and planning, as just outlined when addressing noncompliance, to reduce avoidance and increase engagement in the exposure.

Another reason for lack of habituation may involve failure to tap core OCD features. Review the anxieties triggered by OCD cues to ensure that the treatment plan encompasses the main elements of OCD. Travel may need to be considered, especially if the child's OCD manifests itself in specific environments. Imaginal exposures in the office or bringing items to the office from the home or school may not adequately tap the OCD fears and allow for full habituation. Conducting sessions in the presence of OCD cues in vivo may be required to adequately habituate to the feared cue. Often, we conduct sessions where the fear manifests itself—public bathrooms, hospital lobbies, elevators, churches, cemeteries, parks, homes and schools—to adequately access the core of the feared situation and guide the client through initial exposures to that situation or item. The payoff is that accessing the core features of the OCD fear allows for progress in treatment, rather than core issues remaining unaddressed. With busy schedules, travel out of the office can be accommodated by meeting the child either as the first or last appointment of the day, or by conducting a longer session block and conducting several exposures in vivo at one time.

The parameters of the session may also interfere with habituation. The process may take 45 minutes or longer for distressing cues, and sufficient time must be allowed for habituation. Clinicians may need to consider a double-session for OCD clients to allow sufficient time for homework review, exposure planning, habituation, planning for the week, and reviewing with the parent. The therapist might also refrain from reinforcing the child for completing the exercise, instead reinforcing their efforts. Anxious children may deliberately report decreased anxiety to escape the exposure or to gain the reinforcer sooner. Praise effort at tolerating anxiety and refraining from rituals, noting decreased anxiety as a means of motivating the child to continue rather than the focus of reinforcement. As well, the therapist should have a second exercise planned if the first exposure is completed sooner than anticipated. In that way, the child has the full session to practice their new skills and habituate, rather than ending session early by habituating quickly. A discussion with the child regarding the importance of doing the exercise correctly as moving them towards their long-term goals may help the child be more accurate in their description. Overall, within-session habituation is a critical component for treatment response, and challenges that arise must be addressed immediately.

Habituation Does Not Occur Between Sessions

Despite within-session habituation, children may fail to respond to between-session exercises. In other words, their distress level to identified cues does not decrease over time with repeated exposures. Reasons to explore include inadequate practice at home, reinforcement of OCD from family members, a plateau in response prevention strategies, or failure to generalize practice to daily routines.

Inadequate practice of exposures at home could be due to noncompliance, lack of time management, or opposition. If insufficient time is available to adequately practice OCD, meet with the child and parents to formulate a plan prioritizing OCD treatment, pointing out how the child's goals can be realized with the recommended daily practice. Opposition may result when parents pester their child to do their treatment exercises or patrol their response-prevention practices. These tactics often undermine the child's motivation to conduct the treatment at his or her own pace and choosing, limiting the extent of habituation. It also pits the parent against the child in regards to how to practice the exercises, rather than aligning them together against OCD. Remind the parent that these are recommendations developed for the child to do at his or her own choosing. The parent's role is to oversee practice, support the child, and assist only when asked. If the parent observed mistakes or response prevention practice that was insufficient, suggest they contact you privately (via phone or e-mail) prior to the session rather than starting the session with a report about the week's failures. Opposition may decrease when the parents coach only when requested, with resulting increased practice by the child.

Another cause of inadequate practice between sessions is that the exercises do not engage the child, decreasing motivation to do the homework. Making the exercises fun and/or a game, especially with children and pre-teens, can motivate them to initiate and maintain exposures as planned. For instance, a child can pretend to be Obi-Wan Kenobi and systematically brandish his light saber around a room in the house from which he has chosen to chase away the evil OCD (e.g., the room that he will no longer perform the ritual of ordering things). As well, he will beware the dangerous mind tricks that OCD will try to play on him during the week, and fight back with his inner force. Another example is that a child could play a game of tag in her back yard with the coach (or even the whole family when carefully planned) wherein contaminated items (e.g., the trash can, the back door knob) are the safe bases. A playful attitude in constructing OCD exercises may increase the duration of practice, which allows greater between-session habituation.

Practice can also be more thorough, thereby increasing habituation, by assigning exercises to do things "wrong." If silverware in the dishwasher must be placed just so, an exercise can be to place the knives and forks in different directions (which OCD says is quite bad). If a child always asks a parent a question a certain way, have them instead sing something in another language. Likewise, ritualized washing will be limited by time, but also can be done in an opposite fashion (e.g., starting with the feet). Doing things "incorrectly according to OCD" allows the child to feel the doubt or uncertainty of the situation and to learn to tolerate it, increasing their overall exposure to core OCD features and increasing the chances of habituation.

Family interaction patterns may reinforce OCD and diminish habituation. For instance, the child asks if the curling iron was turned off before everyone left for school. Parents might reassure the child that it is off, tell them not to worry about it (avoiding the thought), or try to reason with him or her that turning it off is part of the morning routine. Each of these responses reinforces the OCD. Instead, advise the parent to recognize this as an obsession and employ their coaching strategies as reviewed in session (e.g., ignoring, not reassuring the child). Parents can coach the child to fight back against the OCD or tune it out. Helping parents change their interactions with children to combat OCD assists in the child's habituation.

Another explanation for lack of between-session habituation is a plateau in ritual-prevention removal. The graduated steps outlined in the treatment plan allow the experience of a choice in delaying or stopping some rituals.

However, the ultimate treatment goal is to remove all rituals. The removal schedule may plateau or move more slowly than is helpful for successful habituation. While rituals remain, there is still negative reinforcement of the anxiety resulting from the obsessions, and the ability to perform certain rituals may be allowing the child to "save up" their anxiety and dispel it at a later time with a ritual performed later in the day. This would prematurely end the anxiety with anticipated negative reinforcement rather than in a habituation process. Asking the child if they "save up" anxiety for later rituals will assess this possibility, as will examining the pattern and pace of response prevention. The timing and structure may need to be altered so that the gradual removal supports habituation, rather than supporting negative reinforcement.

Children must also learn to address obsessions when they intrude during the day, in addition to their exposure homework, to generalize treatment. If the child has difficulty doing this, help the child to interject the choice of either ignoring or "bossing back" the obsession to detach from obsessions between exposures. Ignoring OCD can be analogous to tuning out a radio while it is playing, or not noticing background noises around the home, such as the hum of a refrigerator. Point out to the child that the noise is still there, but he or she is just not paying attention to it. The child can ignore OCD by walking away from it and not getting involved in escalating obsessions. Homework assignments can include preparing a list that helps the child refocus on the bigger picture and diminish OCD's grip on daily life, such as reading a book, exercising, calling a friend, surfing the internet, riding a bike, or skateboarding. The child may alternately choose to combat OCD when it spontaneously occurs by not doing what OCD urges, such as, "I'm not going to go check my homework one more time, I'm going to be brave and keep riding my bike to my friend's house!" These actions retrain the child to think outside the usual OCD mode.

CHALLENGES TO MAINTENANCE
OF TREATMENT GAINS

The successful relief from symptoms often achieved by treatment may give way to the idea that the child is cured. Unfortunately, this is often not the case with OCD. Expectations of being permanently rid of OCD after treatment are not beneficial for long-term maintenance of gains. As a therapist, explain that OCD is better conceptualized as a chronic condition that requires periodic checking, more akin to diabetes or needing glasses than to breaking one's arm and having it mended with a cast. Watching out for OCD is similar to checking blood levels occasionally for signs of diabetes, or in wearing glasses to correct a visual impairment. The child will need a "corrective lens" to watch out for OCD because they have a history of processing anxiety in a manner that increases its distress and using rituals to combat the distress. The therapist can also point out the enormous strides the child and family have made during treatment, and that a chronic condition does not mean chronic disablement, but rather that a radar system will be needed to keep OCD at bay because the child is prone to anxiety of this nature.

Maintenance strategies should include a monthly component of practicing an exposure to the hardest cue from treatment to ensure that it is still easy to do. The child can create a reminder card, computer file, or short video of the steps to take for an exposure and how to combat their OCD to assist in the monthly "tune-up" exercises. The therapist will also plan with the child how to combat OCD if cues become difficult, so that OCD can be managed.

Prepare the child and parent for challenges that may occur that evoke stress from the child, thus increasing vulnerability to anxiety or rituals. Typical events that often place stress on the family include a school transition, exams, illness, a developmental shift, or family discord. Plan with the child to recognize a stressful time period and to be watchful for ways to keep up their resistance to OCD. For instance, when deciding whether to go on a camping trip, the child can plan ways to reduce stress and thus help prevent OCD from recurring. The plan could include getting some extra sleep before the camping trip, as well as eating healthy snacks on the trail. These measures can help make the camping trip a successful experience, rather than a stressor. Planning for occasional lapses and devising exposure exercises to address them is helpful as a means of preventing relapse. This serves to insulate the child from relapse by treating OCD infringements as temporary and treatable.

Overall, the challenges that can present during treatment for OCD are best viewed within a theoretical and clinical framework. Familiarity with the developmental psychopathology of anxiety, theoretical change process, experimental studies of anxiety, and empirically validated treatment techniques allow the clinician to examine any particular case challenge and formulate an action plan. When done within the context of sound clinical training and experience, challenges in treatment will produce opportunities for growth and learning, as well as reach the many children and adolescents in need of intervention.

REFERENCES

Abramowitz, J. S., Franklin, M. E., Schwartz, S. A., & Furr, J. M. (2003). Symptom presentation and outcome of cognitive-behavioral therapy for obsessive-compulsive disorder. *Journal of Consulting and Clinical Psychology, 71*, 1049–1057.

Abramowitz, J. S., Franklin, M. E., Street, G. P., Kozak, M. J., & Foa, E. B. (2000). Effects of comorbid depression on response to treatment for obsessive-compulsive disorder. *Behavior Therapy, 31*, 517–528.

Abramowitz, J. S., Whiteside, S. P., & Deacon, B. J. (2005). The effectiveness of treatment for pediatric obsessive-compulsive disorder: A meta-analysis. *Behavior Therapy, 36*, 55–63.

Araujo, L. A., Ito, L. M., & Marks, I. (1996). Early compliance and other factors predicting outcome of exposure for obsessive-compulsive disorder. *British Journal of Psychiatry, 169,* 747–752.

Black, D. W., Monahan, P., Gable, J., Blum, N., Clancy, G., & Baker, P. (1998). Hoarding and treatment response in 38 nondepressed subjects with obsessive-compulsive disorder. *Journal of Clinical Psychiatry, 59,* 420–425.

Calvocoressi, L., Lewis, B., Harris, M., Trufan, S. J., Goodman, W. K., McDougle, C. J., et al. (1995). Family accommodation in obsessive-compulsive disorder. *American Journal of Psychiatry, 152,* 441–443.

Chambless, D. L., & Steketee, G. (1999). Expressed emotion and behavior therapy outcome: A prospective study with obsessive compulsive and agoraphobic outpatients. *Journal of Consulting and Clinical Psychology, 67,* 658–665.

Cottraux, J., Messy, P., Marks, I. M., Mollard, E., & Bouvard, M. (1993). Predictive factors in the treatment of obsessive-compulsive disorders with fluvoxamine and/or behavior therapy. *Behavioural Psychotherapy, 21,* 45–50.

de Haan, E., van Oppen, P., van Balkom, A. J., Spinhoven, P., Hoogduin, K. A., & Van Dyck, R. (1997). Prediction of outcome and early vs. late improvement in OCD patients treated with cognitive behaviour therapy and pharmacotherapy. *Acta Psychiatrica Scandinavica, 96,* 354–361.

Foa, E. B., Liebowitz, M. R., Kozak, M. J., Davies, S., Campeas, R., Franklin, M. E., et al. (2005). Randomized, placebo-controlled trial of exposure and ritual prevention, clomipramine, and their combination in the treatment of obsessive-compulsive disorder. *American Journal of Psychiatry, 162,* 151–161.

Franklin, M. E., Tolin, D. F., March, J. S., & Foa, E. B. (2001). Treatment of pediatric obsessive-compulsive disorder: A case example of intensive cognitive-behavioral therapy incorporating exposure and ritual prevention. *Cognitive and Behavioral Practice, 8,* 297–304.

Hartl, T. L., & Frost, R. O. (1999). Cognitive-behavioral treatment of compulsive hoarding: A multiple baseline experimental case study. *Behaviour Research and Therapy, 37,* 451–461.

Keijsers, G. P., Hoogduin, C. A., & Schaap, C. P. (1994). Predictors of treatment outcome in the behavioural treatment of obsessive-compulsive disorder. *British Journal of Psychiatry, 165,* 781–786.

Knox, L. S., Albano, A. M., & Barlow, D. H. (1996). Parental involvement in the treatment of childhood obsessive-compulsive disorder: A multiple-baseline examination incorporating parents. *Behavior Therapy, 27,* 93–115.

Kozak, M. J., & Foa, E. B. (1997). *Mastery of obsessive-compulsive disorder: A cognitive-behavioral approach.* San Antonio, TX: The Psychological Corporation.

Leonard, H. L., Swedo, S. E., Lenane, M. C., Rettew, D. C., Hamburger, S. D., Bartko, J. J., et al. (1993). A 2- to 7-year follow-up study of 54 obsessive-compulsive children and adolescents. *Archives of General Psychiatry, 50,* 429–439.

Maltby, N., & Tolin, D. F. (2005). A brief motivational intervention for treatment-refusing OCD patients. *Cognitive Behaviour Therapy, 34,* 176–184.

March, J. S., Frances, A., Carpenter, D., & Kahn, D. A. (1997). The expert consensus guideline series: Treatment of obsessive-compulsive disorder. *Journal of Clinical Psychiatry, 58* (suppl. 4).

March, J. S., & Mulle, K. (1998). *OCD in children and adolescents: A cognitive-behavioral treatment manual.* New York: Guilford.

Mataix-Cols, D., Marks, I. M., Greist, J. H., Kobak, K. A., & Baer, L. (2002). Obsessive-compulsive symptom dimensions as predictors of compliance with and response to behaviour therapy: Results from a controlled trial. *Psychotherapy and Psychosomatics, 71,* 255–262.

Miller, W. R., & Rollnick, S. (1991). *Motivational interviewing: Preparing people to change addictive behaviors.* New York: Guilford.

O'Sullivan, G., Noshirvani, H., Marks, I., Monteiro, W., & Lelliott, P. (1991). Six-year follow-up after exposure and clomipramine therapy for obsessive compulsive disorder. *Journal of Clinical Psychiatry, 52,* 150–155.

Pediatric OCD Treatment Study Team. (2004). Cognitive-behavior therapy, sertraline, and their combination for children and adolescents with obsessive-compulsive disorder: The Pediatric OCD Treatment Study (POTS) randomized controlled trial. *Journal of the American Medical Association, 292,* 1969–1976.

Saxena, S., Maidment, K. M., Vapnik, T., Golden, G., Rishwain, T., Rosen, R. M., Tarlow, G., & Bystritsky, A. (2002). Obsessive-compulsive hoarding: Symptom severity and response to multimodal treatment. *Journal of Clinical Psychiatry, 63,* 21–27.

Steketee, G., & Frost, R. O. (2003). Compulsive hoarding: Current status of the research. *Clinical Psychology Review, 23,* 905–927.

Steketee, G., & Shapiro, L. J. (1995). Predicting behavioral treatment outcome for agoraphobia and obsessive-compulsive disorder. *Clinical Psychology Review, 15,* 315–346.

Tolin, D. F., & Franklin, M. E. (2002). Prospects for the use of cognitive-behavioral therapy in childhood obsessive-compulsive disorder. *Expert Review of Neurotherapeutics, 2,* 89–98.

Tolin, D. F., & Steketee, G. (in press). General issues in psychological treatment for OCD. In M. M. Antony, C. Purdon, & L. J. Summerfeldt (Eds.), *Psychological treatment of OCD: Beyond the basics.* Washington, DC: American Psychological Association.

Van Noppen, B. L., & Steketee, G. (2003). Family responses and multifamily behavioral treatment for obsessive-compulsive disorder. *Brief Treatment and Crisis Intervention, 3,* 231–247.

12

Family-Based Treatment of Early-Onset Obsessive-Compulsive Disorder

Julia M. Berkman
Jennifer B. Freeman
Abbe M. Garcia
Henrietta L. Leonard
Pediatric Anxiety Research Clinic, Bradley/Hasbro Research Center, Brown Medical School

Obsessive-compulsive disorder (OCD) was initially considered to occur only during adolescence or adulthood, but has since been documented as early as 3 years of age. The mean age of onset for individuals who develop OCD prior to adulthood has been estimated at 10 years (Hollingsworth, Tanguay, Grossman, & Pabst, 1980; Swedo, Rapoport, Leonard, Lenane, & Cheslow, 1989). The field to date has generally used the same term, *juvenile onset* to categorize both child and adolescent onset OCD (Geller et al., 1998). However, increasing evidence suggests that there is an early (prepubertal), pubertal, and late adolescent-adult-onset of OCD and that there may be distinct phenomenologic and risk factors of each subtype. Despite a meaningful common core of symptoms observed across the life span (Rettew, Swedo, Leonard, Lenane, & Rapoport, 1992), there are unique features of early-onset OCD that makes consideration of early presentation different from pubertal or late adolescent-onset, and which may have important implications for treatment.

This chapter first reviews the unique features of early-onset OCD, with particular attention to the developmental and familial context of these children's symptoms, including current knowledge about family processes in families of children with OCD. Next, the literature on behavioral family interventions for anxiety disorders is examined, with guidelines for treatment of pediatric OCD, including cognitive-behavioral therapy (CBT) and medication management. Finally, we focus on current evidence-based treatment guidelines, as well as present a new model of family-based treatment for young children with OCD.

DISTINCTIVE FEATURES OF EARLY CHILDHOOD OCD

Gender Distribution

Evidence on gender differences in OCD onset has been mixed. In most research reports to date, children presenting with early childhood-onset OCD (i.e., those with prepubertal-onset) are more likely to be male, whereas the gender difference is reversed in adults (Swedo et al., 1989). Most studies note a male predominance in children (3:2) with the gender distribution becoming more equal in adolescence (Geller et al., 1998; Swedo et al., 1989). However, at least two recent studies failed to find an overrepresentation of boys in their clinically ascertained samples of individuals with early-onset OCD (Chabane et al., 2005; Scahill et al., 2003).

Comorbidity

Children with early onset of symptoms are more likely to have comorbid tic disorders, ADHD, and learning disabilities (Geller et al., 2002; Geller, Biederman, Griffin, Jones, & Lefkowitz, 1996; Geller et al., 1998; Pauls, Alsobrook, Goodman, Rasmussen, & Leckman, 1995). Family studies have established significantly elevated rates of comorbidity between OCD and tic disorders (Pauls et al., 1986). This finding is particularly strong for subjects with an onset of OCD before 9 years of age (Pauls et al., 1995).

Biological/Genetic Features

Individuals with early-onset OCD are more likely to have a family member with the disorder than individuals with late-onset OCD (Nestadt et al., 2000). Higher rates of anxiety disorders have been found in the first-degree relatives of children diagnosed with an anxiety disorder, versus children diagnosed with ADHD and nonpsychiatrically ill children (Last, Hersen, Kazdin, & Orvaschel, 1991). Furthermore, first-degree relatives of individuals with early-onset OCD have been shown to have higher rates of both tic disorders and OCD (Chabane et al., 2005; Pauls et al., 1995). Individuals with early-onset OCD also appear to have a different pattern on SPECT scans than the late-onset OCD patients (Miguel et al., 2000; Rosario-Campos et al., 2001).

Symptom Expression

Early-onset cases have been recently identified as having an atypical pattern of symptom expression (Geller et al., 1996; Geller et al., 1998). In the young child, compulsions without obsessions are common, and the compulsive behaviors themselves may be different than those observed in adolescents or adults (Rosario-Campos et al., 2001; Swedo et al., 1989). Although an adolescent or adult with contamination fears may partake in excessive hand-washing, using abundant amounts of soap, young children whose obsessions revolve around the need for cleanliness have been observed to lick their hands repeatedly as a means of getting them clean. Young children are also more likely to involve their caretakers in self-care rituals, insisting that a parent wash either the child or the child's personal space following a specific routine. Reassurance-seeking (verbal checking) is yet another way in which young children often involve family members in their ritualistic behavior (Rettew et al., 1992). Children may not be in a position to check items (such as the stove or high windows) on their own, thereby involving others by asking them to do the checking or to provide reassurance that everything is as it should be. A final example of reassurance seeking might be a child who comes home from school and tells his mother again and again that he may have said or done something bad that day, looking for her to calm his doubts.

There have also been reports of increased sensory phenomena-related compulsions in younger children (Rosario-Campos et al., 2001). In other words, the feeling or urge to have things be "just right," sometimes described simply as a bodily sensation or as a sense of inner tension, which leads to the performance of a repetitive behavior (Miguel et al., 2000). For example, a child with OCD who touches a counter with one hand, and then needs to touch the counter with the other hand (often back and forth between hands several times) until the tactile sensation is "even." Rosario-Campos and colleagues (2001) found that 100% of the 21 individuals in their study who had early-onset OCD reported that sensory phenomena preceded some of their compulsions, whereas only 67% of the individuals in the late-onset group reported the same trigger for their compulsive behaviors. This association has been found more frequently amongst individuals with OCD who have a comorbid tic disorder or Tourette's syndrome (Miguel et al., 2000).

These differences between children and adults may largely be due to developmental factors, such as the degree of the child's cognitive maturation.

Young children with OCD, unlike older children or adults, may be unable to distinguish obsessional thoughts from other, non-intrusive recurring cognitions or images. Additionally, they may not understand or be able to identify the connection between obsessional thoughts and subsequent compulsions, or to verbally express this pattern to others. Therefore, early-childhood cognitive development is the most likely explanation for why obsessional thoughts are less prominent features in the symptom picture.

Embeddedness in the Family

A prominent feature of early-childhood OCD, in contrast with adult OCD, is the role that the family plays. Young children are "embedded" in the family context in a way that is meaningfully different from that of adolescents or adults. Although adolescents generally start to gain independence, often functioning in social and academic spheres without continuous parent oversight, young children rely on their family for guidance in each area of life. As such, young children spend most of their time in the company of caregivers, who provide assistance in both routine and novel tasks. Parents, therefore, are more likely to play an active role in young children's rituals, as noted previously (Lenane et al., 1990). Empirical investigation of the possible effect of the family's social role in the development and maintenance of childhood OCD is limited. However, clinical evidence suggests that families do have an impact on the presentation and possible course of this disorder with regard to accommodation of, and participation in, rituals and avoidant behaviors (Lenane, 1990; Lenane, 1991; Pollack & Carter, 1999; Steketee, 1997). Patterns of family behavior, parent–child interactions, and parents' own interpretations of potentially anxiety-provoking stimuli, are all likely to affect young children with OCD.

The dependence that young children have on their caregivers also makes them vulnerable to multiple influences over which they have little control. Parental mental health, marital functioning, and family dynamics are just a few of the contextual factors that affect the nature and severity of impairment, treatment progress, and maintenance of treatment gains for children with psychiatric disorders (Kazdin, 1995; Kazdin & Weisz, 1998; Tharp, 1991; Webster-Stratton, 1985; Weisz & Weiss, 1991). Further, the family and the related subsystems are also affected by the child's symptoms of OCD (Lenane, 1989). OCD inflicts emotional distress and functional disruption not only on the child with the disorder, but also on the family members who surround the child and invariably make changes in their own daily activities to manage emerging worries and ritualistic behaviors (Piacentini, Bergman, Keller, & McCracken, 2003). It would be impossible to understand a child's symptoms, and how they are maintained, without approaching them from a family-based framework.

OBSERVATIONAL STUDIES OF FAMILY PROCESS

As stated previously, although we have clinical reason to believe that embeddedness in the family is a key to better understanding the nature of early-onset OCD, empirical investigation of the family's social role in the unfolding development and maintenance of childhood OCD is limited. Particularly given our interest in young children, it is critical to delineate the ways in which family processes (e.g., parent–child interactions that take place when children are anxious) may contribute to symptom development, severity, and maintenance. Using structured experimental paradigms, the following studies have observed parents and children in standardized anxiety-provoking interaction tasks and measured their affect and behavior.

Family Processes in Childhood Anxiety

In a study examining interactions of mother–child dyads, Hudson and Rapee (2001) looked at a sample consisting of clinically anxious children, oppositional defiant children, and children with no clinical diagnosis. Each mother–child pair was asked to complete two challenging cognitive tasks. These researchers found that mothers of anxious children were more intrusive, more involved, and more negative during the tasks, than mothers of nonclinical children. Based on their findings, Hudson and Rapee speculated that parents who overprotect their anxious children might keep them from approaching situations that evoke fear. This, in turn, prevents their children from having experiences that could counteract existing predictions of threat, and help them to overcome their anxiety.

Przeworski and colleagues (1999) examined family conflict and problem solving in OCD-relevant and non-OCD-relevant situations. In 29 mother–child dyads where the child had a current diagnosis of OCD, an OCD-relevant family conflict (e.g., child constantly asks family members for reassurance) and a non-OCD-relevant conflict were discussed and videotaped for 5 minutes each. Mothers and children were told to discuss each situation and to try to generate possible solutions and the discussions were coded. Results indicated that family problem-solving style was generally consistent across OCD and non-OCD situations. Additionally, parent report of increased family accommodation was related to less agreement, less solution-based questions, and more anger during the experimental interactions.

In a more recent study, Barrett and colleagues (2002) investigated whether families with children who have OCD, families with other clinically diagnosed children, and families with nonclinical children looked significantly different in the way they behave during family interactions. The interactions consisted of two videotaped 5-minute family conversations. Both discussions were about ambiguous, hypothetical situations, one involving a physical threat, and one involving a social threat. The researchers observed and coded several behavioral concepts (i.e., control, warmth, doubt, avoidance, positive problem solving, confidence and rewarding, independence) in four different groups of families: those with children affected by OCD, those with anxious children (Generalized Anxiety Disorder, Separation Anxiety Disorder, and Social Phobia), those with externalizing children (Oppositional Defiant Disorder, Conduct Disorder, Attention Deficit/Hyperactivity Disorder), and those with nonclinical children. Results demonstrated that parent and child behaviors during family interactions were substantially different in families with children with OCD, than they were in families with other clinical and nonclinical children. Specifically, parents of children with OCD showed less confidence in their child's ability, were less granting of autonomy, and used less positive problem solving. In addition, children with OCD were less confident, showed less warmth toward their parents, and were less likely to use positive problem solving.

Expressed Emotion (EE) in Childhood OCD

The construct of EE consists of assessment of critical comments, emotional overinvolvement, hostility, warmth, and positive remarks by a relative about a family member/patient (Brown, Birley, & Wing, 1972) and has been used as a predictor of course and relapse in severe psychiatric illness. Although EE has recently received increased attention in adult OCD (Chambless & Steketee, 1999; Steketee, Van Noppen, Lam, & Shapiro, 1998; Van Noppen, 1999), only three studies have examined EE in families of children and adolescents with OCD. Leonard and colleagues (1993) found that children diagnosed with OCD living in high-EE families had poorer global adjustment at 2–7-year follow-up, although EE did not predict their OCD symptom severity. In another study, Hibbs and colleagues (1991) examined EE in families of nonclinical controls and children diagnosed with OCD and disruptive behavior disorders. Relative to the control group, parents in both psychiatric groups were more frequently rated as high-EE, although the OCD and disruptive behavior groups did not differ. Przeworski and colleagues (1999) examined the relationship between EE and child OCD and found that parents were more likely to have high EE profiles for their children with OCD than for non-OCD siblings. High EE was also associated with child OCD symptom severity and greater family accommodation. Thus, high EE may characterize family interactions and serve as a marker of the overall family distress that accompanies the diagnosis of an individual child with OCD.

IMPLICATIONS FOR TREATMENT

Given the findings just outlined, and the degree to which young children are embedded within the family, we believe that there is an ongoing "interactive cycle" between the functioning of the child and the family. The presence of a child with OCD symptoms is likely to impact on the functioning of the family unit and/or subsystems (parent–child, marital relationship). In turn, this "compromised" family functioning is likely to have an impact on the child, and thus his symptoms. The resulting "disequilibrium" in the family needs significant attention in treatment, yet is not typically a primary focus in the traditional individual treatment model. In this regard, it has been suggested that therapy during the early childhood period is by necessity "de facto family context therapy" regardless of the theoretical underpinnings (Kazdin & Weisz, 1998). Essentially, the child cannot be treated outside of the context of the family system.

Additionally, in child mental health care, a family-based approach is advocated to influence enduring changes in the family after the clinician is no longer involved (Fiese & Sameroff, 1989). As the child's predominant recovery environment, the family can play an important role in both maladjustment and in health. Any form of treatment that a child receives becomes stronger when the family participates in treatment—supporting or continuing some of the practices and changes that a clinician initiates within the therapeutic context. Given that parents' own anxiety or emotional expression may be different when interacting with their children who have OCD, it is also critical for the clinician to observe the family system and all of the potential relational factors that may be influencing the child's psychological (mal)adjustment (Geffken et al., 2006). If the therapist is not able to work with the family in helping with the identification and resolution of these potentially detrimental interactions, therapy with the individual child might only be partially successful at best. The family can also provide invaluable information about the child's functioning outside of his OCD symptoms, helping the clinician to understand that child's strengths, not only his vulnerabilities.

It is our hypothesis that cognitive, developmental, and symptom differences, particularly embeddedness in the family context, play a significant role in understanding early-onset OCD and its treatment. A focus on OCD symptomatology alone, without considering involving the family system in treatment, may be insufficient for symptom amelioration and long-term improvement. We propose that the family context is an important vehicle for treatment development and delivery.

BEHAVIORAL FAMILY INTERVENTIONS FOR CHILDHOOD ANXIETY AND OCD

Behavioral family intervention (BFI) has had a major influence in the field of psychopathology and has become an important paradigm in the treatment of childhood disorders (Diamond & Josephson, 2005; Sanders, 1996; Taylor & Biglan, 1998). The core components of BFI involve teaching parents effective child-management strategies (e.g., positive reinforcement, time out) while at the same time teaching the family effective communication and conflict resolution strategies (Taylor & Biglan, 1998). Behavioral family interventions have been empirically shown to benefit a wide range of disruptive behavior problems in children (e.g., AD/HD, ODD, CD; Diamond & Josephson, 2005). The success of BFI has led to its extension to the treatment of other childhood disorders, including chronic illness (Sanders, Shepherd, Cleghorn, & Woolford, 1994; Stark, Owens-Stively, Spirito, & Lewis, 1990), developmental disabilities (Harrold, Lutzker, Campbell, & Touchette, 1992), obesity (Graves, Meyers, & Clark, 1988), and anxiety (Barrett, Dadds, & Rapee, 1996).

The empirical base supports the conclusion that when parents are trained to implement behavior change strategies, there is often a corresponding improvement in their children's behavior and adjustment. The underlying premise of BFI emphasizes the importance of involving parents, teachers, and significant persons as "mediators" or "behavior change agents" to bring about lasting therapeutic change (Sanders, 1996). The BFI model includes interventions targeted at the cognitive, affective, and behavioral dimensions of the parent–child relationship, making it a "cognitive-behavioral family intervention" (Sanders, 1996).

Although behavioral family intervention appears promising for the treatment of other childhood anxiety disorders (Barrett et al., 1996), there is a more limited empirical basis for this strategy in the OCD literature. Although ultimate treatment success is dependent on the child's cooperation, recent studies suggest the importance of including concurrent family intervention, focused on removing parents from their children's rituals, with individual treatment (Piacentini, Gitow, Jaffer, & Graae, 1994; Piacentini, Jacobs, & Maidment, 1997). Interestingly, preliminary evidence also suggests that parents can play a role as co-therapists in the behavioral treatment and still not be "overinvolved" or "enabling" (Knox, Albano, & Barlow, 1996). Family involvement is particularly relevant to the treatment of children with OCD in the early childhood years, yet none of these studies have included children under the age of 8.

It is also important to consider that the requisite cognitive component of CBT protocols for childhood OCD has limited utility during the early childhood period, particularly if applied within an individual therapy modality. Young children have not yet reached the cognitive stage to fully comprehend, utilize, and benefit from cognitive therapy techniques (e.g., abstract thinking, cause and effect, understanding probability). Although adolescents may be able to independently attend a therapy session, understand and retain weekly assignments, and complete between-session homework—all integral steps in existing treatment protocols (discussed further in the following section)—young children cannot. In therapy with young children, caregiver involvement is essential, as they are often required to take on a supportive, or even a primary role, in administering treatment. In addition, parents may themselves learn cognitive techniques that very young children are unable to grasp, such as externalizing or "bossing back" OCD. This will help them not only to better understand their child's experience, but also to provide appropriate support for the child as he attempts to fight OCD. Parents who learn and eventually embrace an externalizing model of OCD (i.e., learn to draw a distinction between the disorder and their child), often provide a less judgmental environment at home. This, in turn, can reduce overall stress for the child, and allow him to feel more comfortable in practicing skills learned in therapy with their parents. Thus, even if the child does not fully grasp the meaning or intent of externalizing OCD, he can still benefit from this technique through his parents. The individual therapy modality is not an optimal mode of treatment delivery for this age group, as it takes away the integral support and ongoing instruction that parents can provide outside of the therapy context.

Finally, given the psychiatric comorbidity in this population, focusing on the OCD symptoms alone is often not sufficient. Young children often have comorbid behavioral issues and are generally more apt to involve their family in their behaviors. Therefore, we propose that expanding current approaches for treatment of pediatric OCD to include the family system is required. This would involve developing OCD-specific behavior modification plans, teaching parents strategies to manage their child's anxiety and distress (often crucial with this population), and teaching parents basic behavior management techniques not specifically related to the OCD per se. The last point refers to parenting skills such as using differential attention to either increase a desired behavior or to decrease an undesired behavior. This coaching may be particularly useful with children who present with oppositional behaviors around completing homework assignments between therapy sessions, and who need additional encouragement or structure for therapeutic intervention to be effective.

CURRENT TREATMENTS FOR PEDIATRIC OCD

It is necessary to review previously investigated interventions for pediatric OCD as we move toward establishing a therapeutic approach that integrates the family into the treatment of young children with this disorder. Currently, two treatment modalities have empirical support for effectively treating OCD: psychotherapy, specifically exposure with response prevention (E/RP), and medication therapy (Serotonin Reuptake Inhibitors/Selective Serotonin Reuptake Inhibitors). In contrast to the adult literature, however, relatively little research has focused on the treatment of pediatric OCD. This section reviews the literature regarding CBT for pediatric OCD, specifically the efficacy of CBT and the combination of CBT and medication. A review of medication therapy alone is not be covered as it is beyond the scope of this chapter.

Psychotherapy Trials

Empirical documentation regarding the efficacy of psychotherapy for children and adolescents with OCD has greatly lagged behind the adult literature (Piacentini, 1999). Although CBT with E/RP has clearly demonstrated usefulness in the treatment of adults with OCD, methodologically rigorous studies in children remain limited.

A limited number of studies published to date have utilized an experimental design with more than one subject and well-documented, reproducible treatment programs. In the first of these, March, Mulle, and Herbel (1994) reported on a sample of fifteen 8–18-year-olds treated with a structured CBT protocol for OCD. Results indicated significant pre- to post-treatment improvement in OCD symptoms for the sample, with a mean reduction in symptom severity by about 50%. The development of a systematic CBT manual for children and adolescents with OCD (8–17 years; March & Mulle, 1998) has provided an important tool that could be exportable, however it is not designed specifically for the very young child with OCD.

The results of the report just discussed (March et al., 1994) suggested that, as in the adult literature, CBT could be a useful treatment modality for youths with OCD. It was clearly the first study in the field to apply reliable and valid measures of treatment outcome to a large sample of patients, assess patients before, after and following treatment, and utilize a manualized treatment protocol. However, some specific issues limited the conclusions that could be drawn. All but one child in the study received adjunctive treatments including medication, family therapy, and supportive individual therapy. Further duration of prior pharmacotherapy and dose adjustments during treatment were not specified and leave open the question as to which factors were responsible for treatment gains. There was no control or comparison condition. Also, this intervention did not specifically target the very young child with OCD, similar to the ages that are discussed in this chapter.

Scahill and colleagues (1996) reported similar findings. These investigators treated seven children between the ages of 8–16 with CBT in the form of E/RP. Results indicated mean symptom improvement of 61% post-treatment, which decreased to 51% at a 3-month follow-up. Although this study did not have a control group, three children who declined CBT were followed for 3 to 6 months, and there was no improvement in their symptoms.

A third study, using CBT with 14 children and adolescents, between 10 and 17 years of age, also yielded findings consistent with the material just discussed (Franklin et al., 1998). Average symptom improvement at post-treatment was 67% and 62% on the Child Yale Brown Obsessive Compulsive Scale (CY-BOCS) at follow-up (average time = 9 months). Further, this study found no difference in outcome measures between CBT applied intensively (i.e., daily sessions) versus weekly.

Most recently, Barrett, Healy-Farrell, and March (2004) examined the relative efficacy of cognitive-behavioral family treatment of childhood OCD administered in an individual versus group therapy setting. This study randomized 77 children, ages 7–17 years, who participated in either the individual or group version of this treatment, or were assigned to a wait list control. Active treatment consisted of a 14-week cognitive-behavioral intervention, with parent and sibling components that included psychoeducation, anxiety management, and skills training around family involvement in the child's OCD behaviors. Results indicated that children in both the individual and group treatments had improvement in diagnostic status and severity of OCD from pre- to post-treatment, with no difference between conditions on improvement ratings. Children in the wait-list control group showed no significant changes in their OCD status during a 4–6 week period.

Although this study did include parents and siblings in treatment, family members participated in sessions that occurred predominantly in parallel to the identified patient's, rather than including the entire family in each meeting. The level of integration of the family system into the child's therapy was therefore limited. Although this approach is undoubtedly helpful in teaching families about OCD and how they can support the child who struggles with the disorder, it does limit a parent's ability to become a co-therapist in those cases where young children need additional guidance on a daily basis.

In sum, although current evidence supports CBT for the treatment of OCD during late childhood and adolescence, and systematic manuals are now available, further empirical documentation is needed. Despite the consistency in results across studies, they contained methodological limitations including small samples, nonstandard application of treatment, ascertainment bias, treatment effects confounded by the presence of concurrent pharmacotherapy, and lack of randomly assigned control groups. Most relevant to this chapter, none were conducted with participating children in the early-childhood age group, and none delivered treatment that consistently included both the child and the family simultaneously. Although there are systematic studies in progress, none to our knowledge specifically focus only on the early-childhood age group or actively involve parents in each component of treatment.

Psychotherapy Versus Medication Versus Combined Treatments

Studies in adults with OCD suggest that combining CBT with medication enhances treatment efficacy (Cottraux et al., 1990; Marks, Stern, Mawson,

Cobb, & McDonald, 1980). Expert consensus panel recommendations for treatment of juvenile and adult OCD also support the combination of CBT and medication (March et al., 1997). In the first published, controlled study comparing behavioral intervention with medication management, de Haan and colleagues (1998) assessed the efficacy of E/RP (plus cognitive restructuring) to clomipramine in 22 youngsters for a 12-week period. Results showed that both treatments produced positive effects, but that E/RP was significantly more effective in terms of both reducing symptom severity and response rate.

The clearest evidence to date of which treatment approaches work best for treating young people with OCD comes from The Pediatric OCD Treatment Study (POTS) Team (2004). This study team evaluated the relative efficacy of medication, of CBT, and their combination in a large randomized controlled trial. One hundred and twelve patients, aged 7 through 17 years, with a primary diagnosis of OCD were randomized to sertraline alone, pill placebo, CBT alone, or combined CBT and sertraline. All three active treatments were each statistically superior to placebo. Importantly, combined treatment proved superior to CBT alone and to sertraline alone. However, CBT alone and sertraline alone did not differ significantly from one another. The remission rate for combined treatment did not differ from that of CBT alone, but was greater than sertraline alone and placebo. Patients treated with CBT either alone, or in combination with medication, showed a substantially higher probability of improvement, with the edge going to combination treatment over CBT alone at one site but not at the other. The authors concluded that children with OCD should begin treatment with the combination of CBT plus an SSRI, or CBT alone.

With the youngest children, outside of the population examined in POTS, concerns about medication efficacy and long-term use have prompted treatment guidelines to recommend CBT as the first-line treatment. Severe presentations and other individual clinical circumstances might suggest a role for medications in some cases (King, Leonard, & March, 1998; March et al., 1997). Thus, CBT would be considered the first-line treatment for the young ages (5–8 years) for whom we have developed a family-based behavioral therapy treatment manual.

Summary of Treatment Outcome Studies

In summary, three treatment modalities (CBT, medication, and combined CBT/medication) have been studied with regard to treatment of OCD in children and adolescents. Evidence supports the efficacy of SRIs/SSRIs in targeting core symptoms of OCD; however, they are not uniformly effective treatments, typically only produce partial symptom remission, and have a high rate of relapse following withdrawal. Although CBT, or CBT with medication, are regarded by many as the psychotherapeutic treatments of choice for children and adolescents with OCD (particularly very young children), solid empirical documentation regarding its efficacy in children under age 7 is lacking. Thus, we have little empirical knowledge about the treatment of OCD in early childhood. For an additional, thorough review on the effectiveness of treatment for pediatric obsessive-compulsive disorder, the reader is directed to a meta-analysis completed by Abramowitz, Whiteside, and Deacon (2005).

PROPOSED TREATMENT APPROACH FOR EARLY-CHILDHOOD OCD

Our specific interest in the treatment of early-onset OCD has led to our team to develop a cognitive-behavioral family intervention that can be used with children who are 4 to 8 years old. Although modified from an existing OCD treatment manual (March & Mulle, 1998), it differs fundamentally by (1) teaching basic behavior management techniques (not specific to OCD); (2) focusing on family accommodation and parental reinforcement of anxiety; and (3) involving parents in implementation of the CBT program at home. The treatment consists of a multicomponent program combining psychoeducation, parent training, family treatment, and cognitive-behavioral strategies including E/RP. Most treatment components are covered in each session.

The goal of the psychoeducation component is to: (a) educate parents about the neurobiology of OCD, (b) correct misattributions about OCD, (c) differentiate between OCD and non-OCD behaviors, and (d) describe the treatment program in detail. The goal of the parent-training component is to: (a) teach parents basic behavior management techniques, such as differential attention; (b) develop a behavior modification plan that will be used throughout treatment to address both OCD and other behaviors; and (c) teach parents strategies to manage their child's anxiety and distress. The goal of the family treatment component is to: (a) reduce family accommodation of child OCD symptoms, (b) reduce criticism and hostility related to child OCD symptoms, (c) promote positive family problem solving related to child OCD, and (d) teach parents to understand the role of their own modeling of anxious interpretations and behaviors. The goal of the cognitive restructuring component is to provide children and parents with some basic and developmentally appropriate tools to cope with E/RP. These tools include learning how to externalize ("boss back") OCD, and using a fear thermometer to rate anxiety. Finally, the goal of the E/RP component is to have parents and children work together to develop a hierarchy and implement E/RP via the behavior modification plan (most often in the form of a reward chart).

Modeled after the March and Mulle (1998) manual, our proposed treatment approach consists of 12 sessions delivered over the course of 14 weeks. The first 10 sessions are delivered weekly with 2-week intervals between the last two sessions. The first two sessions (90 minutes) are conducted with parents alone with the remaining sessions (60 minutes) conducted jointly with both parents and children. The overall focus of treatment is to provide both children and parents with a set of "tools" to help them understand, manage, and reduce OCD symptoms, and to teach them how to integrate these tools into one, coherent approach for fighting OCD. Initial findings from a pilot study implementing this manualized approach suggested that children and parents found the intervention effective in reducing children's OCD symptoms, as well as feasible in terms of the demands placed on the family (Freeman et al., 2003).

CONCLUSION

Young children with OCD differ from older ones, both in their developmental status and in the phenomenology of their symptoms. Intuitively, it makes sense to develop a young child specific behavior therapy that is safe and effective, practical, durable, and exportable. Although manualized treatments exist for older children with OCD, they cannot be simply extrapolated down for the younger ages. Rather than waiting until children with OCD reach an age for which mental health providers currently have reliable treatment, it is imperative to move forward and broaden existing treatments to meet the particular needs of this youngest group. Although they may take a different form from those of adults, the symptoms that young children experience are often highly distressing to them and their families, intrude on various areas of their lives, and may disrupt or compromise the child's developmental course. Evidence that early-onset OCD may be more severe in the long term and more difficult to treat with medication (Rosario-Campos et al., 2001) reinforces our assertion that behaviorally oriented treatment for this specific group is greatly needed. Delaying treatment for a child who is showing symptoms early in life may only prolong their distress, and could be a detriment to their overall development.

REFERENCES

Abramowitz, J. S., Whiteside, S. P., & Deacon, B. J. (2005). The effectiveness of treatment for pediatric obsessive-compulsive disorder: A meta-analysis. *Behavior Therapy, 36*, 55–63.

Barrett, P. M., Dadds, M. R., & Rapee, R. M. (1996). Family treatment of childhood anxiety: A controlled trial. *Journal of Consulting and Clinical Psychology, 64*, 333–342.

Barrett, P., Healy-Farrell, L., & March, J. S. (2004). Cognitive-behavioral family treatment of childhood obsessive-compulsive disorder: A controlled trial. *Journal of the American Academy of Child and Adolescent Psychiatry, 43*, 46–62.

Barrett, P., Shortt, A., & Healy, L. (2002). Do parent and child behaviours differentiate families whose children have obsessive-compulsive disorder from other clinic and non-clinic families? *Journal of Child Psychology and Psychiatry, 43*, 597–607.

Brown, G. W., Birley, J. L. T., & Wing, J. K. (1972). Influence of family life on the course of schizophrenic disorders: A replication. *British Journal of Psychiatry, 121*, 241–258.

Chabane, N., Delorme, R., Millet, B., Mouren, M., Leboyer, M., & Pauls, D. (2005). Early-onset obsessive-compulsive disorder: A subgroup with a specific clinical and familiar pattern? *Journal of Child Psychology and Psychiatry, 46*, 881–887.

Chambless, D. L., & Steketee, G. (1999). Expressed emotion and behavior therapy outcome: A prospective study with obsessive-compulsive and agoraphobic patients. *Journal of Consulting and Clinical Psychology, 65*, 658–665.

Cottraux, J., Mollard, E., Bouvard, M., Marks, I., Sluys, M., Nury, A. M., Douge, R., & Cialdella, P. (1990). A controlled study of fluvoxamine and exposure in obsessive compulsive disorder. *International Clinical Psychopharmacology, 5*, 17–30.

de Haan, E., Hoogduin, K. A., Buitelaar, J. K., & Keijsers, G. P. (1998). Behavior therapy versus clomipramine for the treatment of obsessive-compulsive disorder in children and adolescents. *Journal American Academy of Child and Adolescent Psychiatry, 37*, 1022–1029.

Diamond, G., & Josephson, A. (2005). Family-based treatment research: A 10-year update. *Journal of the American Academy of Child and Adolescent Psychiatry, 44*, 872–887.

Fiese, B. H., & Sameroff, A. J. (1989). Family context in pediatric psychology: A transactional perspective. *Journal of Pediatric Psychology, 14*, 293–314.

Franklin, M. E., Kozak, M. J., Cashman, L. A., Coles, M. E., Rheingold, A. A., & Foa, E. B. (1998). Cognitive-behavioral treatment of pediatric obsessive-compulsive disorder: An open clinical trial. *Journal of the American Academy of Child and Adolescent Psychiatry, 37*, 412–419.

Freeman, J., Garcia, A., Fucci, C., Karitani, M., Miller, L., & Leonard, H. L. (2003). Family-based treatment of early-onset obsessive-compulsive disorder. *Journal of Child and Adolescent Psychopharmacology, 13*(Suppl. 1), 71–80

Geffken, G. R., Storch, E. A., Duke, D. C., Monaco, L., Lewin, A. B., & Goodman, W. K. (2006). Hope and coping in family members of patients with obsessive-compulsive disorder. *Anxiety Disorders, 20*(5), 615–629.

Geller, D., Biederman, J., Faraone, S., Cradock, K., Hagermoser, L., Zaman. N., et al. (2002). Attention-deficit/hyperactivity disorder in children and adolescents with obsessive-compulsive disorder: Fact or artifact? *Journal of the American Academy of Child and Adolescent Psychiatry, 41*, 52–58.

Geller, D. A., Biederman, J., Griffin, S., Jones, J., & Lefkowitz, T. R. (1996). Comorbidity of juvenile obsessive-compulsive disorder with disruptive behavior disorders. *Journal American Academy of Child and Adolescent Psychiatry, 35*, 1637–1646.

Geller, D. A., Biederman, J., Jones, J., Park, K., Schwartz, S., Shapiro, S., et al. (1998). Is juvenile obsessive-compulsive disorder a developmental subtype of the disorder? A review of the pediatric literature. *Journal of the American Academy of Child and Adolescent Psychiatry, 37*, 420–427.

Graves, T., Meyers, A. W., & Clark, L. (1988). An evaluation of parental problem solving training in the behavioral treatment of childhood obesity. *Journal of Consulting and Clinical Psychology, 56*, 246–250.

Harrold, M., Lutzker, J. R., Campbell, R. V., & Touchette, P. E. (1992). Improving parent-child interactions for families with developmental disabilities. *Journal of Behavior Therapy and Experimental Psychiatry, 23*, 89–100.

Hibbs, E. D., Hamburger, S., Lenane, M., Rapoport, J. L., Kruesi, M. J., Keysor, C. S., et al. (1991). Determinants of expressed emotion in families of disturbed and normal children. *Journal of Child Psychology and Psychiatry, 32*, 757–770.

Hollingsworth, C. E., Tanguay, P. E., Grossman, L., & Pabst, P. (1980). Long-term out-come of obsessive-compulsive disorder in childhood. *Journal of the American Academy of Child Psychiatry, 19,* 134–144.

Hudson, J. L., & Rapee, R. M. (2001). Parent–child interactions and anxiety disorders: An observational study. *Behaviour Research and Therapy, 39,* 1411–1427.

Kazdin, A. E. (1995). Child, parent, and family dysfunction as predictors of outcome in cognitive-behavioral treatment of antisocial children. *Behavior Research and Therapy, 33,* 271–281.

Kazdin, A. E., & Weisz, J. R. (1998). Identifying and developing empirically supported child and adolescent treatments. *Journal of Consulting and Clinical Psychology, 66,* 19–36.

King, R. A., Leonard, H. L., & March, J. (1998). Practice parameters for the assessment and treatment of children and adolescents with obsessive-compulsive disorder. *Journal of the American Academy of Child and Adolescent Psychiatry, 37*(Suppl. 10), 27–45.

Knox, L. S., Albano, A. M., & Barlow, D. H. (1996). Parental involvement in the treat-ment of childhood obsessive compulsive disorder: A multiple-baseline examination incorporating parents. *Behavior Therapy, 27,* 93–115.

Last, C., Hersen, M., Kazdin, A., & Orvaschel, H. (1991). Anxiety disorders in children and their families. *Archives of General Psychiatry, 48*(10), 928–934.

Lenane, M. (1989). Families and obsessive-compulsive disorder. In J. L. Rapoport (Ed.), *Obsessive-compulsive disorder in children and adolescents* (pp. 237–249). Washington, DC: American Psychiatric Association Press.

Lenane, M. (1991). Family therapy for children with obsessive-compulsive disorder. In M. T. Pato & M. Zohar (Eds.), *Current treatments of obsessive compulsive disorder—Clinical practice* (pp. 103–113). Washington, DC: American Psychiatric Association Press.

Lenane, M. C., Swedo, S. E., Leonard, H. L., Pauls, D., Sceery, W., & Rapoport, J. L. (1990). Psychiatric disorders in first degree relatives of children and adolescents with obsessive compulsive disorder. *Journal of the American Academy of Child and Adoles-cent Psychiatry, 29,* 407–412.

Leonard, H. L., Swedo, S. E., Lenane, M., Rettew, D. C., Hamburger, S., Bartko, J. J., et al. (1993). A 2- to 7-year follow-up study of 54 obsessive-compulsive children and ado-lescents. *Archives of General Psychiatry, 50,* 429–439.

March, J. S., Frances, A., Carpenter, D., Kahn, D. A., Foa, E. B., Greist, J. H., et al. (1997). Treatment of obsessive-compulsive disorder. *Journal of Clinical Psychiatry, 58*(Suppl. 4), 2–72.

March, J. S., & Mulle, K. (1998). *OCD in children and adolescents: A cognitive-behavioral treatment manual.* New York: Guilford.

March, J., Mulle, K., & Herbel, B. (1994). Behavioral psychotherapy for children and ad-olescents with obsessive-compulsive disorder: An open trial of a new protocol-driven treatment package. *Journal of the American Academy of Child and Adolescent Psychiatry, 33,* 333–341.

Marks, I. M., Stern, R. S., Mawson, D., Cobb, J., & McDonald, R. (1980). Clomipra-mine and exposure for obsessive-compulsive rituals. *British Journal of Psychiatry, 136,* 1–25.

Miguel, E. C., Rosario-Campos, M. C., Prado, H. S., Valle, R., Rauch, S. L., Coffey, B. J., et al. (2000). Sensory phenomena in obsessive-compulsive disorder and Tourette's disorder. *Journal of Clinical Psychiatry, 61,* 150–156.

Nestadt, G., Samuels, J., Riddle, M., Bienvenu, O. J., Liang, K. Y., LaBuda, M., et al. (2000). A family study of obsessive-compulsive disorder. *Archives of General Psychia-try, 57,* 358–363.

Pauls, D., Alsobrook, J. P., Goodman, W. K., Rasmussen, S. A., & Leckman, J. F. (1995). A family study of obsessive-compulsive disorder. *American Journal of Psychiatry, 152,* 76–84.

Pauls, D. L., Hurst, C. R., Kruger, S. D., Leckman, J. F., Kidd, K. K., & Cohen, D. J. (1986). Gilles de la Tourette's syndrome and attention deficit disorder with hyperactivity. *Archives of General Psychiatry, 43,* 1177–1179.

Piacentini, J. (1999). Cognitive behavioral therapy of childhood OCD. *Child and Adolescent Psychiatric Clinics of North America, 8,* 599–616.

Piacentini, J., Bergman, R., Keller, M., & McCracken, J. (2003). Functional impairment in children and adolescents with obsessive-compulsive disorder, *Journal of Child and Adolescent Psychopharmacology, 13*(Suppl. 2), 61–69.

Piacentini, J., Gitow, A., Jaffer, M., & Graae, F. (1994). Outpatient behavioral treatment of child and adolescent obsessive compulsive disorder. *Journal of Anxiety Disorders, 8,* 277–289.

Piacentini, J., Jacobs, C., & Maidment, K. (1997). *Individual CBT and family (ERP/family) treatment: A multicomponent treatment program for children and adolescents with obsessive compulsive disorder.* Unpublished manual.

Pollack, R. A., & Carter, A. S. (1999). The familial and developmental context of obsessive-compulsive disorder. In R. A. King & L. Scahill (Eds.), *Obsessive-compulsive disorder: Child and adolescent psychiatric clinics of North America* (pp. 461–479). Philadelphia: W. B. Saunders.

POTS Team. (2004). Cognitive-behavior therapy, sertraline, and their combination for children and adolescents with obsessive-compulsive disorder. *Journal of the American Medical Association, 292,* 1969–1976.

Przeworski, A., Nelson, A., Zoellner, L., Snyderman, T., Franklin, M., March, J., et al. (1999, November). *Expressed emotion and pediatric OCD.* Poster presented at the annual meeting of the Association for Advancement of Behavior Therapy, Toronto, Canada.

Rettew, D. C., Swedo, S. E., Leonard, H. L., Lenane, M. C., & Rapoport, J. L. (1992). Obsessions and compulsions across time in 79 children and adolescents with obsessive-compulsive disorder. *Journal of the American Academy of Child and Adolescent Psychiatry, 31,* 1050–1056.

Rosario-Campos, M. C., Leckman, J. F., Mercadante, M. T., Shavitt, R. G., Prado, H., Sada, P., et al. (2001). Adults with early-onset obsessive-compulsive disorder. *American Journal of Psychiatry, 158,* 1899–1903.

Sanders, M. R. (1996). New directions in behavioral family intervention with children. In T. H. Ollendick & R. J. Prinz (Eds.), *Advances in clinical child psychology* (pp. 283–330). New York: Plenum.

Sanders, M. R., Shepherd, R. W., Cleghorn, G., & Woolford, H. (1994). The treatment of recurrent abdominal pain in children: A controlled comparison of cognitive-behavioral family intervention and standard pediatric care. *Journal of Consulting and Clinical Psychology, 62,* 306–314.

Scahill, L., Kano, Y., King, R. A., Carlson, A., Peller, A., LeBrun, U., et al. (2003). Influence of age and tic disorders on obsessive-compulsive disorder in a pediatric sample. *Journal of Child and Adolescent Psychopharmacology, 13*(Supp. 1), S7–17.

Scahill, L., Vitulano, L. A., Brenner, E. M., Lynch, K., & King, R. A. (1996). Behavioral therapy in children and adolescents with obsessive-compulsive disorder: A pilot study. *Journal of Child and Adolescent Psychopharmacology, 6,* 191–202.

Stark, L. J., Owens-Stively, J., Spirito, A., & Lewis, A. (1990). Guevremont d: Group behavioral treatment of retentive encopresis. *Journal of Pediatric Psychology, 15,* 659–671.

Steketee, G. (1997). Disability and family burden in obsessive-compulsive disorder. *Canadian Journal of Psychiatry, 42*, 919–928.

Steketee, G., Van Noppen, B. L., Lam, J., & Shapiro, L. (1998). Expressed emotion in families and the treatment of obsessive compulsive disorder. *In Session: Psychotherapy in Practice, 43*, 73–91.

Swedo, S., Rapoport, J., Leonard, H., Lenane, M., & Cheslow, D. (1989). Obsessive compulsive disorders in children and adolescents: Clinical phenomenology of 70 consecutive cases. *Archives of General Psychiatry, 46*, 335–343.

Taylor, T. K., & Biglan, A. (1998). Behavioral family interventions for improving child-rearing: A review of the literature for clinicians and policy makers. *Clinical Child and Family Psychology Review, 1*, 41–60.

Tharp, R. G. (1991). Cultural diversity and treatment of children. *Journal of Consulting and Clinical Psychology, 59*, 799–812.

Van Noppen, B. L. (1999). *The historical development and current status of the expressed emotion construct: A transactional perspective of family processes in obsessive compulsive disorder.* Unpublished manuscript.

Webster-Stratton, C. (1985). Predictors of treatment outcome in parent training for conduct disordered children. *Behavior Therapy, 16*, 223–243.

Weisz, J. R., & Weiss, B. (1991). Studying the "referability" of child clinical problems. *Journal of Consulting and Clinical Psychology, 59*, 266–273.

13

The Function of the Family in Childhood Obsessive-Compulsive Disorder: Family Interactions and Accommodation

Lara J. Farrell
Paula M. Barrett
University of Queensland & Pathways Health and Research Centre

Obsessive-compulsive disorder (OCD) in childhood is a chronic and distressing condition that frequently has a profoundly negative impact on family relationships (Cooper, 1996), peer interactions (Allsopp & Verduyn, 1990), and school performance (Toro, Cervera, Osejo, & Salamero, 1992). This condition in childhood is typically associated with significant functional impairment across multiple areas of a child's life. The time occupied by performing rituals often significantly interferes with a child's daily routine, which inadvertently also disrupts the entire family and family life. As a result of excessive rituals and often uncontrollable anxiety, children and families may become late for school/work or other engagements or completely avoid places or social events due to fears they might trigger symptoms. In addition, they may avoid these situations because getting there simply takes too much time and causes too much distress due to ritualizing, or for fear that friends may become aware of the child's difficulties.

Piacentini and Jaffer (1999) systematically evaluated OCD-related functional impairment in 162 children and adolescents (mean age 11.9 years) with OCD, and found that the most commonly reported areas of interference by parents and children with OCD were doing assigned chores at home (78% of parents, 61% of children), getting ready for bed at night (73% of parents, 56% of children), concentrating on school work (71% of parents, 62% of children), getting along with parents (70% of parents, 56% of children), and getting along with siblings (65% of parents, 53% of children). More than 85% of all informants reported problems across the three domains of functional impairment assessed, including school, social and home or family. The results of this study highlight the great extent to which OCD occurs within the home environment, and the degree to which it interferes in not only the child's life, but also, to a very significant degree the entire family's routine and family relationships.

Childhood OCD is a problem for not only the child or adolescent suffering from the disorder, but for the entire family. More than any other anxiety disorder, this problem, which affects many young people, occurs within the context of a family and family life, and frequently draws the entire family into the disorder. The great extent of functional impairment and distress associated with this disorder is thought to be a primary reason why family members often become a part of the disorder, through accommodation and involvement in symptoms. For these reasons, current approaches to treatment of childhood OCD emphasize the importance of involving families in therapy—including parents and siblings (i.e., Barrett, Healy-Farrell & March, 2004). This chapter examines the role of the family in childhood OCD, specifically examining the familial nature of the disorder, the degree to which parents and siblings become involved in the disorder and frequently accommodate symptoms, current research into observed family interactions, and the role of family factors in predicting treatment outcome and symptomatic relapse.

FAMILIAL NATURE OF OCD

Although research from family studies conducted to date remains largely inconsistent, there is increasing evidence and acceptance that OCD has a strong genetic component. Although there are very few studies of concordance in monozygotic and dizygotic twins, the combined published literature has reported concordance rates of approximately 67% and 31% for monozygotic and dizygotic twins, respectively (Billett, Richter, & Kennedy, 1998). Prevalence rates of OCD in the first-degree relatives of adult probands have also tended to be higher than the general population (Bellodi et al., 1992; Pauls et al., 1995; Rasmussen & Tsuang, 1986; Riddle et al., 1990), although at least three studies have failed to replicate this finding (Insel, Hoover, & Murphy, 1983; McKeon & Murray, 1987; Rosenberg, 1967). Previous studies have demonstrated that other anxiety disorders and depression also occur at higher than expected rates among family members of patients with OCD (e.g., Bellodi, Sciuto, Diaferia, Ronci, & Smeraldi, 1992; Black et al., 1992), suggesting that parental OCD, anxiety, and/or depression may be risk factors for childhood OCD. Although it seems clear from the little available research and from clinical observation that OCD tends to run in families, recent research indicates that this may be even more true for the case for child-onset OCD.

A recent study by Nestadt et al. (2000) examined the familial nature of OCD by comparing the prevalence of OCD in the first-degree relatives of 80 OCD patients and 73 community controls. The relatives of the OCD patients were found to have higher rates of OCD compared to relatives of the controls (11.7% versus 2.7%). Interestingly, age of onset of OCD was strongly related to familiarity. The prevalence of OCD in the relatives of those with early onset OCD (onset between age 5–17 years) was 13.8%; however among the group with late onset OCD (18–41 years) there were no cases of relatives with OCD. These results were consistent with an earlier family study by Pauls, Alsobrook, Goodman, Rasmussen and Leckman (1995), and suggest that childhood onset OCD might have a stronger genetic basis or familial loading than adult onset OCD.

Several earlier family studies of children and adolescents with OCD have been conducted, although results again are largely inconsistent. Flament and Rapoport (1984) found no cases of OCD in the parents of 27 children and youth, whereas other authors have reported a prevalence rate of 20% (Hollingsworth, Tanguay, Grossman, & Pabst, 1980). It has been suggested that the likely prevalence rate of OCD in the parents of affected children is likely to fall somewhere between these two estimates (Allsopp & Verduyn, 1988; Honjo et al., 1989; Last & Strauss, 1989; Riddle et al., 1990). Findings from these early studies however, are inconclusive due to several important limitations, including an absence of diagnostic interviews in most cases, the inclusion of only one parent in the study, and a lack of clear criteria for defining subclinical syndrome (Waters & Barrett, 2000).

In an effort to overcome these limitations, Lenane et al. (1990) conducted a methodologically rigorous investigation of psychopathology in first-degree relatives of 46 children and adolescents with OCD. All parents and siblings (aged greater than 5 years) who took part in the study were screened using structured diagnostic interviews. Subclinical OCD was defined by the presence of obsessions and compulsions without associated significant interference or distress. Obsessive-compulsive personality (OCP) traits were also assessed and defined according to *DSM–III* criteria. The reliability coefficients for each of these diagnostic categories were as follows: 0.88 for OCD, 0.54 for subclinical OCD, 0.24 for OCP, and 0.67 for no diagnosis. The results indicated that 17% of parents met criteria for OCD with fathers almost three times as likely to receive a diagnosis as mothers (25% versus 9%). The rate of OCD in siblings was 5%; however, when this value was corrected for age of risk, the rate increased substantially to 35%. Subclinical OCD was reported in 13% of parents, regardless of gender, and 4% of siblings. Twenty percent of fathers were observed to exhibit obsessive-compulsive personality traits compared to only 2% of mothers—although results for OCP and subclinical OCD should be interpreted with caution due to limited reliability in categorizing cases. The authors of this study also cross-matched childrens' symptoms with that of their parents and found no consistent pattern between the two groups on symptomatology. Although results are somewhat limited in terms of understanding the prevalence of OCP and subclinical OCD, due to only low to moderate diagnostic reliability, the findings for prevalence of parental OCD are consistent with earlier reports, with up to 20% of parents meeting criteria for OCD.

The augmented prevalence of OCD within first-degree relatives, combined with the increased familial clustering of early onset OCD can be explained, in part, by genetics (see Billett, Richter & Kennedy, 1998, for a review) Environmental factors may also contribute, although this has been a neglected area of study to date. A number of authors have speculated about the mechanisms through which parents and family processes may influence the development and/or maintenance of childhood OCD symptoms, for example through parental modelling of extreme caution and fearfulness (Henin & Kendall, 1997) or through modelling of perfectionism and excessive cleanliness (Honjo et al., 1989; McKeon & Murray, 1987; Rachman, 1996; Rasmussen & Tsuang, 1986); however, methodologically sound research investigating family process variables is limited. Although research is minimal, an alternative hypothesis to parental modeling of symptoms that has become widely acknowledged, is that OCD in childhood might be to some degree exacerbated and/or maintained through parental and sibling involvement in symptoms and accommodation of OCD.

FAMILY INVOLVEMENT AND ACCOMMODATION

Many children with OCD are extremely secretive about their symptoms and frequently delay performing their rituals when in front of peers, teachers, or strangers (King, Ollendick, & Montgomery, 1995). Instead, children with OCD "save" their ritualizing behaviors for home, often "erupting" when they arrive home from school. Given that most of their ritualizing occurs within the home environment, it is not surprising that children engage in repetitive reassurance seeking and frequently involve family members in their rituals, probably more so than adults with OCD (Piacentini & Bergman, 2000).

This disorder in childhood profoundly affects the family in a number of ways, causing marked distress and frustration for concerned parents and confused siblings, but also seems to be largely affected by specific family factors, including family involvement in the disorder. Cooper noted that "what distinguishes OCD families from other families of the mentally ill is the inextricable way that they are brought into the illness. OCD symptoms are all-encompassing, and the compulsions involve family members and the home itself" (Cooper, 1996, p. 297). It is thought that families may, in fact, play a critical role in maintaining the symptoms of childhood OCD, through their involvement and accommodation of a child's rituals and OCD demands. Parents and siblings often become involved in a child's OCD demands as an attempt to stop the child from performing rituals, or to decrease the child's obvious distress, or in an effort to hurry the child along.

Cooper (1996) investigated the impact of OCD on parents and siblings, and found that family members reported that OCD-related behaviors caused them personal distress, particularly depression, rumination, and being drawn unwittingly into the rituals. Results from this study also found evidence that family involvement in, and accommodation of OCD, was higher in the caregivers of children and adolescents, than in family members of adults with OCD. Results from the Cooper study (1996) demonstrated that the overall effect of the disorder on family members was deeply negative with the large majority of respondents reporting at least some disturbance in their personal and social lives. Approximately two thirds of families noted hardship to siblings and marital discord as a result of the child's OCD. Allsopp and Verduyn (1990) in their study of OCD and family involvement, found that 70% of parents reported being involved with their adolescent's symptoms. Of these parents, almost three quarters accommodated the young person's rituals, while the remainder reported responding in a hostile manner.

Parents and siblings may become involved in and accommodate a child's OCD through either *direct* involvement in the child's symptoms, and/or through *indirect* approaches, whereby the family member modifies his or her routine and behavior to prevent escalation of symptoms or to reduce a child's distress. Direct accommodation of a child's OCD might include, parents physically assisting the child to wash or clean, wearing sterile gloves while preparing food for the child, or driving the long route home from school to ensure the child's path is exactly the same as the bus route to school. Siblings may open doors for their brother or sister, turn on and off light switches, or answer excessive questions to assist and accommodate the OCD demands, thereby avoiding escalating distress and tantrums from their sibling with OCD. Indirect accommodation to a child's ritualizing typically involves more subtle, yet sometimes considerable, change to a parents or siblings own daily routine to avoid an OCD "moment" for the child. Indirect accommodation might include such things as arranging glasses in the cupboard in an exact and orderly fashion—as the child requires it, ensuring the TV is not turned on in the evening to avoid hearing the news whereby the child might hear stories related to death or dying, not touching the child's personal belongings to avoid contamination, and not entering the child's room in order to ensure the parent or siblings won't move something that has an exact position.

Calvocoressi et al. (1995) interviewed 34 caregivers of adult sufferers, including parents. The results indicated that the degree of accommodation was positively correlated with perceived family dysfunction, personal distress, and negative family attitudes. Shafran, Ralph, and Tallis (1995) also found a high degree of accommodation in a volunteer sample of 95 family members of individuals with self-reported obsessive-compulsive symptoms, with about half of the respondents reporting significant levels of interference in their own lives as a result of the OC symptoms. Calvocoressi and colleagues (1999) developed the Family Accommodation Scale (FAS) for OCD to assess the relationship between family involvement in OCD symptoms and the impact of this on family members (Calvocoressi et al., 1999). The results indicated that 89% of families accommodated the symptoms in some way and that these behaviors were significantly associated with problems such as family stress and burden, disharmony between family members, and rejecting attitudes of the affected individual.

More recently, Amir, Freshman, and Foa (2000) examined the relationships between family members' accommodation of an adult relative's OCD symptoms (e.g., assistance with rituals, modification of family routine), anxiety and depression in those family members, and the severity of the patient's OCD. Their sample comprised 73 OCD patients (aged 11–59 years) and 73 relatives. Family members reported they experienced increased levels of depression and anxiety when they helped with rituals, when they did not help the patient, and when they rejected the patient. Furthermore, family members reported more depression when they had to modify their routine as a result of the patients' OCD. These findings highlight the degree of distress that family members experience when dealing with a relative who has OCD.

Black, Gaffney, Schlosser, and Gabel (1998) reported significant family dysfunction, distress, and hardship to the spouses of 15 adult sufferers. The results indicated that OCD families scored in the "unhealthy" range on the Family Assessment Device (FAD; Epstein, Baldwin, & Bishop, 1983) for communication, affective involvement and general functioning compared to nonclinical controls. At least 50% of spouses rated the sufferers' compulsive rituals, need for reassurance, anxiety, low self-esteem, and indecision as problematic. The disruption to personal and social life was also rated as causing difficulty by more than half of spouses.

Sibling accommodation and distress were examined in a recent qualitative study conducted by Barrett, Rasmussen, and Healy (2001), which involved interviewing siblings of children and youth who were suffering OCD and were part of a treatment program being run by the authors. Barrett and colleagues (2001) found siblings also accommodated the OCD symptoms in both direct and indirect ways, and experienced considerable distress due to the presence of symptoms in their brother or sister. Furthermore, self-reported symptoms of anxiety and depression were higher in siblings of a child with OCD, compared to siblings in a nonclinical comparison group. And finally, this study found that the quality of sibling relationships in OCD families improved following successful treatment of the OCD.

Taken together, these studies of family involvement and accommodation offer consistent evidence that OCD, and particularly childhood OCD, is associated with significant disruption to family members' lives and daily routines. The majority of families affected by this disorder report accommodation of a child's symptoms by both parents and siblings, which not only interferes with the family members' routine, but also causes them considerable distress in most cases. Although the family's accommodation of the symptoms is often well intentioned, this form of involvement in the disorder plays a powerful maintaining role. Specifically, verbal reassurance, the provision of items related to the compulsions (e.g., soap or washing powder), active participation in the rituals, and avoidance of anxiety-provoking stimuli typically provide short-term relief for the child and for the family, thereby reinforcing the continuation of these behaviors and the child's symptoms (Calvocoressi et al., 1995). By all accounts, accommodation and involvement in childhood OCD, lead to negative outcomes for all involved. The involvement of the family in childhood OCD leads to disruption to family life, increased distress for family members, and increased demand by the child for assistance the next time they experience the symptom, hence serving to maintain the disorder and distress. Given that families are so drawn into this disorder, leading to reciprocal negative outcomes for all involved, it is not surprising that observational research of families with a child who has OCD, have time and again found negative behavioral interaction patterns within these families, compared to interactions observed within other families.

FAMILY INTERACTIONS

The accumulating evidence that childhood OCD has an intensely negative impact on family members has led researchers to question whether this, in turn, may affect the quality of family relationships and family interaction patterns. Contemporary models of family processes recognize that behavior within families is reciprocally determined (e.g., coercive patterns of interaction as identified by Patterson, 1982)—that is, one person's behavior is influenced by behaviors of others, as well as the individual's own personal level of functioning, within the family system. Although research investigating family processes and childhood OCD is scant, a number of preliminary family observational studies have provided some evidence to suggest that, relative to others, families with a child who has OCD may be characterized by increased reciprocal negative behavioral interactions among family members. Moreover, preliminary evidence suggests that family environment and interaction style (i.e., families high in expressed emotion) might predict treatment relapse, and further, that negative interactions may be amendable through successful family-based treatment approaches.

Valleni-Basile et al. (1995) in a preliminary investigation of adolescents' perceptions of their family environment, investigated the quality of the family milieu and family interactions, using a self-report questionnaire. In this study, adolescents with OCD reported significantly less emotional support, warmth, and closeness in their family compared to nonclinical controls. Ehiobuche (1988) examined self-report measures of parental rearing practices of 64 nonclinical and 10 clinical college students with OCD, of mixed cultural backgrounds. Regardless of ethnic or cultural background, students with scoring within clinical range for OCD symptoms consistently rated their parents as more rejecting and overprotective and less emotionally warm in their child-rearing practices compared with their normal control counterparts. Findings suggest that OCD exists within the normal population and that parenting style may be associated with this disorder. These studies, although offering some preliminary support to suggest a family environment characterized by less emotional warmth in families with an OCD patient compared to other families, are obviously limited due to subjective biases associated with relying on self-report measures, and the use of nonclinical adult participants.

In a more controlled and reliable approach to assessing family process, Barrett, Shortt and Healy (2002) conducted an observational study examining parent and child behaviors during family interactions, with a sample of families whose child had OCD compared to families who had a child with another anxiety disorder, an externalizing disorder, or no psychiatric diagnosis. The primary goal of this study was to examine whether family interactions could differentiate families with a child who has OCD, from other clinical and nonclinical children. Given the clear lack of literature and existing knowledge about how children with OCD and their parents interact, this study involved macro-coding parent and child behaviors across multiple behavioral and affective dimensions, guided by the limited research to date in the field of OCD, but also by family interaction research with anxious children, and adult cognitive theories of OCD (see Barrett, Shortt, & Healy, 2002). The study involved minute-by-minute macro-coding of mother, father, and child behaviors, during two standardized 5-minute family discussion tasks, with comparisons made across groups of families with a child diagnosed with OCD ($n = 22$), compared to families with a child who had another anxiety disorder ($n = 22$), an externalizing disorder ($n = 21$), or a nonclinical control ($n = 22$). Results from this study indicated that parents and children in the OCD group could be significantly differentiated from families in the other groups based on both parent and child behavior, in that they tended to be less positive in their interactions. Specifically, mothers and fathers of OCD children were less *confident* in their child's ability, less *rewarding of independence*, and less likely to use *positive problem solving*. Children in the OCD group showed less *positive problem solving*, less *confidence* in their ability to solve the problem, and displayed less *warmth* during their interactions with their parents.

Findings from this study suggest that low warmth may be a characteristic of families with OCD children (Barrett, Shortt & Healy, 2002). Mothers in the OCD group displayed less warmth toward their child than mothers in the nonclinic and anxious groups, whereas fathers also showed less warmth relative to fathers in the nonclinical group. Likewise, children with OCD displayed less warmth than children in the anxious and nonclinic groups. These findings support previous studies using questionnaire methodology, which have found demonstrated lack of warmth in families with OCD children and adolescents (Ehiobuche, 1988; Hoover & Insel, 1984; Valleni-Basile et al., 1995). Interestingly, the levels of warmth rated within families in the OCD group most closely paralleled those observed in families with externalizing children. Based on clinical observation, it is not uncommon in both of these clinical groups to see coercive family interactions, with parents commonly drawn into their child's symptoms (Barrett et al., 2001). It may be that parent and child warmth are correlated with parental involvement and accommodation of the child's symptoms—either disruptive or compulsive in nature. Further research investigating the quality of the family environment and family interactions in relation to family involvement and accommodation is warranted to further understand the complexity of the reciprocal relationships between a child's OCD symptomatology and associated family processes.

In follow-up to Barrett and colleagues' observational study (2002), Farrell, Barrett, and Schlup (to be submitted, October 2006) recently conducted an evaluation of treatment outcome on family interactions within families with a child treated for OCD. This study included 44 children and adolescents with OCD and their mothers, who were involved in a controlled treatment outcome trial being conducted by the authors (see Barrett et al., 2004). Families engaged in a 5-minute problem-focused family discussion task at pre- and post-treatment. These family discussions were videotaped and coded by independent raters, blind to the hypotheses of the study, using a standardized macro-coding schedule. Behavioral observational data of these family interactions was compared to a wait-list control group. Participants were rated on behavioral dimensions of criticism, overinvolvement, doubt, avoidance, warmth, confidence, positive problem solving, and rewarding independence. Inter-rater reliability coefficients were obtained for all dimensions, indicating adequate to good reliability overall.

The results of this study demonstrated significant differences between treatment and waitlist conditions on a number of behavioral dimensions, from pre- to post-treatment, with ratings of negative behaviors decreasing and ratings of positive behaviors increasing following treatment for those families who received CBT. Specifically there were significant reductions for the treatment condition in mothers' levels of observed *criticism, over-*

involvement, and *doubt*; with significant increases following treatment on observed ratings of mothers' *warmth, confidence, positive problem solving*, and *rewarding independence* for the treatment condition, in comparison to the wait-list condition, which did not change over time. Similarly, there were significant reductions at post-treatment for the treatment families, on observed child negative behaviors, including *doubt* and *avoidance*; while significant improvements were found for the treatment group on observed child positive behaviors, including *warmth, confidence* and *positive problem solving*. There were no changes over time on observed child behaviors for the families in the waitlist condition.

Interestingly, Farrell and colleagues (to be submitted, October 2006) investigated age-related differences in family interactions, and found that at pretreatment, both mothers and children tended to show more negative and less positive behaviors with increasing age of the child. In terms of treatment outcome, improvements in mother criticism, mother doubt, and child avoidance were greater with increasing age of the child. These results suggest that family interactions may be more negative and less positive with an adolescent sufferer of OCD, compared to a child. Alternatively, it may be that the prospective impact of OCD on the family influences the quality of the family interactions, although this could not be examined given that age of onset of the OCD was not investigated in this study. Given that adolescence is often a time of increased conflict and tension in the family unit (Laursen & Collins, 2004), these results highlight that family-based approaches to OCD treatment, focusing on improving family interactions, may be particularly important for adolescents with OCD.

The results from these studies of family environment and interaction, based on both self-report data and observational research, suggest that families with a child who has OCD might be characterized as displaying less emotional warmth and be less positive in their interactions in the face of problem solving discussions. Importantly, the observational research conducted to date highlights the *reciprocal* nature of these negative interactions patterns, with both children and parents displaying less positive interactions in comparison to control groups. This research suggests that family interaction styles might be associated with the development and/or maintenance of this disorder; however, longitudinal research and further treatment outcome studies are clearly necessary to investigate the exact association between these family processes and OCD symptomatology.

In terms of other studies examining family interactions in childhood OCD, research is very limited, apart from a few investigations examining the process of expressed emotion (EE) within families, and the impact of EE in predicting treatment response. The concept of "expressed emotion" was first introduced to describe a specific type of family environment or family interaction style characteristic of families with a schizophrenic patient. EE refers to a family environment characterized by hostility, criticism, or emotional overinvolvement (Vaughn & Leff, 1976). When at least one family member is observed to display one or all of these characteristics, the family milieu is considered to be high in EE. This attribute has been associated with higher relapse rates in individuals with schizophrenia (Vaughn & Leff, 1976), as well as in several other disorders including bipolar disorder (Miklowitz, Goldstein, Nuechterlein, Snyder, & Mintz, 1988), obesity (Fischmann-Havstead & Marston, 1984), and depression (Hooley 1986).

The literature investigating EE in OCD families is considerably less well developed than with other disorders, although some studies have reported preliminary evidence to suggest that EE may also be characteristic of the family environment in families with an OCD patient. In a sample of four adults with OCD who relapsed following treatment, high expressed emotion was reported for three of the families (Emmelkamp, Kloek, & Blaauw, 1992). Steketee (1993) also found in a study of adults sufferers of OCD, that low levels of social support, high levels of criticism and hostility, and antagonism towards spouses were associated with relapse following treatment for OCD. Research examining EE in the families of children with OCD has also been quite limited. Hibbs and colleagues (1991) investigated 128 families who had a child diagnosed with disruptive behavior problems, OCD, or no clinical disorder. EE was measured via the brief Five-Minute Speech Sample (FMSS-EE; Magana, Goldstein, Karno, Miklowitz, & Falloon, 1986), which involves asking a parent to describe his or her child for a 5-minute period. The dialogue is then coded for criticism and overinvolvement separately for mothers and fathers. When either or both of these characteristics are indicated the family is categorized as high in EE; when these characteristics are not present, the family is assigned to a low EE category. The results indicated that 73% of mothers and 46% of fathers in the OCD group were classified as high in EE, compared to 31% and 22% of nonclinical mothers and fathers, respectively. No differences were found between the two clinical groups; however, high EE was found to be significantly related to the presence of a psychiatric diagnosis in the parents. These results again highlight the apparent similarities in family environment between families with a child who has OCD and families with a child who has disruptive behavioral problems.

Hibbs and colleagues (1992) conducted a further examination of EE in OCD families, specifically examining the relationship between observed parental EE and levels of autonomic arousal in children with OCD. In this study, levels of EE and autonomic arousal (measured by skin conductance) were compared across families with a child who has OCD ($n = 42$), compared to families with a child who has a disruptive behavior disorder ($n = 53$), and nonclinical control families ($n = 24$). The Five-Minute Speech Sample (FMSS-EE: Magana et al., 1986) was used to evaluate parental EE levels, and skin conductance levels were measured during a resting period, by a series of innocuous nonsignal tones and a reaction time procedure. Results demonstrated that high EE in parents was significantly related to elevated autonomic activity in children. Furthermore, levels of autonomic activity in children with OCD were especially associated with fathers' EE, regardless of child's age or gender. The results of this study suggest that the presence of high EE in families may be associated with increased physiological arousal and stress in children (Hibbs et al., 1992).

Leonard and colleagues examined the presence of EE in a cohort of 54 children and adolescents treated for OCD (Leonard et al., 1993), specifically assessing the association between this family process and treatment outcome. All participants were involved in a long-term follow-up study investigating the efficacy of clomipramine in treating childhood OCD. Utilizing the FMSS, each family was classified at intake as either high or low in expressed emotion. Of the 48 mothers and 47 fathers assessed using this method, 77% of mothers and 49% of fathers were assigned high scores. This result mirrors the findings of the Hibbs et al. (1991) study, with 85% of the families overall exhibiting high levels of EE. Interestingly, at 2- to 7-year follow-up, this factor was found to significantly predict poorer global adjustment in the sample, accounting for 35% of the variance in outcome.

Investigations of the impact of familial processes, such as EE, on treatment outcome or prognosis have been very limited. In an uncontrolled case review, Allsopp and Verduyn (1988) reported that familial involvement did not discriminate between 20 adolescents with OCD and those who were asymptomatic at follow-up. It is difficult to draw conclusions from these findings, however, due to the retrospective nature of the data and the lack of control over the implementation of various treatments. Furthermore, the majority of the participants were treated on an inpatient basis, thereby removing the young person from the family environment both during and immediately after treatment.

In a recently published long-term follow-up to a controlled trial of family-based CBT for childhood OCD (Barrett et al., 2004), Barrett and colleagues (Barrett, Farrell, Dadds, & Boutler, 2005) investigated predictors of treatment outcome at 18 months following treatment in samples of children and youth with OCD. Analyses of predictors of long-term treatment indicated that children and adolescents who experience more severe obsessions and compulsions, and live in a family environment characterized by higher dysfunction at pretreatment as measured by mothers' and fathers' self-report on the McMaster Family Adjustment Device (FAD; Epstein et al., 1983), are less likely to respond as well to family-based CBT than others. Piacentini and colleagues (1994) reported similar findings in their case study report of behavior therapy for three children with OCD, finding that children with better social functioning and lower family conflict responded better to CBT. Almost without exception, treatment studies have not analyzed the effect of family involvement and/or the quality of the family environment on the outcome of treatment for childhood OCD. Family processes and the role of such in predicting treatment response clearly warrants further attention in future research.

SUMMARY AND CONCLUSIONS

OCD during childhood both affects and is affected by the family. Based on clinical observation and from what little research exists, it is unquestionable that family members experience distress related to this disorder, are frequently drawn into the symptoms of OCD, and often have to alter their daily routines and lifestyle due to the symptoms of this childhood anxiety disorder (i.e., Amir, Freshman, & Foa, 2000; Barrett, Rasmussen, & Healy, 2001; Calvocoressi et al., 1995; Cooper, 1996). Whether being a sibling or parent of a child who is suffering from OCD, living with this disorder is not easy—for a constellation of reasons. OCD in childhood causes extreme distress and disruption to a child's life, often resulting in complete withdrawal from family and peer activities, and avoidance of school or school-related tasks. For a parent or sibling, it is exceedingly difficult to observe your child or sibling crippled by doubt, intense anxiety, and driven to engage in hours of repetitive and senseless rituals. Presumably it is for these reasons that parents and siblings do what they can believing that it will help the child—even if it does involve assisting with rituals, avoiding triggers to anxiety, and providing constant reassurance to the child. Instances of family involvement and accommodation of childhood OCD are frequent, well-intentioned and quite natural processes for parents and siblings to engage in; however, once started, these attempts to assist the child quickly spiral into a vicious cycle, whereby the youth with OCD desperately depends on this assistance and experiences intense anxiety and distress if s/he is not satisfied by the parent's or sibling's acts of accommodation. There is no doubt that family members' involvement plays a critical role in the maintenance of symptoms and symptomatic distress; and as a result, family members also experience considerable distress and disruption to their lives.

Survey and observational research has provided some evidence that the family environment and family interactions within these families may be characterized as lacking warmth (Barrett, Shortt, & Healy, 2002; Ehiobuche, 1988; Valleni-Basile et al., 1995), displaying increased EE (Hibbs et al., 1991, 1992; Leonard et al., 1993) and generally displaying less positive interactions during family interaction tasks (Barrett, Shortt, & Healy, 2002; Farrell, Barrett, & Schlup, to be submitted, October 2006) when compared with other families. A number of studies have shown similarities between families with a child who has OCD and families with a child who has a disruptive behavior disorder in terms of the observed warmth within the family (i.e., Barrett, Shortt, &

Healy, 2002) and levels of EE (Hibbs et al., 1991). It is indisputable that both of these disorders greatly impact families, causing distress and frustration for family members and disruption to family life, leading to suggestions that the presence of the disorder and associated symptoms might influence family interactions and the family environment over time. Equally as acceptable, is the hypothesis that families characterized by low warmth and high EE might represent increased risk for emotional and behavioral disorders in children and adolescents. Research to date has been unable to answers questions about causality. However, thus far it is clear that the family environment and interaction patterns within families where a child has OCD are generally less positive, less warm, and higher in EE than other families, and that the negative behaviors observed during these interactions are *reciprocal*, in that both the child and parents display these types of behaviors.

Cognitive-behavioral therapy for childhood OCD, including parental involvement in treatment, offers an effective and durable treatment for symptoms (e.g., Barrett, Healy-Farrell, & March, 2004; Franklin et al., 1998; March, 2004; March, Mulle, & Herbel, 1994; Piacentini et al., 1994; Scahill et al., 1996; Waters, Barrett, & March, 2001; Wever & Rey, 1997). The OCD Expert Consensus Guidelines (March et al., 1997) for treating childhood OCD recommend exposure-based CBT as the first-line treatment of choice for all children who present with primary OCD and for adolescents with mild or moderate OCD (i.e., CYBOCS score < 19). For adolescents with more severe OCD symptoms, or for children and youth who do not respond to an initial trial of CBT alone, a combined treatment of CBT and a selective serotonin reuptake inhibitor (SSRI) medication is recommended (March et al., 1997; March, 2004). It is also generally agreed among experts in the field of childhood OCD that, due to the known extent to which OCD impairs with family functioning, treatment should almost always involve family members (i.e., March, 1995). There has been a recent trend to include families in the treatment of childhood OCD (Barrett et al., 2004; Franklin et al., 1998; Knox, Albano, & Barlow, 1996; March & Mulle, 1998; Piacentini et al., 1994; Thienemann, Martin, Cregger, Thompson, & Dyer-Freidman, 2001), however we do not yet know how these interventions might affect family processes associated with maintaining childhood OCD.

Only a few studies to date have examined the effect of treatment outcome on family processes. Waters, Barrett and March (2001) in their open trial of CBT for childhood OCD ($n = 7$), which included parental involvement in all sessions, found significant reductions in family accommodation (based on the Family Accommodation Scale; Calvocoressi et al., 1995) from pre- to post-treatment. Barrett, Rasmussen, and Healy (2001) also found reductions in sibling accommodation of OCD following treatment in a qualitative analysis of the effects of OCD on siblings. The most comprehensive study to date on treatment outcome and family processes is that of Farrell and colleagues (submitted), which examined mother and child behaviors during family interactions pre- and post-treatment, in comparison to a wait-list comparison group. The results of this observational study were encouraging, with significant reductions in negative behaviors and significant increases in positive behaviors for both children and mothers from pre- to post-treatment. Beyond these studies, there are no other evaluations of the impact of treatment on family processes; however, these studies do provide initial support for a positive effect of family-based treatment on improving family interactions and reducing family involvement in OCD symptoms.

Research in the area of adult OCD indicates that improvements in family interactions may be associated with lower rates of relapse at follow-up (e.g., Chambless & Steketee, 1999), highlighting the importance of involving the family in treatment. Barrett, Healy-Farrell, and March (2004) present the only treatment trial to date, which has included not only parents, but also siblings in treatment. Given that research indicates that siblings also accommodate this disorder and are greatly affected by the disorder in terms of their own levels of distress (i.e., Barrett, Rasmussen, & Healy, 2002; Cooper, 1996), it seems logical and essential that treatment approaches for childhood OCD involve the entire family. It is likely that family approaches to treatments do have the potential to improve family interactions and reduce family accommodation of the disorder, thus breaking the cycle of family involvement, which certainly contributes to maintaining OCD symptoms.

Family approaches to treatment involve forming a team approach to supporting the child's fight against OCD, with parent and sibling components typically involving psychoeducation (e.g., removing blame from parents as well as the child suffering from OCD), problem-solving skills, strategies to reduce parental and sibling accommodation and involvement in the child's symptoms, and encouraging family support of home-based exposure and response prevention. From the outset, therapy sessions with children and youth should involve the entire family as much as possible. Each session (1–1.5 hours in duration) should typically involve time with the therapist and child/youth working alone, as well as family review time, whereby the child/youth is joined by their parents at the end of every session to review strategies learned (typically for 15 minutes to half an hour), E/PR goals planned, the role of the parents in supporting the child's weekly goals (i.e., through rewarding efforts, and/or supporting actual E/RP tasks), and family problem solving related to any challenges faced at home in fighting OCD. Involving sibling's in some of the family review sessions is also encouraged (typically involving siblings in 3–4 sessions throughout a 12–14 week program is desirable), so siblings can learn to understand OCD and support their brother/sister in resisting symptoms. Addressing parental and sibling accommodation occurs throughout the therapy program, whereby children and youth are first taught—through psychoeducation techniques and externalizing OCD symptoms—that this type of family involvement is actually a symptom of OCD, which makes the OCD stronger. Following this, the child/youth and parents/siblings work together to monitor and map instances of OCD accommodation and involvement; and finally, as the child becomes stronger in fighting the OCD, they give permission to their parents/siblings—when they feel ready, to slowly withdraw actions of OCD accommodation and/or reassurance, one small step at a time. Once the child has decided to actively resist an instance of accommodation, parents and siblings are instructed to remind the child/youth whenever they seek this kind of accommodation or reassurance—"it is just OCD—you don't need our help—you can do it!" These steps of parental and sibling withdrawal of accommodation are treated in the same way as other E/RP steps, in that the child/youth rates each instance of accommodation in terms of difficulty to resist, making a symptom hierarchy, with withdrawal of accommodation (E/RP) starting with the easiest examples.

Treatment of childhood OCD should involve the entire family, with the exception of family members who may not be cooperative or who are resistant to supporting the child's positive progress. The involvement of the family in therapy is essential given the maintaining role that parental and sibling accommodation plays in the disorder, and because of the typically extreme distress and frustration that family members experience. A positive team approach to the treatment of childhood OCD that includes both parents and siblings, such as Barrett and colleagues family-based CBT protocol (i.e., the FOCUS program: Barrett et al., 2004), offers an empowering approach for families, with positive outcomes likely for not only the child experiencing OCD, but also the entire family.

REFERENCES

Allsopp, M., & Verduyn, C. (1988). A follow up of adolescents with obsessive compulsive disorder. *British Journal of Psychiatry, 154*, 829–834.

Allsopp, M., & Verduyn, C. (1990). Adolescents with obsessive compulsive disorder: A case note review of consecutive patients referred to a provincial regional adolescent psychiatry unit. *Journal of Adolescence, 13*, 157–169.

Amir, N., Freshman, M., & Foa, E. B. (2000). Family distress and involvement in relatives of obsessive-compulsive disorder patients. *Journal of Anxiety Disorders, 14*, 209–217.

Barrett, P. M., Farrell, L. J., Dadds, M., & Boulter, N. A. (2005). Cognitive-behavioral family-based treatment for childhood OCD: Long-term treatment outcome and predictors of response. *Journal of the American Academy of Child and Adolescent Psychiatry, 44*, 1005–1014.

Barrett, P. M., Healy-Farrell, L. J., & March, J. S. (2004). Cognitive-behavioral family treatment of childhood obsessive-compulsive disorder: A controlled trial. *Journal of American Academy of Child and Adolescent Psychiatry, 43*, 46–62.

Barrett, P. M., Rasmussen, P. J., & Healy, L. (2001). The effect of obsessive-compulsive disorder on sibling relationships in late childhood and early adolescence: Preliminary findings. *The Australian Educational and Developmental Psychologist, 17*, 82–102.

Barrett, P. M., Shortt, A., & Healy, L. (2002). Does parent and child behaviors differentiate families whose children have obsessive-compulsive disorder from other clinic and non-clinic children? *Journal of Child Psychology and Psychiatry, 43,* 597–607.

Bellodi, L., Sciuto, G., Diaferia, G., Ronchi, P., & Smeraldi, E. (1992). Psychiatric disorders in the families of patients with obsessive compulsive disorder. *Psychiatry Research, 42,* 111–120.

Billett, E. A., Richter, M. A., & Kennedy, J. L. (1998). Genetics of obsessive-compulsive disorder. In R. P. Swinson, M. M. Antony, S. Rachman, & M. A. Richter (Eds.), *Obsessive-compulsive disorder: Theory, research, and treatment* (pp. 120–140). New York: Guilford.

Black, D. W., Gaffney, G., Schlosser, S., & Gabel, J. (1998). The impact of obsessive-compulsive disorder on the family: Preliminary findings. *Journal of Nervous and Mental Disease, 186,* 440–442.

Calvocoressi, L., Lewis, B., Harris, M., Trufan, S. J., McDougle, C. J., & Price, L. H. (1995). Family accommodation in obsessive compulsive disorder. *American Journal of Psychiatry, 152,* 441–443.

Calvocoressi, L., Mazure, C., Kasl, S. V., Skolnick, J., Fisk, D., Vegso, S. J., Van Noppen, B. L., & Price, L. H. (1999). Family accommodation of obsessive-compulsive symptoms: Instrument development and assessment of family behavior. *Journal of Nervous and Mental Disease, 187,* 636–642.

Chambless, D. L., & Steketee, G. (1999). Expressed emotion and behavior therapy outcome: A prospective study with obsessive-compulsive and agoraphobic outpatients. *Journal of Consulting and Clinical Psychology, 67,* 658–665.

Cooper, M. (1996). Obsessive compulsive disorder: Effects on family members. *American Journal of Orthopsychiatry, 66,* 296–304.

Ehiobuche, I. (1988). Obsessive-compulsive neurosis in relation to parental child-rearing patterns amongst Greek, Italian, and Anglo-Australian subjects. *Acta Psychiatrica Scandinavica, 78*(Suppl. 344), 115–120.

Emmelkamp, P. M. G., Kloek, J., & Blaauw, E. (1992). Obsessive-compulsive disorder in principles and practice of relapse prevention. In P. H. Wilson (Ed.), *Principles and practices of relapse prevention* (pp. 213–234). New York: Guilford.

Epstein, N. B., Baldwin, L. M., & Bishop, D. S. (1983). The McMaster Family Assessment Device. *Journal of Marital and Family Therapy, 9,* 171–180.

Farrell, L. J., Barrett, P. M., & Schlup, B. (to be submitted, October 2006). *Family interactions and childhood OCD: Effects of CBT on parent and child observed behaviors.*

Fischmann-Havstead, L., & Marston, A. (1984). Weight loss maintenance as an aspect of family emotion and process. *British Journal of Clinical Psychology, 23,* 265–271.

Flament, M. F., & Rapoport, J. L. (1984). Childhood obsessive-compulsive disorder. In T. R. Insel (Ed.), *New findings in obsessive-compulsive disorder* (pp. 24–43). Washington DC: American Press.

Franklin, M. E., Kozak, M. J., Cashman, L. A., Coles, M. E., Rheingold, A. A., & Foa, E. B. (1998). Cognitive-behavioral treatment of pediatric obsessive-compulsive disorder: An open trial. *Journal of the American Academy of Child and Adolescent Psychiatry, 37,* 412–419.

Henin, A., & Kendall, P. C. (1997). Obsessive-compulsive disorder in childhood and adolescence. *Advances in Clinical Child Psychology, 19,* 75–131.

Hibbs, E. D., Hamburger, S. D., Lenane, M., Rapoport, J. L., Kruesi, M. J. P., Keysor, C. S., & Goldstein, M. J. (1991). Determinants of expressed emotion in families of disturbed and normal children. *Journal of Child Psychology and Psychiatry, 32,* 757–770.

Hibbs, E. D., Zahn, T., Hamburger, S. D., Krusie, M., & Rapoport, J. (1992). Parental expressed emotion and psychophysiological reactivity inn disturbed and normal children. *British Journal of Psychiatry, 160,* 504–510.

Hollingsworth, C. E., Tanguay, P. E., Grossman, L., & Pabst, P. (1980). Long-term outcome of obsessive compulsive disorder in childhood. *Journal of the American Academy of Child and Adolescent Psychiatry of Child Psychiatry, 19,* 134–144.

Honjo, S., Hirano, C., Murase, S., Kaneko, T., Sugiyama, T., Ohtaka, K., et al. (1989). Obsessive-compulsive symptoms in childhood and adolescence. *Acta Psychiatrica Scandinavica, 80,* 83–91.

Hooley, J. M. (1986). Expressed emotion and depression: Interactions between patients and high- versus low-expressed emotion spouses. *Journal of Abnormal Psychology, 95,* 237–246.

Hoover, C. F., & Insel, T. R. (1984). Families of origin in obsessive-compulsive disorder. *Journal of Nervous and Mental Disease, 172,* 207–215.

Insel, T. R., Hoover, C., & Murphy, D. L. (1983). Parents of patients with obsessive-compulsive disorder. *Psychological Medicine, 13,* 807–811.

King, N. J., Ollendick, T. H., & Montgomery, I. M. (1995). Obsessive-compulsive disorder in children and adolescents. *Behavior Change, 12,* 51–58.

Knox, L. S., Albano, A. M., & Barlow, D. H. (1996). Parental involvement in the treatment of childhood compulsive disorder: A multiple baseline examination incorporating parents. *Behavior Therapy, 27,* 93–114.

Last, C. G., & Strauss, C. C. (1989). Obsessive compulsive disorder in childhood. *Journal of Anxiety Disorders, 3,* 295–302.

Laursen, B., & Collins, W. A. (2004). Parent–child communication during adolescence. In A. L. Vangelisti, (Ed.), *Handbook of family communication* (pp. 333–348). Mahwah, NJ: Lawrence Erlbaum Associates.

Lenane, M. C., Swedo, S. E., Leonard, H., Pauls, D. L., Screry, W., & Rapoport, J. L. (1990). Psychiatric disorders in first-degree relatives of children and adolescents with obsessive compulsive disorder. *Journal of the American Academy of Child and Adolescent Psychiatry, 29,* 407–412.

Leonard, H., Swedo, S. E., Lenane, M. C., Rettew, D. C., Hamburger, S. D., Bartko, J. J., et al. (1993). A 2- to 7-year follow-up study of 54 obsessive-compulsive children and adolescents. *Archives of General Psychiatry, 50,* 429–439.

Magana, A. B., Goldstein, M. J., Karno, D. J., Miklowitz, J. J., & Falloon, I. R. H. (1986). A brief method for assessing expressed emotion in relatives of psychiatric patients. *Psychiatric Research, 17,* 203–212.

March, J. S. (1995). Cognitive behavioral psychotherapy for children and adolescents with OCD: A review and recommendations for treatment. *Journal of the American Academy of Child and Adolescent Psychiatry, 34,* 7–18.

March, J. S. (2004). Cognitive-behavioral therapy, sertraline and their combination for children and adolescents with obsessive-compulsive disorder: The pediatric OCD treatment study (POTS) randomised controlled trial. *Journal of American Medical Association, 292,* 1969–1976.

March, J. S., Frances, A., Carpenter, D., & Kahn, D. (1997). Expert consensus guidelines: Treatment of obsessive-compulsive disorder. *Journal of Clinical Psychology, 58,* 1.

March, J. S., & Mulle, K. (1998). *OCD in children and adolescents: A cognitive-behavioral treatment manual.* New York: Guilford.

March, J. S., Mulle, K., & Herbel, B. (1994). Behavioral psychotherapy for children and adolescents with obsessive-compulsive disorder: An open-trial of a new protocol-driven treatment package. *Journal of the American Academy of Child and Adolescent Psychiatry, 33,* 333–341.

McKeon, P., & Murray, R. (1987). Familial aspects of obsessive-compulsive neurosis. *British Journal of Psychiatry, 151,* 528–534.

Miklowitz, D., Goldstein, M., Nuechterlein, K., Snyder, K., & Mintz, J. (1988). Family factors affecting the course of bipolar affective disorder. *Archives of General Psychiatry, 45,* 225–231.

Nestadt, G., Samuels, J., Riddle, M., Beinvenu, O. J., Liang, K. Y., LaBuda, M., et al. (2000). A family study of obsessive compulsive disorder. *Archives of General Psychiatry, 57,* 358–363.

Patterson, G. R. (1982). *Coercive family process.* Eugene, OR: Castalia.

Pauls, D. L., Alsobrook, J. P., Goodman, W., Rasmussen, S., & Leckman, J. F. (1995). A family study of obsessive compulsive disorder. *American Journal of Psychiatry, 152,* 76–84.

Piacentini, J., & Bergman, R. L. (2000). Obsessive-compulsive disorder in children. *Psychiatric Clinics of North America, 23,* 519–533.

Piacentini, J., Bergman, R. L., Keller, M., & McCracken, J. (2003). Functional impairment in children and adolescents with obsessive-compulsive disorder. *Journal of Child and Adolescent Psychopharmacology, 13*(2, Supplement), s61–s69.

Piacentini, J., Gitow, A., Jaffer, M., Graae, F., & Whitaker, A. (1994). Outpatient behavioral treatment of child and adolescent obsessive compulsive disorder. *Journal of Anxiety Disorders, 8,* 277–289.

Piacentini, J., & Jaffer, M. (1999). *Measuring functional impairment in youngsters with obsessive-compulsive disorder: Manual for the Child OCD Impact Scale (COIS).* Los Angeles, CA: UCLA Department of Psychiatry.

Rachman, S. (1996). A cognitive theory of obsessions. *Behavior Research and Therapy, 36,* 385–401.

Rasmussen, S. A. (1993). Genetic studies of obsessive-compulsive disorder. *Annals of Clinical Psychiatry, 5,* 241–248.

Rasmussen, S. A., & Tsuang, M. T. (1986). Clinical characteristics and family history in DSM-III obsessive-compulsive disorder. *American Journal of Psychiatry, 143,* 317–322.

Riddle, M. A., Scahill, L., King, R., Hardin, M. T., et al. (1990). Obsessive compulsive disorder in children and adolescents: Phenomenology and family history. *Journal of the American Academy of Child and Adolescent Psychiatry, 29,* 766–772.

Rosenberg, C. M. (1967). Familial aspects of obsessional neurosis. *British Journal of Psychiatry, 113,* 405–413.

Scahill, L., Vitulano, L. A., Brenner, E. M., Lynch, K. A., & King, R. A. (1996). Behavioral therapy in children and adolescents with obsessive-compulsive disorder: A pilot study. *Journal of Child and Adolescent Psychopharmacology, 6,* 191–202.

Shafran, R., Ralph, J., & Tallis, F. (1995). Obsessive-compulsive symptoms and the family. *Bulletin of the Menninger Clinic, 59,* 472–479.

Steketee, G. (1993). Social support and treatment outcome of obsessive compulsive disorder at 9-month follow-up. *Behavioral Psychotherapy, 21,* 81–95.

Thienemann, M., Martin, J., Cregger, B., Thompson, H., & Dyer-Friedman, J. (2001). Manual-driven group cognitive-behavioral therapy for adolescents with obsessive-compulsive disorder: a pilot study. *Journal of the American Academy of Child and Adolescent Psychiatry, 40,* 1254–1260.

Toro, J., Cervera, M., Osejo, E., & Salamero, M. (1992). Obsessive compulsive disorder in childhood and adolescence: A clinical study. *Journal of Child Psychology and Psychiatry and Allied Disciplines, 33,* 1025–1037.

Valleni-Basile, L. A., Garrison, C. Z., Jackson, K. L., Waller, J. L., McKeown, R. E., Addy, C. L., et al. (1995). Family and psychosocial predictors of obsessive compulsive disorder in a community sample of young adolescents. *Journal of Child and Family Studies, 4*, 193–206.

Vaughn, C., & Leff, J. (1976). The influence of family and social factors on the course of psychiatric illness: A comparison of schizophrenic and depressed neurotic patients. *British Journal of Psychiatry, 129*, 125–137.

Waters, T. L., & Barrett, P. M. (2000). The role of the family in childhood obsessive-compulsive disorder. *Clinical Child and Family Psychology Review, 3*, 173–184.

Waters, T., Barrett, P., & March, J. (2001). Cognitive-behavioral family treatment of childhood obsessive-compulsive disorder: An open clinical trial. *American Journal of Psychotherapy, 55*, 372–387.

Wever, C., & Rey, J. M. (1997). Juvenile obsessive-compulsive disorder. *Australian and New Zealand Journal of Psychiatry, 31*, 105–113.

14

School Issues in Children With Obsessive-Compulsive Disorder

Deborah Roth Ledley
Temple University

Radhika V. Pasupuleti
University of Rhode Island

Obsessive-compulsive disorder (OCD) is a prevalent psychiatric problem, affecting approximately 2% to 4% of children and adolescents (see Douglass et al., 1995; Zohar, 1999). Approximately one half of adults with OCD report that their symptoms began during childhood (Rasmussen & Eisen, 1990). In children, OCD is more common in boys than in girls, but this gender difference disappears in adolescence (Flament et al., 1988). Due to the intrusive thoughts and distressing behaviors that are characteristic of OCD, it is associated with significant functional impairment in both adults and children (Hollander et al., 1996; Piacentini, Bergman, Keller, & McCracken, 2003).

Controversy remains about whether children with OCD differ intellectually from children without the disorder, with some studies suggesting that they are more intelligent (Apter & Tyano, 1988), some suggesting that they are less intelligent (Heyman et al., 2003) and some showing no difference (Beers et al., 1999). Despite this unresolved issue, there is no doubt that OCD often has a negative impact on school functioning, both in terms of academics and social relationships. In a study carried out by Piacentini and colleagues (2003), almost half of children with OCD and their parents reported that OCD led to significant impairment in academic functioning.

Although social impairment was reported by fewer parents and children in this study, it was still found to be common. Valderhaug and Ivarsson (2005) reported similar findings regarding functional impairment among a sample of Norwegian and Swedish youth with OCD. In this chapter, the specific ways that different presentations of OCD can impact the school environment is discussed.

Before examining the impact of specific subtypes of OCD on the school environment, it is important to take a broader view and consider why academic and social impairment is so common among children with OCD. Throughout the day, children with OCD experience thoughts that are intrusive, distressing, and difficult to stop. In response to these thoughts, children engage in rituals with the goal of decreasing anxiety or preventing feared outcomes. These rituals can be either overt (e.g., hand-washing) or mental (e.g., reviewing something in one's head; saying a special prayer). Given the complexity of the symptoms experienced by children with OCD, it is no surprise that the disorder can lead to a great deal of interference in both academic and social functioning.

In terms of academic functioning, OCD can make it hard to concentrate at school. When children with OCD are more engaged with their obsessions and mental rituals than with lessons, they can suffer academically. OCD can also make children work in unproductive ways. For example, some children with OCD need to make their letters look "just right" and others need to repeatedly check their work to make sure they have not made mistakes. These types of rituals and others like them often cause children to hand in their work late, or to not hand it in at all. Some children with OCD can become so impaired that they are completely unable to attend school.

For a number of reasons, OCD can also interfere significantly in social functioning at school. First, some obsessions and compulsions make it difficult for children to interact with others. For example, a child with contamination concerns might refuse to play after-school sports because he does not want to touch the equipment used by other children. Second, some children with OCD might believe that they do not have time for social activities, needing to spend their after school time on homework or on "catching up" on rituals that they were able to refrain from engaging in at school. Third, some children with OCD are so worn out by their obsessions and compulsions by the end of the school day that they simply do not have the energy to engage in social activities. Finally, OCD can also lead to social impairment simply because children can look quite odd when they engage in their rituals. Even children who do their rituals in relative privacy might elicit attention, like children who leave the classroom frequently to wash their hands. More generally, when children are paying attention to their obsessions and engaging in mental rituals, they can come across as "spacey" and socially disengaged, causing other children to tease them or simply ignore them. A recent study suggests that children with OCD are more frequently victimized by their peers than are nonclinical controls (Storch et al., 2006).

In the remainder of this chapter, the ways in which specific presentations of OCD impact school functioning are reviewed. The role that schools can play in identifying and helping to treat OCD are discussed. Case examples are used throughout to illustrate key points.

THE MANY FACES OF OCD

Although all children and adolescents who suffer from OCD experience obsessions and/or compulsions, the content of the obsessions and the form of the compulsions varies greatly. This heterogeneity means that children diagnosed with OCD will often look very different from one another and will suffer different kinds of impairment in the school environment.

Contamination Concerns

Contamination concerns are very common among children with OCD (see March & Leonard, 1998) and are often relevant in the school setting. The simplest example is children who fear contamination from dirt and germs and therefore wash their hands many times during the school day. These children often miss important information when they are out of the classroom. Avoidance is also prominent. Children might be reluctant to use the bathroom at school, might not want to touch sports equipment, books, or toys used by other children, or might be fearful of classmates themselves for fear of contracting illnesses from them. Some children also fear bringing contaminated schoolbooks into their "clean" homes, preventing them from properly completing homework assignments.

Clinicians and school personnel should be aware that contamination concerns can come in many forms. One child was concerned about being contaminated by his classmates, but his fears were not about contracting illnesses. He feared that if children breathed on him or bumped into him, or if he had to touch something that other children had come in contact with, he would then acquire their distasteful characteristics. For example, he was worried that if he touched the desk of a classmate who picked her nose, he would then begin picking his nose. Similarly, if he bumped into a girl in his class with a physical disability, he worried that he would acquire this disability and no longer be a good athlete. In response to these concerns, this patient frequently wiped his hands on the bottom of his shoes and breathed outward heavily in order to "undo" contamination. If he saw a child heading his way, he also tried to hold his breath so that he would not get contaminated and then have to undo it. By the time this child came for treatment, he was regularly missing school due to anxiety. When he did go to school, he insisted that he sit at a desk sequestered from all of the other children, avoided touching anything that other children had touched, and was so occupied by rituals that his grades had plummeted from straight A's to F's. Not surprisingly, this child was considered quite odd by all of his peers.

As another example, a 12-year-old girl was concerned about contamination from certain chemicals. She worried that she would lose her intelligence if she smelled or came in contact with such things as "smelly" markers, the spray that the teacher used to clean the white-board, or the cleaning products that were used to clean the classroom in the evenings. Her teacher's perfume was also a major trigger for this child's OCD. This patient had elaborate breath-holding rituals and often hid her face in her shirt so that she could not smell the offending substances. Although her grades did not suffer as a result of her OCD, she started to have significant social problems. She frequently yelled at her teacher for using "smelly markers" and white-board spray, which annoyed her teacher and contributed to her fellow students thinking she was odd. Also, some of her peers were becoming interested in nail polish, perfume, and other scented beauty products and she criticized their use of these products. By the time she came for treatment, she had no friends left in her class.

Storch and colleagues (2005) described a fascinating case of a young boy whose OCD onset when he was being severely bullied by his peers at school. Initially, the patient started to shower after school to rid himself of the bullies' taunts. His OCD quickly grew to include other rituals, like clearing his throat whenever he thought about bullying. The patient also became extremely avoidant, refusing to wear clothes that he wore on days that he was bullied and avoiding places where he had bullying-related thoughts. He eventually began to neglect his self-care because his showering rituals were so elaborate that it was easier to simply avoid showering completely. These examples all demonstrate the heterogeneity of OCD symptoms, even within a single symptom cluster.

Aggressive Obsessions

Aggressive obsessions are another common presentation in children with OCD (see March & Leonard, 1998). As with contamination concerns, aggressive obsessions can present in various ways. Some children with this presentation fear that they might accidentally harm a family member or friend. Children with OCD can also develop worries about being responsible for negative events, like fires, burglaries, or floods. A concern that can come up in the school context is the fear of offending others. It is completely normal for children to have negative thoughts about peers, even those whom they really like. Yet, children with OCD may worry that if they think the thoughts, they might blurt them out or that thinking the thoughts is equivalent to actually hurting a person. This phenomenon is referred to as "thought–action fusion" (see Berle & Starcevic, 2005, for a review). Other children may worry that they have offended peers by doing something seemingly benign, like putting their pen down in a certain way or looking at someone in a certain way. These children then tend to seek a great deal of reassurance from peers, or simply avoid talking to peers for fear of offending them. Clearly, both can lead to peer relationship problems.

Sexual Obsessions

Sexual obsessions are particularly difficult for children to talk about with adults, but similar to adult patients with OCD, children can have intrusive thoughts of a sexual nature. For example, a 16-year-old boy worried a great deal that he might be a child molester, even though the idea of engaging in any sexual behavior with a child was greatly distressing to him. In response to his intrusive thoughts, he engaged in elaborate mental reassurance strategies to convince himself he was a "good" person. He also avoided interacting with other children that, not surprisingly, caused considerable impairment. He could not walk through areas of the school where young children might be present, and refused to take part in mandatory tutoring of children that counted as a community service grade on his transcript. This patient told his friends that he "hated" children in order to explain his avoidance of them, but this led to peer relation problems. His friends simply could not understand how someone could hate children to such a degree and wondered whether this patient was not as friendly as he seemed.

Hoarding/Saving Obsessions

In clinical practice, many adult patients who have difficulties with hoarding report that their problems began as soon as they left their parents' home and had the freedom to hold on to things that seemed important, sentimental, or potentially useful. In one unpublished study, patients reported that they started having problems with hoarding at age 18 and that the problem became extreme nearly two decades later, at age 35 (see Steketee & Frost, 2003). When hoarding is observed in children, it tends to be on a more limited scale than is seen with adults. Some patients refuse to throw away any school notes (even after the school year is over) for fear that they might need them again in the future. Other children might fill up their desks or lockers with bits of string, stones, or candy wrappers picked up around the schoolyard. The behavior of picking up bits and pieces of "stuff" can result in children appearing somewhat unusual to their peers, and school personnel might punish children whose lockers or desks are overflowing with junk.

Magical Thoughts/Superstitious Obsessions

Magical thoughts/superstitious obsessions, another common presentation among children with OCD, can also result in children appearing odd or unusual to others (e.g. children who walk in an odd way in order to avoid stepping on cracks). Some children also have certain letters, words, or numbers that are "bad." For example, some children worry that writing the number 3 might make bad things happen to their families. These children might avoid writing "3," even when it is the correct response on a test. Clearly, this type of avoidance can lead to academic impairment.

Somatic Obsessions

Somatic obsessions in OCD typically involve excessive fears of particular illnesses or diseases or concern that there is something wrong with an aspect of one's appearance. Health-related concerns can include fear of having cancer or AIDS. Children might repeatedly seek reassurance from parents or physicians. Alternatively, they may avoid the school nurse or routine physicals altogether for fear of contracting a disease. Children with somatic obsessions might also be concerned about the way a certain part of their body looks or feels. For example, a child was concerned that her stomach would "pop" out. This child was not particularly concerned with her weight and did not meet diagnostic criteria for an eating disorder. Rather, she was concerned that other people would notice her "popped-out" stomach and consider it repulsive and ugly. In order to prevent her stomach from popping, she ate very slowly so as to prevent herself from ingesting air. She also avoided many foods that she felt caused popping. This child spent a great deal of time getting ready for school each day, trying on numerous outfits until she found one that appropriately concealed her abdomen. She remained at her desk for as much of the day as possible and when she did get up, she held her hands over her abdomen to conceal it. This appeared quite odd, leading to ridicule from her peers. She was so preoccupied by her thoughts about her abdomen that her schoolwork began to suffer significantly.

The somatic concerns seen in OCD overlap with other diagnoses— namely, hypochondriasis (in the case of unsubstantiated concerns about having an illness) and body dysmorphic disorder (BDD, in the case of concerns about a physical defect that does not exist). This leaves clinicians with a decision about whether to make a diagnosis of OCD, hypochondriasis/BDD, or both. *The Diagnostic and Statistical Manual of Mental Disorders,* fourth edition (*DSM–IV,* American Psychiatric Association, 1994) offers guidance on this issue. With respect to hypochondriasis, the *DSM–IV* states that, "if recurrent distressing thoughts are *exclusively* related to fears of having, or the idea that one has, a serious disease based on misinterpretation of bodily symptoms, then hypochondriasis should be diagnosed instead of OCD" (APA, 1994, p. 421; italics added for emphasis). When a patient exhibits obsessions and compulsions about illness, *and* about other themes, OCD is a more appropriate diagnosis. Similar rules apply for BDD. Ultimately, cognitive-behavioral treatment will be similar regardless of the diagnosis.

Religious Obsessions

Religious obsessions (also referred to as *scrupulosity*) can present in various guises with some children describing excessive concern about offending God or other religious objects, some worrying a great deal about morality, and others fearing that they are practicing their religion "incorrectly." For example, an Orthodox Jewish child worried very much about keeping kosher "properly." She constantly worried that she had inadvertently eaten nonkosher food, but could not remember doing so. Her OCD became particularly severe during Passover (a Jewish holy week that forbids the eating of leavened bread) when she worried that she might have stepped on some breadcrumbs on the way to school and that they might have gotten into her mouth. Once she got to school, she spent the entire day in the bathroom rinsing out her mouth. When teachers came to check on her and tried to get her back to the classroom, she repeatedly asked for reassurance that she had not "sinned." Thereafter, she became so preoccupied by her concerns about consuming nonkosher foods that her grades plummeted. Rather than paying attention in class, she obsessively reviewed her walk to school to make sure she had not done anything wrong on the way. She also spent a lot of her time seeking reassurance from her teachers, her rabbi, and her parents.

"Just Right" Obsessions

"Just right" obsessions are particularly salient in the school environment. It is quite common to see children with OCD who feel the need to do things "just right" or perfectly. These concerns can lead children to write their letters again and again until they look just right, check their work repeatedly before being able to hand it in, or work extremely slowly to ensure that they do not make mistakes. Other children might need to remember everything they have read, or might need to know everything about a certain topic. For some patients with OCD, the feared consequence of not performing these compulsions is simply that they will not feel right (e.g., the "feeling" of a written letter); for others the fear is making mistakes. When inquiring about feared consequences, it is important for clinicians to get at the *most* feared consequences—for example, by asking the child, "And, what is so bad about making mistakes?" Some will focus on just failing one test or assignment and disappointing themselves and/or their parents. Other children will have much more elaborate consequences where failing one test leads to failing an entire course,which then leads to failing a grade, not graduating, not going to college, never finding a job and ending up on welfare. Understanding the feared consequence of not completing schoolwork correctly is essential to treatment planning.

COMORBIDITY IN OCD

Functional impairment in children with OCD can be compounded by the co-occurrence of other psychiatric disorders. Internalizing disorders including other anxiety disorders, major depressive disorder, and dysthymia are commonly seen in children with OCD (Valleni-Basile et al., 1994). Suicidal ideation is also common, with one study reporting its occurrence in almost one quarter of children with OCD (Valleni-Basile et al., 1994). The presence of these other disorders with OCD can further heighten academic, emotional, and social impairment.

Significant functional impairment is also observed in children with OCD and externalizing disorders, including attention deficit hyperactivity disorder (ADHD; Flament et al., 1988; Geller et al., 1996; Riddle et al., 1990). Children with OCD and ADHD have significantly lower social and academic skills than children with OCD alone and are more likely to be depressed and anxious (Sukhodolsky et al., 2005). Finally, tic disorders commonly co-occur with OCD. Between 26% and 59% of individuals with childhood-onset OCD have a lifetime history of tic disorders (see Eichstedt & Arnold, 2001, for a review). Given the observable nature of tics to peers, these disorders can certainly heighten the social impairment seen in OCD alone.

Although children who suffer from more than one disorder require more of a collaborative effort with families and teachers, exposure and ritual prevention therapy (EX/RP) is still an effective treatment for alleviating the distress associated with anxiety disorders (Kendall, Brady, & Verduin 2001).

HOW SCHOOLS CAN HELP

Identification of OCD

Schools can play a crucial role in identifying OCD in children and adolescents (see Adams, Waas, March, & Smith, 1994), particularly when children have significant difficulties in this environment. The case described of the teenage boy with concerns about molestation had few problems with his OCD at home. Rather, most of his obsessions and compulsions occurred during the school day when he was exposed to children. In a case like this, school personnel might be the first individuals in a child's life to wonder whether OCD is the cause of some of his or her unusual beliefs and behaviors. The key to successfully identifying OCD in schools is to educate classroom teachers and other school personnel on the nature of anxiety disorders. Even a brief, hour-long lecture by the school psychologist or a local clinician can help teachers to learn about the common signs of these highly prevalent disorders.

Accommodations for Children With OCD

Once OCD has been identified, children with the disorder sometimes need accommodations at school to help them to function better. Under The Individuals with Disabilities Education Improvement Act of 2004 (IDEA), all school systems in the United States are required to evaluate any child who may need special education services. Although it is often schools that request such evaluations, parents can request them as well; regardless of who initiates them, parents must give consent prior to them being carried out. Evaluations can include any kind of testing (e.g., intelligence testing, psychological testing) or gathering of information (e.g., discussions with classroom teachers and mental health professionals with whom the child is working) that facilitates an understanding of the child's strengths and needs.

After the evaluation, all of the information that has been compiled is considered by the school district's Individualized Education Program (IEP) Team, comprised of personnel set out by IDEA (e.g., teacher, special education teacher, parents, etc.). The IEP Team reaches a decision about whether the child qualifies as a student with a disability who requires special educational services. If they do, an IEP is created by a team and implemented. The IEP is then reviewed annually to assess whether the child is meeting his or her goals, to set new goals, and to revise the plan as needed.

Section 504 of the Rehabilitation Act of 1973 is also relevant to children with psychiatric conditions. This statute protects the rights of children with disabilities and ensures that they have equal access to education through accommodations and modifications in the school environment. Although IDEA is limited to a defined constellation of disabilities, Section 504 is available to students with any disability that affects their ability to receive an education. In further contrast to IDEA, Section 504 does not require the school to provide a formal IEP but rather permits a more informal "504 plan" to be developed by the parents and school. On the positive side, this means that 504 plans are easier to enact than IEPs. However, the 504 plan has available fewer procedural safeguards for parents and their children than IDEA.

Clinicians may be called on by an IEP team or a classroom teacher to advise them on the nature of OCD, how it can impact school functioning, and what kind of accommodations might benefit the child. These recommendations will likely vary depending on whether or not a child is yet in treatment and on how he or she is doing in treatment. It is important for clinicians to remember that IEPs are typically reviewed only once per year. Because the pace of OCD treatment tends to be quite rapid, clinicians must stay in touch with teachers and other school personnel to coach them on how to adjust plans as OCD symptoms remit.

Involvement in Treatment

School personnel can play a crucial role in the treatment of OCD when a child's OCD symptoms present themselves in the school environment. The psychosocial treatment that has been found to be the most effective in treating children with OCD is called *exposure and ritual prevention therapy* (EX/RP; see March & Mulle, 1998). EX/RP for OCD is a time-limited, problem-focused treatment, typically consisting of about 14 sessions. The strategies employed in EX/RP can be easily integrated into the school environment. Teacher involvement is most practical with younger children who spend most of their time with one teacher throughout the school day. By the time older children and adolescents begin rotating to different classes throughout the day with numerous teachers, most can be quite self-directive with their OCD treatment. Even with older children, however, it can be helpful for parents and/or clinicians to inform teachers of the child's difficulties and let them know how they can help facilitate the treatment plan.

EX/RP for children and adolescents with OCD is clearly described by March and Mulle (1998). To briefly summarize their approach, treatment begins with psychoeducation and with helping children to externalize the OCD (this can include giving the OCD a name like "Germy" or "The Voice") and learn about how to "boss" it back. This sets up the idea that the child is the "good guy" working hard to get rid of OCD, while the OCD is the "bad guy" that needs to be conquered. Early sessions also include detailed treatment planning that includes identifying triggers for OC symptoms, getting a sense of patients' feared consequences if they were to not engage in their rituals, and understanding the role that avoidance plays in symptom maintenance. Subsequent treatment sessions involve helping children to confront cues that trigger their obsessions (exposure) while refraining from engaging in rituals (ritual prevention). At the close of treatment, children are taught skills to help them prevent relapse of their OCD once treatment is over (see chap. 9 for a detailed review of EX/RP components).

The Clinician's Role

The goals of EX/RP are best accomplished when clinicians are flexible about where the treatment is carried out. Outcomes are likely improved by "going where the OCD lives." For children whose OCD "lives" at school, carrying out some treatment sessions at school can be very beneficial. A child was just described, whose OCD centered around being contaminated by other children in his classroom and acquiring negative aspects of their personalities. For initial exposures, the child's mother was asked to "contaminate" pieces of paper towel by wiping them across the desks and chairs of certain children. The mother was very cooperative in doing this and brought the contaminated paper towels into sessions in carefully marked sandwich bags. However, these stimuli did not bring on anxiety for the patient. He explained that their germs had dissipated on the way to treatment sessions. At the same time, this child was far too anxious to do exposures on his own in the classroom. Although parents are often excellent exposure coaches, this patient's mother tended to have very low tolerance for her son's anxiety. She did not think she would be able to coach him through his anxiety and admitted that if he did get anxious during exposures, she would likely discontinue them prematurely.

Rather than give up, the clinician decided to visit the child's classroom. With the mother's permission, she set up a time with the classroom teacher once all the other children had gone home. Both teacher and mom were present at the sessions in order to learn how to be good exposure coaches. Four sessions were held during which the clinician helped the child to touch the desks, chairs, and possessions of contaminated children. Concurrently, he was coached to refrain from engaging in his rituals (blowing outward, holding his breath, and wiping his hands on his shoes). After these sessions, the patient began to see that he would not acquire the negative attributes of other children by being in contact with their "germs." After having observed these initial exposure sessions, his teacher was then able to coach him through exposures when his classmates were present. It is doubtful that this child would have had as much success with treatment had sessions not been carried out in his classroom environment.

More often than actually visiting the school, clinicians become involved in the school environment through collaboration with teachers (see also Adams et al., 1994). Most teachers will be very receptive to such collaboration. Clinicians should be mindful, however, that the child with OCD is just one of the students in a teacher's classroom. Any requests of the teacher should be reasonable in terms of time and effort required. Phone calls to discuss treatment should be arranged around the brief periods of free time that the teacher has in his/her day. Exposure exercises and ritual prevention rules that are to be implemented in the classroom should be kept as simple as possible.

Table 14.1 outlines a plan for clinician–teacher collaboration for the treatment of OCD. Ideally, the first contact between the clinician and the teacher will be relatively lengthy (e.g., 30 minutes). During this conversation, the teacher should describe how the child's OCD plays out in the classroom environment and the clinician should get a sense of ways in which the teacher might serve to maintain the child's OCD symptoms (e.g., by providing reassurance). It is also important to learn whether the child is punished because of OCD symptoms. During this same conversation, the clinician should explain the nature of OCD to the teacher, describe EX/RP, and suggest ways in which the teacher might be able to facilitate the treatment plan. If the teacher agrees to be involved, a plan should be established of how the two parties will communicate (e.g., time of day, frequency of phone calls, etc.).

TABLE 14.1

Plan for Clinician-Teacher Collaboration for Treatment of OCD

Steps in Collaborative Plan	Goals of Each Step
1. Initial phone call with clinician and teacher	a. Teacher to inform clinician of ways OCD interferes in school environment. b. Clinician to inquire about ways teacher might maintain OCD or react negatively toward OCD symptoms (e.g., punishment). c. Clinician to educate teacher on nature and treatment of OCD. d. Clinician and teacher to create a collaborative treatment plan—method of communication, frequency, and a mutually agreeable time.
2. First classroom-based treatment assignment established.	a. To integrate exposure into the classroom environment. b. To establish ritual prevention rules in classroom environment. c. In some cases, to establish a reward system to encourage exposure and ritual prevention. d. To decide on time-frame for this first assignment— when will next contact between teacher and clinician occur?
3. Next contact between teacher and clinician.	a. To discuss the effectiveness of the treatment assignment. To discuss effectiveness of reward system, if established. Specifically, was the patient able to engage in exposure and ritual prevention? Was the teacher able to facilitate the process without undue interference in the classroom? b. To decide if the initial assignment needs to be carried out for longer or if a new assignment needs to be set.
4. Step 3 is repeated throughout treatment. The process is iterative, with progress each week informing the treatment plan for the next week. The treatment plan is a collaboration between patient, parents, clinician, and teacher.	
5. Final phone call at completion of treatment.	a. To review the patient's progress, from the perspective of the clinician and teacher. b. To discuss how the teacher can aid in relapse prevention. c. To encourage teachers to contact clinicians with any concerns or questions in the future.

With this ground-work set, it will then be possible to have much briefer ongoing phone calls (i.e., 15 minutes each). In the second phone call, the clinician should inform the teacher of the plan for that week. This plan will have been agreed on during the treatment session with the child and the parents. The plan typically includes an exposure exercise and a ritual prevention rule. For example, the child who feared inhaling fumes from the teacher's markers agreed in an early treatment session to sit one row closer to where the teacher sat and to try to discontinue her rituals of holding her breath and hiding her face in her shirt. It is important to note that it is not the teacher's job to enforce exposure and ritual prevention. Rather, the teacher can *facilitate* a plan established by the clinician. In this case, the teacher agreed to move some students so that the patient could sit one row closer to the front of the room each week. And, when she saw the student doing a ritual, she agreed to tap the marker on her arm as a "code" to remind the student to try to discontinue the ritual. Teachers should never reprimand a student (either publicly or privately) for failing to do exposures or for doing rituals. It is primarily the patients' responsibility to report to their therapists how they have done with their exposure and ritual prevention homework. If clinicians set up a supportive therapeutic environment, most children will be honest about both their successes and failures. Any ritual prevention violations or inability to do exposures should be discussed and worked through by the clinician and patient. Teachers should also discuss how the child has done with their parents or with the therapist during weekly phone calls. The purpose of these discussions is not to "tattle" on the child, but rather to help inform the ongoing case conceptualization and treatment plan.

After this initial EX/RP assignment, an iterative process ensues. The therapist discusses progress with the teacher, the patient, and the parents and then decides whether the same exercise should be continued for another week, or whether another assignment should be set based on the patient's progress. For example, in the aforementioned example, the patient was instructed to move up a row each time that she was able to spend a few days in a row without doing rituals and feeling only minimal anxiety.

In many cases, children with OCD will willingly do exposure and ritual prevention exercises without undue cajoling from clinicians or parents. At times, however, a reward system can be implemented to help facilitate the process. Although the teacher can play an important role in implementing the reward system, he or she should not be the person who is dispensing rewards. A 7-year-old patient refused to answer any questions in her first-grade classroom for fear of saying the wrong thing. Her teacher agreed to set up a reward system where she received a sticker every time she responded to a question that was asked of her (regardless of if she got the question right or wrong). At the end of the week, if she responded to 80% of the teacher's questions, the patient got to decide what the family would have for dinner on Friday night. The patient loved planning the menu, that usually included her favorite food (macaroni and cheese!). Although the teacher kept track of her classroom participation, it was the child's mother who actually provided the reward. This plan was a great success. Particularly with a child this young, it would be unrealistic to expect her to "fight" her OCD all day at school without guidance. The structure of a reward system and the constant encouragement of her teacher led to significant improvements in her OCD symptoms.

At the end of treatment, once all exposure and ritual prevention goals are accomplished in the classroom, it is helpful for the clinician to hold a concluding phone call with the teacher. During this call, the clinician can educate the teacher on the importance of relapse prevention. When OCD symptoms have been present in the school environment, teachers are often the first to see symptoms re-emerging once they have been resolved. The clinician, parents, patient, and teacher should agree on a plan in the event that this occurs. It is often most practical for the teacher to discuss such observations with the parents and for the parents to then get the clinician involved again if needed. Teachers should also be encouraged to contact clinicians with any future questions or concerns.

The Teacher's Role

Families of children with OCD are often concerned about whether or not to inform the school that the child has OCD and is in treatment. As with any situation, there can be advantages and disadvantages to sharing this information and clinicians should discuss these issues with patients and their families. In many cases, informing teachers can be of great benefit to the child. The most obvious reason to inform teachers is that they can play an important role in facilitating the treatment process. Before teachers know that a student has OCD, they may engage in behaviors that serve to maintain the illness. For example, our clinical experience suggests that teachers commonly provide reassurance to children with OCD when they ask for it. Not only do teachers not like to see their students upset, but they will also learn that it is faster to give reassurance than to try to talk children through their anxiety. Unfortunately, as long as children receive reassurance, their OCD symptoms will be maintained. Similarly, when teachers "allow" a child to engage in any other ritual, they are inadvertently helping to maintain the disorder (e.g., allowing a child with contamination concerns to go and wash her hands many times a day without asking permission).

Other teachers might punish behaviors brought on by OCD, adding to the shame that a child already feels about having the disorder. For example, the child who feared acquiring "negative aspects" of his classmates' personalities came across to his teacher as aggressive, nasty, and unfriendly before he was informed that the child had OCD. This resulted in frequent punishments for the child, including detentions. Ironically, he had to be in detention with all the other misbehaved children in the school and this was terribly stressful for him. Everywhere he turned were children from whom he could "catch" negative attributes. This was so anxiety-provoking for him that on a few occasions, he left school by himself without permission and started to walk home. This resulted in even greater punishments, including suspension from school.

Once a teacher is informed that a student has OCD and is educated about how the disorder is treated, there are various ways that he or she can facilitate the treatment process. First, teachers can play an important role in ritual prevention. They can be coached to discontinue their own behaviors that are serving to maintain the OCD. Although children learn in treatment that they must stop seeking reassurance from others, this can be very difficult for them to do on their own. Adults in their lives, including teachers, need to learn how to appropriately respond to requests for reassurance. Specifically, instead of providing reassurance, adults can say, "Hey, that sounds like your OCD talking. If we answer it, it's not going to go away!" Teachers should be discreet in such discussions so that other children do not overhear. The clinician can work with the teacher and student to come up with a code word or signal that reminds the child (in a supportive way) that the teacher will not be responsive to OCD. For example, when a child asks for reassurance, the teacher might tug her ear to suggest that she hears OCD talking and to remind the child that she refuses to respond to OCD's demands.

Similarly, clinicians can help teachers learn how to stop facilitating other rituals. As already mentioned, the teacher should not be in the role of telling a student to not do rituals. Rather, the teacher can be taught how to facilitate the child's ritual prevention efforts. For example, the child might be told to quietly go up to the teacher and say, "Can you help me get busy with something else?" when having an urge to ritualize. The teacher can then remind the child of some things she can do like reading a book or watering the plants in the classroom until the urge passes.

In addition to ritual prevention, teachers can help children with exposure to feared situations. Obviously, teachers are very busy and cannot spend the entire day helping one student—particularly with tasks that are not academic in nature. However, with the help of the clinician, many teachers will be willing to help integrate exposures into the student's day. This kind of plan worked very well with the student who feared acquiring negative qualities of his classmates. Each Friday, the clinician and teacher had a brief phone call to discuss an exposure for the patient to work on in the classroom the following week that the patient and clinician had designed during their weekly session. Because the child was instrumental in designing his exposures, he did not feel as if they were being forced on him by either the teacher or the clinician. The clinician was mindful of designing exposures that would be easy for the classroom teacher to implement. For example, for many weeks in a row, the child agreed to collect the students' work at the end of a test or assignment. This forced the child to touch things that every other child in the room had touched. These exposures were integral to the child's OCD treatment, but did not interfere with the classroom routine.

The aforementioned examples involved a plan agreed on by clinician, child, parents, and teacher. Sometimes, more "covert" assistance is beneficial. For children who fear doing things imperfectly, teachers can be encouraged by clinicians or parents to give children some leeway without them knowing that this plan is being put in place. If the child's therapy homework is to hand in a story without re-writing it until all the letters are perfect, the teacher should know this so that she does not criticize the child for messiness. The point of an exposure like this is for the child to learn that there are no negative consequences of being imperfect and this can only be accomplished if the teacher is on board with the plan. For most children with OCD who fear being imperfect or making mistakes, it is often the case that even when they stop doing rituals, their work is still very neat and accurate. This means that teachers are rarely put in the position of having to compliment a child's work or give a good grade when a child does not deserve it.

Finally, teachers can help children with OCD function better in the social world. In general, teachers can set a "no-teasing" policy in their classroom and make their best efforts to handle teasing effectively when it occurs. They can also include in their curriculum discussions of children with physical and emotional differences and teach about the importance of being empathic toward such children. For children with OCD specifically, rituals are often so habitual that they might not even notice themselves engaging in them. As was already discussed, teachers can set up a special code or signal to help children refrain from doing rituals that can harm them socially.

CONCLUSION

OCD can significantly impact a child's academic and social functioning in the school environment. When teachers are left in the dark about a student's difficulties, they can inadvertently help to maintain OCD symptoms or they can add to the shame of the disorder by punishing students for engaging in rituals. Teachers can be integral in a child's recovery once they are educated about the nature and treatment of this debilitating disorder. Teachers will be most responsive to playing a role in treatment when clinicians are respectful of the many demands that they have on their time during a typical school day. Yet, when they are involved in treatment in a simple way, the reward is often quite significant both to the child and to the general functioning of the classroom.

REFERENCES

Adams, G. B., Waas, G. A., March, J. S., & Smith, M. C. (1994). Obsessive-compulsive disorder in children and adolescents: The role of the school psychologist in identification, assessment, and treatment. *School Psychology Quarterly, 9,* 274–294.

American Psychiatric Association. (1994). *Diagnostic and statistical manual of mental disorders* (4th ed.). Washington, DC: Author.

Apter, A., & Tyano, S. (1988). Obsessive compulsive disorders in adolescence. *Journal of Adolescence, 11,* 183–194.

Beers, S. R., Rosenberg, D. R., Dick, E. L., Williams, T., O'Hearn, K., Birmaher, B., et al. (1999). Neuropsychological study of frontal lobe function in psychotropic-naive children with obsessive-compulsive disorder. *American Journal of Psychiatry, 156,* 777–779.

Berle, D., & Starcevic, V. (2005). Thought–action fusion: Review of the literature and future directions. *Clinical Psychology Review, 25,* 263–284.

Douglass, H. M., Moffitt, T. E., Dar, R., McGee, R., & Silva, P. (1995). Obsessive-compulsive disorder in a birth cohort of 18-year olds: Prevalence and predictors. *Journal of the American Academy of Child and Adolescent Psychiatry, 34,* 1424–1431.

Geller, D. A., Biederman, J., Griffin, S., Jones, J., & Lefkowitz, T. R. (1996). Comorbidity of juvenile obsessive-compulsive disorder with disruptive behavior disorders. *Journal of the American Academy of Child and Adolescent Psychiatry, 35,* 1637–1646.

Eichstedt, J. A., & Arnold, S. L. (2001). Childhood-onset obsessive-compulsive disorder: A tic-related subtype of OCD? *Clinical Psychology Review, 21,* 137–157.

Flament, M., Whitaker, A., Rapoport, J. L., Davies, M., Berg, C. Z., Kalikow, K., et al. (1988). Obsessive compulsive disorder in adolescence: An epidemiological study. *Journal of the American Academy of Child and Adolescent Psychiatry, 27,* 764–771.

Heyman, I., Fombonne, E., Simmons, H., Ford, T., Meltzer, H., & Goodman, R. (2003). Prevalence of obsessive-compulsive disorder in the British nationwide survey of child mental health. *International Review of Psychiatry, 15,* 178–184.

Hollander, E., Kwon, J. H., Stein, D. J., Broatch, J., Rowland, C. T., & Himelein, C. A. (1996). Obsessive-compulsive and spectrum disorders: Overview and quality of life issues. *Journal of Clinical Psychiatry, 57,* 3–6.

The Individuals with Disabilities Education Act, IDEA: 20 U.S.C 1400 et seq (2004).

Kendall, P. C., Brady, E. U., & Verduin, T. L. (2001). Comorbidity in childhood anxiety disorders and treatment outcome. *Journal of the American Academy of Child and Adolescent Psychiatry, 40,* 787–794.

March, J. S., & Leonard, H. L. (1998). Obsessive-compulsive disorder in children and adolescents. In R. P. Swinson, M. M. Antony, S. Rachman, & M. A. Richter (Eds.), *Obsessive-compulsive disorder: Theory, research and treatment* (pp. 367–394). New York: Guilford.

March, J. S., & Mulle, K. (1998). *OCD in children and adolescents: A Cognitive-behavioral treatment manual.* New York: Guilford.

Piacentini, J., Bergman, L. R., Keller, M., & McCracken, J. (2003). Functional impairment in children and adolescents with obsessive-compulsive disorder. *Journal of Child and Adolescent Psychopharmacology. Special Issue: Obsessive-Compulsive Disorder, 13*(2, Suppl), S61–S69.

Rasmussen, S. A., & Eisen, J. L. (1990). Epidemiology of obsessive compulsive disorder. *Journal of Clinical Psychiatry, 51*(2, Suppl), 10–13.

Riddle, M. A., Scahill, L., King, R., Hardin, M. T., Towbin, K. E., Ort, S. I., et al. (1990). Obsessive compulsive disorder in children and adolescents: Phenomenology and family history. *Journal of the American Academy of Child & Adolescent Psychiatry, 29,* 766–772.

Steketee, G., & Frost, R. (2003). Compulsive hoarding: Current status of the research. *Clinical Psychology Review, 23,* 905–927.

Storch, E. A., Heidgerken, A. D., Adkins, J. W., Cole, M., Murphy, T. K., & Geffken, G. R. (2005). Peer victimization and the development of obsessive-compulsive disorder in adolescence. *Depression and Anxiety, 21,* 41–44.

Storch, E. A., Ledley, D. R., Lewin, A. B., Murphy, T. K., Johns, N. B., Goodman, W. K., & Geffken, G. R. (2006). Peer victimization in children with obsessive-compulsive disorder: Relations with social-psychological adjustment. *Journal of Clinical Child and Adolescent Psychology, 35,* 446–455.

The Rehabilitation Act of, 29 U.S.C. 791 et seq., 1973.

Sukhodolsky, D. G., do Rosario-Campos, M. C., Scahill, L., Katsovich, L., Pauls, D. L. Peterson, B. S., et al. (2005). Adaptive, emotional, and family functioning of children with obsessive-compulsive disorder and comorbid attention deficit hyperactivity disorder. *American Journal of Psychiatry, 162,* 1125–1132.

Valderhaug, R., & Ivarsson, T. (2005). Functional impairment in clinical samples of Norwegian and Swedish children and adolescents with obsessive-compulsive disorder. *European Child and Adolescent Psychiatry, 14,* 164–173.

Valleni-Basile, L. A., Garrison, C. Z., Jackson, K. L., Waller, J. L., McKeown, R. E., Addy, C. L., et al. (1994). Frequency of obsessive-compulsive disorder in a community sample of young adolescents. *Journal of the American Academy of Child and Adolescent Psychiatry, 33,* 782–791.

Zohar, A. H., (1999). The epidemiology of obsessive-compulsive disorder in children and adolescents. *Child and Adolescent Psychiatry Clinics of North America, 8,* 445–460.

15

Obsessive-Compulsive Disorder in the Primary Care Setting

David C. Rettew
University of Vermont, College of Medicine

Obsessive-compulsive disorder (OCD) occurs in approximately 1%–3% of children and adolescents (Flament et al., 1988; Valleni-Basile et al., 1994; Zohar et al., 1992). The disorder's debilitating nature and negative impact on school performance, relationships, and time lost to obsessions and compulsions is well established (AACAP, 1998; Murray & Lopez, 1996). Although OCD can often go undetected, it can be accurately diagnosed and effectively treated. Primary care physicians (PCPs) who are alert to its symptoms can thus affect remarkable changes to an otherwise difficult trajectory.

The objective for this chapter is to summarize briefly some of the core features of OCD and to offer practical guidelines for its assessment and treatment within a primary care setting. The background information is concise and the reader is encouraged to consult other chapters of this book for more in-depth information. The motivation for this particular chapter stems from the concern of many PCPs that they have neither the training nor the time required to manage clinical emotional and behavioral problems in their patients (Williams et al., 2004). In addition, many PCPs describe a much less standardized approach to psychiatric symptoms in contrast to their approach to other medical symptoms. These factors, combined with a critical shortage of child psychiatrists across the country and reimbursement obstacles imposed by managed care companies, can lead to discomfort on the part of the physician, and suboptimal treatment for the patient.

This chapter presents a specific assessment template that can be applied and customized in the primary setting that addresses many of these challenges. Treatment strategies are also outlined, as well as guidelines for refractory cases and consultation to a child psychiatrist or psychologist.

DEFINITIONS

Like other psychiatric disorders, OCD is defined according to the Diagnostic and Statistical Manual–Fourth Edition (*DSM–IV*; APA, 1994), which requires for diagnosis not only the presence of significant obsessions or compulsions, but also a degree of impairment as evidenced by either the amount of time spent in these behaviors (somewhat arbitrarily defined as more than an hour per day), "marked" distress, or "significant" interference with functioning. The obsessions cannot be simply real-life problems that the person thinks about incessantly, and there is a requirement that the individual has tried to resist the obsessions or else perform a compulsion in response to it. The obsessions also need to be recognized as someone's own thoughts, rather than a hallucination or a belief that the thought was inserted from somewhere else. The compulsions (such as washing, checking, counting, arranging) are rigidly performed because the person feels compelled to do so in order to reduce anxiety or prevent some dreaded event or situation. Finally, if another condition such as an eating disorder or hypochondriasis is present, it does not fully account for the content of the obsessions or compulsions.

These criteria were designed mainly for adults, with little explicit modifications for children other than dropping the requirement that the patient realizes that the obsessions or compulsions are excessive or unreasonable. Children may also experience the symptoms as less troubling or alien to them, which can cause a delay in seeking help and reduce compliance to treatment. Younger children especially may have trouble articulating the difference between their own thoughts and a hallucination.

PHENOMENOLOGY

The content of the specific obsessions and compulsions does not dramatically differ between adults and children (Geller et al., 2001). The most common obsessions in children include contamination, aggressive or sexual thoughts, religion, or disturbing images of traumatic events. The most common compulsions, often but not always corresponding to the obsessions, include washing, checking, hoarding, ordering, touching or stepping, counting, and repeating. Children with arranging or touching rituals may not describe a bad event that might happen and instead describe the need to do something "just right." It is also the rule, rather than the exception, that over time there is migration from one type of symptoms to another (Rettew et al., 1992).

There appears to be a bimodal peak with regards to age of OCD onset, with one peak occurring in childhood and another in early adulthood. Additional evidence exists to support the hypothesis that child-onset OCD may represent a somewhat distinct subtype within the disorder, including a different pattern of comorbidity (more associated tics, ADHD, and PDD), male preponderance (especially in prepubescent samples), and greater familiality (Geller et al., 1998). Many children and their parents will also be able to describe particular events that appeared to trigger the onset of OCD symptoms, such as a traumatic event, although the causative role of these events remain in question (Maina et al., 1999).

The natural course of the disorder is one of a long-term illness with waxing and waning episodes. Along with the content of the particular symptoms, the severity of the symptoms, and associated impairment can fluctuate markedly. A recent meta-analysis that pooled available follow-up studies of pediatric OCD (ranging widely from 1 to 15 years) showed a pooled persistence rate of 41% for full OCD and 60% for full or subthreshold OCD (Stewart et al., 2004). Notable for this study, however, is that most patients were treated. Earlier follow-up studies before more effective treatments were available, by contrast, showed evidence of OCD as a more chronic condition with up to 70% of patients still suffering from significant OC symptoms after 6½ years (Hollingsworth et al., 1980).

BRIEF SUMMARY OF NEUROBIOLOGY

Although there remains to be much to be learned about the neuropathophysiology of OCD, there has been a tremendous amount of progress in our understanding of some of the biological mechanisms underlying the disorder. Although it was not that long ago that the disorder was attributed to over-aggressive toilet training, many studies have implicated genetically influenced dysfunction in the cortico-striato-thalamo circuitry (CSTC) involving many structures of the basal ganglia, including the caudate nucleus, and several areas of the frontal lobe such as the orbitofrontal cortex. More specifically, neuroimaging studies, mainly in adults, suggest overactive excitatory CSTC relative to indirect inhibitory pathways (Pittenger et al., 2005). Although serotonin dysfunction has received the majority of attention, in part because of the purported mechanism of its principal treatments, involvement of many other brain chemicals are also likely involved, including neurepinephrine, dopamine, and others. Family studies convincingly show evidence of increased rates of OCD among family members (Pauls et al., 1995), with twin studies showing evidence that this increased risk is conveyed from a combination mainly of additive genetic and unshared environmental influences, with minor effects of shared environments (Hudziak et al., 2004).

One of the most interesting, albeit controversial, developments in OCD research has been the possibility that a subset of children acquire the disorder through an autoimmune mechanism in which antibodies to type A beta-hemolytic streptococcus cross-react to proteins in the brain, similar to the mechanism in rheumatic fever (Swedo, Leonard, & Rapoport, 2004). For a further discussion of this topic, please see chapter 6. Active research in this area continues. Although the possibility of an autoimmune mechanism appears likely in a subset of patients, the specificity of the infectious agent, ensuing symptoms, and specific mechanism remains unclear and in need of further study. Later in this chapter, we address the issue of Pediatric Autoimmune Disorders Associated with Streptococcus (PANDAS) with regards to diagnosis and treatment.

A THREE-STEP APPROACH TO OCD IN PRIMARY CARE

The rest of this chapter is devoted to presenting a systematic approach to the assessment and treatment of obsessive-compulsive symptoms in the primary care setting. Each clinician will need to customize their own approach within the confines of their practice and be flexible with the needs of the individual patient. Notwithstanding, this outline can serve as a starting point for other types of psychiatric symptoms in childhood. An outline of the approach can be found in Table 15.1. This strategy, in a concise manner, incorporates a number of important components including safety assessment, screens for other types of psychopathology, quantitative multi-informant assessment of the primary problem, and follow-up (Rettew, 2005). It can be employed whether or not consultation with a child psychiatrist is anticipated.

Hypothetical Case Background

For the purposes of this section, let us assume that in the course of a busy practice, a family physician has been regularly seeing Megan, an 11-year-old girl, for regular health maintenance. She has been generally healthy but temperamentally anxious her entire life. Her mother, who also often appears anxious, has usually brought Megan for her appointments, and you have only met the father on one occasion. You are somewhat surprised to notice a sick visit appointment in your schedule for "behavioral issues."

Appointment 1

This patient-triggered appointment is usually made with little or no advance notice of the problem. Time constraints are often maximal, especially when the family expects that behavioral questions can be assessed and treated like many other common medical conditions. Under this model the physician for this first visit should focus on four primary areas: (1) The determination that a true problem exists; (2) a quick safety evaluation to assess for the need for urgent action; (3) evaluation for other medical conditions; and (4) discuss-

TABLE 15.1

Three Step Approach to Behavior Problems

Visit 1

Determination of a true problem

Safety evaluation

Assess for other medical conditions

Counsel need to obtain more information and distribute forms

Visit 2

Review broad rating scales

Assess OCD criteria for primary diagnosis

Decision to treat with medication and/or therapy referral

Visit 3 and Beyond

Assess efficacy so far

Making treatment more comprehensive

Referral/consultation to a psychiatrist

---

ing with the family the need for more information. Regarding the question of who to interview (patient alone, parent alone, parent and patient together), it is preferable to spend some time with each person alone and required in the course of assessing for suicidality and abuse.

Is There a Problem or Can the Family Be Provided Reassurance? Younger children especially are often famously rigid and compulsive (Leonard et al., 1990). Many if not most parents are familiar with the young child who insists on particular colors or numbers, specific preparations for a limited number of acceptable foods, and intense need for repetition and routines. Similar traits also can emerge later in life. Anxiety, meanwhile, is also a normal and critical process to alert someone to potential danger and the need to respond accordingly.

Individuals also differ temperamentally on the degree to which they tend to get upset and prefer order and routines to novel and high intensity experiences (Rettew & McKee, 2005; Shiner & Caspi, 2003). Furthermore, OCD has become a more popularized entity as stigma slowly is diminished through popular books like *The Boy who Couldn't Stop Washing* (Rapoport, 1989) and actors portraying people with OCD as eccentric but lovable. Thus, it is not out of the question for very vigilant parents to present to their PCP worried that their normally developing youngster is manifesting early signs of OCD. Because very young children do not have the insight to recognize their obsessions and compulsions as excessive, the clinician also does not have the usual OCD benchmark of the patient herself having insight into these "ego-dystonic" symptoms.

These cases are usually distinguished by a lack of impairment and a quality of the obsessions that fit a predictable context such as a favorite toy or television show, holidays, or upcoming event. Nevertheless, it can be very difficult to draw the line between normal personality or temperamental variation, subclinical symptoms, and OCD (Apter et al., 1996). Complicating matters further is the entity of obsessive-compulsive personality disorder (OCPD), a DSM–IV Axis II disorder characterized by preoccupation with details, perfectionism, rigidity, need for routine, stubbornness, and a lack of spontaneity. As a rule, personality disorders are not diagnosed in children due to the idea that the personality of a child or adolescent is a "work in progress" and thus should not be assessed as disordered. Nevertheless, most adults with OCPD report these symptom traits in childhood, not uncommonly from a very early age.

The hypothesized relations between OCD and OCPD have come nearly full circle over the past 50 years. From the psychodynamic perspective that originally dominated the field, OCD and OCPD were indeed thought to be closely related. As the disorder became increasingly "medicalized" in the late 1980s and 1990s, however, there was a shift in conceptualization so that OCD and OCPD were understood as more distinct entities. This made sense to many clinicians who knew patients with OCD symptoms in the stark absence of an overall obsessive-compulsive personality. A compulsive washer, for example, might be otherwise unkempt. Some studies around this time demonstrated this absence of obsessive compulsive personality in children with OCD, including one study by Leonard and colleagues that showed no evidence of increased superstitions in children with OCD (Leonard et al., 1990).

More recently, however, there has been some evidence that obsessive-compulsive personality or subclinical obsessive-compulsive symptoms may exist on a continuum with full fledged OCD, based on studies showing higher rates of subclinical symptoms in family members of OCD patients (Apter et al., 1996). At the same time, the rate of full OCPD in OCD is low (Albert, Mainer, Forner, & Borgeto, 2004), at least in adults, and there does not appear to be an elevated rate of OCPD in family members of OCD probands (Nestadt et al., 2000). It is possible that within OCD there are multiple subtypes, some of which are more closely linked to personality than others (Rettew & McKee, 2005). As can be surmised, continued study is needed in this interesting and important area.

Safety Evaluation: Can the Patient Leave the Office Today?   If there does indeed appear to be a problem that goes beyond developmental expectations, it is vital to assess whether there is any need for immediate hospitalization to keep the patient safe. Unfortunately, the effects of both psychotherapy and most medications are not immediate, and patients in crisis who are at risk of hurting themselves or others need to have an emergency evaluation, either by a crisis team or through the local emergency department. Although there is not a high risk of suicidal behavior in OCD per se, OCD frequently co-occurs with high-risk disorders such as depression and a safety screen is always indicated. Indeed, some time spent alone with the patient to inquire about suicidality and abuse should be part of all child behavioral assessments. Although patients with OCD often have violent thoughts, most are quick to tell you that they find these thoughts disturbing and have no plans on acting on them. In such instances, hospitalization is rarely necessary.

Assess for Other Medical Conditions.   Although psychiatric disorders are no longer considered to be "diagnoses of exclusion," there are nonpsychiatric conditions that can mimic the symptoms of OCD or complicate its course. Perhaps the most important decision during the first appointment is to screen for evidence of a strep infection that might respond to prompt treatment with an antibiotic. Although there continues to be considerable controversy over the diagnosis of PANDAS, many experts believe that any patient with a history of severe and rapid onset should be tested for a strep infection. Clinical criteria for a PANDAS subtype of OCD requires the abrupt prepubertal onset or course of a tic disorder or OCD in which there is a temporal association between symptom exacerbation and a streptococcal infection (Swedo et al., 2004). The presence of usually subtle neurological abnormalities is also required and can often be elicited by asking the patient to extend his or her arms and observing for fine piano playing movements. Worsening symptoms typically occur 1 to 2 weeks after the infection. Current guidelines issued from the American Academy of Child and Adolescent Psychiatry include testing all children who present with rapid-onset OCD symptoms with a throat culture or, if symptoms have been present over a week, antistreptolysin O (ASO) and anti DNSase B titers, which usually peak around 4–6 weeks (AACAP, 1998). These guidelines stem from the frequent lack of telltale signs of strep infection on physical exam and the documentation of rapid dissolution of OCD symptoms when prompt antibiotic treatment is initiated (Murphy & Pichichero, 2002).

Although a physical exam may reveal few findings related to OCD, except for perhaps dry chafed skin in those with compulsive hand-washing, important signs of comorbid conditions can be seen (Brunell, 1998). In particular, there is an elevated risk of both tics and Tourette's Disorder in childhood OCD that often can be observed and examined in the office. Furthermore, in cases where the differential may include an eating disorder, signs of dehydration and malnutrition may be present and requiring of more immediate intervention.

Counsel on the Need to Obtain More Information to Make a More Thorough Assessment. As much as both families and physicians strive for quick diagnosis and treatment initiation to relieve suffering, there are unfortunately no shortcuts one can take to lessen the considerable investment of time that usually needs to be undertaken. The office presentation of a child can be unrevealing or even misleading, and different people whom know the child well can and often do report very different things (Achenbach, Krukowski, Dumenci, & Ivanova, 2005). Consequently, it is usually wise to resist the temptation to move quickly to either diagnosis or reassurance and instead counsel the family about the need to gather further information so that a more definitive diagnosis can be made and unnecessary and perhaps dangerous treatment is not implemented without due cause.

The habitual use of even one or two rating scales can vastly aid in both the initial assessment of OCD symptoms and in monitoring response to treatment. As part of an overall comprehensive assessment, a general psychopathology rating scale can be used to obtain a complete profile of the patient and ensure that symptoms outside the chief complaint are not being missed. A more specific OCD rating scale can then be used to make a more detailed and quantitative assessment.

Thus, this visit ends with the family being sent home with assessment instruments that can be completed by the patient and multiple people who know the child well, including parents, teachers (one technique is to give two forms to go to both the child's most and least favorite teacher), counselors or therapists, or anyone else who knows the child well. One good choice of instruments is the Achenbach System of Empirically Based Assessment (Achenbach, 2001), including the Child Behavior Checklist, Youth Self Report, and Teacher Report Form (www.aseba.org). These instruments are some of the most widely used and well validated child behavior instruments in use, and are available with both computer and web-based scoring for easy administration. Standardized scales are available from late infancy into the geriatric range. There are, however, other instruments to consider using, such as the Behavioral Assessment Scale for Children (Reynolds & Kamphaus, 1992) or the Symptom Checklist-90-Revised (Derogatis & Lazarus, 1994). Whichever scales are used, these forms should be completed and scored prior to the next visit. If possible, the PCP could attempt to schedule a somewhat longer second appointment, although some of this extra time could be spent with a nurse or other auxiliary staff.

Case Example: Appointment 1

Returning to the case example, Megan's mother reports that over the past year she has gradually noticed that Megan appears more anxious and often seems stuck in repetitive touching behavior. She will often ask family members to repeat themselves over and over. She also insists that certain words, such as "kill" or "pain," not be used in the house. When you interview Megan alone, she confirms the compulsions but reveals that she is actually spending many hours with different obsessions. She also has some additional mental rituals of which her mother is unaware that she performs in her room at night. Some of her obsessions also have a sexual or aggressive content, in which she envisions her mother having a severe car accident. She reassures you that she finds these thoughts very disturbing and has no plan or intent on hurting herself or others. She denies any history of trauma associated with this worsening of symptoms.

Her physical exam is unremarkable, although you do observe what appears to be a blinking tic. There is no evidence of infection either from the exam or from the history to suggest needing to perform a Strep Test.

By the end of the visit, a diagnosis of OCD may be suspected; however, you counsel the family on getting more complete information and send them family home with five ASEBA forms to be completed and returned: one for Megan, one for each of her parents, one for her most favorite teacher, and one for her least favorite teacher. An extended follow-up appointment is scheduled for three weeks.

RELATED ISSUES

Differential Diagnosis

In contrast to classic medical thinking, what is termed *differential diagnosis* may in this case refer more to co-existing or complicating diagnoses rather than a clear "this or that" branch point. Although obsessive-compulsive symptoms have been observed with CNS tumors, infections, trauma or from carbon monoxide poisoning (Wise & Rapoport, 1989), most of the diagnoses required for careful consideration are psychiatric and do not necessarily exclude making an additional diagnosis of OCD.

Tic Disorders. These often occur with OCD, and there is some evidence of a shared genetic diathesis for both conditions (Pauls et al., 1995). What may be puzzling, however, is the patient who presents only with brief rituals in the absence of clear obsessions or other rituals (Mansueto & Keuler, 2005). If this picture is present, these rituals may actually be better conceptualized as a complex tic and if impairing, treated as a tic with an alpha-agonist such as clonidine or guanfacine.

Eating Disorders. There is evidence that OCD and eating disorders may be related and are often seen as co-occurring (Halmi et al., 2003). However, an eating disorder diagnosis should be considered at the exclusion of OCD if the obsessions or perseveration occur primarily about food and body image and the restricting or purging is done to lose or not to gain weight rather due to a different obsession such as a fear of being contaminated by food or from food not being prepared just right.

Trichotillomania.   Trichotillomania refers to persistent and compulsive hair pulling of the head or other body parts that is severe enough to lead to visible alopecia. Although there is some evidence to link it to OCD (Rettew et al., 1991), most children with trichotillomania do not have other characteristic obsessions or compulsions (Swedo, 1993).

Autistic Spectrum Disorders.   From experience, this is one of the trickiest but important decision points to be made because the diagnosis of an autistic spectrum disorder dictates the need for intensive psychosocial intervention in areas that would not likely be covered in regular OCD treatment. Although children with severe autism often are recognized early, some high-functioning autistic children and those with spectrum diagnoses such as Asperger's Disorder or Pervasive Developmental Disorder Not Otherwise Specified can escape detection until late childhood and beyond. Complicating matters is that, in many cases, there may not be much in the way of particular symptom patterns to distinguish PDD from OCD (or comorbid PDD and OCD). The key in these cases is to focus on a developmental history, particularly with regard to social functioning. Screening questions can include asking about whether the child in infancy was able to look at someone and point to what she or he wanted, whether she or he brought others into the play (such as by bringing toys to caretakers) and later on, whether the play had imaginative or symbolic components. A history of a language delay can also be a red flag for an autistic spectrum disorder, although it may not be present in Asperger's Disorder. Other signs of a possible PDD include a history of motor clumsiness and a significant difficulty in the child understanding especially nonverbal aspects of communication. Children with PDD also frequently have preoccupations with unusual things, including parts of objects, and typically are less bothered by their OC symptoms than in children with OCD. They generally have few friends, due either to a lack of interest or great difficulty navigating social encounters. If there is a question of a PDD with or without OCD, consultation with an expert in developmental disorders is strongly recommended.

Appointment 2

The objective of this appointment is to make a specific diagnosis and treatment decision. At this point, the general psychopathology forms have been returned and scored. Armed with data from both the patient and others, the PCP can now get a clearer picture of the severity and scope of the problem and then make a decision either to begin treatment in some form or consult with a child psychiatrist or psychologist. With some advance notice, this appointment could hopefully be a bit longer than the typical visit, perhaps around 30 minutes. Some of this time can be with a nurse or other clinical support staff who may be able to review diagnostic criteria of OCD or administer a specific OCD rating scale.

Reviewing the Broad Psychopathology Instruments. If the ASEBA forms are used, the computer scoring program presents a great deal of output in several formats that are standardized according to the patient's age and gender. This feature allows for the clinician to assess the child's level of achievements and problems relative to his or her peers. The output is summarized in a narrative form that includes the display of any critical items (such as suicidal thought) that the informant endorsed. In addition to the narrative form, several charts are generated for each informant.

1. The competence scores show how well the child is performing socially, academically, and in activities. In general for the CBCL, scores below the 3rd percentile are considered to be in the clinical range and those between the 3rd and 7th percentile are in the borderline range. There is also a total competency score. These ratings are a good indicator of clinical impairment, although one cannot assume that a child's psychiatric symptoms are its sole source.

2. The syndrome scale provides a profile of the level of problems across eight empirically validated domains: anxious/depressed (A/D), withdrawn/depressed (W/D), somatic complaints (SC), social problems (SP), thought problems (TP), attention problems (AP), rule-breaking behavior (RB), and aggressive behavior (AG). The first three scales are considered internalizing problems and the last two externalizing problems. Levels of problems are considered to be in the clinical range if they are above the 97th percentile and in the borderline range between the 93rd and 97th percentile. Although there is no pathonemonic profile for OCD, clinical elevations in anxious/depression and thought problems are common.

3. The internalizing, externalizing, and total problem chart displays the standardized scores in these broader categories.

4. The *DSM*-oriented page reorganizes the instrument items into categories that more closely resemble *DSM–IV* criteria. Although OCD is not one of the categories, an obsessive-compulsive scale has been generated and tested from the ASEBA forms from Items 9, 31, 32, 52, 66, 84, 85, and 112 (Hudziak et al., 2004) and is in consideration for being incorporated in future scoring software (T. Achenbach, personal communication). Summing these items, a score above 5 has been found to be an effective screen for *DSM*-defined OCD.

5. When multiple informants about the same patient are obtained, the output also generates a page of correlations that reflect how well informants agree with each other as well as a page of cross-informant compari-

sons of the problem scales of both the empirically derived and *DSM–IV* oriented categories. These cross-informant comparisons may be the most useful page to examine, especially when time constraints are maximal, as these charts allow the physician a rapid and efficient means of assessing a broad range of psychiatric symptoms from multiple people who know the patient well.

In some cases, all informants will generally agree with each other, providing the clinician with confidence that many people around the patient are seeing the same symptoms and impairments. In many if not most cases, however, there is substantial disagreement about the scope and level of psychopathology. Although these profiles can be confusing, they reflect the complexity of the problems themselves and provide a window of opportunity to clarify key issues in assessment and treatment that could be potential obstacles to treatment.

Discrepancies are primarily due to two broad sources. The first is bias, that is, a distortion in perception that could be due to someone's own level of symptoms, beliefs, denial of problems, or limited contact. Although these reports are, in a sense, "incorrect," they do represent a real perception that needs to be taken into account. More commonly, however, informant discrepancies represent situational specificity—true differences in behavior across settings such as school versus home. Rather than attributing these differences to noise, it is often critical to tackle these discrepancies head-on. If one parent, for example, does not see problem behavior, then obtaining cooperation in treatment may be difficult at best. A slight investment in time from the outset can often avoid significant confusion and conflict down the road.

Narrowing in on OCD. Although the previous discussion has hopefully illustrated the utility of incorporating good general assessment instruments within the primary care setting, these scales do not make diagnoses for *DSM–IV* disorders. Thus, in the case of possible OCD, more specific assessment is needed once the broad picture has been obtained and a review with the patient and family of the *DSM–IV* criteria for OCD is needed to provide the necessary, although oversimplified, yes–no decision. To aid in this process, it is often worthwhile to administer a short-rating scale that specifically targets OCD symptoms. To this aim, probably the most widely used and validated instrument is the Children's Yale-Brown Obsessive-Compulsive Scale (CY-BOCS; Scahill et al., 1997; Storch et al., 2004). This scale can be obtained by contacting the author, Dr. Wayne Goodman at ufocd@psychiatry.ufl.edu. It is administered by a clinician with the patient and parent separately or jointly. At its core, it contains only 10 items and yields an overall score that can provide a good baseline to monitor the effects of treatment

Beginning OCD Treatment. If an OCD diagnosis is made, the PCP should specifically communicate this with the patient and offer some reassurance that a number of effective treatments are available. Spontaneous remission, apart from the PANDAS subtype, is uncommon, although many patients will have a waxing and waning course over time. Consequently, treatment with cognitive-behavioral therapy (CBT), medications, or a combination is recommended.

The decision as to what treatment type to pursue first is based on a number of factors. From a practical standpoint, one of the main determinants will be availability and access to an experienced cognitive-behavioral therapist. CBT also requires the participation of a motivated patient and family. At the same time, many families will have legitimate concerns about the possible risks associated with medications. Many noted experts in OCD have recently gone on record to say that current data leads them to recommend that CBT be at least a component of all first-line OCD treatment (POTS Team, 2004).

Exposure and Response Prevention Therapy

Exposure and response prevention (ERP) therapy is a proven effective treatment for OCD (Franklin et al., 1998). ERP is a component of cognitive-behavioral therapy and has been manualized for treatment in both adults and children (March & Mulle, 1998). This type of psychotherapy tends to be very symptom-focused, relatively brief, and lasting in its effects.

Cognitive-behavioral therapy rests on the premise that although there may be a predisposition to obsessive-compulsive behavior, these symptoms have been reinforced through learning and conditioning and thus can be unlearned. The principal of negative reinforcement is often cited in OCD. For example, a child with an obsessive fear of getting AIDS refuses to touch things in public. Because she or he does not then develop AIDS, these behavior patterns are strengthened. Therapy, consequently, is directed at breaking these patterns—supporting and helping the patient develop skills as she or he risks not performing the ritual within a controlled therapeutic environment. Gradually, the anxiety that occurs in response to blocking the ritual will diminish as the patient realizes that the feared negative event will not occur even if the ritual is not performed.

Research trials conducted in children and adolescents have shown that both individual and group based CBT is an effective treatment for pediatric OCD (Asbahr et al., 2005; Geffken et al., 2004; Lewin et al., 2005) and that gains are maintained at follow-up (Barrett et al., 2005). Some of the trials have also included a strong family component (Barrett, Healy, & March, 2004).

CBT likely works through the same mechanism as medications. A now-classic study by Baxter and colleagues examined PET scan changes prior and after treatment in a group of adults with OCD (Baxter et al., 1992). Half of the subjects were treated with clomipramine and half with ERP. Those patients who responded to treatment, regardless of its type, showed similar normalizations on their post-treatment scan.

In sum, it is difficult to overestimate the value of forming a close working relationship with a number of skilled CBT therapists. Although PCPs routinely work closely with specialists in other areas of medicine, many PCPs struggle to know much more than the fact that a patient is "in counseling." Given the frequent lack of availability of skilled CBT therapists, the decision on finding one of whether or not to share that information with your colleagues is left to your discretion.

Pharmacotherapy

For reasons that are not completely clear, OCD is one of the best-studied anxiety disorders with regards to medication trials. Indeed, in children in adolescents, there are currently four medications (clomipramine, fluoxetine, fluvoxamine, sertraline) with FDA approval to treat pediatric OCD, in contrast to one medication (fluoxetine) with FDA approval to treat pediatric depression.

There are no absolute guidelines as to what would be the first medication to try in a patient with OCD. Geller and colleagues recently conducted a meta-analysis of 12 randomized placebo-controlled double-blind medications trials for pediatric OCD (Geller et al., 2003). The major findings of this study included a clear demonstration of efficacy across trials, although the amount of clinical change was modest compared to placebo. There was little in the way of differential efficacy between SSRIs with the only possible exception being clomipramine, which did show some evidence of a larger treatment effect. Because of its often poor tolerability and potential risks (QT prolongation, lethality in overdose), clomipramine remains a second-line agent despite its effectiveness (Biederman, 1991; DeVeaugh-Geiss et al., 1992). One also needs to keep in mind when switching from an SSRI to clomipramine, especially if there is a period of time that both medicines overlap, that some SSRIs such as paroxetine and fluoxetine can inhibit the CYP 2D6 pathway and increase clomipramine levels to dangerous levels.

Thus, among the SSRIs, it is certainly reasonable to consider other factors in selecting a first agent such as the presence of an FDA indication, cost, half-life, potential interactions with other medications, number of doses per day, comorbid disorders, and patient preference. Table 15.2 shows typical starting and maintenance doses for those medications with documented efficacy in pediatric OCD. Improvement often is gradual and lengthy medication trials of 10 to 12 weeks are required to truly evaluate the efficacy of a particular agent (Pittenger et al., 2005).

TABLE 15.2

Clinically tested medications for pediatric OCD

Generic	Trade	Peds FDA indication	Starting Dose (child/adolescent)	Maintenance	Comments
Fluoxetine	Prozac	Yes	5/10	20-80	Long half life; 2D6 inhibitor
Fluvoxamine	Luvox	Yes	12.5/25	50-300	3A4 inhibitor
Sertaline	Zoloft	Yes	12.5/25	25-200	
Clomipramine	Anafranil	Yes	12.5/25	50-200	Often poorly tolerated; Requires blood levels, baseline and follow-up ECGs
Paroxetine	Paxil	No	5/10	10-60	Some anticholinergic properties; 2D6 inhibitor
Citalopram	Celexa	No	5/10	10-40	

Many primary care physicians have also considered a trial of a benzodiazepine either as monotherapy or as an adjunctive agent with SSRIs. Unfortunately, despite the length of time that benzodiazepines have been available, there is a remarkable paucity of data in children and adolescents in general (Green, 2001), with the literature in child OCD limited to case reports (Leonard et al., 1994; Ross & Piggott, 1993).

Suicidality and Antidepressants. All antidepressants now carry a black-box warning relating to the possible association between suicidal ideation and behavior in pediatric samples and antidepressant use (Leslie et al., 2005). The majority of the data used for the FDA's determination was based on clinical trails of adolescents who were depressed; however, there were pediatric OCD trials that were incorporated into the FDA's analysis.

Although this is an issue that continues to be hotly debated, current FDA recommendations for "ideal" monitoring of a child taking an antidepressant are quite stringent and include having the child seen by a physician weekly for the first month, biweekly for the second, and then again at week 12. Some professional organizations have argued for the need of more customized monitoring to suit the individual family (see www.

parentsmedguide.org). Regardless, physicians should enlist the patient and family to be vigilant for any signs of emerging or worsening suicidality and to contact the prescribing physician immediately. Because of a concern for discontinuation symptoms if antidepressants are stopped abruptly, there is not an automatic recommendation to stop the medication immediately if these symptoms develop.

Combined Psychotherapy and Medication Treatment

Particularly for older children and adolescents with more severe OCD, combining medications and psychotherapy from the outset is a very reasonable option. In 2004, the Pediatric OCD Treatment Study (POTS) was published that compared several treatments of adolescent OCD, including medication alone (sertraline), CBT alone, and combined medications and CBT, to placebo (POTS Team, 2004). The principal finding from this study was that combined treatment was superior to either medications alone or CBT alone in reducing CY-BOCS scores from baseline. The rate of symptom remission (defined as a CY-BOCS score less than 10) was 53.6% for the combined group, 39.3% for CBT alone, 21.4% for sertraline alone, and 3.6% for placebo. The rate of remission was significantly higher for combined treatment versus sertraline but not between combined treatment and CBT alone. The authors concluded that first line treatment of OCD should consist either of CBT or CBT plus an SSRI.

Case Example: Appointment 2

Returning to the case example, the results of all five informants are returned prior to the next visit. The results of the ASEBA scales show evidence of clinical impairment with the competency scales being in the clinical range for activity level and social participation. The cross-informant problem scores are shown in Fig. 15.1. As can be seen, the patient herself and her mother report clinical levels in the anxious/depressed and thought problems scale. The teachers see less of this, although there are some borderline levels of attention problems and rule-breaking behavior. In reviewing these profiles, you discover that, at school, Megan is able to keep many of her rituals in check, although she can be distracted by them and frequently needs to leave class. The teachers are becoming increasingly resentful of this, which may account for the elevations on rule-breaking and attention problems. The father reports fewer symptoms across the board, although Megan reports that she does not confide in him because he is often not home and she fears being ridiculed by him. In summary, the ASEBA forms are consistent with a diagnosis of OCD, but highlight some additional areas of concern such as the re-

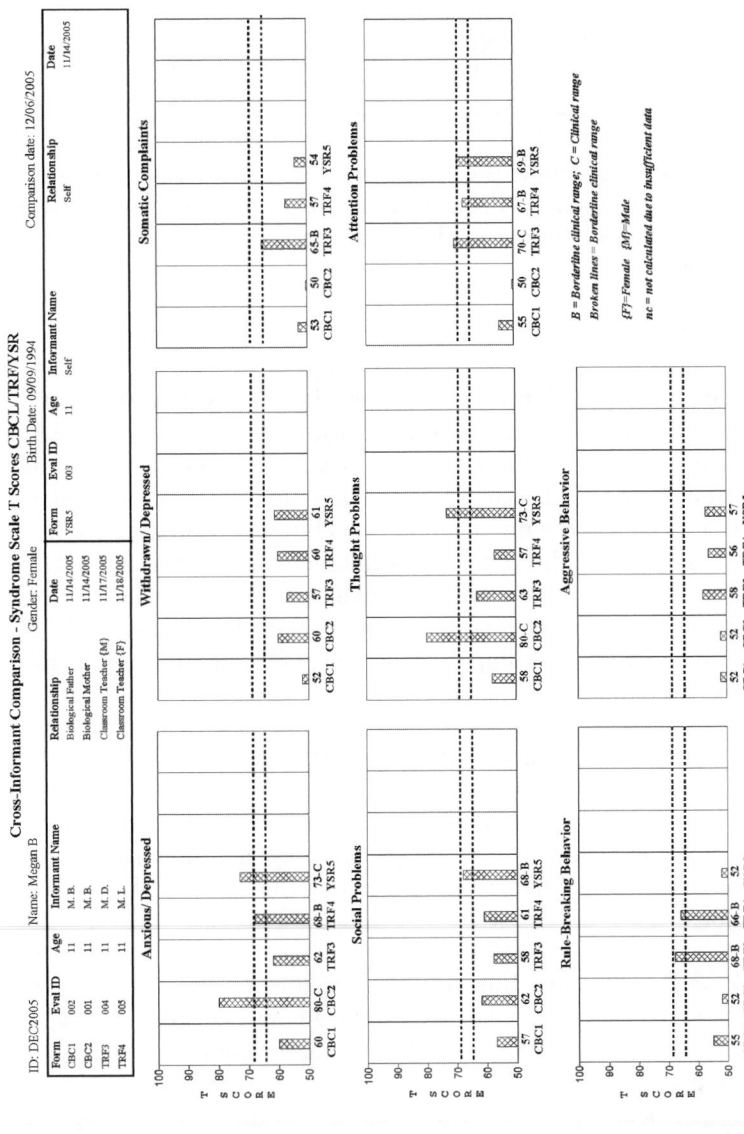

Figure 15.1. ASEBA multi-informant output from hypothetical case. Cross-informant comparison for case example, combining data from parents, teachers, and self-report. This output allows for the rapid integration of multiple sources of data that is standardized by age and gender. The data is consistent with a child suffering from OCD, with clinical elevations (reflecting reported levels of problems above the 97th percentile compared to other girls her age) especially in the anxious/depressed and thought problems areas. Copyright © 2001 ASEBA. All rights reserved. Reprinted with permission.

lationship between Megan and her teachers and father. Although the profile alerts you to the possibility of a comorbid disorder such as ADHD or oppositional defiant disorder (ODD), it appears at this point that the patient's defiance and distractibility is more anxiety-based, and might be expected to attenuate with good anxiety treatment.

Your nurse has seen Megan before you and administered a CY-BOCS, which shows a total score of 22, well within the clinical range. Reviewing the *DSM–IV* criteria, she meets these easily and the symptoms are not better accounted for by another disorder, so at this point a fairly confident diagnosis of OCD can be made. The family is eager to discuss their treatment options, which you review. Together, you decide to refer Megan to a cognitive-behavioral therapist and hold off on medication treatment, at least for now. Follow-up is in two weeks.

Appointment 3 and Beyond

The aim of subsequent appointments is to assess the progress made so far and make a decision about any further treatment adjustments or perhaps, referral to a psychiatrist. Often at Appointment 3, it will be too soon to assess the full impact of either psychotherapy or medications, but there may indeed be some signs that can alert the physician to how things may proceed such as whether the family has made contact with the therapist and has formed an alliance and, if medications are used, whether it appears that it will be tolerated without significant side effects. This appointment also allows the physician to begin looking at other important issues that are part of an overall comprehensive treatment plan.

Filling Gaps and Checking Assumptions

If, after additional time, there appears to be little improvement, a number of issues can be considered. Many of these aspects involve additional efforts towards more comprehensive treatment and testing the veracity of some initial assumptions.

1. *Is the dosing adequate?* Effective OCD treatment often requires robust doses of medication that can exceed the amount needed for depression or other anxiety disorders. See Table 15.2 for guidelines regarding medication dosing.

2. *Is the psychotherapy effective?* As mentioned, the literature support for psychotherapy is mainly for CBT with ERP that adheres closely to published manuals. Although many community psychotherapists and mental health counselor claim to and do draw from cognitive behavioral techniques, this does not necessarily translate into the same CBT found effective in clinical studies. To ascertain whether or not the patient's treatment

truly uses CBT techniques, the physician could ask a number of questions such as whether the child actively confronts their rituals in treatment, if homework is given, or whether the child is taught specific techniques to "talk back" to their OCD symptoms.

3. *Incorporating the family.* Some recent therapy trials have begun to highlight the importance of working with other family members in addition to the patient (Barrett et al., 2005). From experience, it can be critical that families see OCD symptoms as a family-wide concern, deserving of everyone's efforts and not simply as a single individual's problem. Family members may also be suffering from their own psychiatric symptoms (as discussed in the following paragraph).

4. *Medication compliance.* Paying attention to the length of time between medication refills can alert the physician for patients with sporadic compliance. It is sometimes illuminating to ask for detailed information on how and when medications are dispensed. Is there a routine for taking medications every day? Do parents check or give reminders? Where does the pill bottle stay? Understanding these fine points can often allow the physician to recommend specific ways to improve compliance if the problem is a practical one. If there are larger concerns, such as ambivalence about taking the medication altogether, these questions can open an important dialogue.

5. *Is the school providing assistance?* There is tremendous variability between schools in the level of understanding and interventions for children and adolescence with psychiatric disorders. The vast majority of schools, however, are more than willing to provide the reasonable supports and accommodations necessary to help children with OCD and other disorders succeed maximally at school. This is sometimes a difficult decision for parents who want to obtain as many school services as possible but fear the stigma and ridicule than can be directed at children with "special" needs. With the cooperation of the school, however, the implementation of certain modifications for children with OCD can often be done discreetly, such as the allowance of breaks or simply informing teachers of the diagnosis so that other and perhaps more harmful labels (e.g., lazy, difficult) are not applied to the child.

6. *Did you miss a comorbid diagnosis?* Other types of disorders such as disruptive behavior disorders, bipolar disorder, and psychotic disorders carry very different treatment algorithms and may be accounting for the lack of improvement. Reconsidering these possibilities either within your own practice or with the aid of a consultant may be needed.

If these issues do not appear to be a concern and the patient still shows little improvement after an adequate medication trial, current recommendations call for switching to a different SSRI. Should this also prove to be ineffective, the next step may be consider an adjustment to the CBT, a switch to clomipramine, or possible augmentation with clonazepam or atypical antipsychotic (Geller & Spencer, 2003). Combinations of an SSRI and clomipramine have also been used effectively, although extreme care needs to be taken because of the potential drug interactions (Figueroa et al., 1998).

Case Example: Appointment 3

After 3 weeks, there has not been a tremendous amount of improvement, although everyone in the family is somewhat relieved that at least treatment has been initiated. A repeat CY-BOCS is 20. Megan has met the therapist once and has a good connection to her. She has been instructed to keep diaries of her symptoms throughout the week and will present that at the next session. You decide to continue holding off on medications and will reassess this decision if her condition deteriorates or she has not made progress after about 12 weeks of treatment. You encourage the family to speak to the school about implementing some minor accommodations that may help Megan cope with her symptoms better at school and agree to send a letter of support. You also encourage the family to look at the Web site for the Obsessive Compulsive Foundation (www.ocfoundation.org) to obtain more information and support.

OTHER CLINICAL ISSUES

When to Refer?

One of the main goals of this chapter is to increase the comfort level of PCPs to the point where most will feel confident to assess and treat OCD in collaboration with a psychotherapist. Nevertheless, certain factors may encourage consultation with a child psychiatrist sooner rather than later. These issues would include the presence of significant comorbid conditions such as bipolar disorder or a pervasive developmental disorder, failure of two adequate medication trials, consideration of augmentation with atypical antipsychotics or other less evidence-based agents such as benzodiazepines or dual-acting antidepressants, or other specific concerns that the PCP or family might want addressed in consultation.

What to Tell Families About OCD?

Many children and their families are curious to understand as much as possible about the disorder. Effective communication about OCD and its causes can facilitate maximal collaboration between family members. When discussing the cause of OCD, we recommend highlighting a number of important facts.

    1. The important but not nearly exclusive influence of genetics. This point can help reduce blame in both the patient and the family, although it

is critical to point out that the finding of a 40% genetic influence means that much of the symptomatology is due to environmental effects that potentially can be modified.

2. Related to this, some parents will feel guilty that they may have "caused" their child's OCD though their role in a precipitating event. Although these events may be involved in the emergence of symptoms at that point in time, the physician can reassure the family that it is likely that these symptoms would have arisen anyway, triggered by something else.

3. OCD is not just a part of a child's personality. As mentioned, research has shown that most children's OCD symptoms are not congruent with an overall obsessive personality type. Indeed, the symptoms may be covering up other personality traits that are in the process of development.

4. OCD can be treated. Although not wanting to paint an overly rosy picture, it is important to let families know that most children and adolescents will get substantially better with treatment.

Parental Psychopathology

In taking the family history or examining the source of widely discrepant reports of a child, the physician is likely to suspect the existence of psychiatric disorders in other family members. Addressing these parental disorders in a skillful manner can be one of the most important and often overlooked elements in providing care for the child. Given what is now known about the level of genetic influence to most psychiatric disorders, it is very common for similar problems to be present in multiple family members. In anxiety disorders, there is compelling evidence that not only can parents transmit at-risk genes to their offspring, but that their style of interacting and teaching children can often, subtly or more overtly, reinforce anxious tendencies. For example, parents of anxious children have been found to encourage more avoidance strategies in their children rather than supporting efforts to confront their fears (Lenuga & Long, 2002). This can cause a reduction in critical opportunities for exposure and habituation of feared situations. Even non-related psychopathology can have substantial impacts on patient symptoms. A depressed or substance using spouse or parent, for example, can contribute to heightened family conflict and increasing burdens in the higher functioning parent.

Needless to say, this can be a delicate process after family members bring in an identified patient for help and then feel as though the spotlight is turning onto them. It is important that this discussion not be viewed as blaming of parents or spouses. From experience, the discussion of genetic influence of disorders ironically allows many family members to be more open to the idea of having their own symptoms assessed and treated.

Amount of Improvement

Despite the significant advances in OCD treatment, it unfortunately remains true that full symptom remission, especially when using only one treatment modality, occurs less than half the time (Wagner, Cook, Chung, & Messig, 2003), meaning that, even with adequate treatment, most patients will remain somewhat symptomatic. Although some CBT trials have reported higher response rates (Barrett et al., 2005; Barrett et al., 2004), the samples for these studies often are not fully representative of typical patients seeking treatment. Many medication trials show a 30% to 40% reduction in symptoms when measured quantitatively, with the POTS trial showing a 53% reduction with combined medication and CBT. Although this number may be an underestimation of improvement due to the nonlinear methods of the assessment instruments, it remains true that most patients will continue to manifest some degree of troubling symptoms. This presents a dilemma to the treating clinician as to what level of improvement is "good enough," especially when there is no guarantee that switching to another agent will lead to better response and augmentation strategies, such as adding an atypical antipsychotic, can carry a significant degree of risk. One reasonable strategy is to pursue at least partial remission by using the combination of medications and CBT. The decision to attempt riskier and less tested medications remains a personal one and certainly presents a good opportunity to obtain consultation.

Length of Treatment

Due to the fact that OCD is both a typically chronic condition and one that often waxes and wanes in severity, the decision to discontinue treatment remains perplexing to many clinicians and is not aided with a great deal of long-term data. There is good data from placebo discontinuation studies that withdrawing medications before 6 months of treatment can result in a relapse rate of up to 90% (Leonard et al., 1991). The current recommendations for continuing medication treatment calls for treatment for 9 to 18 months after symptom resolution (March et al., 1997). After this time, a slow taper (25% reduction every 1 to 2 months) can be attempted. Some experts have suggested using multiple dosing regimens even in once daily medications to reduce discontinuation effects (Geller & Spencer, 2003).

Cook and colleagues conducted a 1-year open-label sertraline study and found that patients often had additional improvement throughout the year, with some initial nonresponders later improving (Cook et al., 2001). Although the medication was generally well tolerated, weight gain of 10–15 pounds was common (keeping in mind expected growth during that time) and hyperkinesia was the most common reason for medication discontinuation.

Antibiotic Prophylaxis

Although there have been some recent promising results using prophylactic antibiotics to reduce strep infections and neuropsychiatric symptoms (Snider et al., 2005), there are no recommendations at this point for patients even with a suspected PANDAS to be treated with prophylactic antibiotics. Instead, increased vigilance and prompt diagnosis and treatment of possible infections are encouraged to reduce potential OCD exacerbations.

OCD RESOURCES

Another crucial, but often overlooked aspect of treatment is helping patients and their families obtain additional information from reliable sources. Although there is the slight risk of a patient's or family member's identity becoming overly fused with their medical condition, the encouragement of patients to gain additional support and learn more information about OCD can be an extremely useful addition to treatment. Fortunately, there are good sources of information, perhaps most notably the Obsessive Compulsive Foundation (OCF; www.ocfoundation.org) and the Anxiety Disorder Association of America (ADAA; www.adaa.org), both of whom are national organizations devoted to the education and assistance of patients with OCD and the people who care for them. There have also been a number of books than can be read by the lay person about OCD (March & Mulle, 1998; Rapoport, 1989).

SUMMARY AND CONCLUSIONS

OCD is a relatively common condition that exacts a high cost from the children and their families who suffer from it. Fortunately, a number of instruments and treatments now exist that make accurate diagnosis and effective treatment of OCD a realistic goal for the primary care physician. A systematic approach to the evaluation of OCD and other behavioral problems, similar to approaches used with other medical conditions, is strongly encouraged and outlined in this chapter, incorporating the use of established rating scales from multiple informants. Treatment, consisting of cognitive behavior therapy, medications, or both has been shown to provide a clear and lasting benefit, although full symptom remission for most individuals remains an elusive goal.

ACKNOWLEDGMENT

This work was supported by grants K08 MH069562 from the National Institute of Mental Health, Rockville, MD.

REFERENCES

AACAP. (1998). Practice parameters for the assessment and treatment of children and adolescents with obsessive-compulsive disorder. *Journal of the American Academy of Child and Adolescent Psychiatry, 37*(10, Suppl), 27S–45S.

Achenbach, T. M. R. L. A. (2001). *Manual for the ASEBA school-age forms & profiles*. Burlington, VT: University of Vermont, Research Center for Children, Youth, & Families.

Achenbach, T. M., Krukowski, R. A., Dumenci, L., & Ivanova, M. Y. (2005). Assessment of adult psychopathology: Meta-analyses and implications of cross-informant correlations. *Psychological Bulletin, 131*, 361–382.

Albert, U., Maina, G., Forner, F., & Bogetto, F. (2004). *DSM–IV* obsessive-compulsive personality disorder: Prevalence in patients with anxiety disorders and in healthy comparison subjects. *Comprehensive Psychiatry, 45*, 325–332.

American Academy of Child and Adolescent Psychiatry. (1998). Practice parameters for the assessment and treatment of children and adolescents with obsessive-compulsive disorder. *Journal of the American Academy of Child and Adolescent Psychiatry, 37*(10 Suppl), 27S–45S.

American Psychiatric Association. (1994). *Diagnostic and statistical manual of mental disorders, 4th edition (DSM–IV)*. Washington, DC: American Psychiatric Association.

Apter, A., Fallon, T. J., Jr., King, R. A., Ratzoni, G., Zohar, A. H., Binder, M., et al. (1996). Obsessive-compulsive characteristics: From symptoms to syndrome. Journal of the *American Academy of Child and Adolescent Psychiatry, 35*, 907–912.

Asbahr, F. R., Castillo, A. R., Ito, L. M., Latorre, M. R., Moreira, M. N., & Lotufo-Neto, F. (2005). Group cognitive-behavioral therapy versus sertraline for the treatment of children and adolescents with obsessive-compulsive disorder. *Journal of the American Academy of Child and Adolescent Psychiatry, 44*(11), 1128–1136.

Barrett, P., Farrell, L., Dadds, M., & Boulter, N. (2005). Cognitive-behavioral family treatment of childhood obsessive-compulsive disorder: Long-term follow-up and predictors of outcome. *Journal of the American Academy of Child and Adolescent Psychiatry, 44*, 1005–1014.

Barrett, P., Healy-Farrell, L., & March, J. S. (2004). Cognitive-behavioral family treatment of childhood obsessive-compulsive disorder: A controlled trial. *Journal of the American Academy of Child and Adolescent Psychiatry, 43*, 46–62.

Baxter, L. R., Jr., Schwartz, J. M., Bergman, K. S., Szuba, M. P., Guze, B. H., Mazziotta, J. C., et al. (1992). Caudate glucose metabolic rate changes with both drug and behavior therapy for obsessive-compulsive disorder. *Archives of General Psychiatry, 49*, 681–689.

Biederman, J. (1991). Sudden death in children treated with a tricyclic antidepressant. *Journal of the American Academy of Child and Adolescent Psychiatry, 30*, 495–498.

Brunell, W. (1998). Approach to the patient with obsessions or compulsions or an imagined defect in physical appearance. In T. A. Stern, J. B. Herman, & P. L. Slavin (Eds.), *The MGH guide to psychiatry in primary care* (pp. 341–346). New York: McGraw-Hill.

Cook, E. H., Wagner, K. D., March, J. S., Biederman, J., Landau, P., Wolkow, R., et al. (2001). Long-term sertraline treatment of children and adolescents with obsessive-compulsive disorder. *Journal of the American Academy of Child and Adolescent Psychiatry, 40*, 1175–1181.

Derogatis, L. R., & Lazarus, L. (1994). SCL-90-R: Brief symptom inventory and matching clinical rating scales. In administration, scoring, and procedures manual. In M. E. Mariush (Ed.), *The use of psychological testing for treatment planning and outcome assessment* (pp. 217–248). Hillsdale, NJ: Lawrence Erlbaum Associates.

DeVeaugh-Geiss, J., Moroz, G., Biederman, J., Cantwell, D., Fontaine, R., Greist, J. H., et al. (1992). Clomipramine hydrochloride in childhood and adolescent obsessive-compulsive disorder—A multicenter trial. *Journal of the American Academy of Child and Adolescent Psychiatry, 31,* 45–49.

Figueroa, Y., Rosenberg, D. R., Birmaher, B., & Keshavan, M. S. (1998). Combination treatment with clomipramine and selective serotonin reuptake inhibitors for obsessive-compulsive disorder in children and adolescents. *Journal of Child and Adolescent Psychopharmacology, 8,* 61–67.

Flament, M. F., Whitaker, A., Rapoport, J. L., Davies, M., Berg, C. Z., Kalikow, K., et al. (1988). Obsessive compulsive disorder in adolescence: An epidemiological study. *Journal of the American Academy of Child and Adolescent Psychiatry, 27,* 764–771.

Franklin, M. E., Kozak, M. J., Cashman, L. A., Coles, M. E., Rheingold, A. A., & Foa, E. B. (1998). Cognitive-behavioral treatment of pediatric obsessive-compulsive disorder: An open clinical trial. *Journal of the American Academy of Child and Adolescent Psychiatry, 37,* 412–419.

Geffken, G. R., Storch, E. A., Gelfand, K. M., Adkins, J. W., & Goodman, W. K. (2004). Cognitive-behavioral therapy for obsessive-compulsive disorder: Review of treatment techniques. *Journal of Psychosocial Nursing and Mental Health Services, 42*(12), 44–51.

Geller, D., Biederman, J., Jones, J., Park, K., Schwartz, S., Shapiro, S., et al. (1998). Is juvenile obsessive-compulsive disorder a developmental subtype of the disorder? A review of the pediatric literature. *Journal of the American Academy of Child and Adolescent Psychiatry, 37,* 420–427.

Geller, D. A., Biederman, J., Faraone, S., Agranat, A., Cradock, K., Hagermoser, L., et al. (2001). Developmental aspects of obsessive compulsive disorder: Findings in children, adolescents, and adults. *Journal of Nervous and Mental Disease, 189,* 471–477.

Geller, D. A., Biederman, J., Stewart, S. E., Mullin, B., Martin, A., Spencer, T., et al. (2003). Which SSRI? A meta-analysis of pharmacotherapy trials in pediatric obsessive-compulsive disorder. *American Journal of Psychiatry, 160*(11), 1919–1928.

Geller, D. A., & Spencer, T. (2003). Obsessive-compulsive disorder. In A. Martin, L. Scahill, D. S. Charney, & J. F. Leckman (Eds.), *Pediatric psychopharmacology: Principles and practice* (pp. 511–525). Oxford, UK: Oxford University Press.

Green, W. H. (2001). *Child and adolescent clinical psychopharmacology* (Vol. 3). Philadelphia: Lippincott, Williams & Williams.

Halmi, K. A., Sunday, S. R., Klump, K. L., Strober, M., Leckman, J. F., Fichter, M., et al. (2003). Obsessions and compulsions in anorexia nervosa subtypes. *International Journal of Eating Disorders, 33*(3), 308–319.

Hollingsworth, C. E., Tanguay, P. E., Grossman, L., & Pabst, P. (1980). Long-term outcome of obsessive-compulsive disorder in childhood. *Journal of the American Academy of Child and Adolescent Psychiatry, 19*(1), 134–144.

Hudziak, J. J., Van Beijsterveldt, C. E., Althoff, R. R., Stanger, C., Rettew, D. C., Nelson, E. C., et al. (2004). Genetic and environmental contributions to the child behavior checklist obsessive-compulsive scale: A cross-cultural twin study. *Archives of General Psychiatry, 61*(6), 608–616.

Lenuga, L. J., & Long, A. C. (2002). The role of emotionality and self-regulation in the appraisal-coping process: Tests of direct and moderating effects. *Journal of Applied Developmental Psychology, 23,* 471–493.

Leonard, H. L., Goldberger, E. L., Rapoport, J. L., Cheslow, D. L., & Swedo, S. E. (1990). Childhood rituals: Normal development or obsessive-compulsive symptoms? *Journal of the American Academy of Child and Adolescent Psychiatry, 29*(1), 17–23.

Leonard, H. L., Swedo, S. E., Lenane, M. C., Rettew, D. C., Cheslow, D. L., Hamburger, S. D., et al. (1991). A double-blind desipramine substitution during long-term clomipramine treatment in children and adolescents with obsessive-compulsive disorder. *Archives of General Psychiatry, 48*(10), 922–927.

Leonard, H. L., Topol, D., Bukstein, O., Hindmarsh, D., Allen, A. J., & Swedo, S. E. (1994). Clonazepam as an augmenting agent in the treatment of childhood-onset obsessive-compulsive disorder. *Journal of the American Academy of Child and Adolescent Psychiatry, 33*(6), 792–794.

Leslie, L. K., Newman, T. B., Chesney, P. J., & Perrin, J. M. (2005). The food and drug administration's deliberations on antidepressant use in pediatric patients. *Pediatrics, 116*(1), 195–204.

Lewin, A. B., Storch, E. A., Adkins, J., Murphy, T. K., & Geffken, G. R. (2005). Current directions in pediatric obsessive-compulsive disorder. *Pediatric Annals, 34*(2), 128–134.

Maina, G., Albert, U., Bogetto, F., Vaschetto, P., & Ravizza, L. (1999). Recent life events and obsessive-compulsive disorder (OCD): The role of pregnancy/delivery. *Psychiatry Research, 89*(1), 49–58.

Mansueto, C. S., & Keuler, D. J. (2005). Tic or compulsion? It's Tourettic OCD. *Behavior Modification, 29*(5), 784–799.

March, J. S., Frances, A., Carpenter, D., Kahn, D. A. (1997). The expert consensus guideline series: Treatment of obsessive-compulsive disorder. *Journal of Clinical Psychiatry, 58*(Suppl 4), 1–72.

March, J. S., & Mulle, K. (1998). *OCD in children and adolescents: A cognitive-behavioral treatment manual.* New York: Guilford.

Murphy, M. L., & Pichichero, M. E. (2002). Prospective identification and treatment of children with pediatric autoimmune neuropsychiatric disorder associated with group a streptococcal infection (PANDAS). *Archives of Pediatric and Adolescent Medicine, 156*(4), 356–361.

Murray, C. J., & Lopez, A. D. (1996). *The global burden of disease: A comprehensive assessment of mortality and morbidity from diseases, injuries, and risk factors in 1990 and projected to 2020.* Cambridge, MA: Harvard University Press.

Nestadt, G., Samuels, J., Riddle, M., Bienvenu, O. J., III, Liang, K. Y., LaBuda, M., et al. (2000). A family study of obsessive-compulsive disorder. *Archives of General Psychiatry, 57*(4), 358–363.

Pauls, D. L., Alsobrook, J. P., Goodman, W., Rasmussen, S., & Leckman, J. F. (1995). A family study of obsessive-compulsive disorder. *American Journal of Psychiatry, 152*(1), 76–84.

Pediatric OCD Treatment Study (POTS) Team. (2004). Cognitive-behavior therapy, sertraline, and their combination for children and adolescents with obsessive-compulsive disorder: The pediatric OCD treatment study (POTS) randomized controlled trial. *Journal of the American Medical Association, 292*(16), 1969–1976.

Pittenger, C., Kelmendi, B., Bloch, M., Krystal, J. H., & Coric, V. (2005). Clinical treatments of obsessive compulsive disorder. *Psychiatry, 11*(2), 34–43.

Rapoport, J. L. (1989). *The boy who couldn't stop washing: The experience & treatment of obsessive-compulsive disorder.* New York: E. P. Dutton.

Rettew, D. C. (2005, May). *Anxiety disorders and OCD.* Paper presented at the 1st Annual Child Psychiatry for the Primary Care Clinician Conference, Colchester, VT.

Rettew, D. C., Cheslow, D. L., Rapoport, J. L., Leonard, H. L., Lenane, M. C., Black, B., et al. (1991). Neuropsychological test performance in trichotillomania: A further link with obsessive-compulsive disorder. *Journal of Anxiety Disorders, 5*, 225–235.

Rettew, D. C., & McKee, L. (2005). Temperament and its role in developmental psychopathology. *Harvard Review of Psychiatry, 13*(1), 14–27.

Rettew, D. C., Swedo, S. E., Leonard, H. L., Lenane, M. C., & Rapoport, J. L. (1992). Obsessions and compulsions across time in 79 children and adolescents with obsessive-compulsive disorder. *Journal of the American Academy of Child and Adolescent Psychiatry, 31*(6), 1050–1056.

Reynolds, C. R., & Kamphaus, R. W. (1992). *Behavioral assessment system for children manual.* Circle Pines, MN: AGS.

Ross, D. C., & Piggott, L. R. (1993). Clonazepam for OCD. *Journal of the American Academy of Child and Adolescent Psychiatry, 32*(2), 470–471.

Scahill, L., Riddle, M. A., McSwiggin-Hardin, M., Ort, S. I., King, R. A., Goodman, W. K., et al. (1997). Children's Yale-Brown Obsessive Compulsive Scale: Reliability and validity. *Journal of the American Academy of Child and Adolescent Psychiatry, 36*(6), 844–852.

Shiner, R., & Caspi, A. (2003). Personality differences in childhood and adolescence: Measurement, development, and consequences. *Journal of Child Psychology and Psychiatry, 44*(1), 2–32.

Snider, L. A., Lougee, L., Slattery, M., Grant, P., & Swedo, S. E. (2005). Antibiotic prophylaxis with azithromycin or penicillin for childhood-onset neuropsychiatric disorders. *Biological Psychiatry, 57*(7), 788–792.

Stewart, S. E., Geller, D. A., Jenike, M., Pauls, D., Shaw, D., Mullin, B., et al. (2004). Long-term outcome of pediatric obsessive-compulsive disorder: A meta-analysis and qualitative review of the literature. *Acta Psychiatrica Scandinavica, 110*(1), 4–13.

Storch, E. A., Murphy, T. K., Geffken, G. R., Soto, O., Sajid, M., Allen, P., et al. (2004). Psychometric evaluation of the Children's Yale-Brown Obsessive-Compulsive Scale. *Psychiatry Research, 129*(1), 91–98.

Swedo, S. E. (1993). Trichotillomania. *Child and Adolescent Psychiatric Clinics of North America, 2,* 685–694.

Swedo, S. E., Leonard, H. L., & Rapoport, J. L. (2004). The pediatric autoimmune neuropsychiatric disorders associated with streptococcal infection (PANDAS) subgroup: Separating fact from fiction. *Pediatrics, 113*(4), 907–911.

Valleni-Basile, L. A., Garrison, C. Z., Jackson, K. L., Waller, J. L., McKeown, R. E., Addy, C. L., et al. (1994). Frequency of obsessive-compulsive disorder in a community sample of young adolescents. *Journal of the American Academy of Child and Adolescent Psychiatry, 33*(6), 782–791.

Wagner, K. D., Cook, E. H., Chung, H., & Messig, M. (2003). Remission status after long-term sertraline treatment of pediatric obsessive-compulsive disorder. *Journal of Child Adolescent Psychopharmacology, 13*(Suppl 1), S53–60.

Williams, J., Klinepeter, K., Palmes, G., Pulley, A., & Foy, J. M. (2004). Diagnosis and treatment of behavioral health disorders in pediatric practice. *Pediatrics, 114*(3), 601–606.

Wise, S. P., & Rapoport, J. L. (1989). Obsessive-compulsive disorder: Is it basal ganglia dysfunction? In J. L. Rapoport (Ed.), *Obsessive-compulsive disorder in children and adolescents* (pp. 327–344). Washington, DC: American Psychiatric Press.

Zohar, A. H., Ratzoni, G., Pauls, D. L., Apter, A., Bleich, A., Kron, S., et al. (1992). An epidemiological study of obsessive-compulsive disorder and related disorders in Israeli adolescents. *Journal of the American Academy of Child and Adolescent Psychiatry, 31*(6), 1057–1061.

Author Index

Subject Index